Searching for ORDER IN the COMPLEXITY of Evolving Worlds

ACKNOWLEDGMENTS

*The SFI Press would not exist without the support of
William H. Miller and the Miller Omega Program.*

As part of a multi-member global initiative to reimagine political and economic theory, the Santa Fe Institute launched a new research theme on Emergent Political Economies (EPE) in 2022. Funded by the Omidyar Network, this research initiative has sought to develop new interdisciplinary frameworks and methods to better apprehend the core lynchpins that drive our political, economic, and social lives. At a 2023 EPE-sponsored workshop on "Complex-System Approaches to Twenty-First Century Challenges," scholars and practitioners gathered at the Santa Fe Institute to further extend our understanding of the economy as an evolving complex adaptive system. These latest volumes in the EECS series represent both the culmination of those discussions and an invitation to continue the conversation into the twenty-first century and beyond.

https://santafe.edu/EPE

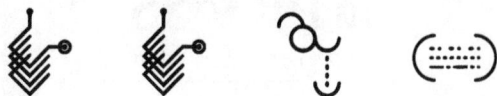

THE ECONOMY AS AN
EVOLVING COMPLEX SYSTEM
IV

Volume Two

R. MARIA DEL RIO-CHANONA
MARCO PANGALLO
JENNA BEDNAR
ERIC D. BEINHOCKER
JAGODA KASZOWSKA-MOJSA
FRANÇOIS LAFOND
PENNY MEALY
ANTON PICHLER
J. DOYNE FARMER

editors

⚡ PR⚡·SS

THE SANTA FE INSTITUTE PRESS

1399 Hyde Park Road
Santa Fe, New Mexico 87501

The Economy as an Evolving Complex System IV, Vol. 2
ISBN (HARDCOVER): 978-1-947864-69-6
Library of Congress Control Number: 2026930870

The SFI Press is made possible by the generous support
of the Miller Omega Program. These volumes were funded by a grant from the
Omidyar Network in support of the Emerging Political Economies theme.

Editorial Note

The order of editors in this book follows standard scientific publishing
conventions. R. Maria del Rio-Chanona and Marco Pangallo are listed first, as
they coordinated the editorial process. J. Doyne Farmer appears last, reflecting
his guidance role. All other editor names are listed in alphabetical order.

"AND IT IMPLIES THAT if we respect truth, we must search for it by persistently searching for our errors: by indefatigable rational criticism, and self-criticism.

KARL POPPER
Conjectures and Refutations: The Growth of Scientific Knowledge (1963)

VOL. 2
TABLE OF CONTENTS

Part III: Macroeconomic Dynamics & Finance

Part IV: Climate & Sustainability

INTRODUCTION

Penny Mealy, University of Oxford, Santa Fe Institute,
and Monash University;
Jenna Bednar, University of Michigan and Santa Fe Institute;
Eric D. Beinhocker, University of Oxford and Santa Fe Institute;
R. Maria del Rio-Chanona, University College London
and Complexity Science Hub;
J. Doyne Farmer, University of Oxford and Santa Fe Institute;
Jagoda Kaszowska-Mojsa, University of Oxford, Narodowy Bank
Polski,
and Institute of Economics, Polish Academy of Sciences;
François Lafond, University of Oxford;
Marco Pangallo, CENTAI Institute; and
Anton Pichler, Vienna University of Economics and Business
and Complexity Science Hub

In 1987, ten economists and ten natural scientists gathered at the Santa Fe Institute (SFI) for a ten-day workshop to explore a provocative idea: Could the global economy be understood as an evolving complex system? Few could have anticipated the significance of this meeting in igniting the development of a brand-new research field, now known as *complexity economics*. In reaching beyond equilibrium formulations to instead analyze the economy as an evolutionary system shaped by the interactions of diverse, adaptive and boundedly rational agents, the field sought to offer a more dynamic, realistic, and empirically grounded approach for understanding economic behavior. This shift in perspective would prove transformative, introducing new ways to understand everything from financial crises to technological change, to inequality and economic development.

What is Complexity Economics?

Complexity economics draws from the science of complex systems to understand the economy as an adaptive system where macro-level patterns emerge from the interaction of many diverse agents, rather than being imposed from above or derived from representative agents. The field shares with modern economics an increasingly empirical orientation but draws on interdisciplinary tools from physics, biology, computer science, and network theory to study economic phenomena across multiple spatial and temporal scales simultaneously. For instance, complexity economists pioneered the use of network analysis to map financial contagion, trace supply chain vulnerabilities, and understand how countries' productive capabilities shape their development paths. This empirical focus extends to uncovering universal patterns like power-law distributions in firm sizes, growth rates, and wealth: regularities that emerge across diverse economic contexts and can be explained through bottom-up mechanisms rather than top-down assumptions.

The emphasis on emergence naturally leads to a different approach to modeling economic behavior and dynamics. While agents in complexity economics may have goals or even utility functions, they are not assumed to achieve optimal outcomes. Instead, agents make decisions with limited information and cognitive capacity, attempting to pursue their goals but often falling short. This marks a conceptual shift: Agents are modeled as boundedly rational decision-makers who learn and adapt, whether through simple heuristics or more sophisticated learning algorithms—a perspective that aligns with behavioral economics research. This bottom-up approach reveals how realistic behavioral rules can generate sophisticated collective outcomes: technological innovation through combinatorial processes, the accumulation of productive capabilities that shape development trajectories (the economic complexity framework), and cascading effects that produce booms, busts, and structural transformations.

Agent-based modeling (ABM) is one of the most widely used tools for studying these dynamics (Axtell and Farmer 2025). These computer-based models simulate economies as constantly evolving processes where individual decisions aggregate into macro patterns that feed back to influence future behavior. Unlike traditional models, ABMs do not have to assume utility maximization. This allows them to simulate millions of interacting agents in complex environments that would be impossible to model with standard mathematical equations. ABMs can also capture economies out of equilibrium as they undergo transformations— whether adapting to technological disruption, navigating financial crises, restructuring in response to climate policies, or reorganizing during pandemics—generating endogenous cycles, tipping points, and regime shifts. Combined with advances in data science and machine learning, these methods are delivering falsifiable predictions and policy-relevant insights precisely when traditional models struggle most: during periods of disruption and transformation (Farmer 2024, 2025). The result is not just a set of different methodologies and techniques but a different way of seeing the economy: as a restless, evolving system whose patterns emerge from the interactions of millions of diverse, boundedly rational agents (Arthur 2021). It is this perspective that sets the stage for the field's contributions explored in this volume.

The History of This Series

The first volume of *The Economy as an Evolving Complex System* (1988) marked a foundational shift in economic thinking. It introduced a pioneering set of ideas and tools drawn from nonlinear dynamics, evolutionary biology, neural networks, and artificial life to analyze economic systems as decentralized, adaptive, and out of equilibrium. Volume II (1997) deepened this approach, expanding its empirical reach and emphasizing features such as path dependence, bounded rationality, networked interactions, and the co-evolution of institutions and behaviors. By volume III (2005), complexity economics had grown into a more sophisticated and multidisciplinary field, offering new insights into finance, technological innovation, macroeconomics, social interaction, and increasingly influencing conversations beyond academia.[1]

Since then, the field has matured significantly (see Beinhocker *et al.* 2026, ch. 2 in this volume, for a brief account of the history of the field). Its intellectual foundations have deepened, its methodological toolkit has become more refined and rigorous, and its practical relevance to real-world policy has grown increasingly evident (Arthur 2021). What began as an exploratory workshop at the Santa Fe Institute has since evolved into an active community of researchers and practitioners engaged in universities, think tanks, central banks, and international institutions all around the world.

Yet just as the field has evolved, so, too, has the complexity of the global challenges it seeks to understand.

An Evolving Complex World: New Challenges,

---

[1] Beinhocker and Bednar (ch. 30 in this volume) provide a comprehensive overview of the intellectual history and evolution of complexity economics, from its founding origins at the Santa Fe Institute to its maturation as a global, multidisciplinary field.

New Imperatives

Today's global economy is undergoing profound structural transformation. The race to reach net-zero emissions is well under way, as devastating climate impacts are becoming more frequent and severe around the world. The pace of technological change has never been faster or more consequential, with advances in areas like artificial intelligence poised to both revolutionize human productivity and upend jobs and sectors across the economy. Meanwhile, shifting balances of economic power are intensifying geopolitical tensions, disrupting global supply chains, and increasing the risk of conflict. At the same time, growing social divides between rich and poor, urban and nonurban dwellers, and those with differing levels of education continue to stretch the social fabric that holds our communities together, an effect amplified by polarizing discourse on social media platforms.

These changes are not marginal or linear processes. They are complex, adaptive, and path-dependent phenomena: precisely the kind of dynamics that complexity economics was designed to illuminate and understand.

This raises urgent questions: Can complexity economics rise to the challenge and meet the moment? To what extent can the field address such pressing global issues? Does viewing and analyzing the economy as an evolving complex system provide unique advantages over more traditional perspectives? And can the analytical approaches the field has heavily invested in— like agent-based models—provide more helpful insights than mainstream economic models?

These questions guided a recent workshop at the Santa Fe Institute, which provided the foundation of this book. Titled "Complex System Approaches to Twenty-First-Century Challenges: Inequality, Climate Change, and New Technologies,"

~ 5 ~

this workshop explored the applicability of the field's recent advances to real-world challenges and discussed key barriers in continuing to become more policy-relevant and impactful.

The workshop was one of the largest in the Santa Fe Institute's history, involving over sixty participants from a diverse range of disciplines and backgrounds. It involved ten sessions on various topics such as "Risk and Resilience in the Twenty-First Century: Are Our Analytical Approaches Up to the Challenge?"; "The Dynamics of Inequality: What Amplifies Unequal Outcomes and What Can Be Done About It?"; "How to Drive an Orderly Rather Than a Disorderly Green Transition"; "Fragmenting or Flourishing: How to Ensure Our Social Fabric Can Address Twenty-First-Century Challenges"; and "What Is the State of the Art in Complexity Economics and What Are the Most Pressing Methodological Challenges?"

This volume contains contributions from the workshop and beyond. The chapters present different perspectives on topics discussed in the workshop, as well as reflections on how the field of complexity economics has evolved and is progressing, and summaries of progress and future outlooks for key research strands within the discipline.

Methodological Advances: Machine Learning and the New Frontier of Agent-Based Models

Since volume III, one of the most significant and exciting methodological advances has been in agent-based modeling. While agent-based models have a long history (Richiardi, van de Ven, and Bronka, ch. 7), much of which has been advanced by researchers at the Santa Fe Institute, their adoption by mainstream economists and policymakers has remained somewhat limited. Early ABMs were often criticized for being overly complicated, containing too many free parameters and arbitrary assumptions, and for being difficult to calibrate or validate. These challenges made them difficult to compare and interpret, particularly against the backdrop of dominant equilibrium-based models (Pangallo, ch. 4).

However, a confluence of developments over the past decade has begun to shift this landscape. Increases in computational power, greater availability of high-resolution micro-level data (Borsos *et al.*, ch. 17), and methodological advances in estimation, calibration, and validation have opened the door to more empirically grounded, data-driven ABMs (Pangallo and del Rio-Chanona, ch. 9). These models increasingly exhibit greater rigor, transparency, and tractability, which is making them more attractive and user-friendly in applied policy settings.

~7~

And, indeed, many chapters in this volume reflect the growing influence and applicability of ABMs across a wide range of real-world contexts. In labor markets, ABMs are helping to model skill mismatches, unemployment, and the impact of technological change on workers (del Rio-Chanona *et al.*, ch. 23). In housing markets, they are offering insights into the emergence of bubbles, lending and borrowing behavior, and household responses to climate-related flood risks (Pangallo and del Rio-Chanona, ch. 9). In finance, ABMs are being used to study the emergence of stock-market crashes, heterogeneous expectations, and systemic risk (Borsos *et al.*, ch. 17). In climate and environmental policy, ABMs are increasingly used to explore the behavioral and network dynamics of risk propagation, insurance uptake, and adaptation strategies under uncertainty (Lamperti, Dosi, and Roventini, ch. 18; Filatova and Akkerman, ch. 21). And in macroeconomics, they are being employed to study production networks, consumption dynamics, inflation, and the coordination challenges inherent in fiscal and monetary policy (Dawid *et al.*, ch. 12; Hommes *et al.*, ch. 13).

Since volume III, these advances in agent-based modeling have been paralleled by dramatic improvements in data science, machine learning, and artificial intelligence. As Arthur Turrell (ch. 10) demonstrates, data-science techniques are transforming how policymakers measure complex economies, from web scraping to tracking price changes for vulnerable households to using computer vision for real-time crisis monitoring. These improvements in machine learning are also directly enhancing ABM capabilities, with algorithms increasingly used to empirically calibrate models (Dyer *et al.* 2022) and studies exploring whether large language models can be used to set realistic agent behaviors (del Rio-Chanona, Pangallo, and Hommes 2025).

Overall, these developments signal a shift in how ABMs are positioned within the field. What were once viewed as exploratory simulations are now becoming serious contenders: powerful tools capable of delivering falsifiable hypotheses, credible forecasts, and actionable policy insights.

Complexity at the Frontlines: Crisis, Contagion, and Criticality

In recent years, a series of global disruptions have thrust complexity economics into the forefront of policymaking. These events have not only tested the limits of traditional economic models but also showcased the unique strengths of complexity-based approaches in times of crisis.

The COVID-19 pandemic was a defining moment. As the virus spread across borders and sectors, policymakers from all nations were forced to grapple with nonlinear contagion dynamics, cascading supply shocks, and the challenge of managing economies through states of profound disequilibrium. In response, the complexity community mobilized rapidly: Within weeks, new out-of-equilibrium models were developed, designed specifically to predict how lockdowns would impact different industries (del Rio-Chanona *et al.* 2020), how these impacts were likely to propagate through economies (Pichler *et al.* 2020; Reissl *et al.* 2022), and how economies could be reopened in a way that reduced infection rates while increasing economic output (Pangallo *et al.* 2024). In addition to providing policymakers with strategic insights that were unattainable by conventional equilibrium-based models of the economy, a later ex-post analysis showed that the forecasts made by the modeling efforts were impressively accurate (Pichler *et al.* 2022).

In the pandemic's aftermath, inflation surged and central banks found themselves navigating unfamiliar terrain. Long reliant on dynamic, stochastic, general equilibrium (DSGE) models and econometric projections, several institutions began to explore alternatives better suited to uncertain, rapidly shifting environments. The Bank of Canada, for example, developed one of the first agent-based models specifically tailored for inflation targeting, macroeconomic forecasting, and policy analysis (Hommes *et al.*, ch. 13). This model, featuring boundedly rational households and firms interacting in a production network calibrated to the Canadian economy, not only outperformed DSGE models in forecasting gross domestic product (GDP) growth and consumption but also yielded unique insights into the key drivers of Canada's inflation surge.

Beyond inflation, complexity-based methods have proven increasingly useful for understanding systemic financial risk. For example, network models of financial contagion have shown how structural properties of interbank networks can amplify the risk of cascading defaults (Caccioli, ch. 15). And in an impressive review of ABM-relevant research and policy outputs of twenty-four central banks and seven related institutions, András Borsos, Adrian Carro, Aldo Glielmo, Marc Hinterschweiger, Jagoda Kaszowska-Mojsa, and Arzu Uluc (ch. 17) document the various contributions such models have made to help central banks perform stress testing, better understand the impacts of macroprudential policies, and monitor and analyze new risks arising from cybersecurity threats, cryptocurrencies, and the net-zero transition.

Complexity economics has also illuminated the vulnerability and criticality of global supply chains. While recent extreme weather events, geopolitical tensions, and disruptions from the COVID-19 pandemic and Russia's invasion of Ukraine have exposed the fragility of these networks, research has also shown that incentives within the system, like just-in-time inventory-management policies, can drive the system toward a highly critical state, such that even a small production delay can cascade through the network, generating major disruptions (Bouchaud, ch. 8). As has also been illustrated in financial systems (Caccioli, ch. 15), an uncomfortable reality facing policymakers is that many interventions aiming to drive greater efficiency may also weaken overall system resilience.

Economic crises may also occur without any external forcing, arising instead from endogenous dynamics of the economy, where each boom contains the seeds of a subsequent bust. Paul Beaudry, Dana Galizia, and Franck Portier (ch. 14) discuss research on endogenous business cycles and present a model that has strongly influenced the revival of the idea that exogenous shocks are not the sole drivers of economic fluctuations. Mathematically, such models exhibit forms of nonlinear dynamics such as limit cycles or chaos, which represent one of the key contributions of complexity-based methods to economics (Brock and Hommes, ch. 5).

Climate Change: Catalyzing the Case for Complexity

Several chapters in this book detail the contributions complexity economics is making to address climate change. Once perceived as a distant concern, climate change is now a defining force shaping lives, livelihoods, and the global economy. Its physical impacts, ranging from floods, fires, and storms to droughts, heat waves, and rising sea levels, are already impacting key sectors like agriculture, fishing, and tourism while placing mounting stress on infrastructure and public health systems.

~ 11 ~

Yet many traditional models in climate economics have struggled to capture the full economic severity of these risks. Standard integrated assessment models often assume gradual, marginal impacts, failing to reflect how shocks propagate through interconnected systems. In reality, damage to a single node, whether a household, firm, or region, can ripple outward through supply chains and financial networks, triggering broader effects such as migration, social unrest, or political destabilization (Filatova and Akkerman, ch. 21).

Moreover, many standard models poorly account for climate tipping points, such as the loss of Arctic sea ice or the thawing of permafrost, which can unleash nonlinear, self-reinforcing feedback loops that rapidly accelerate warming (Battiston and Monasterolo, ch. 19). As a result, these models have often underestimated potential damages. For instance, while prominent economists have suggested that 3.5°C of warming by the end of the century might be "optimal" from a cost–benefit perspective (Nordhaus 2018), most climate scientists argue that such a level would entail catastrophic consequences (Lamperti, Dosi, and Roventini, ch. 18).

New transition risks are also emerging with the introduction of climate policies, green technology investment, and shifting preferences away from emissions-intensive production. These developments can drive abrupt shifts in asset values, sectoral disruption, and major changes in global comparative advantage. Here, too, traditional models struggle to capture path-dependence, technological lock-in, investor uncertainty, asset stranding risks, and associated impacts on financial and labor markets—all of which shape the speed and smoothness of the green transition (Dumas and Andres, ch. 20). However, several new modeling approaches described in this volume better reflect the dynamics of cascading shocks, multiple equilibria, tipping points, and investor uncertainty, offering more realistic assessments of both physical and transition risks (Filatova and Akkerman, ch. 21; Battiston and Monasterolo, ch. 19; and Lamperti, Dosi, and Roventini, ch. 18).

Fortunately—and importantly—there are also solid empirical grounds for optimism. Recent contributions in complexity economics have demonstrated that climate action is not just a story of higher risks and costs but one of immense opportunity. Building on a rich body of work on technological forecasting (Lafond, ch. 25), Rupert Way *et al.* (2022) project that rapid transition to a net-zero energy system could generate $12 trillion in savings when compared to the cost of maintaining current fossil-fuel systems. These findings stand in sharp contrast to projections from many integrated assessment models used by governments and the Intergovernmental Panel on Climate Change, which have historically overestimated the costs of renewable energy and underestimated the pace of technological progress (Farmer *et al.* 2015). As this volume demonstrates, incorporating nonlinear dynamics, tipping points, and empirically grounded technological learning curves can fundamentally reshape how we assess the costs, benefits, and urgency of climate action.

Beyond the Black Box: The Process and Predictability of Technological Evolution

Beyond its role in addressing climate change, technological progress is a powerful driver of economic development and societal transformation. While mainstream economic models often treat it as an exogenous and largely unexplained source of productivity growth, key strands of work within complexity economics have sought to push conceptual, empirical, and modeling frontiers to better understand how technology evolves and how it might be better guided toward societal goals.

On the empirical front, François Lafond (ch. 25) outlines a recent wave of efforts to track cost-improvement trends across technologies and develop forecasting models grounded in observable patterns. Two statistical laws offer alternative lenses: Moore's law predicts costs will decline predictably over time, while Wright's law suggests costs fall with experience (i.e., learning-by-doing). The distinction has important implications for technological investment and innovation strategies. If Moore's law holds, we need to wait for progress; if Wright's law is more accurate, proactive investment and production subsidies can directly accelerate technological advancement. Leveraging World War II as a natural experiment, where production was driven by military necessity rather than market demand, Lafond, Diana Greenwald, and Farmer (2022) find that roughly 50% of cost improvements can be causally attributed to production-driven learning. This finding underscores the role that deliberate policy choices can play in shaping both the pace and the direction of technological progress.

Building on a lineage of important contributions on the nature of technological evolution (Arthur 2009), W. Brian Arthur (ch. 2) sheds new light on the process by which invention occurs. Transformative technologies, such as computers, X-ray machines, or the internet, don't emerge in a vacuum; they evolve through a process of combination and recombination of existing technologies. The global positioning system (GPS), for instance, delivers precise location data by integrating a suite of earlier technologies, including satellites, atomic clocks, radio transmitters, and mathematical algorithms, each of which built on prior technological breakthroughs. Novel technologies are then "encapsulated" and in turn become "modules" or building blocks for future generations of technologies, just as GPS itself has become a foundational building block for further innovations, powering technologies from smartphone navigation to drones.

Arthur describes technological innovation as a "generative system" that operates on two time scales: one fast, where existing elements are routinely combined for immediate purposes, and one slow, where novel elements occasionally enter the toolbox (sometimes from scientific discovery, sometimes from trial and error), driving long-run evolutionary change. This process is recursive, and the combinatorial space of possibility is continually unfolding (autopoietic), branching (or "splintering") into new domains, and effectively unbounded. As such, technological evolution has more in common with other combinatorial systems such as chemical synthesis, mathematical proofs, linguistic neologisms, legal systems, and software development (Valverde, Vidiella, and Duran-Nebreda, ch. 27) than an evolutionary perspective based on biological Darwinian descent with modification (though Arthur notes the combinatorial process is "complementary" with Darwinian evolution, and some evolutionary economists would likely view Arthur's account as providing a mechanism for variation within a broader, algorithmic view of "generalized Darwinism," e.g., Hodgson and Knudsen 2010; Beinhocker 2011).

Pathways to Progress: Capabilities, Complexity and the Dynamics of Growth

A central challenge in translating technological progress into broad-based growth and development outcomes across countries and regions is that innovation is often spatially bounded (Coyle, ch. 26). As a result, the ideas, industries, and infrastructure embedded in a particular place can shape—and often limit—the range of future possibilities. As shown by a rich and growing body of research on economic complexity and economic geography (Frenken and Neffke, ch. 28), places are more likely to generate new innovations, develop new products, or cultivate competitive sectors in areas that are closely related to their existing knowledge base.

~ 15 ~

This path-dependency arises in part because the knowledge required for innovation and industrial development is, as Friedrich Hayek (1945) famously noted, "beyond the span of the control of any one mind." It is instead distributed across networks of people, firms, and institutions. The depth of specialization is limited not just by the extent of the market (as Adam Smith [1775] argued) but also by the costs of coordinating complex, distributed knowledge. Even in an increasingly digital world, spatial proximity continues to play a key role in lowering these costs, enabling dense localized networks to combine and apply distributed expertise more effectively. While economists throughout the ages have, in various ways, articulated the importance of collective know-how embedded in places (Smith 1775; Veblen 1898; Hayek 1945; Lall 1992), only recently has the availability of granular data on patents, products, and skills enabled places' productive capabilities to be empirically analyzed (Neffke *et al.*, ch. 6; del Rio-Chanona *et al.*, ch. 23). Despite ongoing debates about the merits of different measurement approaches, studies within complexity economics consistently show that places with more complex or sophisticated productive activities tend to experience higher rates of economic growth (Neffke *et al.*, ch. 6).

In parallel, complexity economics has advanced new approaches to modeling economic growth and firm dynamics that better reflect observed empirical patterns. Traditional models, such as those following Gibrat's law (Gibrat 1931), assume that firm growth is random and proportional to size. Yet these assumptions often generate predictions, such as lognormal firm size distributions, that diverge from real-world data, which more closely follow heavy-tailed, Pareto-like distributions. To address such discrepancies, Robert Axtell and Omar Guerrero (ch. 11) propose a new stochastic theory of firm growth based not on multiplicative expansion but on labor reallocation dynamics. In their model, workers move between firms in search of better employment opportunities, making one firm's gain another's loss. This labor-flow mechanism departs from the independence assumptions of Gibrat-style models and successfully reproduces empirically observed firm-size distributions. In related work, José Moran and Massimo Riccaboni (ch. 24) explore compositional growth models, which explain aggregate growth by decomposing economies or sectors into smaller, independently evolving components— such as submarkets, firms, or products. These models help account for key empirical regularities, including the fat-tailed distributions of firm sizes and growth rates, that standard aggregate models struggle to replicate.

The Power of Feedback: How Complex Systems can Amplify Inequality and Undermine Democracy

An overarching theme that permeated all topics at the 2023 Santa Fe Institute workshop was the intertwined challenge of political economy, inequality, and democratic resilience.

Power dynamics run rife in many, if not most, twenty-first-century challenges, and even the most carefully designed policy solutions are often constrained or resisted by political realities. And with so many global developments—be it the rapid advance of artificial intelligence, the upheavals of climate change, or shifting geopolitical orders—carrying risks of further widening divides, there is an urgent need to better understand how to promote fairness, inclusion, and the long-term stability of democratic institutions.

Complexity economics offers a unique and powerful lens to understand inequality, not as a static distribution but as a dynamic, endogenous feature of complex adaptive systems. From the earliest agent-based models, such as Joshua Epstein and Robert Axtell's (1996) Sugarscape model, researchers have shown how inequality can emerge not just from differences in individual effort or ability but from the structure and dynamics of the system. A combination of asymmetries (including luck), path dependence, and the compounding processes common in economic systems (e.g., returns on capital, social network effects) can cause individual agent trajectories to diverge, creating emergent distributions with characteristics (e.g., power-law upper tails) that mirror empirical distributions of income and wealth (Yakovenko and Rosser, Jr. 2009; Li, Boghosian, and Li 2019; Palagi *et al.* 2023). Importantly, these disparities can emerge even under conditions of equal opportunity, revealing the limits of simple policy prescriptions that do not address systemic and structural drivers of inequality.

Moreover, complex adaptive systems can act as inequality amplifiers. Small initial differences, whether in wealth, education, or social connections, can be magnified through positive feedback loops and become self-reinforcing over time (Roithmayr 2014;

Trounstine 2018). Steven Durlauf, David McMillon, and Scott Page (ch. 22) show how one form of disadvantage can compound and reinforce others across different spheres, creating "system of system" effects. An unsafe environment may undermine health outcomes, leading to poorer school performance, and increased unemployment risk, which in turn can worsen health outcomes—a vicious cycle that compounds disadvantage. People suffering from poor health and economic prospects are also less likely to place trust in government and social services, further compounding exclusion and making effective policy interventions even harder to deliver.

Reducing inequality therefore requires more than redistribution. It demands interventions that disrupt feedback loops and re-shape institutional structures that perpetuate disparities. As Durlauf, McMillon, and Page discuss, this could take several forms: weakening adverse features of a system (e.g., levying a wealth tax to reduce intergenerational income transfers to disrupt poverty traps in economic systems), dismantling structures that reinforce inequality (e.g., abolishing private prisons), or harnessing positive feedback loops to amplify equality-focused interventions (e.g., a policy that enhances access to capital markets for minorities). And since inequality is often produced by multiple interdependent systems, coordinating policy efforts across multiple domains is critical.

To inform such systemic approaches, policymakers require tools that reliably capture the structural characteristics and reinforcing mechanisms that propagate inequality in an economy. One example is described in Giovanni Dosi, Marcelo Pereira, Andrea Roventini, and Maria Enrica Virgillito (ch. 29), which outlines an extension of a multisector labor-augmented, general-disequilibrium stock-flow consistent ABM to investigate the effect of declining unionization on inequality in the United States. In addition to aligning with several empirical stylized facts in the US, the simulations suggest that declining unionization induces higher macro-level inequality, greater wage dispersion between firms, and stronger polarization in wage growth dynamics. Models like this serve as valuable policy laboratories, enabling governments to test reforms in silico, assess their capacity to disrupt entrenched inequality, and reduce risks before implementing policies in the real world.

Like economies, democracies are also complex adaptive systems, marked by feedback loops, network effects, and emergent dynamics. These systems perspectives help explain why identical constitutions can yield very different political outcomes (Putnam 1994; Elkins, Ginsburg, and Melton 2009; Bednar and Page 2018) and how seemingly stable democracies can be hollowed out and rendered fragile (Acemoglu and Robinson 2005; Ginsburg and Huq 2018). Polarization provides a vivid example: Models of elite opinion dynamics show how asymmetric feedback can drive runaway partisan divergence (Leonard *et al.* 2021), while agent-based simulations demonstrate how intolerance, exposure, and structural inequalities interact to push societies past tipping points into extreme polarization (Axelrod, Daymude, and Forrest 2021). ABMs have also been used to simulate protests and social movements, shedding light on the conditions that can give rise to uprising, civil unrest, and ultimately revolutions (Epstein 2002; Makowsky and Rubin 2013; Moro 2016; Thomas *et al.* 2025).

Democratic robustness depends on many of the same system properties that underpin resilience in other domains. Cross-cutting social ties and integrated information networks cultivate shared understanding and foster a sense of collective fate, while fragmented communication silos erode trust and weaken democratic norms (Horowitz 1985; Centola and Macy 2007; Axelrod, Daymude, and Forrest 2021; Bednar 2021). Diversity of representation expands the menu of solutions, redundancy in overlapping institutions provides important safeguards, and adaptability allows recalibration in response to shocks (Levin 2000; Bednar 2009). And democratic durability cannot rest on institutional design alone. Investing in social infrastructure such as libraries, parks, community centers, and street festivals is critical for sustaining cross-group connections, protecting the integrity of information systems, and building flexible arrangements that evolve as conditions change. Strengthening these elements is essential to ensuring that democracies remain resilient, legitimate, and capable of withstanding mounting pressures.

Shifting the Economic Paradigm: The Future of Complexity Economics

As this volume illustrates, complexity economics has evolved from a provocative workshop into a rich and empirically grounded field—one that is increasingly demonstrating its relevance for understanding and shaping economic issues in the twenty-first century. But the case for complexity economics is not just about better tools for addressing present-day challenges. At its core, it represents an opportunity to rethink the foundations of the economic paradigm.

Eric D. Beinhocker and Jenna Bednar (ch. 30) argue that complexity economics is well-placed to provide the scientific backbone for a new economic paradigm: one that better connects moral values, behavioral realism, systemic understanding, and institutional design. This involves more than refining the assumptions of economic models. In Beinhocker and Bednar's formulation, paradigms can be understood in terms of an "ontological stack"—a set of layered, mutually reinforcing ideas spanning from moral foundations to theories of behavior and economic systems to public narratives and practical policy applications. Complexity economics, they argue, has enormous potential to contribute to scientifically advancing the middle layers of this stack: the theories of behavior, economic systems, and processes of change that are critical for connecting normative goals to real-world outcomes. Without strong explanatory foundations, even the most well-intentioned paradigms falter. Indeed, as history has shown (from socialism to neoliberalism), flawed economic theories can lead to failed systems and unintended harm.

Of course, modern-day economics has changed significantly since the 1987 SFI meeting and is no longer the neoclassical, largely fact-free field that was critiqued in that meeting. Mainstream economics is now far more empirical and is increasingly grappling with the messy complexities of the economy that motivate complexity economics researchers. Yet, as Farmer (2024) argues, complexity economics departs not just in method but in fundamental theoretical foundations—seeking to replace core assumptions like utility maximization, rational expectations, and equilibrium with more realistic representations of economic behavior and dynamics. In this sense, complexity economics represents a revolutionary shift in how we theorize, simulate, and make sense of economic life.

This shift invites a more reflexive, adaptive, and dynamic economics—one capable of tractably grappling with systemic fragility and flexibility, innovation and inequality, and growth within environmental limits. It resonates with political economy movements that seek to move beyond both neoliberal market fundamentalism and rigid state control, and toward more pluralistic, democratic and ecologically responsible economic models. It aligns with contemporary calls for progress metrics beyond simplistic aggregate measures like gross domestic product, for institutions that foster collective intelligence and wisdom, and for public narratives that are grounded in cooperation, dignity, and resilience.

Such a major change won't happen overnight. Paradigm shifts can be generational projects. They require the demanding work of community building, methodological innovation, empirical validation, and interdisciplinary collaboration and synthesis. They also require imagination. The paradigm we build must not only better explain the world, it must help us envision and create a better one.

The chapters in this volume represent building blocks of such a shift. They do not offer a single blueprint. But together they sketch the contours of an emerging economic worldview: one that takes seriously the complexity of our challenges, the diversity of our societies, and the evolutionary nature of change. As we move forward, the task is not simply to refine the research agenda of complexity economics but to advance it as part of a broader effort to reshape the economic paradigm for a complex and uncertain century. ⸙

Acknowledgments

The authors would like to kindly acknowledge the Santa Fe Institute's grant from the Omidyar Network on Emerging Political Economies, as well as funding from Baillie Gifford, the Open Society Foundation, Marie Skłodowska-Curie (H2020) grant no. 101023445, NAWA Bekker grant no. BPN/BEK/2024/1/00240, and the UKRI through ESRC grant PRINZ (ES/W010356/1).

REFERENCES

Acemoglu, D., and J. A. Robinson. 2005. *Economic Origins of Dictatorship and Democracy.* Cambridge, UK: Cambridge University Press.

Anderson, P. W., K. Arrow, and D. Pines, eds. 1988. *The Economy as an Evolving Complex System.* Boston, MA: Addison-Wesley.

Arthur, W. B. 2009. *The Nature of Technology: What it is and How it Evolves.* New York, NY: Free Press.

———. 2021. "Foundations of Complexity Economics." *Nature Reviews Physics* 3:136–145. https://doi.org/10.1038/s42254-020-00273-3.

Arthur, W. B., S. Durlauf, and D. Lane, eds. 1997. *The Economy as an Evolving Complex System II.* Reading, MA: Addison-Wesley.

Axelrod, R., J. J. Daymude, and S. Forrest. 2021. "Preventing Extreme Polarization Of Political Attitudes." *Proceedings of the National Academy of Sciences* 118 (50): e2102139118. https://doi.org/10.1073/pnas.2102139118.

Axtell, R. L., and J. D. Farmer. 2025. "Agent-Based Modeling in Economics and Finance: Past, Present, and Future." *Journal of Economic Literature* 63 (1): 197–287. https://doi.org/10.1257/jel.20221319.

Bednar, J. 2009. *The Robust Federation: Principles of Design.* Cambridge, UK: Cambridge University Press.

———. 2021. "Polarization, Diversity, and Democratic Robustness." *Proceedings of the National Academy of Sciences* 118 (50): e2113843118. https://doi.org/10.1073/pnas.2113843118.

Bednar, J., and S. E. Page. 2018. "When Order Affects Performance: Culture, Behavioral Spillovers, and Institutional Path Dependence." *American Political Science Review* 112 (1): 82–98. https://www.jstor.org/stable/26542118.

Beinhocker, E. D. 2011. "Evolution as Computation: Integrating Self-Organization with Generalized Darwinism." *Journal of Institutional Economics* 7 (3): 393–423. https://doi.org/10.1017/S1744137411000257.

Blume, L., and S. Durlauf, eds. 2005. *The Economy as an Evolving Complex System III.* Oxford, UK: Oxford University Press.

Centola, D., and M. Macy. 2007. "Complex Contagions and the Weakness of Long Ties." *American Journal of Sociology* 113 (3): 702–734. https://doi.org/10.1086/521848.

del Rio-Chanona, R. M., P. Mealy, A. Pichler, F. Lafond, and J. D. Farmer. 2020. "Supply and Demand Shocks in the COVID-19 Pandemic: An Industry and Occupation Perspective." *Oxford Review of Economic Policy* 36 (S1): S94–S137. https://doi.org/10.1093/oxrep/graa033.

del Rio-Chanona, R. M., M. Pangallo, and C. Hommes. 2025. *Can Generative AI Agents Behave Like Humans? Evidence from Laboratory Market Experiments.* arXiv preprint: 2505.07457. https://doi.org/10.48550/arXiv.2505.07457.

Dyer, J., P. Cannon, J. D. Farmer, and S. M. Schmon. 2022. "Calibrating Agent-Based Models to Microdata with Graph Neural Networks." In *ICML Workshop on AI for Agent-Based Modelling.* https://doi.org/10.48550/arXiv.2206.07570.

Elkins, Z., T. Ginsburg, and J. Melton. 2009. *The Endurance of National Constitutions.* Cambridge, UK: Cambridge University Press.

Epstein, J. M. 2002. "Modeling Civil Violence: An Agent-Based Computational Approach." *Proceedings of the National Academy of Sciences* 99 (S3): 7243–7250. https://doi.org/10.1073/pnas.092080199.

Epstein, J. M., and R. L. Axtell. 1996. *Growing Artificial Societies: Social Science from the Bottom Up.* Cambridge, MA: MIT Press.

Farmer, J. D. 2024. *Making Sense of Chaos: A Better Economics for a Better World.* New Haven, CT: Yale University Press.

———. 2025. "Quantitative Agent-Based Models: A Promising Alternative for Macroeconomics." *Oxford Review of Economic Policy,* https://doi.org/10.1093/oxrep/graf027.

Farmer, J. D., C. Hepburn, P. Mealy, and A. Teytelboym. 2015. "A Third Wave in the Economics of Climate Change." *Environmental and Resource Economics* 62 (2): 329–357. https://doi.org/10.1007/s10640-015-9965-2.

Gibrat, R. 1931. *Les Inégalités Économiques.* Paris, France: Sirely.

Ginsburg, T., and A. Z. Huq. 2018. *How to Save a Constitutional Democracy.* Chicago, IL: University of Chicago Press.

Hayek, F. A. 1945. "The Use of Knowledge in Society." *American Economic Review* 35 (4): 519–530. https://www.jstor.org/stable/1809376.

Hodgson, G. M., and T. Knudsen. 2010. *Darwin's Conjecture: The Search for General Principles of Social and Economic Evolution.* Chicago, IL: University of Chicago Press.

Horowitz, D. L. 1985. *Ethnic Groups in Conflict.* Berkeley, CA: University of California Press.

Lafond, F., D. Greenwald, and J. D. Farmer. 2022. "Can Stimulating Demand Drive Costs Down? World War II as a Natural Experiment." *The Journal of Economic History* 82 (3): 727–764. https://doi.org/10.1017/S0022050722000249.

Lall, S. 1992. "Technological Capabilities and Industrialization." *World Development* 20 (2): 165–186. https://doi.org/10.1016/0305-750X(92)90097-F.

Leonard, N. E., K. Lipsitz, A. Bizyaeva, A. Franci, and Y. Lelkes. 2021. "The Nonlinear Feedback Dynamics of Asymmetric Political Polarization." *Proceedings of the National Academy of Sciences* 118 (50): e2102149118. https://doi.org/10.1073/pnas.2102149118.

Levin, S. 2000. *Fragile Dominion: Complexity And The Commons.* Princeton, NJ: Princeton University Press.

Li, J., B. M. Boghosian, and C. Li. 2019. "The Affine Wealth Model: An Agent-Based Model of Asset Exchange That Allows for Negative-Wealth Agents and Its Empirical Validation." *Physica A* 516 (C): 423–442. https://doi.org/10.1016/j.physa.2018.10.042.

Makowsky, M. D., and J. Rubin. 2013. "An Agent-Based Model of Centralized Institutions, Social Network Technology, and Revolution." *PLoS One* 8 (11): e80380. https://doi.org/10.1371/journal.pone.0080380.

Moro, A. 2016. "Understanding the Dynamics of Violent Political Revolutions in an Agent-Based Framework." *PLoS One* 11 (4): e0154175. https://doi.org/10.1371/journal.pone.0154175.

Nordhaus, W. D. 2018. "Projections and Uncertainties About Climate Change in an Era of Minimal Climate Policies." *American Economic Journal: Economic Policy* 10 (3): 333–360. https://doi.org/10.1257/pol.20170046.

Palagi, E., M. Napoletano, A. Roventini, and J.-L. Gaffard. 2023. "An Agent-Based Model of Trickle-Up Growth and Income Inequality." *Economic Modelling* 129:106535. https://doi.org/10.1016/j.econmod.2023.106535.

Pangallo, M., A. Aleta, R. M. del Rio-Chanona, A. Pichler, D. Martín-Corral, M. Chinazzi, F. Lafond, *et al.* 2024. "The Unequal Effects Of The Health–Economy Trade-Off During The COVID-19 Pandemic." *Nature Human Behaviour* 8 (2): 264–275. https://doi.org/10.1038/s41562-023-01747-x.

Pichler, A., M. Pangallo, R. M. del Rio-Chanona, F. Lafond, and J. D. Farmer. 2020. *Production Networks and Epidemic Spreading: How to Restart the UK Economy?* arXiv preprint: 2005.10585. https://doi.org/10.48550/arXiv.2005.10585.

———. 2022. "Forecasting the Propagation of Pandemic Shocks with a Dynamic Input–Output Model." *Journal of Economic Dynamics and Control* 144:104527. https://doi.org/10.1016/j.jedc.2022.104527.

Putnam, R. D. 1994. *Making Democracy Work.* Princeton, NJ: Princeton University Press.

Reissl, S., A. Caiani, F. Lamperti, M. Guerini, F. Vanni, G. Fagiolo, T. Ferraresi, L. Ghezzi, M. Napoletano, and A. Roventini. 2022. "Assessing The Economic Impact Of Lockdowns In Italy: A Computational Input–Output Approach." *Industrial and Corporate Change* 31 (2): 358–409. https://doi.org/10.1093/icc/dtac003.

Roithmayr, D. 2014. *Reproducing Racism: How Everyday Choices Lock In White Advantage.* New York, NY: New York University Press.

Smith, A. 1775. *An Inquiry into the Nature and Causes of the Wealth of Nations.* W. Strahan and T. Cadell.

Thomas, E. F., M. Ye, S. D. Angus, T. J. Mathew, W. Louis, L. Walsh, S. Ellery, M. Lizzio-Wilson, and C. McGarty. 2025. "Repeated And Incontrovertible Collective Action Failure Leads to Protester Disengagement and Radicalisation." *arXiv preprint: 2408.12795,* https://doi.org/10.48550/arXiv.2408.12795.

Trounstine, J. 2018. *Segregation by Design: Local Politics and Inequality in American Cities.* Cambridge, UK: Cambridge University Press.

Veblen, T. 1898. "Why Is Economics Not an Evolutionary Science?" *The Quarterly Journal of Economics* 12 (4): 373–397. https://doi.org/10.2307/1882952.

Way, R., M. C. Ives, P. Mealy, and J. D. Farmer. 2022. "Empirically Grounded Technology Forecasts and the Energy Transition." *Joule* 6 (9): 2057–2082. https://doi.org/10.1016/j.joule.2022.08.009.

Yakovenko, V. M., and J. B. Rosser, Jr. 2009. "Colloquium: Statistical Mechanics of Money, Wealth, and Income." *Reviews of Modern Physics* 81 (4): 1703–1725. https://doi.org/10.1103/revmodphys.81.1703.

A BRIEF HISTORY
OF THE EMERGENCE OF
COMPLEXITY ECONOMICS

Eric D. Beinhocker, University of Oxford and Santa Fe Institute;
J. Doyne Farmer, University of Oxford and Santa Fe Institute;
Jenna Bednar, University of Michigan and Santa Fe Institute;
R. Maria del Rio-Chanona, University College London
and Complexity Science Hub;
Jagoda Kaszowska-Mojsa, University of Oxford, Narodowy Bank
Polski, and Institute of Economics, Polish Academy of Sciences;
François Lafond, University of Oxford;
Penny Mealy, University of Oxford, Santa Fe Institute,
and Monash University;
Marco Pangallo, CENTAI Institute;
Anton Pichler, Vienna University of Economics and Business
and Complexity Science Hub

For readers new to complexity economics, a brief history of how the field emerged may provide useful context for the chapters that follow in this volume. This is not intended to be a complete historical review (for a more in-depth account, see Beinhocker 2006) but instead its purpose is to give readers an overview of key strands of work that provide the foundations for modern complexity economics, as well as some entry points into the historical literature (up to the early 2010s). We have also chosen to focus on the social science foundations and only very briefly mention the immense contributions in ideas and methods that complexity economists have incorporated from the physical sciences. As such, we have inevitably omitted numerous important contributors and works, but the chapters that follow cite a much broader base of scholarship, as well as more recent research.

Complexity economics, a label introduced by W. Brian Arthur in *Science* in 1999, began to emerge as a distinct set of perspectives and methodologies in the mid-1980s, pioneered by a community of scholars associated with the Santa Fe Institute (SFI). As noted in the introduction to this volume, "Complexity economics draws from the science of complex systems to understand the economy as an adaptive system where macro-level patterns emerge from the interaction of many diverse agents, rather than being imposed from above or derived from representative agents (see Mealy *et al.* 2026, ch. 1 in this volume; and Arthur 2021 for a more extended definition). While SFI catalyzed the development of the field in the 1980s, the ideas underpinning complexity economics had deep historical roots in both the social and physical sciences.

Historical Antecedents in the Social Sciences

One could claim that the first complexity economist was the Islamic philosopher Al-Ghazālī (1058–1111) who viewed markets as necessary, self-organizing institutions arising from human interdependence and the division of labor. He observed that order in exchange does not require central design but emerges from decentralized interaction—provided moral and legal norms are in place. While couched in a religious context, his observations anticipate later complexity views (and Friedrich Hayek's) that macroeconomic order arises bottom-up from local interactions rather than from planning (Islahi and Ghazanfar 2011).

While unaware of Al-Ghazālī's thinking, seven centuries later, Western Enlightenment philosophers explored themes of bottom-up emergence. In the eighteenth century, Adam Ferguson (1767 [1979]) argued that social and economic institutions are "The result of human action, but not the execution of any human design." He further saw economies as evolutionary and path dependent, arising from habit, conflict, imitation, and adaptation, and neither optimal nor in equilibrium.

~29~

Ferguson's contemporary Adam Smith was also fascinated by such phenomena. His famous metaphor of the "invisible hand" (Smith [1977]1776) is often misinterpreted as a statement about the pursuit of individual self-interest leading to positive outcomes for society (or in more colloquial terms, greed is good). However, Smith scholars correct this interpretation (Rothschild 1994), noting that Smith was clear that he did not believe that greed is good but rather the metaphor was a comment on the phenomenon of emergence. As Gavin Kennedy (2009, 241) puts it, "Smith's identification of the processes associated with the unintended consequences of individual actions in such diverse phenomena as language, money, moral sentiments, exchange and markets . . . are usefully judged to be an early recognition of evolutionary 'emergent order.'"

Building on this classical liberal tradition, in the twentieth century, economists from the Austrian school such as Joseph Schumpeter ([1911]1934) and Friedrich Hayek (1945) explored ideas of spontaneous order creation, dynamic change, and disequilibrium. Hayek in particular can be seen as a precursor to complexity economics in that he understood the economy as a decentralized, adaptive system in which order emerges from local interactions and dispersed knowledge, rather than from equilibrium optimization or central design (Axtell 2016; Bowles, Kirman, and Sethi 2017).

In addition to ideas of self-organization and emergence, complexity economists have also built on a long history of evolutionary thinking in economics (Hodgson 1993), from Thorstein Veblen (1898) famously asking, "Why is economics not an evolutionary science?" to Richard Nelson and Sidney Winter's landmark *An Evolutionary Theory of Economic Change* (1982). Evolutionary perspectives have been particularly influential in management science, beginning with the behavioral foundations of institutional evolution articulated by Richard M. Cyert and James G. March (1963) and extending to models of organizational adaptation and search (Kauffman 1969; Cohen, March, and Olsen 1972; Beinhocker 1999).

A contemporary of Cyert and March, Herbert Simon is a particularly important inspiration for complexity thinkers. His works "The Architecture of Complexity" (1962) and "The Organization of Complex Systems" (1973) provide theoretical foundations for understanding the hierarchical and modular nature of complex systems and how such structures scale in ways that are stable and adaptable. Simon (1955; 1978) also presents a view of human decision-making as a process of "boundedly rational" heuristic search rather than optimization.

Following Simon's critique of neoclassical rationality, behavioral economists such as Daniel Kahneman and Amos Tversky (1979) and Gerd Gigerenzer (1991; 1999) began to build a substantial body of empirical evidence as to how real human beings make economic decisions, behavioral foundations used extensively by later complexity economists.

Two of the tools most frequently used by modern complexity economists—agent-based modeling and network analysis—also had important antecedents. Barbara Bergmann (1971; 1990) lay early foundations for the complexity perspective and agent-based modeling in her arguments against representative agents (see also Kirman 1992) and their inability to model phenomena such as agent heterogeneity, inequality, power, and discrimination. Thomas Schelling's (1971) model of housing discrimination provides a simple example of emergent phenomena and is one of the earliest and most influential agent-based models in economics (implemented using pennies on a paper grid). The use of network analysis in economics also has historical antecedents, notably Wassily Leontief's examination of the input–output structure of the US economy (1936).

~ 31 ~

Another historically important idea for complexity economists is the view of the economy as an order-creating, metabolic system operating far from equilibrium. This perspective can be traced back to Karl Marx, who in *Capital* (1867, vol. I, ch. 7) described the labor process as "purposeful activity aimed at the production of use-values" and as "the universal condition for the metabolic interaction between man and nature, common to all forms of society in which human beings live." In the 1970s, the economist Nicholas Georgescu-Roegen, while critical of Marx on many points, shared the view that economics had largely ignored the economy's relationship with nature, energy, and fundamental thermodynamic constraints. In *The Entropy Law and the Economic Process* (1971), he argued that the economy is a thermodynamically open, nonequilibrium system, transforming materials, energy, and information into more complex outputs while irreversibly generating waste and entropy. This work laid the foundations for ecological economics (e.g., Daly 1977) and for a complexity-based understanding of economic growth and development as a disequilibrium process embedded in biophysical systems (e.g., Ayres 1994).

Crossing Disciplines and the Emergence of Complexity Economics

While social scientists were exploring these various streams of thought, the twentieth century saw major developments in the physical sciences in understanding what later came to be called "complex systems." These advances cut across multiple disciplines, including work on nonlinear dynamical systems (e.g., Edward Lorenz), statistical physics (e.g., Kenneth Wilson), self-organizing systems (e.g., Lars Onsager and Ilya Prigogine), mathematical evolutionary theory (e.g., Sewall Wright and John Maynard Smith), computation (e.g., Alan Turing and John von Neumann), information theory (e.g., Claude Shannon), fractal geometry and power laws (e.g., Benoît Mandelbrot), and graph theory (e.g., Paul Erdős and Alfréd Rényi).

Thus, when the Nobel economist Kenneth Arrow and Nobel physicist Philip Anderson convened ten economists and ten natural scientists at the now-famous meeting at the Santa Fe Institute in 1987, there was fertile intellectual soil to explore (Waldrop 1992). At that meeting, the eyes of the economists were opened to the powerful concepts and methods employed by the natural scientists for analyzing complex systems, and the eyes of the natural scientists were opened to the challenges the economists faced in developing testable theories and models of a human social system as complex as the global economy.

The meeting yielded the first volume in this series, *The Economy as an Evolving Complex System* (1988), and launched a program of research at SFI, first directed by W. Brian Arthur, with funding support from then-CEO of Citigroup, John Reed.

The program was later directed through the 1990s by John Geanakoplos, Blake LeBaron, Lawrence Blume, and Steven Durlauf, with major contributions from J. Doyne Farmer, Samuel Bowles, and others.

Artificial Economies—the Development of Agent-Based Modeling

Foundational to this movement was the introduction of agent-based modeling (ABM) as a rigorous tool for economic inquiry (for an in-depth review, see Axtell and Farmer 2025). John H. Holland and John H. Miller (1991) offered an early manifesto for "Artificial Adaptive Agents," arguing that complex adaptive systems could model the evolution of economic behavior in ways traditional equilibrium analysis with representative agents could not (consistent with the other critiques mentioned, Bergmann 1971 and Kirman 1992). One of the early outputs of the ABM program was a collaboration between Brian Arthur, John Holland, Blake LeBaron, Richard Palmer, and Paul Tayler to build the Santa Fe Artificial Stock Market model (Arthur *et al.* 1997), demonstrating that ABMs could replicate key statistical emergent features of financial markets from bottom-up simulation of the interactions of heterogeneous agents.

~33~

   Moving from financial markets to more general economic and social phenomena, Joshua M. Epstein and Robert Axtell's *Growing Artificial Societies: Social Science from the Bottom Up* (1996) introduced the influential Sugarscape model. In Sugarscape, simple agents follow local rules for movement, consumption, reproduction, and trade on a spatial landscape, yet generate complex macro phenomena such as wealth inequality, price formation, migration, and social stratification. The book demonstrated that macroeconomic and social regularities can be explained as emergent outcomes of micro-level interaction, without equilibrium assumptions or representative agents, helping motivate a significant body of ABM work in the decades that followed.

During the same period, economists William Brock and Cars Hommes (1998) provided an analytical counterpart to the SFI computational models, examining how the nonlinear dynamics of heterogeneous beliefs in a population of agents could lead to instabilities in financial markets (preceded by related work; see Chiarella 1992). These papers laid the foundation for further work by figures such as J. Doyne Farmer, Thomas Lux, and Jean-Philippe Bouchaud, showing that financial agent-based models could quantitatively replicate the statistical properties of real markets (e.g., Lux and Marchesi 1999; Farmer and Joshi 2002; Giardina and Bouchaud 2003).

In the 2000s, ABM work began to branch from financial markets into macroeconomics. Two economists helped lay important theoretical groundwork for that line of research. Axel Leijonhufvud (1981) reframed macroeconomies as coordination systems operating far from equilibrium, where instability arises endogenously from information failures, decentralized decision-making, and nonlinear adjustment processes rather than solely from exogenous shocks.

Alan Kirman (1992, 2010) systematically criticized the representative-agent paradigm that was foundational in macroeconomics and demonstrated that aggregate economic outcomes emerge from interacting heterogeneous agents, often in ways that cannot be inferred from individual behavior alone. He further showed how coordination failures, herd behavior, and nonlinear dynamics arise endogenously in markets.

Building on this theoretical work, economists including Stefano Cincotti and Herbert Dawid engaged in an ambitious large-scale model building project of the European economy called EURACE (Cincotti, Raberto, and Teglio 2010); Domenico Delli Gatti, Mauro Gallegati, and collaborators worked towards building a general macroeconomic ABM that could challenge widely used dynamic stochastic general equilibrium (DSGE) models (Delli Gatti *et al.* 2005; Delli Gatti *et al.* 2011). Around the same period, another Italian economist, Giovanni Dosi, and colleagues pioneered the use of ABMs to look at questions of economic growth integrating Keynesian demand fluctuations and Schumpeterian growth dynamics (Dosi, Fagiolo, and Roventini 2010).

~ 35 ~

Another early pioneer in agent-based modeling was Leigh Tesfatsion (2002), who articulated a methodology for what she called ACE (agent-based computational economics), set out best practices for model design and validation, and created infrastructure (tutorials, software resources, and edited collections) that made ABM more accessible to economists and students. Tesfatsion's work emphasized the use of ACE for both positive theory (explaining emergence, distributional outcomes, and disequilibrium dynamics) and policy experiments (what-if counterfactuals, regulation, and institutional design), creating a bridge with more orthodox economic methods (Tesfatsion and Judd 2006).

ABMs were also employed to study a variety of microeconomic phenomena. Kirman and Nicolas Vriend (2001) provided one of the earliest empirically grounded agent-based interpretations of market organization with their study of the Marseille fish market. That work showed how real-world markets operate through social learning and repeated interaction, rather than anonymous Walrasian price-taking. Other ABMs of individual markets included the liberalization of electricity markets (Nicolaisen, Petrov, and Tesfatsion 2001) and a detailed study of housing markets (Geanakoplos *et al.* 2012; Axtell *et al.* 2014) that analyzed the endogenous emergence of housing bubbles and tested policies for mitigating them (Baptista *et al.* 2016).

Agent-based models with many agents and realistic institutional complexity also provided motivation for further theoretical work. Game theory is a core tool in economics for exploring strategic interactions. Standard game theory assumes convergence to fixed points such as Nash equilibria, but Yuzuru Sato, Eizo Akiyama, and Farmer (2002) showed that, under bounded rationality, games may fail to converge to fixed-point equilibria and instead follow chaotic trajectories in the strategy space. Subsequently, Marco Pangallo, Torsten Heinrich, and Farmer (2019) revealed that such chaotic behavior is generic for competitive, complicated normal-form games. As most real-world economic phenomena can be characterized as competitive, complex, multiplayer games, this work provides important theoretical foundations for agent-based modeling, which doesn't assume equilibrium convergence and is arguably the only method that can faithfully model such real-world complexity.

Agent Ecologies, Scaling, and Networks

But ABMs were far from the only methodology employed by the growing community of complexity economists. W. Brian Arthur's highly influential "El Farol" paper (1994) demonstrated how a simple deterministic model of agents with heterogeneous expectations could produce complex endogenous fluctuations. The El Farol model was later formalized and generalized by Damien Challet and Yi-Cheng Zhang (1997) into the "minority game," helping launch an "econophysics" analytical literature studying economic fluctuations, phase transitions, and emergent order.

Other researchers demonstrated how "ecologies of expectations" (as Arthur put it) could evolve as agents updated decision rules, learned from their environment and each other, and evolved. Physicist Kristian Lindgren (1991) provided a pioneering example demonstrating how evolving, interacting strategies in a population of agents playing the prisoner's dilemma could generate complex emergent dynamics that never settle to equilibrium. Another example is J. Doyne Farmer's work on market ecologies (Farmer 2002; Scholl, Calinescu, and Farmer 2021) showing how the heterogeneous and evolving strategies of populations of agents in markets interact, and providing explanations for key market dynamics, including market malfunctions.

In many of these systems of dynamically interacting, heterogeneous agents, scaling laws emerged as a macroscopic regularity. Vilfredo Pareto's 1890 characterization of income distributions is usually credited as the first observation of a power law in economics. Linguist George Kingsley Zipf in the 1930s observed that city sizes, firm sizes, and other phenomena follow an inverse rank-size rule known as Zipf's law. The complexity community built on these foundations; Xavier Gabaix (1999, 2009) observed Zipf's law in city size distributions and financial market statistical properties and linked these empirical observations to stochastic growth processes.

Robert Axtell (2001) went on to show empirically that US firm sizes follow a Zipf distribution, and later demonstrated that this regularity holds robustly across countries, industries, and time (2006). He argued that this scaling law is an emergent property of simple, institutionally realistic microeconomic behaviors. It arises from heterogeneous agents interacting through labor reallocation under local increasing returns, generating persistent disequilibrium dynamics rather than convergence to equilibrium.

Scaling laws are familiar territory to physicists; the physicist Geoffrey West, along with an interdisciplinary group of collaborators, showed empirically that cities and other social systems obey systematic scaling laws analogous to those found in biology, revealing deep regularities in how social, economic, and infrastructural quantities grow with system size (West, Brown, and Enquist 1997; Bettencourt *et al.* 2007; West 2017). The work demonstrates strong relationships between social interaction density and economic productivity, innovation, and inequality, with important implications for the role of urbanization in economic development.

The growing complexity-economics community has also embraced the adoption of network-based approaches in economics. This shift led both to detailed empirical characterizations of economic networks (Schweitzer *et al.* 2009) and to formal game-theoretic analyses of network formation and structure (Vega-Redondo 2007; Jackson 2008). An influential early line of research drew on insights from self-organized criticality (Bak, Tang, and Wiesenfeld 1988) and strategic complementarities (Durlauf 1993) to explain how microeconomic shocks can generate aggregate fluctuations through heavy-tailed distributions (Gabaix 2011) and network-mediated amplification mechanisms (Acemoglu *et al.* 2012). Other work (Jackson and Wolinsky 1996; Jackson 2008) formalized how economic networks form, how they shape diffusion and inequality, and how local interactions generate large aggregate effects.

Network-based complexity approaches had an important impact on conceptualizing and modeling financial stability and systemic risk. For example, Michael Boss *et al.* (2004) empirically characterized interbank lending networks as heterogeneous systems with power-law degree distributions, discussing how such structures generate systemic fragility. Network models of systemic risk gained particular prominence in the aftermath of the 2008 global financial crisis (e.g., Battiston *et al.* 2012; Thurner and Poledna 2013; Caccioli *et al.* 2014). For a comprehensive review, see Fabio Caccioli (2026; ch. 16 in this volume).

Another influential research program applies network analysis to the study of economic growth and development. Ricardo Hausmann and César Hidalgo introduced the Economic Complexity Index, which reveals how a country's long-run growth prospects are strongly shaped by its stock of productive knowledge. This knowledge is inferred from the structure of a bipartite network linking countries to the products they export, with greater product diversity and sophistication indicating greater underlying capabilities (Hidalgo *et al.* 2007; Hausmann *et al.* 2011). This framework is synthesized in *The Atlas of Economic Complexity* (Hausmann *et al.* 2014), which formalizes the concept of an economy's "product space"—the set of products a country is able to produce. The analysis emphasizes the path-dependent accumulation of capabilities: countries tend to diversify into products that are closely related to those they already produce, gradually expanding into more complex sectors. Over time, this process is associated with higher value added and rising standards of living, beyond what is explained by traditional factors such as capital accumulation or institutional
quality.

Building on this work, Luciano Pietronero and coauthors developed the fitness–complexity algorithm, offering an alternative network-based measure (Tacchella *et al.* 2012; Cristelli, Tacchella, and Pietronero 2015). Together, these contributions brought concepts of economic complexity and networks of capabilities (or industrial clusters or ecosystems) into discussions of economic growth, development, and policy.

The Meso Level: Technology and Institutions

While pioneering work was done to understand macro phenomena such as growth, instabilities, and distributions, along with micro-level work to understand market function, another group of scholars focused on the meso level, deepening our understanding of technology innovation and the evolution of institutions.

An early contribution is the volume edited by Giovanni Dosi *et al.* (1988), whose papers argue that innovation is an evolutionary, path-dependent, and institutionally embedded process, not a smooth response to prices or incentives, and explicitly challenges equilibrium and representative-agent approaches to modeling technological change.

W. Brian Arthur's *The Nature of Technology* (2009) offers a foundational theory, describing technology as an evolving, combinatorial system in which new technologies arise largely from the recombination of existing components rather than from *de novo* invention. Arthur shows how this recursive, modular process generates path dependence, increasing returns, and structural change, providing a micro-founded basis for theories of endogenous growth and economic evolution (see Arthur 2026, ch. 3 in this volume).

Of course, the other key factor in long-run economic growth is the development of institutions. Complexity researchers have played a central role in reframing cooperation and institutions as endogenous, evolving outcomes of strategic interaction, rather than simply assuming institutions as exogenous constraints or inevitable equilibrium outcomes.

Robert Axelrod (1984) lays important foundations with his work on the evolution of cooperation, most famously through his tournament of agents playing an iterated prisoner's dilemma. This work highlights the importance of reciprocity, reputation, and population structure, showing how adaptive strategies interacting over time can generate stable cooperative norms.

Samuel Bowles and Herbert Gintis have integrated evolutionary game theory, and collaborations with behavioral economists, anthropologists, and biologists, to show that cooperation can be sustained through social preferences, norms, and institutional enforcement, even when standard self-interest models predict defection (Bowles 1998; Bowles and Gintis 2011; Henrich *et al.* 2001; Henrich *et al.* 2004). Bowles combines methods from empirical population genetics and evolutionary game theory to show that a genetic disposition for individuals to behave altruistically towards in-group members could have coevolved with hostility towards "outsiders" and frequent group conflict (Bowles 2006; Choi and Bowles 2007).

Their work demonstrates that preferences themselves are shaped by evolutionary biological and cultural processes, and that markets, states, and communities co-evolve through feedback between incentives and norms (Bowles 2004). This perspective challenges the sharp separation between economics and sociology by treating institutions as adaptive mechanisms that stabilize cooperation in complex societies (Gintis 2016).

A complementary line of research on the evolution of institutions and norms was developed by H. Peyton Young, who provides rigorous game-theoretic foundations for how conventions, norms, and institutional rules emerge (Young 1993, 1998). Young demonstrated that when self-interested agents adjust their behavior through learning, imitation, and experimentation, collective outcomes depend on historical paths rather than converging to a unique equilibrium. This provides a formal explanation for why norms and institutions can be stable across diverse societies.

From 2001 to 2020, an annual SFI working group led by Bowles, Gintis, and Young, along with anthropologist Robert Boyd and economist Larry Blume, explored related themes under the title "The Coevolution of Individual Behaviors and Social Institutions."

Inequalities are an emergent result of institutional arrangements, technologies, and behaviors. Starting in 2006, Bowles and anthropologist Monique Borgerhoff Mulder led the cross-disciplinary "Dynamics of Wealth Inequality" project. This group has used a combination of dynamical-systems methods and network theory along with data from prehistory, recent small-scale societies, and other sources, to better understand the cultural, institutional, and technological forces driving economic disparities in the long run (Borgerhoff Mulder *et al.* 2009; Bowles and Fochesato 2024).

Finally, at the intersection of behavior, cooperation, and institutions, Scott Page has shown that groups of agents with diverse perspectives can outperform homogeneous groups of individually "optimal" decision-makers, challenging representative-agent logic (Page 2007). His work provides rigorous foundations for the role of cognitive diversity and decentralized problem-solving in enhancing institutional performance and system resilience (Page 2010).

From Critique to Innovation, Insight, and Relevance

The trajectory of complexity economics traces a shift from early conceptual critiques of equilibrium, rationality, and representative-agent models toward a mature, empirically grounded science of economic systems. Over several decades, researchers have developed new theoretical frameworks, computational tools, and empirical methods capable of capturing heterogeneity, behavioral and institutional realism, dynamics, path dependence, and emergence—first in stylized models and increasingly in data-rich, empirically validated analysis. What began as an exploratory synthesis of ideas from economics, physics, and other social and physical sciences has now grown into a coherent research program with demonstrated relevance for understanding markets, growth, systemic risk, inequality, institutions, technology, and climate change.

The chapters in this volume build on this intellectual history—and include contributions from a number of figures cited in this review—showcasing recent advances, and pointing toward the next phase of complexity economics: one focused not only on explanation, but also on better prediction, more effective interventions, and supporting the evolution of prosperous, just, and sustainable economic systems. ⚡

REFERENCES

Acemoglu, D., V. M. Carvalho, A. Ozdaglar, and A. Tahbaz-Salehi. 2012. "The Network Origins of Aggregate Fluctuations." *Econometrica* 80 (5): 1977–2016. https://doi.org/10.3982/ECTA9623.

Anderson, P. W., K. J. Arrow, and D. Pines, eds. 1988. *The Economy as an Evolving Complex System*. Reading, MA: Addison-Wesley.

Arthur, W. B. 1994. "Inductive Reasoning and Bounded Rationality." *American Economic Review* 84 (2): 406–411. https://www.jstor.org/stable/2117868.

———. 1999. "Complexity and the Economy." *Science* 284 (5411): 107–109. https://doi.org/10.1126/science.284.5411.107.

Arthur, W. B. 2009. *The Nature of Technology: What It Is and How It Evolves.* New York, NY: Free Press.

———. 2021. "Foundations of Complexity Economics." *Nature Reviews Physics* 3:136–145. https://doi.org/10.1038/s42254-020-00273-3.

———. 2026. "Combinatorial Evolution." In *The Economy as an Evolving Complex System IV,* edited by R. M. del Rio-Chanona, M. Pangallo, J. Bednar, E. D. Beinhocker, J. Kaszowska-Mojsa, F. Lafond, P. Mealy, A. Pichler, and J. D. Farmer. Santa Fe, NM: SFI Press.

Arthur, W. B., J. H. Holland, B. LeBaron, R. Palmer, and P. Tayler. 1997. "Asset Pricing Under Endogenous Expectations in an Artificial Stock Market." In *The Economy as an Evolving Complex System II.* Reading, MA: Addison-Wesley.

Axelrod, R. 1984. *The Evolution of Cooperation.* New York, NY: Basic Books.

Axtell, R. L. 2001. "Zipf Distribution of U.S. Firm Sizes." *Science* 293 (5536): 1818–1820. https://doi.org/10.1126/science.1062081.

———. 2006. *Firm Sizes: Facts, Formulae, Fables and Fantasies.* Technical report 44. Brookings Institution, Center on Social and Economic Dynamics. https://doi.org/10.2139/ssrn.1024813.

———. 2016. "Hayek Enriched by Complexity Enriched by Hayek." In *Revisiting Hayek's Political Economy,* edited by P. J. Boettke and V. H. Storr, vol. 21. Advances in Austrian Economics. Leeds, UK: Emerald Group Publishing Limited. https://doi.org/10.1108/S1529-213420160000021003.

Axtell, R. L., and J. D. Farmer. 2025. "Agent-Based Modeling in Economics and Finance: Past, Present, and Future." *Journal of Economic Literature* 63 (1): 197–287. https://doi.org/10.1257/jel.20221319.

Axtell, R. L., J. D. Farmer, J. Geanakoplos, P. Howitt, E. Carrella, B. Conlee, J. Goldstein, *et al.* 2014. "An Agent-Based Model of the Housing Market Bubble in Metropolitan Washington, DC." *SSRN Electronic Journal,* https://doi.org/10.2139/ssrn.4710928.

Ayres, R. U. 1994. *Information, Entropy, and Progress: A New Evolutionary Paradigm.* Woodbury, NY: American Institute of Physics Press.

Bak, P., C. Tang, and K. Wiesenfeld. 1988. "Self-Organized Criticality." *Physical Review A* 38 (1): 364–374. https://doi.org/10.1103/PhysRevA.38.364.

Baptista, R., J. D. Farmer, M. Hinterschweiger, K. Low, D. Tang, and A. Uluc. 2016. *Macroprudential Policy in an Agent-Based Model of the UK Housing Market.* Bank of England, Working Paper no. 619. https://doi.org/10.2139/ssrn. 2850414.

Battiston, S., M. Puliga, R. Kaushik, P. Tasca, and G. Caldarelli. 2012. "DebtRank: Too Central to Fail? Financial Networks, the FED and Systemic Risk." *Scientific Reports* 2 (1): 541. https://doi.org/10.1038/srep00541.

Beinhocker, E. D. 1999. "Robust Adaptive Strategies." *Sloan Management Review* 40 (3): 95–106.

———. 2006. *The Origin of Wealth: Evolution, Complexity, and the Radical Remaking of Economics.* Boston, MA: Harvard Business School Press.

Bergmann, B. R. 1971. "The Effect on White Incomes of Discrimination in Employment." *Journal of Political Economy* 79 (2): 294–313. https://doi.org/ 10.1086/259744.

———. 1990. "Micro-to-Macro Simulation: A Primer with a Labor Market Example." *Journal of Economic Perspectives* 4 (1): 99–116. https://doi.org/ 10.1257/jep.4.1.99.

Bettencourt, L. M. A., J. Lobo, D. Helbing, C. Kühnert, and G. B. West. 2007. "Growth, Innovation, Scaling, and the Pace of Life in Cities." *Proceedings of the National Academy of Sciences* 104 (17): 7301–7306. https://doi.org/10. 1073/pnas.0610172104.

Borgerhoff Mulder, M., S. Bowles, T. Hertz, A. Bell, J. Beise, G. Clark, I. Fazzio, *et al.* 2009. "Intergenerational Wealth Transmission and the Dynamics of Inequality in Small-Scale Societies." *Science* 326 (5953): 682–688. https://doi.org/10. 1126/science.1178336.

Boss, M., H. Elsinger, M. Summer, and S. Thurner. 2004. "Network Topology of the Interbank Market." *Quantitative Finance* 4 (6): 677–684. https://doi.org/10. 1080/14697680400020325.

Bowles, S. 1998. "Endogenous Preferences: The Cultural Consequences of Markets and other Economic Institutions." *Journal of Economic Literature* 36 (1): 75– 111. https://www.jstor.org/stable/2564952.

———. 2004. *Microeconomics: Behavior, Institutions, and Evolution.* Princeton, NJ: Princeton University Press.

Bowles, S. 2006. "Group Competition, Reproductive Leveling, and the Evolution of Human Altruism." *Science* 314 (5805): 1569–1572. https://doi.org/10.1126/science.1134829.

Bowles, S., and M. Fochesato. 2024. "The Origins of Enduring Economic Inequality." *Journal of Economic Literature* 62 (4): 1475–1537. https://doi.org/10.1257/jel.20241718.

Bowles, S., and H. Gintis. 2011. *A Cooperative Species: Human Cooperation and Its Evolution.* Princeton, NJ: Princeton University Press.

Bowles, S., A. Kirman, and R. Sethi. 2017. "Retrospectives: Friedrich Hayek and the Market Algorithm." *Journal of Economic Perspectives* 31 (3): 215–230. https://doi.org/10.1257/jep.31.3.215.

Brock, W. A., and C. H. Hommes. 1998. "Heterogeneous Beliefs and Routes to Chaos in a Simple Asset Pricing Model." *Journal of Economic Dynamics and Control* 22 (8–9): 1235–1274. https://doi.org/10.1016/S0165-1889(98)00011-6.

Caccioli, F. 2026. "Understanding Financial Contagion: A Complexity-Modeling Perspective." In *The Economy as an Evolving Complex System IV,* edited by R. M. del Rio-Chanona, M. Pangallo, J. Bednar, E. D. Beinhocker, J. Kaszowska-Mojsa, F. Lafond, P. Mealy, A. Pichler, and J. D. Farmer. Santa Fe, NM: SFI Press.

Caccioli, F., M. Shrestha, C. Moore, and J. D. Farmer. 2014. "Stability Analysis of Financial Contagion Due to Overlapping Portfolios." *Journal of Banking & Finance* 46:233–245. https://doi.org/10.1016/j.jbankfin.2014.05.021.

Challet, D., and Y.-C. Zhang. 1997. "Emergence of Cooperation and Organization in an Evolutionary Game." *Physica A* 246 (3–4): 407–418. https://doi.org/10.1016/S0378-4371(97)00419-6.

Chiarella, C. 1992. "The Dynamics of Speculative Behavior." *Annals of Operations Research* 37:101–123. https://doi.org/10.1007/BF02071051.

Choi, J.-K., and S. Bowles. 2007. "The Coevolution of Parochial Altruism and War." *Science* 318 (5850): 636–640. https://doi.org/10.1126/science.1144237.

Cincotti, S., M. Raberto, and A. Teglio. 2010. "Credit Money and Macroeconomic Instability in the Agent-Based Model and Simulator EURACE." *Economics: The Open-Access, Open-Assessment E-Journal* 4 (1): 20100026. https://doi.org/10.5018/economics-ejournal.ja.2010-26.

Chapter 2: A Brief History of the Emergence of Complexity Economics

Cohen, M. D., J. G. March, and J. P. Olsen. 1972. "A Garbage Can Model of Organizational Choice." *Administrative Science Quarterly* 17 (1): 1–25. https://doi.org/10.2307/2392088.

Cristelli, M., A. Tacchella, and L. Pietronero. 2015. "The Heterogeneous Dynamics of Economic Complexity." *PLoS ONE* 10 (2): e0117174. https://doi.org/10.1371/journal.pone.0117174.

Cyert, R. M., and J. G. March. 1963. *A Behavioral Theory of the Firm.* Englewood Cliffs, NJ: Prentice Hall.

Daly, H. E. 1977. *Steady-State Economics.* San Francisco, CA: W. H. Freeman & Co.

Delli Gatti, D., S. Desiderio, E. Gaffeo, P. Cirillo, and M. Gallegati. 2011. *Macroeconomics from the Bottom-Up.* Berlin, Germany: Springer.

Delli Gatti, D., C. Di Guilmi, E. Gaffeo, G. Giulioni, M. Gallegati, and A. Palestrini. 2005. "A New Approach to Business Fluctuations: Heterogeneous Interacting Agents, Scaling Laws and Financial Fragility." *Journal of Economic Behavior & Organization* 56 (4): 489–512. https://doi.org/10.1016/j.jebo.2003.10.012.

Dosi, G., G. Fagiolo, and A. Roventini. 2010. "Schumpeter Meeting Keynes: A Policy-Friendly Model of Endogenous Growth and Business Cycles." *Journal of Economic Dynamics and Control* 34 (9): 1748–1767. https://doi.org/10.1016/j.jedc.2010.06.018.

Dosi, G., C. Freeman, R. Nelson, G. Silverberg, and L. Soete, eds. 1988. *Technical Change and Economic Theory.* London, UK: Pinter.

Durlauf, S. N. 1993. "Nonergodic Economic Growth." *Review of Economic Studies* 60 (2): 349–366. https://doi.org/10.2307/2298061.

Epstein, J. M., and R. Axtell. 1996. *Growing Artificial Societies.* Cambridge, MA: MIT Press.

Farmer, J. D. 2002. "Market Force, Ecology and Evolution." *Industrial and Corporate Change* 11 (5): 895–953. https://doi.org/10.1093/icc/11.5.895.

Farmer, J. D., and S. Joshi. 2002. "Price Dynamics of Common Trading Strategies." *Journal of Economic Behavior & Organization* 49 (2): 149–171. https://doi.org/10.1016/S0167-2681(02)00065-3.

Ferguson, A. 1767 [1979]. *An Essay on the History of Civil Society.* Edinburgh, UK: Edinburgh University Press.

~ 47 ~

Gabaix, X. 1999. "Zipf's Law for Cities: An Explanation." *Quarterly Journal of Economics* 114 (3): 739–767. https://doi.org/10.1162/003355399556133.

———. 2009. "Power Laws in Economics and Finance." *Annual Review of Economics* 1 (1): 255–294. https://doi.org/10.1146/annurev.economics.050708.142940.

———. 2011. "The Granular Origins of Aggregate Fluctuations." *Econometrica* 79 (3): 733–772. https://doi.org/10.3982/ECTA8769.

Geanakoplos, J., R. Axtell, J. D. Farmer, P. Howitt, B. Conlee, J. Goldstein, M. Hendrey, N. M. Palmer, and C.-Y. Yang. 2012. "Getting at Systemic Risk via an Agent-Based Model of the Housing Market." *American Economic Review* 102 (3): 53–58. https://doi.org/10.1257/aer.102.3.53.

Georgescu-Roegen, N. 1971. *The Entropy Law and the Economic Process.* Cambridge, MA: Harvard University Press.

Giardina, I., and J.-P. Bouchaud. 2003. "Bubbles, Crashes and Intermittency in Agent-Based Market Models." *The European Physical Journal B* 31:421–437. https://doi.org/10.1140/epjb/e2003-00050-6.

Gigerenzer, G. 1991. "How to Make Cognitive Illusions Disappear." *European Review of Social Psychology* 2 (1): 83–115. https://doi.org/10.1080/14792779143000033.

Gigerenzer, G., P. M. Todd, and the ABC Research Group. 1999. *Simple Heuristics That Make Us Smart.* Oxford, UK: Oxford University Press.

Gintis, H. 2016. *Individuality and Entanglement: The Moral and Material Bases of Social Life.* Princeton, NJ: Princeton University Press.

Hausmann, R., C. A. Hidalgo, S. Bustos, M. Coscia, S. Chung, J. Jimenez, A. Simoes, and M. A. Yildirim. 2011. *The Atlas of Economic Complexity: Mapping Paths to Prosperity.* Hollis, NH: Puritan Press.

Hausmann, R., C. A. Hidalgo, S. Bustos, M. Coscia, A. Simoes, and M. A. Yildirim. 2014. *The Atlas of Economic Complexity: Mapping Paths to Prosperity.* Cambridge, MA: MIT Press.

Hayek, F. A. 1945. "The Use of Knowledge in Society." *American Economic Review* 35 (4): 519–530. https://www.jstor.org/stable/1809376.

Henrich, J., R. Boyd, S. Bowles, C. Camerer, E. Fehr, and H. Gintis. 2004. *Foundations of Human Sociality: Economic Experiments and Ethnographic Evidence from Fifteen Small-Scale Societies.* Oxford, UK: Oxford University Press.

Henrich, J., R. Boyd, S. Bowles, C. Camerer, E. Fehr, H. Gintis, and R. McElreath. 2001. "In Search of Homo Economicus: Behavioral Experiments in 15 Small-Scale Societies." *American Economic Review* 91 (2): 73–78. https://doi.org/10.1257/aer.91.2.73.

Hidalgo, C. A., B. Klinger, A.-L. Barabási, and R. Hausmann. 2007. "The Product Space Conditions the Development of Nations." *Science* 317 (5837): 482–487. https://doi.org/10.1126/science.1144581.

Hodgson, G. M. 1993. *Economics and Evolution: Bringing Life Back into Economics.* Ann Arbor, MI: University of Michigan Press.

Holland, J. H., and J. H. Miller. 1991. "Artificial Adaptive Agents in Economic Theory." *American Economic Review* 81 (2): 365–371. https://econpapers.repec.org/RePEc:aea:aecrev:v:81:y:1991:i:2:p:365-71.

Islahi, A. A., and S. M. Ghazanfar. 2011. *Economic Thought of al-Ghazālī.* MPRA Paper 53465, University Library of Munich. https://mpra.ub.uni-muenchen.de/53465/.

Jackson, M. O. 2008. *Social and Economic Networks.* Princeton, NJ: Princeton University Press.

Jackson, M. O., and A. Wolinsky. 1996. "A Strategic Model of Social and Economic Networks." *Journal of Economic Theory* 71 (1): 44–74. https://doi.org/10.1006/jeth.1996.0108.

Kahneman, D., and A. Tversky. 1979. "Prospect Theory: An Analysis of Decision Under Risk." *Econometrica* 47 (2): 263–291. https://doi.org/10.2307/1914185.

Kauffman, S. A. 1969. "Metabolic Stability and Epigenesis in Randomly Constructed Genetic Nets." *Journal of Theoretical Biology* 22 (3): 437–467. https://doi.org/10.1016/0022-5193(69)90015-0.

Kennedy, G. 2009. "Adam Smith and the Invisible Hand: From Metaphor to Myth." *Economic Journal Watch* 6 (2): 239–263.

Kirman, A. 1992. "Whom or What Does the Representative Individual Represent?" *Journal of Economic Perspectives* 6 (2): 117–136. https://doi.org/10.1257/jep.6.2.117.

———. 2010. *Complex Economics: Individual and Collective Rationality.* London, UK: Routledge.

Kirman, A. P., and N. J. Vriend. 2001. "Evolving Market Structure: An ACE Model of Price Dispersion and Loyalty." *Journal of Economic Dynamics and Control* 25 (3–4): 459–502. https://doi.org/10.1016/S0165-1889(00)00033-6.

Leijonhufvud, A. 1981. *Information and Coordination.* New York, NY: Oxford University Press.

Leontief, W. 1936. "Quantitative Input and Output Relations in the Economic Systems of the United State." *Review of Economics and Statistics* 18 (3): 105–125. https://doi.org/10.2307/1927837.

Lindgren, K. 1991. "Evolutionary Phenomena in Simple Dynamics." In *Artificial Life II,* edited by C. G. Langton, C. Taylor, J. D. Farmer, and S. Rasmussen, 295–312. Reading, MA: Addison-Wesley.

Lux, T., and M. Marchesi. 1999. "Scaling and Criticality in a Stochastic Multi-Agent Model of a Financial Market." *Nature* 397:498–500. https://doi.org/10.1038/17290.

Mealy, P., J. Bednar, E. D. Beinhocker, R. M. del Rio-Chanona, J. D. Farmer, J. Kaszowska-Mojsa, F. Lafond, M. Pangallo, and A. Pichler. 2026. "Introduction." In *The Economy as an Evolving Complex System IV,* edited by R. M. del Rio-Chanona, M. Pangallo, J. Bednar, E. D. Beinhocker, J. Kaszowska-Mojsa, F. Lafond, P. Mealy, A. Pichler, and J. D. Farmer. Santa Fe, NM: SFI Press.

Nelson, R. R., and S. G. Winter. 1982. *An Evolutionary Theory of Economic Change.* Cambridge, MA: Harvard University Press.

Nicolaisen, J., V. Petrov, and L. Tesfatsion. 2001. "Market Power and Efficiency in a Computational Electricity Market with Discriminatory Double-Auction Pricing." *IEEE Transactions on Evolutionary Computation* 5 (5): 504–523. https://doi.org/10.1109/4235.956714.

Page, S. E. 2007. *The Difference.* Princeton, NJ: Princeton University Press.

———. 2010. *Diversity and Complexity.* Princeton, NJ: Princeton University Press.

Pangallo, M., T. Heinrich, and J. D. Farmer. 2019. "Best Reply Structure and Equilibrium Convergence in Generic Games." *Science Advances* 5 (2): eaat1328. https://doi.org/10.1126/sciadv.aat1328.

Rothschild, E. 1994. "Adam Smith and the Invisible Hand." *American Economic Review* 84 (2): 319–322. https://www.jstor.org/stable/2117851.

Sato, Y., E. Akiyama, and J. D. Farmer. 2002. "Chaos in Learning a Simple Two-Person Game." *Proceedings of the National Academy of Sciences* 99 (7): 4748–4751. https://doi.org/10.1073/pnas.032086299.

Schelling, T. C. 1971. "Dynamic Models of Segregation." *Journal of Mathematical Sociology* 1 (2): 143–186. https://doi.org/10.1080/0022250X.1971.9989794.

Scholl, A., A. Calinescu, and J. D. Farmer. 2021. "How Market Ecology Explains Market Malfunction." *Proceedings of the National Academy of Sciences* 118 (39). https://ideas.repec.org/a/nas/journl/v118y2021pe2015574118.html.

Schumpeter, J. A. [1911]1934. *The Theory of Economic Development*. Cambridge, MA: Harvard University Press.

Schweitzer, F., G. Fagiolo, D. Sornette, F. Vega-Redondo, A. Vespignani, and D. R. White. 2009. "Economic Networks: The New Challenges." *Science* 325 (5939): 422–425. https://doi.org/10.1126/science.1173644.

Simon, H. A. 1955. "A Behavioral Model of Rational Choice." *Quarterly Journal of Economics* 69 (1): 99–118. https://doi.org/10.2307/1884852.

———. 1962. "The Architecture of Complexity." *Proceedings of the American Philosophical Society* 106 (6): 467–482. https://www.jstor.org/stable/985254.

———. 1973. "The Organization of Complex Systems." In *Hierarchy Theory*, edited by H. H. Pattee, 1–27. New York: George Braziller.

———. 1978. "Rationality as Process and as Product of Thought." *American Economic Review* 68 (2): 1–16. https://www.jstor.org/stable/1816653.

Smith, A. [1977]1776. *An Inquiry into the Nature and Causes of the Wealth of Nations*. Chicago, IL: University of Chicago Press.

Tacchella, A., M. Cristelli, G. Caldarelli, A. Gabrielli, and L. Pietronero. 2012. "A New Metrics for Countries' Fitness and Products' Complexity." *Scientific Reports* 2:723. https://doi.org/10.1038/srep00723.

Tesfatsion, L. 2002. "Agent-Based Computational Economics: Growing Economies from the Bottom Up." *Artificial Life* 8 (1): 55–82. https://doi.org/10.1162/106454602753694765.

Tesfatsion, L., and K. L. Judd, eds. 2006. *Handbook of Computational Economics, Volume 2.* Amsterdam, Netherlands: Elsevier.

Thurner, S., and S. Poledna. 2013. "DebtRank-Transparency: Controlling Systemic Risk in Financial Networks." *Scientific Reports* 3 (1): 1888. https://doi.org/10.1038/srep01888.

Veblen, T. 1898. "Why Is Economics Not an Evolutionary Science?" *Quarterly Journal of Economics* 12 (4): 373–397. https://doi.org/10.2307/1882952.

Vega-Redondo, F. 2007. *Complex Social Networks.* Cambridge, UK: Cambridge University Press.

Waldrop, M. 1992. *Complexity: The Emerging Science at the Edge of Order and Chaos.* New York, NY: Simon & Schuster.

West, G. B. 2017. *Scale: The Universal Laws of Growth, Innovation, Sustainability, and the Pace of Life in Organisms, Cities, Economies, and Companies.* New York: Penguin Press.

West, G. B., J. H. Brown, and B. J. Enquist. 1997. "A General Model for the Origin of Allometric Scaling Laws in Biology." *Science* 276 (5309): 122–126. https://doi.org/10.1126/science.276.5309.122.

Young, H. P. 1993. "The Evolution of Conventions." *Econometrica* 61 (1): 57–84. https://doi.org/10.2307/2951778.

———. 1998. *Individual Strategy and Social Structure.* Princeton, NJ: Princeton University Press.

PART III

Macroeconomic Dynamics & Finance

REFLECTIONS ON ECONOPHYSICS' CONTRIBUTIONS TO FINANCE

Rosario N. Mantegna, Università degli Studi di Palermo and Complexity Science Hub

Abstract

This chapter discusses how econophysics, influenced by statistical physics, has shaped its research focus in finance by identifying empirical stylized facts in financial markets and using them to guide model development. I comment on the efficient market hypothesis, noting that it generally holds for short-term return dynamics in mature, liquid markets and that econophysicists view it as an idealized model. By recognizing market heterogeneity and the deviations that can be empirically observed, I suggest that the adaptive market hypothesis offers a more flexible framework that considers the diverse strategies and behaviors of different investors, who adapt to changing market conditions and contribute to price discovery. Econophysics has also promoted granular analysis of individual trading behavior. Such an analysis offers insights into the metaphor of a market ecology. Finland, with its unique daily tracking of financial asset ownership, serves as a valuable "laboratory" for studying investor behavior. Similar granular research helps develop heuristics for price-discovery mechanisms and the ecological characterization of market participants to be used in agent-based models of financial markets.

Introduction

Econophysics (Mantegna and Stanley 1999; Bouchaud and Potters 2003; Slanina 2013) is an interdisciplinary research area at the interface between physics and economics that has developed since the late 1980s (Anderson, Arrow, and Pines

1988; Mantegna 1991; Takayasu *et al.* 1992). An instrumental event for the development of this research area was the first "Evolutionary Paths of the Global Economy" workshop held at the Santa Fe Institute in 1987; the proceedings were published in 1988 with the title *The Economy as an Evolving Complex System.* During the past thirty-five years, researchers in econophysics have developed, adapted, and applied methods and tools based on concepts originating from statistical physics, complexity science, network science, and data mining to social and economic complex systems. The development of econophysics was gradual, characterized by the selection of scientific problems pursued by a group of pioneers, the editorial policies of some academic journals opening their pages to the new approaches, the foundation and development of new journals, and the organization of workshops and congresses that have connected the research community working in the new discipline.

In this chapter I discuss some aspects of the cultural background of econophysics, with a special emphasis on researchers' contributions to finance. First, I discuss the origin of the word econophysics, then I introduce the concept of stylized facts and its role in econophysics and statistical physics. Next, I focus on the information content stored in the return time series and the methods of information filtering that originate from econophysics. I describe a generalization of the efficient market hypothesis compatible with the empirical observation of intrinsic heterogeneity of market participants, then I briefly report on econophysics' contribution to clarifying the process of price discovery and methods of information filtering. I present the type of research done with agent-based models in econophysics before concluding with a brief discussion.

About a Word

The word *econophysics* was first published in a 1996 article in *Physica A* collecting the proceedings of the conference on "Dynamics of Complex Systems" held in Kolkata in 1995 (Stanley *et al.* 1996). The article is associated with Gene Stanley's presentation of studies dealing with different complex systems. The word aimed to describe those studies of complex economic systems performed with tools and concepts from statistical physics. Reciprocal influences between economics and physics have been present since Daniel Bernoulli's introduction of utility function in 1738 (Bernoulli 1954). What was different about the 1980s movement was the cultural background of the physicists, particularly statistical physicists, and the available data. Starting from the 1980s, several sets of detailed financial data become available for research in electronic form. This impacted the process of empirical analysis, allowing for analyses performed not only with classic econometric tools but also with data-mining tools.

Econophysics is an appropriate word for the research efforts that have been pursued in the last forty years by physicists investigating economic complex systems; however, the word has its limits, in particular, the connotation of *physics* with determinist prediction. Physicists today know that the degree of prediction in a physical system can depend on the underlying model and can be valid only under specific limitations originating from various sources, for example, quantum nature of the system, nonlinearities, finite size limit of the system, or equilibrium assumption. These limitations emerge quite naturally in the branch of physics called statistical physics (or statistical mechanics), but their presence is less evident in particle physics or material physics. For these reasons, during the early days of econophysics research, there was a strong debate about the term's appropriateness. For example, at one of the first conferences on econophysics, held in Palermo in 1998 (Mantegna 1999b), the scientific committee was divided in two groups: one supporting the word econophysics and the other preferring *statistical finance*. For this reason, the conference was called "International Workshop on Econophysics and Statistical Finance." In other words, the use of econophysics does not immediately convey that econophysicists' contributions to economics and finance are rooted in statistical physics and data mining.

~ 59 ~

Stylized Facts and Econophysics Methodology

A key concept in economics and finance is that of stylized facts (Kaldor 1961). A stylized fact is a statistical regularity observed in a system that is presenting stochastic dynamics. Econophysicists have investigated many economic and financial complex systems to detect stylized facts. Some were genuinely newly discoveries, whereas others were already known to scholars of other disciplines. The main methodological aspect of the search for stylized facts is related to their use in developing, calibrating, and testing (a) deterministic, (b) probabilistic, (c) agent-based, or (d) data-mining generated models able to produce model predictions compatible with empirically observed stylized facts. One of the most famous stylized facts in finance is the return distribution of a financial asset. It has been shown that in almost all financial markets, asset returns present a highly leptokurtic probability density function (Mantegna and Stanley 1999; Bouchaud and Potters 2003; Slanina 2013). There is no consensus on the shape of the distribution. Most probably, the shape is not universal for all financial assets and markets, but the observation that leptokurtosis is present in different markets, in different time periods, and for different type of assets is a rather robust stylized fact. One crucial point of this stylized fact of asset returns is the empirical observation that the second moment of the return probability density function is indeed finite, in spite of the high degree of leptokurtosis observed (Mantegna and Stanley 1995). Such a conclusion has been used to develop original statistical models such as the truncated Lévy flight (Mantegna and Stanley 1994) and so-called multifractal models (Mandelbrot, Fisher, and Calvet 1997; Bacry, Delour, and Muzy 2001; Calvet and Fisher 2002).

It is worth noting that the methodological approach of focusing on stylized facts, and then developing assumptions and models able to replicate them, is rooted in the methodology used to develop the empirical and theoretical description of phase transitions. In statistical physics, physical laws and statistical regularities such as the spatial correlation of the order parameter (like the magnetization of a ferromagnetic system) were first empirically observed and then theoretically modeled near continuous phase transitions. The universality of some observations, such as the existence of a set of values of so-called critical exponents, was first observed by investigating several, sometimes disparate systems; eventually the knowledge obtained from empirical characterization was used to develop a coherent theory of continuous phase transitions (Stanley 1999). Econophysics has therefore been proposing the use of a methodological approach characterized by a feedback loop cycling from empirical observation to model development and then to model verification through empirical observation.

Information Filtering from Multivariate Time Series

The process of price discovery incorporates shared and idiosyncratic information in return time series of financial assets. Single asset return dynamics is therefore hardly distinguishable from a random walk with an extremely short correlation time. This widespread characteristic of return time series of financial assets is deeply related with the absence of easy and systematic arbitrage opportunities (Samuelson 1965). However, this arbitrage-opportunity constraint doesn't conflict with the incorporation of information in the return time series. In fact, the presence of information in return time series is manifest in several direct and indirect financial indicators. For example, it is present in the structure of covariance and cross-correlation matrices of returns of a financial asset portfolio. The presence of a nontrivial structure in such portfolios has been known since Harry Markowitz's (1952) pioneering work on portfolio optimization.

The information that is relevant for a financial asset portfolio in a given time period is a dynamical entity. This implies that covariance and cross-correlation matrices cannot be estimated using arbitrarily old return records. Moreover, heterogeneity in market participants implies that information concerning the financial assets is mixed with noise originating from idiosyncratic behaviors. These two basic constraints make it challenging to empirically estimate the covariance (correlation) matrix of multivariate return of an asset portfolio.

The problem of estimating sample covariance (correlation) of a multivariate time series with a finite number of records is a classic problem in statistics (Stein 1975). Econophysics has contributed to it in different ways. The first approach is based on the application of random matrix theory (RMT) to the problem of sample correlation estimation (Laloux *et al.* 1999; Plerou *et al.* 1999; Bun, Bouchaud, and Potters 2017). In fact, RMT allows us to introduce and control a well-defined null model, therefore highlighting those empirical characteristics that are not compatible with the precisely defined random model. Multivariate statistical properties affect the nature of predictions obtained with RMT, and therefore a large literature has been produced to highlight the properties associated with Gaussianity or non-Gaussianity of the multivariate time series and the properties associated with so-called rotationally invariant estimators (Bun, Bouchaud, and Potters 2017).

Rotationally invariant estimators have their roots in statistics, and a key assumption is the use of sample eigenvectors in the optimal estimation of covariance. Bulk eigenvectors of sample correlation have the typical property of being delocalized. By contrast, empirical evidence supports the existence of localized eigenvectors. An alternative to the approach of rotationally invariant estimators is the filtering of the correlation matrix by using hierarchical clustering and network theory (Mantegna 1999a; Tumminello *et al.* 2005; Coronnello *et al.* 2005; Tumminello, Lillo, and Mantegna 2010). Hierarchical clustering is a data-mining procedure that clusters a multivariate system. Matrices associated with, for example, single-linkage or average linkage agglomerative hierarchical clustering procedures retain a large amount of information with respect to many difference indicators between pairs of correlation matrices. Examples of these functions are Frobenius distance, Kullback–Leibler divergence, and Stein's loss function.

In summary, it is possible to filter out part of the information that is incorporated in return time series of an asset portfolio. The optimal filtering of this information is not a trivial task, and econophysics studies have contributed significantly in devising methodologies rooted in RMT and hierarchical clustering merged with concepts of network theory.

Generalization of the Efficient Market Hypothesis

The efficient market hypothesis (EMH) is a cornerstone of modern finance (Fama 1970, 1991). It implies that information available to market participants (classified in different categories such as disseminated, publicly accessible, and confidential) is instantly reflected in price time series. In the present context, we only consider informational efficiency. (More complex aspects of efficiency, such as allocative efficiency, are not treated here.) The efficient market hypothesis implies the apparently counterintuitive conclusion that return time series of financial markets must be hardly distinguishable from stochastic processes. One way to reconcile this is to note that random processes have associated no redundancy (here this term is used with the meaning assumed in information theory) and that a time series with minimal redundancy can also be obtained by incorporating a large amount of information from various sources, including idiosyncratic ones.

Econophysics studies have verified that, in most liquid markets, financial assets present return time series with only extremely short autocorrelation time (down to a few milliseconds for the most liquid stocks) and simultaneously present detectable cross-correlation and cointegration with other stocks and financial assets (Mantegna and Stanley 1999; Bouchaud and Potters 2003; Slanina 2013; Chakraborti *et al.* 2011a, 2011b).

When focusing on the short-term dynamics of return time series of liquid financial assets, markets present a quite high degree of informational efficiency. On the other hand, by assuming that markets are able to correctly process all information available to market participants, the validity of the EMH implies that behavioral aspects play no role in price discovery and that the market as an institution is always able

~63~

to perform the correct price discovery, therefore excluding the possibility of so-called bubbles.

Driven by empirical results and by the observation that market participants present a certain degree of heterogeneity, econophysicists have concluded that the efficient market hypothesis is an idealization of real markets, and that deviation from its predictions can be empirically detected and theoretically modeled.

One variant of the efficient market hypothesis takes into account the presence of heterogeneity of participants and the impact of a changing environment in market dynamics. This variant is the so-called adaptive market hypothesis (Farmer and Lo 1999; Farmer 2002; Lo 2004). Within this generalization of the EMH, markets are populated by an ecology of participants collectively concurring with different investing patterns in the process of price discovery. Different categories of market participants are devising, evaluating, and performing distinct trading strategies adapted to the current state of the market.

Granular data concerning trading decisions of different categories of investors have been available for research since the 1990s and have provided empirical support to the presence of different categories of investors in the process of price discovery (Lakonishok and Maberly 1990; Lakonishok, Shleifer, and Vishny 1992; Nofsinger and Sias 1999; Grinblatt and Keloharju 2001; Barber and Odean 2008; Barber et al. 2009).

Heterogeneity and Market Microstructure

Since the 1980s, finance scholars have investigated the process of price discovery down to the basic transaction occurring between the specialist (at the New York Stock Exchange) or jobber (at the London Stock Exchange) and the market participant (Roll 1984; Glosten and Milgrom 1985; Kyle

1985). In fact, during the 1980s, interaction between investors was typically mediated by these institutional figures. Over time, these figures have been progressively replaced with electronic infrastructures such as the electronic order book and/or electronic infrastructures allowing specialized traders, such as high-frequency traders colocated with market venues, constituting what is sometimes called a sociotechnical system.

In other words, specialization of traders in financial markets became more and more explicit due to the continuous introduction of technological innovation in the process of price discovery. However, a basic specialization of traders is intrinsic to the concept of modern financial markets and has always been present.

The most basic description of heterogeneity in the process of price discovery involves three types of traders. In the literature of market microstructure, they are (a) market makers, (b) informed investors, and (c) noise (or idiosyncratic) investors. The market maker is an investor characterized by a very short time horizon and not building up a large inventory of financial assets. The profit they make typically originates from the continuous action of buying and selling a specific financial asset. They are "making" the market, that is, they are providing continuous "liquidity" that otherwise might be absent from time to time in the market. In the past, this figure was institutional (the specialist and jobber cited above); today, in most cases this role is performed by specialized traders, such as the high-frequency traders. Informed investors idealize investors who devote resources and energy to searching for and interpreting information about financial assets. They typically are large, institutional, or professional investors looking for investment opportunities at all time scales. The resources and energy they spend to search and interpret financial and economic information on average gives them a better ability to forecast the direction of price discovery at different time scales. Noise or idiosyncratic investors might act on wrong, misinterpreted, or inappropriate information (the main reason why they are addressed as "noise" traders) or might act for specific idiosyncratic reasons (i.e., reasons that are valid only for a specific investor, such as an illness or some unpredicted relevant expense or occasion).

This is the minimal categorization hypothesized by scholars acting in the field of market microstructure. Econophysics has contributed significantly to the field of market microstructure, primarily in empirical and theoretical modeling of so-called price impact (Lillo, Farmer, and Mantegna 2003; Potters and Bouchaud 2003; Farmer *et al.* 2006; Bouchaud, Farmer, and Lillo 2009; Farmer *et al.* 2013). Price impact is the basic granular process concurring with price discovery in an electronic order book that is observed for each market transaction. It is related to the market movement induced by each transaction by the asymmetric role played by the initiator of a transaction (sometimes called the aggressor) and by a counterpart (typically waiting with offers to buy or sell a given amount of a financial asset in the electronic book). Empirical studies document the presence of a long-range correlated sequence of the type of order (aggressor and counterpart) arriving in the order book (Lillo and Farmer 2004; Lillo, Mike, and Farmer 2005). These long-range correlated time series are difficult to justify without assuming some market-participant heterogeneity, whereas they are more naturally framed in a theoretical framework assuming participants' heterogeneity and some form of market ecology (Farmer and Lo 1999; Farmer 2002; Lo 2004).

A pattern of market ecology distinctly emerges when it is possible to perform empirical analyses down to the trading decisions of individual legal entities (Lakonishok and Maberly 1990; Lakonishok, Shleifer, and Vishny 1992; Nofsinger and Sias 1999; Barber and Odean 2008; Barber *et al.* 2009; Kirilenko *et al.* 2017). Sometimes, these studies are able to detect time scales covering many years (Musciotto *et al.* 2018; Musciotto, Piilo, and Mantegna 2021). Unfortunately, these studies can be done comprehensively only in a few specific markets (Barber *et al.* 2009; Grinblatt and Keloharju 2000) or market trading facilities (Challet and de Lachapelle 2013) and are essentially impossible in large markets. The reason is rooted in the access to investment data of market participants. Investment data are not only hard to access due to confidentiality reasons, but they are typically recorded using nominee registering. This means that the ownership of a specific financial asset is typically taken in the custody of a specific institution (bank or clearinghouse), and therefore only a supervisory agency or the market itself can occasionally reconstruct the trading ownership and activity performed by different legal entities in a market at a given time (Kirilenko *et al.* 2017). The only exception to this among Western countries is Finland (and partially in Sweden and Spain). In fact, Finland is the only country in the Western world where it is legally mandated to track ownership of financial assets issued in Finland on a daily basis at the level of each Finnish investor. Here we use the word "investor" to describe each single legal entity being, for example, a household, a company, or a nonprofit or governmental institution. Finland thus constitutes a "laboratory" for investigating the ecology of market participants acting on multiple time scales in a financial market (Musciotto *et al.* 2018; Grinblatt and Keloharju 2000; Tumminello *et al.* 2012).

Agent-Based Models

Heterogeneous systems are notoriously difficult to model. Starting in the 1970s, statistical physics obtained fundamental results in the theoretical description of heterogeneous models primarily with research focused on idealized models of spin glasses (Edwards and Anderson 1975; Sherrington and Kirkpatrick 1975; Mézard, Parisi, and Virasoro 1987).These idealized models turned out to be highly informative about the role of heterogeneity (mapped in physics in terms of "disorder" present in a physical system) in complex systems. At the same time, the personal computer become widely used in society and specifically in research. The widespread availability of computers made possible the development of a parallel description of heterogeneous complex systems in terms of agent-based models (ABMs). In computer science and statistical physics, ABMs are models in which heterogeneous agents interact with one another and with the environment by using heuristic rules. The system dynamics are therefore obtained by computer simulation and/or by a theoretical description of the model.

An ABM that had a major impact in econophysics is the El Farol bar problem introduced by Brian Arthur (1994). With this model, Arthur illustrated a binary process of rational decision-making for a set of rational agents in the presence of common public information and negative externality. Within the model setting, there is no self-fulfilling equilibrium. This implies that, assuming full rationality and access to public information, the system presents only states that are always frustrating for the agents. Rationality (with the implicit assumption of homogeneity in agents' decisions) therefore produces only a suboptimal (economic) equilibrium. By contrast, with computer simulations, Arthur was able to show that a close-to-optimal allocation of the resource (attendance at the El Farol bar) is reached by the system by hypothesizing a bounded rational inductive reasoning of the agents.

Two econophysicists, Damien Challet and Yi-Cheng Zhang (1997), formalized the El Farol bar model in a mathematical form that allowed a straightforward analytical and numerical investigation. With their reformulation, the statistical physics research community performed several studies on this model highlighting the presence of different phases separated by a phase transition. Specifically, several studies shown that a phase transition was present between two distinct regimes of the deterministic time evolution of the system controlled by a "control parameter." The control parameter is a quantity proportional to the ratio between the number of independent strategies available to each agent and the number of agents. In parallel to this observation, the information that can be extracted from the publicly available time series of the aggregated state of the system is a quantity that can be interpreted as an order parameter of the phase transition. In fact, it discriminates between the two phases observed in the system. In the first phase (characterized by a low number of effective strategies available to agents), public information does not affect strategy selection, whereas in the other phase (presenting an increasing number of effective strategies available to agents), agents can benefit from public information. The first phase is path-dependent (i.e., non-ergodic in the mathematical language), and therefore it depends on the initial conditions; in the other phase, initial conditions play no crucial role. Many theoretical and computational results about the "minority game" can be found in review articles (De Martino and Marsili 2006) or books (Challet, Marsili, and Zhang 2004; Coolen 2005).

In parallel, since the early 1990s there have been many theoretical and computational studies of stylized ABMs mimicking heuristics supposedly used by market participants (Samanidou *et al.* 2007). The first models were quite stylized but already introduced aspects and heuristics observed in real markets. A first pioneering example is the 1989 model of economists Gew-Rae Kim and Harry Markowitz (1989). About the same time, activity at the Santa Fe Institute produced the so-called Santa Fe Artificial Stock Market (Arthur *et al.* 1997). For other classic examples of early ABMs, see Moshe Levy, Haim Levy, and Sorin Solomon (1994) and Thomas Lux and Michele Marchesi (1999). Agent-based models are sometimes focused on specific key financial variables (Bouchaud 2018) or mechanisms of financial markets, such as the order book (Chiarella and Iori 2002). More recently, there has been the tendency to develop large-scale ABMs with the aim of assessing the stability and resilience of the global financial system. Examples of these large-scale agent-based simulations can be found in John Geanakoplos *et al.* (2012), Sebastian Poledna *et al.* (2015), and Poledna *et al.* (2023).

Additional research with ABMs is needed in both physics and economics (Farmer and Foley 2009). I note two recent trends in the study of ABMs. One tendency is to set up economic and financial knowledge, data, and computer infrastructure to allow the study of large-scale ABMs in economics and finance. This type of enterprise has the final goal of achieving a level of knowledge of the systems down to each single agent so that a simulation of the entire system can be replicated to obtain robust predictions at least for the near future. The main problems of this approach concerned the difficulty of taking into account, accessing, and describing all relevant aspects and heuristics of the ABM so that a reliable calibration of the usually large number of control parameters can be successfully performed. A metaphor to support this type of approach cites the improvement in weather forecasting over the last two decades thanks to the increase of computational power and large-scale monitoring of weather-related data. A second approach is primarily focused on stylized ABMs. In this line of thinking the ABM is simplified as much as possible and its large degree of idealization is explicitly acknowledged. However, despite this limitation, the study of these models can be highly informative, not in terms of specific forecasting of a real system modeled by them, but rather in terms of simulated scenarios, in the physics language system phases, that might be strictly put in relation with some variables that the model assumes as "critical."

Discussion

There are deep methodological differences between physics and finance. In the past, major successes in physics have been achieved when scholars can hypothesize, discover, and use conservation laws (e.g., energy, mass, spin) and perform controlled experiments with high signal-to-noise ratios, reducing the need for complex statistical validation. In contrast, finance primarily focuses on microfounded models based on the idealization of a rational agent, assumption of the ability to maximize an agent's utility for all agents, and knowledge and efficient processing of all information regarding states of the world. The two research areas are therefore quite distant from one another. Econophysics attempts to exploit the strengths of the two disciplines by extending tools and concepts from statistical physics to complex systems where conservation laws are only approximate or are absent, and individual and collective optimization are performed by heterogeneous agents processing different pieces of information. In taking this hybrid profile, econophysics has influenced physics by highlighting the need for complex systems to follow rigorous statistical approaches that are more typical in economic modeling. The integration of statistical rigor into the modeling of complex systems will likely help physicists to improve the description of heterogeneous systems of out-of-equilibrium phenomena where emergence, phase transitions occurring at tipping points, power law distributions, and long-range correlations are typical properties. Econophysics has also highlighted the presence of an irreducible heterogeneity in several complex systems. Irreducible heterogeneity means that a representative modeling of the considered system cannot be achieved by subsuming heterogeneity into a global representation obtained through the construction of a representative agent. The answer to the problems raised by the study of systems with irreducible heterogeneity has been the introduction and study of ABMs, both idealized and large-scale.

A key area for advancement in econophysics lies in modeling information production and processing within heterogeneous financial and economic complex systems. In other words, econophysics has yet to fully realize its potential to address information processes in many-agent, open, heterogeneous, and nonequilibrium systems.

Despite the widespread recognition of the importance of interdisciplinary research, its promotion, planning, funding, and organization remains a complex and challenging task. One key challenge is its inherently hybrid nature, involving knowledge, methods, and concepts from different research communities. While this hybridity offers the potential to address complex problems, it can also create uncertainty around researchers' identities. Early-career researchers, in particular, may feel disoriented by the lack of identity and a clear reference research community. Unfortunately, in interdisciplinary research, scholars often understand what they are *not* while struggling to recognize and embrace what they *are*. Luckily, a few prominent research settings genuinely promote interdisciplinarity, although their number and resources are at the moment insufficient for the challenges that are foreseen. I hope that policymakers will convince themselves of the need for and validity of devoting more resources to this type of scientific challenge. ⚕

Acknowledgments

R.N.M. acknowledges financial support by the MIUR PRIN project 2017WZFTZP, Stochastic Forecasting in Complex Systems.

REFERENCES

Anderson, P. W., K. Arrow, and D. Pines. 1988. *The Economy as an Evolving Complex System*. First. Boca Raton, FL: CRC Press.

Arthur, W. B. 1994. "Inductive Reasoning and Bounded Rationality." *The American Economic Review* 84 (2): 406–411. https://www.jstor.org/stable/2117868.

Arthur, W. B., J. H. Holland, B. LeBaron, R. Palmer, and P. Tayler. 1997. "Asset Pricing Under Endogenous Expectations in an Artificial Stock Market." In *The Economy as an Evolving Complex System II*, 15–44. CRC Press. https://doi.org/10.1201/9780429496639-2.

Bacry, E., J. Delour, and J.-F. Muzy. 2001. "Multifractal Random Walk." *Physical Review E* 64 (2): 026103. https://doi.org/10.1103/PhysRevE.64.026103.

Barber, B. M., Y.-T. Lee, Y.-J. Liu, and T. Odean. 2009. "Just How Much do Individual Investors Lose by Trading?" *The Review of Financial Studies* 22 (2): 609–632. https://doi.org/10.1093/rfs/hhn046.

Barber, B. M., and T. Odean. 2008. "All That Glitters: The Effect of Attention and News on the Buying Behavior of Individual and Institutional Investors." *The Review of Financial Studies* 21 (2): 785–818. https://doi.org/10.2139/ssrn.460660.

Bernoulli, D. 1954. "Exposition of a New Theory on the Measurement of Risk." *Econometrica* 22 (1): 23–36. https://doi.org/10.2307/1909829.

Bouchaud, J.-P. 2018. "Agent-Based Models for Market Impact and Volatility." In *Handbook of Computational Economics,* edited by C. Hommes and B. LeBaron, 4:393–436. Elsevier. https://doi.org/10.1016/bs.hescom.2018.02.002.

Bouchaud, J.-P., J. D. Farmer, and F. Lillo. 2009. "How Markets Slowly Digest Changes in Supply and Demand." In *Handbook of Financial Markets: Dynamics and Evolution,* 57–160. Elsevier. https://doi.org/10.1016/B978-012374258-2.50006-3.

Bouchaud, J.-P., and M. Potters. 2003. *Theory of Financial Risk and Derivative Pricing: From Statistical Physics to Risk Management.* Cambridge University Press.

Bun, J., J.-P. Bouchaud, and M. Potters. 2017. "Cleaning Large Correlation Matrices: Tools from Random Matrix Theory." *Physics Reports* 666:1–109. https://doi.org/10.1016/j.physrep.2016.10.005.

Calvet, L., and A. Fisher. 2002. "Multifractality in Asset Returns: Theory and Evidence." *Review of Economics and Statistics* 84 (3): 381–406. http://www.jstor.org/stable/3211559.

Chakraborti, A., I. M. Toke, M. Patriarca, and F. Abergel. 2011a. "Econophysics Review: I. Empirical Facts." *Quantitative Finance* 11 (7): 991–1012. https://doi.org/10.1080/14697688.2010.539248.

———. 2011b. "Econophysics Review: II. Agent-Based Models." *Quantitative Finance* 11 (7): 1013–1041. https://doi.org/10.1080/14697688.2010.539249.

Challet, D., and D. M. de Lachapelle. 2013. "A Robust Measure of Investor Contrarian Behaviour." In *Econophysics of Systemic Risk and Network Dynamics,* edited by F. Abergel, B. K. Chakrabarti, A. Chakraborti, and A. Ghosh, 105–118. Milano: Springer Milan. https://doi.org/10.1007/978-88-470-2553-0_7.

Challet, D., M. Marsili, and Y.-C. Zhang. 2004. *Minority Games: Interacting Agents in Financial Markets.* Oxford, UK: Oxford University Press.

Challet, D., and Y.-C. Zhang. 1997. "Emergence of Cooperation and Organization in an Evolutionary Game." *Physica A: Statistical Mechanics and its Applications* 246 (3): 407–418. https://doi.org/10.1016/S0378-4371(97)00419-6.

Chiarella, C., and G. Iori. 2002. "A Simulation Analysis of the Microstructure of Double Auction Markets." *Quantitative Finance* 2 (5): 346. https://doi.org/10.1088/1469-7688/2/5/303.

Coolen, A. C. C. 2005. *The Mathematical Theory of Minority Games: Statistical Mechanics of Interacting Agents.* Oxford, UK: Oxford University Press.

Coronnello, C., M. Tumminello, F. Lillo, S. Micciché, and R. N. Mantegna. 2005. "Sector Identification in a Set of Stock Return Time Series Traded at the London Stock Exchange." *Acta Physica Polonica. Series B* 36 (9): 2653–2679. https://doi.org/10.48550/arXiv.cond-mat/0508122.

De Martino, A., and M. Marsili. 2006. "Statistical Mechanics of Socio-Economic Systems with Heterogeneous Agents." *Journal of Physics A: Mathematical and General* 39 (43): R465. https://doi.org/10.1088/0305-4470/39/43/R01.

Edwards, S. F., and P. W. Anderson. 1975. "Theory of Spin Glasses." *Journal of Physics F: Metal Physics* 5 (5): 965. https://doi.org/10.1088/0305-4608/5/5/017.

Fama, E. F. 1970. "Efficient Capital Markets." *Journal of Finance* 25 (2): 383–417. https://doi.org/10.2307/2325486.

———. 1991. "Efficient Capital Markets: II." *Journal of Finance* 46 (5): 1575–1617. https://doi.org/10.1111/j.1540-6261.1991.tb04636.x.

Farmer, J. D. 2002. "Market Force, Ecology and Evolution." *Industrial and Corporate Change* 11 (5): 895–953. https://doi.org/10.1093/icc/11.5.895.

Farmer, J. D., and D. Foley. 2009. "The Economy Needs Agent-Based Modelling." *Nature* 460 (7256): 685–686. https://doi.org/10.1038/460685a.

Farmer, J. D., A. Gerig, F. Lillo, and S. Mike. 2006. "Market Efficiency and the Long-Memory of Supply and Demand: Is Price Impact Variable and Permanent or Fixed and Temporary?" *Quantitative Finance* 6 (02): 107–112. https://doi.org/10.1080/14697680600668048.

Farmer, J. D., A. Gerig, F. Lillo, and H. Waelbroeck. 2013. "How Efficiency Shapes Market Impact." *Quantitative Finance* 13 (11): 1743–1758. https://doi.org/10.1080/14697688.2013.848464.

Farmer, J. D., and A. W. Lo. 1999. "Frontiers of Finance: Evolution and Efficient Markets." *Proceedings of the National Academy of Sciences* 96 (18): 9991–9992. https://doi.org/10.1073/pnas.96.18.9991.

Geanakoplos, J., R. Axtell, D. J. Farmer, P. Howitt, B. Conlee, J. Goldstein, M. Hendrey, N. M. Palmer, and C.-Y. Yang. 2012. "Getting at Systemic Risk Via an Agent-Based Model of the Housing Market." *American Economic Review* 102 (3): 53–58. https://doi.org/10.1257/aer.102.3.53.

Glosten, L. R., and P. R. Milgrom. 1985. "Bid, Ask and Transaction Prices in a Specialist Market with Heterogeneously Informed Traders." *Journal of Financial Economics* 14 (1): 71–100. https://doi.org/10.1016/0304-405X(85) 90044-3.

Grinblatt, M., and M. Keloharju. 2000. "The Investment Behavior and Performance of Various Investor Types: A Study of Finland's Unique Data Set." *Journal of Financial Economics* 55 (1): 43–67. https://doi.org/10.1016/S0304-405X(99) 00044-6.

———. 2001. "How Distance, Language, and Culture Influence Stockholdings and Trades." *The Journal of Finance* 56 (3): 1053–1073. https://doi.org/10.1111/ 0022-1082.00355.

Kaldor, N. 1961. "Capital Accumulation and Economic Growth." In *The Theory of Capital: Proceedings of a Conference Held by the International Economic Association*, edited by D. C. Hague, 177–222. Springer.

Kim, G.-R., and H. M. Markowitz. 1989. "Investment Rules, Margin, and Market Volatility." *Journal of Portfolio Management* 16 (1): 45. https://doi.org/10. 3905/jpm.1989.409233.

Kirilenko, A., A. S. Kyle, M. Samadi, and T. Tuzun. 2017. "The Flash Crash: High-frequency Trading in an Electronic Market." *The Journal of Finance* 72 (3): 967–998. https://doi.org/10.1111/jofi.12498.

Kyle, A. S. 1985. "Continuous Auctions and Insider Trading." *Econometrica: Journal of the Econometric Society*, 1315–1335. https://doi.org/10.2307/1913210.

Lakonishok, J., and E. Maberly. 1990. "The Weekend Effect: Trading Patterns of Individual and Institutional Investors." *The Journal of Finance* 45 (1): 231–243. https://doi.org/10.1111/j.1540-6261.1990.tb05089.x.

Lakonishok, J., A. Shleifer, and R. W. Vishny. 1992. "The Impact of Institutional Trading on Stock Prices." *Journal of Financial Economics* 32 (1): 23–43. https: //doi.org/10.1016/0304-405X(92)90023-Q.

Laloux, L., P. Cizeau, J.-P. Bouchaud, and M. Potters. 1999. "Noise Dressing of Financial Correlation Matrices." *Physical Review Letters* 83 (7): 1467. https: //doi.org/10.1103/PhysRevLett.83.1467.

Levy, M., H. Levy, and S. Solomon. 1994. "A Microscopic Model of the Stock Market: Cycles, Booms, and Crashes." *Economics Letters* 45 (1): 103–111. https://doi.org/10.1016/0165-1765(94)90065-5.

Lillo, F., and J. D. Farmer. 2004. "The Long Memory of the Efficient Market." *Studies in Nonlinear Dynamics & Econometrics* 8 (3). https://doi.org/10.48550/arXiv.cond-mat/0311053.

Lillo, F., J. D. Farmer, and R. N. Mantegna. 2003. "Master Curve for Price-Impact Function." *Nature* 421 (6919): 129–130. https://doi.org/10.1038/421129a.

Lillo, F., S. Mike, and J. D. Farmer. 2005. "Theory for Long Memory in Supply and Demand." *Physical Review E* 71 (6): 066122. https://doi.org/10.1103/PhysRevE.71.066122.

Lo, A. W. 2004. "The Adaptive Markets Hypothesis: Market Efficiency from an Evolutionary Perspective." *Journal of Portfolio Management* 30 (5): 15–29. https://doi.org/10.3905/jpm.2004.442611.

Lux, T., and M. Marchesi. 1999. "Scaling and Criticality in a Stochastic Multi-Agent Model of a Financial Market." *Nature* 397 (6719): 498–500. https://doi.org/10.1038/17290.

Mandelbrot, B. B., A. J. Fisher, and L. E. Calvet. 1997. *A Multifractal Model of Asset Returns.* Technical report 1164. Cowles Foundation.

Mantegna, R. N. 1991. "Lévy Walks and Enhanced Diffusion in Milan Stock Exchange." *Physica A: Statistical Mechanics and its Applications* 179 (2): 232–242. https://doi.org/10.1016/0378-4371(91)90061-G.

———. 1999a. "Hierarchical Structure in Financial Markets." *The European Physical Journal B* 11 (1): 193–197. https://doi.org/10.1007/s100510050929.

———. 1999b. "Proceedings of the International Workshop on Econophysics and Statistical Finance held at University of Palermo, Italy 28-30 September 1998-Preface." *Physica A* 269 (1): XIII–XIV. https://www.sudoc.fr/047892013.

Mantegna, R. N., and H. E. Stanley. 1994. "Stochastic Process with Ultraslow Convergence to a Gaussian: The Truncated Lévy Flight." *Physical Review Letters* 73 (22): 2946. https://doi.org/10.1103/PhysRevLett.73.2946.

———. 1995. "Scaling Behaviour in the Dynamics of an Economic Index." *Nature* 376 (6535): 46–49. https://doi.org/10.1038/376046a0.

Mantegna, R. N., and H. E. Stanley. 1999. *Introduction to Econophysics: Correlations and Complexity in Finance.* Cambridge, UK: Cambridge University Press.

Markowitz, H. 1952. "Portfolio Selection." *Journal of Finance* 7 (1): 77–91. https://doi.org/10.2307/2975974.

Mézard, M., G. Parisi, and M. Á. Virasoro. 1987. *Spin Glass Theory and Beyond: An Introduction to the Replica Method and its Applications.* Vol. 9. World Scientific Publishing Company.

Musciotto, F., L. Marotta, J. Piilo, and R. N. Mantegna. 2018. "Long-term Ecology of Investors in a Financial Market." *Palgrave Communications* 4 (1). https://doi.org/10.1057/s41599-018-0145-1.

Musciotto, F., J. Piilo, and R. N. Mantegna. 2021. "High-frequency Trading and Networked Markets." *Proceedings of the National Academy of Sciences* 118 (26): e2015573118. https://doi.org/10.1073/pnas.2015573118.

Nofsinger, J. R., and R. W. Sias. 1999. "Herding and Feedback Trading by Institutional and Individual Investors." *The Journal of Finance* 54 (6): 2263–2295. https://doi.org/10.1111/0022-1082.00188.

Plerou, V., P. Gopikrishnan, B. Rosenow, L. A. N. Amaral, and H. E. Stanley. 1999. "Universal and Nonuniversal Properties of Cross Correlations in Financial Time Series." *Physical Review Letters* 83 (7): 1467–1470. https://doi.org/10.1103/PhysRevLett.83.1471.

Poledna, S., M. G. Miess, C. Hommes, and K. Rabitsch. 2023. "Economic Forecasting with an Agent-Based Model." *European Economic Review* 151:104306. https://doi.org/10.1016/j.euroecorev.2022.104306.

Poledna, S., J. L. Molina-Borboa, S. Martínez-Jaramillo, M. van der Leij, and S. Thurner. 2015. "The Multi-Layer Network Nature of Systemic Risk and its Implications for the Costs of Financial Crises." *Journal of Financial Stability* 20:70–81. https://doi.org/10.48550/arXiv.1505.04276.

Potters, M., and J.-P. Bouchaud. 2003. "More Statistical Properties of Order Books and Price Impact." *Physica A: Statistical Mechanics and its Applications* 324 (1-2): 133–140. https://doi.org/10.48550/arXiv.cond-mat/0210710.

Roll, R. 1984. "A Simple Implicit Measure of the Effective Bid-Ask Spread in an Efficient Market." *The Journal of Finance* 39 (4): 1127–1139. https://doi.org/10.1111/j.1540-6261.1984.tb03897.x.

Chapter 17: *Reflections on Econophysics' Contributions to Finance*

Samanidou, E., E. Zschischang, D. Stauffer, and T. Lux. 2007. "Agent-Based Models of Financial Markets." *Reports on Progress in Physics* 70 (3): 409. https://doi.org/10.1088/0034-4885/70/3/R03.

Samuelson, P. A. 1965. "Proof That Properly Anticipated Prices Fluctuate Randomly." *Management Review* 6 (2). https : / / doi . org / 10 . 1142 / 9789814566926_0002.

Sherrington, D., and S. Kirkpatrick. 1975. "Solvable Model of a Spin-Glass." *Physical Review Letters* 35 (26): 1792. https://doi.org/10.1103/PhysRevLett.35.1792.

Slanina, F. 2013. *Essentials of Econophysics Modelling.* Oxford University Press.

Stanley, H. E. 1999. "Scaling, Universality, and Renormalization: Three Pillars of Modern Critical Phenomena." *Reviews of Modern Physics* 71 (2): S358. https://doi.org/10.1103/RevModPhys.71.S358.

Stanley, H. E., V. Afanasyev, L. A. N. Amaral, S. V. Buldyrev, A. L. Goldberger, S. Havlin, H. Leschhorn, *et al.* 1996. "Anomalous Fluctuations in the Dynamics of Complex Systems: From DNA and Physiology to Econophysics." *Physica A: Statistical Mechanics and its Applications* 224 (1-2): 302–321. https://doi.org/10.1016/0378-4371(95)00409-2.

Stein, C. 1975. *Estimation of a Covariance Matrix.* Rietz lecture, 39th Annual Meeting IMS, Atlanta, GA, 1975.

Takayasu, H., H. Miura, T. Hirabayashi, and K. Hamada. 1992. "Statistical Properties of Deterministic Threshold Elements—the Case of Market Price." *Physica A: Statistical Mechanics and its Applications* 184 (1-2): 127–134. https://doi.org/10.1016/0378-4371(92)90161-I.

Tumminello, M., T. Aste, T. Di Matteo, and R. N. Mantegna. 2005. "A Tool for Filtering Information in Complex Systems." *Proceedings of the National Academy of Sciences* 102 (30): 10421–10426. https://doi.org/10.1073/pnas.0500298102.

Tumminello, M., F. Lillo, and R. N. Mantegna. 2010. "Correlation, Hierarchies, and Networks in Financial Markets." *Journal of Economic Behavior & Organization* 75 (1): 40–58. https://doi.org/10.1016/j.jebo.2010.01.004.

Tumminello, M., F. Lillo, J. Piilo, and R. N. Mantegna. 2012. "Identification of Clusters of Investors from Their Real Trading Activity in a Financial Market." *New Journal of Physics* 14 (1): 013041. https : / / doi . org / 10 . 1088 / 1367 - 2630/14/1/013041.

AGENT-BASED MODELING AT CENTRAL BANKS: RECENT DEVELOPMENTS AND NEW CHALLENGES

*András Borsos, Magyar Nemzeti Bank,
Complexity Science Hub, and University of Oxford;
Adrian Carro, University of Oxford and Banco de España;
Aldo Glielmo, Banca d'Italia;
Marc Hinterschweiger, Bank of England;
Jagoda Kaszowska-Mojsa, University of Oxford, Narodowy Bank
Polski, and Institute of Economics, Polish Academy of Sciences; and
Arzu Uluc, Bank of England*

Abstract

Over the past decade, agent-based models (ABMs) have been increasingly employed as analytical tools within economic policy institutions. This chapter documents this trend by surveying the ABM-relevant research and policy outputs of central banks and other related economic policy institutions. We classify these studies and reports into three main categories: (1) applied research connected to the mandates of central banks; (2) technical and methodological research supporting the advancement of ABMs; and (3) examples of the integration of ABMs into policy work. Our findings indicate that ABMs have emerged as effective complementary tools for central banks in carrying out their responsibilities, especially after the extension of their mandates following the global financial crisis of 2007–2009. While acknowledging that room for improvement remains, we argue that integrating ABMs into the analytical frameworks of central banks can support more effective policy responses to both existing and emerging economic challenges, including financial innovation and climate change.[1]

Introduction

Over the last decade, there has been increasing interest in developing and using agent-based models (ABMs) at central banks. This chapter sheds light on the drivers of this trend and reviews these models.

Historically, the main functions of central banks have consisted of ensuring price stability; providing liquidity during crises, that is, being the lender of last resort; supervising financial institutions; and providing payment systems. In the last fifteen years, these functions have expanded considerably for two main reasons. First, the global financial crisis (GFC) of 2007–2009 revealed the need for a holistic understanding of the financial system in order to ensure financial stability. Hence, many jurisdictions expanded the remits and responsibilities of their central banks in order to address systemic risks by introducing, for instance, macroprudential regulations, macro stress testing, central clearing, restrictions on remuneration, and resolution powers over failing or failed institutions.

Second, a large number of potential new challenges— not directly linked to the GFC—have emerged or increased in relevance. A nonexhaustive list of these risks includes cybersecurity, such as the disruption of a large financial institution, a financial market, or a critical third-party provider; climate change, including both physical impacts and those derived from the transition to a net-zero economy; cryptocurrencies, including their potential for competing with

~81~

[1] Any views expressed in this chapter are solely those of the authors and should not be attributed to the Magyar Nemzeti Bank, the Banco de España, the Narodowy Bank Polski, the Banca d'Italia, the Eurosystem, the Bank of England, or any of their committees.

or destabilizing traditional sectors of the financial system as well as the role of central bank digital currencies (CBDCs); and an increase in economic inequality. In many of these areas, central banks have already gained new powers to address these challenges. All of these developments have led to an increased demand for analytical tools to help policymakers understand how to best use these newly acquired powers. Given the novelty, variety, and potential complexity of the policies under consideration, policymakers increasingly rely on a broad range of models and methodologies, including ABMs.

Over this period, steadily increasing computational power and major advancements in data availability have enabled the development of large-scale, data-driven, and policy-oriented ABMs. At the same time, the potential for applying this methodology in economics has increased due to the growing trend of interdisciplinary research within this field, in particular in conjunction with computer and data science. There are several advantages for central banks to use ABMs to address policy-relevant questions. First, ABMs offer a high level of heterogeneity across multiple dimensions and allow for complex interactions between heterogeneous agents. Second, they can generate nonlinear dynamics similar to those observed in the real world, such as boom and bust cycles. Third, ABMs provide a flexible framework not only for assessing the impact of various policy scenarios on multiple aggregate measures, such as gross domestic product (GDP) and unemployment, but also for evaluating the distributional effects of these policies on, for instance, different segments of the economy. Finally, this flexibility also allows for capturing both the particularities of a given country and the details of real-world policies, as well as for promptly adapting the model to changing economic circumstances.

Table 1. List of central banks and other relevant institutions cited in this chapter.

ACRONYM	CENTRAL BANK	JURISDICTION
BCB	Banco Central de Bolivia	Bolivia
BCBr	Banco Central do Brasil	Brazil
BCL	Banque Centrale du Luxembourg	Luxembourg
BCRP	Banco Central de Reserva del Perú	Peru
BCU	Banco Central del Uruguay	Uruguay
BdE	Banco de España	Spain
BdF	Banque de France	France
BdI	Banca d'Italia	Italy
BdM	Banco de México	Mexico
BoC	Bank of Canada	Canada
BoE	Bank of England	United Kingdom
BoG	Τράπεζα της Ελλάδος	Greece
BoR	Банк России	Russian Federation
BRC	Banco de la República	Colombia
CBI	Central Bank of Ireland	Ireland
DBB	Deutsche Bundesbank	Germany
DN	Danmarks Nationalbank	Denmark
DNB	De Nederlandsche Bank	Netherlands
ECB	European Central Bank	Euro Area
MNB	Magyar Nemzeti Bank	Hungary
NBP	Narodowy Bank Polski	Poland
OeNB	Oesterreichische Nationalbank	Austria
RBNZ	Reserve Bank of New Zealand	New Zealand
SP	Suomen Pankki	Finland

ACRONYM	OTHER RELEVANT INSTITUTIONS	JURISDICTION
BCBS	Basel Committee on Banking Supervision	Member countries
CEMLA	Centro de Estudios Monetarios Latinoamericanos	Member countries
DGT	Direction Générale du Trésor	France
ESRB	European Systemic Risk Board	European Union
IMF	International Monetary Fund	Member countries
OFR	Office of Financial Research	United States of America
WB	World Bank	Member countries

~ 83 ~

Several policymakers have explicitly addressed the key features and advantages of ABMs in their speeches and publications, calling for more research and attention to be devoted to this approach or even advocating for its inclusion as part of a broader suite of modeling techniques available to central banks. Two prominent examples are Jean-Claude Trichet while he was president of the European Central Bank (Trichet 2010; 2011; 2013, ECB) and Andrew Haldane while he was chief economist of the Bank of England (Haldane 2016; 2019; Haldane and Turrell 2018, BoE). Stress testing is one of the areas where the potential contributions of ABMs were acknowledged early on, including in several working papers by various international policy institutions related to central banking (Henry *et al.* 2013, ECB; Bookstaber *et al.* 2014, OFR; Demekas 2015, IMF; Basel Committee on Banking Supervision 2015).

In the last decade, the development of policy-oriented ABMs has significantly accelerated, due to their increased recognition and the involvement of more researchers and material resources. In this chapter, we review research that has been undertaken at central banks and, to some degree, at other government bodies and international organizations with a similar policy focus.[2] We assign a research publication to a central bank or related institution if at least one author was affiliated with it at the time of publication.[3] The institutions covered in this

---

[2]For a more in-depth historical account of the emergence and growth of ABM research in the specific case of the Bank of England, see Plassard (2020). For a broader review of ABM research in economics, mostly conducted in academia, see Axtell and Farmer (2025).

[3]Since the aim of this chapter is to highlight the increasing interest in ABMs in central banks and related policy institutions, we focus on research conducted at least partially in this type of organizations. It should be noted, however, that this research does not necessarily represent the official views of the respective central banks or other organizations. For the sake of simplicity, we may still refer to it as research by or at central banks.

chapter are listed in alphabetical order by the acronym used to refer to them in table 1. Furthermore, we adopt a broad interpretation of what an ABM entails, and we focus on the fundamental similarities between modeling approaches rather than the small variations in the terminology used to describe them. Following J. Doyne Farmer and Duncan Foley (2009), an ABM can be broadly defined as "a computerized simulation of a number of decision-makers (agents) and institutions, which interact through prescribed rules." As such, we consider most network models and systemwide stress tests, among others, to be within the scope of this chapter.

~ 85 ~

The rest of this chapter is organized as follows: The second section outlines ABM research developed by central banks in relation to their various mandates. The third section focuses instead on the technical research central banks have conducted on the methodology itself. The fourth section presents a few examples of the application of ABMs for central bank policy work. In the final section we draw the main conclusions of this review and point at future research avenues for ABMs at central banks.

Research Related to Central Bank Mandates

Recent changes in the economy, financial system, and society have been leading to shifts in the role and mandate of central banks. At the same time, there is a need to search for new methods that could help researchers comprehend the complexity of the ongoing processes and inform policymakers on how to effectively design, calibrate, and implement policies. Figure 1 provides an overview of how central bank research using ABMs has evolved over time. Research on payment systems was one of the first use cases; however, following the GFC, financial stability ABMs have become predominant. Several

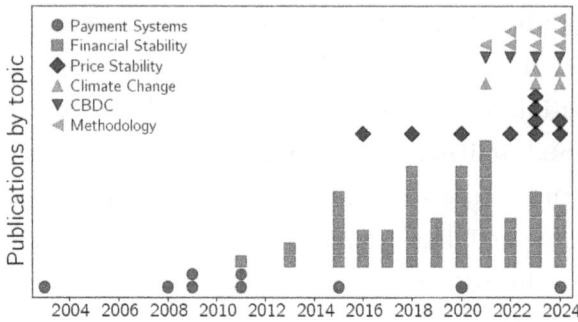

Figure 1. A timeline of publications from central banks and related institutions using agent-based models. Different application domains are highlighted by different shades and symbols and are discussed in detail in the respective sections. For example, publications related to climate change are indicated via a light gray upward-pointing triangle and are discussed in the "Climate Change" subsection below.

studies on price stability and climate change have emerged since 2016, while work on CBDCs only began in 2021.

FINANCIAL STABILITY

This section explores the application of ABMs for analyzing and mitigating systemic risk, which poses a threat to financial stability. Systemic risk "can be defined as a risk of disruption to financial services that is caused by an impairment of all or parts of the financial system and has the potential to have serious negative consequences for the real economy" (Caruana 2010, BIS). As the GFC has shown, risks can emerge in corners of the financial system that are considered to be relatively insignificant before they materialize. However, risks can spread rapidly and engulf institutions at the core of the system, which can then further propagate and amplify these risks. In the following subsections, we categorize these models into five areas: (1) interbank market; (2) financial markets; (3) interaction between financial and real sectors; (4) the housing market; and (5) climate change.

Interbank Market

Numerous central bank research projects have contributed greatly to the development and application of network models that feature contagion processes within the banking system. This rich branch of the literature provides advancements along several strands, most importantly regarding (1) the formation and reconstruction of bank networks and (2) the spreading of shocks via different contagion channels in the banking system. Although most of the works listed in this section have contributed to both of these topics, we have categorized them into these two groups based on their primary focus.

~87~

Modeling the incentives behind the formation of bank networks can help central banks better understand the emergence of systemic risk in the interbank market. This can be used as a basis for designing policies aimed at lowering such risks. Grzegorz Hałaj and Christoffer Kok (2013, ECB) propose a network reconstruction method that provides a way to assess the resilience of the banking system without observing its actual topology. Christoph Aymanns and Co-Pierre Georg (2015, DBB), Hałaj and Kok (2015, ECB), Marcin Wolski and Michiel van de Leur (2016, ECB), and Jorge Chan-Lau (2017, IMF) focus instead on modeling the endogenous development of networks in the interbank market.

Regarding contagion channels, many central bank studies on bank networks consider only a single channel. Paolo Barucca *et al.* (2020, BoE) build a model in which the value of the non-interbank assets of banks is uncertain, while Marco Bardoscia *et al.* (2019, BoE) extend this work with the possibility for banks to default at any point in time rather than at fixed maturity. Parallel to these developments, Anqi Liu *et al.* (2020, OFR) build an ABM consisting of thousands of banks together with their empirically observed decision rules, while Hałaj (2020,

BoC) uses the ABM of Hałaj (2018, BoC) calibrated to empirical data from Canada to model contagion on the interbank market. Lastly, Adrian Carro and Patricia Stupariu (2024, BdE) also consider the incomplete information and the heterogeneous expectations of agents in interbank contagion.

Several central bank studies also attempt to combine multiple contagion channels in order to capture the overall extent of systemic risks more comprehensively. Sebastian Poledna *et al.* (2015, BdM), Walter Cuba *et al.* (2021, BCRP) and Eduardo Yanquen *et al.* (2022, BRC) use the multilayer version of the DebtRank model (a pivotal work by Battiston *et al.* 2012) to combine different types of exposures, such as credit, derivatives, foreign exchange, and securities, for the Mexican, Peruvian, and Colombian banking systems, respectively. Georg (2013, DBB), Mattia Montagna and Kok (2016, ECB), Alan Roncoroni *et al.* (2021a, BoC, ECB, ESRB), and Poledna *et al.* (2021, BdM, CEMLA) consider another critical contagion channel, the overlapping portfolios of banks, while Montagna, Gabriele Torri, and Giovanni Covi (2021, BoE) define three separate contagion layers based on whether banks are affected through solvency, liquidity, or fire sales. Regarding some of the applications of these models, Anne-Caroline Hüser *et al.* (2018, ECB, DBB) and Christoph Siebenbrunner *et al.* (2024, OeNB) use multilayer contagion models to analyze the consequences of bail-in policies, while Farmer *et al.* (2020, BoE) propose a stress-testing framework for the European financial system with multiple network layers and interactions among the different channels.

Financial Markets

Given their relevance for the stability of the financial system, as well as for the effective transmission of monetary policy, financial markets are closely monitored by central banks. In this context, ABMs have been used to study different risks emerging in financial markets as well as to explore the impact of various policies to address such risks.

First, limit order book models have been developed at various institutions to study the emergence of flash crashes in financial markets.[4] These models have been able to reproduce important stylized facts of financial asset returns, such as fat tails (leptokurtic distribution), volatility clustering, and a decaying autocorrelation over moderate time lags. For instance, Richard Bookstaber, Michael D. Foley, and Brian F. Tivnan (2015, OFR) show that heterogeneity in trading decision cycles can have a strong impact on the provision of liquidity and market stability, thereby increasing the likelihood of extreme price movements. This provides support for regulator-imposed pauses in trading (circuit breakers), as they reduce the heterogeneity of the decision cycles. In line with this conclusion, Geir-Are Kårvik *et al.* (2018, BoE) also show that an increase in the trading speed of high-frequency market participants leads to more prevalent flash episodes, while implementing circuit breakers, which are triggered by large price movements, reduces the magnitude and frequency of such episodes. Mark Paddrik *et al.* (2017, OFR) demonstrate that financial stability metrics using more detailed market microstructure data, which is usually available only to regulators and exchanges, have the greatest predictive power as early-warning indicators of impending market destabilization in the form of flash crashes. Bookstaber and Paddrik (2015, OFR) extend this model by introducing sequential auctions, which produce more realistic market dynamics.

---

[4]A flash crash is a swift, steep, and highly volatile drop in the price of a security that happens in a very short time and is quickly followed by a rapid recovery.

Second, in order to understand the dynamics observed in real financial markets, central bank researchers have also explored the use of heterogeneous agent models with adaptive expectations. In particular, Cars Hommes and Joris Vroegop (2019, BoC) provide an explanation for the co-movement in asset markets by extending the seminal asset-pricing model of William Brock and Hommes (1998) to the case of two different (though *ex ante* identical) asset markets with spillover effects between them. In a single market setting, Tommaso Di Francesco and Hommes (2023, BoC) propose the inclusion of agents with perfect foresight, which can be approximated by using a machine learning algorithm. Furthermore, they develop a measure of investor bias based on natural language processing of Twitter data. Using a similar methodology to model the dollarization of household deposits, Ramis Khabibullin and Alexey Ponomarenko (2022, BoR) are able to capture the varying sensitivity of dollarization to exchange rate developments in a context of heightened volatility.

A third focal point of central bank research about financial markets has been on the specific risks posed by various forms of leverage. For instance, building on a model of leveraged asset purchases with margin calls, Stefan Kerbl (2011, OeNB) studies the implications of several regulatory measures on market liquidity and stability. In particular, he finds that a short selling ban reduces volatility but increases tail risk; a transaction tax reduces the occurrence of crashes but increases volatility; only a mandatory risk limit is beneficial for both liquidity and volatility; and there are non-negligible interactions between these regulations. Thomas Breuer *et al.* (2015, OeNB) focus instead on the exchange of leveraged assets and bonds in a model with a continuous double auction mechanism. They validate recent general equilibrium theory results regarding endogenous leverage and its impact on asset pricing, and they highlight the critical role played by the institutional details of the exchange. Building on previous models of leverage targeting among banks, Eva Levelt, Kostas Mavromatis, and Hommes (2021, BoC, DNB) allow banks to repeatedly choose between leverage targeting and an expected utility optimization strategy. They find that, while cycles are still observed, their amplitude decreases as compared to a system of fully leverage targeting banks.

Fourth, central bank research has also explored the consequences of the rise in passive investment strategies among funds investing in the corporate bond market. In particular, Karen Braun-Munzinger, Zijun Liu, and Arthur Turrell (2018, BoE) show that a larger fraction of passive investment funds can increase the tail risk of larger yield dislocations. Furthermore, they also show that spreading redemptions over longer time periods can mitigate the impact of shocks during stressed periods, when investor outflows are unusually large.

Finally, several strands of the literature have built network models of financial contagion similar to those described above for the interbank market, although crucially including other types of financial institutions, such as asset managers, investment funds, insurance companies, or central counterparties (CCPs). Importantly, these institutions are allowed to interact with each other in various markets. Fabio Caccioli, Gerardo Ferrara, and Amanah Ramadiah (2024, BoE) model fire sales contagion through common asset holdings between banks, open-ended investment funds, and insurance companies in the United Kingdom. Matthias Sydow *et al.* (2024, ECB, BdI, BoE, BoG, BCL, BdF, CBI, DNB, DBB), Hałaj (2018, ECB), and Susanna Calimani, Hałaj, and Dawid Żochowski (2022, ECB, BoC) explicitly include other types of financial institutions, such as asset managers or investment funds. A common finding of these studies is that banks that are active in both the interbank and the securities market have a central role in propagating shocks. Bookstaber, Paddrik, and Brian Tivnan (2018, OFR) include prime brokers, hedge funds, and cash providers, among others, in their ABM and assess the risk of fire sales on both the asset and funding sides. Artur Kotlicki *et al.* (2022, BoE) focus on the counterparty credit risk stemming from reinsurance contracts for both life and nonlife insurers, which can act as a source of financial contagion in the UK reinsurance sector. The Bank of England (2021) and Stathis Tompaidis (2017, OFR) propose supervisory stress tests for CCPs.

Interaction Between the Financial and Real Sectors

An increasing number of studies focus on financial stability concerns originating from network connections outside of the financial system. Thiago Christiano Silva, Michel Alexandre da Silva, Benjamin Miranda Tabak (2017; 2018, BCBr) use a network framework to analyze the feedback effects between the Brazilian financial sector and the real economy by observing not only the bank network but also the loan contracts between the banks and their clients. Both Silva *et al.* (2020, BCBr) and Alexandre *et al.* (2023, BCBr) investigate the impact of monetary policy shocks on the Brazilian economy by using similar network model setups. Victoria Landaberry *et al.* (2021, BCU, BdM, CEMLA) take into account not only bank–firm links but also the intrafirm network in Uruguay using a survey about these connections. In a similar manner, András Borsos and Bence Mérő (2020, MNB) build a simulation model of shock propagation based on the observation of the entire Hungarian multilayer bank network, the bank–firm loan connections, and the firm-level supplier network of the country. Jagoda Kaszowska-Mojsa and Mateusz Pipień (2020, NBP) also represent bank–firm interactions in a general macroeconomic ABM environment designed to simulate the economic consequences of macroprudential policies. Lastly,

Ponomarenko and Andrey Sinyakov (2018, BoR) examine the impacts of different regulatory regimes in a model that also includes interactions between the financial and real sectors. However, these interactions are defined in a more general manner, without explicitly addressing the topology of the loan and deposit markets.

Housing Market

The GFC has shown how a downturn in the housing market can destabilize the financial system and the real economy. Since then, several countries have implemented prudential tools such as loan-to-value (LTV), loan-to-income (LTI), and debt-service-to-income limits to help contain risks originating in the housing market. ABMs provide a natural setting to investigate the potential impacts of these housing tools on the housing market. First of all, ABMs are able to capture the high degree of heterogeneity in the housing market, such as households with varying ages, incomes, and wealth profiles, as well as housing stock with different qualities. Second, ABMs can generate nonlinear dynamics similar to those observed in real housing markets, such as housing booms and busts. Importantly, these dynamics emerge endogenously from the complex interactions between different types of households based, for instance, on their housing tenure, that is, on whether they are renters, first-time buyers, home movers, or buy-to-let investors. Finally, ABMs enable researchers to incorporate potentially complex policy interventions, such as policies targeting a certain segment of the market (e.g., residential mortgages) and/or involving thresholds (e.g., a soft LTI limit).

The model by Rafa Baptista *et al.* (2016, BoE) was the first housing ABM developed by central bank researchers to study the impact of housing tools on the housing and mortgage markets. This model builds on the groundbreaking work of Robert Axtell *et al.* (2014) by incorporating realistic lifecycle dynamics, both a buy-to-let sector and an autonomous rental market, as well as a more realistic double-auction market mechanism. With these new features, the authors are able to analyze the impact of housing policies on different types of households in the United Kingdom, such as renters, first-time buyers, home movers, and buy-to-let investors. This model has been extended and improved in various directions, as well as adapted and calibrated to different national housing markets: in Denmark by Graeme Cokayne (2019, DN; 2024, DN, RBNZ, BoE); in Italy by Gennaro Catapano *et al.* (2021, BdI) and Catapano (2023, BdI); in Spain by Carro (2023, BdE); and in the UK by Carro *et al.* (2023, BdE, BoE). These models are used to conduct counterfactual analyses in order to understand the impact of different LTV and LTI limits on credit and house price cycles. These studies find a dampening effect of these housing tools on mortgage lending and house price cycles. Some other key findings from these studies can be summarized as follows: housing tools lead to a reduction in household indebtedness, loan riskiness, mortgage default, and negative equity, and an increased demand for lower-quality houses; first-time buyers are affected more by these policy interventions; policies targeting the owner–occupier mortgage market can have spillover effects to buy-to-let mortgages/house purchases, and therefore affect the rental market as well; when calibrating an individual housing tool, the calibration of other policies and the joint distribution of risk characteristics should be taken into account.

Building on Baptista *et al.* (2016, BoE), though significantly departing from it, Mérő *et al.* (2023, MNB) develop a 1:1 scale model of the Hungarian residential housing market, incorporating detailed characteristics of four million households and the entire housing stock. This type of very granular and detailed ABM is useful for studying the impact of a range of policies, from macroprudential tools to family support programs. Furthermore, this high level of granularity allows for close monitoring of the effects of these policies across, for instance, different regions of the country. Dimitrios Laliotis *et al.* (2020, ECB) and Arthur Bauer and Nicolas Krakovitch (2021, DGT) build on the original model of Axtell *et al.* (2014) to develop housing ABMs for European economies and the French housing market, respectively. These models are then used to evaluate the impact of various housing tools. Based on a simpler approach, Wilko Bolt *et al.* (2019, DNB) and Ugochi Emenogu, Hommes, and Mikael Khan (2021, BoC) introduce a small ABM component into a standard user cost of capital housing model in order to represent endogenous switching between heterogeneous expectations. While Bolt *et al.* (2019, DNB) use this model to identify housing bubbles and crashes across different countries, Emenogu, Hommes, and Khan (2021, BoC) use it to build indicators of housing exuberance for a broad set of Canadian cities.

~ 95 ~

It is important to note that all the models described above are partial, in the sense that they all focus exclusively on the housing and mortgage markets, thereby neglecting the multiple feedback effects between these sectors and the rest of the economy. A major breakthrough in this regard is the model recently proposed by Bardoscia *et al.* (2025, BoE, BdE), which incorporates Carro *et al.*'s (2023, BdE, BoE) housing ABM into Lilit Popoyan, Mauro Napoletano, and Andrea Roventini's (2017) macroeconomic ABM. By properly accounting for these feedback effects in a stock-flow consistent manner, this model enables researchers to understand the impact of housing tools on the broader economy as well as to conduct comprehensive cost and benefit analyses.

Climate Change

In recent years, an increasing number of central banks and financial supervisors have come to identify climate change as a potential source of risk to financial stability (Carney 2015; Gros *et al.* 2016; Network for Greening the Financial System 2019; Dunz and Power 2021; Basel Committee on Banking Supervision 2021; Brunetti *et al.* 2021). On the one hand, regulatory changes aimed at fostering the transition to a low-carbon economy may entail important shifts in the use of energy, with potential macroeconomic consequences, as well as a sudden revaluation of carbon-intensive assets (transition risk). On the other hand, the increased exposure to natural hazards driven by climate change can lead to significant financial costs for companies and households, such as repair and replacement expenses for damaged infrastructure, as well as to losses due to the disruption that these hazards cause to businesses (physical risk).

Most of the ABMs developed by central banks to study the impact of climate change have focused on transition risks. In this context, Roncoroni *et al.* (2021b, BdM, CEMLA) expand on Barucca *et al.*'s (2020, BoE) interbank network contagion model by also considering the indirect contagion between banks and investment funds via common asset exposures, and they use this expanded model to focus on transition-related shocks derived from various climate policy scenarios. They find that, during a disorderly low-carbon transition, stronger market conditions enable the adoption of more ambitious climate policies without increasing systemic risk. Expanding on Hałaj (2018; 2020, BoC), Gabriel Bruneau *et al.*'s (2023, BoC) network contagion model includes banks, investment funds, insurance companies, and pension funds, and it also considers various contagion channels, such as interbank lending, common asset exposures, and fire sales. They find that certain types of entities, such as investment funds, are more likely to amplify transition shocks within the financial system, while others, such as pension funds, tend to dampen them. Focusing on the real economy, Johannes Stangl *et al.* (2024, MNB) build a model of shock propagation through supply chains, which they calibrate using the entire firm-level production network of the Hungarian economy. With this model, they are able to identify optimal emission reduction strategies with a minimum of additional unemployment and economic losses. In particular, they find that, for a given emission reduction (20%), the most effective strategy minimizes job and output losses (both 2%), while a naive approach targeting the largest emitters results in significantly higher losses (28% in jobs, 33% in output).

Considering both transition and physical risks, Régis Gourdel and Sydow (2023) develop a model of short-term stress propagation in the investment fund sector that takes into account both cross-holdings of fund shares and overlapping exposures. In terms of transition risk, they find that the diverse sustainability investment strategies of funds act as a limiting factor for contagion and network amplification. Physical risk, on the contrary, is found to be more equally distributed across funds, also leading to more substantial contagion losses. Also taking into account both transition and physical risks, Gourdel *et al.* (2024, WB, ECB) build a stock-flow consistent behavioral model (based on Monasterolo and Raberto 2018) in order to examine the reciprocal influence between climate, the real economy, and the financial system. They find that an orderly transition yields early benefits by lowering emissions and promoting economic growth, while a disorderly transition worsens economic output and financial stability. Furthermore, if coupled with a higher degree of physical risk, a disorderly transition can also lead to a strong economic contraction (12% fall in GDP).

Finally, they find that climate policy credibility plays an important role in accelerating the transition to a low-carbon economy and in decreasing the risk of carbon-stranded assets for investors.

PRICE STABILITY

This section explores ABMs that have been used to investigate the implications of monetary policy. Since the 1990s, central banks have primarily relied on dynamic stochastic general equilibrium (DSGE) models and econometric analyses for this task. Recently, however, central banks have made increasing efforts to incorporate alternative modeling approaches such as ABMs into their toolkits.

One of the most important contributions in this regard is the paper by Poledna *et al.* (2023, BoC), who develop a macroeconomic ABM of the small open economy of Austria that can compete with benchmark vector autoregression and DSGE models in out-of-sample forecasting of macro variables. Crucially, the model not only serves as a competitive forecasting framework for aggregate variables but also enables detailed sector-level forecasts due to its agent-based nature. As an application, the authors present projections for the medium-term macroeconomic impacts resulting from the lockdown measures implemented in Austria in response to the COVID-19 pandemic. Hommes *et al.* (2024, BoC) build on this model by adapting and recalibrating it to the Canadian economy, as well as by extending it in three main directions: increased household heterogeneity (e.g., heterogeneous incomes); a dynamic monetary policy; and a more sophisticated price-setting rule for firms allowing for a decomposition of inflation into demand-pull, expectations, and cost-push factors. With this extended model, the authors are able to explore the main drivers behind the postpandemic inflation surge in Canada and analyze the uneven impact of the lockdown across households and industries (see Hommes *et al.* 2026, ch. 14 of this volume, for additional details). Using this same model, Jakob Grazzini *et al.* (2023, BoC) delve deeper into the dynamics of postpandemic inflation in Canada, tracing its origins back to the lifting of economic restrictions in mid-2020, which triggered demand-pull inflation. Finally, Hommes and Poledna (2023, BoC) extend the original model by Poledna *et al.* (2023, BoC) with a financial accelerator mechanism, which paves the way for its application in analyzing and potentially forecasting financial crises in the absence of any exogenous shock. In particular, they calibrate this extended model to the euro area and focus on three recent economic crises: the financial crisis of 2007–2009 and the subsequent Great Recession; the European sovereign debt crisis; and the COVID-19 recession. Importantly, the out-of-sample forecasts produced by this model are, in general, significantly better than those of the benchmark vector autoregression and DSGE models.

~99~

Several other ABMs investigate issues relevant to monetary policy. Paul De Grauwe and Eddie Gerba (2016, BdE) develop a behavioral macroeconomic framework with bounded rationality and provide a comparison of impulse responses to monetary policy shocks against a DSGE model with rational expectations. Their findings indicate that the impulse responses of the bounded rationality model are more closely aligned with the empirical evidence on the effects of monetary policy shocks. Alexandre *et al.* (2023, BCBr) also study the impact of monetary policy shocks, in particular to enhance our understanding of the financial network channel of monetary policy transmission. Although the model does not consider a fully endogenous monetary policy, it helps to assess how exogenous shocks to the policy interest rate affect some key topological measures of the bank–firm credit network through simulations. Ramis Khabibullin, Ponomarenko, and Sergei Seleznev (2018, BoR) develop an ABM that includes a realistic mechanism of money creation and assumes different scenarios of foreign reserve accumulation in Russia.

The evolution of central bank mandates has led to increased research on the interplay between monetary policy frameworks and financial stability regulations (see the "Financial Stability" subsection above). In this context, Alexandre and Gilberto Tadeu Lima (2020, BCBr) study the impact of various combinations of monetary policy and prudential regulation frameworks on macroeconomic and financial stability. In particular, they focus on several rules for setting interest rates as well as various capital requirement regulations (specifically, different types of cyclical buffers). They find that the effectiveness of a given policy (e.g., interest rate rule) depends on the specification of the other policy it is combined with (e.g., capital requirement rule); interest rate smoothing is more effective than the traditional Taylor rule and a leaning against the wind rule; and there is no trade-off between achieving monetary and financial stability. At the intersection of monetary policy and financial stability analysis, Elena Deryugina, Maria Guseva and Ponomarenko (2022, BoR) use ABMs and New Keynesian models to generate artificial credit cycle episodes. They show that the decrease in the measures of the natural rate of interest so widely discussed in the literature does not always reflect changes in macroeconomic fundamentals but rather reflects the effect of the measurement technique around peaks in the credit cycle.

To summarize, while the use of ABMs in monetary policy is not yet widespread, the papers discussed above demonstrate the value of this approach. In particular, these studies have highlighted ABMs' ability to provide useful insights even during periods of high uncertainty, such as the COVID-19 pandemic. ABMs have also proven useful in enhancing our understanding of the interaction between monetary policy and other policies, such as fiscal, macroprudential, and even social policies, provided we consider the potential redistributive effects of monetary policy (Gleiser *et al.* 2024, NBP). Further research on this topic is crucially needed.

PAYMENT SYSTEMS AND CENTRAL BANK DIGITAL CURRENCIES

With the rapid rise of digital technologies in the early 2000s, central banks have been compelled to evaluate the opportunities and risks associated with new forms of digital payments. Computer simulations have proven particularly suited for this task, given their natural ability to reproduce specific payment flows under controlled conditions. In this context, the decentralized modeling approach of ABMs offers the additional advantage of permitting the analysis of emergent macroscopic patterns from detailed microscopic behavioral changes.

The first wave of research in payment systems simulations revolved around the study of real-time gross settlement (RTGS) systems. RTGS simulations were pioneered by the Bank of Finland through the development and use of the general software Bank of Finland Payment and Settlement Simulator (BoF-PSS), which also encompasses simulators based on ABMs (Leinonen and Soramäki 2003; Leinonen 2009, SP). Notably, the simulation software created by the Bank of Finland (2024) has been licensed to more than ninety central banks and continues to be enhanced. Following this, other central banks have proposed ABMs for similar purposes. Amadeo Alentorn *et al.* (2011, BoE) develop an ABM for assessing the risks and costs associated with different payment systems design choices. Marco Galbiati and Kimmo Soramäki (2011, BoE) use ABMs to study the properties of the game-theoretic equilibria that are achieved when banks try to optimize liquidity costs within an RTGS system. Luca Arciero *et al.* (2008, BdI) set up an ABM to simulate and analyze the macroscopic impact of a disruptive event that happens at the level of a single bank. Jonnathan Caceres-Santos *et al.* (2020, BCB, BdM, CEMLA) assess the systemic risk of the Bolivian high-value payment system and interbank market by characterizing the properties of both networks and performing stress-testing experiments. The advent of electronic payments for retail use also led to an interest in ABM simulations for these payment technologies. Biliana Alexandrova-Kabadjova and Jose Luis Negrín (2009, BdM) and Alexandrova-Kabadjova, Sara Castellanos-Pascacio, and Alma García-Almanza (2015, BdM) use ABMs to assess how network effects and payment fees impact the growth of card payment networks.

Recently, with the rise of native digital-asset technologies, central banks have begun to explore the potential for issuing direct liabilities in the form of central bank digital currencies (CBDCs). Researchers at central banks and other policy institutions have analyzed the potential effects of this novel means of payment using ABM simulations. Marco Gross and Siebenbrunner (2022, IMF) study how bank loans could be granted in a CBDC-dominated financial system where all money is digital and directly issued by the central bank. Martens (2021, DNB) studies the crowding-out effects of CBDCs on traditional cash and deposits across various scenarios, including simulations of deposit-like and cash-like CBDCs, to examine the impact of CBDC competitiveness and the critical role of network effects. Gross and Elisa Letizia (2023, IMF) quantitatively explore the potential implications of a CBDC on banking profitability through an ABM that encompasses banks modeled as learning agents setting the remuneration rates in a competitive game. Marco Benedetti *et al.* (2024, BdI) simulate a scaled-down hypothetical European CBDC based on blockchain technologies for studying its trade-offs between liquidity, payment success rate, throughput, and latency.

Technical and Methodological Research

Agent-based models are highly computational tools and, for this reason, can greatly improve over time through the ever-growing availability of data and computational power. However, this also means that technical and methodological research efforts are particularly important for their success and to progressively mitigate their limitations. In this section, we review some directions of methodological progress that are currently being investigated and point at relevant contributions from central banks and related institutions.

A first direction of methodological progress lies in the development of very large-scale models. Following the categorization of Axtell and Farmer (2025), we can divide ABMs into three broad classes: (1) "small-scale" models that qualitatively reproduce some stylized facts; (2) "medium-scale" models that quantitatively reproduce aggregate economic data and serve to link micro and social levels; (3) "large-scale" models in which microdata are used to quantitatively identify the behavior of individuals through calibration or estimation procedures in order to recreate or predict important economic phenomena. Significant improvements in data availability and computational capabilities, coupled with the increased prevalence of interdisciplinary research in economics (especially in conjunction with computer and data science), are leading to a rapid progression of the field toward the latter category, and even toward models that aim for a 1:1 representation. These models have the advantage of often being directly calibrated using microdata and could lead to authentic digital twins of the real economy, as was also advocated in Haldane (2019, BoE). Key contributions in this area include the work of Mérő *et al.* (2023, MNB), which establishes the first central banking model at a 1:1 scale with the real world. Furthermore, Zsuszanna Hosszú *et al.* (2024, MNB) present an in-depth analysis of the implications of downscaling economic ABMs, concluding that optimal model size is often larger than previously imagined. Lastly, in Aldo Glielmo *et al.* (2025, BdI), researchers introduce an open-source software package designed to support the development of large-scale macroeconomic models.

A second direction of methodological progress involves the exploitation of machine learning algorithms and software tools for model calibration on large volumes of data. This could enable more accurate and more efficient calibrations and, at the same time, eliminate the need for the lengthy, human-driven trial-and-error process that would otherwise be required. A prominent contribution in this area is the work of Benedetti *et al.* (2022, BdI), which introduces a software package specifically designed for ABM calibration encompassing, for example, search methods based on machine learning surrogates, genetic algorithms, or low-discrepancy sequences. The software was originally designed to calibrate the ABM of the Italian housing market (Catapano *et al.* 2021, BdI) and was later expanded, reengineered, and made available in open source. Additionally, Glielmo *et al.* (2023, BdI) explore how reinforcement learning algorithms can accelerate the calibration process of ABMs.

A third direction of methodological progress is motivated

by the rapid rise of artificial intelligence (AI). In the future, AI software agents with complex decision-making behavior could be integrated within ABMs, thereby ensuring realism and lifting the modeler's need to specify precise behavioral rules in advance. Important contributions in this area include the work of Tohid Atashbar and Rui (Aruhan) Shi (2022, IMF), which investigates the application of reinforcement learning to enhance traditional macroeconomic models with learning agents. The work suggests that, combined with this technique, ABMs can be used to simulate complex economies featuring numerous learning and interacting economic agents. Complementarily, Simone Brusatin *et al.* (2024, BdI) expand a traditional macro ABM by incorporating reinforcement learning agents that derive behavioral rules from the rational maximization of a reward function. Additionally, Edward Hill, Bardoscia, and Turrell (2021, BoE) leverage reinforcement learning to solve a hybrid model that combines features of both macro ABMs and general equilibrium models. Looking ahead, we can imagine large language models (LLMs) to be used as models for human decision-making in ABMs, as also suggested by Andrea Coletta *et al.* (2024, BdI) in their assessment of the capability of existing LLMs to effectively capture subrational human behavior.

~ 105 ~

A final promising future development lies in the exploitation of recent advancements in automatic differentiation coming from the deep learning community to build ABMs that can be differentiated algorithmically. Having access to the derivative of the simulation results with respect to any model parameter would facilitate conducting a sensitivity analysis, ultimately improving the interpretability and trustworthiness of the resulting ABMs even for researchers and policymakers who are not experts in the field. This area of research is only now beginning to attract researchers from the ABM community and has not yet been pursued at central banks.

Applications in Policy Work

Agent-based approaches have been used by several central banks to inform actual policy processes. While the specific analytical tools and methodologies used by central banks in their policy work are sometimes not explicitly mentioned, we collect in this section examples where such use of ABMs has been publicly disclosed.

The European Central Bank was among the first to recognize the value of this methodology and to use it to inform some of its policy work and assessments, particularly in relation to the contagion of distress in financial networks and systemic risk monitoring. For instance, it has highlighted the importance of understanding the financial system as a complex and dynamic network, and it has advocated for the development of contagion models with behavioral features to gain a deeper understanding of systemic risk and improve the identification of systemically important institutions (ECB, 2010; Adam *et al.* 2019, ECB). Furthermore, a number of its policy reports in the last decade have included contributions based on the use of such models. For example, ECB (2012) and Hałaj, Kok, and Montagna (2013) address the emergence of the network of interbank exposures, as well as the potential effect of macroprudential policies on the structure of the resulting network. Lorenzo Cappiello, Linda Fache Rousová, and Montagna (2015, ECB), Giovanni Covi, Kok, and Barbara Meller (2018, ECB), and Covi, Montagna, and Torri (2019, ECB) focus on measuring systemic risk and identifying systemically important institutions based on network models that account for different subsets of contagion channels (from direct exposures to overlapping portfolios and fire sales). Finally, Tomasz Dubiel-Teleszynski *et al.* (2022, ECB) use a systemwide stress-testing framework with multiple contagion channels and various types of institutions (banks, investment funds, and insurance companies) to analyze the impact of a severe climate-change stress scenario (disorderly transition) on the financial system.

The Bank of England was also an early adopter of agent-based modeling, incorporating it into some of its policy analyses and evaluations (Plassard 2020; Turrell 2016, BoE). It has used systemwide stress tests in which banks and nonbank financial institutions, such as insurers, central counterparties, pension funds, hedge funds, and other types of managed funds, have participated (Bank of England 2023). It has also used its housing ABM, among other evidence, to inform its analysis of financial stability risks stemming from the UK buy-to-let market (Zemaityte, Hughes, and Blood 2023, BoE).

The Magyar Nemzeti Bank, the central bank of Hungary, has also extensively used the methodology. Specifically, it has used its housing market ABM to assist in answering several questions of financial stability, such as the impact of loan-to-value ratio limits, financial support, or increased utility costs on households (see, e.g., MNB, 2021aa, 2021cc, 2022bb). It has also used the same model for questions related to the housing market more specifically, such as the impact of increases in home construction costs and in the base interest rate on housing and credit markets (see, e.g., MNB, 2021bb, 2022aa). Additionally, the Magyar Nemzeti Bank has also embedded a version of the Borsos and Mérő (2020, MNB) network model into its liquidity stress-testing framework to represent various contagion channels in the banking system. The results of this stress test exercise have been regularly published in the Financial Stability Reports of the Magyar Nemzeti Bank since 2016 (MNB, 2016).

Another example is the Bank of Canada, which has been a pioneer in incorporating ABMs into its general toolkit for macroeconomic projections and policy analysis. In fact, it recently became the first central bank to formally acknowledge a role for this methodological approach within its official modeling strategy. In particular, Don Coletti (2023, BoC) outlines a strategic plan for developing a suite of models to better support a risk management approach to monetary policy that recognizes the significant uncertainties in how the economy functions. In this context, ABMs are explicitly included within the category of specialty models, which are defined as models whose goal is to consider "alternative plausible economic structures that are too complex to include in the core model or its variants." The role played by ABMs within the modeling strategy of the Bank of Canada has been further discussed by Marc-André Gosselin and Sharon Kozicki (2023, BoC), who address the challenges involved in adapting research-oriented models for policy use. Specifically, they highlight that the macroeconomic ABM by Hommes *et al.* (2024, BoC), described above in "Price Stability," has been particularly informative during the COVID-19 lockdowns and subsequent supply-chain issues.

Finally, it is worth emphasizing that, over time, a growing number of central banks are incorporating agent-based modeling into their policy analysis toolkit, as a complement to their existing tools. For instance, the most recent Financial Stability Report of the Banco de España employs a network contagion model for the first time to evaluate the potential contagion losses resulting from a severe shock to the Spanish banking system (BdE, 2024).

Conclusion

We have reviewed the literature on the use of ABMs by central banks and related policy institutions over the last decade, focusing particularly on how these models have helped to address traditional central bank mandates—such as price and financial stability—as well as the new challenges that emerged following the global financial crisis and the COVID-19 pandemic.

The strengthening and consolidation of this relatively novel tool of economic investigation seems particularly timely in relation to the new challenges that central banks will have to face in the coming years, and for which a range of modern instruments will certainly be needed. We have already described some of these challenges and how ABMs could be used to address them. For example, we referred to the proliferation of digital assets and the potential introduction of a CBDC, and described how ABMs can serve as valuable analytical tools in this context due to their ability to simulate individual monetary transactions within structured and realistic payment networks. Another relevant challenge concerns the analysis and regulation of nonbank financial intermediaries. This growing sector already accounts for more than 50% of total financial assets in the euro area, and while it is difficult to include within traditional modeling frameworks, it can be easily modeled in an ABM along with its interaction with the banking sector. In recent decades, economic inequality has increased considerably in almost all advanced economies. This phenomenon also poses a challenge for central banks, both because of its macroeconomic impact on inflation and growth and for the analysis of any potential unintended redistributive consequences of monetary and financial stability policies. ABMs' ability to naturally model heterogeneity in both wealth and income makes them particularly suitable for these studies. Finally, it is also worth mentioning that some global processes that are not strictly economic or financial in nature still appear to be of interest to central banks for their potential disruption of certain markets. For example, climate change and the green energy transition can have significant effects on the energy or housing markets, digital innovation and the rise of AI are likely to cause significant changes to the labor market, and geopolitical tensions can cause disruptions of global supply chains.

Given their key strengths, ABMs could be valuable tools for analyzing each of the described trends. First, intrinsically nonequilibrium shocks—for example, an abrupt suspension of certain supply chains—can be difficult to model accurately within traditional equilibrium frameworks, while ABMs are well suited for this purpose. Second, the granular and heterogeneous nature of ABMs is a highly valuable feature for providing practical policy advice, for example, for differentiating the specific job categories that are most vulnerable to being replaced by AI. Third, ABMs have the potential to be coupled with simulation models from disciplines other than economics in order to provide a richer and timelier picture of the phenomenon being studied. For example, the effects of climate change on house prices could be examined by coupling a housing market model with geographical or environmental models. Similarly, the economic effects of another possible pandemic could be studied by coupling an economic ABM with a detailed model of the transmission of infectious diseases.

The advantages of ABMs come with some challenges. The granular and heterogeneous nature of ABMs, while enabling rich and diverse agent behaviors, also presents difficulties.

Defining the behavioral rules that govern agent interactions can be complex, particularly when deviating from standard economic assumptions, and often requires novel approaches at the frontier of economic theory. Precise calibration of parameters is challenging, especially when empirical data is scarce. Simulating large numbers of heterogeneous agents in a dynamic environment makes the model computationally intensive and complex. Due to the nonlinear nature of agent interactions, tracing the pathways from specific behaviors or rules to emergent outcomes demands significant time and effort. Moreover, large-scale ABMs require specialized skills, such as programming, data processing, and simulation modeling, which often necessitate interdisciplinary research teams. While these challenges limit the widespread use of ABMs in some institutions, continuous technological and methodological advancements are gradually reducing these barriers. Alleviating computational constraints, in particular, could help address modeling challenges, especially in the crucial calibration phase of ABMs.

~III~

To summarize, agent-based modeling has proven to be an effective analytical tool for central banks in carrying out their responsibilities, especially after the expansion of their mandates following the global financial crisis. While there is still significant room for improvement, ongoing advancements in the methodology provide a solid foundation for the future. Considering the many challenges that modern economies will face in the coming years, from digital currencies to climate risks, ABMs represent a unique opportunity for central banks to enrich their analytical frameworks to promptly provide informed policy responses.

REFERENCES

Adam, M., P. Bochmann, M. Grodzicki, L. Mingarelli, M. Montagna, C. Rodriguez d'Acri, and M. Spaggiari. 2019. *Assessing the Systemic Footprint of Euro Area Banks.* Financial Stability Review, Special Feature B. https://www.ecb.europa. eu/press/financial-stability-publications/fsr/special/html/ecb.fsrart201911_02~5fd45e4b5a.en.html.

Alentorn, A., S. Markose, S. Millard, and J. Yang. 2011. *Designing Large Value Payment Systems: An Agent-Based Approach.* Discussion Paper, No. 700, November 2011. Department of Economics, University of Essex. https://repository.essex.ac.uk/3714/1/dp700.pdf.

Alexandre, M., and G. T. Lima. 2020. "Combining Monetary Policy and Prudential Regulation: An Agent-Based Modeling Approach." *Journal of Economic Interaction and Coordination* 15:385–411. https://doi.org/10.1007/s11403-017-0209-0.

Alexandre, M., G. T. Lima, L. Riccetti, and A. Russo. 2023. "The Financial Network Channel of Monetary Policy Transmission: An Agent-Based Model." *Journal of Economic Interaction and Coordination* 18 (3): 533–571. https://doi.org/10.1007/s11403-023-00377-w.

Alexandrova-Kabadjova, B., S. G. Castellanos-Pascacio, and A. L. García-Almanza. 2015. "The Adoption Process of Payment Cards: An Agent-Based Approach." In *Banking, Finance, and Accounting: Concepts, Methodologies, Tools, and Applications,* edited by Information Resources Management Association, 1228–1252. IGI Global. https://doi.org/10.4018/978-1-4666-6268-1.ch066.

Alexandrova-Kabadjova, B., and J. L. Negrín. 2009. *What Drives the Network's Growth? An Agent-Based Study of the Payment Card Market.* Working Paper 1143. European Central Bank. https://doi.org/10.2139/ssrn.1522034.

Arciero, L., C. Biancotti, L. D'Aurizio, and C. Impenna. 2008. "Exploring Agent-Based Methods for the Analysis of Payment Systems: A Crisis Model for Starlogo TNG." *Temi di Discussione (Working Paper)* 686. https://doi.org/10.2139/ssrn.1290520.

Atashbar, T., and R. Shi. 2022. *Deep Reinforcement Learning: Emerging Trends in Macroeconomics and Future Prospects.* IMF Working Paper WP/22/259. International Monetary Fund. https://doi.org/10.5089/9798400224713.001.

Chapter 18: Agent-Based Modeling at Central Banks

Axtell, R. L., and J. D. Farmer. 2025. "Agent-Based Modeling in Economics and Finance: Past, Present, and Future." *Journal of Economic Literature* 63 (1): 197–287. https://doi.org/10.1257/jel.20221319.

Axtell, R. L., J. D. Farmer, J. Geanakoplos, P. Howitt, E. Carrella, B. Conlee, J. Goldstein, *et al.* 2014. "An Agent-Based Model of the Housing Market Bubble in Metropolitan Washington, DC." In *Deutsche Bundesbank's Spring Conference on "Housing Markets and the Macroeconomy: Challenges for Monetary Policy and Financial Stability"*, 5–6. https://doi.org/10.2139/ssrn.4710928.

Aymanns, C., and C.-P. Georg. 2015. "Contagious Synchronization and Endogenous Network Formation in Financial Networks." *Journal of Banking & Finance* 50:273–285. https://doi.org/10.1016/j.jbankfin.2014.06.030.

Banco de España. 2024. *Financial Sector Risks and Resilience*. Financial Stability Report, Autumn 2024. https://www.bde.es/f/webbe/Secciones/Publicaciones/InformesBoletinesRevistas/InformesEstabilidadFinancera/24/FSR_2024_2_Ch2.pdf.

Bank of England. 2021. *Supervisory Stress Testing of Central Counterparties*. Discussion Paper Discussion Paper 1000. Bank of England. https://www.bankofengland.co.uk/paper/2021/supervisorystress-testing-of-central-counterparties.

———. 2023. *The Bank of England's System-Wide Exploratory Scenario Exercise*. https://www.bankofengland.co.uk/financial-stability/boe-system-wideexploratory-scenario-exercise/boe-swes.

Bank of Finland. 2024. *BoF-PSS Simulator*. https://www.suomenpankki.fi/en/financial-stability/bof-pss-simulator/.

Baptista, R., J. D. Farmer, M. Hinterschweiger, K. Low, D. Tang, and A. Uluc. 2016. *Macroprudential Policy in An Agent-Based Model of the UK Housing Market*. Staff Working Paper 619. Bank of England. https://doi.org/10.2139/ssrn.2850414.

Bardoscia, M., P. Barucca, A. B. Codd, and J. Hill. 2019. "Forward-Looking Solvency Contagion." *Journal of Economic Dynamics and Control* 108:103755. https://doi.org/10.1016/j.jedc.2019.103755.

~113~

Bardoscia, M., A. Carro, M. Hinterschweiger, M. Napoletano, L. Popoyan, A. Roventini, and A. Uluc. 2025. "The Impact of Prudential Regulations on the UK Housing Market and Economy: Insights from an Agent-Based Model." *Journal of Economic Behavior & Organization* 229:106839. https://doi.org/ 10.1016/j.jebo.2024.106839.

Barucca, P., M. Bardoscia, F. Caccioli, M. D'Errico, G. Visentin, G. Caldarelli, and S. Battiston. 2020. "Network Valuation in Financial Systems." *Mathematical Finance* 30 (4): 1181–1204. https://doi.org/10.1111/mafi.12272.

Basel Committee on Banking Supervision. 2015. *Making Supervisory Stress Tests More Macroprudential: Considering Liquidity and Solvency Interactions and Systemic Risk.* Working Paper 29. BCBS. https://www.bis.org/bcbs/publ/ wp29.htm.

———. 2021. *Climate-Related Risk Drivers and Their Transmission Channels.* Report April 2021. BCBS. https://www.bis.org/bcbs/publ/d517.htm.

Battiston, S., M. Puliga, R. Kaushik, P. Tasca, and G. Caldarelli. 2012. "DebtRank: Too Central to Fail? Financial Networks, The FED and Systemic Risk." *Scientific Reports* 2 (1): 1–6. https://doi.org/10.1038/srep00541.

Bauer, A., and N. Krakovitch. 2021. *Macroprudential Mortgage Lending Measures.* Tresor-Economics No. 277. Direction générale du Trésor, Ministère de l'Économie, des Finances, et de la Relance. https://www.tresor.economie. gouv.fr/Articles/dacc9963-8021-48f9-8b34-3b125e5bf291/files/a11a4da9-9784-4ea0-8838-b8bd1ac37188.

Benedetti, M., G. Catapano, F. De Sclavis, M. Favorito, A. Glielmo, D. Magnanimi, and A. Muci. 2022. "Black-it: A Ready-to-Use and Easy-to-Extend Calibration Kit for Agent-Based Models." *Journal of Open Source Software* 7 (79): 4622. https://doi.org/10.21105/joss.04622.

Benedetti, M., F. De Sclavis, M. Favorito, G. Galano, S. Giammusso, A. Muci, and M. Nardelli. 2024. "Self-Balancing Semi-Hierarchical Payment Channel Networks for Central Bank Digital Currencies." In *2024 IEEE International Conference on Pervasive Computing and Communications Workshops and other Affiliated Events (PerCom Workshops),* 530–536. https://doi.org/10.1109/ PerComWorkshops59983.2024.10503409.

Bolt, W., M. Demertzis, C. Diks, C. Hommes, and M. van der Leij. 2019. "Identifying Booms and Busts in House Prices Under Heterogeneous Expectations." *Journal of Economic Dynamics and Control* 103:234–259. https://doi.org/ 10.1016/j.jedc.2019.04.003.

Bookstaber, R., J. Cetina, G. Feldberg, M. Flood, and P. Glasserman. 2014. "Stress Tests to Promote Financial Stability: Assessing Progress and Looking to the Future." *Journal of Risk Management in Financial Institutions* 7 (1): 16–25. https://doi.org/10.69554/SVZG1421.

Bookstaber, R., M. Paddrik, and B. Tivnan. 2018. "An Agent-Based Model for Financial Vulnerability." *Journal of Economic Interaction and Coordination* 13:433–466. https://doi.org/10.1007/s11403-017-0188-1.

Bookstaber, R. M., M. Foley, and B. Tivnan. 2015. *Market Liquidity and Heterogeneity in the Investor Decision Cycle.* Working Paper 15-03. Office of Financial Research. https://doi.org/10.2139/ssrn.2648459.

Bookstaber, R. M., and M. E. Paddrik. 2015. *An Agent-Based Model for Crisis Liquidity Dynamics.* Working Paper 15-18. Office of Financial Research. https://doi.org/10.2139/ssrn.2664230.

Borsos, A., and B. Mérő. 2020. *Shock Propagation in the Banking System with Real Economy Feedback.* MNB Working Papers 2020/6. Magyar Nemzeti Bank. https://www.mnb.hu/letoltes/mnb-wp-2020-6-final.pdf.

Braun-Munzinger, K., Z. Liu, and A. E. Turrell. 2018. "An Agent-Based Model of Corporate Bond Trading." *Quantitative Finance* 18 (4): 591–608. https://doi.org/10.1080/14697688.2017.1380310.

Breuer, T., M. Jandačka, M. Summer, and H.-J. Vollbrecht. 2015. "Endogenous Leverage and Asset Pricing in Double Auctions." *Journal of Economic Dynamics and Control* 53:144–160. https://doi.org/10.1016/j.jedc.2015.02.004.

Brock, W. A., and C. H. Hommes. 1998. "Heterogeneous Beliefs and Routes to Chaos in a Simple Asset Pricing Model." *Journal of Economic Dynamics and Control* 22 (8): 1235–1274. https://doi.org/10.1016/S0165-1889(98)00011-6.

Bruneau, G., J. Ojea-Ferreiro, A. Plummer, M.-C. Tremblay, and A. Witts. 2023. *Understanding the Systemic Implications of Climate Transition Risk: Applying a Framework Using Canadian Financial System Data.* Staff Discussion Paper 2023-32. Bank of Canada. https://doi.org/10.34989/sdp-2023-32.

Brunetti, C., B. Dennis, D. Gates, D. Hancock, D. Ignell, E. K. Kiser, G. Kotta, A. Kovner, R. Rosen, and N. K. Tabor. 2021. *Climate Change and Financial Stability.* FEDS Notes 2021-03-19. Board of Governors of the Federal Reserve System. https://doi.org/10.17016/2380-7172.2893.

Brusatin, S., T. Padoan, A. Coletta, D. Delli Gatti, and A. Glielmo. 2024. *Simulating the Economic Impact of Rationality Through Reinforcement Learning and Agent-Based Modelling.* arXiv preprint:2405.02161. https://doi.org/10.1145/3677052.3698621.

Caccioli, F., G. Ferrara, and A. Ramadiah. 2024. "Modelling Fire Sale Contagion Across Banks and Non-Banks." *Journal of Financial Stability* 71:101231. https://doi.org/10.1016/j.jfs.2024.101231.

Caceres-Santos, J., A. Rodriguez-Martinez, F. Caccioli, and S. Martinez-Jaramillo. 2020. "Systemic Risk and Other Interdependencies Among Banks in Bolivia." *Latin American Journal of Central Banking* 1 (1): 100015. https://doi.org/10.1016/j.latcb.2020.100015.

Calimani, S., G. Hałaj, and D. Żochowski. 2022. "Simulating Fire Sales in a System of Banks and Asset Managers." *Journal of Banking & Finance* 138:105707. https://doi.org/10.1016/j.jbankfin.2019.105707.

Cappiello, L., L. F. Rousová, and M. Montagna. 2015. *Systemic Risk, Contagion, and Financial Networks.* Financial Stability Review, Special Feature C. European Central Bank. https://www.ecb.europa.eu/pub/pdf/fsr/art/ecb.fsrart201511_03.en.pdf.

Carney, M. 2015. *Breaking the Tragedy of the Horizon—Climate Change and Financial Stability.* Speech given at Lloyd's of London, 29 September. Available at https://www.bankofengland.co.uk/speech/2015/breaking-the-tragedy-of-the-horizon-climate-change-and-financial-stability.

Carro, A. 2023. "Taming the Housing Roller Coaster: The Impact of Macroprudential Policy on the House Price Cycle." *Journal of Economic Dynamics and Control* 156:104753. https://doi.org/10.1016/j.jedc.2023.104753.

Carro, A., M. Hinterschweiger, A. Uluc, and J. D. Farmer. 2023. "Heterogeneous Effects and Spillovers of Macroprudential Policy in an Agent-Based Model of the UK Housing Market." *Industrial and Corporate Change* 32 (2): 386–432. https://doi.org/10.1093/icc/dtac030.

Carro, A., and P. Stupariu. 2024. "Uncertainty, Non-Linear Contagion and the Credit Quality Channel: An Application to the Spanish Interbank Market." *Journal of Financial Stability* 71:101226. https://doi.org/10.1016/j.jfs.2024.101226.

Caruana, J. 2010. *Systemic Risk: How to Deal With It?* Other publications. Bank for International Settlements (BIS). https://www.bis.org/publ/othp08.htm.

Chapter 18: Agent-Based Modeling at Central Banks

Catapano, G. 2023. *Borrower Based Measures Analysis via a New Agent Based Model of the Italian Real Estate Sector.* Questioni di Economia e Finanza (Occasional Papers) 822. Bank of Italy. https://doi.org/10.2139/ssrn.4849455.

Catapano, G., F. Franceschi, M. Loberto, and V. Michelangeli. 2021. *Macroprudential Policy Analysis via an Agent Based Model of the Real Estate Sector.* Temi di Discussione (Working Paper) 1338. Bank of Italy. https://doi.org/10.2139/ssrn.3891583.

Chan-Lau, J. A. 2017. "ABBA: An Agent-Based Model of the Banking System." *IMF Working Papers* 17 (136): 1. https://doi.org/10.5089/9781484300688.001.

Cokayne, G. 2019. *The Effects of Macro-Prudential Policies on House Price Cycles in an Agent-Based Model of the Danish Housing Market.* Working Paper 138. Danmarks Nationalbank. https://www.nationalbanken.dk/media/dafdshbq/working-paper-nr-138.pdf.

Cokayne, G., E. Gerba, A. Kuchler, and R. Pank Roulund. 2024. ""Thank Me Later": Why is (Macro)prudence Desirable?" *Journal of Financial Stability* 71:101227. https://doi.org/10.1016/j.jfs.2024.101227.

Coletta, A., K. Dwarakanath, P. Liu, S. Vyetrenko, and T. Balch. 2024. *LLM-Driven Imitation of Subrational Behavior: Illusion or Reality?* arXiv preprint:2402.08755. https://doi.org/10.48550/arXiv.2402.08755.

Coletti, D. 2023. *A Blueprint for the Fourth Generation of Bank of Canada Projection and Policy Analysis Models.* Staff Discussion Paper 2023-23. Bank of Canada. https://doi.org/10.34989/sdp-2023-23.

Covi, G., C. Kok, and B. Meller. 2018. *Using Large Exposure Data to Gauge the Systemic Importance of SSM Significant Institutions.* Macroprudential Bulletin No. 5. European Central Bank. https://www.ecb.europa.eu/press/financial-stability-publications/macroprudential-bulletin/html/ecb.mpbu201804_01.en.html.

Covi, G., M. Montagna, and G. Torri. 2019. *Economic Shocks and Contagion in the Euro Area Banking Sector: A New Micro-Structural Approach.* Financial Stability Review, Special Feature B. European Central Bank. https://www.ecb.europa.eu/press/financial-stability-publications/fsr/special/html/ecb.fsrart201905_2~073bba7192.en.html.

Cuba, W., A. Rodriguez-Martinez, D. A. Chavez, F. Caccioli, and S. Martinez-Jaramillo. 2021. "A Network Characterization of the Interbank Exposures in Peru." *Latin American Journal of Central Banking* 2 (3): 100035. https://doi.org/10.1016/j.latcb.2021.100035.

De Grauwe, P., and E. Gerba. 2016. *Stock Market Cycles and Supply Side Dynamics: Two Worlds, One Vision?* Documento de Trabajo 1626. Banco de España. https://doi.org/10.2139/ssrn.2859977.

Demekas, D. 2015. *Designing Effective Macroprudential Stress Tests: Progress So Far and the Way Forward.* IMF Working Papers 2015/146. International Monetary Fund. https://doi.org/10.5089/9781513513621.001.

Deryugina, E., M. Guseva, and A. Ponomarenko. 2022. "The Credit Cycle and Measurement of the Natural Rate of Interest 1." *Journal of Central Banking Theory and Practice* 11 (1): 87–104. https://doi.org/10.2478/jcbtp-2022-0004.

Di Francesco, T., and C. H. Hommes. 2023. "Sentiment-Driven Speculation in Financial Markets with Heterogeneous Beliefs: A Machine Learning Approach." *Available at SSRN 4429858,* https://doi.org/10.2139/ssrn.4429858.

Dubiel-Teleszynski, T., F. Franch, G. Fukker, D. Miccio, M. Pellegrino, and M. Sydow. 2022. *System-Wide Amplification of Climate Risk.* Macroprudential Bulletin No. 17. European Central Bank. https://www.ecb.europa.eu/press/financial-stability-publications/macroprudential-bulletin/html/ecb.mpbu202206_2~1bec56088f.en.html.

Dunz, N., and S. Power. 2021. *Climate-Related Risks for Ministries of Finance: An Overview.* Note May 2021. Coalition of Finance Ministers for Climate Action. https://www.financeministersforclimate.org/sites/cape/files/inline-files/Climate-Related%20Risks%20for%20Ministries%20of%20Finance%20-%20An%20Overview%20(CFMCA)_1.pdf.

Emenogu, U., C. Hommes, and M. Khan. 2021. *Detecting Exuberance in House Prices Across Canadian Cities.* Staff Analytical Note 2021-9. Bank of Canada. https://doi.org/10.34989/san-2021-9.

European Central Bank (ECB). 2010. *Financial Networks and Financial Stability.* Financial Stability Review, Special Feature D. https://www.ecb.europa.eu/pub/pdf/fsr/art/ecb.fsrart201006_04.en.pdf.

———. 2012. *Evaluating Interconnectedness in the Financial System on the Basis of Actual and Simulated Networks.* Financial Stability Review, Special Feature C. https://www.ecb.europa.eu/pub/pdf/fsr/art/ecb.fsrart201206_03.en.pdf.

Farmer, J. D., and D. Foley. 2009. "The Economy Needs Agent-Based Modelling." *Nature* 460 (7256): 685–686. https://doi.org/10.1038/460685a.

Farmer, J. D., A. M. Kleinnijenhuis, P. Nahai-Williamson, and T. Wetzer. 2020. *Foundations of System-Wide Financial Stress Testing with Heterogeneous Institutions.* Staff Working Paper 861. Bank of England. https://doi.org/10.2139/ssrn.3601846.

Galbiati, M., and K. Soramäki. 2011. "An Agent-Based Model of Payment Systems." *Journal of Economic Dynamics and Control* 35 (6): 859–875. https://doi.org/10.1016/j.jedc.2010.11.001.

Georg, C.-P. 2013. "The Effect of the Interbank Network Structure on Contagion and Common Shocks." *Journal of Banking & Finance* 37 (7): 2216–2228. https://doi.org/10.1016/j.jbankfin.2013.02.032.

Gleiser, I., J. D. Farmer, J. Kaszowska-Mojsa, and S. Bydlon. 2024. *How Agent-Based Models Powered by HPC are Enabling Large Scale Economic Simulations.* https://aws.amazon.com/blogs/hpc/how-agent-based-models-powered-by-hpc-are-enabling-large-scale-economic-simulations/.

Glielmo, A., M. Devetak, A. Milgrana, and S. Poledna. 2025. *BeforeIT.jl: High-Performance Agent-Based Macroeconomics Made Easy.* arXiv preprint: 2502.13267 [cs.MA]. https://doi.org/10.48550/arXiv.2502.13267.

Glielmo, A., M. Favorito, D. Chanda, and D. Delli Gatti. 2023. "Reinforcement Learning for Combining Search Methods in the Calibration of Economic ABMs." In *Proceedings of the Fourth ACM International Conference on AI in Finance,* 305–313. ICAIF '23. New York, NY: Association for Computing Machinery. https://doi.org/10.1145/3604237.3626889.

Gosselin, M.-A., and S. Kozicki. 2023. *Making It Real: Bringing Research Models into Central Bank Projections.* Staff Discussion Paper 2023-29. Bank of Canada. https://doi.org/10.34989/sdp-2023-29.

Gourdel, R., I. Monasterolo, N. Dunz, A. Mazzocchetti, and L. Parisi. 2024. "The Double Materiality of Climate Physical and Transition Risks in the Euro Area." *Journal of Financial Stability* 71:101233. https://doi.org/10.1016/j.jfs.2024.101233.

Gourdel, R., and M. Sydow. 2023. "Non-Banks Contagion and the Uneven Mitigation of Climate Risk." *International Review of Financial Analysis* 89:102739. https://doi.org/10.1016/j.irfa.2023.102739.

Grazzini, J., C. H. Hommes, S. Poledna, and Y. Zhang. 2023. "Understanding Post-Pandemic Inflation Dynamics with a Behavioral Macroeconomic Model of the Canadian Economy." *SSRN Electronic Journal*, https://doi.org/10.2139/ssrn. 4381235.

Gros, D., P. R. Lane, S. Langfield, S. Matikainen, M. Pagano, D. Schoenmaker, and J. Suarez. 2016. *Too Late, Too Sudden: Transition to a Low-Carbon Economy and Systemic Risk.* Report of the Advisory Scientific Committee No 6 / February 2016. European Systemic Risk Board. https://doi.org/10.2849/703620.

Gross, M., and E. Letizia. 2023. *To Demand or Not to Demand: On Quantifying the Future Appetite for CBDC.* IMF Working Paper WP/23/009. International Monetary Fund. https://doi.org/10.5089/9798400228780.001.

Gross, M., and C. Siebenbrunner. 2022. "Money Creation and Liquid Funding Needs are Compatible." Chap. 6 in *Central Banking, Monetary Policy and the Future of Money*, 154–186. Cheltenham, UK: Edward Elgar Publishing. https://doi.org/10.4337/9781800376403.00013.

Hałaj, G. 2018. "System-Wide Implications of Funding Risk." *Physica A: Statistical Mechanics and its Applications* 503:1151–1181. https://doi.org/10.1016/j. physa.2018.08.060.

———. 2020. "Resilience of Canadian Banks to Funding Liquidity Shocks." *Latin American Journal of Central Banking* 1 (1): 100002. https://doi.org/10.1016/ j.latcb.2020.100002.

Hałaj, G., and C. Kok. 2013. "Assessing Interbank Contagion Using Simulated Networks." *Computational Management Science* 10:157–186. https://doi. org/10.1007/s10287-013-0168-4.

———. 2015. "Modelling the Emergence of the Interbank Networks." *Quantitative Finance* 15 (4): 653–671. https://doi.org/10.1080/14697688.2014.968357.

Hałaj, G., C. Kok, and M. Montagna. 2013. *Gauging the Effectiveness of Cross-Sectional Macroprudential Tools Through the Lens of Interbank Networks.* Financial Stability Review, Special Feature C. European Central Bank. https://www.ecb.europa.eu/pub/pdf/fsr/art/ecb.fsrart201311_03.en.pdf.

Haldane, A. G. 2016. *The Dappled World.* Speech given at the GLS Shackle Biennial Memorial Lecture, 10 November. https : / / www . bankofengland . co . uk / speech/2016/the-dappled-world.

———. 2019. *Is All Economics Local?* Speech given at the Sheffield Political Economy Research Institute (SPERI) Annual Lecture, University of Sheffield, 7 May. https://www.bankofengland.co.uk/speech/2019/andy-haldane-sheffield-political-economy-research-institute-annual-lecture-2019.

Haldane, A. G., and A. E. Turrell. 2018. "An Interdisciplinary Model for Macroeconomics." *Oxford Review of Economic Policy* 34 (1-2): 219–251. https: //doi.org/10.1093/oxrep/grx051.

Henry, J., C. Kok, A. Amzallag, P. Baudino, I. Cabral, M. Grodzicki, M. Gross, *et al.* 2013. *A Macro Stress Testing Framework for Assessing Systemic Risks in the Banking Sector.* Occasional Paper 152. European Central Bank. https://doi. org/10.2139/ssrn.2337894.

Hill, E., M. Bardoscia, and A. Turrell. 2021. *Solving Heterogeneous General Equilibrium Economic Models with Deep Reinforcement Learning.* arXiv preprint: 2103.16977 [econ.GN]. https://doi.org/10.48550/arXiv.2103. 16977.

Hommes, C., M. He, S. Poledna, M. Siqueira, and Y. Zhang. 2024. "CANVAS: A Canadian Behavioral Agent-Based Model for Monetary Policy." *Journal of Economic Dynamics and Control* 172:104986. https://doi.org/10.1016/j. jedc.2024.104986.

Hommes, C., S. Kozicki, S. Poledna, and Y. Zhang. 2026. "How an Agent-Based Model Can Support Monetary Policy in a Complex Evolving Economy." In *The Economy as an Evolving Complex System IV,* edited by R. M. del Rio-Chanona, M. Pangallo, J. Bednar, E. D. Beinhocker, J. Kaszowska-Mojsa, F. Lafond, P. Mealy, A. Pichler, and J. D. Farmer. Santa Fe, NM: SFI Press.

Hommes, C., and J. Vroegop. 2019. "Contagion Between Asset Markets: A Two Market Heterogeneous Agents Model with Destabilising Spillover Effects." *Journal of Economic Dynamics and Control* 100:314–333. https://doi.org/ 10.1016/j.jedc.2018.10.005.

Hommes, C. H., and S. Poledna. 2023. "Analyzing and Forecasting Economic Crises with an Agent-Based Model of the Euro Area." *SSRN Electronic Journal,* https: //doi.org/10.2139/ssrn.4381261.

~ 121 ~

Hosszú, Z., A. Borsos, B. Mérő, and N. Vágó. 2024. "The More the Merrier? The Optimal Choice of Scaling in Economic Agent-Based Models." *SSRN Electronic Journal,* https://doi.org/10.2139/ssrn.4751602.

Hüser, A.-C., G. Hałaj, C. Kok, C. Perales, and A. van der Kraaij. 2018. "The Systemic Implications of Bail-In: A Multi-Layered Network Approach." *Journal of Financial Stability* 38:81–97. https://doi.org/10.1016/j.jfs.2017.12.001.

Kårvik, G.-A., J. Noss, J. Worlidge, and D. Beale. 2018. *The Deeds of Speed: An Agent-Based Model of Market Liquidity and Flash Episodes.* Staff Working Paper 743. Bank of England. https://doi.org/10.2139/ssrn.3222692.

Kaszowska-Mojsa, J., and M. Pipień. 2020. "Macroprudential Policy in a Heterogeneous Environment—An Application of Agent-Based Approach in Systemic Risk Modelling." *Entropy* 22 (2): 129. https://doi.org/10.3390/e22020129.

Kerbl, S. 2011. *Regulatory Medicine Against Financial Market Instability: What Helps And What Hurts?* Working Paper 174. Oesterreichische Nationalbank. https://www.oenb.at/dam/jcr:aefbbe58-021b-4514-b96c-6ffb4aaefc0a/wp174_tcm16-240232.pdf.

Khabibullin, R., and A. Ponomarenko. 2022. "An Empirical Behavioral Model of Household's Deposit Dollarization." *Journal of Economic Interaction and Coordination* 17 (3): 827–847. https://doi.org/10.1007/s11403-022-00345-w.

Khabibullin, R., A. Ponomarenko, and S. Seleznev. 2018. *Forecasting the Implications of Foreign Exchange Reserve Accumulation with an Agent-Based Model.* Working Paper Series 37. Bank of Russia. https://doi.org/10.2139/ssrn.3282108.

Kotlicki, A., A. Austin, D. Humphry, H. Burnett, P. Ridgill, and S. Smith. 2022. *Network Analysis of the UK Reinsurance Market.* Staff Working Paper 1000. Bank of England. https://www.bankofengland.co.uk/-/media/boe/files/working-paper/2022/network-analysis-of-the-uk-reinsurance-market.pdf.

Laliotis, D., A. Buesa, M. Leber, and J. Población. 2020. "An Agent-Based Model for the Assessment of LTV Caps." *Quantitative Finance* 20 (10): 1721–1748. https://doi.org/10.1080/14697688.2020.1733058.

Landaberry, V., F. Caccioli, A. Rodriguez-Martinez, A. Baron, S. Martinez-Jaramillo, and R. Lluberas. 2021. "The Contribution of the Intra-Firm Exposures Network to Systemic Risk." *Latin American Journal of Central Banking* 2 (2): 100032. https://doi.org/10.1016/j.latcb.2021.100032.

Leinonen, H., ed. 2009. *Simulation Analyses and Stress Testing of Payment Networks.* Scientific Monographs, E:42. Bank of Finland. https://publications.bof.fi/handle/10024/45688.

Leinonen, H., and K. Soramäki. 2003. *Simulating Interbank Payments and Securities Settlement Mechanism with the BoF-PSS2 Simulator.* Research Discussion Paper 23, Bank of Finland. https://doi.org/10.2139/ssrn.3016759.

Levelt, E., K. Mavromatis, and C. H. Hommes. 2021. *Leverage Cycles When Banks Have a Choice.* https://doi.org/10.2139/ssrn.3882467.

Liu, A., M. Paddrik, S. Y. Yang, and X. Zhang. 2020. "Interbank Contagion: An ~123~ Agent-Based Model Approach to Endogenously Formed Networks." *Journal of Banking & Finance* 112:105191. https://doi.org/10.1016/j.jbankfin.2017.08.008.

Magyar Nemzeti Bank (MNB). 2016. *Box 10: Modelling Channels of Contagion in the Banking Sector.* Financial Stability Report. https://www.mnb.hu/letoltes/financial-stability-report-2016-may.PDF.

———. 2021a. *Box 2: Agent-Based Housing Market Model: Impacts of the Regulation Regarding the Loan-to-Value Ratio and of the COVID Crisis.* Financial Stability Report. https://www.mnb.hu/letoltes/financial-stability-report-2021-june.pdf.

———. 2021b. *Box 2: Impact of a Rise in Home Construction Costs on the Housing Market Based on an Agent-Based Housing Market Model.* Housing Market Report November 2021. https://www.mnb.hu/letoltes/laka-spiaci-jelente-s-2021-november-eng.pdf.

———. 2021c. *Box 6: Effects of Family Support Measures on the Housing Loan Market on the Basis of an Agent-Based Model.* Financial Stability Report. https://www.mnb.hu/letoltes/financial-stability-report-december-2021.pdf.

———. 2022a. *Box 3: Impacts of the Rise in the Base Rate on Housing and Credit Markets.* Housing Market Report. https://www.mnb.hu/letoltes/laka-spiaci-jelente-s-2022-ma-jus-eng.pdf.

———. 2022b. *Special Topic: Manageable Risks in the Vulnerable Loan Portfolios.* Financial Stability Report. https://www.mnb.hu/letoltes/financial-stability-report-november-2022.pdf.

Martens, M. 2021. "Adoption and Implications of CBDC: An Agent-Based Modelling Approach." Master's thesis, University of Twente. https://essay.utwente.nl/89014/.

Mérő, B., A. Borsos, Z. Hosszú, Z. Oláh, and N. Vágó. 2023. "A High-Resolution, Data-Driven Agent-Based Model of the Housing Market." *Journal of Economic Dynamics and Control,* 104738. https://doi.org/10.1016/j.jedc.2023.104738.

Monasterolo, I., and M. Raberto. 2018. "The EIRIN Flow-of-Funds Behavioural Model of Green Fiscal Policies and Green Sovereign Bonds." *Ecological Economics* 144:228–243. https://doi.org/10.1016/j.ecolecon.2017.07.029.

Montagna, M., and C. Kok. 2016. *Multi-Layered Interbank Model for Assessing Systemic Risk.* Working Paper 1944. European Central Bank. https://doi.org/10.2866/38986.

Montagna, M., G. Torri, and G. Covi. 2021. *On the Origin of Systemic Risk.* Staff Working Paper 906. Bank of England. https://doi.org/10.2139/ssrn.3778199.

Network for Greening the Financial System. 2019. *A Sustainable and Responsible Investment Guide for Central Banks' Portfolio Management.* Technical document October 2019. Network for Greening the Financial System (NGFS). https://www.ngfs.net/sites/default/files/medias/documents/ngfs-a-sustainable-and-responsible-investment-guide.pdf.

Paddrik, M., R. Hayes, W. Scherer, and P. Beling. 2017. "Effects of Limit Order Book Information Level on Market Stability Metrics." *Journal of Economic Interaction and Coordination* 12:221–247. https://doi.org/10.1007/s11403-015-0164-6.

Plassard, R. 2020. *Making a Breach: The Incorporation of Agent-Based Models into the Bank of England's Toolkit.* GREDEG Working Paper No. 2020-30. Groupe de REcherche en Droit, Economie, Gestion (GREDEG CNRS), Université Côte d'Azur, France. https://ideas.repec.org/p/gre/wpaper/2020-30.html.

Poledna, S., S. Martinez-Jaramillo, F. Caccioli, and S. Thurner. 2021. "Quantification of Systemic Risk from Overlapping Portfolios in the Financial System." *Journal of Financial Stability* 52:100808. https://doi.org/10.1016/j.jfs.2020.100808.

Poledna, S., M. G. Miess, C. Hommes, and K. Rabitsch. 2023. "Economic Forecasting with an Agent-Based Model." *European Economic Review* 151:104306. https://doi.org/10.1016/j.euroecorev.2022.104306.

Poledna, S., J. L. Molina-Borboa, S. Martinez-Jaramillo, M. van der Leij, and S. Thurner. 2015. "The Multi-Layer Network Nature of Systemic Risk and its Implications for the Costs of Financial Crises." *Journal of Financial Stability* 20:70–81. https://doi.org/https://doi.org/10.1016/j.jfs.2015.08.001.

Popoyan, L., M. Napoletano, and A. Roventini. 2017. "Taming Macroeconomic Instability: Monetary and Macro-Prudential Policy Interactions in an Agent-Based Model." *Journal of Economic Behavior & Organization* 134:117–140. https://doi.org/10.1016/j.jebo.2016.12.017.

Roncoroni, A., S. Battiston, M. D'Errico, G. Hałaj, and C. Kok. 2021a. "Interconnected Banks and Systemically Important Exposures." *Journal of Economic Dynamics and Control,* 104266. https://doi.org/10.1016/j.jedc.2021.104266.

Roncoroni, A., S. Battiston, L. O. L. Escobar-Farfán, and S. Martinez-Jaramillo. 2021b. "Climate Risk and Financial Stability in the Network of Banks and Investment Funds." *Journal of Financial Stability* 54:100870. https://doi.org/10.1016/j.jfs.2021.100870.

Siebenbrunner, C., M. Hafner-Guth, R. Spitzer, and S. Trappl. 2024. "Assessing the Systemic Risk Impact of Bank Bail-ins." *Journal of Financial Stability* 71:101229. https://doi.org/10.1016/j.jfs.2024.101229.

Silva, T. C., M. Alexandre da Silva, and B. M. Tabak. 2017. "Systemic Risk in Financial Systems: A Feedback Approach." *Journal of Economic Behavior & Organization* 144:97–120. https://doi.org/10.1016/j.jebo.2017.09.013.

———. 2018. "Bank Lending and Systemic Risk: A Financial-Real Sector Network Approach with Feedback." *Journal of Financial Stability* 38:98–118. https://doi.org/10.1016/j.jfs.2017.08.006.

Silva, T. C., S. M. Guerra, M. Alexandre da Silva, and B. M. Tabak. 2020. "Micro-Level Transmission of Monetary Policy Shocks: The Trading Book Channel." *Journal of Economic Behavior & Organization* 179:279–298. https://doi.org/10.1016/j.jebo.2020.09.013.

Sinyakov, A., and A. Ponomarenko. 2018. "Impact of Banking Supervision on Banking System Structure: Conclusion from Agent-Based Modelling." *Russian Journal of Money and Finance* 77 (1): 26–50. https://doi.org/10.31477/rjmf.201801.26.

Stangl, J., A. Borsos, C. Diem, T. Reisch, and S. Thurner. 2024. "Firm-Level Supply Chains to Minimize Unemployment and Economic Losses in Rapid Decarbonization Scenarios." *Nature Sustainability,* 1–9. https://doi.org/10.1038/s41893-024-01321-x.

Sydow, M., A. Schilte, G. Covi, M. Deipenbrock, L. Del Vecchio, P. Fiedor, G. Fukker, *et al.* 2024. "Shock Amplification in an Interconnected Financial System of Banks and Investment Funds." *Journal of Financial Stability* 71:101234. https://doi.org/10.1016/j.jfs.2024.101234.

Tompaidis, S. 2017. "Measuring Systemwide Resilience of Central Counterparties." *Journal of Financial Market Infrastructures* 6 (4): 41–54. https://doi.org/10.21314/JFMI.2018.098.

Trichet, J.-C. 2010. *Reflections on the Nature of Monetary Policy Non-standard Measures and Finance Theory.* Speech given as an opening address at the ECB Central Banking Conference, Frankfurt, 18 November. https://www.ecb.europa.eu/press/key/date/2010/html/sp101118.en.html.

———. 2011. "Intellectual Challenges to Financial Stability Analysis in the Era of Macroprudential Oversight." *Banque de France Financial Stability Review,* no. 15, 139–149. https://publications.banque-france.fr/sites/default/files/medias/documents/financial-stability-review-15_2011-02.pdf.

———. 2013. "Unconventional Monetary Policy Measures: Principles-Conditions-Raison d'etre." *International Journal of Central Banking* 9 (1): 229–250. https://www.ijcb.org/journal/v9supplement-1/unconventional-monetary-policy-measures-principles-conditions-raison-detre.

Turrell, A. 2016. *Agent-Based Models: Understanding the Economy from the Bottom Up.* Quarterly Bulletin Q4. Bank of England. https://www.bankofengland.co.uk/quarterly-bulletin/2016/q4/agent-based-models-understanding-the-economy-from-the-bottom-up.

Wolski, M., and M. van de Leur. 2016. *Interbank Loans, Collateral and Modern Monetary Policy.* Working Paper 1959. European Central Bank. https://doi.org/10.2139/ssrn.2839816.

Yanquen, E., G. Livan, R. Montañez-Enriquez, and S. Martinez-Jaramillo. 2022. "Measuring Systemic Risk for Bank Credit Networks: A Multilayer Approach." *Latin American Journal of Central Banking* 3 (2): 100049. https://doi.org/10.1016/j.latcb.2022.100049.

Zemaityte, G., E. Hughes, and K. Blood. 2023. "The Buy-to-Let Sector and Financial Stability." *Bank of England Quarterly Bulletin,* https://www.bankofengland.co.uk/quarterly-bulletin/2023/2023/the-buy-to-let-sector-and-financial-stability.

PART IV

Climate & Sustainability

A COMPLEX-SYSTEMS PERSPECTIVE ON THE ECONOMICS OF CLIMATE CHANGE, BOUNDLESS RISK, AND RAPID DECARBONIZATION

Francesco Lamperti, Sant'Anna School of Advanced Studies, RFF-CMCC
European Institute on Economics and the Environment, and
Euro-Mediterranean Center on Climate Change (CMCC);
Giovanni Dosi, Sant'Anna School of Advanced Studies;
and Andrea Roventini, Sant'Anna School of Advanced Studies
and OFCE Sciences Po

Abstract

Climate change stands as one of the most formidable challenges in the twenty-first century. Despite this, our understanding of the unfolding and interconnection of climate-related physical and transitional risks, and their implications for socioeconomic dynamics along various transition pathways, remains insufficient. This deficit of understanding echoes throughout the formulation of effective climate change policies. In this context, our chapter emphasizes the need for a comprehensive and interdisciplinary approach to address climate change. Such an approach must (1) credibly encompass the immense risks that global warming exerts on the Earth system; (2) account for the intricate processes of technical change and technology diffusion that are at the core of the low-carbon transition; (3) allow the percolation of risks and opportunities across sectors and regions; (4) account for behavioral change in consumption dynamics; and (5) allow testing of a wide range of climate policies and their robustness. Complex-systems science offers distinct vantage points for framing the intricate climate challenge. While outlining current research gaps, we argue that the current generation of climate–economy models rooted in complex systems provides a promising starting point to fill these gaps. We delve into a series of findings that evaluate the material impact of climate risks on economic and financial stability and explore alternative trajectories for policy implementation. Our analysis underscores the ability of complex-systems models to account for the extreme costs of climate change and the emergence of critical tipping points, wherein unmitigated emissions lead to free-falling declines in long-term growth and catalyze financial and economic instability. Given such findings, we argue that a complex-systems perspective on climate change advocates for stricter and earlier policy interventions than do traditional climate economy models. These policies can transform the seemingly antithetical objectives of decarbonization and economic growth in standard models into complementary ones. We assert that a combination of regulation and green industrial policies can nurture eco-friendly investments and foster technological innovation, thus steering the economy onto a zero-carbon sustainable growth pathway. These results challenge conventional precepts in the realm of cost–benefit climate economics and offer the building blocks for a more robust and realistic framing of the climate challenge.

Introduction

Addressing climate change is one of the most daunting challenges of the twenty-first century. It requires a systemic turn in production and consumption modes at all scales. New technologies must be developed and deployed; novel sectors must rise, and established ones transform or be phased out. Different lifestyles must emerge, the capacity to adapt to unmitigable risks must be developed, and we must find a more conscious and respectful relationship between nature and human activities.

Further, to avoid catastrophic and irreversible impacts on ecosystems and societies, all these processes must be timely and adequately sustained by regional, national, and global policy architectures. At the time of writing, the remaining carbon budget for a 50% likelihood to limit global warming to 2°C has reduced to 315 GtC, equivalent to around twenty-eight years at 2023 emissions levels (Friedlingstein *et al.* 2023). For a target of 1.5°C with the same likelihood, only seven years are left. While natural scientists have made enormous progress in assessing the climate system and the risks it poses under uncontrolled emissions, much less understood are the socioeconomic effects of global warming and the strategies needed to rapidly decarbonize the world economy.

The traditional lens used to analyze the relationship between the climate and socioeconomic activities is at best grounded on a stylized representation of the basic elements: the economy, the process of growth, the carbon cycle, the damages induced by global warming, the means to decarbonize production, the role of states and governments (Pindyck 2013; but see Stern, Stiglitz, and Taylor 2022). The basic architecture was motivated by an interpretation of climate change as a simple externality created by greenhouse gas emissions. The implied solution boiled down to the determination of a desirable Pigouvian tax, internalizing the "costs" of emissions through a monetary incentive and restoring the welfare-maximizing equilibrium (Nordhaus 1992). After more than thirty years, a good deal of research in climate economics is still concerned with the same issue, adopts the same interpretation of global warming, and uses the same tools—somehow stretched to incorporate novel elements and evidence (e.g., new values for discount rates)—to provide ever-changing estimates of the optimal carbon tax (Barrage and Nordhaus 2024; Tol 2024). Though potentially helpful in building tractable relationships between extremely complex phenomena, these models grossly failed to understand the socioeconomic repercussions of climate change or provide clear policy guidance toward rapid decarbonization (Ackerman and Stanton 2012; Stern 2016; Stern, Stiglitz, and Taylor 2022). In his 2018 Nobel lecture, William Nordhaus advocated for a desirable global warming of about +3.5°C (Nordhaus 2019), in stark contrast with natural scientists' worries and Intergovernmental Panel on Climate Change (IPCC) reports. Climate damages were underestimated by an order of magnitude with respect to most recent empirical evidence (Kotz, Levermann, and Wenz 2024; Palagi *et al.* 2022; Tol 2018), and policymakers have largely discarded the plea for carbon taxes as the silver-bullet climate policy (Peñasco, Anadón, and Verdolini 2021). Motivated by these failures, alternative approaches to the economics of climate change have emerged in the last decade (see, e.g., the discussion in Balint *et al.* 2017; Farmer *et al.* 2015; Stern, Stiglitz, and Taylor 2022). Many of them have implicitly or explicitly adopt a complex system perspective to inform the analysis of global warming, its sources, its effects in the short and long runs, and the range of remedies that should be considered to avoid or limit adverse impacts.

This chapter builds on these studies and advocates for a comprehensive and interdisciplinary approach to addressing the complex challenges posed by global warming. Such an approach must consider the intricate processes of technological change and diffusion, the fundamental drivers of economic growth, the structure of production and consumption across sectors and regions, and the basic statical properties of climate-related events. As Nicholas Stern, Joseph Stiglitz, and Charlotte Taylor (2022) put it, addressing global warming requires an economics of immense risk, radical changes, and urgent policy intervention. In this direction, a comprehensive framework (see fig. 1) is needed that addresses (1) large impacts and potentially irreversible dynamics induced by sector- and region-specific risks to nature and the climate; (2) the percolation of shocks across input–output networks of production, investment, and financing relationships; (3) emerging new technologies, firms, and sectors as fundamental drivers of the transition (and incumbents as obstacles to change); (4) the heterogeneity of behaviors and the determinants of their mutation; and (5) the possibility of jointly assessing public policies in their full complexity. Approaches rooted in complex-systems science—nonlinear dynamical systems, network models, and agent-based simulations—are uniquely positioned to integrate knowledge from different fields (such as climate, network science, machine learning, and evolutionary theories) and develop the necessary framework for a reliable economics of climate change.

First, we will discuss climate risks in the context of complex economies and outline the need to better integrate them into complex-systems modeling. Then we will delve into technological change as the core process behind any credible decarbonization trajectory before moving the focus to decarbonization, highlighting the contributions of agent-based and network models.

Climate Risks for Complex Economies

First and foremost, climate risks are those associated with the impacts of climate change. These risks—typically labeled as *physical*—are determined by the dynamics of the Earth system (see, e.g. Steffen *et al.* 2018) and can be either event-driven (acute) or associated with longer-term shifts in climate patterns (chronic). A key question that has rapidly gained momentum at the top of the policy agenda concerns how large these risks can be for modern economies, especially when accounting

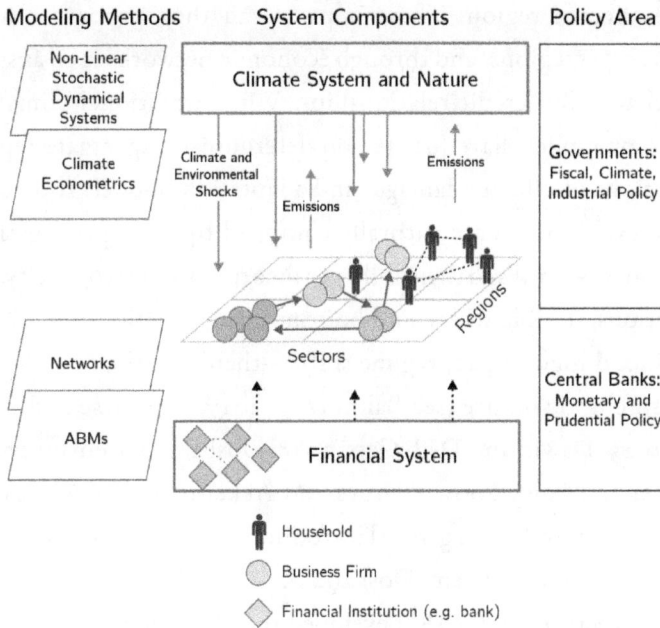

Figure 1. A complex-systems perspective on the economics of climate change, merging impact assessment and the design of mitigation pathways supported by public policies.

for tipping points and irreversible dynamics (Wunderling *et al.* 2024).

Modeling the impact of the weather on the macroeconomy presents significant challenges. Weather conditions are geographically clustered, can encompass a wide range of hazards (from floods and heat waves to droughts and compound events), and show return times (i.e., the average period between one event and another of equal or greater magnitude) that may shift abruptly with climate change. Further, the weather's effects on human activities depend highly on adaptation capacities, which vary widely among firms, households, regions, and societies. Consequently, physical risks inherently produce effects that are localized, strongly nonstationary, and heterogeneous across economic agents within the same affected region. These impacts can then propagate over time, across regions, and through economic networks such as supply chains and credit relationships. While traditional climate-economy models have focused on deterministic aggregate representations of climate damages and adaptation, models rooted in complexity science are naturally equipped to study propagation dynamics—thanks to their ability to incorporate heterogeneity, interactions, flexible scales, and bottom-up aggregation—and low-likelihood high-impact regime shifts—thanks to their nonlinear and stochastic nature (see Balint *et al.* 2017; Coronese and Luzzati 2025; Dawid and Delli Gatti 2018; Dosi and Roventini 2019; Farmer and Foley 2009; Filatova and Akkerman 2026, ch. 21 in this volume; and, for a general introduction to the economics of a complex evolving system, Dosi 2023).

Lamperti *et al.* (2018) developed the Dystopian Schumpeter Meeting Keynes (DSK) agent-based integrated assessment model to study the macroeconomic effects of climate-related shocks on economic dynamics over the short, medium, and long runs. The DSK model is the first attempt to employ a genuine bottom-up approach to assess climate damages in complex economies. It models the impacts of changing climatic conditions as micro shocks hitting workers' labor productivity and firms' energy efficiency, capital stock, or inventories. To do this, it introduces a stochastic microscopic damage-generating function, which models the direct impact of the weather on individual economic activities. At the end of each period, a random sample of climate-related shocks—which mirrors both acute events (e.g., floods) and chronic exposure (e.g., gradual temperature increases)—is constructed to affect agents though a multiplicative process. In particular, in most applications, the microscopic damage-generating function takes the form of a beta distribution (from which shocks are sampled), whose location and scale parameters are calibrated to reflect the shifts in likelihood of impacts due to global warming and its variability (Coronese *et al.* 2019; Kiley 2024). Simulating the unfolding of climate–economy interactions along carbon-intensive futures—as mirrored by business-as-usual scenarios compatible with a Representative Concentration Pathway 8.5 delivering global warming at the end of the century beyond 3°C—returns way higher economic risks than those of the standard impact assessment literature. The century-long growth in income is about one-third of the counterfactual scenario without global warming, but, more relevant, climate change is found to affect the short-, medium-, and long-run growth trajectory of the economy, rather than simply cutting the level of gross domestic product. Further, the negative impacts of climate change are magnified by the financial system via firms' bankruptcies possibly triggering instability in the banking sector (Lamperti *et al.* 2021; Lamperti *et al.* 2019). Results provide evidence of a substantial lack of isomorphism between the effects of micro- and macro-level shocks, as is typical of complex systems. Different types of shocks exert different effects on output growth, the unemployment rate, financial instability, and the likelihood of economic crises. Most relevantly, simulating the DSK model shows that uncontrolled warming may induce emergent tipping points in the dynamics growth, which appear as shifts in the growth trajectory of the economy toward a regime characterized by stagnation and high volatility in which the economy locks in even if emissions are (too lately) mitigated (Lamperti *et al.* 2019; Tàbara *et al.* 2018; Wunderling *et al.* 2024).

A micro-to-macro approach to the macroeconomic assessment of climate change has been incorporated in other models beyond DSK, showing that weather events may affect the aggregate economy by altering the agglomeration dynamics of production activities (Taberna *et al.* 2022; Coronese *et al.* 2023), as well as the uncertainty of business cycles (Bazzana *et al.* 2024). However, there is a relevant dimension that most macroeconomic agent-based models grossly miss that is relevant to study the propagation of climate impacts: region and sector cross-dependencies in production and consumption. Indeed, different sectors have different exposure to the weather (e.g., construction vs. information and communication technology), and climatic conditions are most often region (or even location) specific. While traditional approaches have focused on computable general equilibrium models to study such dynamics, there is no *ex ante* reason to believe that imbalances in production and trade across regions and sectors are fully solved by relative prices, especially when large weather events disrupt businesses, infrastructures and credit relationships. By contrast, production network models rooted in complexity science offer flexible environments to study the out-of-equilibrium, scarring, and path-dependent adjustment of a "shocked" input–output economic structure, at least in the short run (Di Noia *et al.* 2024; Poledna *et al.* 2018; Willner, Otto, and Levermann 2018). These analyses are crucial to inform policymakers about the most vulnerable (and resilient) parts of the production system and to evaluate the shape, length, and geographical heterogeneity of the postdisaster recovery.

Beyond physical risk, there is another large class of climate-related risks whose assessment deeply benefits from a complexity-based perspective. Transition risks are business-related risks that follow societal and economic shifts toward a low-carbon and more climate-friendly future. The systemic turn to a low-carbon economy will inevitably produce winners and losers, and assessing where opportunities and risks are created—and how they percolate in the economy—is pivotal to guide decarbonization policies. For instance, studies embracing network analysis have shown that aggressive shifts toward low-carbon energy sources may create stranded assets, underutilized capital stocks, and losses in financial actors percolating within the financial system and back to the real economy (Battiston *et al.* 2021; Cahen-Fourot *et al.* 2021; Mercure *et al.* 2018a). Using different macro ABMs, Ciola *et al.* (2023), Kremer *et al.* (2025), and Fierro *et al.* (2024). (2024) pointed out that transition imbalances most likely induce adverse distributional effects calling for stabilization and counterbalancing policies. Indeed, the materiality of transition risks largely depends on how the transition is initiated and managed. Lamperti *et al.* (2024) rely on the DSK agent-based model to show that—in a complex evolving economy in which economic agents are relatively insensitive to price signals—decarbonization may create either large frictions or opportunities spurring growth and job creation, depending on the actual policy mix used to foster the transition. And, last but not least, successfully mitigating climate change will have an enormous impact on living conditions, health, life expectancy, and social welfare in general (Carleton and Hsiang 2016; van Daalen *et al.* 2024).

Though they are mostly treated as stand-alone categories, there is increasing evidence that physical and transition risks are strongly intertwined. For instance, Lamperti *et al.* (2020) use the DSK model to show that the low-carbon transition of the energy sector may be affected by climatic conditions. Indeed, when climate damages are factored in, the likelihood of the green transition depends on how climate change affects agents in the economy. Global warming may lead to increases in energy demand that—at the prevailing energy mix in most economies—may favor carbon-intensive technologies and delay the transition. A comprehensive assessment of climate risks would need to incorporate both physical impacts and transition imbalances to design robust decarbonization trajectories and help actual policymaking.

Overall, merging methods in complexity science (e.g., network and agent-based models) with robust evidence from climate science and climate econometrics—which would deliver a realistic picture of future climates and their micro-level impacts—appears to be a promising avenue to solve current modeling gaps and build the next generation of climate–economy models.

Technological Change as the Basic Building Block of the Low-Carbon Transition

Reducing carbon emissions to limit global warming to 1.5°C above preindustrial levels also requires the application of climate technologies that are not yet available. Many sectors—from freight, water, and air transportation to metallurgy and cement production—still rely on fossil fuels, with green alternatives either nonexistent or unavailable on the necessary scale. To give a sense of the current technological gaps, consider that 99% of the mitigation scenarios employed in IPCC reviews that comply to the 1.5°C target rely at least to some extent on technologies that are still at the testing stage and need time, research, and financial support to reach maturity and adequate diffusion. Overall, a wide range of climate-friendly technologies still need to be discovered, developed, and upscaled. It is unrealistic to expect that markets alone will coordinate all the economic actors involved through price signals. Governments and public agencies will play a major role, and they need to build the necessary state capacities to support and guide the process, eventually creating and shaping markets rather than following them (see Mazzucato *et al.* 2015; Dosi *et al.* 2023).

Evolutionary economics and complexity science are in a unique position to offer the theoretical background and the modeling tools to understand the process of technical change that is needed to operationalize the low-carbon transition and to assess the drivers and barriers to its unfolding.

Theories on the emergence, development, and shifts of technological paradigms and technological trajectories can provide the bulk of the architecture (Dosi 1982, 2023). Indeed, contrary to what the majority of climate–economy models assume (Mercure *et al.* 2019; Pasqualino *et al.* 2024), technologies do not develop from scratch, nor they are pushed by markets. Rather, they emerge from the accumulation of technical knowledge and the development of routines embedding it. In this process, a novel technological paradigm stems from the interplay among scientific advances, economic factors, institutional variables, and unsolved difficulties on established technological paths (Dosi 1988, 1982). The history of a technology is then contextual to the history of the industrial structures associated with it. The emergence of a new paradigm is often related to novel companies arising through Schumpeterian creative destruction, while its establishment typically relates to a process of oligopolistic stabilization. The direction of technological change is set by the emergence of industrial structures and technological paradigms supporting a given technological trajectory. While the unfolding of a technological trajectory makes the pattern of innovation more incremental and predictable, the exhaustion of an established path is associated with large and irreducible uncertainty, which can be only partially mitigated by policy interventions and is only solved by the emergence of the next paradigm (Dosi 2023).

First and foremost, the process of decarbonization is linked to the emergence of an ensemble of technological paradigms and trajectories enabling the full development and diffusion of alternative technologies in currently carbon-intensive sectors. In stark contrast, traditional models employed to assess mitigation pathways (including the so-called process-based integrated assessment models used in IPCC reviews) overlook the role of industrial structures, institutions, radical uncertainty, and path-dependence. They tend to depict mitigation as an optimal process of adopting available technological options (eventually ameliorating over time at exogenous and fixed rates) operated in perfectly competitive markets and guided by policies altering their costs—typically, a carbon tax. In such a context, technological change is mostly limited to walking through learning curves. Indeed, these models have little to say about how different low-carbon technologies can be developed and diffused, which is a major current challenge.

By contrast, agent-based and system dynamics models that take technical change seriously have existed for decades (Dawid 2006). These models embed the theoretical setting (briefly) described above into realistic simulations of the evolution of technologies and industrial structures, shedding light on the emergence of novel technological trajectories and novel sectors, the diffusion pattern of innovations, and the possible lock-ins in inferior technologies. Further, macroeconomic models rooted in the evolutionary tradition put technical change at the core of long-run growth (Dosi and Roventini 2019). In this context, the economy's development is mostly set by the direction of technological change, which in turn coevolves with the emergence of firms, sectors, coherent demand, and the institutional setting (Dosi *et al.* 2022). As such, the direction of innovation can be influenced by public policies and, possibly, predicted (especially within technological trajectories; see also Farmer and Lafond 2016 and Lafond 2026, ch. 25 in this volume).

All these elements should be gradually translated into macroeconomic models for the transition to provide a realistic assessment of the available trajectories for decarbonation, including their drivers and obstacles, and to assess if, when, and how full decoupling between growth, emissions, and resource use is viable. Currently, this is the most promising avenue to study the long-run prospects of growth, its sustainability, and the eventual consequences of postgrowth trajectories (Stern and Stiglitz 2023). As we shall see in the next section, such a process has already started and has delivered successful results.

~ 143 ~

Modeling Climate Change and Decarbonization through Agent-Based and Network Models

Agent-based models (ABMs) have increasingly been recognized as promising alternatives to traditional climate–economy frameworks, not only for assessing climate risks but also for designing realistic and robust mitigation pathways that align with ambitious climate targets (Balint *et al.* 2017; Farmer *et al.* 2015; Stern 2016). These models offer at least five key distinctive advantages: (1) they typically account for endogenous technical change and the diffusion of new technologies; (2) they incorporate heterogeneity in consumption dynamics and behavior change; (3) they naturally address distributional issues, which are mostly overlooked in other modeling approaches; (4) they can easily incorporate climate impacts at the micro level; and (5) they flexibly allow for a wide array of policies and their combination, from price incentives to regulation on quantities, from relative standard to nudges (see also Savin *et al.* 2023).

Several ABMs have been developed over the past decade, providing valuable insights into the complex processes underlying the transition to a low-carbon economy (see Balint *et al.* 2017; Castro *et al.* 2020, for two reviews) and highlighting key gaps to be filled in future research.

The DSK model—the first agent-based integrated-assessment model—was developed to account for the coevolution of the economy and the climate at global scale, allowing for endogenous and path-dependent technological change, the diffusion of low-carbon technologies in multiple sectors, the dynamics of electrification and the phasing out of carbon-intensive capital stock (see Lamperti and Roventini 2022 for a review). The model—which has undergone a detailed empirical validation (Martinoli, Moneta, and Pallante 2024)—accommodates climate, innovation, industrial, fiscal, monetary, and prudential policies. Using DSK as a policy simulation laboratory, Lamperti *et al.* (2024) have shown the fallacy of carbon taxation as the major climate policy instrument. Indeed, while carbon taxes are often seen as the key tool for reducing greenhouse gas emissions, their effectiveness and consequences are far from straightforward. The results show that rapid and uncoordinated implementation of high carbon taxes can lead to significant economic disruptions, including sharp increases in energy prices, reduced investment, rising bankruptcy rates, and potential spikes in unemployment. Indeed, as economic agents behave through adaptive routines, their sensitivity to relative prices is far less pronounced than equilibrium-based models rooted in the expected utility framework assume. As a consequence, the price signal needed to guide a transition might be excessively high not to exert adverse and potentially long-lasting effects on the macroeconomy (on this matter, see also the empirical results of Känzig 2023). And this holds when carbon taxes increase over time, as suggested by the cost-benefit literature à la Nordhaus (2019) or in the form of rebates to households and firms. These results suggest that relying solely on carbon taxes to drive decarbonization is not only insufficient but potentially harmful to economic stability. To the contrary, complexity-based climate–economy models robustly show that navigating the transition more effectively requires a combination of policy approaches. In the DSK model, this translates into a policy mix focused on green industrial policies (Lamperti *et al.* 2024; Lamperti, Dosi, and Roventini 2024). Indeed, regulatory measures, such as command-and-control policies, can set clear standards and enforce compliance across different sectors, ensuring that emissions are reduced consistently and systematically moving the system toward different technological trajectories. These regulations can be complemented by green industrial and innovation policies that promote the development and adoption of sustainable technologies. By fostering innovation and guiding investment toward green industries, these policies can help build the foundation for a sustainable economy without placing undue strain on incumbent firms, which need to rapidly shift their technology and electrify production. While carbon taxes can still play a role in this policy mix, their application should be more strategic and measured: a moderate carbon tax could be levied to generate revenues for funding the transition to a low-carbon economy. This approach would help neutralize the impact of climate policy on the public budget while providing an incentive for businesses and consumers to reduce their carbon footprints. The policy mix designed with the DSK model turns decarbonization and sustainable economic growth into complementary objectives answering the plea of Stern and Stiglitz (2023), for which the only possible story of economic growth for the twenty-first century is a green growth story. These results align with the broader evidence coming from the complexity-based literature on the centrality of industrial policies to effective decarbonization (see Dafermos and Nikolaidi 2019; Lamperti *et al.* 2021; Mercure *et al.* 2018b; Rengs, Scholz-Wäckerle, and Bergh 2020; Nieddu *et al.* 2024).

Moreover, the transition must be managed in a way that accounts for the dynamic interactions between different sectors of the economy (see also Dumas and Andres 2026, ch. 20 in this volume). The shift to a low-carbon economy will affect not just energy production and consumption but also industries such as transportation, manufacturing, and finance. A holistic approach that considers these interconnections is essential for ensuring a smooth and sustainable transition. In the aftermath of the 2007 financial crisis, macroeconomic ABMs have been extended to incorporate real-financial interactions (Fagiolo and Roventini 2017; Farmer and Foley 2009). Further, recent developments in input–output network modeling have shown the centrality of accounting for microscopic entities and their relationships to correctly capture the structure of production and consumption activities (Pichler *et al.* 2023; Diem *et al.* 2024). Indeed, the sectoral dimension is often too coarse. Thanks to such developments, ABMs and network models are ideally situated to offer the necessary framework to study the percolating risks and opportunities that can materialize during a rapid decarbonization process (see fig. 1). In that, one key area in which future development is needed concerns extensions to multiple energy sources and the inclusion of additional low-carbon technologies (e.g., negative emission technologies and carbon removal methods, which are increasingly represented in computable general equilibrium climate–economy models). Indeed, for most climate–economy ABMs to generate mitigation pathways that meet the inclusion criteria for IPCC reports, a more fine-grained representation of the transition is needed in most emission-intensive sectors (e.g., power, transportation, buildings, industry; see also del Rio-Chanona *et al.* 2026, ch. 23 in this volume). Further, these developments must integrate into a multiregion framework to differentiate the trajectories of technological and structural change across key areas and to accommodate international flows of technologies, labor, and funds within the design of climate policy. To gain policy relevance, this should be a key objective for the next generation of climate–economy ABMs.

Another crucial factor in accelerating the transition involves behavioral changes, public attitudes toward policies (such as policy credibility), and how these attitudes spread through society. This becomes even more significant in light of the growing body of evidence showing the vast disparity in emissions across different income and wealth levels (Chancel 2022). Agent-based and network models have a long-standing tradition of studying how individual behaviors emerge, adapt, survive, or cease in an ecology of interacting entities. For example, they have proved a powerful tool to represent the complexities and behavioral aspects of energy demand. By contrast, traditional climate-economic models struggle to account for heterogeneity and change in households' and firms' behavior. Notwithstanding such "natural" advantages, macroeconomic ABMs employed to study the transition tend to miss elements such as heterogeneous consumption patterns, behavioral changes in energy use, drivers of adoption of sustainable transportation modes, and changing attitudes toward public policies. Though exceptions exist (see, e.g., D'Orazio and Valente 2019; Rengs, Scholz-Wäckerle, and Bergh 2020; Safarzyńska and van den Bergh 2017), future research should better integrate climate–economy modeling with household heterogeneity (e.g., social classes), changing consumption patterns, and consumers' views on the credibility of future policy (see, e.g., Campiglio, Lamperti, and Terranova 2024). A deeper understanding of the evolution of demand for polluting products would open the door to coupling climate policies targeting the supply side of the economy with demand and investment patterns (on the importance of altering current consumption regimes, see IPCC 2022; Lamperti, Palagi, and Perniola 2025). Along these lines, policies addressing distributional issues could be designed to be synergic to emission mitigation (Guzzardi *et al.* 2023).

~148~

In summary, assessing the conditions that lead to successful and unsuccessful transitions requires integrating many elements, including climate impacts, a rigorous process of technical change, sufficient sectoral disaggregation, and behavioral changes determining the state of demand, that are overlooked by traditional analyses of decarbonization pathways. Theories, methods, and models rooted in complexity science are already filling these gaps. The next generation of climate–economy models can complete the process by integrating elements that are currently spread over different fields and applications in a coherent and synergic novel family of platforms.

Conclusions

We have provided a complex-systems perspective on the economics of climate change and its currents gaps and highlighted the need for a complex-systems approach to address the multifaceted challenges of climate change. Traditional economic models fall short in capturing the extreme costs of climate change impacts, intricacies of technological change, sectoral dynamics, the distributional roots of carbon emissions, and the required policy combinations to deliver sustainable growth. Hence, we advocate for the integration of complex system science, particularly agent-based and network models, to provide a more realistic and comprehensive understanding of the climate–economy relationship. These models are better equipped to simulate the emergence of new technologies, the percolation of risks across sectors and regions, the drivers and obstacles of behavioral change, and the impact of different ensembles of policies, ultimately guiding more effective and robust climate policy combinations. Looking at climate change from the lens of complex systems provides an interdisciplinary framework that can estimate the huge costs of climate change inaction and the many benefits stemming from the decarbonization of the economy. In a complexity framework, timely and stringent climate policies can support the fast-decarbonization pathway required to stay well below 2°C while avoiding transition risks and fostering long-run sustainable growth. Further, such a perspective allows the analysis of the coevolution of the techno-economic domains and social dynamics. A complexity perspective allows the full appreciation of the possibility that continuing—rather than transforming—current trends could lead into the abyss the entire humankind. ⸙

Acknowledgments

FL and AR acknowledge financial support from PRIN 2021 project "ECLIPTIC" and PRIN 2022 PNRR project "NEWS." GD acknowledges financial support from PRIN 2022 project "TELI"; FL also acknowledges financial support of the European Research Council (ERC) under the European Union's Horizon Europe Programme (Grant agreement No. 101117427 – "FIND").

REFERENCES

Ackerman, F., and E. Stanton. 2012. "Climate Risks and Carbon Prices: Revising the Social Cost of Carbon." *Economics: The Open-Access, Open-Assessment E-Journal* 6:10. https://doi.org/10.5018/ECONOMICS-EJOURNAL.JA. 2012-10.

Balint, T., F. Lamperti, A. Mandel, M. Napoletano, A. Roventini, and A. Sapio. 2017. "Complexity and the Economics of Climate Change: A Survey and a Look Forward." *Ecological Economics* 138:252–265. https://doi.org/10.1016/j. ecolecon.2017.03.032.

Barrage, L., and W. Nordhaus. 2024. "Policies, Projections, and the Social Cost of Carbon: Results from the DICE-2023 Model." *Proceedings of the National Academy of Sciences* 121:e2312030121. https://doi.org/10.1073/pnas. 2312030121.

Battiston, S., I. Monasterolo, K. Riahi, and B. J. van Ruijven. 2021. "Accounting for Finance is Key for Climate Mitigation Pathways." *Science,* https://doi.org/10. 1126/science.abf3877.

Bazzana, D., M. Rizzati, E. Ciola, E. Turco, and S. Vergalli. 2024. "Warming the MATRIX: Uncertainty and Heterogeneity in Climate Change Impacts and Policy Targets in the Euro Area." *Energy Economics* 134:107585. https://doi. org/10.1016/j.eneco.2024.107585.

Cahen-Fourot, L., E. Campiglio, A. Godin, E. Kemp-Benedict, and S. Trsek. 2021. "Capital Stranding Cascades: The Impact of Decarbonisation on Productive Asset Utilisation." *Energy Economics* 103:105581. https://doi.org/10.1016/j. eneco.2021.105581.

Campiglio, E., F. Lamperti, and R. Terranova. 2024. "Believe Me when I Say Green! Heterogeneous Expectations and Climate Policy Uncertainty." *Journal of Economic Dynamics and Control* 165:104900. https://doi.org/10.1016/j. jedc.2024.104900.

Carleton, T. A., and S. M. Hsiang. 2016. "Social and Economic Impacts of Climate." *Science* 353 (6304): aad9837. https://doi.org/10.1126/science.aad9837.

Castro, J., S. Drews, F. Exadaktylos, J. Foramitti, F. Klein, T. Konc, I. Savin, and J. van den Bergh. 2020. "A Review of Agent-Based Modeling of Climate–Energy Policy." *WIREs Climate Change* 11:e647. https://doi.org/10.1002/wcc.647.

Chancel, L. 2022. "Global Carbon Inequality over 1990–2019." *Nature Sustainability* 5 (11): 931–938. https://doi.org/10.1038/s41893-022-00955-z.

Ciola, E., E. Turco, A. Gurgone, D. Bazzana, S. Vergalli, and F. Menoncin. 2023. "Enter the MATRIX Model: A Multi-Agent Model for Transition Risks with Application to Energy Shocks." *Journal of Economic Dynamics and Control* 146:104589. https://doi.org/10.1016/j.jedc.2022.104589.

Coronese, M., F. Lamperti, K. Keller, F. Chiaromonte, and A. Roventini. 2019. "Evidence for Sharp Increase in the Economic Damages of Extreme Natural Disasters." *Proceedings of the National Academy of Sciences* 116:21450–21455. https://doi.org/10.1073/pnas.1907826116.

Coronese, M., and D. Luzzati. 2025. "Economic Impacts of Natural Hazards and Complexity Science: A Critical Review." In *Routledge International Handbook of Complexity Economics,* edited by P. Chen, W. Elsner, and A. Pyka, 461–485. New York, NY: Routledge.

Coronese, M., M. Occelli, F. Lamperti, and A. Roventini. 2023. "AgriLOVE: Agriculture, Land-Use and Technical Change in an Evolutionary, Agent-Based Model." *Ecological Economics* 208:107756. https://doi.org/10.1016/j.ecolecon.2023.107756.

D'Orazio, P., and M. Valente. 2019. "The Role of Finance in Environmental Innovation Diffusion: An Evolutionary Modeling Approach." *Journal of Economic Behavior & Organization* 162:417–439. https://doi.org/10.1016/j.jebo.2018.12.015.

Dafermos, Y., and M. Nikolaidi. 2019. "Fiscal Policy and Ecological Sustainability: A Post-Keynesian Perspective." In *Frontiers of Heterodox Macroeconomics,* edited by P. Arestis and M. Sawyer, 277–322. Cham, Switzerland: Springer International Publishing. https://doi.org/10.1007/978-3-030-23929-9_7.

Dawid, H. 2006. "Agent-Based Models of Innovation and Technological Change." In *Handbook of Computational Economics,* edited by L. Tesfatsion and K. L. Judd, 2:1235–1272. Amsterdam, Netherlands: Elsevier. https://doi.org/10.1016/S1574-0021(05)02025-3.

Dawid, H., and D. Delli Gatti. 2018. "Agent-Based Macroeconomics." In *Handbook of Computational Economics,* edited by C. Hommes and B. LeBaron, 4:63–156. Amsterdam, Netherlands: Elsevier. https://doi.org/10.1016/bs.hescom.2018.02.006.

del Rio-Chanona, R. M., M. R. Frank, P. Mealy, E. Moro, and L. Nedelkoska. 2026. "Beyond Efficiency: Labor-Market Resilience in an Age of AI and Net Zero." In *The Economy as an Evolving Complex System IV,* edited by R. M. del Rio-Chanona, M. Pangallo, J. Bednar, E. D. Beinhocker, J. Kaszowska-Mojsa, F. Lafond, P. Mealy, A. Pichler, and J. D. Farmer. Santa Fe, NM: SFI Press.

Di Noia, J., A. Caiani, L. Cesarini, and B. Monteleone. 2024. *A High Resolution Input–Output Model to Assess the Economic Impact of Floods.* https://doi.org/10.2139/ssrn.4728894.

Diem, C., A. Borsos, T. Reisch, J. Kertész, and S. Thurner. 2024. "Estimating the Loss of Economic Predictability from Aggregating Firm-Level Production Networks." *PNAS Nexus* 3 (3): pgae064. https://doi.org/10.1093/pnasnexus/pgae064.

Dosi, G. 1982. "Technological Paradigms and Technological Trajectories: A Suggested Interpretation of the Determinants and Directions of Technical Change." *Research Policy* 11:147–162. https://doi.org/10.1016/0048-7333(82)90016-6.

———. 1988. "Sources, Procedures, and Microeconomic Effects of Innovation." *Journal of Economic Literature* 26:1120–1171. https://www.jstor.org/stable/2726526.

———. 2023. *The Foundations of Complex Evolving Economies.* Oxford, UK: Oxford University Press.

Dosi, G., F. Lamperti, M. Mazzucato, M. Napoletano, and A. Roventini. 2023. "Mission-Oriented Policies and the "Entrepreneurial State" at Work: An Agent-Based Exploration." *Journal of Economic Dynamics and Control* 151:104650. https://doi.org/10.1016/j.jedc.2023.104650.

Dosi, G., M. C. Pereira, A. Roventini, and M. E. Virgillito. 2022. "Technological Paradigms, Labour Creation and Destruction in a Multi-Sector Agent-Based Model." *Research Policy* 51:104565. https://doi.org/10.1016/j.respol.2022.104565.

Dosi, G., and A. Roventini. 2019. "More is Different ... and Complex! The Case for Agent-Based Macroeconomics." *Journal of Evolutionary Economics* 29:1–37. https://doi.org/10.1007/s00191-019-00609-y.

Chapter 19: The Economics of Climate Change

Dumas, M., and P. Andres. 2026. "Decarbonizing a Complex System." In *The Economy as an Evolving Complex System IV*, edited by R. M. del Rio-Chanona, M. Pangallo, J. Bednar, E. D. Beinhocker, J. Kaszowska-Mojsa, F. Lafond, P. Mealy, A. Pichler, and J. D. Farmer. Santa Fe, NM: SFI Press.

Fagiolo, G., and A. Roventini. 2017. "Macroeconomic Policy in DSGE and Agent-Based Models Redux: New Developments and Challenges Ahead." *Journal of Artificial Societies and Social Simulation* 20:1. https://doi.org/10.18564/jasss.3280.

Farmer, J. D., and D. Foley. 2009. "The Economy Needs Agent-Based Modelling." *Nature* 460:685–686. https://doi.org/10.1038/460685a.

Farmer, J. D., C. Hepburn, P. Mealy, and A. Teytelboym. 2015. "A Third Wave in the Economics of Climate Change." *Environmental and Resource Economics* 62:329–357. https://doi.org/10.1007/s10640-015-9965-2.

Farmer, J. D., and F. Lafond. 2016. "How Predictable is Technological Progress?" *Research Policy* 45:647–665. https://doi.org/10.1016/j.respol.2015.11.001.

Fierro, L. E., S. Reissl, F. Lamperti, E. Campiglio, L. Drouet, J. Emmerling, and M. Tavoni. 2024. "Safeguarding Macro-Financial Stability under Carbon Pricing and Rapid Energy Transition." Forthcoming, *Communications Earth & Environment*.

Filatova, T., and J. Akkerman. 2026. "Complexity Economics' View on Physical Climate Change Risks and Adaptation." In *The Economy as an Evolving Complex System IV*, edited by R. M. del Rio-Chanona, M. Pangallo, J. Bednar, E. D. Beinhocker, J. Kaszowska-Mojsa, F. Lafond, P. Mealy, A. Pichler, and J. D. Farmer. Santa Fe, NM: SFI Press.

Friedlingstein, P., *et al.* 2023. "Global Carbon Budget 2023." *Earth System Science Data* 15:5301–5369. https://doi.org/10.5194/essd-15-5301-2023.

Guzzardi, D., E. Palagi, T. Faccio, and A. Roventini. 2023. "In Search of Lost Time: An Ensemble of Policies to Restore Fiscal Progressivity and Address the Climate Challenge." In *Financing Investment in Times of High Public Debt*, 169. Cambridge, UK: Open Book Publishers.

IPCC. 2022. *Chapter 5: Demand, Services and Social Aspects of Mitigation.* https://www.ipcc.ch/report/ar6/wg3/chapter/chapter-5/.

Känzig, D. R. 2023. *The Unequal Economic Consequences of Carbon Pricing.* Working Paper Series. https://doi.org/10.3386/w31221.

Kiley, M. T. 2024. "Growth at Risk from Climate Change." *Economic Inquiry* 62:1134–1151. https://doi.org/10.1111/ecin.13206.

Kotz, M., A. Levermann, and L. Wenz. 2024. "The Economic Commitment of Climate Change." *Nature* 628:551–557. https://doi.org/10.1038/s41586-024-07219-0.

Kremer, E., S. Reissl, L. E. Fierro, J. Emmerling, F. Lamperti, and A. Roventini. 2025. "Energy Price Shocks in the European Union: Macroeconomic Impacts, Distributional Effects and Policy Responses." *Energy Economics* 152:108979. https://doi.org/10.1016/j.eneco.2025.108979.

Lafond, F. 2026. "Forecasting Technological Progress." In *The Economy as an Evolving Complex System IV*, edited by R. M. del Rio-Chanona, M. Pangallo, J. Bednar, E. D. Beinhocker, J. Kaszowska-Mojsa, F. Lafond, P. Mealy, A. Pichler, and J. D. Farmer. Santa Fe, NM: SFI Press.

Lamperti, F., V. Bosetti, A. Roventini, and M. Tavoni. 2019. "The Public Costs of Climate-induced Financial Instability." *Nature Climate Change* 9:829–833. https://doi.org/10.1038/s41558-019-0607-5.

Lamperti, F., V. Bosetti, A. Roventini, M. Tavoni, and T. Treibich. 2021. "Three Green Financial Policies to Address Climate Risks." *Journal of Financial Stability*, 100875. https://doi.org/10.1016/j.jfs.2021.100875.

Lamperti, F., G. Dosi, M. Napoletano, A. Roventini, and A. Sapio. 2018. "Faraway, So Close: Coupled Climate and Economic Dynamics in an Agent-Based Integrated Assessment Model." *Ecological Economics* 150:315–339. https://doi.org/10.1016/j.ecolecon.2018.03.023.

———. 2020. "Climate Change and Green Transitions in an Agent-Based Integrated Assessment Model." *Technological Forecasting and Social Change* 153:119806. https://doi.org/10.1016/j.techfore.2019.119806.

Lamperti, F., G. Dosi, and A. Roventini. 2024. "Climate Change, Transition Risk and Policies for Green Growth: Insights from the DSK Integrated-Assessment Agent-Based Model." In *Festschrift Volume: 80 Years of Joseph Stiglitz*. Forthcoming.

Lamperti, F., E. Palagi, and T. Perniola. 2025. *The Emission-Inequality Nexus Across Stages of Development*. Laboratory of Economics and Management (LEM), Sant'Anna School of Advanced Studies, Pisa, Italy.

Lamperti, F., and A. Roventini. 2022. *Beyond Climate Economics Orthodoxy: Impacts and Policies in the Agent-Based Integrated-assessment* DSK *model.* https://doi.org/10.4337/ejeep.2022.0096.

Lamperti, F., C. Wieners, G. Dosi, and A. Roventini. 2024. *Macroeconomic Policies for Rapid Decarbonization, Steady Economic Transition and Employment Creation.* https://doi.org/10.21203/rs.3.rs-4637209/v1.

Martinoli, M., A. Moneta, and G. Pallante. 2024. "Calibration and Validation of Macroeconomic Simulation Models by Statistical Causal Search." *Journal of Economic Behavior & Organization* 228:106786. https://doi.org/10.1016/j. jebo.2024.106786.

Mazzucato, M., M. Cimoli, G. Dosi, J. E. Stiglitz, M. A. Landesmann, M. Pianta, R. Walz, and T. Page. 2015. "Which Industrial Policy Does Europe Need?" *Intereconomics* 50:120–155. https://doi.org/10.1007/s10272-015-0535-1.

Mercure, J.-F., F. Knobloch, H. Pollitt, L. Paroussos, S. S. Scrieciu, and R. Lewney. 2019. "Modelling Innovation and the Macroeconomics of Low-Carbon Transitions: Theory, Perspectives and Practical Use." *Climate Policy* 19:1019–1037. https://doi.org/10.1080/14693062.2019.1617665.

Mercure, J.-F., H. Pollitt, N. R. Edwards, P. B. Holden, U. Chewpreecha, P. Salas, A. Lam, F. Knobloch, and J. E. Vinuales. 2018a. "Environmental Impact Assessment for Climate Change Policy with the Simulation-Based Integrated Assessment Model E3ME-FTT-GENIE." *Energy Strategy Reviews* 20:195–208. https://doi.org/10.1016/j.esr.2018.03.003.

Mercure, J.-F., H. Pollitt, J. E. Viñuales, N. R. Edwards, P. B. Holden, U. Chewpreecha, P. Salas, I. Sognnaes, A. Lam, and F. Knobloch. 2018b. "Macroeconomic Impact of Stranded Fossil Fuel Assets." *Nature Climate Change* 8:588–593. https://doi.org/10.1038/s41558-018-0182-1.

Nieddu, M., M. Raberto, L. Ponta, A. Teglio, and S. Cincotti. 2024. "Evaluating Policy Mix Strategies for the Energy Transition Using an Agent-Based Macroeconomic Model." *Energy Policy* 193:114276. https://doi.org/10.1016/j.enpol.2024.114276.

Nordhaus, W. D. 1992. "An Optimal Transition Path for Controlling Greenhouse Gases." *Science* 258:1315–1319. https://doi.org/10.1126/science.258.5086.1315.

Nordhaus, W. D. 2019. "Climate Change: The Ultimate Challenge for Economics." *American Economic Review* 109 (6): 1991–2014. https://doi.org/10.1257/aer. 109.6.1991.

Palagi, E., M. Coronese, F. Lamperti, and A. Roventini. 2022. "Climate Change and the Nonlinear Impact of Precipitation Anomalies on Income Inequality." *Proceedings of the National Academy of Sciences* 119:e2203595119. https://doi. org/10.1073/pnas.2203595119.

Pasqualino, R., C. Peñasco, P. Barbrook-Johnson, F. S. De Moura, S. Kolesnikov, S. Hafner, F. J. M. M. Nijsse, *et al.* 2024. "Modelling Induced Innovation for the Low-Carbon Energy Transition: A Menu of Options." *Environmental Research Letters* 19:073004. https://doi.org/10.1088/1748-9326/ad4c79.

Peñasco, C., L. D. Anadón, and E. Verdolini. 2021. "Systematic Review of the Outcomes and Trade-Offs of Ten Types of Decarbonization Policy Instruments." *Nature Climate Change* 11:257–265. https://doi.org/10.1038/ s41558-020-00971-x.

Pichler, A., C. Diem, A. Brintrup, F. Lafond, G. Magerman, G. Buiten, T. H. Choi, V. Carvalho, J. D. Farmer, and S. Thurner. 2023. "Building an Alliance to Map Global Supply Networks." *Science* 382 (6668): 270–272. https://doi.org/10. 1126/science.adi7521.

Pindyck, R. S. 2013. "Climate Change Policy: What Do the Models Tell Us?" *Journal of Economic Literature* 51:860–872. https://doi.org/10.1257/jel.51.3.860.

Poledna, S., S. Hochrainer-Stigler, M. G. Miess, P. Klimek, S. Schmelzer, J. Sorger, E. Shchekinova, *et al.* 2018. *When does a Disaster Become a Systemic Event? Estimating Indirect Economic Losses from Natural Disasters.* ArXiv preprint: 1801.09740. https://doi.org/10.48550/arXiv.1801.09740.

Rai, V., and A. D. Henry. 2016. "Agent-Based Modelling of Consumer Energy Choices." *Nature Climate Change* 6:556–562. https://doi.org/10.1038/ nclimate2967.

Rengs, B., M. Scholz-Wäckerle, and J. van den Bergh. 2020. "Evolutionary Macroeconomic Assessment of Employment and Innovation Impacts of Climate Policy Packages." *Journal of Economic Behavior & Organization* 169:332–368. https://doi.org/10.1016/j.jebo.2019.11.025.

Safarzyńska, K., and J. C. J. M. van den Bergh. 2017. "Integrated Crisis-Energy Policy: Macro-Evolutionary Modelling of Technology, Finance and Energy Interactions." *Technological Forecasting and Social Change* 114:119–137. https://doi.org/10.1016/j.techfore.2016.07.033.

Savin, I., F. Creutzig, T. Filatova, J. Foramitti, T. Konc, L. Niamir, K. Safarzynska, and J. van den Bergh. 2023. "Agent-Based Modeling to Integrate Elements from Different Disciplines for Ambitious Climate Policy." *WIREs Climate Change* 14:e811. https://doi.org/10.1002/wcc.811.

Steffen, W., *et al.* 2018. "Trajectories of the Earth System in the Anthropocene." *Proceedings of the National Academy of Sciences* 115:8252–8259. https://doi.org/10.1073/pnas.1810141115.

Stern, N. 2016. "Economics: Current Climate Models are Grossly Misleading." *Nature* 530:407. https://doi.org/10.1038/530407a.

Stern, N., J. Stiglitz, and C. Taylor. 2022. "The Economics of Immense Risk, Urgent Action and Radical Change: Towards New Approaches to the Economics of Climate Change." *Journal of Economic Methodology* 29:181–216. https://doi.org/10.1080/1350178X.2022.2040740.

Stern, N., and J. E. Stiglitz. 2023. "Climate Change and Growth." *Industrial and Corporate Change* 32:277–303. https://doi.org/10.1093/icc/dtad008.

Tàbara, J. D., N. Frantzeskaki, K. Hölscher, S. Pedde, K. Kok, F. Lamperti, J. H. Christensen, J. Jäger, and P. Berry. 2018. "Positive Tipping Points in a Rapidly Warming World." *Current Opinion in Environmental Sustainability* 31:120–129. https://doi.org/10.1016/j.cosust.2018.01.012.

Taberna, A., T. Filatova, A. Roventini, and F. Lamperti. 2022. "Coping with Increasing Tides: Evolving Agglomeration Dynamics and Technological Change Under Exacerbating Hazards." *Ecological Economics* 202:107588. https://doi.org/10.1016/j.ecolecon.2022.107588.

Tol, R. S. J. 2018. "The Economic Impacts of Climate Change." *Review of Environmental Economics and Policy* 12:4–25. https://doi.org/10.1093/reep/rex027.

———. 2024. "Trends and Biases in the Social Cost of Carbon." *Annals of the New York Academy of Sciences* 1548 (1): 248–259. https://doi.org/10.1111/nyas.15340.

van Daalen, K. R., C. Tonne, J. C. Semenza, J. Rocklöv, A. Markandya, N. Dasandi, R. Lowe, *et al.* 2024. "The 2024 Europe Report of the Lancet Countdown on Health and Climate Change: Unprecedented Warming Demands Unprecedented Action." *The Lancet Public Health.*

Willner, S. N., C. Otto, and A. Levermann. 2018. "Global Economic Response to River Floods." *Nature Climate Change* 8:594–598. https://doi.org/10.1038/s41558-018-0173-2.

Wunderling, N., *et al.* 2024. "Climate Tipping Point Interactions and Cascades: A Review." *Earth System Dynamics* 15:41–74. https://doi.org/10.5194/esd-15-41-2024.

CLIMATE RISK THROUGH THE LENS OF COMPLEXITY ECONOMICS AND FINANCE

Stefano Battiston, University of Zurich, Ca'Foscari,
University of Venice, and CEPR; and
Irene Monasterolo, Utrecht University, CEPR,
and Wirtschaftsuniversität Wien

Abstract

This chapter aims to clarify the contributions of complexity-based approaches to the analysis of climate financial risk, in its physical and transition dimensions. First, it discusses the defining characteristics of climate risk—deep uncertainty, nonlinearity, and endogeneity—and why they pose challenges to standard economic and finance modeling approaches. Second, it critically presents the limits of standard approaches in macroeconomics and financial economics used in research, as well as by central banks and financial institutions, to analyze climate financial risks. Third, it discusses an approach to climate finance that is able to capture these key aspects of complexity and is increasingly used by financial authorities. The chapter concludes by discussing new avenues for research in climate finance based on complexity, and the conditions for complexity-based approaches to support and strengthen decision-making in the context of climate risk.

1 Introduction

Climate risk has been recognized by several financial authorities in the world, including central banks and financial supervisors, as a new source of financial risk (see, e.g., NGFS 2019; EBA 2020; Alogoskoufis *et al.* 2021). Since 2020, over 140 central banks and financial authorities have joined the Network for Greening the Financial System (NGFS) and started to develop climate scenarios to support the assessment of climate-related financial risks (Bertram *et al.* 2021), either internally or in collaboration with researchers. In the past fifteen years, both academics (see, e.g., Farmer *et al.* 2015; Mercure *et al.* 2016; Monasterolo, Roventini, and Foxon 2019) and financial institutions (Ranger, Mahul, and Monasterolo 2022), including recently the NGFS (NGFS 2023), have acknowledged the need to complement traditional modeling with approaches capable of capturing the complexity of climate risks. Indeed, traditional macroeconomic and financial models developed in academia and used at several central banks face major challenges in embedding the key characteristics of climate risk: endogeneity, nonlinearities and tipping points, and deep uncertainty (see sec. 2).

Therefore, we need to better understand the limits of standard modeling approaches and the extent to which complexity approaches can contribute to them. This chapter addresses this issue from a conceptual and methodological point of view, focusing in particular on two key aspects of complexity. The first concerns multiple equilibria and tipping points, which is a fundamental aspect of the earth's climate system, and the socioeconomic and financial system. Together, they form a coupled system, hereafter referred to as a CSEF system. The second aspect is the multidimensionality of the notion of well-being (Stiglitz, Sen, and Fitoussi 2009), which modelers and decision-makers should take into account in the context of climate risk.

We start by reviewing some of the main approaches to climate finance. Then, in sections 3 and 4, we discuss why the approaches building on either standard macroeconomic models or standard financial economics models fail to capture these two aspects of complexity, and thus may lead to inadequate policy recommendations. In section 5, we discuss an alternative approach—the complexity climate finance (CCF) approach—that acknowledges complexity and builds on the risk management approach that inspired the Paris Agreement. The CCF approach is now well-established in academia (Battiston *et al.* 2017; Dunz, Naqvi, and Monasterolo 2021; Battiston *et al.* 2023) and increasingly used among practitioners (Battiston *et al.* 2018; Roncoroni *et al.* 2021; Ranger, Mahul, and Monasterolo 2022). Finally, in section 6, we discuss future research avenues (e.g., nature-climate and biodiversity risk, compound risk) for complexity-based approaches and some implications for the design of monetary policies and prudential regulation.

2 Climate-Related Financial Risks and Complexity

The climate system, coupled with the socioeconomic and financial system—CSEF—can be regarded as a complex system, characterized by several reinforcing feedback loops.

A first key aspect of complexity that characterizes the CSEF can be referred to, with some simplifications, as multiple equilibria and tipping points (Lenton *et al.* 2008). On the one hand, once a tipping point for one or more key variables (e.g., greenhouse gas emissions [GHG] concentration in the atmosphere) is reached, it may be impossible to revert to the initial system equilibrium (Rocha, Peterson, and Biggs 2015). On the other hand, under some conditions and before reaching the tipping points, economic policies can steer the system from one equilibrium to another, with possibly large effects on achieving a carbon-neutral society (Otto *et al.* 2020). For instance, investments in climate mitigation and adaptation can help to decrease future risks and increase preparedness. This is particularly relevant insofar as climate risks do not happen in isolation but often compound, including with other risks, leading to an amplification of the magnitude and persistence of the shock (Zscheischler *et al.* 2018; Ranger, Mahul, and Monasterolo 2021; Dunz *et al.* 2023). In addition, multiple interacting tipping points could give rise to a domino effect (Steffen *et al.* 2015), with key feedback mechanisms underlying tipping dynamics across systems and scales.

A second aspect has to do with the criteria to design and assess policies in relation to climate change. The impacts of climate change are unprecedented in human history and affect multiple societal dimensions, ranging from inequality of access to water and other key resources to inequality of exposure to impacts of extreme weather events (IPCC 2022). As a result, designing economic policies that aim to be consistent with the nature of the climate problem requires recognizing the role of complexity and the adoption of a multidimensional notion of well-being (Stiglitz, Sen, and Fitoussi 2009). Similarly, these aspects need to be taken into account in climate finance, especially in the methodologies used to assess climate-related financial risk, which in turn support the design of financial policies and regulations to preserve financial stability.

Two main channels of climate risk transmission to the economy and finance have been identified (Carney 2015; NGFS 2019): physical risk and transition risk.

Physical climate risks entail the damage to tangible assets of firms, the depletion of natural capital, and threats to human well-being due to acute risks (hazards such as floods, droughts, and hurricanes) and chronic risks (e.g., temperature rise, sea-level rise and biodiversity loss). Physical climate risks tend to reduce the profitability of companies that own productive plants and activities that are exposed and vulnerable to hazards and chronic risks, and thus lead to negative adjustments on the value of the financial securities associated (e.g., equity and bonds) and loans repayment.

Transition risks arise from changing expectations of market participants about the future profitability of economic activities. These changes can be triggered by the sudden or unanticipated introduction of new climate policies (e.g., a carbon tax or more stringent environmental targets), by technological shocks, or by changes in consumers' preferences (e.g., for low-carbon goods). Climate policies tend to reduce the profitability of fossil fuels and high-carbon companies and thus lead to negative adjustments on the value of the financial securities associated (e.g., equity and bonds) and loans repayment.

A key feature of transition risk is its endogeneity; that is, agents' perception of climate-related risk impacts the materialization of risk itself (Battiston *et al.* 2021). This circularity is related to the presence of multiple equilibria in the CSEF system and may induce a path dependence in the complex dynamics leading to lock-in effects similar to those described in models of technology diffusion. In this context, the credibility of climate policies is key for the policy to perform the steering function described earlier (see more details in sec. 2).

3   Limitations of Climate Finance Approaches Building on Standard Macroeconomic Models

Some climate finance approaches combine asset pricing with a cost–benefit analysis of climate economics based on the DICE model (Nordhaus 1993), an aggregate integrated assessment models (IAM). For simplicity, we refer hereafter to cost–benefit climate economic (CBCE) and cost–benefit climate finance (CBCF). The cost–benefit climate economic (CBCE)

~164~

Coupled Climate–Economic System **without Complexity**

Coupled Climate–Economic–Finance System **with Complexity**

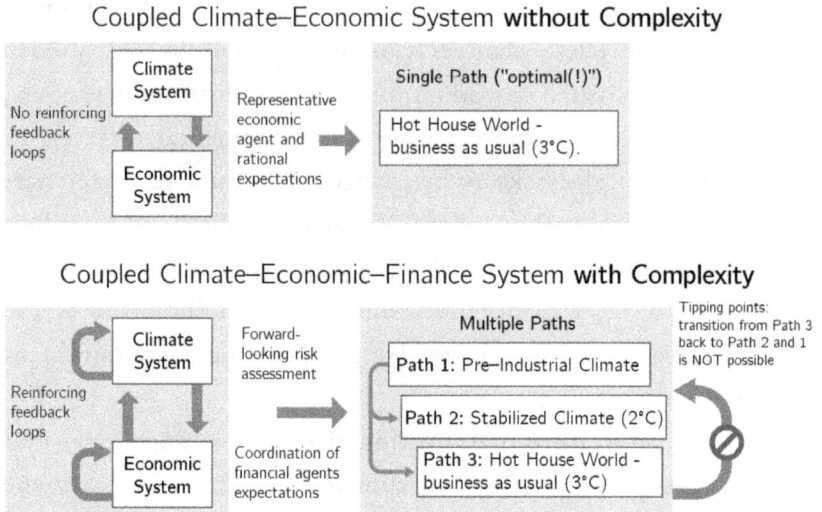

Figure 1. Accounting for complexity (multiple equilibria and tipping points) in the coupled climate-economic-finance system. Top: Standard models (e.g., DICE) couple the climate and economic systems. However, ignoring reinforcing feedback loops and assuming representative agents and rational expectations leads to a single path (referred to as "equilibrium" for simplicity). This path is often presented as "optimal" but in fact it corresponds to a hot-house world scenario leading to over 3° Celsius by 2100 and thus to irreversible and very adverse climate impacts. Bottom: The complexity approach couples the climate system with the economic *and* financial systems. Taking into account reinforcing feedback loops, forward-looking risk assessment, and coordination dynamics of agents' expectations leads to multiple possible paths and tipping points. Here, a transition from the preindustrial climate system to the hot-house world path takes place over time if climate variables evolve as per business-as-usual trends. Climate policies can enable the transition to a stabilized 2°C path, but only if climate tipping points are not reached. Source: authors' own elaborations.

approach typically treats climate change as an intertemporal optimization problem of aggregate consumption and gross domestic product (GDP) and aims to identify an optimal policy response (e.g., carbon price). The DICE model is among the most well-known examples of CBCE approaches. DICE is a neoclassical economic model coupled with a simplified climate module that describes the relation between cumulative GHG emissions and the average temperature.

Recently, some asset pricing models started to use the aggregate GDP losses from DICE to derive the prices of assets today as a function of adjustment in consumption. This is what we call the CBCF approach. While DICE is widely known in the economic profession, it has been criticized by both economists and natural scientists. A systematic analysis of the shortcomings of DICE is beyond the scope of this chapter, so we will focus on those most relevant for our analysis, which are inherited by the CBCF building on it.

In the CBCE approach, multiple equilibria are ruled out by construction, and tipping points are not considered. Indeed, the relation between climate and the economy is limited to a stabilizing feedback loop: more economic output leads to more GHG emissions and thus higher impact of climate-related hazards, which reduce economic output. Moreover, the economy consists of a representative agent that maximizes intertemporal utility. The model structure does not allow for the distinction between fossil fuels and renewable energy technologies, meaning that it is not possible to assess the impact of climate policies on the development of the green sector. Since there is only one possible path of the economy and only one technology, the model does not allow us to investigate climate transition risk.

The "optimal policy" recommended by William Nordhaus's DICE prescribes that the world should not take climate action until the second half of the twenty-first century and let the planet warm as much as 3°C. This prescription is, however, highly sensitive to the chosen discount rate (typically 5–7% in the classic DICE implementations). Since there is no scientific basis for choosing the discount rate, as it reflects ethical considerations (Arrow *et al.* 2013), there is also no scientific basis for the recommended policy.

The optimal policy is also highly dependent on the damage function, that is, the function that translates temperature increases into economic average aggregate losses on GDP. In the context of DICE, the calibration of the damage function has been criticized because it ignores nonlinearities and heterogeneity across time and regions of the world (Keen *et al.* 2022). Overall, these shortcomings limit the practical relevance of estimates of climate financial risks obtained with the CBCF approach.

Another approach used in the literature aims to integrate the impact of carbon taxes in the standard dynamic stochastic general equilibrium (DSGE) models (see, e.g., Annicchiarico and Di Dio 2017; Diluiso *et al.* 2021; Carattini, Heutel, and Melkadze 2023) traditionally used internally by central banks to assess macrofinancial dynamics. We refer to this as climate DSGE, or CDSGE. This approach shares the limitations of the CBCE approach. Multiple equilibria are ruled out by construction because the assumption of rational expectations imposes the uniqueness of the equilibrium.

Neither of these approaches considers the multidimensional nature of well-being. Indeed, both DICE and DSGE carry out an intertemporal optimization of consumption, and the externalities of climate change do not consider extra-economic dimensions such as public health, ecosystems, or intergenerational equity.

Aggregate IAM and cost–benefit analysis versus process-based IAM and target-based analysis.

In addition to the class of aggregate IAM, there is a different class, known as process-based IAMs, which provide a detailed representation of how energy is transformed and used throughout the economy by means of all available technologies. While the aggregate IAM are typically used for cost–benefit analysis, the process-based IAM are used for target-based analysis. In the latter, a cost-efficient trajectory of economy is computed, conditional to the constraints of reaching a given target in terms of carbon budget and thus likely level of global warming. This approach implicitly acknowledges that multiple paths of the economy (e.g., in terms of economic composition and restructuring) are possible to achieve a given decarbonization scenario. Further, while the path to reach, for example, 2°C is still computed as an optimal path from the point of view of consumption, it is an optimization that comes as a secondary objective, after reaching the temperature target. This enables a decision-maker to evaluate and choose the target on the basis of a set of independent criteria of well-being (e.g., societal risks, conflicts, access to basic natural resources, inequality), and to optimize for consumption later. The target-based approach is more consistent with a risk-management approach, and indeed is the one used to develop the NGFS climate scenarios used by central banks, financial supervisors, and investors for climate financial risk assessment and climate stress-test. Importantly, the international negotiations on climate and the 2°C objective of the Paris Agreement, and the investors' climate pledges (e.g., Net-Zero Banking Alliance) are based on the target-based approach and not on the cost–benefit approach.

~ 167 ~

4 Limitations of Climate Finance Approaches Building on Standard Financial Economic Models

In the field of financial economics, many works follow the market-based climate finance (MBCF) approach. By applying econometric techniques to the historical prices of financial instruments, they estimate to what extent climate risk is already priced in financial markets. The findings show that both physical risk (see, e.g., Bernstein, Gustafson, and Lewis 2019; Acharya *et al.* 2022) and transition risk command an impact on asset prices that varies in magnitude depending on the type of security, issuer, and market, but remains of the order of few basis points (Monasterolo and de Angelis 2020; Pástor, Stambaugh, and Taylor 2022; Bolton and Kacperczyk 2021; Alessi, Ossola, and Panzica 2021; Beyene *et al.* 2021; Zerbib 2019; Ilhan, Sautner, and Vilkov 2021; Ardia *et al.* 2023; Sautner *et al.* 2023; Giglio, Kelly, and Stroebel 2021). All these works estimate markets' perception of past climate risk but do not address the question of what is the potential climate risk for the financial sector in relation to future risk (Battiston *et al.* 2023).

Two problematic assumptions are somewhat implicit in these analyses. The first assumption is that past price return distributions are a good representation of future distributions. This does not hold if climate change leads to structural breaks (in a statistical sense). There are several reasons why this can be the case. On the one hand, the transition to a low-carbon economy would require large and fast changes in business models across the sectors, such as energy, transportation and buildings, which represent a substantial portion of market capitalization. On the other hand, the impact of physical risk is only now becoming evident and it is expected to increase in a nonlinear way in the future, even in the most optimistic case of the world agreeing on Paris Agreement–aligned climate-mitigation policies.

The second assumption is that markets are able and willing to incorporate into prices all the information about future climate impacts and future climate policies. However, climate impacts are characterized by tail risk, which is difficult to estimate because of data limitation and evolving scientific evidence on tipping points. Moreover, vulnerability of physical assets depends on investments in adaptation, which in turn depend on policy makers and investors' risk assessment (Monasterolo *et al.* 2024). At the same time, the climate policy landscape is also evolving, often intertwined with geopolitical developments (see e.g. the recent election of Trump as POTUS, which led to the US exiting the Paris Agreement again). Thus, assuming that financial markets are able to make reliable forecasts requires a big leap of faith.

The MBCF approach neglects the possibility of multiple equilibria because it assumes rational expectations and it also neglects the multidimensionality of well-being, since it only examines asset prices.

Some remarks apply to a specific stream of work that aims to conduct "market-based climate stress tests" (Jung, Engle, and Berner 2021; Acharya *et al.* 2023). These works estimate losses on banks' capital based on the sensitivity of banks' stock prices to variations on stock prices of high-carbon firms in their loan portfolio. This approach measures markets' past perception of climate risk for banks. However, this perception does necessarily reflect the risks that could materialize in reality. For instance, in the lead-up to the great financial crisis, until mid-2008, markets had a perception of very low risk on a horizon of five years (e.g., in terms of five-year credit default swap spreads) about the very financial institutions that got into distress (and in some cases defaulted) just six months later. Several more recent events, such as shifts in US climate policy, Brexit, and European Union elections, have also shown that investors sometimes misjudge the economic risks resulting from policy developments, lending support to the idea that climate risk should be estimated based on genuinely forward-looking metrics (Battiston *et al.* 2023). Market-based risk metrics could have the undesired effect of giving policymakers the illusion that climate risk is lower than it is. Further, in case transition risk materializes, even in the case in which markets would correctly anticipate that, governments would bail out the systemically important firms affected, and the cost to taxpayers could be very substantial. Therefore, from the perspective of financial supervision in the broad sense, the results of market-based climate stress tests are to be taken with large caution.

5   The Complexity Climate Finance Approach

The complexity climate finance approach, which is well-established in academia (Battiston *et al.* 2017; Battiston *et al.* 2021; Battiston *et al.* 2023) and used among practitioners (Battiston *et al.* 2018; Roncoroni *et al.* 2021; Ranger, Mahul, and Monasterolo 2022), acknowledges complexity and builds on the risk-management approach that inspired the Paris Agreement.

The CCF approach computes financial risk measures that are conditional to a given scenario as opposed to the standard asset pricing models that aim to assess a pricing of instruments unconditional to future climate outcomes. CCF is compatible with the notion of multiple equilibria in CSEF and with the multidimensionality of well-being. Indeed, the desirability of each scenario could be assessed in terms of metrics that go beyond intertemporal consumption. In each scenario, investors' expectations about climate risk (also known as climate sentiments; Dunz, Naqvi, and Monasterolo 2021) depend on climate policy credibility and can give rise to self-defeating prophecies.

Climate policy credibility can trigger the change of beliefs in a coordinated fashion, giving it a crucial role in steering the system from one equilibrium to another, provided that tipping points are not reached. If investors do not trust the policy to be carried forward, they would not adjust their risk assessment for high-carbon and low-carbon activities (by increasing the risk profile for the former and decreasing it for the latter), and thus the cost of capital for high-carbon and low-carbon firms, respectively. This, in turn, can lead to a gap between the level of climate investments actually carried out by investors and those assumed to be carried out in the scenario used in the climate stress test (Battiston *et al.* 2021). Implications include a potential underestimation of investors' exposure to climate risks, which could amplify risks for financial stability; an overoptimistic assessment of the role of private climate finance and thus an underestimation of public action, including the investment needs; a poor understanding of the economic and financial policy response to climate change; and missed opportunities for mitigation and adaptation.

Figure 2 illustrates the approach by coupling the climate financial risk (CFR) model with a process-based IAM. The process-based IAM generates trajectories of output across sectors and technologies and does not contain finance nor financial actors. However, the coupling of the two models can be implemented through the value of the interest rate paid by firms in different sectors. The interest rate is computed by the CFR at a given date and for a given firm or sector on the basis of the future trajectory of that firm or sector.

This approach enables the quantitative assessment of both climate physical and transition risk, conditional to the adjustment in expectations on future scenarios. It also captures the impact of investors' risk perception on their decision-making on levels of investments into low- or high-carbon activities. Thus, by capturing the complexity of the problem,

IAM $\left\{ \begin{array}{l} \text{Carbon Price: } p_s(t) \\ \text{Investment: } I_{s,k}(t) = I_{s,k}^{(\text{IAM})}(p_s(t)) + \Delta I_{s,k}^{(\text{CFR})}(r_{c,k}(t)) \\ \text{Output: } Y_{s,k}(I_{s,k}(t), p_s(t)) \end{array} \right.$

Output from CFR to IAM:
Interest rates and capital allocation across technologies based on expectations

Output from IAM to CFR:
Carbon price, investment, output trajectories across scenarios

CFR $\left\{ \begin{array}{l} \text{Expectations: } \beta(t) \\ \text{Interest Rate: } r_{s,k}(Y_{s,k}(t), p_s(t), \beta(t)) \\ \text{Capital Allocation: } h(\text{ClimateVaR}(Y_{s,k}(t), \beta(t)) \end{array} \right.$

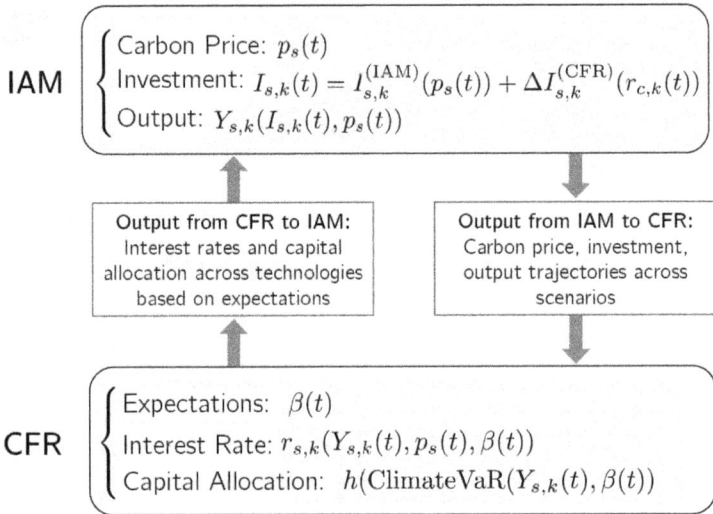

Figure 2. The feedback between the process-based integrated assessment model (IAM) and the climate financial risk (CFR) model in the complexity climate finance approach. The approach acknowledges the existence of multiple equilibria in the CSEF system and thus carries out a valuation of financial instruments conditional to any given path (as opposed to approaches that assume ex-ante a unique equilibrium). Further, the approach allows one to see how a given equilibrium path can be affected by the feedback loop of investors' expectations about the risk along the path and the materialization of the path. This feedback loop is implemented as follows. First, in the CFR, investors assess climate financial risk based on climate scenarios. The credibility of climate policies affects investors' expectations (denoted by β), which in turn concur to determine the adjustment of the cost of capital (denoted by r). The adjusted r is then fed back to the IAM, resulting in new investment decisions (denoted by I) of the firms and thus in new output scenarios. Source: authors' own elaborations.

the CCF approach is more coherent with the objectives of addressing the societal challenges of climate risk.

This approach has also been extended to couple the CFR with stock-flow consistent (SFC) models to capture the distributive effects of climate policies, the interplay between fiscal and financial (e.g., monetary and macroprudential) policy, and the potential resulting trade-offs in socioeconomic and financial systems. These dimensions are usually not considered in standard macroeconomic models and yet they are crucial to understand the role of finance and financial policy.

In particular, the coupling of the CFR, implemented with the CLIMACRED model (Battiston *et al.* 2023) and the EIRIN SFC model (Dunz *et al.* 2023) was used to develop the NGFS short-term climate scenarios for climate stress tests (NGFS 2023).

The SFC macrofinancial model EIRIN can represent the out-of-equilibrium macrofinancial response of the economy considering a range of fiscal and monetary policies and their interaction. Agents are characterized by bounded rationality and adaptive expectations, and are subject to incomplete information. This implies that shocks such as sudden changes in the carbon price are not fully anticipated, and the magnitude of the shock in the economy not dampened, as compared to fully rational agents with perfect information.

The climate credit-risk model CLIMACRED provides climate-scenario-contingent estimates of credit risk, costs of capital, and asset values. For transition risk, CLIMACRED takes as inputs firms' climate risk exposure, business and financial characteristics, the projections of sectoral economic trajectories and the policy rate from the EIRIN model. It then derives the dynamic evolution of the firms' balance sheets, and from that the climate-scenario-contingent changes in asset values and financial risk characteristics (e.g., the probability of default, PD). For physical risk, the difference stands in the input of CLIMACRED, which takes the country- and sector-level distribution of impacts (e.g., capital destruction, business interruption, and productivity losses).

Overall, these blocks withstand the framework for climate stress test, shown in figure 3. For a detailed description of the climate stress test methodology, see Battiston and Monasterolo (2024). In the climate stress test, CLIMACRED (c. block of 3) can be fed by network effects in order to consider the reverberation of losses (e.g., second, third round, etc.) on the balance sheet of individual investors, within the financial network.[1]

6 Future Directions in Complexity Economics and Finance Research

The emergent field of complexity economics and finance continually unveils new research avenues, particularly as they pertain to the multifaceted challenges posed by climate change. This section identifies open questions in the field and potential areas of investigation, such as the financial implications of nature and biodiversity loss, systemic risks that precipitate substantial financial downturns, regulatory oversights, and the intersection of climate change with geopolitical dynamics.

In this regard, a key open methodological question in complexity economics and finance that arises when dealing with practical applications is: How much complexity do we need to address our research or policy question? Parsimonious modeling—that is, trying to capture only the complexity that is essential to the problem at hand—is particularly important in the context of climate change, where the impact of policies

---

[1] Network effects are analyzed in a financial network model of contagion that considers the exposures of individual investors to climate risk via the securities and financial contracts held in their portfolio (Battiston *et al.* 2017; Roncoroni *et al.* 2021).

a. NGFS Scenarios Framework in Phase IV

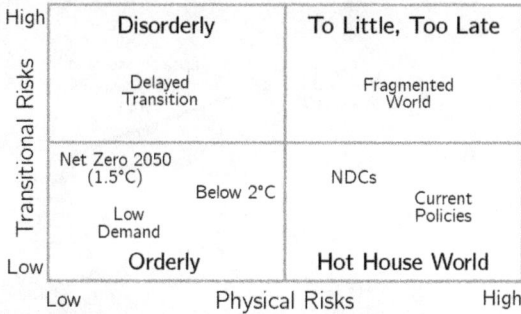

b. Output Trajectories Process-Based IAM

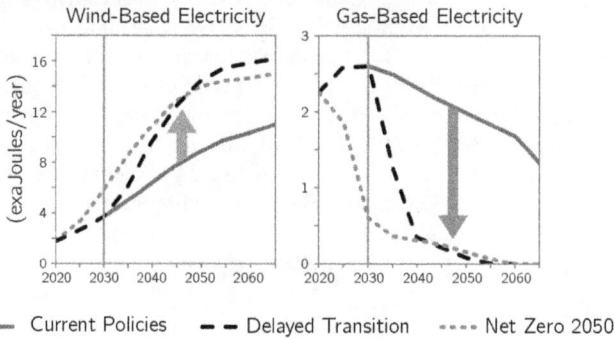

—— Current Policies   – – Delayed Transition   ···· Net Zero 2050

c. Climate Credit Risk Model: Correlated Defaults Under NGFS

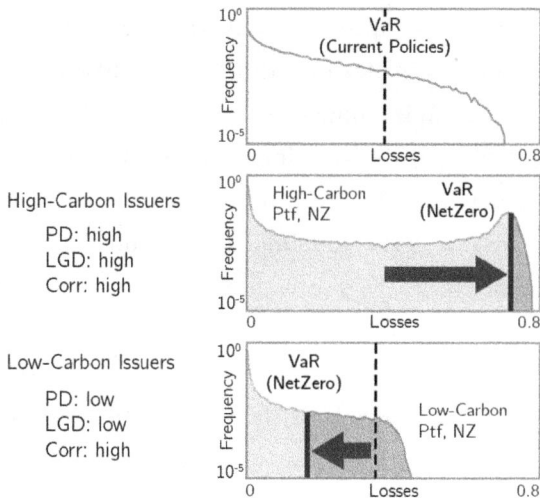

High-Carbon Issuers

PD: high
LGD: high
Corr: high

Low-Carbon Issuers

PD: low
LGD: low
Corr: high

d. Financial Network Effects

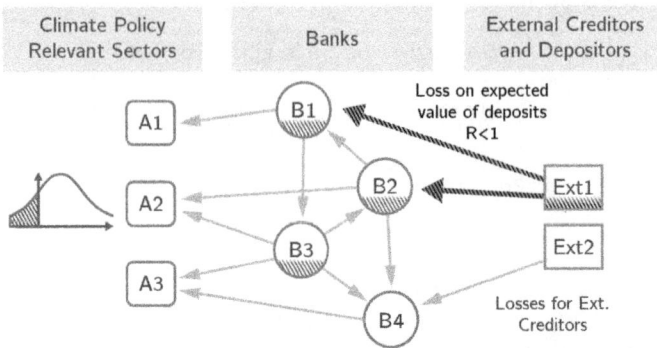

Figure 3. Methodological framework of a science-based climate stress-test (example of transition risk). Step 1 (a): Select the relevant climate scenarios (e.g., NGFS 2023 phase IV). Step 2 (b): Extract output trajectories by type of energy technology from the NGFS scenarios. Step 3 (c): Adjust the financial valuation of individual securities and loans conditioned to the scenarios' trajectories (CLIMACRED, Battiston *et al.* 2023) and compute the adjustments in financial risk measures (e.g., the Climate Value at Risk (VaR)) at portfolio level (see, e.g., Battiston and Monasterolo 2020). Step 4 (d): Consider financial network effects (e.g., contagion and fire sales; Roncoroni *et al.* 2021). Source: Authors' own elaborations.

or their absence has to be communicated to a broad range of stakeholders. Methodological advancements must navigate the fine line between capturing essential details and avoiding overcomplexity that obfuscates actionable insights. In addition, the validation of complex models against real-world data remains a significant challenge, necessitating comprehensive datasets that are often difficult to obtain or create.

In this regard, the modeling innovation used for the development of the NGFS short-term climate scenarios (NGFS 2025), which couple an SFC model (EIRIN, Monasterolo and Raberto 2018) with a climate credit-risk model (CLIMACRED, Battiston *et al.* 2023; Mandel, Battiston, and Monasterolo 2025) and a CGE model (GEME3, Fragkos *et al.* 2017), represent a promising way ahead.

Research extension involves the consideration of the relation between climate and nature risks, including biodiversity and ecosystem losses, in financial risk assessment (Ranger *et al.* 2024; NGFS 2024). Indeed, our economic system is highly dependent on the health of ecosystems, which is in turn negatively affected by anthropogenic climate change. Including ecosystem and biodiversity risk scenarios could lead to an amplification of economic and financial losses, with relevant implications on asset price volatility and financial stability. This, in turn, is relevant for risk assessment at central banks and financial regulators with supervisory mandate, and to inform the design of prudential regulation aimed at strengthening the climate resilience of the financial system.

Overall, incorporating complexity science in economic and financial research can support robust decision-making, enhancing strategic planning for climate action and fostering an adaptive, informed, and proactive approach to both climate mitigation and adaptation strategies. In particular, it can provide relevant information about where to invest in climate mitigation and in adaptation, how (financial instruments, public/private governance), and how much. This information is important for policymakers who have to decide how to allocate tight budgets in times of fiscal constraint and growing public debts. In this regard, future research should help to find a balance between model complexity, empirical validation, and the practical application of findings to guide effective climate finance policy. ✤

REFERENCES

Acharya, V. V., R. Berner, R. Engle, H. Jung, J. Stroebel, X. Zeng, and Y. Zhao. 2023. "Climate Stress Testing." *Annual Review of Financial Economics* 15 (1): 291–326. https://doi.org/10.1146/annurev-financial-110921-101555.

Acharya, V. V., T. Johnson, S. Sundaresan, and T. Tomunen. 2022. *Is Physical Climate Risk Priced? Evidence from Regional Variation in Exposure to Heat Stress.* Technical report. National Bureau of Economic Research. https://doi.org/10.3386/w30445.

Alessi, L., E. Ossola, and R. Panzica. 2021. "What Greenium Matters in the Stock Market? The Role of Greenhouse Gas Emissions and Environmental Disclosures." *Journal of Financial Stability* 54 (10086): 9. https://doi.org/10.1016/j.jfs.2021.100869.

Alogoskoufis, S., N. Dunz, T. Emambakhsh, T. Hennig, M. Kaijser, C. Kouratzoglou, M. A. Muñoz, L. Parisi, and C. Salleo. 2021. *ECB Economy-Wide Climate Stress Test: Methodology and Results.* 281. ECB Occasional Paper.

Annicchiarico, B., and F. Di Dio. 2017. "GHG Emissions Control and Monetary Policy." *Environmental and Resource Economics* 67:823–851. https://doi.org/10.1007/s10640-016-0007-5.

Ardia, D., K. Bluteau, K. Boudt, and K. Inghelbrecht. 2023. "Climate Change Concerns and the Performance of Green vs. Brown Stocks." *Management Science* 69 (12): 7607–7632. https://doi.org/10.1287/mnsc.2022.4636.

Arrow, K., M. Cropper, C. Gollier, B. Groom, G. Heal, R. Newell, W. Nordhaus, et al. 2013. "Determining Benefits and Costs for Future Generations." *Science* 341 (6144): 349–350. https://doi.org/10.1126/science.1235665.

Battiston, S., P. Jakubik, I. Monasterolo, K. Riahi, and B. van Ruijven. 2018. "Climate Risk Assessment of the Sovereign Bond Portfolio of European Insurers." *EIOPA Financial Stability Report.*

Battiston, S., A. Mandel, I. Monasterolo, and A. Roncoroni. 2023. "Climate Credit Risk and Corporate Valuation." *SSRN Electronic Journal,* https://doi.org/10.2139/ssrn.4124002.

Battiston, S., A. Mandel, I. Monasterolo, F. Schütze, and G. Visentin. 2017. "A Climate Stress-Test of the Financial System." *Nature Climate Change* 7 (4): 283–288. https://doi.org/10.1038/nclimate3255.

Battiston, S., and I. Monasterolo. 2020. "On the Dependence of Investor's Probability of Default on Climate Transition Scenarios." *SSRN Electronic Journal*, https://doi.org/10.2139/ssrn.3743647.

———. 2024. *Enhanced Scenarios for Climate Stress Tests*. Technical report. The INSPIRE Sustainable Central Banking Toolbox, Policy Briefing Paper 16. https://www.lse.ac.uk/granthaminstitute/wp-content/uploads/2024/04/INSPIRE-Sustainable-Central-Banking-Toolbox-Paper-16.pdf.

Battiston, S., I. Monasterolo, K. Riahi, and B. J. van Ruijven. 2021. "Accounting for Finance is Key for Climate Mitigation Pathways." *Science* 372 (6545): 918–920. https://doi.org/10.1126/science.abf3877.

Bernstein, A., M. T. Gustafson, and R. Lewis. 2019. "Disaster on the Horizon: The Price Effect of Sea Level Rise." *Journal of Financial Economics* 134 (2): 253–272. https://doi.org/10.1016/j.jfineco.2019.03.013.

Bertram, C., J. Hilaire, E. Kriegler, T. Beck, D. Bresch, L. Clarke, R. Cui, *et al.* 2021. "NGFS Climate Scenario Database: Technical Documentation V2. 2," https://pure.iiasa.ac.at/17511.

Beyene, W., M. D. Delis, K. de Greiff, and S. Ongena. 2021. "Too-Big-to-Strand? Bond Versus Bank Financing in the Transition to a Low-Carbon Economy," https://ssrn.com/abstract=3960296.

Bolton, P., and M. Kacperczyk. 2021. "Do Investors Care About Carbon Risk?" *Journal of Financial Economics* 142 (2): 517–549. https://doi.org/10.1016/j.jfineco.2021.05.008.

Carattini, S., G. Heutel, and G. Melkadze. 2023. "Climate Policy, Financial Frictions, and Transition Risk." *Review of Economic Dynamics* 51:778–794. https://doi.org/10.1016/j.red.2023.08.003.

Carney, M. 2015. "Breaking the Tragedy of the Horizon—Climate Change and Financial Stability." Speech given at Lloyd's of London by the Governor of the Bank of England, https://www.bankofengland.co.uk/speech/2015/breaking-the-tragedy-of-the-horizon-climate-change-and-financial-stability.

Diluiso, F., B. Annicchiarico, M. Kalkuhl, and J. C. Minx. 2021. "Climate Actions and Macro-Financial Stability: The Role of Central Banks." *Journal of Environmental Economics and Management* 110:102548. https://doi.org/10.1016/j.jeem.2021.102548.

~179~

Dunz, N., A. H. Essenfelder, A. Mazzocchetti, I. Monasterolo, and M. Raberto. 2023. "Compounding COVID-19 and Climate Risks: The Interplay of Banks' Lending and Government's Policy in the Shock Recovery." *Journal of Banking & Finance* 152:106306. https://doi.org/10.1016/j.jbankfin.2021.106306.

Dunz, N., A. Naqvi, and I. Monasterolo. 2021. "Climate Sentiments, Transition Risk, and Financial Stability in a Stock-Flow Consistent Model." *Journal of Financial Stability* 54:100872. https://doi.org/10.1016/j.jfs.2021.100872.

EBA. 2020. *Risk Assessment of the European Banking System—December 2020.* https://www.eba.europa.eu/risk-and-data-analysis/risk-analysis/risk-monitoring/risk-reports-and-other-thematic-work/risk-assessment-reports.

Farmer, J. D., C. Hepburn, P. Mealy, and A. Teytelboym. 2015. "A Third Wave in the Economics of Climate Change." *Environmental and Resource Economics* 62:329–357. https://doi.org/10.1007/s10640-015-9965-2.

Fragkos, P., N. Tasios, L. Paroussos, P. Capros, and S. Tsani. 2017. "Energy System Impacts and Policy Implications of the European Intended Nationally Determined Contribution and Low-Carbon Pathway to 2050." *Energy Policy* 100:216–226. https://doi.org/10.1016/j.enpol.2016.10.023.

Giglio, S., B. Kelly, and J. Stroebel. 2021. "Climate Finance." *Annual Review of Financial Economics* 13 (1): 15–36. https://doi.org/10.1146/annurev-financial-102620-103311.

Ilhan, E., Z. Sautner, and G. Vilkov. 2021. "Carbon Tail Risk." *The Review of Financial Studies* 34 (3): 1540–1571. https://doi.org/10.1093/rfs/hhaa071.

IPCC. 2022. "Summary for Policymakers." In *Climate Change 2022: Impacts, Adaptation, and Vulnerability,* edited by H.-O. Pörtner, D. C. Roberts, E. S. Poloczanska, K. Mintenbeck, M. Tignor, A. Alegría, M. Craig, *et al.*, 3–33. Cambridge, UK: Cambridge University Press. https://doi.org/10.1017/9781009325844.001.

Jung, H., R. F. Engle, and R. Berner. 2021. "CRISK: Measuring the Climate Risk Exposure of the Financial System." *FRB of New York Staff Report,* no. 977, https://doi.org/10.1016/j.jfineco.2025.104076.

Keen, S., T. M. Lenton, T. J. Garrett, J. W. B. Rae, B. P. Hanley, and M. Grasselli. 2022. "Estimates of Economic and Environmental Damages from Tipping Points cannot be Reconciled with the Scientific Literature." *Proceedings of the National Academy of Sciences* 119 (21): e2117308119. https://doi.org/10.1073/pnas.2117308119.

Lenton, T. M., H. Held, E. Kriegler, J. W. Hall, W. Lucht, S. Rahmstorf, and H. J. Schellnhuber. 2008. "Tipping Elements in the Earth's Climate System." *Proceedings of the National Academy of Sciences* 105 (6): 1786–1793. https://doi.org/10.1073/pnas.0705414105.

Mandel, A., S. Battiston, and I. Monasterolo. 2025. "Mapping Global Financial Risks under Climate Change." *Nature Climate Change* 15:329–334. https://doi.org/10.1038/s41558-025-02244-x.

Mercure, J.-F., H. Pollitt, A. M. Bassi, J. E. Viñuales, and N. R. Edwards. 2016. "Modelling Complex Systems of Heterogeneous Agents to Better Design Sustainability Transitions Policy." *Global Environmental Change* 37:102–115. https://doi.org/10.1016/j.gloenvcha.2016.02.003.

Monasterolo, I., and L. de Angelis. 2020. "Blind to Carbon Risk? An Analysis of Stock Market Reaction to the Paris Agreement." *Ecological Economics* 170 (10657): 1. https://doi.org/10.1016/j.ecolecon.2019.106571.

Monasterolo, I., A. Pacelli, M. Pagano, and C. Russo. 2024. "A European Climate Bond." *Economic Policy,* eiae065. https://doi.org/10.1093/epolic/eiae065.

Monasterolo, I., and M. Raberto. 2018. "The EIRIN Flow-of-Funds Behavioural Model of Green Fiscal Policies and Green Sovereign Bonds." *Ecological Economics* 144:228–243. https://doi.org/10.1016/j.ecolecon.2017.07.029.

Monasterolo, I., A. Roventini, and T. J. Foxon. 2019. "Uncertainty of Climate Policies and Implications for Economics and Finance: An Evolutionary Economics Approach." *Ecological Economics* 163:177–182. https://doi.org/10.1016/j.ecolecon.2019.05.012.

NGFS. 2019. *Network for Greening the Financial System—A Call for Action Climate Change as a Source of Financial Risk.* First Comprehensive Report. https://www.ngfs.net/sites/default/files/medias/documents/ngfs_first_comprehensive_report_-_17042019_0.pdf.

———. 2023. *Network for Greening the Financial System Technical Document: Conceptual Note on Short-Term Climate Scenarios.* Technical report. https://www.ngfs.net/system/files/import/ngfs/medias/documents/conceptual-note-on-short-term-climate-scenarios.pdf.

———. 2024. *Nature-Related Financial Risks: A Conceptual Framework to Guide Action by Central Banks and Supervisors.* Technical report. NGFS. https://www.ngfs.net/system/files/import/ngfs/medias/documents/ngfs-conceptual-framework-nature-risks.pdf.

NGFS. 2025. *Network for Greening the Financial System Short-Term Climate Scenarios for Central Banks and Supervisors.* Technical report. https://www.ngfs.net/en/publications-and-statistics/publications/ngfs-short-term-climate-scenarios-central-banks-and-supervisors.

Nordhaus, W. D. 1993. "Optimal Greenhouse-Gas Reductions and Tax Policy in the "DICE" Model." *The American Economic Review* 83 (2): 313–317. https://www.jstor.org/stable/2117683.

Otto, I. M., J. F. Donges, R. Cremades, A. Bhowmik, R. J. Hewitt, W. Lucht, J. Rockström, et al. 2020. "Social Tipping Dynamics for Stabilizing Earth's Climate by 2050." *Proceedings of the National Academy of Sciences* 117 (5): 2354–2365. https://doi.org/10.1073/pnas.1900577117.

Pástor, L., R. F. Stambaugh, and L. A. Taylor. 2022. "Dissecting Green Returns." *Journal of Financial Economics* 146 (2): 403–424. https://doi.org/10.1016/j.jfineco.2022.07.007.

Ranger, N., T. Oliver, J. Alvarez, S. Battiston, S. Bekker, H. Killick, I. Hurst, et al. 2024. *Assessing the Materiality of Nature-Related Financial Risks for the UK.* Technical report. Green Finance Institute. https://nora.nerc.ac.uk/id/eprint/537627/.

Ranger, N. A., O. Mahul, and I. Monasterolo. 2021. "Managing the Financial Risks of Climate Change and Pandemics: What We Know (and Don't Know)." *One Earth* 4 (10): 1375–1385. https://doi.org/10.1016/j.oneear.2021.09.017.

———. 2022. *Assessing Financial Risks from Physical Climate Shocks: A Framework for Scenario Generation.* Washington, DC: World Bank. https://climateinstitute.edhec.edu/publications/assessing-financial-risks-physical-climate-shocks-framework-scenario-generation.

Rocha, J. C., G. D. Peterson, and R. Biggs. 2015. "Regime Shifts in the Anthropocene: Drivers, Risks, and Resilience." *PloS One* 10 (8): e0134639. https://doi.org/10.1371/journal.pone.0134639.

Roncoroni, A., S. Battiston, L. O. L. Escobar-Farfán, and S. Martinez-Jaramillo. 2021. "Climate Risk and Financial Stability in the Network of Banks and Investment Funds." *Journal of Financial Stability* 54:100870. https://doi.org/10.1016/j.jfs.2021.100870.

Sautner, Z., L. van Lent, G. Vilkov, and R. Zhang. 2023. "Pricing Climate Change Exposure." *Management Science* 69 (12): 7540–7561. https://doi.org/10.1287/mnsc.2023.4686.

Chapter 20: Climate Risk

Steffen, W., W. Broadgate, L. Deutsch, O. Gaffney, and C. Ludwig. 2015. "The Trajectory of the Anthropocene: The Great Acceleration." *The Anthropocene Review* 2 (1): 81–98. https://doi.org/10.1177/2053019614564785.

Stiglitz, J. E., A. K. Sen, and J.-P. Fitoussi. 2009. *Report by the Commission on the Measurement of Economic Performance and Social Progress.* Commission on the Measurement of Economic Performance and Social Progress, Paris.

Zerbib, O. D. 2019. "The Effect of Pro-Environmental Preferences on Bond Prices: Evidence from Green Bonds." *Journal of Banking & Finance* 98:39–60. https://doi.org/10.1016/j.jbankfin.2018.10.012.

Zscheischler, J., S. Westra, B. J. J.M. van den Hurk, S. I. Seneviratne, P. J. Ward, A. Pitman, A. AghaKouchak, *et al.* 2018. "Future Climate Risk from Compound Events." *Nature Climate Change* 8 (6): 469–477. https://doi.org/10.1038/s41558-018-0156-3.

DECARBONIZING
A COMPLEX SYSTEM

Marion Dumas, London School of Economics and Political Science, and
Pia Andres, Durham University and Centre for Economic Performance

Abstract

Meeting the challenge of climate-change mitigation involves a rapid and comprehensive transformation of the global economy away from high-emitting production systems toward low-carbon ones. This chapter illustrates how complex-systems approaches are uniquely well suited to understanding the drivers, barriers, and risks arising from such a technological transformation. We first consider the dynamics at play in growing new technological systems. We contrast two empirically well-documented cases (solar photovoltaics and electric vehicles) to show the central importance of technological interdependencies in shaping the dynamics of innovation and in crafting effective policy strategies. In particular, we argue that promoting low-carbon technologies that are less modular may require a more targeted and coordinated approach than is standard in innovation policy. We then turn to the dynamics at play in phasing out old technological systems. A central question is whether the progress of low-carbon technologies can on its own displace fossil-fuel-based technologies without policies that actively phase out or discourage these technologies. We highlight the different feedback processes that are key to answering this question (including the interaction between changes in technology costs, the rebound effect and the green paradox, and the role of heterogeneous expectations), some areas where better modeling is needed, and open policy questions. Finally, we argue that accounting for the heterogeneous nature of capital assets, skills, and regional capabilities, as well as understanding systemic interdependencies, is essential to anticipating disruption and asset stranding and crafting policies to mitigate transition risks.

Introduction

For decades, climate change was implicitly viewed as a static problem. Internationally, this problem consisted of allocating a fixed carbon budget among countries. Domestically, the problem consisted of reducing emissions along a fixed, or exogenously changing, marginal abatement curve, which represented the ongoing costs. The principal task of policy analysis was to find a cost-minimizing way of abating up to the desired point, which led economists to argue that pricing carbon was the most efficient approach to decarbonization, as it would allow the market to find the most efficient allocation of abatement effort. Today, the paradigm has changed, thanks to the realization that the problem is one of spurring transitions in path-dependent systems, from high-emitting systems (of technologies and associated behaviors) to low-emitting ones. Once the transition is complete, the costs of abating will have become limited, and the new systems may even be superior in some respects.[1] The challenge is then to orchestrate technological transitions at a fast pace, across many sectors and services, and in all (or most) locations. This involves "growing" new technological systems and phasing out old ones.

~185~

Here, we highlight how a complexity lens that emphasizes dynamics and system interdependencies can help us catalyze these transitions and anticipate some of their consequences, as well as navigate their fundamental uncertainties. We focus on the technological transition, while Francesco Lamperti, Giovanni Dosi, and Andrea Roventini (2026, ch. 19 in this volume) provide a review of how complexity approaches can inform the economics of climate of change more broadly.

---

[1] For example, they may be characterized by lower pollution and lower energy costs.

Growing the New

SOURCES AND CONSEQUENCES OF
PATH DEPENDENCE

What does it take and how difficult is it to initiate and sustain the development of new low-carbon technological systems?

To answer this question, imagine the simplest approach that could be proposed by Economics 101. In this baseline, the government funds R&D, in the most neutral way, and puts a price on greenhouse gases. This double policy is meant to encourage the production of new ideas and knowledge (underprovided by the market alone). These ideas are then meant to be picked up and selected by a market that adequately rewards lower-emission technologies thanks to the carbon price (Jaffe, Newell, and Stavins 2005). With this technology-neutral policy, the creative forces of the market are free to identify and further invest in the "best" solutions (Pless and Srivastav 2025).

This baseline model assumes a great capacity for technological systems to reconfigure themselves through the decentralized search and risk-taking of economic agents, guided only by price signals (and drawing on a publicly nurtured store of knowledge and ideas). This is not incompatible with W. Brian Arthur's (2010) groundbreaking account of technological systems, which he depicts as highly dynamic. In Arthur's words, inventors "continually create the new by combining the old." As they try novel combinations of existing ideas, innovators sometimes identify radically new technologies with better or new functionalities. Through ripple effects, these lead others to modify their practices of production and consumption, often in far reaching ways: In this way, Arthur writes, "the economy disrupts itself from within."

Yet historical examples of renewal, disruption, and change are usually linked to the diffusion of something entirely new, such

~186~

as the internet, or the replacement by something vastly better performing, such as cars replacing horses (Grübler, Nakićenović, and Victor 1999). Low-carbon technologies, instead, are meant to substitute existing high-emitting technologies in order to achieve a public good, rather than offering a performance increase for private users:[2] They have to break through in systems that are mature and highly functional.

Most mature technological systems are highly inert, due to mechanisms that create path dependence.[3] As we will see, because of this path dependence, the baseline model is too simplistic. To grow radically new alternatives in these mature systems, we need to understand and overcome the mechanisms that create path dependence. These mechanisms include: (1) possible increasing returns to knowledge on a given technology (Acemoglu *et al.* 2012); (2) relative increasing returns to fixing and then refining complex technological architectures (Murmann and Frenken 2006); (3) a network of technology-specific, long-lived complements (infrastructure, other technologies, behaviors, regulatory systems) that make technologies incompatible with that network unattractive (Cowan and Gunby 1996; Seto *et al.* 2016);[4] and (4) political organization to resist replacement of one industry by another (Seto *et al.* 2016). The implication of this path dependence is that market competition (based on

---

[2] Co-benefits may emerge, but tend to materialize later and often are themselves externalities (e.g., reducing air pollution).

[3] In his 2006 essay on path dependence, Scott Page highlights that this term captures a range of processes by which history matters in shaping the future. Our discussion here relates to what he calls "phatdependence," in which the accumulation of past choices shapes the probability of future choices, rather than their exact sequence.

[4] Although increasing returns are often equated with path dependence or seen as its main underlying mechanism, Page (2006) alerts us that, in most cases, it is instead negative externalities that engender path dependence: Due to constraints (spatial, budgetary, attentional, etc.), as one option is developed, there are fewer resources available to later develop another.

price) is more likely to reward innovation and investments in refinements of the existing system than innovation on an entirely new substitute system (Murmann and Frenken 2006). Empirical research on low-carbon innovation provides some evidence for the increasing return to innovation mechanism (Aghion *et al.* 2016), as well as for the prediction that carbon prices will favor incremental technological change (e.g., energy efficiency) rather than radical innovations (Grubb *et al.* 2021; Lilliestam, Patt, and Bersalli 2022), and that incumbents try to politically undermine radically new technologies (Geels 2014).

Instead of the economy disrupting itself from within with the help of a carbon price, the engines of disruption that have proven most effective have been innovative institutions and policies that target and nurture new technologies.

THE SUCCESS OF SOLAR PHOTOVOLTAIC AND THE EMERGING MODEL FOR CRAFTING NEW TECHNOLOGICAL PATHWAYS

The most studied example of successful targeting of a low-carbon technology is that of solar photovoltaic (PV). It has become the poster child of clean technology innovation and deployment because of the astonishing rate at which its performance and cost improved roughly 15,000-fold from 1975 to 2020 (Nemet 2019; Way *et al.* 2022), shattering all forecasts along the way and making the prospect of affordable clean power a reality. Based on numerous studies and a synthesis account of the technology's life history by Gregory Nemet, the case of solar PV has helped shore up a heuristic model of how policy can enable a radically new energy technology to break through in a highly locked-in system.[5]

---

[5] Similar heuristic models are articulated in multiple contributions, such as Roger Fouquet (2010), Arnulf Grübler *et al.* (2012), and Grubb *et al.* (2021). They are of course not just based on the case of solar PV; detailed studies of many past technology transitions have helped build this understanding.

This model, which we call the *innovation chain model* following Michael Grubb, Will McDowall, and Paul Drummond (2017), starts with public R&D directly targeted at the new technology, which is soon deployed in niche markets. These niche markets are areas of application where the new technology offers a key advantage that offsets the higher price and lower overall performance. Solar PV, for example, provided electricity off-grid. Niche markets can also be created by public procurement. The niche market enables innovators and policymakers to test the technology and assess its potential. This on its own can encourage further private innovation and investment. However, as was the case for solar PV, niche markets are often saturated before the new technology can compete with mature technologies. Hence, the critical policy lever in addition to public R&D are market-expanding policies such as targeted public subsidies (e.g., feed-in-tariffs for rooftop solar). This subsidized market expansion sets in motion positive feedbacks: Costs come down thanks to innovation and learning-by-doing; this encourages more innovation and new adopters; and then economies of scale set in. Eventually, the new technology becomes cost-competitive—with the help of a politically acceptable level of carbon pricing toward the end of the journey (Meckling, Sterner, and Wagner 2017). Increasingly, the view is that sustained technology support policy can in this way allow a technology to reach the point of cost parity, which many view as a key tipping point in the transition to the new system (Beinhocker 2017; Sharpe and Lenton 2021; Winkelmann *et al.* 2022).

Thanks to a bottom-up model of PV costs, Goksin Kavlak, James McNerney, and Jessika Trancik (2018) have quantified the channels of PV's cost reduction, offering a good test of this model. Their estimates attribute 30% of cost reduction to public R&D and 60% to targeted market-expanding policies. Half of that 60% was due to private R&D stimulated by the market-expanding policies, and half to more recent investments in large plants and routinized processes.. Thus, both public R&D and market-expanding policies proved to be crucial and generated global spillovers in innovation and adoption (Gerarden 2023). Crucially, technology push and demand pull worked in tandem rather than sequentially. In a review covering all types of clean technologies, Grubb *et al.* (2021) confirm the key role of targeted market-expanding policies in the development of clean technology, whilst François Lafond, Diana Greenwald, and J. Doyne Farmer (2022) buttress the causal evidence that public demand can induce innovation, using World War II as an exogenous shock.

LESS MODULAR SYSTEMS MAY REQUIRE A MORE COORDINATED APPROACH

How general is the innovation chain model described above, and how reproducible is the case of solar PV? An important hypothesis has come out of complex-systems research, namely that the modularity of solar PV is an important structural feature that enabled solar PV's astonishing improvement rate (Malhotra and Schmidt 2020). Modularity may be playing two roles. First, modularity allows the same basic technological building block to be deployed at different scales, as they can be assembled in smaller or larger configurations. In the case of solar, this allowed rapid iteration and exploration of a diverse set of niche markets, enabling fast learning in a variety of contexts (Nemet 2019). Second, modularity implies lower complexity in system architecture (Baldwin and Clark 2000; Fink and Reeves 2019): The components don't interact too much, so improvements in one component do not compromise the performance of other components, and they can be improved upon in parallel. McNerney *et al.* (2011) show theoretically that more modular technologies should enjoy a higher learning rate. Charlie Wilson *et al.* (2020) provide broader evidence for this hypothesis by looking at many technologies and showing a suggestive set of correlations between modularity and transition outcomes, notably learning and diffusion rates.

Solar PV is modular, too, in a broader sense illustrated by figure 1. Here, an individual technology z, such as solar PV, sits in the center and is surrounded by elements of the economic system it interacts with (denoted $X = \{x_i\}$): (a) a network of other novel technologies that the nascent technology may require to function; and (b) nontechnological complements (denoted $Y = \{y_i\}$), such as complementary infrastructure, key material inputs and skills, consumer tastes and habits, and institutional frameworks that enable the technology to be deployed in markets. The figure depicts a buffer zone between an individual technology z and an interacting system element (x_i, y_i). A large buffer between z and (x_i, y_i) indicates that (x_i, y_i) is not a binding constraint for the initial stages of z's development. Conversely, a small buffer between z and (x_i, y_i) indicates that (x_i, y_i) are required elements of z's development from the get-go: It is difficult to find a functional use for z without simultaneously developing or modifying (x_i, y_i).

In this framework, solar PV is modular in the sense that it could take its baby steps in the system without being constrained by missing or incompatible elements of X such as demand response, smart grids, storage and long-range transmission. Now that solar PV has improved, people see the value of further supporting the technology itself, but also of developing solutions to the integration of PV with the wider economic system. Thus, modularity allows distributed decision-making, as well as distributed and gradual expansion of the set of actors investing in supporting systems. This is how the innovation chain model described earlier views these transitions more generally: The technology goes through a succession of phases in which integration with the broader system happens gradually and in later stages (Geels 2002; Grubb *et al*. 2021).

Hence, for solar PV, as may be the case for many technologies that have successfully entered and thrived in the broader economic system, the buffers in figure 1 were large: that is, the initial barriers to entry were low. However, to decarbonize, we must grow a large number of new technologies across a variety of sectors, and they may not all enjoy this propitious characteristic.

Case Study: Lightweight Electric Vehicles

The case of lightweight vehicles offers a contrasting story of low-carbon transition. Over time, policymakers and industrialists have focused on two technologies: fuel-cell electric vehicles (FCEVs) and battery electric vehicles (BEVs). As with solar PV, governments had been making public R&D investments in both fuel cells and batteries since the mid-1990s[6] and deployed a number of market-expanding policies. Yet, it was not until 2010 that BEVs or FCEVs started being produced for commercialization. This stands in contrast to solar PV, where public R&D and market support policies translated into deployment, refinement, and further R&D, in a cycle of positive feedbacks in which the technology improved and the market expanded (Bettencourt, Trancik, and Kaur 2013). An additional oddity of the car transition story is that the BEV eventually broke through, even though carmakers had largely been focusing on FCEVs (Melton, Axsen, and Sperling 2016; Dugoua and Dumas 2024).

Eugenie Dugoua and Marion Dumas (2024) propose that the dynamics of the EV transition have to be interpreted in

---

[6]These investments were on a similar scale to those for solar PV. For example, in the United States, both were on the order of $100 million per year (Gallagher and Anadon 2021).

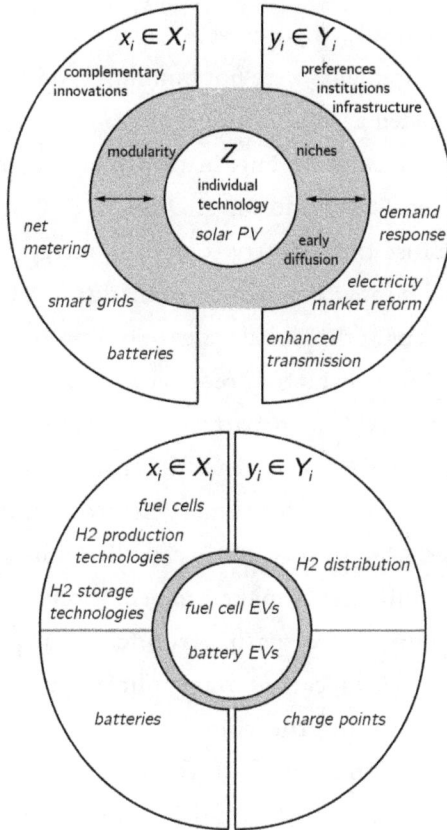

Figure 1. Schematic representation of the context in which nascent technologies develop. The figure contrasts the case of solar PV, with a large initial buffer between the individual technology and broader system components, and the bottom depicts the case of electric vehicles (EVs), where broader system components were critical in the initial stages, leaving little buffer zone for the individual technologies to develop without those complements in place.

light of the interdependencies shown in figure 1: Without their respective complementary innovations and infrastructure, either car technology is useless even in the initial stages (illustrated by the very thin buffer between the technology and complementary elements). As a result, there were no major niche applications where these requirements were not binding: Production of these technologies needed a simultaneous growth in the availability of the relevant complements. This in turn required that a choice be made between FCEVs and BEVs. Dugoua and Dumas (2024) argue that, because the industry is globally integrated—in both its markets and supply chains—coordination on technological choices must occur at the global scale to spur production.

A combination of factors reduced the initial barriers for BEVs but not for FCEVs. In particular, a wave of innovation in lithium-ion batteries in the electronics sector, driven by the need to power consumer electronics, created the know-how and the supply chain for lithium-ion batteries needed in cars, shifting carmakers expectations' regarding the most likely technological path. Around 2010, policymakers in all major markets carved out policies supporting BEVs (including support for the complementary infrastructure), and commercial production of these vehicles was able to start, setting off the learning and innovation dynamics that would bring the cost down and performance up. In the case of the transition to EVs, we thus see another type of tipping point playing a role: the point at which the expectations of major players, both on the policy and the industry sides, align on a common technological trajectory, which allows them to coordinate investments in z as well as the comple-ments (x_i, y_i).

According to this analysis of the dynamics, FCEV is an example of a technology that would have required a much more coordinated form of innovation policy to have a chance to succeed than that proposed in the "innovation chain model." Innovation policy would have had to carve out niche markets that address not just fuel cells but also hydrogen production and distribution at the right scale to allow initial deployment, and across enough markets to align expectations on a FCEV trajectory. Unlike solar PV, this technology could not advance through local niche expansion and fragmented national innovation policies. Other needed low-carbon technologies such as net-zero shipping or aviation may have the same characteristics.

INTERDEPENDENCIES AND DISRUPTION

Systemwide interdependencies can thus block the baby steps of a nascent technology and skew the search for clean technologies toward more system-compatible ones. On the other hand, they can also open the door for destabilizing factors to come into play and accelerate change. These destabilizing factors could be knowledge spillovers, as in the case of the growth of the consumer electronics industry bringing down the cost and up the performance of lithium-ion batteries, or the destabilizing role of artificial intelligence (AI; see Andres, Dugoua, and Dumas 2022). Analyses of the patent citation network have shown that the growth rate in patenting of downstream technologies is largely predictable by the growth rate in patenting of upstream technologies, which underscores the very key role of knowledge spillovers in technological dynamics far beyond the targeted technology (Pichler, Lafond, and Farmer 2020). Another type of destabilizing factor especially relevant when the interdependencies are global is the arrival on the innovation scene of emerging economies. With fewer legacy systems to worry about, they may invest heavily in a new clean technology and its complements, thus accelerating its evolution. In the case of EVs, China's choice of the BEV technology and targeted support to all critical parts of the supply chain may have helped tip the global industry.

THE ART OF CRAFTING TECHNOLOGY POLICIES FOR DECARBONIZATION

The basic innovation chain model described earlier says that to develop a technology that can eventually vie with well-established systems, technology policies need to provide *targeted* R&D support and *targeted* support for market expansion. This simple recipe is an excellent building block, which should be enriched after considering a broader set of dynamics.

First, one needs to be aware of the set of interdependencies and their scale that affect the next stage of progress of the technology. Policy needs to encourage innovating on all the binding parts of the system (Geels 2002). Innovation policy may be seen as niche construction or finding very unique niches that relax these constraints.

A striking example is that of Norway. Because of its numerous fjords, regional airports are very close to each other, making Norway's airport network a unique niche to test new low-carbon fuels and engines (Kallbekken and Victor 2022).

One can push the logic of niche construction further and thereby expand the toolbox of innovation policy. For example, some innovations require a simultaneous change in consumer habits (e.g., meat alternatives): Consumers should perhaps then become part of the innovation process (Baldwin and von Hippel 2011). When local infrastructure matters early on, cities can be used as laboratories, as China has done to develop BEVs.

Second, since interdependent actors need to coordinate, expectations matter. In the case of strong interdependencies, innovation policymakers may wish to focus on creating common expectations for the direction of change, possibly beyond the national scale (Sharpe 2023).

Third, innovation tends to skew toward more system-compatible innovations. Some complex-systems scholars have studied the properties of innovation search strategies in different fields, generally finding that they tend to be too local, exploiting known solutions rather than exploring more radical options (Rzhetsky *et al.* 2015; Foster, Rzhetsky, and Evans 2015). It would be fruitful to apply these approaches to the problem of decarbonization and to study how innovation policy (and its governance) can shape the boldness of search strategies. Finally, innovation policy can ride the waves of external disruptors, and in particular collaborate with emerging markets where the new is easier to create and grow.

Phasing Out the Old

We now turn from the development of cleaner technologies to the other aspect of the transition: phasing out fossil fuel–based systems. Understanding this process and its impacts requires models which can account for heterogeneity, interdependencies, and system dynamics.

ADDITIVE OR SUBSTITUTIVE?

Several low-carbon energy technologies are starting to diffuse rapidly. Does this imply that an energy transition away from fossil fuels is under way? Not necessarily. Historically, technologies allowing us to harness new energy sources have, in aggregate, all been additive rather than substitutive (York and Bell 2019): Although energy sources have, in waves, come to replace each other as the dominant source in the energy mix, all sources (whether biomass, coal, oil, etc.) have grown overall, pushed by a great expansion of overall energy consumption (Fouquet 2016). So far, the same pattern can be observed in the low-carbon energy "transition," with fossil-fuel use continuing to rise even as the share of renewables in the global energy mix has tripled over the past fifty years (Ritchie and Rosado 2020). Why is it rare to see a net withdrawal of an old energy technology? Should we, based on this history, expect that new clean technologies that succeed in becoming competitive will grow alongside continued growth of fossil fuel–based technologies? This question is particularly relevant as some countries have focused exclusively on policies that "grow the new," implicitly leaving us to hope that this is enough to displace the old.

Roger Fouquet (2016) reminds us that the aggregate evolution of a primary energy source is the result of many underlying technology transitions: in each energy service (light, heat, power), in each sector (residential, industrial, transport), and in each country, a new energy source can replace an old one only if adequate complementary technologies and institutions are developed. Each location may be held back by different missing elements in figure 1, causing lags or tilting choices toward the legacy system, thereby increasing the stock of dirty assets. For example, although solar PV electricity is now very cheap, there may still be too many local barriers for a steel company to prefer building a solar-powered steel plant over a conventional one. Several low-income Asian countries saw a period of fast growth over 2010–2020, when and where coal was still cheaper than solar, which has led to an extraordinary renaissance of coal (Steckel, Edenhofer, and Jakob 2015). It is thus key to model these transitions in a very granular way, with fine-grained data that can help identify the levers that lift local constraints to make low-carbon technologies the most attractive option.

Besides this heterogeneity in local context affecting the diffusion rate, we must also take into account dynamic feedbacks working through prices and demand. An expansion in energy production from the use of a new source of energy should at some point translate into lower energy prices. Especially at lower levels of economic development, we can expect this to increase overall energy demand through both income effects and price effects.[7] This would contribute to the new energy source being additive rather than substitutive.

~199~

There are also feedbacks on the supply side. First, as clean technologies are scaled up, the prices of key inputs such as critical minerals could increase, at least in the medium-term, as capacity expansion takes time (Moerenhout, Lee, and Glynn 2023; Nijsse *et al.* 2023) and will face higher environmental and labor standards. Supply chains for critical minerals could become key bottlenecks if demand is increased too rapidly for supply to keep up; and are also subject to other vulnerabilities such as local and geopolitical conflict (Lee *et al.* 2020).[8] Second, owners of fossil resources could strategically increase their extraction and lower the price of fossil fuels in response to increased expectations of a transition—the green paradox (Sinn 2012; Jensen *et al.* 2015). In theory, stronger expectations of a transition could form because of an expected increase in competition from renewables or an expected tightening of phase-out policies (carbon prices, bans, etc.). Few tests exist of this very worrisome negative feedback on the transition to

---

[7] In developed economies, energy consumption is relatively inelastic (Fouquet 2016), and we therefore expect a weaker feedback on overall consumption.
[8] There is, of course, a role for technological change to reduce reliance on such inputs; this, however, also takes time.

low-carbon systems. Maya Norman and Wolfram Schlenker (2024) do find evidence that the anticipation of a US carbon-pricing policy[9] depressed oil prices. The result of this policy anticipation was a net increase in current oil consumption. Suggestively, they also find that increases in the media salience of renewable-energy policy do not reduce oil prices, implying that oil producers have not to date seen the expansion of renewables as a real threat to the future profitability of oil reserves.

Skepticism that merely pushing the supply of low-carbon technologies is enough to bring about a transition should be particularly high given that 760 million people globally still lack access to electricity, 80% of whom live in Sub-Saharan Africa, where improvements in access have thus far been outstripped by population growth (IEA 2023). In this context of expanding demand, if price declines in renewables slow down at a certain scale (or cannot be achieved to the same degree in some subsectors because the required complementary investments are not made or face insurmountable challenges) and prices from low-cost suppliers fall sufficiently for fossil fuels to remain competitive in those subsectors, then the system could settle on a new equilibrium in which the transition is more or less additive, absent strong phase-out policies.

On the other hand, it is important to remember how asymmetric the competition between the new and the old is: Renewable-energy technologies (as well as other net-zero technologies such as batteries and electrolyzers) are following qualitatively different technological learning rates (Way *et*

---

[9] The Waxman-Markey Bill, eventually defeated.

al. 2022).[10] Their costs are falling dramatically, whilst those of fossil fuel–based incumbent technologies remain stable. Moreover, they are fueled by resources which are—as the name suggests—renewable: unlike coal, oil, or gas, solar irradiation does not become increasingly scarce and difficult to harness, the more we use it. Renewables are thus poised to become universally cheaper (Way *et al.* 2022), leading to net savings in a transition scenario (see also Heal 2022).

The small amount of knowledge we have about some key feedbacks on the transition path means that there is still a lot of uncertainty about the fundamental dynamics of the transition away from fossil fuel–based systems, both with and without various phase-out policies. Many of the feedbacks described above are not well captured in integrated assessment models, nor are the positive feedbacks that have been endogenously driving down prices and increasing the rate of diffusion (Grubb, Wieners, and Yang 2021). The nonequilibrium integrated assessment model E3ME-FTT-Genie is one of the few models that brings some of these different dynamic processes together (Mercure *et al.* 2018a).[11] Simulations based on recent data suggest that solar PV is now cheap enough to lead to a displacement of coal and natural gas in the power sector globally, even without new policies (Mercure *et al.* 2021). Other sectors require additional policies to see a displacement of fossil fuel–based systems by low-carbon ones. Under a

---

[10]Lafond (2026, ch. 26 in this volume) offers a detailed account of different approaches to technological forecasting.

[11]It captures the endogenous dynamics of technology diffusion using a Lotka–Volterra competition equation: Diffusion is influenced by its own history and gains substantial momentum as it grows. This is counterbalanced by limits to the number of sites for renewable generation and endogenous power system integration constraints. The model also includes endogenous fossil fuel extraction and production decisions by producers with geographically resolved marginal costs of production.

net-zero scenario, the model shows that OPEC countries may capture most future oil and gas demand, by increasing their production and decreasing their prices, leading to fossil-fuel asset stranding in all other producing regions. This in turn leads to a fundamental restructuring of the incentives of different countries to decarbonize, with all current energy importers now being net winners of a transition irrespective of the damages of climate change. Moving forward, model plurality and comparison across modeling traditions will be key to understanding the transition that is unfolding.

The high level of uncertainty in the dynamics of the transition means that there is a high potential for divergent expectations about it, especially among investors and lenders. These heterogeneous expectations may feed back into the dynamics in nontrivial ways via the financial system. Indeed, financial actors' perception of the relative risk of investing in high-carbon versus low-carbon firms affects the flow of investments in these alternative asset classes. If they expect the transition to be gradual, they may not see high-carbon firms to be very risky and therefore not reallocate capital to low-carbon firms, impeding the transition (Battiston *et al.* 2021). If they see the transition as disorderly with potential abrupt changes, they may on the contrary reallocate capital away from high-carbon firms seen as increasingly risky. Incorporating financial actors in modeling of the transition is therefore a high priority (for current efforts, see Battiston *et al.* 2021; Dunz, Naqvi, and Monasterolo 2021). Heterogeneous expectations also add to the current indeterminacy of the transition, as the climate policy cycle influences these expectations, which in turn influence the political feasibility of climate policy, leading to multiple equilibria.

What policies then can ensure that clean technologies lead to a net move away from fossil fuels? Answering this question cognizant of nonlinear transition dynamics, Simon Sharpe (2023) proposed a rethinking of the role of carbon prices. This alternative view is not yet well explored by researchers. Recall that the standard (Pigouvian) view is that the most efficient policy is a universal carbon price across all sectors and countries to find the lowest cost abatement opportunities. However, Sharpe (2023) makes the point that the same carbon price may be sufficient in one sector and one economy to make a given fossil technology unprofitable and tip the system to favor a clean substitute, but be grossly insufficient in another sector to fundamentally drive technology choices. He cites the example of the carbon levy in the UK power sector, which was just sufficient to make coal-fired power plants unprofitable and drive them out of the energy system. A possible approach, then, is to start by supporting clean substitutes, and once they become more competitive, use a carbon price *targeted at that sector* to "tip it away" from a dirty incumbent (see also Burke, Byrnes, and Fankhauser 2019). This strategy takes a targeted and differentiated approach to carbon pricing, recognizing the different stages of technological transition in different sectors and countries (see also Hallegatte, Meunier, and Vogt-Schilb 2012). This echoes a recent contribution by Geoffrey Heal (2022), who points out that the carbon price needed to move away from oil is many times higher than that needed to move away from coal. The latter is in a range that seems politically acceptable, but not the former. Whether such a piecemeal and differentiated approach to carbon pricing is compatible with creating a stable policy framework that encourages smooth asset-value adjustments in the financial sector is unknown. Here too, a greater plurality of models is needed to break the dominance of the Pigouvian framework.

THE RISKS OF A FAST TRANSITION

If the transition is successful (i.e., substitutive), incumbent fossil-fuel-based sectors will decline and disappear. As a result, capital and other assets related to those sectors are likely to see downward revisions in their profitability, economic lifetime and capacity utilization, leading to write-offs of economic value—commonly referred to as stranding (van der Ploeg and Rezai 2020).

The displacement of an incumbent technology with a new, superior one and the subsequent stranding of assets associated with the declining sector is not new (Zenghelis, Fouquet, and Hippe 2018)—in fact, it is a central feature of capitalism's creative destruction. However, the speed, scale, and pervasiveness at which this must happen in order to mitigate climate change may well be unprecedented. Louison Cahen-Fourot *et al.* (2021) show that activities which depend on integrated networks—such as energy or transport—are particularly vulnerable to large-scale asset stranding when a new technology displaces the old, a key concern in the transition to a low-carbon economy. Thus, the very features which create the path dependencies hampering the development and diffusion of a new technology also increase the level of disruption we must expect if a new technology does succeed. Moreover, shortsighted efforts to protect incumbent industries can cement the inevitability of their demise, by preventing effective and timely adaptation to the new system. Dimitri Zenghelis, Roger Fouquet, and Ralph Hippe (2018) give the example of Britain's canals, which failed to be integrated into railway systems arriving in the nineteenth century due to policy designed to shield these waterways from new railway companies. In the current low-carbon energy transition, we can point—for example—to the failure of German car manufacturers to shift to electric vehicles early on, while relying on government to delay stringent climate policy in the name of protecting jobs.

Assets and capabilities that are at risk of stranding include fossil fuel reserves themselves, financial investments therein, and physical capital built for the purpose of extracting, refining, or burning fossil fuels. Other productive capabilities affected— which can be thought of as a kind of intangible asset— are the skills and knowhow developed by workers in fossil fuel industries, as well as, at a larger scale, broader regional capabilities related to those same industries. They vary along multiple dimensions: first, the ease and speed with which they can be repurposed (if at all); second, where they are located geographically; and third, the systemwide implications of failing to repurpose them in a timely manner.

Predicting and managing the disruption from the transition requires methodological approaches which can incorporate both geographical and sectoral heterogeneity and dynamics, and account for the non-homogeneous nature of capital. One of the key insights that economic complexity methods highlight is that factors of production are imperfectly mobile across sectors and activities (Hidalgo 2023; Balland *et al.* 2022). In the context of the low-carbon transition this raises the question: Which factors can be repurposed, and at what rate? Which factors cannot be repurposed adequately, and how much stranding at any given time and in any given place can be mitigated by developing new capabilities and assets? Are there skills, knowledge, and tasks required in declining sectors which are so specialized as to become completely redundant in the new economic order—such as the skills of lamplighters following the advent of electric street lighting (Frey 2019)—or can the capital assets and know-how underlying fossil fuel–related activities be recombined and put to other uses?

Current fossil fuel reserves and the current value of fossil fuel assets are not in line with climate goals: Either they will be stranded, or climate goals will be missed by a large margin. An estimate by Christophe McGlade and Paul Ekins (2015) suggests that reaching the Paris Agreement's 2°C target requires 80% of global coal reserves, 50% of gas reserves, and 33% of oil reserves to remain unused. Frederick van der Ploeg and Armon Rezai (2020) argue that up to 80% of declared reserves owned by largest fossil fuel companies and sovereign states could become stranded. Gregor Semieniuk *et al.* (2022) estimate that under plausible changes in expectations about climate policy, the present value of future lost profits in the upstream oil and gas sectors could be in excess of $1 trillion, with market risk falling primarily on private investors in OECD countries. While some financial capital currently invested in fossil fuels could potentially be shifted to other assets, the financial loss must be borne by whoever is eventually left holding these assets.

Physical capital devoted to the extraction, processing, and usage of fossil fuels may, in some cases, be transferable to other uses (such as carbon capture and storage). However, most estimates suggest that a transition consistent with global climate goals requires premature retiring and decommissioning of fossil-based assets (Mercure *et al.* 2021; Trout *et al.* 2022), even after considering retrofitting and end-of-pipe abatement technologies (Lu *et al.* 2022). More broadly, fossil fuels form part of highly interdependent and integrated production systems. In the absence of adaptive changes and complementary investments throughout the supply chain, a much broader set of capital goods could be at risk of stranding (Cahen-

Fourot *et al.* 2021). Fossil fuel–related assets also constitute a central component of a highly integrated financial system. Negative shocks to fossil-fuel activities and their financial valuations could therefore have significant impacts on the broader financial system (Semieniuk *et al.* 2021; Campiglio *et al.* 2018; Campiglio and van der Ploeg 2022; van der Ploeg and Rezai 2020) and through it, the broader macroeconomy (Semieniuk *et al.* 2021; Mercure *et al.* 2018b; Campiglio and van der Ploeg 2022).

Besides physical assets, the skills of workers in affected sectors may be more or less specialized and more or less transferable. While the transition to a low-carbon economy will not only destroy jobs in declining sectors, but also create employment in emerging ones—in fact, most studies suggest that, in aggregate, the latter outweighs the former (Bücker *et al.* 2025)—new jobs tend to be created in different locations (Lim, Aklin, and Frank 2023) and require a different set of skills and qualifications (Saussay *et al.* 2022) than those lost. Mark Curtis, Layla O'Kane, and R. Jisung Park (2024) show that, although transitions from dirty to green jobs are increasing in the US, less than 1% of workers in carbon-intensive jobs transition to green ones. Starting from the empirical observation that workers (much like geographical regions) more easily transition between occupations which use similar skills, Joris Bücker *et al.* (2025) analyze the employment dynamics of decarbonizing the US power sector by 2035. Their results suggest that in the absence of appropriate policy to smooth the transition—such as careful planning and retraining programs in anticipation of changes in skills demand—considerable labor-market frictions are likely to arise in relation to the energy transition. These include both labor shortages in some sectors and displaced labor in others—even

~207~

when geographical mismatches are not taken into account. However, they argue that job losses combined with a lack of suitable new vacancies are more prevalent in the later "scale-down" phase of the transition (following an initial "scale-up" phase involving a significant investment push in low-carbon infrastructure). Further research on the distance workers can travel within the skills space and the time required to do so would be useful in informing policy to ease these frictions. R. Maria del Rio-Chanona *et al.* (2026, ch. 24 in this volume) propose a complexity approach to model labor markets' resilience in the face of structural change.

At a larger scale, entire regions and nation-states have built their livelihoods on fossil fuels. Like workers having an easier time transitioning into positions which require similar skills, countries and regions are more likely to develop new comparative advantages in economic activities which are similar to those they already specialize in. Koen Frenken and Frank Neffke (2026, ch. 29 in this volume) offer a rich discussion of local economic capabilities and the path dependence of regional development. Pia Andres *et al.* (2023) develop measures of transition risk based on what can be inferred about countries' productive capabilities from trade data, and find that nations heavily dependent on fossil fuel exports for a large share of export volume are likely to find it difficult to diversify into climate-compatible sectors. Countries such as the United States or Canada, while exposed to financial losses if priced out of the global market for oil and gas (Mercure *et al.* 2021), have fairly diverse, complex economic structures. Many of the high-emitting activities they specialize in—such as manufacturing conventional vehicles, or carbon-intensive industrial processes—are located in dense areas of the product space and therefore likely to require capabilities which can be recombined and devoted to low-emitting activities with relative ease. Meanwhile, many OPEC members depend on fossil fuels for an extremely high share of their export volume (more than 90%, in some cases), and have few nearby diversification opportunities within the product space network. These countries could find it difficult to adapt to a global low-carbon economy (Andres *et al.* 2023).

What do we know about the possibilities and the time scales of economic diversification? While the "principle of relatedness"—the observation that regions diversify into related activities with much higher probability than into unrelated ones—is very well documented (Hidalgo 2021; Balland *et al.* 2022), path-defying diversification is much more poorly understood, despite its potentially key role in solving the problem that the principle of relatedness diagnoses for countries stuck in low-complexity development pathways. Flávio Pinheiro *et al.* (2022) tackle a key aspect of this by studying the timing and implications of so-called unrelated diversification. They argue that unrelated diversification, while more likely at higher levels of economic complexity,[12] is key to allowing countries to escape the middle income trap. At lower levels of development, countries tend to diversify into more related activities—however, those which have been successful in industrial upscaling seem to do so in a more strategic way which allows them to move into more complex activities later on. Countries such as South Korea and China have managed to increase their Economic Complexity Index (ECI) by about one standard deviation from the mean over a period of only two decades, with South Korea moving from ECI -0.6 in 1985 to 0.4 in 2005, and China moving from an ECI of -0.8 in 1995 to about 0.2 in 2015 (Pinheiro *et al.* 2022).

---

[12] This insight is somewhat built into the "relative relatedness" measures used, as the same "relative relatedness" will correspond to a much higher absolute relatedness in a high-complexity country than a low-complexity one.

Nevertheless, major fossil fuel exporters tend to exhibit income levels which are much higher than the usual relationship between economic complexity and income predicts. Sufficient foresight to anticipate the demise of the fossil fuel industry and a well-executed multidecade diversification strategy may be necessary to prevent a sudden and rapid deterioration in living standards as fossil fuel assets suddenly lose their value in international trade. Research on effective industrial policy is urgently needed—luckily, academic interest in the topic seems to be experiencing a renaissance (e.g. Aiginger and Rodrik 2020; Juhász *et al.* 2022; Juhász, Lane, and Rodrik 2023; Evenett *et al.* 2024; Goldberg *et al.* 2024).

Conclusion

Mitigating climate change requires a rapid transition from high- to low-emitting energy sources and production methods within a highly inert technological system. Economic complexity approaches allow us to model the economy in a granular and dynamic way—accounting for geographical and sectoral heterogeneity and systemic interdependencies. This is crucial for understanding the barriers to innovation in and diffusion of new technologies, as well as the disruption that could follow the decline of the displaced incumbents.

Nevertheless, a technological transformation at the scale and speed required could push the boundaries of established methods and knowledge even within the paradigm of economic complexity, which accounts for existing relationships between sectors and makes predictions about factors such as future cost declines or changes in regional comparative advantages using historical data. However, sudden, multisectoral technological change could fundamentally reshape some of these relationships in ways that are currently hard to predict. For example, the relationships between different economic activities in the product, technology or skills space networks could shift (and do so faster than usual), potentially compromising predictive approaches incorporating what is known about these networks. The transition therefore calls for novel research drawing on complex systems in these areas. ✐

Acknowledgments

We gratefully acknowledge the following funding sources: the London School of Economics Grantham Research Institute on Climate Change and the Environment, and the ESRC Programme on Productive and Inclusive Net Zero (PRINZ, reference ES/W010356/1).

REFERENCES

Acemoglu, D., P. Aghion, L. Bursztyn, and D. Hémous. 2012. "The Environment and Directed Technical Change." *American Economic Review* 102 (1): 131–66. https://doi.org/10.1257/aer.102.1.131.

Aghion, P., A. Dechezleprêtre, D. Hémous, R. Martin, and J. Van Reenen. 2016. "Carbon Taxes, Path Dependency, and Directed Technical Change: Evidence from the Auto Industry." *Journal of Political Economy* 124 (1): 1–51. https://doi.org/10.1086/684581.

Aiginger, K., and D. Rodrik. 2020. "Rebirth of Industrial Policy and an Agenda for the Twenty-First Century." *Journal of Industry, Competition and Trade* 20:189–207. https://doi.org/10.1007/s10842-019-00322-3.

Andres, P., E. Dugoua, and M. Dumas. 2022. *Directed Technological Change and General Purpose Technologies: Can AI Accelerate Clean Energy Innovation?* Centre for Climate Change Economics and Policy Working Paper No. 403 and Grantham Research Institute on Climate Change and the Environment Working Paper No. 378.

Andres, P., P. Mealy, N. Handler, and S. Fankhauser. 2023. "Stranded Nations? Transition Risks and Opportunities Towards a Clean Economy." *Environmental Research Letters* 18 (4): 045004. https://doi.org/10.1088/1748-9326/acc347.

Arthur, W. B. 2010. *The Nature of Technology: What It Is and How It Evolves.* London, UK: Penguin UK.

Baldwin, C., and E. von Hippel. 2011. "Modeling a Paradigm Shift: From Producer Innovation to User and Open Collaborative Innovation." *Organization Science,* https://doi.org/10.1287/orsc.1100.0618.

Baldwin, C. Y., and K. B. Clark. 2000. *Design Rules: The Power of Modularity.* Vol. 1. Cambridge, MA: MIT Press.

Balland, P.-A., T. Broekel, D. Diodato, E. Giuliani, R. Hausmann, N. O'Clery, and D. Rigby. 2022. "The New Paradigm of Economic Complexity." *Research Policy* 51 (3): 104450. https://doi.org/10.1016/j.respol.2021.104450.

Battiston, S., I. Monasterolo, K. Riahi, and B. J. van Ruijven. 2021. "Accounting for Finance is Key for Climate Mitigation Pathways." *Science* 372 (6545): 918–920. https://doi.org/10.1126/science.abf3877.

Beinhocker, E. D. 2017. *The Tipping Point: How America Can Lead the Transition to a Prosperous Clean Energy Economy.* Prepared for the Aspen Institute Congressional Program, Energy for America: Challenges, Opportunities and Solutions, Oslo, Norway, 9–15 August, 2017. INET Oxford Working Papers 2017-11.

Bettencourt, L. M. A., J. E. Trancik, and J. Kaur. 2013. "Determinants of the Pace of Global Innovation in Energy Technologies." *PloS One* 8 (10): e67864. https://doi.org/10.1371/journal.pone.0067864.

Bücker, J., R. M. del Rio-Chanona, A. Pichler, M. C. Ives, and J. D. Farmer. 2025. "Employment Dynamics in a Rapid Decarbonization of the Power Sector." *Joule* 9 (2): 101803. https://doi.org/10.1016/j.joule.2024.12.004.

Burke, J., R. Byrnes, and S. Fankhauser. 2019. *How to Price Carbon to Reach Net-Zero Emissions in the UK.* Technical report. London, UK: Grantham Research Institute on Climate Change and the Environment.

Cahen-Fourot, L., E. Campiglio, A. Godin, E. Kemp-Benedict, and S. Trsek. 2021. "Capital Stranding Cascades: The Impact of Decarbonisation on Productive Asset Utilisation." *Energy Economics* 103:105581. https://doi.org/10.1016/j.eneco.2021.105581.

Campiglio, E., Y. Dafermos, P. Monnin, J. Ryan-Collins, G. Schotten, and M. Tanaka. 2018. "Climate Change Challenges for Central Banks and Financial Regulators." *Nature Climate Change* 8 (6): 462–468. https://doi.org/10. 1038/s41558-018-0175-0.

Campiglio, E., and F. van der Ploeg. 2022. "Macrofinancial Risks of the Transition to a Low-Carbon Economy." *Review of Environmental Economics and Policy* 16 (2): 173–195. https://doi.org/10.1086/721016.

Cowan, R., and P. Gunby. 1996. "Sprayed to Death: Path Dependence, Lock-in and Pest Control Strategies." *The Economic Journal* 106 (436): 521–542. https:// doi.org/10.2307/2235561.

Curtis, E. M., L. O'Kane, and R. J. Park. 2024. "Workers and the Green-Energy Transition: Evidence from 300 Million Job Transitions." *Environmental and Energy Policy and the Economy* 5 (1): 127–161. https://doi.org/10.3386/ w31539.

del Rio-Chanona, R. M., M. R. Frank, P. Mealy, E. Moro, and L. Nedelkoska. 2026. "Beyond Efficiency: Labor-Market Resilience in an Age of AI and Net Zero." In *The Economy as an Evolving Complex System IV,* edited by R. M. del Rio-Chanona, M. Pangallo, J. Bednar, E. D. Beinhocker, J. Kaszowska-Mojsa, F. Lafond, P. Mealy, A. Pichler, and J. D. Farmer. Santa Fe, NM: SFI Press.

Dugoua, E., and M. Dumas. 2024. "Coordination Dynamics Between Fuel Cell and Battery Technologies in the Transition to Clean Cars." *Proceedings of the National Academy of Sciences* 121 (27). https://doi.org/10.1073/pnas. 2318605121.

Dunz, N., A. Naqvi, and I. Monasterolo. 2021. "Climate Sentiments, Transition Risk, and Financial Stability in a Stock-Flow Consistent Model." *Journal of Financial Stability* 54:100872. https://doi.org/10.1016/j.jfs.2021.100872.

Evenett, S., A. Jakubik, F. Martín, and M. Ruta. 2024. "The Return of Industrial Policy in Data." *The World Economy* 47 (7): 2762–2788. https://doi.org/10. 1111/twec.13608.

Fink, T. M. A., and M. Reeves. 2019. "How Much Can We Influence the Rate of Innovation?" *Science Advances* 5 (1). https://doi.org/10.1126/sciadv.aat6107.

Foster, J. G., A. Rzhetsky, and J. A. Evans. 2015. "Tradition and Innovation in Scientists' Research Strategies." *American Sociological Review* 80 (5): 875–908. https://doi.org/10.1177/0003122415601618.

Fouquet, R. 2010. "The Slow Search for Solutions: Lessons from Historical Energy Transitions by Sector and Service." *Energy Policy* 38 (11): 6586–6596. https://doi.org/10.1016/j.enpol.2010.06.029.

———. 2016. "Historical Energy Transitions: Speed, Prices and System Transformation." *Energy Research & Social Science* 22:7–12. https://doi.org/10.1016/j.erss.2016.08.014.

Frenken, K., and F. Neffke. 2026. "Economic Geography and Complexity Theory." In *The Economy as an Evolving Complex System IV,* edited by R. M. del Rio-Chanona, M. Pangallo, J. Bednar, E. D. Beinhocker, J. Kaszowska-Mojsa, F. Lafond, P. Mealy, A. Pichler, and J. D. Farmer. Santa Fe, NM: SFI Press.

Frey, C. B. 2019. "The Technology Trap: Capital, Labor, and Power in the Age of Automation." In *The Technology Trap.* Princeton, NJ: Princeton University Press.

Gallagher, K. S., and L. D. Anadon. 2021. *DOE Budget Authority for Energy Research, Development, and Demonstration Database.* https://www.belfercenter.org/publication/database-us-department-energy-doe-budgets-energy-research-development-demonstration-1.

Geels, F. W. 2002. "Technological Transitions as Evolutionary Reconfiguration Processes: A Multi-Level Perspective and a Case-Study." *Research Policy* 31 (8-9): 1257–1274. https://doi.org/10.1016/S0048-7333(02)00062-8.

———. 2014. "Regime Resistance Against Low-Carbon Transitions: Introducing Politics and Power into the Multi-Level Perspective." *Theory, Culture & Society* 31 (5): 21–40. https://doi.org/10.1177/0263276414531627.

Gerarden, T. D. 2023. "Demanding Innovation: The Impact of Consumer Subsidies on Solar Panel Production Costs." *Management Science* 69 (12). https://doi.org/10.1287/mnsc.2022.4662.

Goldberg, P. K., R. Juhász, N. J. Lane, G. L. Forte, and J. Thurk. 2024. "Industrial Policy in the Global Semiconductor Sector." *NBER Working Paper 32651,* https://doi.org/10.3386/w32651.

Grubb, M., P. Drummond, A. Poncia, W. McDowall, D. Popp, S. Samadi, C. Penasco, *et al.* 2021. "Induced Innovation in Energy Technologies and Systems: A Review of Evidence and Potential Implications for CO2 Mitigation." *Environmental Research Letters* 16 (4): 043007. https://doi.org/10.1088/1748-9326/abde07.

Grubb, M., W. McDowall, and P. Drummond. 2017. "On Order and Complexity in Innovations Systems: Conceptual Frameworks for Policy Mixes in Sustainability Transitions." *Energy Research & Social Science* 33:21–34. https://doi.org/10.1016/j.erss.2017.09.016.

Grubb, M., C. Wieners, and P. Yang. 2021. "Modeling Myths: On DICE and Dynamic Realism in Integrated Assessment Models of Climate Change Mitigation." *WIREs Climate Change* 12 (3): e698. https://doi.org/10.1002/wcc.698.

Grübler, A., N. Nakićenović, and D. G. Victor. 1999. "Dynamics of Energy Technologies and Global Change." *Energy Policy* 27 (5): 247–280. https://doi.org/10.1016/S0301-4215(98)00067-6.

Grübler, F., A. Aguayo, K. Gallagher, M. Hekkert, K. Jiang, L. Mytelka, L. Neij, G. Nemet, *et al.* 2012. "Chapter 24: Policies for the Energy Technology Innovation System (ETIS)." (Cambridge, UK), 1665–1744. https://doi.org/10.1017/CBO9780511793677.030.

Hallegatte, S., G. Meunier, and A. C. Vogt-Schilb. 2012. *How Inertia and Limited Potentials Affect the Timing of Sectoral Abatements in Optimal Climate Policy.* Policy Research Working Paper 6154. Washington, DC: World Bank. http://documents.worldbank.org/curated/en/730421468330048560.

Heal, G. 2022. "Economic Aspects of the Energy Transition." *Environmental & Resource Economics* 83 (1): 5–21. https://doi.org/10.1007/s10640-022-00647-4.

Hidalgo, C. A. 2021. "Economic Complexity Theory and Applications." *Nature Reviews Physics* 3 (2): 92–113. https://doi.org/10.1038/s42254-020-00275-1.

———. 2023. "The Policy Implications of Economic Complexity." *Research Policy* 52 (9): 104863. https://doi.org/10.1016/j.respol.2023.104863.

IEA. 2023. "World Energy Outlook 2023." *International Energy Organization,* https://www.iea.org/reports/world-energy-outlook-2023.

Jaffe, A. B., R. G. Newell, and R. N. Stavins. 2005. "A Tale of Two Market Failures: Technology and Environmental Policy." *Ecological Economics* 54 (2–3): 164–174. https://doi.org/10.1016/j.ecolecon.2004.12.027.

Jensen, S., K. Mohlin, K. Pittel, and T. Sterner. 2015. "An Introduction to the Green Paradox: The Unintended Consequences of Climate Policies." *Review of Environmental Economics and Policy* 9 (2): 246–265. https://doi.org/10.1093/reep/rev010.

Juhász, R., N. Lane, E. Oehlsen, and V. C. Pérez. 2022. "The Who, What, When, and How of Industrial Policy: A Text-Based Approach." *What, When, and How of Industrial Policy: A Text-Based Approach (August 15, 2022)*, https://doi.org/10.2139/ssrn.4198209.

Juhász, R., N. Lane, and D. Rodrik. 2023. "The New Economics of Industrial Policy." *Annual Review of Economics* 16. https://doi.org/10.1146/annurev-economics-081023-024638.

Kallbekken, S., and D. G. Victor. 2022. "A Cleaner Future for Flight—Aviation Needs a Radical Redesign." *Nature*, 673–675. https://doi.org/10.1038/d41586-022-02963-7.

Kavlak, G., J. McNerney, and J. E. Trancik. 2018. "Evaluating the Causes of Cost Reduction in Photovoltaic Modules." *Energy Policy* 123:700–710. https://doi.org/10.1016/j.enpol.2018.08.015.

Lafond, F. 2026. "Forecasting Technological Progress." In *The Economy as an Evolving Complex System IV*, edited by R. M. del Rio-Chanona, M. Pangallo, J. Bednar, E. D. Beinhocker, J. Kaszowska-Mojsa, F. Lafond, P. Mealy, A. Pichler, and J. D. Farmer. Santa Fe, NM: SFI Press.

Lafond, F., D. Greenwald, and J. D. Farmer. 2022. "Can Stimulating Demand Drive Costs Down? World War II as a Natural Experiment." *The Journal of Economic History* 82 (3): 727–764. https://doi.org/10.1017/S0022050722000249.

Lamperti, F., G. Dosi, and A. Roventini. 2026. "A Complex System Perspective on the Economics of Climate Change, Boundless Risk, and Rapid Decarbonization." In *The Economy as an Evolving Complex System IV*, edited by R. M. del Rio-Chanona, M. Pangallo, J. Bednar, E. D. Beinhocker, J. Kaszowska-Mojsa, F. Lafond, P. Mealy, A. Pichler, and J. D. Farmer. Santa Fe, NM: SFI Press.

Lee, J., M. Bazilian, B. Sovacool, K. Hund, S. M. Jowitt, T. P. Nguyen, A. Månberger, et al. 2020. "Reviewing the Material and Metal Security of Low-Carbon Energy Transitions." *Renewable and Sustainable Energy Reviews* 124 (C). https://ideas.repec.org/a/eee/rensus/v124y2020ics136403212030085x.html.

Lilliestam, J., A. Patt, and G. Bersalli. 2022. "On the Quality of Emission Reductions: Observed Effects of Carbon Pricing on Investments, Innovation, and Operational Shifts. A Response to van den Bergh and Savin (2021)." *Environmental & Resource Economics* 83 (3): 733–758. https://doi.org/10.1007/s10640-022-00708-8.

Lim, J., M. Aklin, and M. R. Frank. 2023. "Location is a Major Barrier for Transferring US Fossil Fuel Employment to Green Jobs." *Nature Communications* 14 (1): 5711. https://doi.org/10.1038/s41467-023-41133-9.

Lu, Y., F. Cohen, S. M. Smith, and A. Pfeiffer. 2022. "Plant Conversions and Abatement Technologies Cannot Prevent Stranding of Power Plant Assets in 2°C Scenarios." *Nature Communications* 13 (1): 806. https://doi.org/10.1038/s41467-022-28458-7.

Malhotra, A., and T. S. Schmidt. 2020. "Accelerating Low-Carbon Innovation." *Joule* 4 (11): 2259–2267. https://doi.org/10.1016/j.joule.2020.09.004.

McGlade, C., and P. Ekins. 2015. "The Geographical Distribution of Fossil Fuels Unused When Limiting Global Warming to 2°C." *Nature* 517 (7533): 187–190. https://doi.org/10.1038/nature14016.

McNerney, J., J. D. Farmer, S. Redner, and J. E. Trancik. 2011. "Role of Design Complexity in Technology Improvement." *Proceedings of the National Academy of Sciences* 108 (22): 9008–9013. https://doi.org/10.1073/pnas.1017298108.

Meckling, J., T. Sterner, and G. Wagner. 2017. "Policy Sequencing Toward Decarbonization." *Nature Energy* 2 (12): 918–922. https://doi.org/10.1038/s41560-017-0025-8.

Melton, N., J. Axsen, and D. Sperling. 2016. "Moving Beyond Alternative Fuel Hype to Decarbonize Transportation." *Nature Energy* 1 (3): 1–10. https://doi.org/10.1038/nenergy.2016.13.

Mercure, J.-F., H. Pollitt, N. R. Edwards, P. B. Holden, U. Chewpreecha, P. Salas, A. Lam, F. Knobloch, and J. E. Vinuales. 2018a. "Environmental Impact Assessment for Climate Change Policy with the Simulation-Based Integrated Assessment Model E3ME-FTT-GENIE." *Energy Strategy Reviews* 20:195–208. https://doi.org/10.1016/j.esr.2018.03.003.

Mercure, J.-F., H. Pollitt, J. E. Viñuales, N. R. Edwards, P. B. Holden, U. Chewpreecha, P. Salas, I. Sognnaes, A. Lam, and F. Knobloch. 2018b. "Macroeconomic Impact of Stranded Fossil Fuel Assets." *Nature Climate Change* 8 (7): 588–593. https://doi.org/10.1038/s41558-018-0182-1.

Mercure, J.-F., P. Salas, P. Vercoulen, G. Semieniuk, A. Lam, H. Pollitt, P. B. Holden, *et al.* 2021. "Reframing Incentives for Climate Policy Action." *Nature Energy* 6 (12): 1133–1143. https://doi.org/10.1038/s41560-021-00934-2.

Moerenhout, T., L. Y. Lee, and J. Glynn. 2023. *Critical Mineral Supply Constraints and Their Impact on Energy System Models.* Center on Global Energy Policy at Columbia University SIPA: New York, NY, USA.

Murmann, J. P., and K. Frenken. 2006. "Toward a Systematic Framework for Research on Dominant Designs, Technological Innovations, and Industrial Change." *Research Policy* 35 (7): 925–952. https://doi.org/10.1016/j.respol.2006.04.011.

Nemet, G. F. 2019. *How Solar Energy Became Cheap: A Model for Low-Carbon Innovation.* New York, NY: Routledge.

Nijsse, F. J. M. M., J.-F. Mercure, N. Ameli, F. Larosa, S. Kothari, J. Rickman, P. Vercoulen, and H. Pollitt. 2023. "The Momentum of the Solar Energy Transition." *Nature Communications* 14 (1): 6542. https://doi.org/10.1038/s41467-023-41971-7.

Norman, M. A., and W. Schlenker. 2024. *Empirical Tests of the Green Paradox for Climate Legislation.* Technical report, Working Paper Series 32405. National Bureau of Economic Research. https://doi.org/10.3386/w32405.

Page, S. E. 2006. "Path Dependence." *Quarterly Journal of Political Science* 1 (1): 87–115. https://doi.org/10.1561/100.00000006.

Pichler, A., F. Lafond, and J. D. Farmer. 2020. *Technological Interdependencies Predict Innovation Dynamics.* arXiv preprint:2003.00580. https://doi.org/10.48550/arXiv.2003.00580.

Pinheiro, F. L., D. Hartmann, R. Boschma, and C. A. Hidalgo. 2022. "The Time and Frequency of Unrelated Diversification." *Research Policy* 51 (8): 104323. https://doi.org/10.1016/j.respol.2021.104323.

Pless, J., and S. Srivastav. 2025. "Unintended Consequences of Tech-Neutrality: Evidence from Environmental and Innovation Policy Interactions." http://jacquelynpless . com / wp - content / uploads / 2025 / 01 / PlessSrivastav_PolIntInnov_Jan2025.pdf.

Ritchie, H., and P. Rosado. 2020. "Energy Mix." *Our World in Data,* https://ourworldindata.org/energy-mix.

Rzhetsky, A., J. G. Foster, I. T. Foster, and J. A. Evans. 2015. "Choosing Experiments to Accelerate Collective Discovery." *Proceedings of the National Academy of Sciences* 112 (47): 14569–14574. https://doi.org/10.1073/pnas.1509757112.

Saussay, A., M. Sato, F. Vona, and L. O'Kane. 2022. *Who's Fit for the Low-Carbon Transition? Emerging Skills and Wage Gaps in Job and Data.* https://doi.org/10.2139/ssrn.4260227.

Semieniuk, G., E. Campiglio, J.-F. Mercure, U. Volz, and N. R. Edwards. 2021. "Low-Carbon Transition Risks for Finance." *WIREs Climate Change* 12 (1): e678. https://doi.org/10.1002/wcc.678.

Semieniuk, G., P. B. Holden, J.-F. Mercure, P. Salas, H. Pollitt, K. Jobson, P. Vercoulen, U. Chewpreecha, N. R. Edwards, and J. E. Viñuales. 2022. "Stranded Fossil-Fuel Assets Translate to Major Losses for Investors in Advanced Economies." *Nature Climate Change* 12 (6): 532–538. https://doi.org/10.1038/s41558-022-01356-y.

Seto, K. C., S. J. Davis, R. B. Mitchell, E. C. Stokes, G. Unruh, and D. Ürge-Vorsatz. 2016. "Carbon Lock-In: Types, Causes, and Policy Implications." *Annual Review of Environment and Resources* 41 (October): 425–452. https://doi.org/10.1146/annurev-environ-110615-085934.

Sharpe, S. 2023. *Five Times Faster.* Cambridge, UK: Cambridge University Press.

Sharpe, S., and T. M. Lenton. 2021. "Upward-Scaling Tipping Cascades to Meet Climate Goals: Plausible Grounds for Hope." *Climate Policy* 21 (4): 421–433. https://doi.org/10.1080/14693062.2020.1870097.

Sinn, H.-W. 2012. *The Green Paradox: A Supply-Side Approach to Global Warming.* Cambridge, MA: MIT Press.

Steckel, J. C., O. Edenhofer, and M. Jakob. 2015. "Drivers for the Renaissance of Coal." *Proceedings of the National Academy of Sciences* 112 (29): E3775–81. https://doi.org/10.1073/pnas.1422722112.

Trout, K., G. Muttitt, D. Lafleur, T. Van de Graaf, R. Mendelevitch, L. Mei, and M. Meinshausen. 2022. "Existing Fossil Fuel Extraction Would Warm the World Beyond 1.5°C." *Environmental Research Letters* 17 (6): 064010. https://doi.org/10.1088/1748-9326/ac6228.

van der Ploeg, F., and A. Rezai. 2020. "Stranded Assets in the Transition to a Carbon-Free Economy." *Annual Review of Resource Economics* 12:281–298. https://doi.org/10.1146/annurev-resource-110519-040938.

Way, R., M. C. Ives, P. Mealy, and J. D. Farmer. 2022. "Empirically Grounded Technology Forecasts and the Energy Transition." *Joule* 6 (9): 2057–2082. https://doi.org/10.1016/j.joule.2022.08.009.

Wilson, C., A. Grübler, N. Bento, S. Healey, S. De Stercke, and C. Zimm. 2020. "Granular Technologies to Accelerate Decarbonization." *Science* 368 (6486): 36–39. https://doi.org/10.1126/science.aaz8060.

Winkelmann, R., J. F. Donges, E. K. Smith, M. Milkoreit, C. Eder, J. Heitzig, A. Katsanidou, M. Wiedermann, N. Wunderling, and T. M. Lenton. 2022. "Social Tipping Processes Towards Climate Action: A Conceptual Framework." *Ecological Economics: The Journal of the International Society for Ecological Economics* 192:107242. https://doi.org/10.1016/j.ecolecon.2021. 107242.

York, R., and S. E. Bell. 2019. "Energy Transitions or Additions?: Why a Transition from Fossil Fuels Requires More than the Growth of Renewable Energy." *Energy Research & Social Science* 51:40–43. https://doi.org/10.1016/j. erss.2019.01.008.

Zenghelis, D., R. Fouquet, and R. Hippe. 2018. "Stranded Assets: Then and Now." In *Stranded Assets and the Environment*, 23–54. New York, NY: Routledge.

COMPLEXITY ECONOMICS' VIEW ON PHYSICAL CLIMATE-CHANGE RISKS AND ADAPTATION

Tatiana Filatova, Faculty of Technology, Policy, and Management, Delft University of Technology; and Joos Akkerman, Faculty of Technology, Policy, and Management, Delft University of Technology

Abstract

Climate change increases physical risks—damages from floods, storms, wildfires, droughts, heatwaves, and sea level rise. These globally accelerating risks pose a fundamental threat to economies and societies. Conventional economic analysis of climate change focuses on damages and costs/benefits of climate actions (mitigation and adaptation), relying on models that assume perfect rationality, homogeneity, and unique equilibrium. Yet, this approach falls short of capturing the complexity of physical climate risks, their inherent uncertainty, feedbacks, and adaptation responses by boundedly rational actors. Complexity economics recognizes the economy as a dynamic, adaptive system in which aggregate dynamics emerge from interactions of many boundedly rational agents who learn and update their expectations about climate and economic consequences of their actions. This chapter discusses why embracing complexity matters for the assessment of physical climate risks and climate change adaptation strategies. Using illustrative examples from agent-based computational economics, we show how relaxing traditional economic assumptions enables us to study distributional impacts and the emergence of structural shifts in markets as agents learn and interact. We highlight the importance of tracing out-of-equilibrium dynamics triggered by climate

*damages and adaptation responses, focusing on potential
nonlinearities, including socioeconomic tipping points and
potential systemic risks posed by the changing climate.*

Introduction

Globally, climate change already manifests via *physical risks*—
damages arising from hazards like floods, storms, wildfires,
heatwaves, droughts, and sea level rise. The new climate, unlike
any seen for millennia (Calvin *et al.* 2023), poses a fundamental
threat to global socioeconomic development. Yet, over the past
decades, economic choices have led to increased clustering of
people and assets in areas prone to climate-induced hazards
(IPCC 2022), further escalating physical risks. Despite growing
recognition that these physical risks will have more severe
impacts than the risks associated with transitions toward a
decarbonized economy (Bank of England 2021), progress in
economic assessments of physical risks and climate change
adaptation lags behind the analysis of transition risks and
climate change mitigation policies. To adequately prepare
for the inevitable climate changes resulting from past and
present carbon-dioxide emissions, we must study the impacts
of physical risks on the economy in more detail.

Most physical climate risk assessments focus on quantifying
direct impacts of climate-induced shocks, relying on the solid
literature in environmental sciences, engineering, and economics
that studies how various environmental hazards cause damages.
However, the primary gap lies in estimating *complex* physical
climate risks, where compounding or cascading risks generate
indirect or *higher-order* effects of shocks (Simpson *et al.* 2021),
which cannot simply be inferred from first-order impacts. Such
shocks can propagate from directly affected households and firms
toward others through market interactions, supply relations,
opinion dynamics, migration, banking networks, and even social

unrest and political turmoil. Moreover, when experiencing increasing hazards, economic actors respond by adapting their behavior and the environment. This can reduce both direct and indirect exposure and vulnerability, as well as hazard probabilities, but can also lead to unforeseen path-dependent consequences, maladaptation, or inequitable outcomes (Chambwera *et al.* 2014). Since economies are complex adaptive systems, we should ideally account for interactions, feedbacks, adaptive expectations, and adaptive behavior beyond relying on past trends alone. Furthermore, with climate justice and equity being jeopardized (Berrang-Ford *et al.* 2021; IPCC 2022), it is imperative to quantify the distributional impacts of physical risks across and within groups of economic agents.

This chapter discusses how complexity economics can support physical climate risk assessments, with a focus on computational agent-based economic modeling (ABM). The next section provides a basic overview of how physical risks are defined and modeled. We then briefly describe how these physical risks have been traditionally incorporated in economic models, and the strengths and pitfalls of this conventional approach. Using several ABM examples, we then illustrate how complexity models can be employed to study physical climate risks. Lastly, we conclude with a discussion and possible directions for future research.

Direct and Indirect Damages from Climate-Induced Hazards

Conventionally, physical climate risks are differentiated into *direct* and *indirect* impacts. *Direct* impacts are the immediate tangible damages incurred from a hazard shock, such as injuries or fatalities; loss of ecosystems, crops, or livestock; and the destruction of assets like buildings and infrastructure. Various climate-induced hazards impact the economy via different channels. For example, heat waves typically reduce labor productivity, while storms destroy capital and inventories. Incurred damages depend on exposure, that is, land use[1] and asset location and elevation, which are contingent on the assumed socioeconomic development pathway (shared socioeconomic pathways, or SSP).[2] The share of capital and labor affected depends on vulnerability, often operationalized in the form of a damage curve that could vary across economic sectors and geographical regions (Huizinga, de Moel, and Szewczyk 2016; Wing *et al.* 2020). Furthermore, hazard probability and severity vary greatly across climate scenarios (IPCC 2022), demanding physical climate risk assessments for various Representative Concentration Pathways (RCP).[3] Given the depth and diversity of interdisciplinary expertise required to assemble these data across climate-induced hazards, most physical climate risk assessments stop at quantifying only direct damages as a product of exposure, hazard, and vulnerability. Luckily, open-access datasets providing direct physical climate risks assessments have increasingly become available.[4] Sometimes, fine-resolution physical climate risk assessments require complementary datasets on the exact location of economic assets, which are increasingly within reach (Cortés Arbués *et al.* 2024).

~224~

---

[1]Various land use datasets have become available globally, including open-access land use data projected under various Shared Socioeconomic Pathways and Representative Concentration Pathways climate scenarios (Chen *et al.* 2020).

[2]SSP scenarios dataset: https://iiasa.ac.at/models-tools-data/ssp, https://ourworldindata.org/explorers/ipcc-scenarios.

[3]RCP scenarios dataset: https://iiasa.ac.at/models-tools-data/rcp, leading to datasets on geographic patterns under various climates (e.g., Gao, Sokolov, and Schlosser 2023).

[4]For example, via CLIMADA globally: https://wcr.ethz.ch/research/climada.html, or via COACCH for Europe: https://www.scenarioxplorer.coacch.eu/.

The *indirect* impacts are secondary and higher-order effects that ripple through the economy, beyond the directly affected economic actors, sectors, and regions. Typical indirect damages include (i) business interruption leading to income and productivity drop and cascading supply chain disruptions; (ii) distortions in markets for goods, services, assets, or labor, triggering price adjustments; (iii) loss of jobs due to business bankruptcies or long-term loss of livelihood options causing migration; (iv) adverse effects on long-term economic growth, debt-to-GDP ratio, collateral fiscal damages, and changes in credit ranking; and (v) shocks to the financial system, including decreasing investments in affected areas, readjustments of the insurance system, increased risk to financial portfolios, and the emergence of stranded assets or even systemic risk to the financial system. Such indirect damages can substantially amplify the total physical climate risks beyond the initial direct damages (Hallegatte, Hourcade, and Dumas 2007). The assessment of indirect damages from climate-induced hazards relies on sophisticated economic models.

Mainstream Economic Models for Physical Climate Risk Assessment

A wide range of economic models have been developed to capture how economic systems react to climate-induced hazards. Most of these models developed in environmental economics have inherited the traditional economic assumptions: rational homogeneous agents with perfect foresight and markets reaching a unique equilibrium in the absence of externalities or information asymmetries, or focused on finding an optimal solution. Notably, these assumptions are constantly challenged, particularly in post-disaster situations (Safarzyńska, Brouwer, and Hofkes 2013) and in climate economics in general (Farmer *et al.* 2015; Pindyck 2013; Stern, Stiglitz, and Taylor 2022).

Integrated assessment models (IAMs) are the key family of climate-economy policy models, initially developed to identify optimal climate mitigation policies. Despite a variety of types (see them reviewed by Fisher-Vanden and Weyant 2020), IAMs typically combine economic and climate modules and explicitly model feedbacks between them. Climate conditions are mapped to economic losses through a damage function that has to capture both direct and indirect impacts, and all costs and benefits of adaptation that occur in equilibrium (Auffhammer 2018). This damage function is usually a stylized estimation of economic climate-induced damages at global or supranational scales as a GDP loss contingent on a certain global mean temperature under various RCP–SSP scenarios. A marginal change in such crudely estimated physical risks is also known as the social costs of carbon. Both the functional relationship between GDP losses and temperature, as well as the empirical basis, are highly debated (Diaz and Moore 2017; Ortiz and Markandya 2010; van der Wijst *et al.* 2023), making the IAM damage function one of the key sources of uncertainty and one of the main among many critiques of IAMs (Stern 2013; Weitzman 2009). Some IAMs anchor climate-induced damages to empirical, typically econometrically estimated losses, resulting in physical risks in orders of magnitude higher, for example, up to 23% (Burke, Hsiang, and Miguel 2015) compared to conservative 1–3% GDP loss (Kahn *et al.* 2021).

While IAMs collapse direct and indirect damages into one function, indirect climate damages can be explicitly modeled using *input–output* (IO) or *computable general equilibrium* (CGE) *models*. IO models link various economic sectors, and often many regions/countries, connected by trade relations and grounded in econometrically estimated relationships. The input–output table that describes the extent of these connections is traditionally static. This means that prices, quantities, and trade relations do not adapt to shocks. Furthermore, production does not allow for the substitution of inputs (i.e., Leontief production), and technology is typically stable. This means IO models are most suitable for capturing dynamics in the very short term when agents cannot adjust to new conditions. CGE models are similarly detailed at the sectoral and often regional level but also add a microeconomic behavioral component based on the general equilibrium theory. Consequently, prices, supply, demand, and trade relations adjust optimally in response to shocks to facilitate Walrasian market clearing in an economy with a representative firm and a representative household. Due to their structure, both models uniquely capture the indirect propagation of shocks to other sectors and regions/countries explicitly, typically quantifying type (i), (ii), and (iv) indirect effects described above. However, the static nature of IO models means they likely overestimate indirect effects, because adaptive behaviors are omitted (Hallegatte 2008). Conversely, in CGE models rational representative agents adapt guided optimally to a new equilibrium, which means they likely underestimate indirect effects (Farmer *et al.* 2015).

IO and CGE models, due to their explicit representation of economic linkages, have a long history of being employed to analyze detailed direct and indirect physical risks from various climate-induced hazards, which the aggregated nature of the IAM damage functions does not allow for. IO and CGE models have also been employed to analyze climate change adaptation options to attenuate these risks (Bosello, Roson, and Tol 2007; Kondrup *et al.* 2022; Parrado *et al.* 2020), often relying on conventional cost-benefit analysis of public adaptation strategies. However, so far little attention has been paid to the economic analysis of autonomous adaptation of businesses and households, to uneven impacts of physical climate risks across sectors or actors, to distributional impacts of climate change adaptation, or to the role of risk (mis)perception potentially leading to stranded assets or even systemic risks in the economy. Systemic physical climate risks are increasingly discussed in finance (for insurance, managing bank portfolios, and risk transmission in bank networks; e.g., Lamperti *et al.* 2019) as well as in resilience engineering with respect to critical infrastructure (Koks *et al.* 2019; Verschuur, Koks, and Hall 2023). However, potential adverse cascading damages to economic actors—diverse households, businesses, and governments—remain understudied.

The Complexity Perspective on Physical Climate Risks

The latest Intergovernmental Panel on Climate Change (IPCC) cycle (Calvin *et al.* 2023) highlights the urgency of accounting for *complexity* in physical climate risk assessments (Simpson *et al.* 2021). This complexity perspective recognizes that physical climate risks are shaped by:

- An interplay among the direct risk components—hazard, exposure, vulnerability—highlighting the importance of explicitly modeling economic drivers of changing exposure (e.g., via investment choices), vulnerability (e.g., via private adaptation, changing economic well-being), and hazard (e.g., via public adaptation).

- Feedbacks triggered by actors' socioeconomic responses to direct damages, including market adjustments (e.g., prices, wages, reorganization of trade networks), changes to financial rules (e.g., for insurance, mortgages or credit), economic restructuring (e.g., change in sectoral compositions of economies in climate-sensitive areas), and investments (e.g., in climate adaptation or mitigation).

- Interactions among actors and across sectors, regions, and countries that over time give rise to compounding/cascading risks or to path-dependence potentially leading to stranded assets. Cumulatively, such processes could over-strain economic capacities—uneven among households, businesses, and governments—to recover from or adapt to physical climate risks.

These recognized complexity aspects highlight the importance of systems thinking and of tracing processes instead of only optimal equilibrium endpoints. Moreover, they demand explicit modeling of responses of various interconnected actors, acknowledging the existence of temporal lags, subjective risk perceptions, and iteratively revised expectations about future physical risks and/or the state of the economy.

Computational agent-based economics (Arthur 2021, Tesfatsion and Judd 2006) sets the stage by considering economies as evolving complex systems consisting of heterogeneous boundedly rational agents who learn and adapt over time, giving rise to emergent macrophenomena through interactions with each other and their environments (physical, social, economic, and other institutional). Designed to trace out-of-equilibrium dynamics, complexity economics models can relax many of the assumptions required to keep equilibrium-based models tractable. This creates flexibility that, on the agent level, allows for heterogeneity, bounded rationality, imperfect information, learning, and different types of (cross-scale) interactions. In turn, this allows for out-of-equilibrium dynamics, emergence, self-organization, and nonlinearities on the system level. As a rule, ABMs applied to study physical climate risks would start with linking to direct damages or climate hazard maps (bottom layer, fig. 1, typically under specific RCP–SSP scenarios). Consequently, they introduce agent-level boundedly rational behavior (including risk perceptions, per-

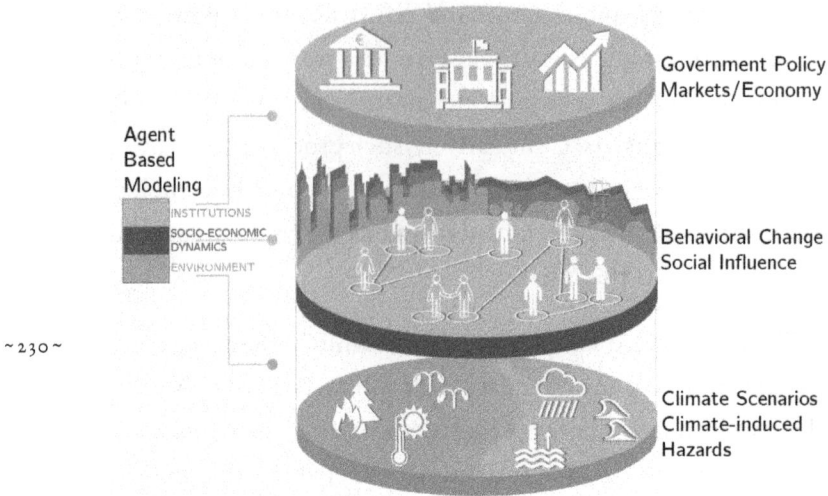

Government Policy
Markets/Economy

Agent
Based
Modeling

INSTITUTIONS
SOCIO-ECONOMIC
DYNAMICS
ENVIRONMENT

Behavioral Change
Social Influence

Climate Scenarios
Climate-induced
Hazards

Figure 1. Schematic overview of the components in a typical ABM applied to studying physical climate risks, combining the physical, microbehavioral, and institutional layers that shape aggregate outcomes.

ceived efficacy of coping actions, past hazard experience affecting choices) and social networks (middle layer, fig. 1), increasingly relying on microlevel data from surveys and other behavioral data. Last, contemporary ABMs for physical climate risk assessments accommodate institutions, with much attention paid to integrating interconnected markets into complex risk assessments (top layer, fig. 1), tapping into macro trade data. Using a range of examples, we illustrate how ABMs enabled the integration of various complexity aspects relevant to physical climate risk assessments.

Bounded Rationality and Adaptive Economic Expectations

By design, ABMs allow economic agents to accommodate *bounded rationality* (Simon 1990)—an alternative to perfect rationality, which denotes rational optimization behavior with complete information about all possible outcomes in the future. In the context of physical climate risks, bounded rationality typically comes in the form of myopia, satisficing, or behavioral biases. First, decisions about possible future outcomes are often *myopic*, which means an agent's perception of the world may not incorporate all relevant information. For example, agents may underestimate perceived probabilities of damages in the new climate if they rely on past hazard experiences. In ABMs, agents may have a memory of the performance of their strategies in the past, for example, under scenarios of drought occurrence and adaptation behavior (van Duinen *et al.* 2016), to model myopic behavior. Second, ABMs applied to physical climate risks often model *satisficing behavior*, when in the absence of complete information economic agents do not aim for the global maximum for their goal functions (utility/profit). Instead, they settle with an option that satisfies a threshold (usually agent-specific) or search for a local optimum in a limited choice set. Last, economic choices are affected by *social norms* (e.g., in private climate adaptation behavior; Wilson *et al.* 2020) and *behavioral biases*, like subjective risk perception, framing of decisions depending on a reference point, or information asymmetry among agents (De Koning, Filatova, and Bin 2017; Haer, Botzen, and Aerts 2016). In the presence of bounded rationality, agents employ diverse models of expectation formation (Magliocca *et al.* 2011) about future prices, resources, strategies of others, or risks. Bounded rationality is prevalent in hazard-prone housing markets, where empirical evidence reveals that, for example, flood risk is not adequately capitalized in current property prices due to heterogeneity in climate beliefs, subjective risk perceptions, and fading memory (Beltrán, Maddison, and Elliott 2018; Bin and Landry 2013; Mutlu, Roy, and Filatova 2023). The RHEA ABM (Filatova 2015) models a decentralized housing market populated by households with heterogeneous preferences and behavioral biases, and by real-estate agents forming adaptive price expectations under changing climate risks. De Koning and Filatova (2020) use RHEA to show how empirically defined boundedly rational behavior of traders leads to housing price collapse in flood-prone areas and the emergence of stranded assets under repetitive floods. Amplified by path dependence and market sorting, this leads to climate gentrification, where well-off households move to safe areas and drive up property prices there. Low-income households are trapped in high-risk areas because their mortgage debt is higher than the collapsed housing price of flood-prone properties and because they are outpriced from safety.

As agents are boundedly rational, expectation formation and update play an important role. Early economic ABMs (Tesfatsion and Judd 2006) have already been testing the effects of alternative expectation models on economic outcomes. For example, Nicholas Magliocca *et al.* (2011) tested six price expectation models for future housing prices. In application to physical climate risks, in Filatova (2015) and Koen De Koning and Filatova (2020) we use the RHEA ABM with dynamic price expectations for flood-prone properties. Here, price expectations update with changing demand (i.e., driven by evolving risk perceptions of boundedly rational traders) and housing characteristics (tracked via hedonic analysis that accounts for hazard probabilities). Boundedly rational firms and households update their economic expectations about prices and wages driven by changing location preferences, unemployment, and market opportunities in an economy prone to coastal hazards in the CRAB ABM (Taberna *et al.* 2022).

Agents' Heterogeneity

Understanding distributional impacts is critical for climate damages and adaptation assessments. Virtually every ABM applied to study physical climate impacts embraces agents heterogeneous in economic *roles* (e.g., households, businesses, governments, insurers, banks; Taberna *et al.* 2020), in *attributes* (e.g., incomes, behavioral biases, social networks) or *strategies* (e.g., decision-making grounded in expected utility vs. prospect theory; see De Koning, Filatova, and Bin 2017; Magliocca and Walls 2018). Agents could also *alternate their behavioral strategies endogenously.* For example, farmers choose among four empirically grounded behavioral strategies as their performances update based on agents' past economic decisions, taken adaptation measures, and droughts affecting individual farmers in the ABM developed by Rianne van Duinen *et al.* (2016).

~233~

Another study explores the impact of heterogeneity in sociobehavioral adaptation constraints on the distribution of flood damages among households in the CRAB ABM by Alessandro Taberna *et al.* (2023a). Households heterogeneous in education/income are embedded in the macroeconomic ABM where they interact with heterogeneous firms via goods and labor markets, giving rise to endogenous agglomeration dynamics. Connecting the macroeconomy with the survey-grounded behavior of households allows us to trace emerging distributions of damages driven by indirect impacts, such as post-flood unemployment and income decrease of low-educated households, and by social norms that hinder middle-level households from investing in adaptation. Mass private adaptation diffusion strengthens long-run macroeconomic performance, reducing both direct and indirect damages (Taberna *et al.*, 2023b). Tailored interventions such as subsidies (Taberna *et al.*, 2023b) and informational policies (Taberna *et al.*, 2023a) could improve post-flood recovery time and long-run economic output.

Asjad Naqvi and Miriam Rehm (2014) use the SHELscape ABM to show the distributional effects of flood shocks. Their model represents a low-income economy, consisting of multiple cities and villages, where (agricultural) goods are produced and agents interact through trade and migration. They trace the propagation of a flood-induced supply shock, which sharply increases prices and decreases incomes, disproportionately affecting low-income workers. Both the SHELscape and CRAB ABMs show how floods affect prices and wages, triggering migration that affects wages and prices in other regions, further inducing migration and creating ripple effects through the wider economy.

Agents' Interaction and Learning

Interactions and learning leading to adaptive behavior are at the core of any ABM. Notably, besides conventional economic interactions via markets, and spatial interactions with the environment (e.g., via hazard maps) common for physical risk assessments, ABMs explicitly model social interactions and evolving social norms. These market, spatial, and social interactions and subsequent learning are especially important when agents make decisions under uncertain physical climate risks. Here, individual households and businesses, communities, and governments may need to discover new probabilities and severity of climate-induced hazards, and these probabilities need to be updated using past trends and new individual experiences (Haer, Botzen, and Aerts 2016; Taberna *et al.* 2020). However, these learning processes are imperfect, as shown by the growing evidence of markets incorrectly pricing physical climate risks (Beltrán, Maddison, and Elliott 2018; Bin and Landry 2013; Mutlu, Roy, and Filatova 2023), potentially leading to a "climate

Minsky moment" (Miller and Dikau 2022)—a market tipping and collapse due to a sudden materialization of unrecognized climate-related risks. Furthermore, individual changes in preferences and valuations of climate-induced hazards lead to behavioral changes, which, when taken by critical masses, lead to shifts in social norms (Taberna *et al.*, 2023a) or structural shifts in markets (De Koning and Filatova 2020).

Agents can learn by receiving information from their peers, or *social* learning. Here, social networks enable opinion dynamics on physical risks and on (effectiveness of) adaptation options, and as such have been incorporated in many climate economics ABMs. By employing different opinion dynamics models (Bayesian or non-Bayesian; Acemoglu and Ozdaglar 2011) and different social networks (Will *et al.* 2020), these ABMs can be used to study how information spreads, and when and how agents influence each other. In the domain of physical risks and climate adaptation, there is strong empirical evidence that social norms shape economic choices (van Valkengoed and Steg 2019), but nearly no data detailed enough to specify such social influences. Representation of social networks and opinion dynamics about climate risks/adaptations in ABMs often rely on parameterized stylized networks (Tierolf *et al.* 2023), sometimes testing the sensitivity of, say, private adaptation diffusion and regional damage reduction to social influence (Wagenblast *et al.* 2024). Emerging big social data enables progress in empirical social network and norms evolution analysis, with impacts for physical climate risks and adaptation tested in ABM (Bell *et al.* 2021).

Learning—individual and social—becomes particularly essential when the distribution of climate-induced hazards is nonstationary. While initial (subjective) climate risk perceptions may be incorrect, agents in ABMs routinely learn from hazard experiences and adjust their beliefs, affecting economically relevant outcomes like housing prices, production in a specific sector and location, GDP, or unemployment. ABMs often utilize rule-based learning, such as when farmer agents mimic past strategies of successful peers (Gotts and Polhill 2009; van Duinen *et al.* 2016). Bayesian learning about changing physical risks in economic ABMs already relies on survey data, integrating past hazard experiences of traders and their peers in flood-prone property markets (De Koning and Filatova 2020). These insights are crucial to understanding how novel climate information affects agents' behavior and how, in turn, society's exposure and vulnerability may develop.

Out-of-Equilibrium Dynamics and Self-Organization

Complexity-economics models are "agnostic" about equilibrium, which means they require less restrictive assumptions to be solvable (Arthur 2006). As such, ABMs can capture dynamics where a system is not in equilibrium but moving *back toward* or *in between* equilibria (or permanently *out-of-equilibrium*). This is instrumental when responses of various economic agents exhibit time lags, and the economic system is unable to recover in the (very) short term. Especially in the aftermath of (large) climate-induced shocks, such out-of-equilibrium periods may take a long time and be very costly, and agents' decisions could lead to path dependencies. Notably, ABMs are not necessarily in disequilibrium but can generate statistical equilibria under certain conditions (Gintis 2007), with equilibrium being a region of relative stability, a plateau in the temporal trend of an aggregated variable of interest, potentially with small noise occurring around the trend (Axtell, Guerrero, and López 2019). In fact, complex adaptive systems are often *self-organizing*, as agents perpetually adapt their behaviors and collectively reach a (new) equilibrium (Holland 1992). This means that in the presence of multiple equilibria, ABMs can be used to explore alternative pathways to either of those equilibria (Arthur 2006; Farmer *et al.* 2015). Naturally, ABMs can capture nonlinear shifts, such as endogenous transitions between equilibria or tipping in economic systems.

One example where climate-shocked economic systems can self-organize is in trade networks with different spatial exposure, as presented in the SHELscape ABM (Naqvi and Rehm 2014). Before disasters, endogenous spatial trade networks tend to highly localize due to uneven trade costs across locations triggering agglomeration processes. However, once floods create a negative supply shock or change wages/unemployment in an affected region, trade connections restructure between regional markets and unaffected locations farther away. Thus, as economic agents react to postshock economic signals, the overall trade network become less localized, reducing future direct/indirect damages.

Another case of self-organization to reduce disaster impacts was found in production networks. The Acclimate ABM by Christian Otto *et al.* (2017) combines global production network with adaptive agents representing economic sectors. When a climate shock pushes the economy out of equilibrium, the agents can adapt their behaviors to limit disaster damages. With the price mechanism as an organizing mechanism, agents shift demand within the trade network between producers or adjust the quantities they produce. As such, they decrease the extent of aggregate damages in the short run. This presents a more realistic estimate of how damages propagate than does a static IO outcome or the optimal CGE outcome. However, it also shows how self-organization is not absolute, with indirect damages being as high as direct damages and much more persistent. Another approach that studies climate shocks in production networks is presented by Sebastian Poledna *et al.* (2018). They use a large-scale macroeconomic ABM with millions of agents and sixty-four industries to model flood shock propagation. This setup allows them to showcase not only macroeconomic impacts on growth, employment, and fiscal deficits but also the distributional effects *between* sectors. Furthermore, they show how for large enough shocks, the economy loses its resilience, causing a drop in output that is no longer recovered. Both examples show how economies can autonomously recover from shocks, but that this ability to self-organize may break down under large enough shocks. Such a loss of self-organization is called a *corridor effect* (Leijonhufvud 1973), and understanding it is crucial to understanding how and if economic systems recover after a climate shock.

Agents adapting to changing risks can also lead to unforeseen consequences, eventually increasing physical climate risks. One vivid empirical example is the safe development paradox, which is caused by public protection reducing risk perceptions, and therefore attracting more people into exposed areas. Then, while there are fewer smaller events, a large event will affect more people than before the protection. A model that exhibits an endogenous safe development paradox is presented by Toon Haer *et al.* (2020), who use a large-scale socio-hydrological model at the European Union level, with adaptation actions taken by households and the government. In their model, regional population growth adjusts to the level of government protection, and households base private adaptation decisions on public protection levels. This recursive loop, where agents base their decisions on the decisions of other agents, leads to an endogenous increase of physical risk. It showcases how self-organization does not always lead to socially optimal outcomes, even if agents act in their own best interest.

Discussion and Future Research Agenda

The economic analysis of physical climate risks and climate change adaptation is still in its early stages relative to the analysis of climate change mitigation and transition risks (see Battiston and Monasterolo 2026, ch. 20 in this volume for a discussion of transition risks). Preliminary assessments indicate that physical risks are of a larger magnitude than transition risks (Bank of England 2021) and, hence, are critical for informing climate policy. Yet the analysis of physical climate risks from the systems perspective remains understudied (Simpson *et al.* 2021), and quantitative public and private adaptation goals, let alone monitoring progress toward them, are underdeveloped (Berrang-Ford *et al.* 2021). Furthermore, climate-change adaptation needs a more location-specific approach, which requires new data, particularly on exposed assets (Bank of England 2021) and on the effectiveness of adaptation measures (Berrang-Ford *et al.* 2021). Luckily, efforts to study how physical climate risks affect the economy and society are growing. This chapter has highlighted some aspects where complexity economics, and ABMs in particular, are providing valuable insights.

There are several further research directions where complexity economics can support quantitative analysis of physical climate risks. There is still a need for better insights into the higher-order impacts of physical shocks, in particular systemic risks. This calls for identifying channels through which risk is transmitted, with the inclusion of "constructed" risks due to private and public actions (economic choices, private/public climate adaptation). For instance, how are physical climate risks in the economy passed to the financial system? Do feedbacks between economic and financial systems amplify or attenuate physical climate risks? Could the cascading effects of stranded assets, like properties in climate-sensitive areas, potentially lead to wider systemic financial and economic risks? Which assets could suddenly lose much or all of their value due to changing climate or due to evolving expectations? Think of houses or firms in climate-sensitive locations and cannot be protected. These stranded assets are projected to have a significant impact on financial and economic stability (Bank of England 2021; Battiston, Dafermos, and Monasterolo 2021). Notably, such assets cannot exist in a world with rational expectations and perfect information, but a complexity approach helps to identify them and to explore risk attenuation strategies. Furthermore, ABMs started to explore economic tipping mainly outside climate applications (Gualdi *et al.* 2015), with simple models of physical risk (van Ginkel, Haasnoot, and Botzen 2022). Yet, much work remains to be done on specifying solid theoretical and empirical microfoundations for tipping processes as well as on their statistical identification in multidimensional model outputs. Last, while contemporary ABMs focused on physical risks have strong empirical foundations for both hazard quantification and agents' behavior, collecting data on expectations about new climate—with no precedent in the past—remains a fundamental challenge not just for ABMs but for climate change economics and climate adaptation in general.

Agent-based modeling is a powerful method to complement traditional economic methods of analysis, especially for studies of socioenvironmental systems. However, ABMs are not a silver bullet to solve all the challenges of physical climate risks and climate change adaptation assessments. Therefore, we argue for a more pluralistic approach that integrates the strengths of and insights from conventional economic models and complexity models. Here, the flexibility of ABMs can be used to test behavioral assumptions, evolving expectations, bounded rationality, and heterogeneity, enabling targeted policy interventions and novel mixes of policy interventions (e.g., market and information policies jointly). First examples of combining ABMs with IAM and CGE models for physical climate risks are being developed (Filatova *et al.* 2025). These integrated models offer possibilities for tracing out-of-equilibrium dynamics under adaptive expectations, shaped by behavioral biases and social influences, while leveraging the cross-sectoral and cross-regional interconnectedness offered by conventional models. Combining the insights from equilibrium and complexity approaches will give a more complete picture of the issues at hand, enabling complex risk assessments with various direct and indirect damages quantified at both agent and system levels, offering novel information for future policy design. ✦

~241~

Acknowledgments

This work was supported by the NWO VIDI (grant number 191015) and the European Research Council (ERC) under the European Union's Horizon 2020 Research and Innovation Program (grant numbers 758014 and 101171568). The authors are thankful to Susanna Boietti for her help with the illustration.

REFERENCES

Acemoglu, D., and A. Ozdaglar. 2011. "Opinion Dynamics and Learning in Social Networks." *Dynamic Games and Applications* 1 (1): 3–49. https://doi.org/10.1007/s13235-010-0004-1.

Arthur, W. B. 2006. "Out-of-Equilibrium Economics and Agent-Based Modeling." In *Handbook of Computational Economics,* edited by L. Tesfatsion and K. L. Judd, 2:1551–1564. Elsevier. https://doi.org/10.1016/S1574-0021(05)02032-0.

Arthur, W. B. 2021. "Foundations of Complexity Economics." *Nature Reviews Physics* 3 (2): 136–145. https://doi.org/10.1038/s42254-020-00273-3.

Auffhammer, M. 2018. "Quantifying Economic Damages from Climate Change." *Journal of Economic Perspectives* 32 (4): 33–52. https://doi.org/10.1257/jep. 32.4.33.

Axtell, R. L., O. A. Guerrero, and E. López. 2019. "Frictional Unemployment on Labor Flow Networks." *Journal of Economic Behavior & Organization* 160:184–201. https://doi.org/10.1016/j.jebo.2019.02.028.

Bank of England. 2021. *Key Elements of the 2021 Biennial Exploratory Scenario: Financial Risks from Climate Change.* Retrieved August 30, 2024. https:// www.bankofengland.co.uk/stress-testing/2021/key-elements-2021biennial-exploratory-scenario-financial-risks-climate-change.

Battiston, S., Y. Dafermos, and I. Monasterolo. 2021. "Climate Risks and Financial Stability." *Journal of Financial Stability* 54:100867. https://doi.org/10.1016/ j.jfs.2021.100867.

Battiston, S., and I. Monasterolo. 2026. "Climate Risk through the Lens of Complexity Economics and Finance." In *The Economy as an Evolving Complex System IV,* edited by R. M. del Rio-Chanona, M. Pangallo, J. Bednar, E. D. Beinhocker, J. Kaszowska-Mojsa, F. Lafond, P. Mealy, A. Pichler, and J. D. Farmer. Santa Fe, NM: SFI Press.

Bell, A. R., D. J. Wrathall, V. Mueller, J. Chen, M. Oppenheimer, M. Hauer, H. Adams, *et al.* 2021. "Migration Towards Bangladesh Coastlines Projected to Increase with Sea-Level Rise Through 2100." *Environmental Research Letters* 16 (2): 024045. https://doi.org/10.1088/1748-9326/abdc5b.

Beltrán, A., D. Maddison, and R. J. R. Elliott. 2018. "Is Flood Risk Capitalised Into Property Values?" *Ecological Economics* 146:668–685. https://doi.org/10. 1016/j.ecolecon.2017.12.015.

Berrang-Ford, L., A. R. Siders, A. Lesnikowski, A. P. Fischer, M. W. Callaghan, N. R. Haddaway, K. J. Mach, *et al.* 2021. "A Systematic Global Stocktake of Evidence on Human Adaptation to Climate Change." *Nature Climate Change* 11 (11): 989–1000. https://doi.org/10.1038/s41558-021-01170-y.

Bin, O., and C. E. Landry. 2013. "Changes in Implicit Flood Risk Premiums: Empirical Evidence from the Housing Market." *Journal of Environmental Economics and Management* 65 (3): 361–376. https://doi.org/10.1016/j. jeem.2012.12.002.

Bosello, F., R. Roson, and R. S. J. Tol. 2007. "Economy-Wide Estimates of the Implications of Climate Change: Sea Level Rise." *Environ Resource Econ* 37:549–571. https://doi.org/10.1007/s10640-006-9048-5.

Burke, M., S. M. Hsiang, and E. Miguel. 2015. "Global Non-Linear Effect of Temperature on Economic Production." *Nature* 527 (7577): 235–239. https://doi.org/10.1038/nature15725.

Calvin, K., D. Dasgupta, G. Krinner, A. Mukherji, P. W. Thorne, C. Trisos, J. Romero, et al. 2023. *Climate Change 2023: Synthesis Report. Contribution of Working Groups I, II and III to the Sixth Assessment Report of the Intergovernmental Panel on Climate Change.* Geneva, Switzerland: Intergovernmental Panel on Climate Change (IPCC). https://doi.org/10.59327/IPCC/AR6-9789291691647.

Chambwera, M., G. Heal, C. Dubeux, S. Hallegatte, L. Leclerc, A. Markandya, B. A. McCarl, et al. 2014. "Economics of Adaptation." In *Climate Change 2014: Impacts, Adaptation, and Vulnerability. Part A: Global and Sectoral Aspects. Contribution of Working Group II to the Fifth Assessment Report of the Intergovernmental Panel on Climate Change,* edited by C. B. Field, V. R. Barros, D. J. Dokken, K. J. Mach, M. D. Mastrandrea, T. E. Bilir, M. Chatterjee, et al., 945–977. Cambridge, United Kingdom and New York, NY, USA: Cambridge University Press.

Chen, M., C. R. Vernon, N. T. Graham, M. Hejazi, M. Huang, Y. Cheng, and K. Calvin. 2020. "Global Land Use for 2015–2100 at 0.05° Resolution under Diverse Socioeconomic and Climate Scenarios." *Scientific Data* 7 (1): 320. https://doi.org/10.1038/s41597-020-00669-x.

Cortés Arbués, I., T. Chatzivasileiadis, O. Ivanova, S. Storm, F. Bosello, and T. Filatova. 2024. "Distribution of Economic Damages Due to Climate-Driven Sea-level Rise Across European Regions and Sectors." *Scientific Reports* 14. https://doi.org/10.1038/s41598-023-48136-y.

De Koning, K., and T. Filatova. 2020. "Repetitive Floods Intensify Outmigration and Climate Gentrification in Coastal Cities." *Environmental Research Letters* 15 (3). https://doi.org/10.1088/1748-9326/ab6668.

De Koning, K., T. Filatova, and O. Bin. 2017. "Bridging the Gap Between Revealed and Stated Preferences in Flood-Prone Housing Markets." *Ecological Economics* 136:1–13. https://doi.org/10.1016/j.ecolecon.2017.01.022.

Diaz, D., and F. Moore. 2017. "Quantifying the Economic Risks of Climate Change." *Nature Climate Change* 7:774–782. https://doi.org/10.1038/nclimate3411.

Farmer, J. D., C. Hepburn, P. Mealy, and A. Teytelboym. 2015. "A Third Wave in the Economics of Climate Change." *Environmental and Resource Economics*, https://doi.org/10.1007/s10640-015-9965-2.

Filatova, T. 2015. "Empirical Agent-Based Land Market: Integrating Adaptive Economic Behavior in Urban Land-Use models." *Computers, Environment, and Urban Systems* 54:397–413. https://doi.org/10.1016/j.compenvurbsys. 2014.06.007.

Filatova, T., J. Akkerman, F. Bosello, T. Chatzivasileiadis, I. Cortés Arbués, A. Ghorbani, O. Ivanova, *et al.* 2025. "The Power of Bridging Decision Scales: Model Coupling for Advanced Climate Policy." *Proceedings of the National Academy of Sciences* 122 (38): e2411592122. https://doi.org/10.1073/pnas. 2411592122.

Fisher-Vanden, K., and J. Weyant. 2020. "The Evolution of Integrated Assessment: Developing the Next Generation of Use-Inspired Integrated Assessment Tools." *Annual Review of Resource Economics* 12 (October). https://doi.org/ 10.1146/annurev-resource-110119-030314.

Gao, X., A. Sokolov, and C. A. Schlosser. 2023. "A Large Ensemble Global Dataset for Climate Impact Assessments." *Scientific Data* 10 (1): 801. https://doi.org/ 10.1038/s41597-023-02708-9.

Gintis, H. 2007. "The Dynamics of General Equilibrium." *The Economic Journal* 117 (523): 1280–1309. https://doi.org/10.1111/j.1468-0297.2007.02083.x.

Gotts, N. M., and J. G. Polhill. 2009. "When and How to Imitate Your Neighbours: Lessons from and for FEARLUS." *Journal of Artificial Societies and Social Simulation* 12 (3): 2. https://www.jasss.org/12/3/2.html.

Gualdi, S., M. Tarzia, F. Zamponi, and J.-C. Bouchaud. 2015. "Tipping Points in Macroeconomic Agent-Based Models." *Journal of Economic Dynamics and Control* 50:29–61. https://doi.org/10.1016/j.jedc.2014.08.003.

Haer, T., W. J. W. Botzen, and J. C.J.H. Aerts. 2016. "The Effectiveness of Flood Risk Communication Strategies and the Influence of Social Networks—Insights from an Agent-Based Model." *Environmental Science & Policy* 60:44–52. https://doi.org/10.1016/j.envsci.2016.03.006.

Haer, T., T. G. Husby, W. J. W. Botzen, and J. C. J. H. Aerts. 2020. "The Safe Development Paradox: An Agent-Based Model for Flood Risk under Climate Change in the European Union." *Global Environmental Change* 60:102009. https://doi.org/10.1016/j.gloenvcha.2019.102009.

Hallegatte, S. 2008. "An Adaptive Regional Input-Output Model and Its Application to the Assessment of the Economic Cost of Katrina." *Centre International de Recherche sur l'Environnment et le Développement, Paris,* 779–799. https://doi.org/10.1111/j.1539-6924.2008.01046.x.

Hallegatte, S., J.-C. Hourcade, and P. Dumas. 2007. "Why Economic Dynamics Matter in Assessing Climate Change Damages: Illustration on Extreme Events." Special Section: Ecological-economic Modelling for Designing and Evaluating Biodiversity Conservation Policies, *Ecological Economics* 62 (2): 330–340. https://doi.org/10.1016/j.ecolecon.2006.06.006.

Holland, J. H. 1992. "Complex Adaptive Systems." *Daedalus* 121 (1): 17–30. http://www.jstor.org/stable/20025416.

Huizinga, J., H. de Moel, and W. Szewczyk. 2016. *Global Flood Depth-Damage Functions – Methodology and the Database with Guidelines.* Publications Office of the European Union. https://doi.org/10.2760/16510.

IPCC. 2022. *Climate Change 2022—Impacts, Adaptation and Vulnerability: Working Group II Contribution to the Sixth Assessment Report of the Intergovernmental Panel on Climate Change.* Cambridge, UK: Cambridge University Press. https://doi.org/10.1017/9781009325844.

Kahn, M. E., K. Mohaddes, R. N. C. Ng, M. Pesaran, M. Raissi, and J.-C. Yang. 2021. "Codes and Data Package: Long-Term Macroeconomic Effects of Climate Change: A Cross-Country Analysis." *IMF Working Papers* V1 (19). https://doi.org/10.17632/hytzz8wftw.1.

Koks, E. E., J. Rozenberg, C. Zorn, M. Tariverdi, M. Vousdoukas, S. A. Fraser, J. W. Hall, and S. Hallegatte. 2019. "A Global Multi-hazard Risk Analysis of Road and Railway Infrastructure Assets." *Nature Communications* 10 (1). https://doi.org/10.1038/s41467-019-10442-3.

Kondrup, C., P. Mercogliano, F. Bosello, J. Mysiak, E. Scoccimarro, A. Rizzo, R. Ebrey, M. de Ruiter, A. Jeuken, and P. Watkiss, eds. 2022. *Climate Adaptation Modelling.* Cham, Switzerland: Springer Nature. https://doi.org/10.1007/978-3-030-86211-4.

Lamperti, F., V. Bosetti, A. Roventini, and M. Tavoni. 2019. "The Public Costs of Climate-Induced Financial Instability." *Nature Climate Change* 9 (11). https://doi.org/10.1038/s41558-019-0607-5.

Leijonhufvud, A. 1973. "Effective Demand Failures." *The Swedish Journal of Economics* 75 (1): 27–48. http://www.jstor.org/stable/3439273.

Magliocca, N., E. Safirova, V. McConnell, and M. Walls. 2011. "An Economic Agent-Based Model of Coupled Housing and Land Markets (CHALMS)." *Computers, Environment, and Urban Systems* 35 (3): 183–191. https://doi.org/10.1016/j.compenvurbsys.2011.01.002.

Magliocca, N. R., and M. Walls. 2018. "The Role of Subjective Risk Perceptions in Shaping Coastal Development Dynamics." *Computers, Environment and Urban Systems* 71:1–13. https://doi.org/10.1016/j.compenvurbsys.2018.03.009.

Miller, H., and S. Dikau. 2022. *Preventing a 'Climate Minsky Moment': Environmental Financial Risks and Prudential Exposure Limits.* Technical report. London, UK: Grantham Research Institute on Climate Change, the Environment, London School of Economics, and Political Science.

Mutlu, A., D. Roy, and T. Filatova. 2023. "Capitalized Value of Evolving Flood Risks Discount and Nature-Based Solution Premiums on Property Prices." *Ecological Economics* 205:107682. https://doi.org/10.1016/j.ecolecon.2022.107682.

Naqvi, A. A., and M. Rehm. 2014. "A Multi-Agent Model of a Low Income Economy: Simulating the Distributional Effects of Natural Disasters." *Journal of Economic Interaction and Coordination* 9 (2): 275–309. https://doi.org/10.1007/s11403-014-0137-1.

Ortiz, R., and A. Markandya. 2010. *Literature Review of Integrated Impact Assessment Models of Climate Change with Emphasis on Damage Functions.* Working Papers 2009-06. BC3, April. https://ideas.repec.org/p/bcc/wpaper/2009-06.html.

Otto, C., S. N. Willner, L. Wenz, K. Frieler, and A. Levermann. 2017. "Modeling Loss-Propagation in the Global Supply Network: The Dynamic Agent-Based Model Acclimate." *Journal of Economic Dynamics and Control* 83:232–269. https://doi.org/10.1016/j.jedc.2017.08.001.

Parrado, R., F. Bosello, E. Delpiazzo, J. Hinkel, D. Lincke, and S. Brown. 2020. "Fiscal Effects and the Potential Implications on Economic Growth of Sea-Level Rise Impacts and Coastal Zone Protection." *Climatic Change* 160:283–302. https://doi.org/10.1007/s10584-020-02664-y.

Pindyck, R. S. 2013. "Climate Change Policy: What Do the Models Tell Us?" *Journal of Economic Literature* 51 (3): 860–72. https://doi.org/10.1257/jel.51.3.860.

Poledna, S., S. Hochrainer-Stigler, M. G. Miess, P. Klimek, S. Schmelzer, J. Sorger, E. Shchekinova, *et al.* 2018. *When Does a Disaster Become a Systemic Event? Estimating Indirect Economic Losses from Natural Disasters.* arXiv preprint: 1801.09740. https://doi.org/10.48550/arXiv.1801.09740.

Safarzyńska, K., R. Brouwer, and M. Hofkes. 2013. "Evolutionary Modelling of the Macro-Economic Impacts of Catastrophic Flood Events." Transaction Costs and Environmental Policy, *Ecological Economics* 88:108–118. https://doi.org/10.1016/j.ecolecon.2013.01.016.

Simon, H. A. 1990. "Bounded Rationality." In *Utility and Probability,* edited by J. Eatwell, M. Milgate, and P. Newman, 15–18. London, UK: Palgrave Macmillan UK. https://doi.org/10.1007/978-1-349-20568-4_5.

Simpson, N. P., K. J. Mach, A. Constable, J. Hess, R. Hogarth, M. Howden, J. Lawrence, *et al.* 2021. "A Framework for Complex Climate Change Risk Assessment." *One Earth* 4 (4): 489–501. https://doi.org/10.1016/j.oneear.2021.03.005.

Stern, N. 2013. "The Structure of Economic Modeling of the Potential Impacts of Climate Change: Grafting Gross Underestimation of Risk onto Already Narrow Science Models." *Journal of Economic Literature* 51 (3): 838–59. https://doi.org/10.1257/jel.51.3.838.

Stern, N., J. Stiglitz, and Charlotte Taylor. 2022. "The Economics of Immense Risk, Urgent Action and Radical Change: Towards new Approaches to the Economics of Climate Change." *Journal of Economic Methodology* 29 (3): 181–216. https://doi.org/10.1080/1350178X.2022.2040740.

Taberna, A., T. Filatova, A. Hadjimichael, and B. Noll. 2023a. "Uncertainty in Boundedly Rational Household Adaptation to Environmental Shocks." *Proceedings of the National Academy of Sciences* 120 (44). https://doi.org/10.1073/pnas.2215675120.

Taberna, A., T. Filatova, S. Hochrainer-Stigler, I. Nikolic, and B. Noll. 2023b. "Economic Implications of Autonomous Adaptation of Firms and Households in a Resource-Rich Coastal City." *Scientific Reports* 13 (1). https://doi.org/10.1038/s41598-023-46318-2.

Taberna, A., T. Filatova, A. Roventini, and F. Lamperti. 2022. "Coping with Increasing Tides: Evolving Agglomeration Dynamics and Technological Change under Exacerbating Hazards." *Ecological Economics* 202:107588. https://doi.org/10.1016/j.ecolecon.2022.107588.

Taberna, A., T. Filatova, D. Roy, and B. Noll. 2020. "Tracing Resilience, Social Dynamics and Behavioral Change: A Review of Agent-Based Flood Risk Models." *Socio-Environmental Systems Modelling* 2:17938. https://doi.org/10.18174/sesmo.2020a17938.

Tesfatsion, L., and K. L. Judd, eds. 2006. *Handbook of Computational Economics. Volume 2, Agent-Based Computational Economics.* Amsterdam, Netherlands: North Holland.

Tierolf, L., T. Haer, W. J. W. Botzen, J. A. de Bruijn, M. J. Ton, L. Reimann, and J. C. J. H. Aerts. 2023. "A Coupled Agent-Based Model for France for Simulating Adaptation and Migration Decisions under Future Coastal Flood Risk." *Scientific Reports* 13 (1): 4176. https://doi.org/10.1038/s41598-023-31351-y.

van der Wijst, K.-I., F. Bosello, S. Dasgupta, L. Drouet, J. Emmerling, A. Hof, M. Leimbach, *et al.* 2023. "New Damage Curves and Multimodel Analysis Suggest Lower Optimal Temperature." *Nature Climate Change* 13 (5): 434–441. https://doi.org/10.1038/s41558-023-01636-1.

van Duinen, R., T. Filatova, W. Jager, and A. van der Veen. 2016. "Going Beyond Perfect Rationality: Drought Risk, Economic Choices and the Influence of Social Networks." *The Annals of Regional Science* 57 (2): 335–369. https://doi.org/10.1007/s00168-015-0699-4.

van Ginkel, K. C. H., M. Haasnoot, and W. J. Botzen. 2022. "A Stepwise Approach for Identifying Climate Change Induced Socio-Economic Tipping Points." *Climate Risk Management* 37:100445. https://doi.org/10.1016/j.crm.2022.100445.

van Valkengoed, A. M., and L. Steg. 2019. "Meta-Analyses of Factors Motivating Climate Change Adaptation Behaviour." *Nature Climate Change* 9 (2): 158–163. https://doi.org/10.1038/s41558-018-0371-y.

Verschuur, J., E. E. Koks, and J. W. Hall. 2023. "Systemic Risks from Climate-Related Disruptions at Ports." *Nature Climate Change* 13 (8): 804–806. https://doi.org/10.1038/s41558-023-01754-w.

Wagenblast, T., T. Filatova, L. Grimley, A. Sebastian, and N. Goyal. 2024. *From Opinion to Action: Impact of Social Networks and Information Policy on Private Flood Adaptation.* SSRN Electronic Journal. https://doi.org/10.2139/ssrn.4763672.

Weitzman, M. L. 2009. "On Modeling and Interpreting the Economics of Catastrophic Climate Change." *Review of Economics and Statistics* 91 (1): 1–19. https://doi.org/10.1162/rest.91.1.1.

Will, M., J. Groeneveld, K. Frank, and B. Muller. 2020. "Combining Social Network Analysis and Agent-Based Modelling to Explore Dynamics of Human Interaction: A Review." *Socio-Environmental Systems Modelling* 2:16325. https://doi.org/10.18174/sesmo.2020a16325.

Wilson, R. S., A. Herziger, M. Hamilton, and J. S. Brooks. 2020. "From Incremental to Transformative Adaptation in Individual Responses to Climate-Exacerbated Hazards." *Nature Climate Change* 10 (3): 200–208. https://doi.org/10.1038/s41558-020-0691-6. 10.1038/s41558-020-0691-6.

Wing, O. E. J., N. Pinter, P. D. Bates, and C. Kousky. 2020. "New Insights into US Flood Vulnerability Revealed from Flood Insurance Big Data." *Nature Communications* 11 (1): 1444. https://doi.org/10.1038/s41467-020-15264-2.

PART V
Inequality, Labor &
Structural Resilience

COMPLEXITY THEORY AND ECONOMIC INEQUALITY

Steven N. Durlauf, University of Chicago;

David McMillon, Emory University; and

Scott E. Page, University of Michigan–Ann Arbor

and Santa Fe Institute

Abstract

We analyze the potential for complexity theory to produce insights that elucidate the evolution of socioeconomic inequality and point toward effective policies. We position complexity theory as a complement to more traditional economic approaches. Economic models of inequality can fall into four broad categories: models based on individual attributes and technologies, social interaction models, intergenerational models of transfer, and models of institutional and social structure. Within each of these categories, complexity theory can enhance traditional theory. It is of particular value in helping to distinguish between bottom-up systemic and top-down structural causes of inequality. Complexity theory can further enrich our understanding of economic inequality by adopting a complex adaptive system of systems approach in which economic, social, political, and psychosocial systems interact with one another and with institutional and social structures to produce robust inequality, particularly on racial lines.

Introduction

In this chapter, we describe four categories of models that attempt to provide causal explanations of economic inequality. We then interpret these models through the lens of complexity science. Our modest overarching goal is to call attention to how the core ideas from complexity science can add to our understanding of inequality and aid in the development of policies and interventions that might reduce it.

Our specific contributions are fourfold. First, we show how the connections between the four common classes of inequality models overlap with complexity theory. Second, we highlight a distinction between bottom-up *systemic* causes and contributors to inequality and (mostly) top-down *structural* causes. Third, we argue that our understanding of inequality could be improved by adopting a *complex adaptive system of systems* approach that more deeply interrogates the interdependent effects of economic, political, educational, health, environmental, and psychological systems on inequality (Page and Zelner 2020). Last, we suggest that the addition of a complexity lens can result in better policies.

The concern with inequality is hardly new. The standard objectives of economic policies have long been efficiency, growth, and equality. Ideally, an economic system produces goods and services efficiently and then allocates both relatively equally, or at least with limited envy across individuals, with an understanding that the need to incentivize effort often results in differences in allocations.

Economists care about growth for good reason. Increases in productive capacity over time have enormous implications for individual and social well-being. A mere 3% annual growth over a century produces a sixteenfold increase in the output.

Producing efficient outcomes—both static and temporal— along with equality has historically been thought to involve tradeoffs (Okun 1975; Meade 1975). While it is true that some policies that reduce inequality can reduce growth, there is no necessary tradeoff. A standard example involves education, where increases in supply of skills, as produced by expanding educational opportunities, can be growth enhancing and inequality inducing; the complexities of these dynamics underlie the work of Claudia

Goldin and Lawrence Katz. A second important example involves the effects of reductions in discrimination on growth. Chang-Tai Hsieh *et al.* (2019) argue that a 20 to 40% in increase in per capita market output in the United States since 1960 may be attributed to increased opportunities for women and African Americans.

Complex systems represent one class of environments in which one can formally model evolving sectional distributions to understand how efficiency, growth and inequality coevolve, and by implications reveal what sorts of interventions produce tradeoffs and what sorts do not. One example on how systems thinking reveals novel ways to promote equality and efficiency is demonstrated by Lu Hong and Scott Page (2001, 2004), who show how diverse groups can outperform homogeneous ones; Page (2017) provides a broad synthesis of these ideas. These findings imply that reductions of inequalities in the compositions of groups can be efficiency enhancing. As such, they speak to broad issues in what Steven Durlauf (2002, 2006) has called the memberships theory of inequality, which captures the general role of socioeconomic segregation as a fundamental source of contemporary inequalities.

Inequality remains a pressing issue because nations have not been successful at reducing it. Internationally, much of the story of post–World War II economies is one of growth. In Western Europe, the United States, and Canada, per capita gross domestic product has increased sixfold, so the advanced economies have sustained growth. In Eastern Europe and South America, country-level increases vary from four- to sixfold, and in East Asia, increases have been more than tenfold. Africa is a more complicated story, where much of the postwar period has involved stagnation.

Progress on inequality has been far less impressive. Economists measure inequality by dispersion of income, lifetime earnings, or wealth across a population; sociologists often focus on occupations. These inequality measures are typically calculated nationally, although some focus on differences at regional levels. Global inequality has always been a concern as well, though it is more difficult to measure given differences in purchasing power and variations in market penetration across countries.

Over the past forty years, inequality in Europe and the Americas has not lessened. Nor, in the postwar period, does one find that national per capita income inequalities between the developed and developing economies are converging (see Johnson and Papageorgiou 2020, for an overview of the evidence). Such regularities, of course, mask important heterogeneities. For example, extraordinary growth exhibited by East Asian economies coexists with persistent differences between Europe and China. Paul Johnson and Chris Papageorgiou illustrate the nuances of measuring inequality by the fact that while countries may not be converging, population differences between countries are such that, at the individual level, income inequality has been declining worldwide.

Human well-being can also be measured by social connectedness, income, wealth, health status, life expectancy, or life satisfaction. These measures also vary substantially across peoples and places. Some people live socially integrated lives while others live in isolation; some people earn millions per year in salary while others live in poverty; and some people can expect to live healthily into their 80s or 90s whereas others are fortunate to reach 70 years of age (Gee and Ford 2011).

Empirical analysis of economic inequality reveals clustering by place and differences across racial and ethnic groups. While we should expect some variation to arise due to differences in natural capacities, effort, luck, and circumstances, the extent of variation and its spatial concentration within particular communities suggests the presence of compounded disadvantages that limit the prospects for many (Perkins and Sampson 2015).

Compounded disadvantages create *system of system effects.* Each disadvantage reinforces others: An unsafe environment contributes to poor health, which in turn contributes to worse performance in school; high school dropouts are more likely to be unemployed and to lead less healthy lifestyles (Last *et al.* 2018). In addition, people suffering from poor health and poor economic prospects are less likely to place trust in government and social services, contributing to a system of forces that make life difficult.

~256~

Within these systems, we can distinguish *bottom-up systemic* forces that operate on features relating to interactions across individuals and/or their outcomes that generate population-level patterns from more *top-down structural* forces that result from features embedded in institutions, laws, or social structures that influence the preferences, beliefs, and constraints of individuals' choices. For example, healthcare provided by employers as opposed to the government is a structural feature that produces systemic effects: Poorer health among the unemployed leads to less ability to find and hold a job and reduced educational performance. On the other hand, the fact that racial wealth gaps contribute to racial differences in educational performance is a systemic feature that can have structural effects. White parents pulling their children from increasingly diverse but lower-performing schools (a social, systemic effect) results in segregation in both schools and communities. In turn, this can lead to less funding for schools (a structural effect).

This example, and others like it, demonstrates the complex dynamics that link equality and efficiency and how policy outcomes can depend upon the contexts in which they are implemented. As we have just suggested, if initial conditions are unequal, then well-intentioned movements toward structural fairness could amplify systemic disparities.

Systemic thinking about inequality also has important normative implications. Institutional structures that are *prima facie* fair will not necessarily reduce inequality if the contexts in which they are placed exhibit systemic and structural forces. These can combine to make inequalities robust. Consider meritocratic college admissions and firm hiring policies. These can exacerbate existing inequalities if winners of these competitions receive sufficiently high rewards and then pass on these benefits to their children by giving them more opportunities to excel (Jayakumar and Page 2021). As a result, their children become the likely winners of future competitions (Markovits 2019). Complexity science refers to this as a *positive feedback*. Ironically, it is one with negative consequences. Steven Durlauf (2008) argues that these forces need to be accounted in intertemporally efficient admissions and hiring rules. Doing so changes the meaning of merit in ways that can break claims that meritocracy and equality work at cross purposes.

Neoclassical and Complexity Economics

The motivation for this chapter was to explore what complexity has added or can add to our understanding of inequality. Scholars at the Santa Fe Institute have been thinking of the economy as a complex system for more than thirty years. Early proponents of complexity economics highlighted the stark differences between its assumptions and those of neoclassical economics. Those comparisons painted neoclassical economics as making unrealistic assumptions about the world: optimizing, homogeneous agents interacting at a single place in a single moment in time in well-defined, separable strategic environments who always achieve equilibria.

In stark contrast, complexity economics makes far more realistic assumptions: diverse agents who learn are situated in networks and interact over time in environments rife with systems effects and externalities. In complex-systems models, macro-level patterns emerge from the bottom up. These patterns include stock market crashes, technological clustering, and segregation by race and income. These patterns become relevant parts of the economic landscape. They impact behavior and outcomes.

These provocative comparisons initially played a role in bolstering the field of complexity economics. Viewed from a broader perspective, they were one of many empirical and theoretical challenges to neoclassical economics. Those challenges have been successful. Present-day economics makes more realistic assumptions about the capacities of actors and the spaces in which they operate. Current mainstream economic models include heterogeneous, boundedly rational agents who learn. Economic models even include network effects, peer effects, and altruistic preferences.

The incorporation of the various assumptions of complexity science did not, however, result in a paradigmatic shift. Neoclassical economics has not become complexity economics. Instead, we argue that the economics profession has become more expansive in the types of assumptions it makes about how people act and how the world works.

On the whole, the evidence suggests that some economic phenomena can be explained quite well with the minimalistic version of neoclassical economics, while others require moving in the direction of complexity economics and taking seriously the many dimensions of human diversity (not just preferences, but perspectives, belief systems, and culture), bounded rationality, peer effects, and self-organization. Economists, while still searching for general theories of human behavior, now pick and choose models based on context. Actors in large firms and sophisticated financial investors who operate in high stakes, repeated settings may well optimize, or come close to it. Students deciding on whether to take out college loans decidedly do not.

To summarize, in our view economics has evolved in directions that show there is no fundamental incapability of adapting ideas from complexity theory. The irreducible core of economic theory involves reasoning about purposeful agents who make choices given preferences, monetary and time constraints, information, and beliefs, and whose choices interact via various socioeconomic structures ranging from markets to polities to social networks. Assumptions about the determinants of choices and features of institutions are the loci in which complex-systems thinking may be introduced.

We therefore see little current value in attacking economics from a complexity perspective or in positioning complexity economics as somehow correct and neoclassical economics as wrong. These are two classes of models. Individually, each is useful and wrong. Collectively, they are more useful and less wrong (Page 2018).

That said, moving in the direction of complexity economics differs from adopting the paradigm as a whole. One can construct equilibrium models of agents who learn strategies in a game played on a network. Or one can construct a dynamic general equilibrium growth model with heterogeneous agents. Though neither should be considered a model of a complex system, both move in that direction. And, as stated, our strong belief is that viewing inequality as resulting from multiple interacting complex systems operating within political structures offers powerful insights into the causes of and corrections for inequality.

A Taxonomy of Models

Models of inequality, especially those that have been brought to data, reflect the aforementioned blurring between neoclassical and complexity economics. To demonstrate that claim, we categorize models based on their core assumptions. Inequality models can be loosely partitioned into four types of explanations: *individual characteristics models, social interaction models, institutional and social structure models,* and *intergenerational models*. These category boundaries will vary in the extent to which they explicitly include complex processes. We first describe them and then discuss their implications when inequality dynamics are considered.

INDIVIDUALISTIC MODELS

Individualistic models assume a population of agents who differ on a single attribute or combination of attributes. An agent's income is a function of that attribute. A simple example would be a model that explains individual i's income, y_i, as a function of some measure of ability a_i. That function could be linear, $y_i = \beta_0 + \beta_a a_i + \epsilon_i$, where β_a represents economic returns to ability, β_0 is baseline income for someone with no ability, and ϵ_i captures the many unobserved contributions to income. Of course, the function need not be linear. Income could exhibit increasing or decreasing returns to ability. The functional form will depend on how ability has been measured.

Income will also depend on the supply of labor and the technology (Goldin and Katz 2008). Positing income as a function of something called ability also ignores the role of parental investment, individual effort, and beliefs about the returns to investments.

As should be obvious, these models can quickly become complicated as an individual chooses an effort level and their parent (most economic models assume parents that act as a single rational actor) makes investments in education based on their beliefs about the return to education and effort, and (in some models) on general equilibrium effects.

We note with a touch of irony that almost no social scientist would describe this class of models as complex. These are canonical neoclassical models. Such models assume that everyone optimizes given their attributes, resources, beliefs, and, most critically, the actions of everyone else.

As limited in scope as it seems, the model just discussed captures five possible causes of inequality: differences in ability, differences in returns to effort, differences in parental wealth, differences in parental preferences toward offsprings' future income, and differences in beliefs. Individual models take variation on these variables as features of the world. But these variations and their consequences also depend on large social and structural factors, to which we now turn.

SOCIAL INTERACTION MODELS

Individual characteristics and choices do not arise *de novo* but rather occur within social systems. Social influences can range from peer effects to neighborhood effects to network effects and racial and cultural effects. For example, an individual's returns to education depend on how much other individuals believe in the value of education. This in turn will influence their and others' investments in education. In our view, this is a *systemic* effect.

In social interaction models such as this, an outcome of interest such as educational attainment depends not just on a person's own characteristics but on the actions and beliefs of their peers and their larger community. One important dimension involves identity. What constitutes an ideal behavior depends upon a person's peer group, their attitudes, and how those attitudes align with the school's culture (Steele 2018; Akerlof and Kranton 2000, 2002).

Models in this category often assume local interactions, a feature of complexity models but not the canonical neoclassical models. In local interaction models, an individual's beliefs, actions, and returns can all depend on the people with whom they interact. An individual who belongs to a peer group that believes education offers few opportunities, who don't put forth effort in school, and who sanction the individual's attempts to succeed will have lower income than a person with similar characteristics placed in a more supportive neighborhood.

Once network structures are introduced (cf. Calvó-Armengol and Jackson 2004), then the rates of diffusion of information will depend on social distance between individuals. It follows that the introduction of social influences creates correlations in outcomes between individuals and can produce theories of group-level inequalities. Further, interdependences between individuals mean that changes in one individual's characteristics will affect others as well. Collectively, social interactions produce a social multiplier, whereby initial inequalities are amplified by the interdependences between individuals.

Social influences not only produce inequalities, they can result in persistent inequalities (Page 2011). One cause of persistence is that interdependences between individuals can lead to multiple self-consistent choices. If one's peer works hard, hard work is a best choice; if one's peers shirk, shirking becomes a best choice. The key formal condition for multiplicity is strong complementarities in individual choices, which means that the benefits of one person's choice increase when others make the same or similar choices.

A second reason is that social interactions create incentives for individuals to segregate themselves. Affluent parents have incentives to choose neighborhoods with other affluent parents, which can produce equilibrium configurations of income segregation.

In other cases, the rules by which public goods are produced can induce segregation. Local finance of education is an obvious example. Other examples derive from decisions on what a policymaker deems the optimal way to assign individuals and environments. Educational sorting rules ranging from ability grouping in classrooms to admissions rules that condition on grades and test scores can have multiplier effects that amplify individual ability differences. In fact, Daniel Markovits (2019) challenges meritocracy as a social goal because of the inequalities it can induce. These mechanisms, in turn, can be amplified by neighborhood effects. Beliefs in the value of education can depend on local information and on the ways that one's social environment shape aspirations. In a remarkable study, Caroline Hoxby and Christopher Avery (2013) show that there are thousands of adolescents with high test scores who, despite eligibility for scholarships, fail to apply to elite schools. Finally, there are basic differences in exposure to neighborhood ills, such as exposure to lead and exposure to violence, that can profoundly inhibit education. Robert Manduca and Robert Sampson (2019) document how, for the city of Chicago, Black and White children are deeply segregated in levels of exposures.

Considered collectively, social models provide multiple mechanisms that can explain poverty and affluence traps. A poor community finds itself stuck in what dynamical-systems theorists would call a large "basin of attraction." Imagine a ball sitting at the bottom of a bowl. Policies intended to improve health status and socioeconomic well-being push the ball up the side of the bowl, but only temporarily. The forces within the system, in the form of level effects and negative feedback loops, pull the ball back down to the bottom. A large basin corresponds to a large bowl. Getting the ball out requires a large push.

In these models, social and individual sources of disadvantage are interdependent, not additive, a distinction that must be front of mind if we hope to reduce inequalities. In a complex system, single isolatable interventions generally do not produce large, persistent improvements. Reinforcing loops within the system pull it back to its status quo. Evidence from fifty years of randomized controlled trials testing policies to reduce crime reveals that few prove replicable and those that do have effects of small magnitude at best (Stevenson 2024).

By intergenerational persistence, we mean low levels of income across generations of the same family. Social and structural effects will influence every variable and coefficient in the production of skills. Educational sorting rules ranging from ability grouping in classrooms to admissions rules that condition on grades and test scores can have multiplier effects that amplify individual ability differences. Differences in parental incomes can produce these skill differences both via direct investments and via access to better schools.

When one integrates individual and social mechanisms, one can produce more elaborate models of inequality. These models can produce inequality as an emergent phenomenon. Levels of socioeconomic and racial segregation are emergent properties of (constrained) individual choices. The classic Schelling model of racial segregation shows how complete segregation can emerge in environments where individuals prefer some levels of integration but do not wish to be completely isolated from their in-group. It is unsurprising that complexity scientists developed variants of this framework to show how it can also produce segregation by income and segregation by race and income.

POLITICAL INSTITUTIONS AND STRUCTURAL CAUSES

The first two classes of models demonstrate how individual attributes and social (systemic) interactions can produce and maintain inequality. They take the institutional structure as given. Within that structure, individual choices can be amplified and reinforced by social forces to produce persistent inequality. That persistence is not intended. It is an emergent phenomenon.

This view must be complemented with considerations of how institutions support and reinforce inequalities. Racial inequality in America is an obvious context. Jim Crow laws are the most obvious example of postbellum structures inducing inequalities, but they are hardly unique. Richard Rothstein (2017) delineates the long history of government policies, such as the exclusion of Black people from receiving Federal Housing Administration loans to public housing that promoted segregation; Daniel Aaronson, Daniel Hartley, and Bhashkar Mazumder (2021) demonstrate how far just one of these policies—loan exclusion— can explain contemporary segregation patterns.

Beyond the explicit introduction of unjust inequalities via discrimination, there are powerful ways that democratic institutions potentially amplify inequalities. The simplest model of equilibrium voting patterns is the so-called median voting model, in which policies are implemented in accordance with the median preferences among voters, since alternatives to the policy would be defeated in a head-to-head election against them. This implies that changes in the income distribution will change redistributive policies such as taxes and transfers.

John Roemer (2006) offers a clear demonstration on how democratic choices may not eliminate poverty when voters are self-interested. Further, differentials in political power associated with wealth can distort voting outcomes in ways that perpetuate

~ 265 ~

inequalities (see Acemoglu *et al.* 2015, for a survey). All of these can lead to distributional instabilities.

INTERGENERATIONAL MODELS

Intergenerational models build from the previous models by considering lineages. Rather than consider an individual i at a single moment in time, these models assume a lineage of individual is and a sequence of generations indexed by t. Income for lineage i at time t, written as y_{it}, is a function of variables that include the income of the lineage at time $t-1$. Intergenerational mobility is studied via lineage models. These models typically have a Markovian structure where t denotes generations. These models are capable of producing persistent inequalities.

Social and structural factors are a natural route to these. When neighborhood and school factors are combined, one can see how a system in which families choose neighborhoods subject to constraint generated by house or rental prices and the unmeasured costs of social acceptance or antipathy, combined with the sorting rules for education, can create deep distributional instabilities as parental inequalities induce inequalities in children that amplify initial inequalities. Durlauf (1996a, 1996b) demonstrates that, in theory, these social factors can produce a nonergodic system in which the descendants of the rich and poor never alter their relative positions in society.

Raj Chetty *et al.* (2014) launched a research program demonstrating large spatial heterogeneity in intergenerational mobility, as predicted by such models. Here as well, the implicit interpretations very much align with a complex systems view of the economy, but the formal model does not. It estimates fixed racial differences in the slopes and intercepts of a linear dynamic model, implying a significant Black–White steady-state difference in average income rank. The approach here systematically controls for a number of factors in a linear fashion (including some that are endogenously related to parent and child income, such as parental wealth), finding the steady state difference is driven by males and segregation. However, Black–White inequality remains in 99% of census tracts. The only areas that reach parity are those with low levels of anti-Black bias among Whites, high Black father presence, and low poverty rates. Very few Black children grow up in such unique areas, hindering intergenerational mobility.

~267~

Our discussion of systems and intergenerational inequality speaks to an important empirical regularity that has been found, namely, that greater cross-sectional inequality is associated with greater intergenerational persistence of socioeconomic status across generations. The regularity, which has been dubbed the Great Gatsby Curve, was first identified at a global level by Miles Corak (2013). This finding has been replicated within countries as well. An analogous finding holds for intergenerational mobility: Greater inequality across parents reduces mobility. Durlauf, Kourtellos, and Tan (2022) survey theory and evidence for this relationship. Our vision of an evolving cross-sectional distribution in which family, social, and institutional systems create nonlinearities in individual level transmission provides the microfoundations. Alessandra Fogli and Veronica Guerrieri (2019) show how these ideas can replicate important aspects of US inequality.

INTERGENERATIONAL MODELS AND SYSTEMIC INEQUALITY

The intergenerational models add dynamics to the other three classes of models, allowing us to capture how systemic inequality emerges. Once these are embedded in contexts where individual and social interactions operate under distinct rules, one can think about inequality as the outcome of a system as opposed to being a consequence of individual differences.

Our reading of the evidence is that systemic inequality can be best understood as the translation of initial individual-level inequalities into equilibrium levels of inequality through contemporary and dynamic interdependences. In our judgment, these differ from structural causes that can be traced to political institutions and collective choices and laws. That said, systemic and structural causes of inequality mutually reinforce each other.

To see how to operationalize this type of reasoning, consider one essential dimension of American inequality: discrimination. How would one model individual acts of discrimination by employers? First, one would specify the decision-making process of those committing the acts. It is standard to think of discrimination, individual actions, as driven by two factors: animus toward Black people and statistical discrimination, the formation of beliefs about Black people that lead to differential treatment from White people of equal ability. Individual actions will, however, have social roots. Some factors are structural. Jim Crow laws structured individual employment outcomes. Alternatively, one can think of unequal educational opportunities for Black people and White people, which means that even if equally productive individuals are hired, the distribution of skills is the product of discrimination.

Beyond this, systemic factors need to be modeled. Animus is the outcome of social processes. Beliefs about the potential of Black job applicants will be conditioned on the information sets of potential employers. Hence, employers' lack of interactions with Black people can lead to an inability to discern skills due to cultural capital deficits. Alternatively, suppose that White employers possess adverse priors—prejudices—about Black applicants. Employers must receive information so that their posterior beliefs become accurate. This need not happen. Every failure to hire a Black applicant is a loss of information about the potential of Black applicants. Generally, when individuals segregate themselves due to adverse priors, they shut off the potential for these priors to evolve.

Social multipliers will emerge as individual acts of discrimination amplify equilibrium racial inequality. One reason is that information about job opportunities flows through networks (see Calvó-Armengol and Jackson 2004, for a formalization). Hence, every act of discrimination against one Black person can affect everyone in their network. Further, every act of discrimination means that information about Black people's potential is lost to all employers. It is possible for inequalities to become permanent when these feedback effects are strong enough so that prejudice-based priors are not overcome by adequate data. Further, discrimination can damage incentives for educational attainment and hence prejudices are confirmed *ex post*, not because of intrinsic differences but because prejudices put into motion chains of decisions from which *ex post* confirmation emerges.

Complexity Theory and Policy Interventions

A complexity-theory perspective on inequality assumes that the compounded disadvantages are interdependent, not additive. This distinction should be front of mind as we consider how a complexity-theory lens would influence policy that aims to reduce inequalities. In an additive system, inequality is caused by a collection of mostly independent factors with a smattering of interactive terms. It follows that the most effective policy will identify the most important variables and enact policies that change their values. If math education has the largest return on investment in the estimated equation, then money should be allocated there.

The idea that we can gather data, fit models with lots of linear terms and a few interaction terms, and then allocate resources to key variables has guided a large share of government and philanthropic spending. This approach to evidence-based policymaking has had limited success. A complexity-theory approach would not expect isolated interventions to succeed in systems that contain mutually reinforcing or balancing feedbacks.

Nonetheless, scholars have often relied exclusively on reduced-form approaches when evaluating interventions rather than considering the effects of interventions through a complexity lens. This evaluative narrowness is surprising in the field of education, given that a large empirical and qualitative literature demonstrates that educational success and failure results from a system of political, social, economic, and psychological factors (Ladson-Billings and Tate 2006; Lee 2008).

A complexity lens can help anticipate unintended consequences and clarify empirical puzzles, such as why educational interventions sometimes fade out and sometimes persist. It can also identify key features of complex systems—such as reinforcement processes—that can be disrupted or leveraged to produce lasting intervention effects. For example, the feedback between low self-concept, low effort, and low achievement might be disrupted with growth mindset interventions or exploited with self-concept-improving self-affirmation interventions (McMillon 2024a).

The causes of racial inequalities also include discrimination. This, too, can become systemic when the initial effects of an injustice become amplified through social multipliers, reinforcement processes, and complementarities (McMillon 2024b). When an economic shock hits, poor households rationally engage in sharp reductions in welfare-relevant consumption. Hence, racial wealth inequalities make Black Americans more vulnerable to economic shocks (Ganong *et al.* 2020; De *et al.* 2021).

Amplification mechanisms also occur within other systems. This is especially true for health. Biological mechanisms that make people with heart disease more susceptible to COVID-19 result in increased risk for Black Americans, who face preexisting differences in heart disease (Wadhera *et al.* 2021).

Health disparities, as well as educational disparities, can then spill over into the economic system. David McMillon (2024b) refers to these as *intersectoral spillovers*. Often, a given inequality will have systemic effects both within and across systems. Disparate treatment in charging decisions within the criminal justice system spills over into disparities in sentencing outcomes (Rehavi and Starr 2014). These differences create an intersectoral spillover into labor market outcomes (Agan and Starr 2018).

A complex-systems perspective leads organically to three policy insights. First, we might seek to disrupt the mechanisms that amplify inequalities. This could mean reducing the impact of a feature within a system (e.g., levying a wealth tax to effect income transfers to disrupt poverty traps in economic systems) or demolishing a structure that reinforces systemic effects (e.g., abolishing private prisons).

Second, policies might attempt to exploit systems effects to amplify equality-focused interventions (e.g., a policy that enhances access to capital markets for minorities). Second, policies might attempt to exploit systems effects to amplify equality-focused interventions (e.g., a policy that enhances access to capital markets for minorities). In either case, we are leveraging the same systemic processes that produced systemic discrimination and inequality to eradicate them. That is, "using the mechanics of systemic discrimination against itself" (McMillon 2024b).

Third, adopting a complex adaptive system of systems perspective and representing inequality as being produced by multiple, interdependent systems with reinforcing and amplifying loops implies the need to coordinate policies across systems. Multiple levers must be activated simultaneously at the community level if any are to have their full effect. Attempts to improve a local economy without also putting resources in the health system and the educational system may not succeed because the failure of one system will prevent progress in others. Poorly educated people living in unsafe communities with little access to health services cannot take full advantage of economic opportunities.

The failure to think systemically may not only produce ineffective policies, but also lead to misleading inferences. A recent large-scale test of universal basic income that targeted individuals and not entire communities found only modest effects (Vivalt *et al.* 2024). This experiment, which had enormous cost, tells us little about what would happen if every member of a single community were given a basic income. Evidence from a second unconditional cash transfer program that found significant indirect spillover effects on ineligible individuals (Angelucci and De Giorgi 2009) suggests the possibility that, had the entire community been given transfers, these spillovers might have become synergies.

John List, Fatemeh Momeni, and Yves Zenou (2019) find similar results in the context of early childhood education interventions, which are traditionally randomized at the individual level, within school districts. Students given additional resources have positive effects on untreated students, and thus the true overall effect would be underestimated were spillovers not taken into account. Under traditional assumptions in economic experiments, treated and control units do not influence one another. If they do, then treatment effects may be underestimated.

This observation also holds for other contexts in which social interactions matter, such as the spread of crime (McMillon, Simon, and Morenoff 2014) and wealth transfer networks under a reparations policy for slavery and Jim Crow. Within-community experiments of reparations policies may underestimate the extent of persistence compared with cross-community experiments due to social multipliers (McMillon 2024b). A large-scale reparations policy would leverage the economic interdependence of recipients to enhance persistence. Within-community experiments of reparations policies may underestimate the extent of persistence compared with cross-community experiments due to social multipliers (McMillon 2024b). A large-scale reparations policy would leverage the economic interdependence of recipients to enhance persistence.

To summarize, traditional economic models have provided deep insights into the causes of economic inequality. They demonstrate that inequality results from differences in individual attributes—often resulting from historical injustices, social interactions, and political institutions. Those differences are then often magnified in the labor market and within the criminal justice system.

Intertemporal models further explain why inequality persists and proves robust to interventions. Neither of these classes of models are antithetical to a complexity approach. To the contrary, both embed, at least implicitly, ideas and concepts from complexity economics. And, when viewed through a complexity lens, we can distinguish between bottom-up systemic features and top-down structural features that produce and maintain inequality.

What economic models emphasize less explicitly is how economic inequalities are amplified and reinforced by other systems. Many economic models include social, educational, political, health, and psychological variables, but few include them as separate, interdependent systems.

We see the value of adopting a complex adaptive system approach as potentially significant. It should lead to better policies and to more informative policy experiments in three ways: first, by recognizing that effective policies must improve communities as well as give assistance to individuals; second, by connecting economic disparities to health, educational, and social disparities and encouraging coordination; and third, by generating more support for enacting policies to reduce inequality. When people view racial inequalities as due to systemic and structural effects and not individual shortcomings, they become more likely to advocate for reform (Rucker and Richeson 2021).

We end, therefore, on an optimistic note. A greater emphasis on the complexity of inequality and how it results from systemic and structural causes across multiple, interdependent systems may not only result in deeper, more accurate understandings and better policies, it may also produce greater social support and political will to make the coordinated efforts and investments necessary to reduce inequality. ✤

Chapter 23: Complexity Theory and Economic Inequality

REFERENCES

Aaronson, D., D. Hartley, and B. Mazumder. 2021. "The Effects of the 1930s HOLC 'Redlining' Maps." *American Economic Journal: Economic Policy* 13:355–392. https://doi.org/10.1257/pol.20190414.

Acemoglu, D., S. Naidu, P. Restrepo, and J. Robinson. 2015. "Democracy, Redistribution, and Inequality." In *Handbook of Income Distribution Vol. 2,* edited by A. Atkinson and F. Bourguignon. Amsterdam, Netherlands: Elsevier. https://doi.org/10.1016/B978-0-444-59429-7.00022-4.

Agan, A., and S. Starr. 2018. "Ban the Box, Criminal Records, and Racial Discrimination: A Field Experiment." *Quarterly Journal of Economics* 133:191–235. https://doi.org/10.1093/qje/qjx028.

Akerlof, G., and R. Kranton. 2000. "Economics and Identity." *Quarterly Journal of Economics* 115 (3): 715–753. https://doi.org/10.1162/003355300554881.

———. 2002. "Identity and Schooling: Some Lessons for the Economics of Education." *Journal of Economic Literature* 40:1167–1201. https://doi.org/10.1257/002205102762203585.

Angelucci, M., and G. De Giorgi. 2009. "Indirect Effects of an Aid Program: How Do Cash Transfers Affect Ineligibles' Consumption?" *American Economic Review* 99:486–508. https://doi.org/10.1257/aer.99.1.486.

Calvó-Armengol, A., and M. Jackson. 2004. "The Effects of Social Networks on Employment and Inequality." *American Economic Review* 94:426–454. https://doi.org/10.1257/0002828041464542.

Chetty, R., N. Hendren, P. Kline, and E. Saez. 2014. "Where is the Land of Opportunity? The Geography of Intergenerational Mobility in the United States." *Quarterly Journal of Economics* 129:1553–1623. https://doi.org/10.1093/qje/qju022.

Corak, M. 2013. "Income Inequality, Equality of Opportunity, and Intergenerational Mobility." *Journal of Economic Perspectives* 27 (3): 79–102. https://doi.org/10.1257/jep.27.3.79.

De, K., R. Compton, D. Giedeman, and G. Hoover. 2021. "Macroeconomic Shocks and Racial Labor Market Differences." *Southern Economic Journal* 88:680–704. https://doi.org/10.1002/soej.12534.

Durlauf, S. 1996a. "A Theory of Persistent Income Inequality." *Journal of Economic Growth* 1:75–93. https://www.jstor.org/stable/40215882.

Durlauf, S. 1996b. "Neighborhood Feedbacks, Endogenous Stratification, and Income Inequality." In *Dynamic Disequilibrium Modelling*, edited by W. Barnett, G. Gandolfo, and C. Hillinger. New York, NY: Cambridge University Press.

———. 2002. "The Memberships Theory of Poverty: The Role of Group Affiliations In Determining Socioeconomic Outcomes." In *Understanding Poverty in America*, edited by S. Danziger and R. Haveman. Cambridge, MA: Harvard University Press. https://doi.org/10.4159/9780674030176-014.

———. 2006. "Groups, Social Influences, and Inequality: A Memberships Theory Perspective on Poverty Traps." In *Poverty Traps*, edited by S. Bowles, S. Durlauf, and K. Hoff. Princeton, NJ: Princeton University Press. https://doi.org/10.1515/9781400841295.141.

———. 2008. "Affirmative Action, Meritocracy, and Efficiency." *Politics, Philosophy & Economics* 7:131–158. https://doi.org/10.1177/1470594X08088726.

Durlauf, S., A. Kourtellos, and C. M. Tan. 2022. "The Great Gatsby Curve." *Annual Review of Economics* 14:571–605. https://doi.org/10.1146/annurev-economics-082321-122703.

Fogli, A., and V. Guerrieri. 2019. *The End of the American Dream? Inequality and Segregation in US Cities*. Working Paper 26143. National Bureau of Economic Research. https://doi.org/10.3386/w26143.

Ganong, P., D. Jones, P. Noel, D. Farrell, F. Greig, and C. Wheat. 2020. *Wealth, Race, and Consumption Smoothing of Typical Income Shocks*. Working Paper 27552. National Bureau of Economic Research, July. https://doi.org/10.3386/w27552.

Gee, G., and C. Ford. 2011. "Structural Racism and Health Inequities: Old Issues, New Directions." *Du Bois Review* 8:115–132. https://doi.org/10.1017/S1742058X11000130.

Goldin, C., and L.F. Katz. 2008. *The Race Between Education and Technology*. Cambridge, MA: Harvard University Press. https://doi.org/10.2307/j.ctvjf9x5x.

Hong, L., and S. Page. 2001. "Problem Solving by Heterogeneous Agents." *Journal of Economic Theory* 97 (1): 123–163. https://doi.org/10.1006/jeth.2000.2709.

———. 2004. "Groups of Diverse Problem Solvers Can Outperform Groups of High-Ability Problem Solvers." *Proceedings of the National Academy of Sciences* 101:16385–16389. https://doi.org/10.1073/pnas.0403723101.

Hoxby, C., and C. Avery. 2013. "The Missing 'One-Offs': The Hidden Supply of High-Achieving, Low-Income Students." *Brookings Papers on Economic Activity* 1:1–65. https://doi.org/10.3386/w18586.

Hsieh, C.-T., E. Hurst, C. Jones, and P. Klenow. 2019. "The Allocation of Talent and U.S. Economic Growth." *Econometrica* 87:1439–1474. https://doi.org/10.3982/ECTA11427.

Jayakumar, U. M., and S. E. Page. 2021. "Cultural Capital and Opportunities for Exceptionalism: Bias in University Admissions." *The Journal of Higher Education* 92 (7): 1109–1139. https://doi.org/10.1080/00221546.2021.1912554.

Johnson, P., and C. Papageorgiou. 2020. "What Remains of Cross-Country Convergence?" *Journal of Economic Literature* 58:129–175. https://doi.org/10.1257/jel.20181207.

Ladson-Billings, G., and W. Tate. 2006. *Education Research in the Public Interest: Social Justice, Action, and Policy.* New York, NY: Teachers College Press.

Last, B., G. Lawson, K. Breiner, L. Steinberg, and M. Farah. 2018. "Childhood Socioeconomic Status and Executive Function in Childhood and Beyond." *PLoS One* 13. https://doi.org/10.1371/journal.pone.0202964.

Lee, C. 2008. "The Centrality of Culture to the Scientific Study of Learning and Development: How an Ecological Framework in Education Research Facilitates Civic Responsibility." *Educational Researcher* 37:267–279. https://doi.org/10.3102/0013189X08322683.

List, J., F. Momeni, and Y. Zenou. 2019. "Are Estimates of Early Education Programs Too Pessimistic? Evidence from a Large-Scale Field Experiment that Causally Measures Neighbor Effects." *SSRN Electronic Journal,* https://doi.org/10.2139/ssrn.3385107.

Manduca, R., and R. Sampson. 2019. "Punishing and Toxic Neighborhood Environments Independently Predict the Intergenerational Social Mobility of Black and White Children." *Proceedings of The National Academy of Sciences* 116:7772–7777. https://doi.org/10.1073/pnas.1820464116.

Markovits, D. 2019. *The Meritocracy Trap.* New York, NY: Penguin.

McMillon, D. 2024a. "The Self-Reinforcing Effects of Temporary Interventions: Systems Thinking to Reduce Systemic Disadvantage." *SSRN Electronic Journal,* https://doi.org/10.2139/ssrn.4694354.

McMillon, D. 2024b. *What Makes Systemic Discrimination, 'Systemic'? Exposing the Amplifiers of Inequity.* Technical report 2403.11028. arXiv.org. https://doi.org/10.48550/arXiv.2403.11028.

McMillon, D., C. Simon, and J. Morenoff. 2014. "Modeling the Underlying Dynamics of the Spread of Crime." *PLoS One* 9. https://doi.org/10.1371/journal.pone.0088923.

Meade, J. E. 1975. *The Intelligent Radical's Guide to Economic Policy.* London, UK: George Allen & Unwin.

Okun, A. 1975. *Equality and Efficiency: The Big Tradeoff.* Washington, DC: Brookings Institution Press.

Page, S. 2011. *Diversity and Complexity.* Princeton, NJ: Princeton University Press.

———. 2017. *The Diversity Bonus.* Princeton, NJ: Princeton University Press.

———. 2018. *The Model Thinker.* New York, NY: Basic Books.

Page, S., and J. Zelner. 2020. "Population Health as a Complex Adaptive System of Systems," https://doi.org/10.1093/oso/9780190880743.003.0003.

Perkins, K., and R. Sampson. 2015. "Compounded Deprivation in the Transition to Adulthood: The Intersection of Racial and Economic Inequality among Chicagoans, 1995-2013." *RSF: The Russell Sage Foundation Journal of the Social Sciences* 1 (1): 35–54. https://doi.org/10.7758/RSF.2015.1.1.03.

Rehavi, M. M., and S. B. Starr. 2014. "Racial Disparity in Federal Criminal Sentences." *Journal of Political Economy* 122 (6): 1320–1354. https://doi.org/10.1086/677255.

Roemer, J. 2006. *Democracy, Education, and Equality.* New York, NY: Cambridge University Press.

Rothstein, R. 2017. *The Color of Law.* New York, NY: Liveright.

Rucker, J., and J. Richeson. 2021. "Toward an Understanding of Structural Racism: Implications for Criminal Justice." *Science* 374:286–290. https://doi.org/10.1126/science.abj7779.

Steele, C. 2018. "Stereotype Threat and African American Student Achievement." In *The Inequality Reader: Contemporary and Foundational Readings in Race, Class, and Gender.* New York, NY: Routledge. https://doi.org/10.4324/9780429494468-31.

Stevenson, M. 2024. "Cause, Effect, and the Structure of the Social World." *Boston University Law Review* 103:2001–2047. https://doi.org/10.2139/ssrn.4445710.

Vivalt, E., E. Rhodes, A. Bartik, D. Broockman, P. Krause, and S. Miller. 2024. *The Employment Effects of a Guaranteed Income: Experimental Evidence from Two U.S. States.* Working Paper 32719. National Bureau of Economic Research. https://doi.org/10.3386/w32719.

Wadhera, R., J. Figueroa, F. Rodriguez, M. Liu, W. Tian, D. Kazi, Y. Song, R. W. Yeh, and K. Joynt Maddox. 2021. "Racial and Ethnic Disparities in Heart and Cerebrovascular Disease Deaths During the COVID-19 Pandemic in the United States." *Circulation* 143:2346–2354. https://doi.org/10.1161/CIRCULATIONAHA.121.054378.

BEYOND EFFICIENCY: LABOR-MARKET RESILIENCE IN AN AGE OF AI AND NET ZERO

R. Maria del Rio-Chanona, University College London
and Complexity Science Hub;
Morgan R. Frank, University of Pittsburgh;
Penny Mealy, University of Oxford, Santa Fe Institute,
and Monash University;
Esteban Moro, Northeastern University
and Massachusetts Institute of Technology; and
Ljubica Nedelkoska, Complexity Science Hub and
Central European University

Abstract

The future of work is increasingly uncertain. With new technologies such as generative artificial intelligence (AI) and the transition to a green economy driving unprecedented change, workers are navigating an evolving labor market that is constantly being pushed out of equilibrium. While labor economics has traditionally emphasized the importance of labor-market efficiency, this chapter stresses the importance of analyzing the resilience of labor markets in the face of disruption. We discuss how a complexity-based approach opens up new and important avenues for studying the labor market from an evolutionary perspective, and we highlight recent work that has combined increasingly granular occupational data with network analysis, agent-based modeling, machine learning, and other techniques to provide important and policy-relevant insights into labor-market resilience. This approach is especially advantageous for modeling transition periods of significant job disruption when labor markets are constantly changing. During economic change, these models can simulate policy outcomes before they are implemented, thus offering the best opportunity to shape resilience through policy interventions.

From Efficiency to Resilience: Why Labor Markets Need Complex-Systems Thinking

Today's workforce is navigating an economy undergoing rapid transformation, driven by technological advancements and the shift toward a net-zero future.   ~281~

For some, these changes present exciting career prospects: Generative AI and large language models (LLMs) promise to automate routine tasks and boost productivity (Korinek 2024), while the green economy is expected to create numerous new jobs across a variety of sectors (Saussay *et al.* 2022). However, for others, the future of work is fraught with uncertainty. Robotics have already displaced many physical jobs in manufacturing and agriculture (Acemoglu and Restrepo 2020; Autor, Katz, and Kearney 2008; Acemoglu 2002) and even high-skill professions—such as data science, social sciences, and creative fields—are increasingly competing with sophisticated AI technologies (Eloundou *et al.* 2024; Manning, Zhu, and Horton 2024; Epstein, Hertzmann, and The Investigators of Human Creativity 2023; Teutloff *et al.* 2025). Additionally, the green transition is likely to reduce demand for workers in emissions-intensive industries, with many of their skills not easily transferable to newly created green jobs (Bücker *et al.* 2025; Lim, Aklin, and Frank 2023). In this rapidly changing landscape, critical questions arise: How should workers decide which skills to invest in? How should firms adapt their hiring strategies and manage talent? And what policies could improve overall labor market outcomes? While traditional labor economics has often prioritized market efficiency, we argue that focusing on strategies to enhance labor market resilience is increasingly crucial for today's dynamic economy.

The resilience of complex systems to disruptions has been studied in a variety of different settings. For example, network analysis and agent-based modeling have been applied to analyze the resilience of power grids, financial markets, transport networks and supply chains, and other key infrastructure systems (Vespignani 2010; Buldyrev *et al.* 2010; Caccioli *et al.* 2014; Elliott, Golub, and Jackson 2014). More recently, these approaches have been applied to predict how economic systems respond to external shocks from lockdowns during the COVID-19 pandemic (del Rio-Chanona *et al.* 2020), and the propagation of these shocks throughout the United Kingdom economy (Pichler *et al.* 2022). A follow-up study (Pangallo *et al.* 2024) further predicted the unequal effects of COVID lockdowns on employment and wages in New York City. In each of these examples, the interactions between granular elements within the system—whether person-to-person contact, inter-industry relationships, or the structure of energy networks—significantly influence the system's overall resilience to disruptions.

This chapter makes the case for applying a complex-systems approach to study the labor market and its resilience to various disruptions. The labor market exhibits several key characteristics that make it particularly well-suited for analysis through the lens of complex systems. For example, it comprises many heterogeneous and interconnected agents (e.g., workers and firms) whose interactions shape macro-level outcomes like unemployment, wage inequality and labor shortages. These agents are always adapting to changes in demand, technologies, and various economic shocks. For workers, this could mean re-skilling or switching industries, while for firms, it could entail changing their hiring strategies or business models.

Recent research has begun to lay the groundwork for a complexity-based approach to understanding how shocks and economic transformations affect labor markets. Complex-systems work pioneered breaking away from categorizing occupations and skills into broad groups (e.g., high vs. low skill or blue vs. white collar; see Acemoglu and Autor 2011) and instead used network analysis on granular data about skills and work activities to understand what enables workers to switch jobs (Alabdulkareem *et al.* 2018; Mealy, del Rio-Chanona, and Farmer 2018) and how labor demand shocks propagate through these networks to impact workers' employment (Moro *et al.* 2021; del Rio-Chanona *et al.* 2021). Network analysis also reveals skill and geographical mobility frictions (Lim, Aklin, and Frank 2023; Fair and Guerrero 2025; Berryman *et al.* 2025) that constrain job transitions during labor demand shocks. This granular approach may explain why AI automation predictions have not consistently predicted actual job displacement or unemployment increases (Frank, Ahn, and Moro 2025), since technologies typically alter tasks within jobs rather than eliminating entire occupations (Brynjolfsson and Mitchell 2017; Frank *et al.* 2019; Nedelkoska and Quintini 2018; Nedelkoska *et al.* 2021).

Beyond mapping network structures, understanding labor-market resilience requires modeling how workers and firms adapt during transitions. Recent agent-based models have advanced this by building on foundational approaches (Richiardi 2006; Dawid *et al.* 2008) while incorporating network structures to capture how unemployment outcomes depend not just on a single occupation's vulnerability to disruption, but also on the supply and demand dynamics of related occupations and regions that displaced workers could transition into (del Rio-Chanona *et al.* 2021; Fair and Guerrero 2025; Berryman *et al.* 2025). Similarly, foundational models on the firm side established realistic hiring behaviors and integration with the economy (Fagiolo, Dosi, and Gabriele 2004; Dosi *et al.* 2018).

In this chapter, we first discuss the value of taking an evolutionary perspective on the labor market, where one can analyze workers' career pathways in a similar way to species' evolutionary trajectories. In the same way that species need to adapt to changing ecological conditions, workers respond to evolving labor demands, either by switching into occupations that require similar skills to their current role,[1] or by learning new skills to remain relevant to the changing fitness landscape. With granular data on occupational characteristics and worker attributes becoming increasingly available, it is now possible to make such analogies more empirically grounded and leverage analytical techniques from evolutionary biology to glean new insights on the evolution of the labor market.

Second, we emphasize the importance of being able to study and analyze out-of-equilibrium dynamics in the labor market. Traditional labor and macroeconomic models often struggle to capture these dynamics, but agent-based models offer a more flexible and natural framework for analyzing them. We discuss recent advances in this area, highlighting their applicability to modeling the impact of key technological and climate-related shocks on the labor market.

Third, we consider what the application of a complex-systems approach to the labor market means from a causality perspective. When considering policy applications of research on labor market resilience, being able to identify causal mechanisms is often important. While on the one hand, causality is difficult to identify in complex systems in general, on the other hand,

---

[1] For a more in-depth discussion of how capabilities and the principle of relatedness affect countries and workers' development, see Frank Neffke *et al.* 2026, ch. 7 in this volume.

greater availability of granular data, improved computational power, and advances in machine learning are opening up new avenues for causal inference. We discuss both the obstacles and the new opportunities for identifying causal relationships relevant to the labor market, emphasizing how these developments can help address the well-known limitations of traditional methods such as randomized controlled trials.

Finally, we conclude with a reflection on both the challenges and exciting possibilities that advancing a complexity-based research agenda on labor-market resilience is likely to entail. Much can be gained by leveraging increasingly available granular datasets and applying data-science and machine-learning tools to uncover patterns in these large datasets. Additionally, we highlight the potential for fine-grained calibration of agent-based models and incorporating insights from behavioral economics. We also emphasize the importance of causal inference and closer collaboration with labor economists and policymakers in guiding just and inclusive transitions. All these opportunities rely on new data, advanced statistical methods, and emerging areas of research, making developments in complexity economics particularly promising for labor markets.

An Evolutionary Approach to the Labor Market

Granular labor data and a complexity approach empower an analogy between workers' career trajectories and species' evolutionary trajectories. Workers' skills, preferences, and social connections act as the unobservable genetic material—the genotype—that underlies their career development (see fig. 1a). These professional attributes shape individuals' abilities, guiding their growth and potential just as genes guide a species' characteristics and biological fitness. The career mobility and job transition rates then represent the phenotypes—the observable outcomes of those underlying "genetic" factors (see fig. 1b). In typical analysis, job transitions become the career equivalents of a species' observable traits, like an animal's fur color or a plant's height. Evolution in nature occurs through the gradual adaptation and change in genetic compositions, while career evolution happens through the acquisition and honing of skills, gaining experience, and building networks. The labor market environment *selects* among groups with different phenotypes based on desirable observable performance, resulting in successful phenotypes (here career trajectories) being retained and proliferated.[2]

However, recent advances in social-media data and wide-ranging skill data enable researchers to quantify labor genotypes directly. Research has focused on either phenotypic labor dynamics or genotypic labor factors but connecting the two could improve labor market predictions, elucidate worker adaptability, and reveal the resilience of labor markets to economic shocks. Complexity affords the ability to model interactions both within each abstraction as well as between abstractions (e.g., skill complementarity is a within-genotype interaction). The challenges have been tracking individuals' careers over time and measuring skills directly. While reskilling and upskilling are theoretical mechanisms for adaptation, job transitions are the manifestation of adaptations and are easier to measure through large cross-sectional surveys (vom Lehn, Ellsworth, and Kroff 2022; Neffke, Nedelkoska, and Wiederhold 2024). In contrast, skills are amorphous and do not correspond to events, but are usually observed through job descriptions or expert surveys (e.g., O*NET or the German BIBB/BAuA).

---

[2] This way of thinking is akin to the neo-Schumpeterian thinking in economics, where firms' collective routines are metaphorically referred to as genotypes, and their observable behavior on the market as phenotypes (Dosi, Nelson, and Winter 2000; Witt 2008).

a. Genotypes

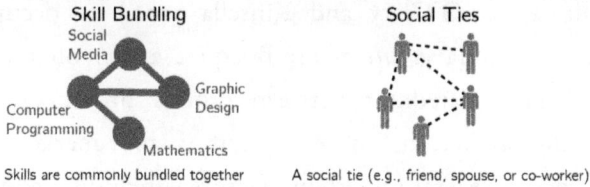

Skill Bundling

Social Ties

Social Media

Computer Programming

Graphic Design

Mathematics

Skills are commonly bundled together

A social tie (e.g., friend, spouse, or co-worker)

b. Phenotypes

Career Mobility

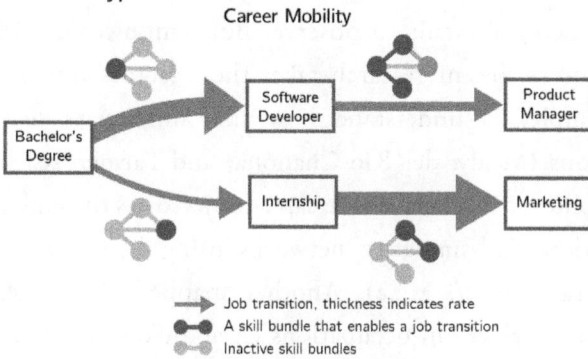

Bachelor's Degree

Software Developer

Product Manager

Internship

Marketing

⟶ Job transition, thickness indicates rate

● A skill bundle that enables a job transition

● Inactive skill bundles

c.

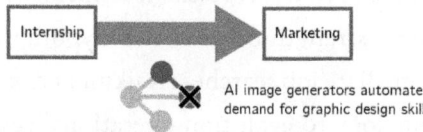

Internship

Marketing

AI image generators automate demand for graphic design skill

d.

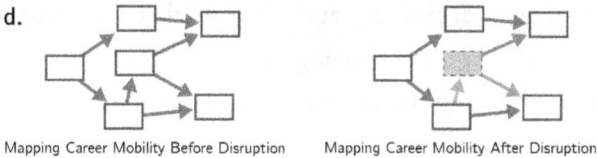

Mapping Career Mobility Before Disruption

Mapping Career Mobility After Disruption

Figure 1. Mapping the genotypes and phenotypes of labor. (a) Workers' skills, preferences, and social connections act as the genetic material—the genotype—that underlies their career development. These professional attributes shape individuals' abilities, guiding their growth and potential just as genes guide a species' characteristics and biological fitness. (b) The career mobility and job transition rates then represent the phenotypes—the observable characteristics or outcomes of those underlying "genetic" factors. (c) Disruptions to genotypes can reshape phenotypic outcomes. For example, automating skills with technology might impact how workers use their skills to progress their career. (d) In large disruptions, the removal of career pathways and/or occupations can reshape career mobility, thus leaving some workers isolated from opportunities they may have had previously.

Job transitions (e.g, between industries; see Neffke and Henning 2013; O'Clery and Kinsella 2022) or occupations (del Rio-Chanona *et al.* 2021; Bocquet 2022) offer a proxy for the skill relatedness between groups of workers while prioritizing prediction and description of labor markets as they are. However, several underlying factors—including education, skills, and social connections—shape these career outcomes despite being difficult to observe. But, empowered with new data sources, recent research takes these factors into account, for example, to understand how skill differences shape job transitions (Mealy, del Rio-Chanona, and Farmer 2018). One study followed workers' entire career trajectories through a city's occupation skill-similarity networks using large-scale résumé data (Frank *et al.* 2024). Another mapped the patterns of skill bundling within occupations (Alabdulkareem *et al.* 2018; Aufiero *et al.* 2024). Other research confirmed Mark Granovetter's longstanding strength-of-weak-ties hypothesis describing how social ties mediate job searches (Rajkumar *et al.* 2022).

This analogy to evolution operationalizes key concepts that shape workers' adaptability and labor market resilience. Just as species must adapt to changing ecological conditions, workers respond to changing labor demands. In cases of persistent change (e.g., due to technology or global trade), workers learn new skills to remain relevant (e.g., through reskilling)—similar to changes in a species' genetic makeup over long periods of time (see fig. 1c). However, technological change does not uniformly reshape skill demands across occupations; instead, it can simultaneously make some expertise more valuable while rendering other expertise obsolete, creating a "bifurcation" in the evolutionary fitness landscape of skills (Autor and Thompson 2025). In cases of sudden disruption (e.g., a global pandemic or a housing-market crash), disrupted workers must use their existing skills and labor-market conditions to find their next employment opportunity—similar to how organisms respond in real time to a natural disaster rather than a multigenerational genetic evolution. Many concepts from evolutionary biology have analogies in the labor market and are now measurable. For example, mapping the "mutualism" between occupations or firms in a local economy based on skill relatedness (see fig. 1d; Moro *et al.* 2021). Or, certain occupations may act as "keystone species" that are necessary in a labor market to support the existence of other occupations (e.g., information technology consultants, police, baristas); recent research (Hong *et al.* 2020) suggests that United States cities recapitulate predictable patterns of industrial development where specific occupations act as stepping stones toward other occupations. Advances in text embeddings now allow researchers to measure the expertise requirements of different occupational tasks (Autor and Thompson 2025).

Modeling cities as labor markets offers an analogy to ecosystems whose resources shape and limit employment levels according to the systems' carrying capacity. As epicenters of our economy, geographical labor markets centered about urban areas play an increasing role in our economy. Only ten countries in the world (including, of course, the United States) have a larger GDP than the New York City area. Large cities lead to more job opportunities in aggregate but also by specialization, creating more skilled jobs. This creates a thicker labor market, where workers can easily transition to new jobs, acquire new skills, and adapt to economic shocks. But excessive specialization in medium-to-small cities can create less resilient job markets, where workers in a particular sector or industry might find no similar jobs to transition to after an automation or economic shock (Moro *et al.* 2021). Even within large cities, not all workers benefit from the "city" effect. Jobs and learning opportunities are not equally distributed around urban areas, and low-income and less-skilled workers traditionally live in areas with reduced access to those job opportunities (Shen 1998), which makes them more vulnerable to unemployment shocks or less-skilled jobs (Autor 2019).

This analogy between careers and biological evolution is helpful for explaining why recent granular data will enable advances in labor economics. But the analogy is not perfect. First, our focus on skills and social connections misses many other "genotypes" that shape career outcomes. For example, structural biases in society and the economy shape hiring decisions independent of these factors and can mediate the career success of truly "fit" individuals. However, we believe that continued analysis and use of newly available skills data can actually combat some bias. For example, employers could use objective measures of workers' abilities in hiring decisions. Second, skills and social ties are themselves the outcomes of other functions. For example, workers with a college education have distinctive skills from those who do not. Similarly, social ties are heavily influenced by where a person grew up. Still, skills and social ties have historically been treated as unobservable features in labor economics, but they are now observable through new large-scale data. As similar large-scale data emerge, reflecting the functions that cause skills and social ties (e.g., data on skills taught across college majors and universities), and new data-science and machine-learning tools enable us to study these datasets, the present list of labor genotypes will need to expand and new insights into career mobility will surely be revealed.

Modeling Adaptation Dynamics in Labor Market Transitions

Granular data and tools like network analysis allow us to map the landscape of skills (Alabdulkareem *et al.* 2018; Mealy, del Rio-

Chanona, and Farmer 2018; Teutloff *et al.* 2025)—essentially, the playing board of the labor market. To understand how the net-zero transition, new technologies, and policies will affect employment and wages, we need to define the rules of the game and how players move through time—this is where modeling comes in. We argue that agent-based models have the flexibility to capture two critical elements: realistic behavioral rules and dynamic time steps that allow for path dependence. [3]

Figure 2 illustrates why these two elements matter. Traditional equilibrium models (a) assume agents optimize intertemporally—making decisions once while perfectly anticipating all future conditions and others' responses. Workers and firms instantly adjust to shocks, jumping from one equilibrium to another. In contrast, agent-based models (b) incorporate bounded rationality, where agents use simple heuristics and myopic decision-making at discrete time steps. Workers might follow rules like "If the job pays enough and I have the skills, take it," while firms adjust hiring based on recent demand patterns rather than perfect foresight.

In figure 2a, the economy is initially in equilibrium—no agent (worker, investor, or employer) has an incentive to deviate from their chosen action. A shock—a rapid improvement in the dark gray technology—causes all agents to re-optimize simultaneously, each anticipating the others' best responses, as depicted by the individuals computing equations and circular arrows. The economy then shifts from the original equilibrium (dominated by light gray technology) to a new equilibrium (dominated by dark gray technology). In figure 2b, agents update decisions over discrete time steps using heuristics and boundedly rational rules. As the dark gray technology advances quickly (time = 2), that sector sees some growth but is constrained by a lack of sufficiently

---

[3] Another related and flexible approach is microsimulation, which is discussed in more detail in Richiardi and van de Ven (2026, ch. 8 in this volume)

skilled workers, while some light gray–sector workers may be displaced. By time = 3, workers begin acquiring new skills, which in turn spurs investment in the improving technology. Eventually (time = T), the workforce and technology align, and the dark gray sector expands accordingly.

Figure 2c shows why these modeling differences matter for policy. The left-hand panel captures changes in unemployment and vacancies by transitioning from one equilibrium state to another, while the panel on the right reveals how agent-based models trace gradual adjustment paths where skill mismatches temporarily raise both unemployment and vacancies. Although this example shows the two approaches converging to a similar endpoint, path dependence can fundamentally alter outcomes. For instance, during a net-zero energy transition, temporary high unemployment could prompt social or political shifts that change the entire policy trajectory, leading to a change of government and preventing any return to the intended equilibrium. Feedback loops also affect optimal policy choices, as demand for AI-related skills grows (Teutloff *et al.* 2025), workers contribute to AI improvement through open-source software and usage data that trains these systems, creating continuous co-evolution between technology and workforce capabilities. This ongoing adaptation may result in static, one-time training programs insufficient as they cannot account for how today's skill investments shape tomorrow's technology development.

Several works have paved the way for building labor-market agent-based models (Neugart and Richiardi 2018). For example, Jean-Daniel Kant, Gérard Ballot, and Olivier Goudet (2020) model firms that predict demand with a limited horizon, using these predictions to set job vacancy levels. Similarly, in Giovanni Dosi *et al.* (2018), firms adjust their hiring practices based on demand expectations and current productivity, while, in del Rio-

a. Equilibrium & Comparative Statics

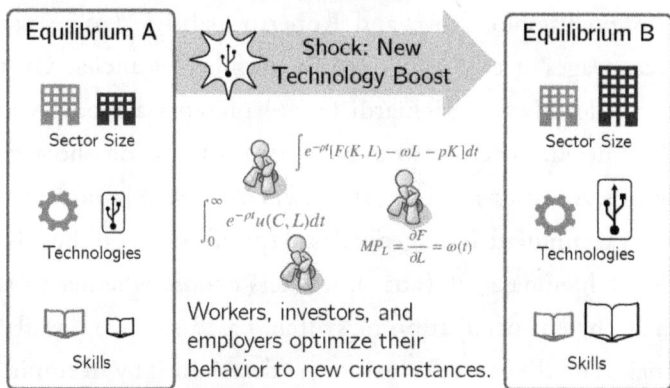

Equilibrium A

Shock: New Technology Boost

Sector Size

Technologies

Skills

$$\int e^{-\rho t}[F(K,L) - \omega L - pK]dt$$

$$\int_0^\infty e^{-\rho t} u(C,L)dt$$

$$MP_L = \frac{\partial F}{\partial L} = \omega(t)$$

Workers, investors, and employers optimize their behavior to new circumstances.

Equilibrium B

Sector Size

Technologies

Skills

~293~

b. Agent-Based Modeling

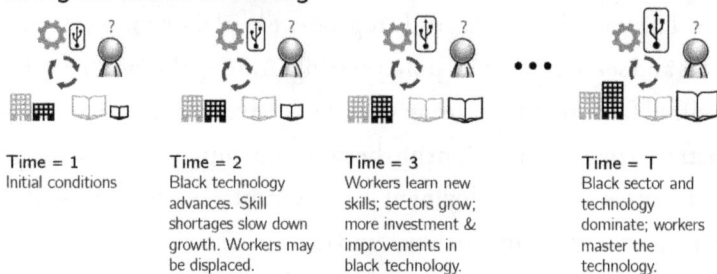

Time = 1
Initial conditions

Time = 2
Black technology advances. Skill shortages slow down growth. Workers may be displaced.

Time = 3
Workers learn new skills; sectors grow; more investment & improvements in black technology.

Time = T
Black sector and technology dominate; workers master the technology.

c. Example: Beveridge Curve

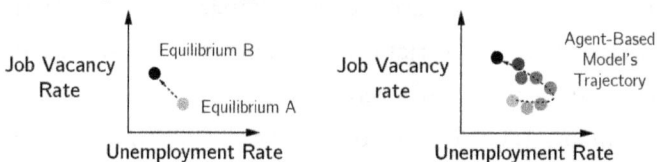

Job Vacancy Rate

Equilibrium B

Equilibrium A

Unemployment Rate

Job Vacancy rate

Agent-Based Model's Trajectory

Unemployment Rate

Figure 2. Illustration of equilibrium and agent-based modeling approaches. We consider a simplified two-sector economy denoted by buildings of different shades. Each sector benefits from its own technology (shown by gears and electronics) and employs a specialized workforce (represented by books). The size of each building denotes sector output, the size of the technology icons indicates capabilities, and the volume of books corresponds to the number of workers proficient in that technology. We examine how the economy responds to a sudden boost in the dark gray technology.

Chanona *et al.* (2021), firms adapt sluggishly to external factors like automation. Wage dynamics have also been modeled without assuming global utility or profit maximization. Instead, firms in Giorgio Fagiolo, Dosi, and Roberto Gabriele (2004; 2008) increase wages at each time step for unfilled vacancies. On the worker side, Matteo Richiardi (2006) presents a model where workers decide whether to apply for jobs based on short-term trade-offs. Additionally, Herbert Dawid *et al.* (2008) consider how workers accumulate both general and specific skills on the job. In del Rio-Chanona *et al.* (2021), workers choose whether to stay in their current occupation or switch, based solely on available vacancies and the ease of transition, as determined by an empirical network of job transitions covering hundreds of occupations.

These models successfully reproduce key labor-market stylized facts and serve as tools for policy testing. Among the most common stylized facts are the wage curve and the Beveridge curve, which illustrate a negative relationship between unemployment and wages, and between unemployment and vacancy rates, respectively (Richiardi 2006; Fagiolo, Dosi, and Gabriele 2004; Dosi *et al.* 2018). By modeling job-mobility frictions through networks, Robert L. Axtell, Omar A. Guerrero, and Eduardo López (2019) demonstrated that these frictions can shift the Beveridge curve outward, leading to higher levels of both unfilled vacancies and unemployment. Agent-based models have also contributed to ongoing debates about the counter-clockwise cyclicity of the Beveridge curve, often observed during "jobless recoveries" when unemployment remains high for a given vacancy rate after a crisis. For example, del Rio-Chanona *et al.* (2021) showed that focusing on time-step adaptation dynamics rather than comparative statics[4] can explain this phenomenon without assuming that work-

---

[4] Comparative statics analyzes changes in equilibrium outcomes resulting from different initial conditions, policy scenarios, or shocks.

ers adjust to economic changes within just one month (Michaillat and Saez 2021) [5]; J. Doyne Farmer (2024) is studying this phenomenon further. On a broader scale, studies have integrated labor market search models with macroeconomic models, reproducing a wider range of stylized facts (Dosi *et al.* 2018). These models are also practical for policy testing, including policies related to hiring and firing flexibility, temporary contracts, production-based layoffs, increasing-protection work contracts (Dosi *et al.* 2018), minimum wage (Dosi and Virgillito 2024), and retraining programs (Neugart 2008; del Rio-Chanona *et al.* 2021).

While these models provide a foundation, opportunities remain to integrate behavioral economics literature and enhance out-of-sample forecasting ability. Existing ABMs often incorporate bounded rationality, drawing on Herbert Simon's concepts of satisficing and myopic forecasts. However, experimental and empirical research offer new insights into worker and firm behavior. Laboratory simulations of firm-vacancy postings demonstrate the emergence of the Beveridge curve and the tendency to underpost vacancies (Duffy and Jenkins 2024). Experiments reveal how wage announcements influence job search, sometimes resulting in fewer applications for higher-paying jobs perceived as more competitive (Belot, Kircher, and Muller 2022). Studies document how search behavior—including reservation wages, commute choices, and job search effort—varies by gender, race, and age (McGee and McGee 2025; Le Barbanchon, Rathelot, and Roulet 2021; Pager and Pedulla 2015). Workers' willingness to retrain is influenced by risk preferences and perceptions (Caliendo *et al.* 2023; Innocenti and Golin 2022). While most labor-market ABMs rely on reproducing stylized facts for validation, advances in modeling techniques and data

---

[5] This assumption contrasts with research suggesting that adaptation times are closer to ten months (Bocquet 2022).

availability now allow for more robust validation through out-of-sample forecasting. As discussed in the next section, this approach provides stronger validation of causality, which is crucial for policymaking.

Causal Inference in Complex Labor Markets

Designing policies that help labor markets adapt to the net-zero transition and new technologies is by nature a causal question, but detecting causality in complex systems presents unique empirical challenges (Wagner 1999).

Complex systems exhibit a high degree of interconnectedness, which makes it difficult to isolate the effect of a single variable. For one, the number of relevant variables affecting a phenomenon of interest—and the number of relevant interactions between them—may be large. Simple evaluations of causal effects, which ignore the complex multilayer structure of labor markets, are bound to miss spillover effects or hidden treatments (Rothstein and von Wachter 2017). For example, data aggregation can mask subgroup effects on employment, skill restructuring, and wages in labor market studies (Card 1990). Simple causal studies can fail to reach causal identification in the presence of omitted-variable bias (Dippel et al. 2017). The most common approaches to studying causality in complex systems broadly fall into two groups: statistical inference and ABMs.

Statistical inference uses econometrics, including, more recently, machine learning (ML). Larger availability of granular data, increases in computational power, and the advent of ML have enabled these approaches to better identify causal effects on the labor market. In the case of statistical inference, a plethora of new methods emerged in recent decades, including behavioral experiments, synthetic controls, instrumental variable methods, difference-in-difference, and regression discontinuity, among others (Thaler 2016; Abadie 2021; Angrist and Pischke 2009). Most recently, scholars have successfully integrated machine learning into more standard econometrics, in methods such as causal forests (Davis and Heller 2017) or regression discontinuity with LASSO (Kreiss and Rothe 2023). Each of these methods has specific advantages in addressing endogeneity issues. Randomized control trials (RCTs) and behavioral experiments reduce the number of potential confounders by controlling the environment in which a treatment is applied. Instrumental variable methods parse the identifying variation of the system into an exogenous and endogenous part. Machine-learning methods bring about several new advantages in causal identification. Double or debiased machine learning can control for a large number of covariates without overfitting (Chernozhukov *et al.* 2018; Knaus 2022). All ML methods allow for more flexible functional forms, avoiding biases commonly induced by fitting simple functions (Hernán 2021). ML methods have also greatly advanced our ability to estimate heterogeneous effects—conditional, individualized, personalized average treatment (Knaus, Lechner, and Strittmatter 2021; Knaus 2022; Nie and Wager 2021).

At the same time, ABMs have unique advantages for the study of complex systems, that observational approaches have a hard time addressing. ABMs can model emerging macro-level behavior (e.g., unemployment and vacancy rates (del Rio-Chanona *et al.* 2021) or wage inflation (Fagiolo, Dosi, and Gabriele 2004) from micro-level interactions of heterogeneous agents (employees, job seekers, consumers, firms; see Neugart and Richiardi 2018). They can model feedback loops, where agent behavior impacts labor-market outcomes, and where labor-market outcomes, in turn, impact agent behavior (Farmer and Foley 2009; Pangallo *et al.* 2024). Such models can help us better understand two-way causality—a phenomenon that is hard to tackle in causal modeling. The growing availability of data allows for increasingly better calibration of ABMs (see Pangallo and del Rio-Chanona 2026, ch. 10 in this volume), expanding the possibilities of their validation and their relevance for real-world complex systems.

When it comes to studying causality in the labor-market context, recent and future progress is threefold: First, more data about the dynamics of skills, jobs, sectors, and cities in the presence of shocks allow us to gain better understanding of the complex structure of the market, and help us design better experiments and interventions, and better detect counterfactuals in quasi-experimental designs (Rothstein and von Wachter 2017; Abadie 2021). Similar to the study of systems with network spillovers, such as experiments in social networks, causal inference in labor markets can employ techniques suited for network experiments (Aral 2016; Rajkumar *et al.* 2022).

Second, more granular data, and its combination with ML methods can help researchers study effect heterogeneity much better. Groups of different socio-demographic background or geography all have different skills, jobs, and educational levels. This is extremely important for policy. One reason why traditional labor-market studies are of limited use for public policy is because the estimated effects are for an average individual, an individual who is seldom found in the real world. Today, however, we are much better positioned to study the effects on people with various socio-demographic characteristics.

Finally, methodological advancements and the availability of granular data at the individual level help us learn more from natural experiments or quasi-experimental designs in contrast to RCTs and lab experiments. We can now expand the causal analysis of interventions when lab experiments or RCTs cannot be designed. In most labor-market situations, conducting RCTs is not possible due to ethical concerns, significant costs, or time limitations. RCTs can also only answer a limited set of questions that can comply with controlled environments. New statistical and ML techniques developed recently have transformed those methods into tools that substitute and complement RCTs in labor markets (Ceritoglu *et al.* 2017; Hirvonen, Stenhammar, and Tuhkuri 2022), increasing the relative value of quasi-experimental designs.

Outlook and Challenges in Complexity Labor Economics

The transition to new technologies and a net-zero economy will significantly reshape the labor market. While these shifts can boost productivity and create better jobs, ensuring an inclusive and equitable transition requires strengthening labor-market resilience and supporting workers' adaptation. By leveraging granular data, simulation, and econometric tools, complexity economics can assess policy interventions that strengthen resilience and promote inclusive development pathways for workers.

Looking ahead, the growing availability of new data sources and advanced analytical tools presents significant opportunities for understanding labor-market disruptions and adaptation. Real-time data from online labor markets (Kässi and Lehdonvirta 2018; Teutloff *et al.* 2025), such as job postings (Das *et al.* 2020) and résumés (Frank *et al.* 2024), offer faster information compared to traditional government statistics. Similarly, social-media data can help track intangible factors, such as the role of work-related stress in the rise of job quits during the Great Resignation (del Rio-Chanona *et al.* 2023). To fully capitalize on these developments, future research in complexity economics should focus on harnessing large datasets using machine-learning and data-science techniques such as networks, graph neural networks, and natural language processing. These tools hold the potential to reveal hidden structures in labor-market dynamics, providing a more detailed description of the labor market, increasing chances for predictive models and designing effective policy interventions.

Agent-based models can leverage the complexity of granular data, building on empirical networks and data-driven high-dimensional spaces to capture worker adaptation dynamics. While they sacrifice the mathematical tractability of equilibrium models, agent-based models offer a complementary tool to study transition paths. However, there is still room for improvements in calibration and initialization methods specifically tailored for these models could increase their reliability in policy applications. Few agent-based models have been validated through out-of-sample predictions, which limits their reliability for policy assessments. Furthermore, while many models incorporate basic behavioral rules like satisficing, few reflect recent insights from behavioral economics. Addressing these gaps would strengthen agent-based models for evaluating policy interventions, making them more effective tools for labor-market analysis and policy evaluation.

Complexity economics can benefit from integrating advanced econometric tools to address causal questions in complex systems, accounting for interactions among various factors. Advances in machine learning can aid in this by enabling causal inference in networked complex systems with many variables, thus offering one potential pathway forward. In turn, labor economics should balance the need for specific causal insights (e.g., the value of education) with a holistic approach to modeling labor markets, particularly during disruptions. While traditional economics has provided valuable insights into structural transformations and is becoming more empirical (Angrist *et al.* 2017), it often struggles when disruptions push labor markets out of equilibrium. To guide effective policy during these times, labor economics must shift from analyzing isolated economic factors to modeling the entire system to predict labor outcomes, even if the roles of individual factors remain unclear. This transition requires collaboration among complexity researchers, labor economists, and policymakers, along with equipping future researchers with tools for studying causal inference in equilibrium and modeling market adaptations in nonequilibrium situations.

AI and climate change create unprecedented labor-market challenges that require new analytical approaches. Complexity economics is uniquely positioned to address these disruptions, as the same technological advances that reshape work also provide better tools for understanding it. The rapid development of AI, while disrupting traditional employment, generates vast amounts of real-time data about skills, transitions, and adaptation patterns. Combined with growing computational power and machine-learning techniques, these data enable better modeling of labor-market dynamics. The expanding field of behavioral economics provides additional insights into how workers and firms actually make decisions during transitions. Each advancement in these areas—data availability, computational methods, and behavioral understanding—enhances our ability to model feedback loops, path dependence, and adaptation in real time. As workers navigate an economy in constant flux, complexity economics offers the tools to understand not just where markets might settle, but how to guide them through the turbulent paths between equilibria. The challenge now is developing these approaches quickly enough to inform the policy decisions shaping the transitions already underway. 🌿

Acknowledgments

We would like to thank Stefania Inoccenti and Ebba Mark for discussions on behavioral economics and Labor economics.

REFERENCES

Abadie, A. 2021. "Using Synthetic Controls: Feasibility, Data Requirements, and Methodological Aspects." *Journal of Economic Literature* 59 (2): 391–425. https://doi.org/10.1257/jel.20191450.

Acemoglu, D. 2002. "Technical Change, Inequality, and the Labor Market." *Journal of Economic Literature* 40 (1): 7–72. https : / / doi . org / 10 . 1257 / 0022051026976.

Acemoglu, D., and D. Autor. 2011. "Skills, Tasks, and Technologies: Implications for Employment and Earnings." In *Handbook of Labor Economics,* edited by D. Card and O. Ashenfelter, vol. 4B, 1043–1171. Amsterdam, Netherlands: North Holland. https://doi.org/10.1016/S0169-7218(11)02410-5.

Acemoglu, D., and P. Restrepo. 2020. "Robots and Jobs: Evidence from US Labor Markets." *Journal of Political Economy* 128 (6): 2188–2244. https://doi.org/10.1086/705716.

Alabdulkareem, A., M. R. Frank, L. Sun, B. AlShebli, C. Hidalgo, and I. Rahwan. 2018. "Unpacking the Polarization of Workplace Skills." *Science Advances* 4 (7). https://doi.org/10.1126/sciadv.aao6030.

Angrist, J., P. Azoulay, G. Ellison, R. Hill, and S. F. Lu. 2017. "Economic Research Evolves: Fields and Styles." *American Economic Review* 107 (5): 293–297. https://doi.org/10.1257/aer.p20171117.

Angrist, J. D., and J.-S. Pischke. 2009. *Mostly Harmless Econometrics: An Empiricist's Companion.* Princeton, NJ: Princeton University Press.

Aral, S. 2016. "Networked Experiments." In *The Oxford Handbook of the Economics of Networks,* edited by Y. Bramoullé, A. Galeotti, and B. W. Rogers, 376–411. New York, NY: Oxford University Press.

Aufiero, S., G. De Marzo, A. Sbardella, and A. Zaccaria. 2024. "Mapping Job Fitness and Skill Coherence into Wages: An Economic Complexity Analysis." *Scientific Reports* 14 (1): 11752. https://doi.org/10.1038/s41598-024-61448-x.

Autor, D., and N. Thompson. 2025. "Expertise." *Journal of the European Economic Association* 23 (4): 1203–1271. https://doi.org/10.1093/jeea/jvaf023.

Autor, D. H. 2019. "Work of the Past, Work of the Future." *AEA Papers and Proceedings* 109:1–32. https://doi.org/10.1257/pandp.20191110.

Autor, D. H., L. F. Katz, and M. S. Kearney. 2008. "Trends in US Wage Inequality: Revising the Revisionists." *The Review of Economics and Statistics* 90 (2): 300–323. https://doi.org/10.1162/rest.90.2.300.

Axtell, R. L., O. A. Guerrero, and E. López. 2019. "Frictional Unemployment on Labor Flow Networks." *Journal of Economic Behavior & Organization* 160:184–201. https://doi.org/10.1016/j.jebo.2019.02.028.

Belot, M., P. Kircher, and P. Muller. 2022. "How Wage Announcements Affect Job Search—A Field Experiment." *American Economic Journal: Macroeconomics* 14 (4): 1–67. https://doi.org/10.1257/mac.20200116.

Berryman, A. K., J. Bücker, F. S. de Moura, P. Barbrook-Johnson, M. Hanusch, P. Mealy, J. D. Farmer, and R. M. del Rio-Chanona. 2025. *Skill and Spatial Mismatches for Sustainable Development in Brazil.* ArXiv preprint:2503.05310. https://doi.org/10.48550/arXiv.2503.05310.

Bocquet, L. 2022. "The Network Origin of Slow Labor Reallocation." PSE Working Papers No. 2022-17. https://shs.hal.science/halshs-03703862.

Brynjolfsson, E., and T. Mitchell. 2017. "What Can Machine Learning Do? Workforce Implications." *Science* 358 (6370): 1530–1534. https://doi.org/10.1126/science.aap8062.

Bücker, J., R. M. del Rio-Chanona, A. Pichler, M. C. Ives, and J. D. Farmer. 2025. "Employment Dynamics in a Rapid Decarbonization of the US Power Sector." *Joule* 9 (2): 101803. https://doi.org/10.1016/j.joule.2024.12.004.

Buldyrev, S. V., R. Parshani, G. Paul, H. E. Stanley, and S. Havlin. 2010. "Catastrophic Cascade of Failures in Interdependent Networks." *Nature* 464 (7291): 1025–1028. https://doi.org/10.1038/nature08932.

Caccioli, F., M. Shrestha, C. Moore, and J. D. Farmer. 2014. "Stability Analysis of Financial Contagion Due to Overlapping Portfolios." *Journal of Banking & Finance* 46:233–245. https://doi.org/10.1016/j.jbankfin.2014.05.021.

Caliendo, M., D. A. Cobb-Clark, C. Obst, and A. Uhlendorff. 2023. "Risk Preferences and Training Investments." *Journal of Economic Behavior & Organization* 205:668–686. https://doi.org/10.1016/j.jebo.2022.11.024.

Card, D. 1990. "The Impact of the Mariel Boatlift on the Miami Labor Market." *ILR Review* 43 (2): 245–257. https://doi.org/10.2307/2523702.

Ceritoglu, E., H. B. Gurcihan Yunculer, H. Torun, and S. Tumen. 2017. "The Impact of Syrian Refugees on Natives' Labor Market Outcomes in Turkey: Evidence from a Quasi-Experimental Design." *IZA Journal of Labor Policy* 6:1–28. https://doi.org/10.1186/s40173-017-0082-4.

Chernozhukov, V., D. Chetverikov, M. Demirer, E. Duflo, C. Hansen, W. Newey, and J. Robins. 2018. "Double/Debiased Machine Learning for Treatment and Structural Parameters." *The Econometrics Journal* 21 (1): C1–C68. https://doi.org/10.1111/ectj.12097.

Das, S., S. Steffen, W. Clarke, P. Reddy, E. Brynjolfsson, and M. Fleming. 2020. "Learning Occupational Task-Shares Dynamics for the Future of Work." In *Proceedings of the AAAI/ACM Conference on AI, Ethics, and Society*, 36–42. Washington, DC: AAAI Press.

Davis, J. M. V., and S. B. Heller. 2017. "Using Causal Forests to Predict Treatment Heterogeneity: An Application to Summer Jobs." *American Economic Review* 107 (5): 546–550. https://doi.org/10.1257/aer.p20171000.

Dawid, H., S. Gemkow, P. Harting, K. Kabus, M. Neugart, and K. Wersching. 2008. "Skills, Innovation, and Growth: An Agent-Based Policy Analysis." *Jahrbücher für Nationalökonomie und Statistik* 228 (2-3): 251–275. https://doi.org/10.1515/jbnst-2008-2-307.

del Rio-Chanona, R. M., A. Hermida-Carrillo, M. Sepahpour-Fard, L. Sun, R. Topinkova, and L. Nedelkoska. 2023. "Mental Health Concerns Precede Quits: Shifts in the Work Discourse During the Covid-19 Pandemic and Great Resignation." *EPJ Data Science* 12 (1): 49. https://doi.org/10.1140/epjds/s13688-023-00417-2.

del Rio-Chanona, R. M., P. Mealy, M. Beguerisse-Díaz, F. Lafond, and J. D. Farmer. 2021. "Occupational Mobility and Automation: A Data-Driven Network Model." *Journal of The Royal Society Interface* 18 (174): 20200898. https://doi.org/10.1098/rsif.2020.0898.

del Rio-Chanona, R. M., P. Mealy, A. Pichler, F. Lafond, and J. D. Farmer. 2020. "Supply and Demand Shocks in the COVID-19 Pandemic: An Industry and Occupation Perspective." *Oxford Review of Economic Policy* 36 (Supplement_1): S94–S137. https://doi.org/10.1093/oxrep/graa033.

Dippel, C., R. Gold, S. Heblich, and R. Pinto. 2017. *Instrumental Variables and Causal Mechanisms: Unpacking the Effect of Trade on Workers and Voters.* Technical report. Working Paper 23209. National Bureau of Economic Research. https://doi.org/10.3386/w23209.

Dosi, G., R. R. Nelson, and S. G. Winter. 2000. *The Nature and Dynamics of Organizational Capabilities.* Oxford, UK: Oxford University Press.

Dosi, G., M. C. Pereira, A. Roventini, and M. E. Virgillito. 2018. "The Effects of Labour Market Reforms upon Unemployment and Income Inequalities: An Agent-Based Model." *Socio-Economic Review* 16 (4): 687–720. https://doi.org/10.1093/ser/mwx054.

Dosi, G., and M. E. Virgillito. 2024. "Minimum Wage for Italy: From Social Justice to Productive Efficiency." *Intereconomics* 59 (4): 231–235. https://www.intereconomics.eu/contents/year/2024/number/4/article/minimum-wage-for-italy-from-social-justice-to-productive-efficiency.html.

Duffy, J., and B. C. Jenkins. 2024. "Search, Unemployment, and the Beveridge Curve: Experimental Evidence." *Labour Economics* 87:102518. https://doi.org/10.1016/j.labeco.2024.102518.

Elliott, M., B. Golub, and M. O. Jackson. 2014. "Financial Networks and Contagion." *American Economic Review* 104 (10): 3115–3153. https://doi.org/10.1257/aer.104.10.3115.

Eloundou, T., S. Manning, P. Mishkin, and D. Rock. 2024. "GPTs are GPTs: An Early Look at the Labor Market Impact Potential of Large Language Models." *Science* 384 (6702): 1306–1308. https://doi.org/10.1126/science.adj0998.

Epstein, Z., A. Hertzmann, and The Investigators of Human Creativity. 2023. "Art and the Science of Generative AI." *Science* 380 (6650): 1110–1111. https://doi.org/10.1126/science.adh4451.

Fagiolo, G., G. Dosi, and R. Gabriele. 2004. "Matching, Bargaining, and Wage Setting in an Evolutionary Model of Labor Market and Output Dynamics." In *Advances in Complex Systems,* 7:157–186. 02. Singapore: World Scientific.

Fair, K. R., and O. A. Guerrero. 2025. "Endogenous Labour Flow Networks." *EPJ Data Science* 14 (1): 39. https://doi.org/10.1140/epjds/s13688-025-00539-9.

Farmer, J. D. 2024. *Making Sense of Chaos: A Better Economics for a Better World.* New Haven, CT: Yale University Press.

Farmer, J. D., and D. Foley. 2009. "The Economy Needs Agent-Based Modelling." *Nature* 460 (7256): 685–686. https://doi.org/10.1038/460685a.

Frank, M., Y.-Y. Ahn, and E. Moro. 2025. "AI Exposure Predicts Unemployment Risk." *PNAS Nexus* 4 (4): pgaf107. https://doi.org/10.1093/pnasnexus/pgaf107.

Frank, M. R., D. Autor, J. E. Bessen, E. Brynjolfsson, M. Cebrian, D. J. Deming, M. Feldman, *et al.* 2019. "Toward Understanding the Impact of Artificial Intelligence on Labor." *Proceedings of the National Academy of Sciences* 116 (14): 6531–6539. https://doi.org/10.1073/pnas.190094911.

Frank, M. R., E. Moro, T. South, A. Rutherford, A. Pentland, B. Taska, and I. Rahwan. 2024. "Network Constraints on Worker Mobility." *Nature Cities* 1 (1): 94–104. https://doi.org/10.1038/s44284-023-00009-1.

Hernán, M. A. 2021. "Methods of Public Health Research—Strengthening Causal Inference from Observational Data." *New England Journal of Medicine* 385 (15): 1345–1348. https://doi.org/10.1056/NEJMp2113319.

Hirvonen, J., A. Stenhammar, and J. Tuhkuri. 2022. *New Evidence on the Effect of Technology on Employment and Skill Demand.* Working Paper No. 93. The Research Institute of the Finnish Economy (ETLA), Helsinki. https://hdl.handle.net/10419/273019.

Hong, I., M. R. Frank, I. Rahwan, W.-S. Jung, and H. Youn. 2020. "The Universal Pathway to Innovative Urban Economies." *Science Advances* 6 (34): eaba4934. https://doi.org/10.1126/sciadv.aba4934.

Innocenti, S., and M. Golin. 2022. "Human Capital Investment and Perceived Automation Risks: Evidence from 16 Countries." *Journal of Economic Behavior & Organization* 195:27–41. https://doi.org/10.1016/j.jebo.2021.12.027.

Kant, J.-D., G. Ballot, and O. Goudet. 2020. "WorkSim: An Agent-Based Model of Labor Markets." *Journal of Artificial Societies and Social Simulation* 23 (4). https://doi.org/10.18564/jasss.4396.

Kässi, O., and V. Lehdonvirta. 2018. "Online Labour Index: Measuring the Online Gig Economy for Policy and Research." *Technological Forecasting and Social Change* 137:241–248. https://doi.org/10.1016/j.techfore.2018.07.056.

Knaus, M. C. 2022. "Double Machine Learning-based Programme Evaluation Under Unconfoundedness." *The Econometrics Journal* 25 (3): 602–627. https://doi.org/10.1093/ectj/utac015.

Knaus, M. C., M. Lechner, and A. Strittmatter. 2021. "Machine Learning Estimation of Heterogeneous Causal Effects: Empirical Monte Carlo Evidence." *The Econometrics Journal* 24 (1): 134–161. https://doi.org/10.1093/ectj/utaa014.

Korinek, A. 2024. *Economic Policy Challenges for the Age of AI.* Working Paper 32980. National Bureau of Economic Research. https://doi.org/10.3386/w32980.

Kreiss, A., and C. Rothe. 2023. "Inference in Regression Discontinuity Designs with High-dimensional Covariates." *The Econometrics Journal* 26 (2): 105–123. https://doi.org/10.1093/ectj/utac029.

Le Barbanchon, T., R. Rathelot, and A. Roulet. 2021. "Gender Differences in Job Search: Trading off Commute Against Wage." *The Quarterly Journal of Economics* 136 (1): 381–426. https://doi.org/10.1093/qje/qjaa033.

Lim, J., M. Aklin, and M. R. Frank. 2023. "Location is a Major Barrier for Transferring US Fossil Fuel Employment to Green Jobs." *Nature Communications* 14 (1). https://doi.org/10.1038/s41467-023-41133-9.

Manning, B. S., K. Zhu, and J. J. Horton. 2024. *Automated Social Science: Language Models as Scientist and Subjects.* Working Paper 32381. National Bureau of Economic Research. https://doi.org/10.3386/w32381.

McGee, A., and P. McGee. 2025. "Gender Differences in Reservation Wages in Search Experiments." *Labour Economics* 94:102698. https://doi.org/10.1016/j.labeco.2025.102698.

Mealy, P., R. M. del Rio-Chanona, and J. D. Farmer. 2018. "What You Do at Work Matters: New Lenses on Labour." *SSRN Electronic Journal,* https://doi.org/10.2139/ssrn.3143064.

Michaillat, P., and E. Saez. 2021. "Beveridgean Unemployment Gap." *Journal of Public Economics Plus* 2:100009. https://doi.org/10.1016/j.pubecp.2021.100009.

Moro, E., M. R. Frank, A. Pentland, A. Rutherford, M. Cebrian, and I. Rahwan. 2021. "Universal Resilience Patterns in Labor Markets." *Nature Communications* 12 (1): 1972. https://doi.org/10.1038/s41467-021-22086-3.

Nedelkoska, L., S. G. Matha, J. McNerney, A. Assumpcao, D. Diodato, and F. Neffke. 2021. *Eight Decades of Changes in Occupational Tasks, Computerization and the Gender Pay Gap.* CID Working Papers 151, Center for International Development at Harvard University.

Nedelkoska, L., and G. Quintini. 2018. "Automation, Skills Use and Training." *OECD Social, Employment and Migration Working Papers,* no. 202, https://doi.org/10.1787/2e2f4eea-en.

Neffke, F., and M. Henning. 2013. "Skill Relatedness and Firm Diversification." *Strategic Management Journal* 34 (3): 297–316. https://doi.org/10.1002/smj.2014.

Neffke, F., L. Nedelkoska, and S. Wiederhold. 2024. "Skill Mismatch and the Costs of Job Displacement." *Research Policy* 53 (2): 104933.

Neffke, F., A. Sbardella, U. Schetter, and A. Tacchella. 2026. "Economic Complexity Analysis." In *The Economy as an Evolving Complex System IV*, edited by R. M. del Rio-Chanona, M. Pangallo, J. Bednar, E. D. Beinhocker, J. Kaszowska-Mojsa, F. Lafond, P. Mealy, A. Pichler, and J. D. Farmer. Santa Fe, NM: SFI Press.

Neugart, M. 2008. "Labor Market Policy Evaluation with ACE." *Journal of Economic Behavior & Organization* 67 (2): 418–430. https://doi.org/10.1016/j.jebo.2006.12.006.

Neugart, M., and M. Richiardi. 2018. "Agent-Based Models of the Labor Market." In *The Oxford Handbook of Computational Economics and Finance*, edited by S.-H. Chen, M. Kaboudan, and Y.-R. Du, 667–687. https://doi.org/10.1093/oxfordhb/9780199844371.013.24.

Nie, X., and S. Wager. 2021. "Quasi-Oracle Estimation of Heterogeneous Treatment Effects." *Biometrika* 108 (2): 299–319. https://doi.org/10.1093/biomet/asaa076.

O'Clery, N., and S. Kinsella. 2022. "Modular Structure in Labour Networks Reveals Skill Basins." *Research Policy* 51 (5): 104486. https://doi.org/10.1016/j.respol.2022.104486.

Pager, D., and D. S. Pedulla. 2015. "Race, Self-Selection, and the Job Search Process." *American Journal of Sociology* 120 (4): 1005–1054. https://doi.org/10.1086/681072.

Pangallo, M., A. Aleta, R. M. del Rio-Chanona, A. Pichler, D. Martín-Corral, M. Chinazzi, F. Lafond, *et al.* 2024. "The Unequal Effects of the Health--Economy Trade-Off During the COVID-19 Pandemic." *Nature Human Behaviour* 8 (2): 264–275. https://doi.org/10.1038/s41562-023-01747-x.

Pangallo, M., and R. M. del Rio-Chanona. 2026. "Data-Driven Economic Agent-Based Models." In *The Economy as an Evolving Complex System IV*, edited by R. M. del Rio-Chanona, M. Pangallo, J. Bednar, E. D. Beinhocker, J. Kaszowska-Mojsa, F. Lafond, P. Mealy, A. Pichler, and J. D. Farmer. Santa Fe, NM: SFI Press.

Pichler, A., M. Pangallo, R. M. del Rio-Chanona, F. Lafond, and J. D. Farmer. 2022. "Forecasting the Propagation of Pandemic Shocks with a Dynamic Input–Output Model." *Journal of Economic Dynamics and Control* 144:104527. https://doi.org/10.1016/j.jedc.2022.104527.

Rajkumar, K., G. Saint-Jacques, I. Bojinov, E. Brynjolfsson, and S. Aral. 2022. "A Causal Test of the Strength of Weak Ties." *Science* 377 (6612): 1304–1310. https://doi.org/10.1126/science.abl4476.

Richiardi, M. 2006. "Toward a Non-Equilibrium Unemployment Theory." *Computational Economics* 28 (4): 421–446. https://doi.org/10.1007/s10614-005-9019-x. ~309~

Richiardi, M., and J. van de Ven. 2026. "Back to the Future: Agent-Based Modeling and Dynamic Microsimulation." In *The Economy as an Evolving Complex System IV,* edited by R. M. del Rio-Chanona, M. Pangallo, J. Bednar, E. D. Beinhocker, J. Kaszowska-Mojsa, F. Lafond, P. Mealy, A. Pichler, and J. D. Farmer. Santa Fe, NM: SFI Press.

Rothstein, J., and T. von Wachter. 2017. "Social Experiments in the Labor Market." In *Handbook of Economic Field Experiments,* edited by A. V. Banerjee and E. Duflo, 2:555–637. Amsterdam, Netherlands: Elsevier. https://doi.org/10.1016/bs.hefe.2016.10.001.

Saussay, A., M. Sato, F. Vona, and L. O'Kane. 2022. *Who's Fit for the Low-Carbon Transition? Emerging Skills and Wage Gaps in Job Ad Data.* Centre for Climate Change Economics and Policy Working Paper No. 406 and Grantham Research Institute on Climate Change and the Environment Working Paper No. 381. https://www.frbsf.org/wp-content/uploads/working-paper-381-Saussay-et-al.pdf.

Shen, Q. 1998. "Location Characteristics of Inner-City Neighborhoods and Employment Accessibility of Low-Wage Workers." *Environment and Planning B: Planning and Design* 25 (3): 345–365. https://doi.org/10.1068/b250345.

Teutloff, O., J. Einsiedler, O. Kässi, F. Braesemann, P. Mishkin, and R. M. del Rio-Chanona. 2025. "Winners and Losers of Generative AI: Early Evidence of Shifts in Freelancer Demand." *Journal of Economic Behavior & Organization,* 106845. https://doi.org/10.1016/j.jebo.2024.106845.

Thaler, R. H. 2016. "Behavioral Economics: Past, Present, and Future." *American Economic Review* 106 (7): 1577–1600. https://doi.org/10.1257/aer.106.7.1577.

Vespignani, A. 2010. "The Fragility of Interdependency." *Nature* 464 (7291): 984–985. https://doi.org/10.1038/464984a.

vom Lehn, C., C. Ellsworth, and Z. Kroff. 2022. "Reconciling Occupational Mobility in the Current Population Survey." *Journal of Labor Economics* 40 (4): 1005–1051. https://doi.org/10.1086/718563.

Wagner, A. 1999. "Causality in Complex Systems." *Biology and Philosophy* 14:83–101. https://doi.org/10.1023/A:1006580900476.

Witt, U. 2008. "What is Specific about Evolutionary Economics?" *Journal of Evolutionary Economics* 18:547–575. https://doi.org/10.1007/s00191-008-0107-7.

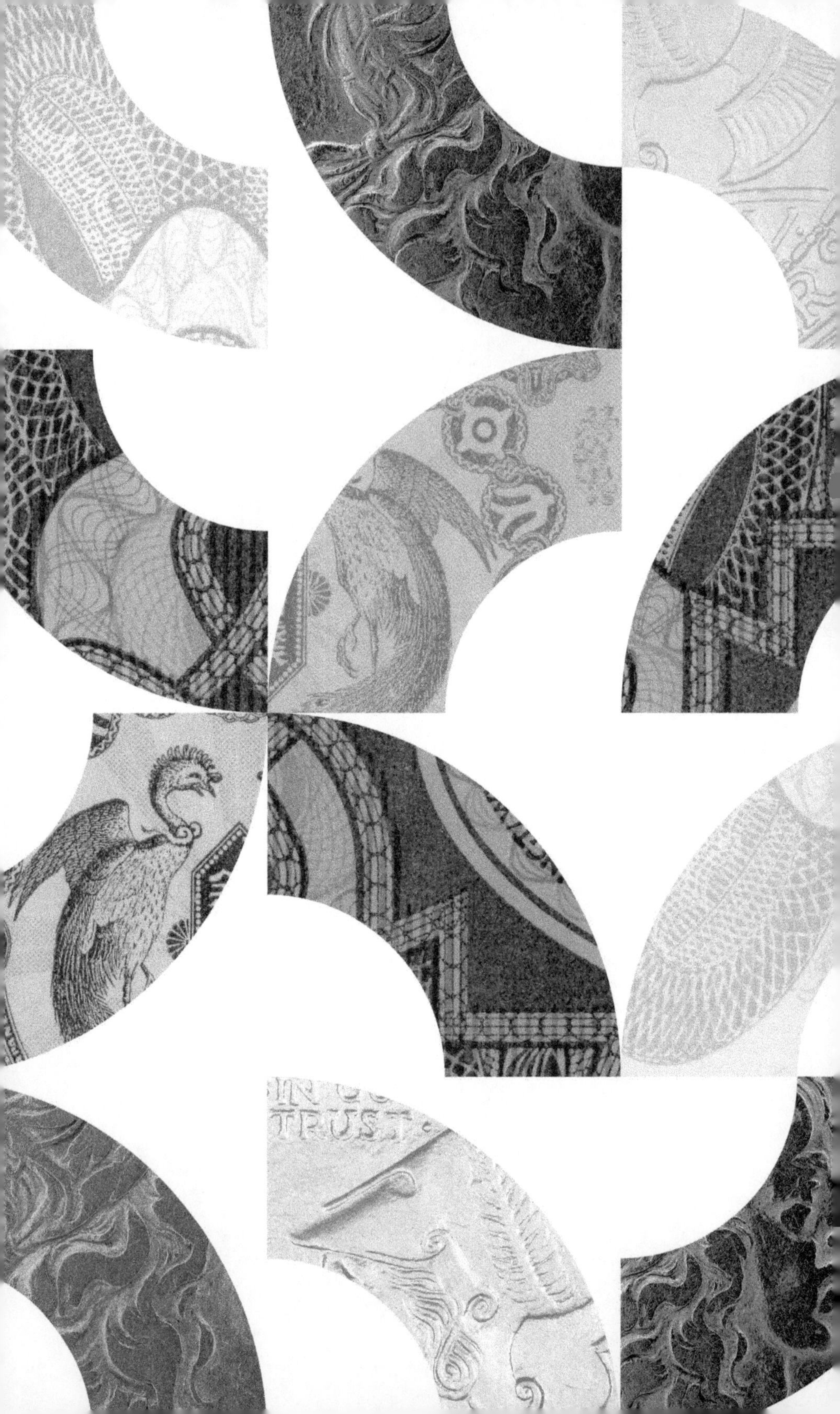
TRUST

PART VI

Innovation &
Technological Disruption

COMPOSITIONAL GROWTH MODELS

José Moran, Macrocosm Inc.,
University of Oxford, and Complexity Science Hub;
Massimo Riccaboni, IMT School for Advanced Studies Lucca
and Scuola Superiore IUSS

Abstract

Compositional models are increasingly used for the microfoundation of economic growth models. This approach has gained empirical support with the growing availability of detailed microdata. In these models, aggregate entities are decomposed into units that grow almost independently of each other, such as a firm's sales across different markets or products. The growth rate of the aggregate entities is therefore the sum of the growth rates of a changing set of constituent units, weighted by their importance. We offer a comprehensive overview of compositional models and demonstrate how they can be interpreted within a unified theoretical framework based on Gaussian scale mixtures. Finally, we explore their practical applications and outline promising directions for future research.

Introduction

Over the past twenty years, compositional growth models have played a central role in economic analysis, from industrial organization to international trade, and from economic theory to macroeconomics. The scaling properties of economic systems have been fundamentally rethought. A key feature of compositional models is the granular hypothesis: Economic systems cannot be broken down into units of approximately equal size. Some products are blockbusters, others are fiascoes; a few customers are much more important than others, a handful of countries and companies dominate the global economy. This is a distinctive feature of complex systems whose components exhibit a skewed size distribution across levels of aggregation. At the firm level, compositional models help explain deviations from Robert Gibrat's growth model. At the macro level, these models provide an explanation for the excessive volatility of composite economies whose effective diversification is bounded away from the predictions of the law of large numbers (Gabaix 2011; Yeh 2025).

Traditionally, market equilibrium analysis has been based on single-product firms. However, single-product firms are "more the exception than the rule" (Hottman, Redding, and Weinstein 2016), with multi-product firms dominating both domestic (Hottman, Redding, and Weinstein 2016) and international markets (Bernard *et al.* 2018). As early as the 1950s, Joan Robinson noted that: "Dropping the fiction of one-commodity firms destroys the simplicity of the analysis . . . but enlarges its scope" (Robinson 1953), but it was not until the late 1970s that an interdisciplinary trend in the literature developed models for firms consisting of multiple, almost independent, units. At that time, however, the models for multiproduct firms largely neglected strategic interaction in order to maintain tractability. John Sutton vividly described these models as island models: Markets are small islands on which only a single firm fits (Sutton 1997, 2001). The companies grow by conquering the island markets and behaving like local monopolists. The island economies are independent of each other and there is no local competition. Despite their simplicity, island models provide useful insights for understanding firm growth, market concentration, and aggregate dynamics.

A significant advance in this direction was made at the turn of the twenty-first century following the seminal contribution of Gene Stanley and coworkers (Stanley *et al.* 1996), with compositional models that consider both the intensive and extensive margins of firm growth (Klette and Kortum 2004; Fu *et al.* 2005). The intensive margin is a measure of the size of the company in a given market. The simplest model for this case goes back to Gibrat (1931). By *extensive margin* we mean the number of almost independent markets in which a company operates. The allocation of business opportunities to firms is usually modeled as a Bose–Einstein process (Ijiri and Simon 1977). For example, if you assume that national markets are almost independent, the size of a multinational firm is the sum of its sales in the national markets in which the firm operates (Armenter and Koren 2014; Bernard *et al.* 2018). Similarly, the growth of diversified companies with a portfolio of products in different markets is subject to almost independent product-specific shocks (Sutton 2002). This is a robust stylized fact that is well rooted in oligopoly theory, as substitution effects have been used to define market boundaries (Tirole 1988). Across markets, substitution effects are negligible, but within markets they play a fundamental role, both within and between firms (Hottman, Redding, and Weinstein 2016; Argente, Lee, and Moreira 2024). This decomposition of economic activity has been generalized and applied to different levels of aggregation of economic systems. At the finer level, there is the number of transactions (extensive margin) and the value of the good sold in a single transaction (intensive margin). In business-to-business networks, the intensive margin can be represented by the number of customers of a company, while the extensive margin is the amount of revenue per customer (Bernard *et al.* 2022). At the macro level, gross domestic product (GDP) growth shocks are influenced by firm-specific shocks and the diversification argument does not hold in compositional models of the economy (Gabaix 2011). Therefore, in compositional models, shocks at the micro level can have a persistent effect on performance at the aggregate level from firms to the national economies (the so-called *granular* hypothesis).

This chapter summarizes the main advances in the literature dealing with compositional growth models and points to promising future research directions. The compositional models we describe in this chapter are included in a companion GitHub repository.[1]

Compositional Models of Growth

Consider the size of a firm i at time t, $S_i(t)$, which is defined as follows

$$S_i(t) = \sum_{j=1}^{K_i(t)} x_{ij}(t),\qquad(1)$$

where $K_i(t)$ is the number of units and $x_{ij}(t)$ is the size of the unit j. The number of units within a firm (i.e., the extensive margin) and the size of each unit (i.e., the intensive margin) are independent and evolve in time *a priori*. In a compositional model, the growth of an aggregated entity, as measured by $S_i(t)$, depends on the evolution of the number of units $K_i(t)$ and their sizes $x_{ij}(t)$.

We define the logarithmic growth rate of the firm as $g_i(t) = \log S_i(t+1) - \log S_i(t)$ and the percentage growth as $r_i(t) = \exp(g_i(t)) - 1$.[2] We can define the logarithmic g_{ij} and percentage

~317~

---

[1] https://github.com/jose-moran/firm_growth.
[2] For the sake of simplicity, we neglect the effect of firm-wide and macroeconomic shocks here. The compositional effect must be combined with aggregate effects to get a complete picture.

r_{ij} growth rates of the subunits by replacing S with x in the above equations.

In this case, if we assume for simplicity that $K_i(t+1) = K_i(t)$ we can write

$$r_i(t) = \sum_{i=1}^{K_i(t)} \frac{x_{ij}(t)r_{ij}(t)}{S_i(t)} - 1, \qquad (2)$$

where it is clear that the growth rate of the whole firm is a weighted average of the growth rates of its units. If the number of units K fluctuates, then an additional term must be added to account for this change in size. We will first focus on models where the assumption that K is static in the relevant time frame is justified, and later look at models that explain growth by fluctuations in K.

If we assume that the growth rates r_{ij} are independent Gaussian random variables, then r_i is a weighted sum of Gaussian variables and therefore also normally distributed, with variance

$$\sigma_i^2 = \sum_{j=1}^{K_i} \frac{x_{ij}^2 \sigma_{ij}^2}{S_i^2}, \qquad (3)$$

where σ_{ij}^2 is the variance of the unit growth rates.[3] In other words, conditional on the value of σ_i^2, the growth rate of the firm is Gaussian.

In practice, most models study the *logarithmic* growth rather than the percentage growth. However, outside of the tails of the distribution one can approximate $r_i \approx g_i$, and it is often

---

[3] The Gaussian assumption for the r_{ij}s can be relaxed to requiring only that they have a finite variance if K_i is large: The sum in equation 2 is Gaussian because of the central limit theorem.

found numerically that many of the statistical properties hold for both objects.[4]

Because σ_i is related to the internal structure of a firm, considering the distribution of r_i across all firms means looking at the superposition of Gaussians with different variances and thus different scales. This is the case, for example, if the firms have a different number of units K. This leads to what is known as a scale mixture of Gaussians, and the shape of the distribution depends on the distribution of the scales σ_i. Specifically, this means that the distribution of r_i reads $P(r_i) = \int d\sigma_i \, P(\sigma_i)P(r_i|\sigma_i)$, where $P(r_i|\sigma_i)$ is a Gaussian with variance σ_i^2.

Scale mixtures of Gaussians can give distributions with varying characteristics. For example, if the distribution of volatilities is fat-tailed, with $P(\sigma) \underset{\sigma\gg1}{\sim} \sigma^{-1-\mu}$ for large σ and for some $\mu > 0$, then this results in a fat-tailed distribution with the same exponent, $P(r) \sim r^{-1-\mu}$. Similarly, if $P(\sigma) \underset{\sigma\ll1}{\sim} \sigma^k$ with $k > 0$, then the distribution is generally more peaked than a Gaussian, and can even present a profile that is not smooth at 0 if $k < 2$. This is the case for a choice $P(\sigma) = \sigma e^{-\sigma^2} \mathbf{1}_{\sigma>0}$, which leads to $P(r) \propto e^{-|r|}$, the Laplace distribution, which is incidentally also more fat-tailed than a Gaussian.

What is a Unit? Conceptually, and when taking this to the data, we are faced with the problem of defining what a unit is (Simon 1962). In the literature, alternative definitions have been used, with market-driven (products or submarkets), production-driven (establishments or plants), assets (like in portfolio theory) or organizational (divisions or business) units. The most common approach is to consider independent submarkets (the so-called island model; see Sutton 1997). In this

---

[4]This excludes the cases of entry/exit or extreme events where the firm's size drops to 0, leading to $r_i = -1$ and $g_i = -\infty$.

case, the size of a unit is determined by the revenues of the firm in a submarket. This is considered a reliable measure in the case of monopolistic competition. However, the growth rates of the units may be correlated if products are substitutes. Therefore, possible interdependencies between units both within and between companies must be carefully considered.

Given some arbitrary partition of the firm into units, the growth rate of firm i has a contribution of the form $\sum_j x_{ij} r_{ij}(t)$ with a correlation structure that is, for example, $C_{i,jk} = \mathrm{Cov}(x_{ij} r_{ij}(t), x_{ik} r_{ik}(t))$. This matrix may be diagonalized, with eigenvalues we call λ, so that $\sum_j x_{ij} r_{ij}(t) = \sum_k \sqrt{\lambda_{ik}} r'_{ik}(t)$, where the r'_{ik} random variables are now decorrelated. Because the management has incentives to split the company into independent partitions, we expect that $C_{i,jk} = \delta_{jk} +$ small corrections, that is, that the partition makes the units' growth roughly independent, up to corrections (Sutton 2002). This then leads to $\sqrt{\lambda_{ij}} \approx x_{ij}$, and to a firm volatility that does indeed behave as the formula defined above.[5]

Traditionally, the size of the firm S has been considered to be proportional to the number of units K: $S_i = \bar{x} K_i$. Given a finite variance of x_{ij}, when the number of units is sufficiently large, the variance of a firm's growth tends to zero approximately as $K^{-1} \propto S^{-1}$ for the law of large numbers. However, this approximation works only if units are about the same size $\bar{x}$. Empirically, high heterogeneity has been observed to be persistent in time and across different scales of economic systems (Buldyrev *et al.* 2020; Riccaboni *et al.* 2008; Stanley *et al.* 1996). Furthermore, the variance of the growth rates conditioned on size is empirically found to decrease much slower, as $S^{-2\beta}$ with $2\beta < 1$.

---

[5] This is in line with the empirical findings of Luca Mungo and Moran (2023) and Riccaboni *et al.* (2008).

The hypothesis that the units are of roughly the same size is therefore not true. This is captured by the Herfindahl index of a firm, which measures how concentrated it is across its subunits (Buldyrev *et al.* 2020). This quantity is defined as $\mathcal{H}_i = \sum_{j=1}^{K_i} \frac{x_{ij}^2}{S_i^2}$, and is equal to $1/K_i$. If all the units have the same size, but of order ≈ 1 if a single unit concentrates all the size. In the case where the growth rates of units have all the same volatility, which we take to be for simplicity $\sigma_{ij} = \sigma$, then this yields a relationship between volatility and the Herfindahl index that is $\sigma_i = \sigma \mathcal{H}_i$ (Gabaix 2011).

This leads to the intuitive concept of the *effective* number of independent units, $K_{\text{eff},i} := \mathcal{H}_i^{-1}$, and implies that the volatility goes to 0 as the inverse of this number rather than the actual number of units.

Thus, there is a clear relationship between the volatility distribution and the distribution of the aggregate growth rate in the context of compositional models, and since there is a clear link between the structure of firms and their volatility, it is obvious that models specifying different firm structures lead to different distributions of growth rates. We will therefore attempt to explain the different hypotheses in compositional models within a unifying Gaussian scale mixture framework and emphasize how they translate into volatility distributions and thus in different propositions for a growth rate distribution.

Gabaix and Wyart–Bouchaud Models. The models introduced by Xavier Gabaix (2011) and Matthieu Wyart and Jean-Philippe Bouchaud (2003) imagine a setup where aggregate entities have a fixed number of units K, and these units have sizes distributed according to a stationary distribution. In this framework, it is assumed that the number and size of units are independent. The main difference between the two models is that Gabaix (2011) studies these properties at fixed K, while Wyart and Bouchaud (2003) consider the possibility that the number of units also fluctuates across firms. In this case and from the discussion above, it is clear that the growth volatility of an aggregate entity is directly related to its Herfindahl, as $\sigma_i = \sqrt{\mathcal{H}_i}$.

In both cases, the unit size is distributed with a fat-tailed distribution: $P(x_{ij}) \sim x^{-1-\mu}$ for large x and with $1 < \mu < 2$. This means that the average unit size is well defined, but that its second moment is divergent. As a consequence, when considering the Herfindahl index of a firm $\mathcal{H}_i = \sum_{j=1}^{K_i} \left(\frac{x_{ij}}{S_i} \right)^2$, the largest element of the sum $\sum_j x_{ij}^2$ scales as $K_i^{\frac{2}{\mu}}$ while the denominator $S_i^2 \sim K_i^2 \mathbb{E}[x]^2$. In other words, the typical value of the Herfindahl scales as $\mathcal{H}_{i,\text{typ}} \sim K_i^{2\left(\frac{1-\mu}{\mu}\right)}$, and since $S_i \approx K_i \mathbb{E}[x]$ one has directly that $\mathcal{H}_i \sim S_i^{2\left(\frac{1-\mu}{\mu}\right)}$.

In fact, for a fixed value of K_i it is possible to compute the entire Herfindahl distribution $P(\mathcal{H}|K)$, as done in Moran, Secchi, and Bouchaud (2024), to see that it is indeed peaked at $\mathcal{H}_i \approx \mathcal{H}_{i,\text{typ}}$ but that it is distributed as a truncated power law, that is, $P(\mathcal{H}|K) \sim \mathcal{H}^{-1-\frac{\mu}{2}}$ for $\mathcal{H}_{\text{typ}} \ll \mathcal{H} \ll 1$ and equal to 0 for $\mathcal{H} > 1$. This implies that the volatility at fixed K has a truncated power law tail with exponent μ.

Thus, the *average* Herfindahl is dominated by rare observations of firms that have their size concentrated in just a handful of subunits, which therefore have a much larger concentration than the typical Herfindahl index. Altogether, the average Herfindahl has a contribution $\mathbb{E}[\mathcal{H}|K] \sim K^{1-\mu} \gg \mathcal{H}_{\text{typ}}$, a fact that was overlooked by Wyart and Bouchaud (2003) and Gabaix (2011) but picked up by Moran, Secchi, and Bouchaud (2024). However, it is still the case that $\mathbb{E}[\sqrt{\mathcal{H}}|K] \sim \sqrt{\mathcal{H}_{\text{typ}}}$. Going back to firm volatility, this means that one must be careful when defining the object one is working with, as $\sqrt{\mathbb{E}[\sigma^2|K]} \neq \mathbb{E}[\sigma|K]$.

All in all, one can obtain the growth-rate distribution by integrating the Gaussian mixture induced by the Herfindahl distribution. In this case, because the Herfindahl and, therefore, the volatility have a distribution that is a truncated power law, the growth-rate distribution conditional on the number of subunits K also shares the same features, and it is given by a Lévy alpha-stable distribution that is truncated at $g \sim 1$, as shown by Wyart and Bouchaud.

Retrieving the entire growth-rate distribution is done by integrating over the distribution of subunits. Wyart and Bouchaud assume that this number K is itself power law distributed, as $P(K) \sim K^{-1-\alpha}$ with $1 < \alpha < \mu < 2$. This results in nontrivial size/ volatility relations, with $\mathbb{E}[\sigma|S] \propto S^{\frac{\mu-1}{\mu}}$ but with $\sqrt{\mathbb{E}[\sigma^2|S]} \propto S^{\frac{\alpha-\mu}{2}}$. Note that this second form comes from a contribution where K is not proportional to S, since with a probability of order $S^{\alpha-\mu}$ a firm in this model can have a large size S but be made up of only a handful of units, leading to $K \sim 1$ and therefore mechanically to $\mathcal{H} \approx 1$.

Because of its structure, the model is *scale invariant*, in the sense that one can aggregate two firms with K_1 and K_2 units into one larger super-firm with $K_1 + K_2$ units, and the growth statistics of that *super-firm* remain well described by the model. This also has a consequence that the firm size distribution in the model has a tail $P(S) \sim S^{-1-\alpha}$. Integrating the K-conditional growth rate distribution, one obtains a mixture of truncated Lévy alpha-stable distributions, namely a growth rate distribution with a power law tail $P(g) \sim g^{-1-\mu}$.

The Generalized Proportional Growth Framework by Stanley and Coworkers. These models, summarized in Sergey Buldyrev *et al.* (2020), postulate that the number of elementary units grows according to the so-called Simon process (Ijiri and Simon 1977). Keeping with the language of firms, the model imagines $1 \leq i \leq N$ firms, each of which has $K_i(t)$ units at time t.

Between times $t \to t+1$, a new unit arrives in the economy. It becomes a new independent firm with probability b, or it is added to an existing firm with probability $1 - b$. The unit is then added to firm i with a probability $\propto K_i(t)$. At long times, if the process starts in a setting where there are no firms at all, the distribution of K converges to a power-law distribution with an exponential cutoff, that is, $P(K) \propto K^{-\varphi} f(K)$ where $\varphi = 2 + \frac{b}{1-b}$ and $f(K) \xrightarrow[K\to\infty]{} 0$ exponentially (Yamasaki *et al.* 2006).

However, when $b \to 0$ the picture is different, and the distribution at long times is given by an exponential distribution. This is similar to the Wyart–Bouchaud model, but with a unit distribution $P(K) = \lambda e^{-\lambda K}$ for some λ. Thus, this is also a simple scenario for a Gaussian mixture. In the model of Dongfeng Fu *et al.* (2005), the distribution of unit sizes is assumed to be log-normal as it results from a random Gibrat-like process. It can then be shown that the *logarithmic* growth rate of a firm with K subunits is given by a Gaussian with a variance $\propto K^{-1/2}$, namely $P(g|K) \propto \exp\left(-\frac{g^2 K}{2\sigma^2}\right)$.

This therefore also leads to a Gaussian mixture. In this case, the entire growth-rate distribution reads

$$P(g) \propto \int dK \, e^{-\lambda K} e^{-\frac{Kg^2}{2\sigma^2}}, \qquad (4)$$

which can be solved to find a distribution that satisfies $P(g) \sim e^{-|g|}$ for $g \ll 1$ and $P(g) \sim g^{-3}$ for $g \gg 1$. For the case $b > 0$ there is no close form solution for the Gaussian mixture, but in Fu *et al.* (2005) it was shown that the resulting distribution is very similar. In a recent contribution (Buldyrev *et al.* 2020), the model was extended in several directions, for example, to take into account a stable economy, the contribution of the change in the number of units K_i, and multiple levels of aggregation. For the scaling law of variance of growth conditioned on size, the model predicts a crossover with a variance that does not depend on size for small firms to $S^{-1/2}$ in the limit $S \to \infty$ (Riccaboni *et al.* 2008).

This model can be extended to *exponential mixtures of Gaussians* (Buldyrev *et al.* 2007). This corresponds to the case where $P(K) = \lambda e^{-\lambda K}$, but where the variance is set to be a general power of K, so that $P(g|K) \propto \exp\left(-\frac{g^2}{2\sigma^2 K^\psi}\right)$. The case $\psi = -1$ corresponds to the situation described above, but other distributions can be obtained.

For instance, the choice $\psi = -2$ would lead to a distribution behaving as $P(g) \sim g^{-2}$ for large g, and more generically power law tails are obtained for $\psi < 0$. The choice $\psi = 1$ leads directly to a Laplace distribution, and corresponds to a different firm growth model that is not a compositional model and that was studied by Giulio Bottazzi and Angelo Secchi (2010). In this model, firms are made up of one single unit, but at each time step a fixed number of growth opportunities are available to them. These growth opportunities are attributed at random, leading to a Bose–Einstein distribution, which has an exponential tail. Therefore, the number of company-wide growth shocks a firm receives per time unit has an approximately exponential distribution, but now the growth volatility scales with the number of growth shocks and leads to the exponent $\psi = 1$. This can be understood by saying that the volatility of a company's growth scales directly with the number of growth shocks per unit of time it receives, but inversely with its number of units.

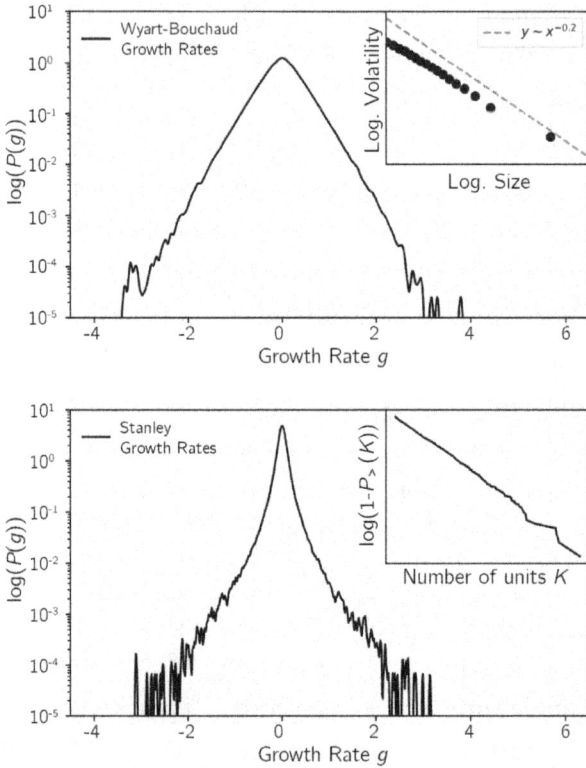

Figure 1. Top: Results for a simulation of the Wyart–Bouchaud model with $\alpha = 1.2$ and $\mu = 1.4$, resulting in $\frac{\alpha - \mu}{2} = 0.2$. The main plot shows the density using a Gaussian kernel density estimator, showing fatter-than-Gaussian tails, while the inset shows the size volatility relation, which decays to 0 slower than $S^{-1/2}$. Bottom: Results for a simulation of the Stanley group's model with $b = 0$. The main plot shows a Gaussian kernel density estimation of the density, with fat tails. The inset shows the distribution of the number of units per firm in the simulation of the model.

Sutton's Model. The goal of John Sutton's model (2002) is to explain the anomalous scaling between size and volatility. To this end, he imagines a *microcanonical* model where a firm is taken to be of an integer size S_i, and is partitioned into K units with sizes x_{ij} such that $\sum x_{ij} = S_i$. Sutton assumes that all partitions (both in terms of number and in terms of size) are equiprobable, and uses results on partitions of the number of integers to compute his result. The same results are obtained in a very succinct fashion in Wyart and Bouchaud (2003).

~327~

The result is that, conditional on firm size, a firm has on average $\exp(a\sqrt{S_i})$ units, with $a > 0$, and that their sizes are distributed according to a Bose–Einstein distribution, with $p(x_{ij}) \propto \left(\exp\left(\frac{b}{2}x_{ij}/\sqrt{S_i}\right) - 1\right)$. Because this is again a compositional model, the unit size distribution can be used directly to compute the variance of the percent growth conditional on size. The result is that the variance scales as $\sigma(S)^2 \propto S^{-1/2}$, providing an explanation to the anomalous scaling with an exponent $\beta = 1/4$.

Rescaling the growth rate of a firm as $r/\sigma(S)$, one finds that the distribution of this quantity approaches a Gaussian distribution as $S \to \infty$ regardless of the distribution of the growth rates of individual subunits. However, it can be shown that the excess kurtosis decays very slowly with S, so that important corrections to the Gaussian asymptotic case can be seen for finite S.

Farmer–Axtell–Schwarzkopf Model. The model proposed by Yonathan Schwarzkopf, Robert L. Axtell, and J. Doyne Farmer is different than others in that it explains growth not by varying the size of the subunits in time, but by varying their number (Schwarzkofp, Axtell, and Farmer 2010). In this model, all the units have a constant size and the equality $S_i(t) = K_i(t)$ holds up to a constant multiplicative factor, which we set to 1 for simplicity. Thus, the percentage growth reads $r_i(t) = K_i(t + 1)/K_i(t) - 1$, and the entire process is explained through the dynamics of $K_i(t)$.

The idea of the process is that, at each time step, a unit is replaced by n new units drawn at random from some distribution $P(n)$. Thus, for a fixed $K_i(t)$, the value of $K_i(t+1)$ is the sum of a series of draws from the distribution $P(n)$, and $r_i(t) = \frac{1}{K_i(t)} \sum_{j=1}^{K_i(t)} n_{ij} - 1$. If one picks a fat-tailed distribution, that is, $P(n) \sim n^{-1-\mu}$ with $0 < \mu \le 2$ for large n, then under the generalized central limit theorem the distribution of $K_i(t)^{-\frac{1-\mu}{\mu}} r_i(t)$ converges to a Lévy alpha-stable distribution with parameter α.

This model is then used to derive the volatility–size scaling relationship. The key idea is that $K_i(t + 1)$ is dominated by the largest draw from $P(n)$, which scales as $K_i(t)^{1/\mu}$. Taking the square, we get the scaling $\mathbb{E}[K_i(t+1)^2] \sim K_i(t)^{2/\mu}$, which can be reworked easily to yield $\sqrt{\mathbb{V}[r_i(t)^2]} \sim K_i(t)^{\frac{1-\mu}{\mu}}$ and therefore to the size-volatility scaling relation $\sqrt{\mathbb{E}[\sigma^2|S]} \sim S^{\frac{1-\mu}{\mu}}$.

On the surface, this size–volatility scaling relation looks similar to the one obtained for the Wyart–Bouchaud model, although here the model is not a Gaussian mixture. The trajectory of firm growth is wildly different between the two models, since the model proposed by Schwarzkopf, Axtell, and Farmer (2010) says that the growth rate of a single individual firm is a Lévy flight, and therefore implies that from one period to the next the size of a firm can fluctuate by various orders of magnitude, which seems unrealistic. In contrast, the family of Gaussian mixture models, which includes the models described before, suggests that the growth rate of a single firm would follow something closer to a standard geometric Brownian motion, with fluctuations that are approximately Gaussian but have a firm-dependent volatility. This leads to more tamed and realistic trajectories, and the anomalous statistics observed in firm data are the result of wild fluctuations in firm heterogeneity rather than wild fluctuations in firm trajectories.

Concluding Discussion

Despite recent progress in analyzing firms and other aggregate entities in economic systems consisting of varying numbers of nearly independent units of different sizes, there are still some promising research directions to explore. First and foremost, the impact of strategic interaction, substitution effects, and constraints on the growth of units needs to be adequately addressed. In compositional models, the entry of new products into a market implies that products from different companies are displaced (Klette and Kortum 2004). However, several products may be on the market at the same time and their market shares may be interdependent (see Sutton 2007, for an interesting contribution in this direction). Recent work using barcodes as units addresses this issue by considering cannibalization (substitution within a firm) and product life cycles (Hottman, Redding, and Weinstein 2016; Argente, Lee, and Moreira 2024). In general, cross-price elasticity and interdependencies at the product level need to be taken into account. There are also some technological interdependencies in the product space, as emphasized in the economic complexity literature. This interaction between firm size, number of products (scope), products' appeal, sales, and prices may also induce correlations between the variables denoted by K and x, which were neglected in the models we considered.

A natural extension of compositional models is the consideration of more complex dynamics of corporate growth, such as mergers and acquisitions (M&As).[6] One way to include M&As is to consider the possibility of companies acquiring more than one unit at a time in order to take over (parts of) existing companies. Another possible extension is the integration of compositional models and firm-to-firm networks (Riccaboni and Pammolli 2002). Currently, compositional models are based on simplifying assumptions about the production function that firms use to convert inputs into outputs. Accordingly, with rare exceptions, the change in company size is usually measured by the number of employees or total turnover. In reality, firms are embedded in a production network and have complex production dynamics that use multiple inputs. The input composition itself has its own dynamics. Although there is ample theoretical and empirical evidence (Acemoglu *et al.* 2012; Herskovic *et al.* 2020; Bernard *et al.* 2022) suggesting that network features have an influence on aggregate dynamics, further work needs to be done to establish the link between the production network and the individual dynamics of firms.

We must also consider the evolution of firm sizes in a shrinking economy. Compositional growth models were initially developed for expanding economies with a growing number of individuals, products, and firms. More recently, versions of these models have considered stable economies with steady-state distributions of firm sizes. However, given the demographic, digital, and environmental transitions, we need to develop models for business dynamics in shrinking economies.

Similarly, a proper mapping of the various stylized facts that determine firm growth can be useful in narrowing

---

[6]See Sandro Claudio Lera and Didier Sornette (2017) for first steps in that direction.

down the various ingredients and mechanisms that should be incorporated into agent-based models (ABMs) so that they can accurately reproduce the behavior observed in real data. Since ABMs are explicitly dynamic non equilibrium models, their main motivation and focus is to capture dynamic features of the economy. This line of thought was started with Domenico Delli Gatti *et al.* (2005), and compositional growth models suggest that it should be extended to constrain the structure of the productive sector in ABMs. In this sense, the role of cross-sectional correlations of firm growth and their connection with production relationships, as in Mungo and Moran (2023), should also be investigated in more detail.

Another important line of research concerns the use of machine-learning methods to predict firm growth and aggregate dynamics (Bargagli-Stoffi, Niederreiter, and Riccaboni 2021). The increasing availability of fine-grained datasets at the unit level across different industries and countries makes it possible to combine machine learning with compositional models to improve economic forecasting and nowcasting. On a broader note, macroeconomic forecasting can take advantage of data-driven agent-based methods, and compositional models enable the derivation of aggregate forecasts using ensemble models of different unit-level learners. ⸙

REFERENCES

Acemoglu, D., V. M. Carvalho, A. Ozdaglar, and A. Tahbaz-Salehi. 2012. "The Network Origins of Aggregate Fluctuations." *Econometrica* 80 (5): 1977–2016. https://doi.org/10.3982/ECTA9623.

Argente, D., M. Lee, and S. Moreira. 2024. "The Life Cycle of Products: Evidence and Implications." *Journal of Political Economy* 132 (2): 337–390. https://doi.org/10.1086/726704.

Armenter, R., and M. Koren. 2014. "A Balls-and-Bins Model of Trade." *American Economic Review* 104 (7): 2127–2151. https://doi.org/10.1257/aer.104.7.2127.

Bargagli-Stoffi, F. J., J. Niederreiter, and M. Riccaboni. 2021. "Supervised Learning for the Prediction of Firm Dynamics." In *Data Science for Economics and Finance: Methodologies and Applications,* 19–41. Cham, Switzerland: Springer International Publishing. https://doi.org/10.1007/978-3-030-66891-4_2.

Bernard, A. B., E. Dhyne, G. Magerman, K. Manova, and A. Moxnes. 2022. "The Origins of Firm Heterogeneity: A Production Network Approach." *Journal of Political Economy* 130 (7): 1765–1804. https://doi.org/10.1086/719759.

Bernard, A. B., J. B. Jensen, S. J. Redding, and P. K. Schott. 2018. "Global Firms." *Journal of Economic Literature* 56 (2): 565–619. https://doi.org/10.1257/jel.20160792.

Bottazzi, G., and A. Secchi. 2010. "Explaining the Distribution of Firm Growth Rates." *The RAND Journal of Economics* 37 (2): 235–256. https://doi.org/10.1111/j.1756-2171.2006.tb00014.x.

Buldyrev, S. V., J. Growiec, F. Pammolli, M. Riccaboni, and H. E. Stanley. 2007. "The Growth of Business Firms: Facts and Theory." *Journal of the European Economic Association* 5 (2–3): 574–584. https://doi.org/10.1162/jeea.2007.5.2-3.574.

Buldyrev, S. V., F. Pammolli, M. Riccaboni, and H. E. Stanley. 2020. *The Rise and Fall of Business Firms: A Stochastic Framework on Innovation, Creative Destruction and Growth.* Cambridge, UK: Cambridge University Press. https://doi.org/10.1017/9781316798539.

Delli Gatti, D., C. D. Guilmi, E. Gaffeo, G. Giulioni, M. Gallegati, and A. Palestrini. 2005. "A New Approach to Business Fluctuations: Heterogeneous Interacting agents, Scaling Laws and Financial Fragility." *Journal of Economic Behavior & Organization* 56 (4): 489–512. https://doi.org/10.1016/j.jebo.2003.10.012.

Fu, D., F. Pammolli, S. V. Buldyrev, M. Riccaboni, K. Matia, K. Yamasaki, and H. E. Stanley. 2005. "The Growth of Business Firms: Theoretical Framework and Empirical Evidence." *Proceedings of the National Academy of Sciences* 102 (52): 18801–18806. https://doi.org/10.1073/pnas.0509543102.

Gabaix, X. 2011. "The Granular Origins of Aggregate Fluctuations." *Econometrica* 79 (3): 733–772. https://doi.org/10.3982/ECTA8769.

Gibrat, R. 1931. *Les Inégalités Économiques: Applications aux Inégalités des Richesses, à la Concentration des Entreprises... D'une loi Nouvelle, la loi de L'effet Proportionnel.* Libr. du Recueil Sirey.

Herskovic, B., B. Kelly, H. Lustig, and S. Van Nieuwerburgh. 2020. "Firm Volatility in Granular Networks." *Journal of Political Economy* 128 (11): 4097–4162. https://doi.org/10.1086/710345.

Hottman, C. J., S. J. Redding, and D. E. Weinstein. 2016. "Quantifying the Sources of Firm Heterogeneity." *The Quarterly Journal of Economics* 131 (3): 1291–1364. https://doi.org/10.1093/qje/qjw012.

Ijiri, Y., and H. A. Simon. 1977. *Skew Distributions and the Sizes of Business Firms.* Vol. 24. Amsterdam, Netherlands: North-Holland.

Klette, T. J., and S. Kortum. 2004. "Innovating Firms and Aggregate Innovation." *Journal of Political Economy* 112 (5): 986–1018. https://doi.org/10.1086/422563.

Lera, S. C., and D. Sornette. 2017. "Quantification of the Evolution of Firm Size Distributions Due to Mergers and Acquisitions." *PLoS One* 12 (8): e0183627. https://doi.org/10.1371/journal.pone.0183627.

Moran, J., A. Secchi, and J.-P. Bouchaud. 2024. *Revisiting Granular Models of Firm Growth.* arXiv preprint: 2404.15226. https://doi.org/10.48550/arXiv.2404.15226.

Mungo, L., and J. Moran. 2023. *Revealing Production Networks from Firm Growth Dynamics.* arXiv: 2302.09906. https://doi.org/10.48550/ARXIV.2302.09906.

Riccaboni, M., and F. Pammolli. 2002. "On Firm Growth in Networks." *Research Policy* 31 (8-9): 1405–1416. https://doi.org/10.1016/S0048-7333(02)00071-9.

Riccaboni, M., F. Pammolli, S. V. Buldyrev, L. Ponta, and H. E. Stanley. 2008. "The Size Variance Relationship of Business Firm Growth Rates." *Proceedings of the National Academy of Sciences* 105 (50): 19595–19600. https://doi.org/10.1073/pnas.0810478105.

Robinson, J. 1953. "Imperfect Competition Revisited." *The Economic Journal* 63 (251): 579–593. https://doi.org/10.2307/2226447.

Schwarzkopf, Y., R. L. Axtell, and J. D. Farmer. 2010. *The Cause of Universality in Growth Fluctuations.* arXiv: 1004.5397. https://doi.org/10.48550/ARXIV.1004.5397.

Simon, H. A. 1962. "The Architecture of Complexity." *Proceedings of the American Philosophical Society* 106 (6): 467–482. https://www.jstor.org/stable/985254.

Stanley, M. H. R., L. A. N. Amaral, S. V. Buldyrev, S. Havlin, H. Leschhorn, P. Maass, M. A. Salinger, and H. E. Stanley. 1996. "Scaling Behaviour in the Growth of Companies." *Nature* 379 (6568): 804–806. https://doi.org/10.1038/379804a0.

Sutton, J. 1997. "Gibrat's Legacy." *Journal of Economic Literature* 35 (1): 40–59. https://www.jstor.org/stable/2729692.

———. 2001. *Technology and Market Structure: Theory and History.* Cambridge, MA: MIT Press.

———. 2002. "The Variance of Firm Growth Rates: The 'Scaling' Puzzle." *Physica A: Statistical Mechanics and its Applications* 312 (3–4): 577–590. https://doi.org/10.1016/s0378-4371(02)00852-x.

———. 2007. "Market Share Dynamics and the 'Persistence of Leadership' Debate." *American Economic Review* 97 (1): 222–241. https://doi.org/10.1257/aer.97.1.222.

Tirole, J. 1988. *The Theory of Industrial Organization.* Cambridge, MA: MIT Press.

Wyart, M., and J.-P. Bouchaud. 2003. "Statistical Models for Company Growth." *Physica A: Statistical Mechanics and its Applications* 326 (1-2): 241–255. https://doi.org/10.1016/S0378-4371(03)00267-X.

Yamasaki, K., K. Matia, S. V. Buldyrev, D. Fu, F. Pammolli, M. Riccaboni, and H. E. Stanley. 2006. "Preferential Attachment and Growth Dynamics in Complex Systems." *Physical Review E* 74 (3): 035103. https://doi.org/10.1103/PhysRevE.74.035103.

Yeh, C. 2025. "Revisiting the Origins of Business Cycles with the Size-Variance Relationship." *Review of Economics and Statistics* 107 (3): 864–871. https://doi.org/10.1162/rest_a_01374.

FORECASTING TECHNOLOGICAL PROGRESS

François Lafond, University of Oxford

Abstract

After a brief history of technological forecasting, I synthesize our work at the Institute for New Economic Thinking (INET) over the last decade developing time-series models for performance curves. I conclude with ongoing efforts and a research agenda.

Introduction

Technology forecasting is essential for solving global problems and limiting exposure to catastrophic risks. Humanity's fate often depends on what are, essentially, technological bets. Can we risk emitting more carbon dioxide because we think that carbon-capture technologies will become scalable and cheap? Should we pause the development of generative artificial intelligence (AI) and its promises of great productivity gains because we worry about catastrophic risks associated with it, as advocated by Y. Bengio *et al.* (2023)? Should we spend billions of dollars changing our encryption methods because we think that quantum technologies will make progress quickly and make it possible to break current cryptographic protocols? Should we strictly regulate synthetic biology, stifling medical innovation, because it can create serious biohazard and terrorist threats?

In this chapter, I review recent attempts at predicting technological progress, focusing on predictions of technological performance and unit costs, exposing some key technical issues.

I also briefly discuss other approaches, including predictions of technology diffusion and patenting rates. Before diving into these, I provide a brief motivation and history of technology forecasting.

A BRIEF HISTORY OF TECHNOLOGY FORECASTING

Why is technology forecasting done? Historically, the main reasons have been (i) war, as the military "played a disproportionate role in the emergence of technological forecasting as a serious professional activity" (Ayres 1969); (ii) industrial policy, as evidenced by the popularity of national foresights exercises (Harper 2013); (iii) financial gain, as there is a clear business advantage to knowing the future of technology better than competitors; (iv) survival, as I have already hinted at biohazards and rogue AI, but nuclear technologies also made their fair contribution to that motivation; and last but not least (v) fun—this should be evident from the popularity of the science-fiction genre.

~337~

But while fears, hopes, and fantasies about technology are indeed entertaining, technology forecasting is now a very serious activity. It developed as such in the twentieth century. Before World War II, technology-forecasting methods remained qualitative. As R. Ayres (1969, 144) quipped, "The first major forecasting effort by a panel, the 1937 study by the Natural Resources Committee of the National Research Council, was a very sober and responsible document which missed virtually all of the major developments of its decade, including antibiotics, radar, jet engines, and atomic energy."

After World War II, "technological forecasting emerged as a recognised management discipline" (Jantsch 1967). This makes sense, as missed opportunities may cost companies dearly. In two famous examples, the inventor of xerography "pounded the pavement for years in a fruitless search for a company that would develop his invention into a useful product,"[1] and the CEO of IBM is said to have declared in 1943 that there was a market for only a few computers (though this may be apocryphal).[2]

Beyond these eye-catching examples of rather spectacular failure, however, early attempts at technological foresights appear to have been pretty decent. An early study by S. C. Gilfillan (1937), found that 60% of 75-year-ahead forecasts from a 1920 *Scientific American* were realized or almost so sixteen years later. Ayres (1969, 9–14) reports broadly similar success rates for a number of other public predictions of future inventions. More recently, R. Albright (2002) found that half of Kahn and Wiener (1967)'s "one hundred technical innovations very likely in the last third of the twentieth century" were realized.

In the 1970s and '80s, technology forecasting became increasingly integrated with planning, leading to the development of foresights and scenarios for strategic planning (Martino 1993), sometimes using semi-quantitative approaches such as Delphi (see below). In the 1990s and 2000s, the term "tech mining" (Porter and Cunningham 2005) appeared, shifting the emphasis to data-based prediction. In the 2010s, larger datasets (web-based data, patents and publications, etc.) triggered a new era of technology forecasting, with new analytical techniques.

[1] According to Xerox's own account: https://www.xerox.com/downloads/usa/en/innovation/innovation_storyofxerography.pdf.
[2] The Wikipedia page of Thomas J. Watson, section "Famous attribution" (accessed 1 August 2024), fails to track down a reliable source. Peter Schwartz, a well-known scenario planner, does document a 1981 IBM forecast that shipments of the X1000 would peak in 1983, calling it "the costliest slide in business history" (https://longnow.org/ideas/scenario-planning-for-the-long-term/).

In the early 2020s, the growing availability of large language models makes it possible to deal with text data in a much easier and much more effective way, opening new avenues for rigorous or automated approaches to issues that have hitherto been seen as requiring more qualitative or expert-based insights, ranging from data collection to direct predictions of technological milestones. The next section provides a very succinct overview of currently used methods.

METHODS OF TECHNOLOGY FORECASTING

While this chapter focuses primarily on my and my colleagues' work in the Complexity Economics group at INET Oxford, I first offer a list of the key methods in technology forecasting (for more complete reviews, see Ayres 1969; Jantsch 1967; Martino 1993; Ciarli, Coad, and Rafols 2016).

Progress curves and learning curves. This method is based on the idea that a key feature of a technology, such as its unit cost or performance along a key metric, follows trends either as a function of time or as a function of "experience." I will discuss this extensively in "Performance Curves and Learning Curves."

Growth curves: diffusion and substitution. This branch of work starts from the observation that there are predictable patterns in which technology diffuses, specifically, "S-shaped" patterns. I will discuss this in "S-curve Diffusion."

Patent networks. Since the early 2000s, we have seen the development of very large, easy-to-use databases of patents and scientific publications that include metadata that are relational in nature, making it possible to construct networks of technologies, such as citation networks between patents, or networks of similarities between patent categories. I will discuss this in "Patents."

Expert elicitation. These methods, such as the well-known Delphi method, do not just query "experts," but try to avoid or even correct known expert biases: overconfidence, anchoring, unwillingness to back down from the publicly announced positions, peer effects, bandwagon effects, overcompensation for past errors, vested interest, etc. Recent expert-elicitation studies include an explicit process of expert debiasing (e.g., Verdolini *et al.* 2018). P. E. Tetlock and D. Gardner (2016) have documented how experts often do not perform better than laypeople, except for a few "superforecasters". Expert elicitations remain popular—see K. Grace *et al.* (2024) for an interesting example of AI experts' predictions about future AI capabilities.

Prediction markets. These are closely related to expert elicitation but with a stronger focus on quantitatively leveraging the "wisdom of crowds." While some platforms have developed, they are not as popular or successful as was hoped a couple of decades ago (Arrow *et al.* 2008). A number of recent studies have used large language models as "experts" (or aids to experts) and evaluate performance against human-level performance on prediction platforms. Early results are very encouraging (Halawi *et al.* 2024; Schoenegger *et al.* 2024) and make it possible to address technological forecasts that are more qualitative than is possible with the time-series methods reviewed here, while still using a rigorous evaluation framework, including in evaluating errors quantitatively.

Foresight, scenarios, and road maps. This refers to more general exercises than a single expert elicitation study. Foresight exercises constitute "an approach for collectively exploring, anticipating and shaping the future" (Harper 2013). Most advanced economies regularly produce technology foresights and road maps, generally produced by groups of civil servants aided by experts and consultants.

Evolutionary dynamics and taxonomies. The literature on cultural evolution is starting to accumulate considerable data on technology phylogenies (Solé *et al.* 2013), typically constructed by carefully mapping how one design evolved from a previous one (in this volume, see ch. 28, fig. 3, for an example in software). I am not aware that these techniques have been used for forecasting, but this would be an interesting avenue of research, as it is one of the rare approaches that has a shot at predicting qualitative change. F. Lafond and D. Kim (2019) studied the evolution of the US patent classification system, arguing that radical innovations are by definition *sui generis* and should thus be reflected by the creation of new categories. Patent reclassification indeed appears related to quality, as measured by future citations. There have been some attempts at predicting the emergence of new patent categories (Érdi *et al.* 2013). While the work on economic complexity, reviewed in this volume by Neffke *et al.* (2026, ch. 7), Frenken and Neffke (2026, ch. 29), and Diane (2026, ch. 27), does predict the probability that an entity adopts a new technology, it does so under a fixed classification scheme, making clear the need for techniques that predict the *expansion* of the technological space. W. B. Arthur (2026, ch. 3), in this volume, proposes combinatorial evolution as a mechanism through which the technological space expands.

Total factor productivity. In economics, time-series forecasting is highly developed, and it is well acknowledged that long-run economic growth originates mostly in technological change. Thus, we can think of most long-term forecasts of gross domestic product (GDP) as technology forecasts. However, there seems to be almost no work on directly forecasting long-term total factor productivity growth. An exception is T. Philippon (2023), who finds that total factor productivity growth is better predicted using linear than exponential growth. I. Goldin *et al.* (2024) discuss how predictions of future of productivity growth revolves around "optimists" and "pessimists," with few quantitative forecasts being made.

So, what works best? I have not seen many studies comparing methods, as they usually predict different things. An area that has attracted attention, however, is the cost of energy technologies. This is important: the costs of the "backstop" technology in integrated assessment models (IAMs) are key to determine the "optimal choice of abatement." Unfortunately, R. Way *et al.* (2022) documented that IAMs have systematically used too pessimistic forecasts of the costs of some renewables, such as solar and wind. J. Meng *et al.* (2021) concluded that for key energy technologies, time series models outperformed experts.

I will come back to multi-method approaches and forecast combination in the conclusion; for now, let us look in detail at time-series models.

Performance Curves and Learning Curves

Here I review recent work on "performance" or "cost curves" (as a function of time) and "learning curves" or "experience curves" (as a function of experience).

VARIABLES AND DATASETS

Different studies use different concepts of performance, and when explaining performance using a learning-curve approach, different studies use difference concepts for experience.

For performance, some authors use technical performance records along one metric (Koh and Magee 2006, 2008), and study different metrics separately; others try to construct scores, merging different metrics, based on engineering/expert knowledge (Martino 1993; Benson, Triulzi, and Magee 2018). Statistical offices producing price indices try in principle to produce quality-adjusted prices, often using hedonic regressions; that is, they construct scores by inferring the relative importance of various performance characteristics directly from the data by observing which ones contribute most to price differences (Gordon 1990). Other studies use productivity metrics, either labor productivity (Lafond, Greenwald, and Farmer 2022) or total factor productivity (Nordhaus 2014).

In the case of learning curves, for experience, some studies use installed capacity (that is, excluding retired capacity), or, similarly, account for obsolescence (Argote and Epple 1990). Typically, the variable under consideration is production, but sometimes, as in Arrow's 1962 original paper, it is investment.

Finally, defining scope is a real problem. Even if we can find a good definition for what technology is—simplifying Arthur (2010), a technology is a specific set of means (typically from a particular techno-scientific domain) for a specific end—because technologies are recursively made of other technologies, one needs to decide on a "level" or "boundary," such as energy technologies/solar energy/photovoltaic/thin-film and, in parallel, technology components (e.g., solar photovoltaic module cost vs. installed system cost vs. levelized cost of electricity). This matters because neither Wright's law nor Moore's law have nice aggregative properties: if they are true at one level, they would in general not hold true at another (see, e.g., Nordhaus 2014). In practice, intuition appears to dictate primary data collection, and data availability dictates data analysis.

Here our discussion is based on thinking about performance as unit costs, and about experience as cumulative production, as in B. Nagy *et al.* (2013).

MOORE'S LAW, WRIGHT'S LAW, AND SAHAL'S IDENTITY

Many studies have observed that technical performance or unit cost tend to follow an exponential trend.[3] Denoting unit cost of technology i by c, we have

$$c_t = c_0 \exp(\mu t), \qquad (1)$$

where μ is the rate of exponential growth, c_0 is a constant, and t is time. Because G. Moore's predicted the number of transistors on integrated circuits would double every two years, Nagy *et al.* (2013) called this Moore's law. Similarly, since T. Wright's study of airplane manufacturing, many studies have observed unit costs falling with cumulative production. Denoting production by q, cumulative production z is

$$z_t = \sum_{j=t_0}^{t} q_j, \qquad (2)$$

where t_0 is the time at which production started.[4] Then, "Wright's law" is

$$c_t = c_0 z_t^{\omega}, \qquad (3)$$

---

[3] See Nagy *et al.* (2011) for a study of detection of super-exponential trends in information technologies.

[4] An important issue empirically is that one typically observes production only several years after t_0. It is then necessary to estimate initial cumulative production to construct experience. When production grows exponentially at rate g, one may use the formula $z_{init} = q_{init}/\hat{g}$ (Lafond *et al.* 2018). Otherwise, one does need to try to carefully reconstruct the initial stock; see Lafond, Greenwald, and Farmer (2022) for a practical example using World War II military equipment.

where ω is the experience exponent[5]. D. Sahal (1979) noted that Moore's law and Wright's law are highly related, in the sense that if experience grows exponentially at rate r,

$$z_t = z_0 \exp(rt), \qquad (4)$$

substituting equation (4) into equation (3) gives equation (1) with $\mu = \omega r$. The growth rate of cost is, trivially, the elasticity of cost to experience times the growth rate of experience.

Nagy *et al.* (2013) pioneered a systematic study of Moore's and Wright's laws, building the Santa Fe Performance Curve Database and demonstrating that the relationship $\mu = \omega r$ holds well when the three parameters are estimated independently. They showed that, in practice, Moore's law and Wright's laws tend to perform relatively similarly out-of-sample, and using an encompassing model $c_t = c_0 z_t^{\omega} \exp(\mu t)$ does not work very well. The next section will explain why, providing considerable details on when *stochastic* Wright's law and Moore's law are observationally equivalent, what we can and cannot deduce from this, and why it is so hard to test which one is best.

STATISTICAL STRUCTURE AND DISTRIBUTIONAL FORECASTS

So far, we have assumed that the relationships described are deterministic. It is crucial to determine a sound statistical basis for these models, not only to get better parameter estimates but also because the statistical structure strongly determines the properties of the forecast errors and, therefore, of prediction

~345~

---

[5] The parameter ω can be thought of as an elasticity. The literature also often refers to the "learning rate" (LR), which represents the percentage decline on cost for a doubling a experience. If experience doubles, the new cost c' is $c' = c_0(2z)^{\omega} = 2^{\omega} c$, so the learning rate is usually defined as $LR \equiv 1 - 2^{\omega}$. For instance, a rule of thumb is that for $\omega \approx -1/3$ (roughly what has been found in the classic cases of WWII airplanes, or solar PV), costs fall by around 20% for each doubling of experience.

intervals. In Farmer and Lafond (2016) and in Lafond *et al.* (2018), we addressed this problem for Moore's and Wright's law respectively.[6]

Moore's Law

For Moore's law, an option would be a "deterministic trend" or "mean reversion" model such as $\ln c_t = \alpha + \mu t + \eta_t$, perhaps with autocorrelated η_t. Instead, in Farmer and Lafond (2016) we propose using a geometric random walk with drift, where the growth rate at each period is drawn from a distribution centered on μ,

$$\Delta \ln c_t \equiv \ln c_t - \ln c_{t-1} = \mu + \eta_t, \tag{5}$$

where for simplicity $\eta_t \sim$ i.i.d. $\mathcal{N}(0, \sigma_\eta^2)$. The parameter estimates $\hat{\mu}$ and $\hat{\sigma}_\eta^2$ are simply the sample mean and variance of the growth rates. I denote the number of time periods by $m+1$, and thus the sample size (the number of growth rates) by m.

Having estimated the average growth rate, our best forecast is just that this growth rate will repeat every period, so, for τ-steps ahead,

$$\ln \hat{c}_{m+\tau} = \ln c_m + \hat{\mu}\tau. \tag{6}$$

If the data-generating process (DGP) is indeed equation (5), and we have made forecasts using (6), we can calculate explicitly the forecast errors

$$\mathcal{E}_\tau \equiv \ln c_{m+\tau} - \ln \hat{c}_{m+\tau} \sim \mathcal{N}\Big(0, \mathrm{Var}(\mathcal{E})\Big),$$

where

$$\mathrm{Var}(\mathcal{E}_\tau) = \sigma_\eta^2 \Big(\tau + \frac{\tau^2}{m}\Big). \tag{7}$$

~346~

---

[6]Appendix A provides an in-depth analysis of the distribution of forecast errors, including proofs of all the results stated here.

Knowing the distribution of the errors is useful because we can make a distributional forecast as

$$\Pr(\ln \tilde{c}_{m+\tau}) = \ln \hat{c}_{m+\tau} + \Pr(\mathcal{E}) \sim \mathcal{N}\left(\ln c_m + \hat{\mu}\tau, \sigma_\eta^2\left(\tau + \frac{\tau^2}{m}\right)\right).$$
$$(8)$$

The formula for the variance of forecast errors, equation (7), is well worth pausing. It shows that (squared) errors (i) do not depend on the drift; (ii) increase with volatility; (iii) increase with the forecast horizon; and (iv) are composed of two terms. The linear term τ is due to the fact that unforecastable noise accumulates in the future. The second term is due to error in estimating the drift; while it tends to zero as sample size m increases, for a small sample size and long horizon it is likely to be the dominant source of errors—more precisely, when $\tau^2/m > \tau$, that is, when the horizon is greater than the sample size. Perhaps counterintuitively, the farther ahead in the future we try to predict, the more the error is dominated by mistakes in understanding the past, rather than by unpredictable future shocks.

~ 347 ~

Equation (7) is also extremely useful for model validation, because if different technologies have different volatilities $\sigma_{\eta,i}$, we can renormalize the errors as $\mathcal{E}_{i,\tau}/\sigma_{\eta,i}$ to get a distribution that is, in principle, the same for all technologies, so that forecast errors for all technologies can be pooled together for testing the validity of the model. Further, we can also construct renormalized errors $\mathcal{E}_{i,\tau}/\left[\sigma_{\eta,i}\left(\tau + \frac{\tau^2}{m}\right)\right]$ to pool together errors at various forecast horizons.

In Farmer and Lafond (2016), we computed empirical forecast errors on more than fifty technologies, using various sample sizes and forecast horizons, and used the normalization above to pool the errors and test whether they followed the expected distribution. We found that they did not; however, if instead of assuming i.i.d. noise, we assumed an MA(1) process

$\eta_t = \epsilon_t + \rho \epsilon_{t-1}$ with i.i.d. ϵ, the empirical forecast errors were well aligned with what we expected them to be if the DGP was true. Under that null hypothesis, the formula for the variance of the forecast errors is a little unsightly,[7] but its large τ, large m approximation reads

$$\text{Var}\big(\mathcal{E}_\tau\big) \approx \sigma_\eta^2 \frac{(1+\rho)^2}{1+\rho^2} \Big(\tau + \frac{\tau^2}{m}\Big). \tag{9}$$

To test this using empirically constructed forecast errors, in Farmer and Lafond (2016) (and in Lafond *et al.* 2018, for Wright's law), we faced two additional issues. First, when forecast errors are computed by rolling windows, they are correlated, and this is not taken into account into the formulas. Second, in practice σ_η^2 and ρ need to be estimated. To tackle these two issues, instead of testing whether empirically derived forecast errors have the theoretically predicted distribution, we tested whether empirically derived forecast errors on real data have the same distribution as empirically derived forecast errors on surrogate datasets, that is, datasets with the same unbalanced panel structure and generated using the assumed DGP with parameters as estimated on the real data.

For the parameter ρ, which is very hard to estimate on short time series, we assumed a universal value and found that using $\rho = 0.6$ allowed a good match between the distributions of forecast errors on empirical versus surrogate datasets.

While the method for making these distributional forecasts has been derived from substantial analysis and testing, ultimately it is extremely easy to implement—it requires estimating the mean and variance of the growth rates of the data, and code one formula: the probability distribution function of the normal distribution with mean equal to the point forecast

---

[7] See appendix A.

(eq. 6), and variance equal to the variance of forecast errors (eq. 9, or rather the exact version in appendix A).

One can even *make a distributional forecast after observing only two values for costs*: with two observations, it is possible to compute $\hat{\mu} = \ln(y_m/y_0)/m$, and knowing $\hat{\mu}$ one can guess the standard deviation using the relation $\hat{\sigma}_\eta = 0.02 - 0.76\hat{\mu}$, which was empirically derived in Farmer and Lafond (2016) ($R^2 = 0.87$; they also report a log–log fit).

Before I turn to Wright's law, one final remark. The prediction equation (8) is for the *logarithm* of the cost, or, since the distribution is normal, the median of the distributional forecast for cost.[8] What about the expected cost? Using properties of lognormals,

$$E[\hat{c}_{m+\tau}] = \hat{c}_m \exp\left(\hat{\mu}\tau + \frac{1}{2}\sigma_\eta^2\left(\tau + \frac{\tau^2}{m}\right)\right). \qquad (10)$$

Thus, as the forecast horizon goes to infinity, no matter how negative the drift, the mean of the distribution of predicted values for cost is (positive) infinity, a somewhat disturbing result. If the estimated drift is not negative enough, $(-\hat{\mu}) < \sigma_\eta^2/2$, then the expected value of future cost is always higher than today's cost and keeps rising. If it is negative enough, $(-\hat{\mu}) > \sigma_\eta^2/2$, expected cost goes down initially but plateaus at some forecast horizon $\tau^* = m((-2\hat{\mu} - \sigma_\eta^2)/(2\sigma_\eta^2))$, reaches the same level as today's costs at $2\tau^*$, and exceeds it more and more after that. In practice, it is better to think in terms of point forecasts (the median) and forecast error uncertainty (from

[8]To be clear, this is a distributional forecast for the concept of cost that underlies the data. Usually, the data is for *average* costs, so the point forecast is the median of the predicted distribution of average costs in the future. Put differently, the average cost is observed as a scalar and treated as a known value, but an interesting avenue for further research would be to model the empirical distribution of costs. So far, too little data has been available. This may change as microdata underlying aggregate price indices becomes available.

the percentiles); the mean itself drifts farther and farther away into upper percentiles—it is not a good indicator of "central tendency" (see Mandelbrot 1997, for an insightful discussion of the moments of lognormals). It is possible that for long-term forecasts, a model with mean reversion would be more appropriate, but the data available so far has not allowed us to explore this.

Wright's Law

Typically, learning curves are estimated using the "level" model, $\ln c_t = \alpha + \omega \ln z_t + \epsilon$. As we did in Farmer and Lafond (2016) for the Moore's law model, in Lafond *et al.* (2018) we proposed to use instead a model where the noise follows a random walk, that is

$$\Delta \ln c_t = \omega \Delta \ln z_t + \eta_t, \qquad (11)$$

where again for simplicity $\eta_t \sim \text{i.i.d.} \mathcal{N}(0, \sigma_\eta^2)$. The parameters ω and σ_η can be estimated by ordinary least squares (OLS) (being careful to run a regression through the origin, that is, without intercept). The forecasts are then made *conditional* on future values of experience,

$$\ln \hat{c}_{m+\tau} = \ln c_m + \hat{\omega}\left(\ln z_{m+\tau} - \ln z_m \right), \qquad (12)$$

where $\hat{\omega}$ is the estimated value of ω. This formulation of the stochastic model has the advantage, like for Moore's law as a random walk, that the forecast origin corresponds to the actual observed data point (setting $\tau = 0$ gives $\ln \hat{c}_m = \ln c_m$). The forecast errors are again mean zero and

$$\text{Var}(\mathcal{E}_\tau) = \sigma_\eta^2 \left(\tau + \frac{\left(\sum_{i=m+1}^{m+\tau} \Delta \ln z_i \right)^2}{\sum_{i=0}^{m} (\Delta \ln z_i)^2} \right). \qquad (13)$$

If experience grows deterministically, $\Delta \ln z_t = r, \forall t$, and we see again a manifestation of "Sahal's identity," as Wright's law equation (11) becomes Moore's law equation (5) with $\mu = \omega r$ and the same noise terms, Moore and Wright's laws are observationally equivalent; the forecast errors are also the same, as equation (13) becomes equation (7). An insightful way to rewrite equation (13) is

$$\text{Var}(\mathcal{E}_\tau) = \sigma_\eta^2 \left(\tau + \frac{\tau^2}{m} \cdot \frac{\hat{r}_{(f)}^2}{\hat{\sigma}_{z,(p)}^2 + \hat{r}_{(p)}^2} \right), \qquad (14)$$

where $\hat{\sigma}_{z,(p)}^2$ and $\hat{r}_{(p)}$ are the sample mean and variance of experience growth rates in the past data $(0\ldots m)$, and $\hat{r}_{(f)}$ is the sample mean of future experience growth rates.

This can be compared directly to the equivalent for Moore's law, equation (7), where the only difference is the final ratio within the parentheses. It is instructive to look at it in detail. First, note that it is associated with the τ^2/m term, that is, it is linked to forecast errors resulting from errors in parameter estimation. Second, the fluctuations of experience (high $\sigma_{z,(p)}^2$) reduce the forecast errors. This is because a high variance of the regressor makes the estimates of the slope more precise (lower standard errors of ω). Third, a high growth rate of experience in the past (high $r_{(p)}$) also reduces the forecast errors, as experience spans a larger range, making estimation of the slope easier. Fourth, when experience in the future grows very fast (high $r_{(f)}$), costs are going down faster so the target to predict is farther away on the learning curve, and therefore any error in the estimated slope leads to larger error (said differently, if experience does not increase much, it is easy to predict that costs don't change much). Finally, since the predictions are conditional on observed experience in the future, fluctuations around the future trend (which I would have denoted $\sigma_{z,(f)}$) do not appear in the formula, as expected.

This discussion is helpful to understand whether and when, assuming that Wright's law is correct, we expect Wright's law to actually perform better than Moore's law out-of-sample. This will be the case when there has been a lot of accumulated experience in the past (fast growth, i.e., high $r_{(p)}$), but not a strong acceleration in the future (low $r_{(f)}$); and, crucially, cumulative production growth rates should have fluctuated a lot (high $\sigma_{z,(p)}$). This latter point is critical because this is typically not the case, simply because experience is a *cumulative* variable. Indeed, in Lafond *et al.* (2018) we were able to derive the following important result. Let production follow a geometric random walk with drift g and volatility σ_q. Then, cumulative production (experience) has the same average growth rate ($E[\Delta \ln z] \equiv r \approx q$),[9] but its volatility is

$$\sigma_z^2 \approx \sigma_q^2 \tanh(g/2) \approx \sigma_q^2(g/2), \qquad (15)$$

where tanh is the hyperbolic tangent function, and the second approximation is very good for growth rates of the magnitude typically observed (less than 0.3, say). This is a remarkable formula as it makes it clear that the volatility of cumulative production is expected to be very small; when production grows at 5% per year, the volatility of cumulative production is $\sqrt{0.05/2} \approx 16\%$ of the volatility of production, more than six times smaller. This approximation holds very well for $\sigma_q \geq 0.1$, see appendix B for further discussion of this and related formulas, which have applicability well beyond experience curves. The appendix also shows that, perhaps surprisingly, while cumulative production is much less volatile, it is as uncertain as production, in the sense that its cross-sectional (ensemble) dispersion is almost the same.

For completeness, in Lafond *et al.* (2018) we found that to give a good fit to the forecast errors, as in the case of Moore's

---

[9] This reflects the fact that the exponential function is defined as the only one whose derivative is itself.

law, we had to extend the model to allow for (moving average) autocorrelation. In this case, it is possible to derive a formula that extends equation (14) in the same way that for Moore's law, equation (9) extends equation (7). More specifically, as derived in the appendix,

$$\mathrm{Var}(\mathcal{E}_T) = \sigma_\eta^2 \frac{(1+\rho)^2}{1+\rho^2} \left(\tau + \frac{\tau^2}{m} \cdot \frac{\hat{r}_{(f)}^2}{\hat{r}_{(p)}^2 + \hat{\sigma}_{z,(p)}^2} \right), \qquad (16)$$

where ρ is the moving average autocorrelation parameter. Appendix A shows the exact formula and discusses implementation. In Lafond *et al.* (2018), based on testing on pooled data, we suggested using $\rho = 0.19$.

CAUSALITY

An important criticism of experience curves is that they are used to predict costs conditional on experience, thereby assuming a clear causal relation, while they may only be a statistical relationship with no causal underpinning. While it is plausible that output (cumulative or not) causes lower cost, it is also very plausible that lower costs drive demand up. To examine this issue, we have looked at military production during World War II, when it was clear that the demand for weapons was driven by battlefield needs, relatively independently of cost considerations. But before diving into this, let us discuss a more direct source of concern: spurious regressions.

Spurious Regressions. We have assumed that log costs follow a random walk, that is, are integrated of order 1, I(1). Testing for unit roots is fraught with difficulties, particularly in small samples, but this appears to be a reasonable assumption. Similarly, it is reasonable to assume that log experience is I(1). It is well known that, when two variables are I(1), regressing one on the other in levels will produce non-sense, that is, it will pick up a highly significant relationship between the two, with high R^2, even when none exists.

More formally, when the random walks have drifts, H. Entorf (1997) showed that the coefficient tends to the ratio of the drifts. If costs have a drift μ and experience has a drift r, and if they are completely independent, running the regression $\ln c_t = \alpha + \omega \ln z_t + \epsilon$ will give $\hat{\omega} \approx \mu/r$ even though by assumption $\omega = 0$.

The well-known solution is to estimate the relation in first differences, but *with an intercept*. In other words, running the regression $\Delta \ln c_t = \alpha + \omega \Delta \ln z_t + \epsilon$ will produce $\hat{\omega} \approx 0$, as desired. But there is an important problem with this solution. Adding an intercept corresponds to estimating another model, in fact a mix of Moore's and Wright's laws, of the form $c_t = c_0 e^{\mu t} z_t^{\omega}$. In principle, adding an irrelevant variable does not bias OLS estimates, but it makes them less precise; this turns out to be a huge problem here, because, as discussed in the previous section, $\Delta \ln z_t$ has very low variance, so this regression will typically have huge standard errors and be untrustworthy. What if we omit the intercept, then?

In this case, one can show (appendix C) that the expected value of the first-difference estimator *without a constant* is $\hat{\omega} \approx \frac{\mu/r}{1+(\sigma_z/r)^2}$. Thus, the estimate $\hat{\omega}$ goes to the "spurious" result $\hat{\omega} = \mu/r$ as the volatility of experience $\sigma_z \to 0$, and goes to the correct result $\hat{\omega} = 0$ if $\sigma_z \to \infty$. If the variance of the growth rate of cumulative production is high, we can safely do a regression in first differences without a constant; but as I have emphasized, σ_z tends to be very low. This makes it almost impossible to test whether the relation is spurious ($\omega = 0$). First differences regressions with a constant do not produce a definite answer because the standard errors are too large; first difference regressions without a constant produce an answer biased toward the spurious regression result.

Of course, an alternative solution would exist if the two time series were co-integrated, but we have not found good evidence that this is the case (although acknowledging again the difficulty of testing in small samples). In any case, from a theoretical point of view, there are no *a priori* good reasons to expect a co-integrated relationship, which would assume that there is an intrinsic relationship between the variables *in level*, so that short-term departures from this long-run relation would be corrected over time.[10] Instead, because experience curves may be based on learning, there are good reasons to think that a first difference relationship is appropriate. What we are postulating here is a relationship between technological *progress* (the *growth rate* of unit costs, not unit costs) and the *accumulation* of experience (not the *level* of experience per se).

While this discussion gives a somewhat disillusioned treatment of "learning curves," it turns out that a deeper concern (reverse causality) has led us on a path toward datasets that do have high fluctuations of experience, and thus make it possible to also estimate a separate exogenous time trend.

Are learning curves just flipping the axes of a demand curve? W. D. Nordhaus (2014) criticized learning curves by noting the issue of reverse causality. Let's assume that unit costs depend on both experience and an exogenous time trend, with the form

$$c_t = c_0 z_t^{-b} e^{-at}. \tag{17}$$

The parameters a and b are expected to be positive. Assume that production is equal to demand and that price is equal to unit cost, and let demand be a constant elasticity function of cost, with an

---

[10]Note also that the growth rate of experience should remain non-negative, so the error-correction equations may need to be amended.

additional exponentially growing exogenous demand at rate d,

$$q_t = D_t = D_0 c_t^{-\epsilon} e^{dt}, \tag{18}$$

with demand elasticity $\epsilon > 0$. Taking logs and first differences of equations (17) and (18), assuming $\Delta \ln q \approx \Delta \ln z$, and solving the system gives

$$\Delta \ln c = \frac{-a - bd}{1 - b\epsilon}, \tag{19}$$

$$\Delta \ln z = \Delta \ln q = \frac{a\epsilon + d}{1 - b\epsilon}. \tag{20}$$

Nordhaus (2014)'s critique is that experience curve studies typically assume that experience is the single explanatory factor for costs, that is, they assume that

$$\omega = \frac{\Delta \ln c}{\Delta \ln z} = \frac{-a - bd}{a\epsilon + d}. \tag{21}$$

It is clear that in general $\hat{\omega}$ does not identify the effect of experience, or learning parameter $-b$. However, we can recover b from simple regressions in two cases. First, if there is no exogenous technological progress ($a = 0$), then equation (21) becomes $\omega = -b$. Second, if demand is exogenous ($\epsilon = 0$), then equation 21 becomes $\omega = -(a/d) - b$, that is, since in this case $\Delta \ln z = b$, $\Delta \ln c = -a - b\Delta \ln z$. In other words, if demand is exogenous a simple regression of costs on experience will retrieve both the rate of exogenous technological progress and the experience coefficient.

In Lafond, Greenwald, and Farmer (2022), we studied learning curves during World War II, following a long tradition but with a renewed emphasis on the specific natural experiment aspect of this data: We can argue that demand was exogenous, dictated by battlefield needs. While there may have been some substitutions between different plants or kinds of weapons depending on their changing relative costs, costs were not a big factor overall in deciding output, as the goal was often simply to produce as much as possible. While the war solves the issue of reverse causality, exogenous demand in such a context has another benefit: It is far from simply exponential, exhibiting an increase, plateau, and decline as the war ended. This means that the volatility of production and cumulative production tended to be higher than in modern datasets, allowing a better identification.

In Lafond, Greenwald, and Farmer (2022) we studied three different datasets: one with plant-level data and long time series, but limited to a few categories of products; one with almost all products but only two time-series points per product; and one with long time series covering all types of products but very aggregated. None of these datasets is perfect, but they differ in their drawbacks and advantages. Lafond, Greenwald, and Farmer (2022) estimate $\Delta \ln c_{it} = \alpha + \beta \Delta \ln z_{it} + \epsilon$, that is, assuming constant exogenous and endogenous learning parameters across technologies. The key question is: in a context where demand is exogenous, and the variance in the data makes it possible to estimate both α ad β, is $\beta \neq 0$? In all three datasets, they found that roughly $\hat{\alpha} \approx \Delta \ln c_{it}/2$, that is, exogenous technological progress accounts for about only half of technological progress— the rest can be attributed to the effects of experience.

MOORE'S LAW VS. WRIGHT'S LAW

While this is good evidence that there is some causality from experience to costs, defenders of Moore's law over Wright's law have found evidence of cases where costs decreased in absence of increased experience (Funk and Magee 2015).

It is unclear how externally valid the World War II results are, and whether precommercial rapid improvement implies that a pure Moore's law would be more predictive than Wright's law once deployment has started. However, given the impossibility of separating the effect of a time trend from that of deployment in most existing datasets, the "half–half" result provides a useful prior; in fact, rather than choosing between Moore and Wright, it may be useful to attempt an estimation of the mixed model using the half–half result to center a prior in a Bayesian setting.

Moore's law is much simpler to implement. To recall, using Wright's law requires knowing not only some of the past data on production but in fact having an estimate of initial cumulative production and a good prediction for future production.

The case for Wright's law rests on its usefulness for policy evaluation to capture the endogenous effects of our decisions on technology costs. A case in point is the construction of a technology portfolio.

TECHNOLOGY PORTFOLIOS

An important application of stochastic experience curves is for constructing technology portfolios. Consider a set of technologies that produce a perfectly substitutable product, and follow Wright's law but perhaps with different parameters. Now imagine that a policy maker has a fixed budget to invest. Investing in a technology brings down its cost, so they have an incentive to invest everything into one technology—this is the classic "increasing returns imply lock-in" argument (Arthur 1989), well known in the literature on technological change. However, because experience curves are stochastic, a risk-averse decision-maker may prefer to hedge their bets and invest in different technologies, as their "noise realizations" will average out—this is a classic "diversification reduces risks" argument (Markowitz 1952), well known in the finance literature.

In R. Way *et al.* (2019), we studied this trade-off theoretically, in the simple case of two technologies for two periods. The solution exhibits a cusp bifurcation. When risk aversion is high, it is always better to diversify—there is a single local minimum, and it is for a diversified portfolio. But when risk aversion is low, there are two local minima, one for each technology being highly dominant in the portfolio.

In perhaps the most useful and comprehensive application of stochastic experience curves so far, Way *et al.* (2022) compared the costs of various energy portfolios. Energy systems are complicated, as different sources are not perfectly substitutable (mostly due to intermittency and the need for electricity storage, and the difference between primary, final and useful energy), so optimizing is not practical. However, they showed that the expected present discounted cost of a fast transition scenario is trillions of dollars lower than that of a business as usual scenario— at least $5–15 trillion cheaper over a fifty-year horizon for any plausible discount rate. This is because fossil fuels have a zero learning rate, while some renewables are very likely to become cheaper and cheaper as we invest in them.

~359~

One area that has received little attention is the issue of cross-sectional dependence. In Way *et al.* (2019), we showed that, as expected, increasing correlation between the noise of competing technologies limits the benefits of diversification. However, real data is so scarce that there has been very limited empirical investigation of this issue.

Ongoing Work and Research Agenda

COST CURVES

An important issue with cost curves is that they are typically based on world-level data. For highly standardized and commoditized products that are manufactured and sold globally, such as solar cells, this is justified. However, in practice, what matters for users are other elements of costs that are substantially local in nature, such as installation cost or, to some extent, the cost of capital. L.

Baumgärtner and Farmer (n.d.) are investigating cost curves for solar PV and onshore wind at the national level, decomposing levelized costs of electricity into its components. Their key finding is that solar and wind technologies behave quite differently, with "balance-of-system" costs consistently declining for solar, but not for wind. They argue that this implies that wind energy will approach a floor cost around $35/MWh, whereas solar will continue declining for some time, reaching a likely cost around $3–15/MWh by mid-century.

There are many other interesting avenues for further research. A first is to consider panel data rather than independent time series, and model cross-sectional correlations. Very little has been done so far to evaluate the covariance matrix of technologies. This is relevant for forecasting and also for technology portfolio construction, as positive correlations reduce the benefits of diversification (Way *et al.* 2019). Relatedly, for portfolios an interesting question arises of whether it is easier to predict the aggregate directly, or predict the components and aggregate the forecasts. The theoretical answer to this is that it depends on the statistical structure of the data (relative noise variances, weights, etc.), and therefore this should be examined empirically in specific cases.

A second is to predict observed *distributions*. Consider, for instance, hydropower: We may be able to observe the costs of several projects in a given year, and they may vary a lot. We might thus not be very interested in making a distributional for the average cost, but rather we would like to predict the distribution of costs of various projects in the future.

A third avenue for research is to consider the associated decision theory seriously; the forecast methods presented so far are typically optimal under mean square loss for the log of the cost, essentially for convenience. However, decision-makers may care more about the risk that carbon capture and storage does *not* make progress, or that artificial intelligence makes too much progress. The forecasting and decision-theory literature offers tools to deal with asymmetric loss.

S-CURVE DIFFUSION

We have seen that production and cumulative production often grow so closely to exponentially that this creates estimation issues. This is somewhat surprising, as a large literature has studied "S-curves" for technology diffusion, including a long research program at the International Institute for Applied Systems Analysis to understand technology substitution in energy systems (e.g., Grübler, Nakićenović, and Victor 1999). Here I describe ongoing research efforts in our group to analyze technology diffusion. The classic approach is to assume a logistic curve, that is,

$$Y_t = \frac{L}{1 + \exp(-k(t - t_0))}, \qquad (22)$$

where Y_t is the global stock of a technology in year t (e.g., the global installed capacity of solar PV), L is the asymptotic level of diffusion, k is a parameter that tunes the speed of the diffusion and corresponds to the rate of exponential growth in the initial phase, and t_0 is the year in which diffusion has reached 50% of the total, that is, one can easily check that $Y_{t_0} = L/2$. We have experimented with other S-curve models, starting from the most general (Richard's curve), and found that this classic, simple model works as well as more complex models, although the Gompertz model works well too.

Distributional forecasts. In B. Wagenvoort *et al.* (2025), we are developing a method to make distributional forecasts for S-curves. This involves building a method to pool the data from various technologies so that we can create a good model for the structure of the errors; developing parameter-estimation methods, as naive estimates of S-curve based on technologies that have not passed the inflection point can be highly biased; and testing that out-of-sample distributional forecasts are well calibrated.

Is technology diffusion accelerating? B. Tankwa (2024) shows that the same countries always tend to be early adopters of new technologies, and that technology diffusion has accelerated over time, in the sense that more recent technologies tend to have a faster diffusion speed k.

In addition to these ongoing efforts, there are a number of further avenues for research. One is the hope that collecting data where diffusion is *not* exponential will help settle the Moore versus Wright debate. Another is the development of multivariate models, which predict both series simultaneously.

PATENTS

Patents are one of the most widely used indicators of technological change in the academic literature, because they constitute a large and very well-documented record.

A particularly interesting feature of patent data is that it has a lot of metadata and relational data that can be used to perform network analysis. We briefly discuss technology codes and citations.

Technology codes and their combination. Patents are classified into one or more technology classes (or codes),[11] which can be used for several tasks. For instance, D. Strumsky and J. Lobo (2015) and H. Youn *et al.* (2015) document that while

---

[11] The classification system changes substantially over time, and patents are reclassified so that they are always all classified in the latest vintage of the classification system. Lafond and Kim (2019) document the development of the US patent classification system, propose a model for its development, provide examples of key changes, and explain how using the latest vintage of the system biases historical analysis.

early patents tend to introduce new classes, more recent patents tend to introduce new recombinations of existing classes. A large literature has developed to quantify the novelty of patents or scientific publications based on how atypical code combinations are, which can help predict future impact (Kim *et al.* 2016) or future combinations (Tacchella, Napoletano, and Pietronero 2020; Shi and Evans 2023). More generally, this points to the underlying idea that technologies (codes or patents) can be represented as points in a high-but-not-so-high-dimensional space where clusters and distances can be computed for downstream tasks, including prediction.

~ 363 ~

Citations. Another key metadata in patents is the citations between them, which makes it possible to construct networks between patents or between patent categories. Citations were less common in the early decades of the patent system, and are thus harder to parse, so citation networks typically cover only a more limited time span. Nevertheless, patent citations have been very popular for technology forecasting because they allow us to see an objective, direct relationship between patents; as in scientific papers, one may assume that highly cited patents are more influential. For instance, in Mariani, Medo, and Lafond (2019) we showed that patents that are at the top of their cohort in terms of citations received early are more likely to become part of a list of "significant" patents, as defined by Strumsky and Lobo (2015).

In contrast to networks constructed based on coclassification, networks constructed based on patent citations have a clear direction (see Alstott *et al.* 2017, for a discussion of the various ways of constructing and normalizing patent networks), from the citing category to the cited category, suggesting that technologies rely on others for their development. This is appealing from a complex-systems point of view, and indeed one can study, for instance, the auto-catalytic properties of this network (Napolitano *et al.* 2018). The idea is that if a technology is developing fast, the technologies that tend to depend on it will also be able to develop faster in the future. Thus, the structure of the network should help predict future patenting rates.

D. Acemoglu, Akcigit, and Kerr 2016 constructed an influence network between technology classes based on citations and used this to predict future patenting rates. They predicted the number of future patents in a given technology class, showed that including past patenting rates from related classes improved their results, and argued that this demonstrates the existence of network effects.

Because patenting rates are very persistent, however, these results require careful interpretation. The number of patents granted in a given class in a given year tends to be very similar to the number of patents that were granted in that class in previous years. As is well known in the spurious regression literature, a persistent time series can be an excellent predictor of other persistent yet independent time series. Thus, to demonstrate the existence of network effects, one must first establish a careful benchmark. As shown in A. Pichler (2021), however, the network-based predictions of Acemoglu, Akcigit, and Kerr (2016) are substantially worse than network-independent predictions made from simple random walks with drifts.

Motivated by this observation, in Pichler, Lafond, and Farmer (2020) we developed a network-based model and carefully established its predictive over and above that of a random walk. The model resembles a spatial econometrics model and is very similar to production network models. The growth rate of a technology depends on the growth rates of its neighbors,

$$g_{it} = \beta \sum_j W_{ji,t} g_{jt} + \epsilon_{it} \Rightarrow \boldsymbol{g}_t = (\boldsymbol{I} - \beta \boldsymbol{W}'_t)^{-1} \epsilon_t \qquad (23)$$

where g_t is a vector of growth rates of patents, and $\mathbf{W}_t$ is a matrix where column j gives the "recipe" of technology j, that is, the share of the citations it makes that go to each of the other technologies.

An issue with these models is that, if the shocks ϵ are independent across technologies, this assumes that all co-movement comes from the network. When there is observed co-movement, an alternative hypothesis that is equally compelling *a priori* but fundamentally different conceptually is that there is a common factor, exogenous to all technologies. The factor model says that all technologies move together because they are driven by a common external force, while the network model says that they move together because they are interdependent. Econometrically, common factors represent strong cross-sectional dependence because the dependence between two nodes does not really depend on how many other nodes are present, while network dependence is weak because two randomly chosen nodes are less likely to be close as network size goes to infinity. That said, details matter and it is usually difficult to distinguish between the two sources of co-movement.

A. T. Foerster, P.-D. G. Sarte, and M. W. Watson (2011) proposed an encompassing model, in the context of production networks, keeping equation (23) but assuming that the noise follows a factor model, $\epsilon_t = \lambda f_t + \nu_t$, where λ is a vector of loadings, ν_t is a vector of idiosyncratic shocks and f_t is a scalar, the common factor. In ongoing work, we are investigating the source of cross-sectional dependence to establish whether predictability arises from common trends in the patent system, or from the endogenous dynamics inherent to systems with strong network-based interdependencies. Of course, this approach remains very parametric or highly model-based, and one could likely do a better job at a pure prediction task by using black-box machine-learning methods.

Conclusion: Toward a Technology Observatory

In many cases, it is very hard to collect historical data on costs, but patent data exists and is straightforwardly available. Can we relate patent data on a technology with progress rates of that technology, for the cases where both are available, so that we can predict improvement rates in cases where only patent data is available? In a potentially important study, G. Triulzi, J. Alstott, and C. L. Magee (2020) argue that centrality in a carefully crafted network (using citations, technology codes, and careful normalization) is predictive of the Moore's law technological progress rate. More generally, it is tempting to think that the positions of technologies in an abstract, latent technological space determine their progress rate.

An alternative approach to the same problem is to predict progress rates using properties of a technology; for instance, A. Malhotra and T. S. Schmidt (2020) classify technologies according to their degree of design complexity and the need for customization, arguing that this determines progress rates—actually, in their case, Wright's law exponents. Simple technologies like solar PV have higher learning rates than nuclear power, because their granularity implies large economies of scale and learning; when each project is huge, and highly specific, these benefits are harder to materialize.

This suggests an ambitious research agenda to construct a technology observatory, combining data on costs, deployment, technical performance, design characteristics, latent demand indicators, patents, scientific publications, products, associated companies, etc. This would make it possible to better understand the fundamental drivers of progress rates, why they are so diverse, and improve predictions when they are most helpful, that is, for technologies in very early stages of deployment.

This is likely to be a lively and exciting area of future research, as it is very important but remains difficult, with the application of new data and analytical methods having a genuine potential to improve over existing approaches. ⟆

Acknowledgments

I would like to thank all my collaborators on this research program, and in particular Doyne Farmer, as well as Lorenzo Agnelli, Lennart Baumgärtner, Joel Dyer, José Moran, Anton Pichler, Rupert Way, Benjamin Wagenvoort, and Owen Westfold for comments and stimulating discussions. The usual disclaimer applies. This research was funded by Baillie Gifford and the UKRI through ESRC grant PRINZ (ES/W010356/1).

REFERENCES

Acemoglu, D., U. Akcigit, and W. R. Kerr. 2016. "Innovation Network." *Proceedings of the National Academy of Sciences* 113 (41): 11483–11488. https://doi.org/10.1073/pnas.1613559113.

Albright, R. E. 2002. "What Can Past Technology Forecasts Tell Us about the Future?" *Technological Forecasting and Social Change* 69 (5): 443–464. https://doi.org/10.1016/S0040-1625(02)00186-5.

Alstott, J., G. Triulzi, B. Yan, and J. Luo. 2017. "Mapping Technology Space by Normalizing Patent Networks." *Scientometrics* 110:443–479. https://doi.org/10.1007/s11192-016-2107-y.

Argote, L., and D. Epple. 1990. "Learning Curves in Manufacturing." *Science* 247 (4945): 920–924. https://doi.org/10.1126/science.247.4945.920.

Arrow, K. J. 1962. "The Economic Implications of Learning by Doing." *The Review of Economic Studies* 29 (3): 155–173. https://doi.org/10.2307/2295952.

Arrow, K. J., R. Forsythe, M. Gorham, R. Hahn, R. Hanson, J. O. Ledyard, S. Levmore, *et al.* 2008. "The Promise of Prediction Markets." *Science* 320 (5878): 877–878. https://doi.org/10.1126/science.1157679.

Arthur, W. B. 1989. "Competing Technologies, Increasing Returns, and Lock-In by Historical Events." *The Economic Journal*, 116–131. https://doi.org/10.2307/2234208.

———. 2010. *The Nature of Technology: What It Is and How It Evolves.* New York, NY: Free Press.

———. 2026. "Combinatorial Evolution." In *The Economy as an Evolving Complex System IV,* edited by R. M. del Rio-Chanona, M. Pangallo, J. Bednar, E. D. Beinhocker, J. Kaszowska-Mojsa, F. Lafond, P. Mealy, A. Pichler, and J. D. Farmer. Santa Fe, NM: SFI Press.

Ayres, R. U. 1969. *Technological Forecasting and Long-Range Planning.* Maidenhead, NY: McGraw-Hill Book Company. https : / / archive . org / details / technologicalfor0000ayre_l4a1/.

Baumgärtner, L., and J. D. Farmer. n.d. "Empirical Basis for National Renewable Cost Forecasts." In progress.

Bengio, Y., S. Russell, E. Musk, S. Wozniak, Y. N. Harari, E. Mostaque, A. Yang, *et al.* 2023. *Pause Giant AI Experiments: An Open Letter.* Future of Life Institute. https://futureoflife.org/open-letter/pause-giant-ai-experiments/.

Benson, C. L., G. Triulzi, and C. L. Magee. 2018. "Is There a Moore's Law for 3D Printing?" *3D Printing and Additive Manufacturing* 5 (1): 53–62. https:// doi.org/10.1089/3dp.2017.0041.

Ciarli, T., A. Coad, and I. Rafols. 2016. "Quantitative Analysis of Technology Futures: A Review of Techniques, Uses and Characteristics." *Science and Public Policy* 43 (5): 630–645. https://doi.org/10.1093/scipol/scv059.

Clements, M., and D. F. Hendry. 1998. *Forecasting Economic Time Series.* Cambridge, UK: Cambridge University Press.

Diane, C. 2026. "Why Are New Ideas Getting Harder to Use?" In *The Economy as an Evolving Complex System IV,* edited by R. M. del Rio-Chanona, M. Pangallo, J. Bednar, E. D. Beinhocker, J. Kaszowska-Mojsa, F. Lafond, P. Mealy, A. Pichler, and J. D. Farmer. Santa Fe, NM: SFI Press.

Entorf, H. 1997. "Random Walks with Drifts: Nonsense Regression and Spurious Fixed-Effect Estimation." *Journal of Econometrics* 80 (2): 287–296. https://doi.org/10.1016/S0304-4076(97)00041-9.

Érdi, P., K. Makovi, Z. Somogyvári, K. Strandburg, J. Tobochnik, P. Volf, and L. Zalányi. 2013. "Prediction of Emerging Technologies based on Analysis of the US Patent Citation Network." *Scientometrics* 95 (1): 225–242. https://doi.org/10.1007/s11192-012-0796-4.

Farmer, J. D., and F. Lafond. 2016. "How Predictable is Technological Progress?" *Research Policy* 45 (3): 647–665. https://doi.org/10.1016/j.respol.2015.11.001.

Foerster, A. T., P.-D. G. Sarte, and M. W. Watson. 2011. "Sectoral versus Aggregate Shocks: A Structural Factor Analysis of Industrial Production." *Journal of Political Economy* 119 (1): 1–38. https://doi.org/10.1086/659311.

Frenken, K., and F. Neffke. 2026. "Economic Geography and Complexity Theory." In *The Economy as an Evolving Complex System IV,* edited by R. M. del Rio-Chanona, M. Pangallo, J. Bednar, E. D. Beinhocker, J. Kaszowska-Mojsa, F. Lafond, P. Mealy, A. Pichler, and J. D. Farmer. Santa Fe, NM: SFI Press.

Funk, J. L., and C. L. Magee. 2015. "Rapid Improvements with No Commercial Production: How Do the Improvements Occur?" *Research Policy* 44 (3): 777–788. https://doi.org/10.1016/j.respol.2014.11.005.

Gilfillan, S. C. 1937. "The Prediction of Inventions." *Journal of the Patent and Trademark Office Society* 19:623.

Goldin, I., P. Koutroumpis, F. Lafond, and J. Winkler. 2024. "Why is Productivity Slowing Down?" *Journal of Economic Literature* 62 (1): 196–268. https://doi.org/10.1257/jel.20221543.

Gordon, R. J. 1990. *The Measurement of Durable Goods Prices.* Chicago, IL: University of Chicago Press.

Grace, K., H. Stewart, J. F. Sandkühler, S. Thomas, B. Weinstein-Raun, J. Brauner, and R. C. Korzekwa. 2024. "Thousands of AI Authors on the Future of AI." arXiv preprint: 2401.02843, https://doi.org/10.48550/arXiv.2401.02843.

Grübler, A., N. Nakićenović, and D. G. Victor. 1999. "Dynamics of Energy Technologies and Global Change." *Energy Policy* 27 (5): 247–280. https://doi.org/10.1016/S0301-4215(98)00067-6.

Halawi, D., F. Zhang, C. Yueh-Han, and J. Steinhardt. 2024. *Approaching Human-Level Forecasting with Language Models.* arXiv preprint: 2402.18563. https://doi.org/10.48550/arXiv.2402.18563.

Harper, J. C. 2013. *Impact of Technology Foresight.* Compendium of Evidence on the Effectiveness of Innovation Policy Intervention Project, Nesta Working Paper no. 13/16. Compendium of Evidence on the Effectiveness of Innovation Policy Intervention, Manchester Institute of Innovation Research. https://www.nesta.org.uk/wp13-16.

Jantsch, E. 1967. *Technological Forecasting in Perspective.* OECD.

Kahn, H., and A. J. Wiener. 1967. "The Next Thirty-Three Years: A Framework for Speculation." *Daedalus* 96 (3): 705–732. https://www.jstor.org/stable/20027066.

Kim, D., D. B. Cerigo, H. Jeong, and H. Youn. 2016. "Technological Novelty Profile and Invention's Future Impact." *EPJ Data Science* 5:1–15. https://doi.org/10.1140/epjds/s13688-016-0069-1.

Koh, H., and C. L. Magee. 2006. "A Functional Approach for Studying Technological Progress: Application to Information Technology." *Technological Forecasting and Social Change* 73 (9): 1061–1083. https://doi.org/10.1016/j.techfore.2006.06.001.

———. 2008. "A Functional Approach for Studying Technological Progress: Extension to Energy Technology." *Technological Forecasting and Social Change* 75 (6): 735–758. https://doi.org/10.1016/j.techfore.2007.05.007.

Lafond, F., A. G. Bailey, J. D. Bakker, D. Rebois, R. Zadourian, P. McSharry, and J. D. Farmer. 2018. "How Well Do Experience Curves Predict Technological Progress? A Method for Making Distributional Forecasts." *Technological Forecasting and Social Change* 128:104–117. https://doi.org/10.1016/j.techfore.2017.11.001.

Lafond, F., D. Greenwald, and J. D. Farmer. 2022. "Can Stimulating Demand Drive Costs Down? World War II as a Natural Experiment." *The Journal of Economic History* 82 (3): 727–764. https://doi.org/10.1017/S0022050722000249.

Lafond, F., and D. Kim. 2019. "Long-Run Dynamics of the US Patent Classification System." *Journal of Evolutionary Economics* 29 (2): 631–664. https://doi.org/10.1007/s00191-018-0603-3.

Malhotra, A., and T. S. Schmidt. 2020. "Accelerating Low-Carbon Innovation." *Joule* 4 (11): 2259–2267. https://doi.org/10.1016/j.joule.2020.09.004.

Mandelbrot, B. 1997. "A Case Against the Lognormal Distribution." In *Fractals and Scaling in Finance: Discontinuity, Concentration, Risk,* 252–269. New York, NY: Springer. https://doi.org/10.1007/978-1-4757-2763-0_9.

Mariani, M. S., M. Medo, and F. Lafond. 2019. "Early Identification of Important Patents: Design and Validation of Citation Network Metrics." *Technological Forecasting and Social Change* 146:644–654. https://doi.org/10.1016/j. techfore.2018.01.036.

Markowitz, H. 1952. "Portfolio Selection." *Journal of Finance* 7 (1): 77–91. https://doi.org/10.1111/j.1540-6261.1952.tb01525.x.

Martino, J. P. 1993. *Technological Forecasting for Decision Making.* New York, NY: McGraw-Hill, Inc.

Meng, J., R. Way, E. Verdolini, and L. Díaz Anadón. 2021. "Comparing Expert Elicitation and Model-Based Probabilistic Technology Cost Forecasts for the Energy Transition." *Proceedings of the National Academy of Sciences* 118 (27): e1917165118. https://doi.org/10.1073/pnas.1917165118.

Nagy, B., J. D. Farmer, Q. M. Bui, and J. E. Trancik. 2013. "Statistical Basis for Predicting Technological Progress." *PloS One* 8 (2): 1–7. https://doi.org/10.1371/journal.pone.0052669.

Nagy, B., J. D. Farmer, J. E. Trancik, and J. P. Gonzales. 2011. "Superexponential Long-Term Trends in Information Technology." *Technological Forecasting and Social Change* 78 (8): 1356–1364. https://doi.org/10.1016/j.techfore.2011. 07.006.

Napolitano, L., E. Evangelou, E. Pugliese, P. Zeppini, and G. Room. 2018. "Technology Networks: The Autocatalytic Origins of Innovation." *Royal Society Open Science* 5 (6): 172445. https://doi.org/10.1098/rsos.172445.

Neffke, F., A. Sbardella, U. Schetter, and A. Tacchella. 2026. "Economic Complexity Analysis." In *The Economy as an Evolving Complex System IV,* edited by R. M. del Rio-Chanona, M. Pangallo, J. Bednar, E. D. Beinhocker, J. Kaszowska-Mojsa, F. Lafond, P. Mealy, A. Pichler, and J. D. Farmer. Santa Fe, NM: SFI Press.

Nordhaus, W. D. 2014. "The Perils of the Learning Model for Modeling Endogenous Technological Change." *The Energy Journal* 35 (1): 1–14. https://doi.org/10. 5547/01956574.35.1.1.

Pfeiffer, A., C. Hepburn, A. Vogt-Schilb, and B. Caldecott. 2018. "Committed Emissions from Existing and Planned Power Plants and Asset Stranding Required to Meet the Paris Agreement." *Environmental Research Letters* 13 (5): 054019. https://doi.org/10.1088/1748-9326/aabc5f.

Philippon, T. 2023. *Additive Growth*. Technical report. Leonard N. Stern School of Business. https://pages.stern.nyu.edu/~tphilipp/papers/AddGrowth_macro. pdf.

Pichler, A. 2021. "Network-Dependent Dynamics of Innovation and Production." PhD diss., University of Oxford.

Pichler, A., F. Lafond, and J. D. Farmer. 2020. "Technological Interdependencies Predict Innovation Dynamics." arXiv preprint: 2003.00580, https://doi.org/ 10.48550/arXiv.2003.00580.

Porter, A. L., and S. W. Cunningham. 2005. "Tech Mining." *Competitive Intelligence Magazine* 8 (1): 30–36.

Sahal, D. 1979. "A Theory of Progress Functions." *AIIE Transactions* 11 (1): 23–29. https://doi.org/10.1080/05695557908974396.

Sampson, M. 1991. "The Effect of Parameter Uncertainty on Forecast Variances and Confidence Intervals for Unit Root and Trend Stationary Time-Series Models." *Journal of Applied Econometrics* 6 (1): 67–76. https://doi.org/10. 1002/jae.3950060106.

Schoenegger, P., I. Tuminauskaite, P. S. Park, and P. E. Tetlock. 2024. *Wisdom of the Silicon Crowd: LLM Ensemble Prediction Capabilities Match Human Crowd Accuracy*. https://doi.org/10.48550/arXiv.2402.19379.

Shi, F., and J. Evans. 2023. "Surprising Combinations of Research Contents and Contexts are Related to Impact and Emerge with Scientific Outsiders from Distant Disciplines." *Nature Communications* 14 (1): 1641. https://doi.org/ 10.1038/s41467-023-36741-4.

Solé, R. V., S. Valverde, M. R. Casals, S. A. Kauffman, J. D. Farmer, and N. Eldredge. 2013. "The Evolutionary Ecology of Technological Innovations." *Complexity* 18 (4): 15–27. https://doi.org/10.1002/cplx.21436.

Strumsky, D., and J. Lobo. 2015. "Identifying the Sources of Technological Novelty in the Process of Invention." *Research Policy* 44 (8): 1445–1461. https://doi. org/10.1016/j.respol.2015.05.008.

Tacchella, A., A. Napoletano, and L. Pietronero. 2020. "The Language of Innovation." *PloS One* 15 (4): e0230107. https://doi.org/10.1371/journal.pone.0230107.

Tankwa, B. 2024. *Is Technology Diffusion Accelerating?* In progress.

Tetlock, P. E., and D. Gardner. 2016. *Superforecasting: The Art and Science of Prediction.* New York, NY: Random House.

Triulzi, G., J. Alstott, and C. L. Magee. 2020. "Estimating Technology Performance Improvement Rates by Mining Patent Data." *Technological Forecasting and Social Change* 158:120100. https://doi.org/10.1016/j.techfore.2020.120100.

Verdolini, E., L. Díaz Anadón, E. Baker, V. Bosetti, and L. A. Reis. 2018. "Future Prospects for Energy Technologies: Insights from Expert Elicitations." *Review of Environmental Economics and Policy,* https://doi.org/10.1093/reep/rex028.

Wagenvoort, B., J. Dyer, F. Lafond, and J. D. Farmer. 2025. "Universality and Predictability of Technology Diffusion." *in progress* x (x): x–x.

Way, R., M. C. Ives, P. Mealy, and J. D. Farmer. 2022. "Empirically Grounded Technology Forecasts and the Energy Transition." *Joule* 6 (9): 2057–2082. https://doi.org/10.1016/j.joule.2022.08.009.

Way, R., F. Lafond, F. Lillo, V. Panchenko, and J. D. Farmer. 2019. "Wright Meets Markowitz: How Standard Portfolio Theory Changes When Assets are Technologies Following Experience Curves." *Journal of Economic Dynamics and Control* 101:211–238. https://doi.org/10.1016/j.jedc.2018.10.006.

Youn, H., D. Strumsky, L. M. A. Bettencourt, and J. Lobo. 2015. "Invention as a Combinatorial Process: Evidence from US Patents." *Journal of the Royal Society Interface* 12 (106): 20150272. https://doi.org/10.1098/rsif.2015.0272.

Zadourian, R. 2018. "Model-Based and Empirical Analyses of Stochastic Fluctuations in Economy and Finance." PhD diss., Technische Universität Dresden.

Zadourian, R., and A. Klümper. 2018. "Exact Probability Distribution Function for the Volatility of Cumulative Production." *Physica A: Statistical Mechanics and its Applications* 495:59–66. https://doi.org/10.1016/j.physa.2017.12.003.

Appendix

The code to reproduce the figures in this appendix (and a little more) can be downloaded from https://francoislafond.info/research/.

A Forecast Errors

We consider the general model

$$\ln \frac{c_t}{c_{t-1}} = \omega \ln \frac{z_t}{z_{t-1}} + \eta_t, \tag{24}$$

$$\eta_t = \epsilon_t + \rho \epsilon_{t-1}, \tag{25}$$

$$\epsilon_t \sim \mathcal{N}(0, \sigma_\epsilon^2). \tag{26}$$

For future reference, the variance of η is

$$\sigma_\eta^2 = (1 + \rho^2)\sigma_\epsilon^2. \tag{27}$$

Throughout, we will assume for simplicity that we know the autocorrelation parameter ρ and the variances. While we will carefully distinguish between ω and its estimated counterpart $\hat{\omega}$, we will always use σ^2 and ρ without a hat, and use true values in our simulations.

Table 1 shows the various restrictions we consider below. It is useful to start from the simple random walk with drift with no autocorrelated noise, and work our way up.

Table 1. Restrictions of the general model equations (24)–(25) in each specific model, and associated section.

MODEL	EXPERIENCE	AUTOCORRELATION	SECTION
Moore	$\Delta \ln z_t = r$	$\rho = 0$	A.1
Moore + MA(1)	$\Delta \ln z_t = r$	$-1 < \rho < 1$	A.2
Wright	unrestricted	$\rho = 0$	A.3
Wright + MA(1)	unrestricted	$-1 < \rho < 1$	A.4

Throughout, we assume that the process starts at $t = 0$ (although noise starts at $t = -1$), and we observe data for $m + 1$ periods, that is, until $t = m$. We normalize to $c_0 = z_0 = 1$. We seek to predict τ steps ahead, to $t = m + \tau$.

This is a detailed treatment of highly specific cases; in particular, even when we assume that the noise is autocorrelated, we do not use this to make better forecasts. See M. Sampson (1991) and M. Clements and D. Hendry (1998) for more general treatments.

THE RANDOM WALK WITH DRIFT AKA "MOORE'S LAW"

We call "Moore's law" the random walk with drift. This corresponds to equation (24), where experience grows at exactly the same rate every period, $\Delta \ln z_t = r$. In other words, if experience grows at exactly the same rate every period, its effects are indistinguishable from simply time ticking.

Starting from the case with no autocorrelation, equation (25) with $\rho = 0$, our model here is

$$\ln c_t - \ln c_{t-1} \equiv Y_t = \mu + \eta_t, \qquad (28)$$

where $\mu \equiv \omega r$. We estimate it from a sample of the first $m + 1$ periods (i.e., m growth rates) as the simple mean

$$\hat{\mu} = \frac{1}{m} \sum_{i=1}^{m} Y_i = \mu + \frac{1}{m} \sum_{i=1}^{m} \eta_i \sim \mathcal{N}\left(\mu, \frac{\sigma_\eta^2}{m}\right), \qquad (29)$$

where the last step follows from a direct application of rules for summing up independent random normal variables.

Considering the data-generating process (28), since future noise is not predictable, and since we do not know μ but we have the estimate $\hat{\mu}$ from (29), the forecast for τ-periods ahead is

$$\ln \hat{c}_{m+\tau} = \ln c_m + \hat{\mu}\tau. \qquad (30)$$

The forecast error then is

$$\mathcal{E} \equiv \ln c_{m+\tau} - \ln \hat{c}_{m+\tau} = (\mu - \hat{\mu})\tau + \sum_{i=m+1}^{m+\tau} \eta_i,$$

$$\sim \mathcal{N}\left(0, \tau^2 \frac{\sigma_\eta^2}{m}\right) + \mathcal{N}\left(0, \tau \sigma_\eta^2\right),$$

$$\sim \mathcal{N}\left(0, \sigma_\eta^2\left(\tau + \frac{\tau^2}{m}\right)\right). \qquad (31)$$

The third step follows from assuming independence, which is correct in this case: noise from the past, which affects parameter estimation, is independent from noise in the future. This calculation makes clear that the prediction variance is the sum of two terms—a term τ is associated with future noise, and a term τ^2/m is associated with parameter estimation; both are premultiplied by the variance of the noise.

To get a distributional forecast at horizon τ using data until time m, denoted $\mathcal{P}_{m,\tau}$, one usually uses the point forecast (30) plus the forecast error (31), that is,

$$\mathcal{P}_{m+\tau} = \ln \hat{c}_{m+\tau} + \mathcal{E} \sim \mathcal{N}\left(\ln c_m + \hat{\mu}\tau, \sigma_\eta^2\left(\tau + \frac{\tau^2}{m}\right)\right), \quad (32)$$

see, for example, Sampson (1991) for the same specific case of the geometric random walk with drift.[12]

An alternative derivation of formula (32) arises if we proceed as in R. Way *et al.* (2022) have done for Wright's law. We will call this "the simulation method." Way *et al.* (2022) are interested

---

[12]Note that this derivation conditions on past data, but treats the estimated parameter as stochastic, which may appear contradictory. Here, one considers the ensemble for the entire time series $(0 \ldots m \ldots (m+\tau))$, rather than just for the future conditional on one specific realization of the past (a single realization $(0 \ldots m)$ and an uncertain future $((m+1) \ldots (m+\tau))$). In terms of simulations, it means drawing one full time series, splitting into train and test, evaluating one forecast, and repeating by drawing an entirely new full time series at the next iteration. This is different from drawing one time series until m, making a forecast, and comparing it to the distribution of possible futures conditional on that one specific realization.

in making predictions, but do not always have access to the raw data, so they sometimes have to pick parameter values from the literature. Let us start from the last observed value, and project forward by first drawing a drift parameter from its distribution, taken to be

$$\tilde{\mu} \sim \mathcal{N}(\hat{\mu}, \sigma^2/m), \qquad (33)$$

where σ^2/m can directly be a standard error reported in the literature, and then draw a set of future noises from

$$\eta_{m+\tau} \sim \mathcal{N}(0, \sigma^2).$$

Now let us denote a future value generated in this way by $\ln \tilde{c}_{m+\tau}$. Instead of simulating, we can actually compute its probability exactly as

$$\Pr(\ln \tilde{c}_{m+\tau} = x) = \int \Pr(\ln \tilde{c}_{m+\tau}|\tilde{\mu}) \Pr(\tilde{\mu})d\tilde{\mu}, \qquad (34)$$

where the first factor in the integral is $\mathcal{N}(\ln c_m + \tilde{\mu}\tau, \sigma_\eta^2\tau)$ by well-known properties of random walks, and the second factor is from equation 33. Inserting the formulas for the Gaussian probability densities with the appropriate means and variances, and performing the integral gives (32) as expected. Note that this is essentially a Bayesian calculation; in fact, it can be shown that the same formula arises in a Bayesian framework with an improper prior on μ.

While this is intuitive, we shall now see that a complication arises when one introduces autocorrelated noise. The reason to show this is that in practice, to make a forecast, we may have to pick the parameters (drift and its standard error, and variance of the noise) from the literature. In these cases we do not have the luxury to estimate all the parameters ourselves, including in a Bayesian way. Reassuringly, we will find that the predictions from the "simulation method" reproduce very well the exact distribution of forecast errors.

MOORE'S LAW WITH MOVING AVERAGE NOISE

When noise is autocorrelated, the realizations of the noise in the latest periods of the estimation sample affect the parameter estimation (of course), *but also future noise,* since future noise depends on past noise.

In Farmer and Lafond (2016), we chose an MA(1) process for the noise (eq. 25). The reason was that it worked well for our purpose—it increased the theoretical variance of the forecast errors in a way that made it more similar to the empirical forecast errors; we used it a bit as a fudge factor, providing us with a powerful parametric model for the forecast errors. It is quite possible that more complex autoregressive moving-averages ARMAs would be more appropriate,[13] but the MA(1) makes analytical calculations very simple because noise at time t depends only on noise at time $t - 1$.

Starting again from (31) and using (29), the forecast error is

$$\mathcal{E} = (\mu - \hat{\mu})\tau + \sum_{i=m+1}^{m+\tau} \eta_i = \left(\frac{-1}{m} \sum_{i=1}^{m} \eta_i\right)\tau + \sum_{i=m+1}^{m+\tau} \eta_i. \quad (35)$$

We will now see three methods to compute or approximate the variance of (35).

Method 1: Exact calculation from independent noise terms.
The first method is to painstakingly separate all the independent

---

[13] Data-generation processes (DGPs) with fat tail or long memory noise did not work as well as DGPs with ARMA noise to imply forecast errors similar to those we had empirically, but these two possibilities could be re-investigated with more and better data.

noise terms ϵ_i in equation 35. Substituting in (25),

$$\mathcal{E} = \underbrace{\left\{ \frac{-\tau}{m} \sum_{i=1}^{m} [\epsilon_i + \rho\epsilon_{i-1}] \right\}}_{\text{due to parameter estimation}} + \underbrace{\left\{ \sum_{i=m+1}^{m+\tau} [\epsilon_i + \rho\epsilon_{i-1}] \right\}}_{\text{due to future noise}}$$

$$= \left\{ \frac{-\tau}{m} \left(\rho\epsilon_0 + \frac{\tau}{m} \sum_{i=1}^{m-1} (1+\rho)\epsilon_i + \epsilon_m \right) \right\}$$

$$+ \left\{ \rho\epsilon_m + \sum_{i=m+1}^{m+\tau-1} (1+\rho)\epsilon_i + \epsilon_{m+\tau} \right\}$$

$$= \frac{-\tau}{m} \left(\rho\epsilon_0 + \frac{\tau}{m} \sum_{i=1}^{m-1} (1+\rho)\epsilon_i \right) + \underbrace{\left(\rho - \frac{\tau}{m} \right)\epsilon_m}_{\text{"mixed" term}}$$

$$+ \sum_{i=m+1}^{m+\tau-1} (1+\rho)\epsilon_i + \epsilon_{m+\tau}.$$

The term ϵ_m has gathered a prefactor from parameter estimation (τ/m), and another from future noise (ρ); we will see below that this creates non-null covariance between $\hat{\mu}$ and future noise. For now, now that we have our fully independent noise terms we can get the variance as

$$\text{Var}(\mathcal{E})_{\text{exact}} = \sigma_\epsilon^2 \Bigg[\left(\frac{\tau}{m}\rho \right)^2 + (m-1)\left(\frac{\tau}{m}(1+\rho) \right)^2$$
$$+ \left(\rho - \frac{\tau}{m} \right)^2 + (\tau-1)(1+\rho)^2 + 1 \Bigg],$$

and, while the algebra is a little tedious, this simplifies to

$$\text{Var}(\mathcal{E})_{\text{exact}} = \sigma_\epsilon^2 \left[-2\rho + \left(1 + 2\frac{m-1}{m}\rho + \rho^2 \right)\left(\tau + \frac{\tau^2}{m} \right) \right].$$
$$(36)$$

In this formula, we cannot neatly separate a "τ term associated with future noise" from a "τ^2/m term associated with parameter estimation" since the τ term is multiplied by a factor that includes the sample size for parameter estimation m. In more general settings, this is one of the reasons why forecast error taxonomies are only approximate (Clements and Hendry 1998, section 7.2, p. 163).

However, assuming that m is large enough (that is, $(m - 1)/m \approx 1$) and τ is large enough (-2ρ can be neglected), we get the approximation quoted in the main text,

$$
\begin{aligned}
\mathrm{Var}(\mathcal{E})_{\mathrm{exact}} &\approx \sigma_\epsilon^2 (1 + \rho)^2 \left(\tau + \frac{\tau^2}{m} \right) \\
&= \sigma_\eta^2 \frac{(1 + \rho)^2}{1 + \rho^2} \left(\tau + \frac{\tau^2}{m} \right) \equiv \mathrm{Var}(\mathcal{E})_{\mathrm{approx}}.
\end{aligned}
\tag{37}
$$

Since the only issue preventing us from separating the two effects is a single noise term that affects parameter estimation and future noise (ϵ_m), its overall influence decreases if we increase the sample size and the number of future periods. It is good to keep in mind that the problem will be worse the stronger and the longer the autocorrelation is (e.g., more general autoregressive integrated moving averages with "high" parameters).

Method 2: Evaluating the variance due to parameter estimation and future noise separately. The following preliminary is useful. Recall from equation (27) that the MA(1) process from equation (25) has variance $(1 + \rho^2)\sigma_\epsilon^2$. However, if we sum the noise, say m times, the variance is not $m\sigma_\eta^2$, but instead

$$
\begin{aligned}
\mathrm{Var}\left(\sum_{i=1}^m \eta_i \right) &= \mathrm{Var}\left(\sum_{i=1}^m (\epsilon_i + \rho\epsilon_{i-1}) \right) = \mathrm{Var}\left(\rho\epsilon_0 + \sum_{i=1}^{m-1} \epsilon_i + \epsilon_m \right) \\
&= \sigma_\epsilon^2 \left(\rho^2 + (m - 1)(1 + \rho)^2 + 1 \right) \tag{38} \\
&= \sigma_\epsilon^2 \left(m(1 + \rho)^2 - 2\rho \right). \tag{39}
\end{aligned}
$$

Note the useful approximation

$$
\mathrm{Var}\left(\sum_{i=1}^m \eta_i \right) \approx \sigma_\epsilon^2 m(1 + \rho)^2. \tag{40}
$$

Now, we can compute the variance of the forecast error starting from (35), which is exact, as

$$\mathrm{Var}(\mathcal{E}) = \mathrm{Var}\left(\tau(\mu - \hat{\mu})\right) + \mathrm{Var}\left(\sum_{i=m+1}^{m+\tau} \eta_i\right)$$

$$+ \, 2\,\mathrm{Cov}\left(\tau(\mu - \hat{\mu}), \sum_{i=m+1}^{m+\tau} \eta_i\right)$$

$$= \tau^2 \mathrm{Var}(\hat{\mu}) + \mathrm{Var}\left(\sum_{i=m+1}^{m+\tau} \eta_i\right)$$

$$- \, 2\tau\,\mathrm{Cov}\left(\hat{\mu}, \sum_{i=m+1}^{m+\tau} \eta_i\right)$$

$$= \tau^2 \mathrm{Var}\left(\frac{1}{m}\sum_{i=1}^{m} \eta_i\right) + \mathrm{Var}\left(\sum_{i=m+1}^{m+\tau} \eta_i\right)$$

$$- \, 2\tau\,\mathrm{Cov}\left(\frac{1}{m}\sum_{i=1}^{m} \eta_i, \sum_{i=m+1}^{m+\tau} \eta_i\right).$$

Using equation (39), we compute easily the two variances as

$$\mathrm{Var}(\hat{\mu}) = \mathrm{Var}\left(\frac{1}{m}\sum_{i=1}^{m} \eta_i\right)$$

$$= \sigma_\epsilon^2 \left(\frac{1}{m}\right)^2 \left(\rho^2 + (m-1)(1+\rho)^2 + 1\right) \qquad (41)$$

and

$$\mathrm{Var}\left(\sum_{i=m+1}^{m+\tau} \eta_i\right) = \sigma_\epsilon^2 \left(\rho^2 + (\tau-1)(1+\rho)^2 + 1\right). \qquad (42)$$

The covariance term is, indeed, not zero,

$$\mathrm{Cov}\left(\frac{1}{m}\sum_{i=1}^{m} \eta_i, \sum_{i=m+1}^{m+\tau} \eta_i\right)$$

$$= E\left[\frac{\epsilon_m}{m}\rho\epsilon_m\right] = \frac{\rho}{m}\sigma_\epsilon^2, \qquad (43)$$

that is, if $\rho > 0$, there is positive correlation between $\hat{\mu}$ and future noise. Substituting equations (41), (42) and (43) back into (41) gives the exact formula derived using method 1, equation (36).

If instead of the exact formulas for the variance (using 39), we use the approximation (40), and assume that the covariance is equal to zero, we retrieve the approximation for the forecast errors derived earlier, equation (37).

Method 3: Simulation. The third method consists in drawing a value from the distribution of $\hat{\mu}$, and then drawing values from an MA(1) process for the future noise, and repeating this experiment many times to obtain a distributional forecast. The simulation method effectively generates

$$\ln c_{m+\tau} = \ln c_m + \tilde{\mu}\tau + \sum_{i=m+1}^{m+\tau} \eta_i,$$

where

$$\tilde{\mu} \sim \mathcal{N}\left(\hat{\mu}, \mathrm{Var}(\hat{\mu})\right).$$

with $\mathrm{Var}(\hat{\mu})$ from equation (41). The variance of the predicted log cost in the simulation method is thus

$$\mathrm{Var}(\mathcal{E})_{\mathrm{sim}} \equiv \mathrm{Var}(\ln c_{m+\tau}) = \tau^2 \mathrm{Var}(\hat{\mu}) + \mathrm{Var}\left(\sum_{i=m+1}^{m+\tau} \eta_i\right),$$

using equations (41) and (42) for an explicit formula.

Put differently, the simulation method is better than the approximation because it produces exact values for the variances (in the limit of infinitely many simulations), but it is not as good as the exact method because it omits the covariance between the distribution of the estimated parameter and the distribution of future noise.

To sum up, we have

$$\begin{aligned}
\mathrm{Var}(\mathcal{E})_{\mathrm{sim}} &= \mathrm{Var}(\mathcal{E})_{\mathrm{exact}} - 2\tau \mathrm{Cov}\left(\hat{\mu}, \sum \text{future noise}\right) \\
&= \mathrm{Var}(\mathcal{E})_{\mathrm{exact}} - 2\sigma_\epsilon^2 \frac{\tau}{m}\rho.
\end{aligned} \tag{44}$$

A note on bias. An unbiased forecast of a MA(1) process would use the estimated past noise to make a forecast of future noise

$$E[\eta_{m+1}|\hat{\epsilon}_m] = \rho\hat{\epsilon}_m.$$

For any particular realization of a time series, our forecast for time $m+1$ is biased because it does not account for this. However, on average over the ensemble, where we cannot condition on a specific realization of ϵ_m, the forecasts are unbiased.

WRIGHT'S LAW WITHOUT AUTOCORRELATION

Starting again from the general model (24) but with $\rho = 0$, and using shorthands Y and X for growth rates of costs and experience, respectively, we have

$$Y_t = \omega X_t + \eta_t. \tag{45}$$

We estimate the learning exponent as

$$\hat{\omega} = \frac{\sum_{i=1}^m Y_i X_i}{\sum_{i=1}^m X_i^2} = \omega + \frac{\sum_{i=1}^m X_i \eta_i}{\sum_{i=1}^m X_i^2}, \tag{46}$$

where the last step comes from substituting in (45). This is an ordinary least squares (OLS) regression through the origin (omitting the intercept is important because the intercept would estimate an exponential time trend; see the main text for an informal discussion and section C for additional discussion in the context of spurious regressions). Note that here and throughout, I treat experience as given (i.e., as "non-stochastic").

Note for later that, since the noise terms η_t are independent,

$$\hat{\omega} \sim \mathcal{N}\left(\omega, \frac{\sigma_\eta^2}{\sum_{i=1}^m X_i^2}\right). \tag{47}$$

The predictions are made as

$$\ln \hat{c}_{m+\tau} = \ln c_m + \hat{\omega} \ln \frac{z_{m+\tau}}{z_m} = \ln c_m + \hat{\omega} \sum_{i=m}^{m+\tau} X_i. \tag{48}$$

The forecast error then is

$$\mathcal{E} \equiv \ln c_{m+\tau} - \ln \hat{c}_{m+\tau} = (\omega - \hat{\omega}) \sum_{i=m}^{m+\tau} X_i + \sum_{i=m+1}^{m+\tau} \eta_i.$$

Using (47), we can see that the forecast is unbiased ($E[\mathcal{E}] = 0$), and the variance can be computed as

$$\mathrm{Var}(\mathcal{E}) = \left(\sum_{i=m+1}^{m+\tau} X_i \right)^2 \frac{\sigma_\eta^2}{\sum_{i=1}^m X_i^2} + \tau \sigma_\eta^2,$$

$$= \sigma_\eta^2 \left(\tau + \frac{\left(\sum_{i=m+1}^{m+\tau} X_i \right)^2}{\sum_{i=1}^m X_i^2} \right),$$

$$= \sigma_\eta^2 \left(\tau + \frac{\tau^2}{m} \mathcal{W} \right),$$

where

$$\mathcal{W} \equiv \frac{r_{(f)}^2}{r_{(p)}^2 + \sigma_{z,(p)}^2} \qquad (49)$$

is defined from the "sample moments" of experience: $r_{(f)}$ is the mean growth in the future $(1 \ldots \tau)$, and $r_{(p)}$ and $\sigma_{z,(p)}$ are the mean and standard deviation in the past $(1 \ldots m)$, noting that $\hat{\sigma}_{z,(p)}$ must be calculated without the "Bessel" degrees of freedom correction. I put "sample moments" in quotation marks because experience is taken as nonstochastic—all further derivations are conditioned on one specific realization of (past and future) experience.

Equation (49) now looks very similar to the equivalent equation for Moore's law, equation (31), and the main text provides intuition into the differences.

WRIGHT'S LAW WITH AUTOCORRELATION

Finally, we arrive at the more complex model,

$$Y_t = \omega X_t + \eta_t, \qquad \eta_t = \epsilon_t + \rho \epsilon_{t-1}, \qquad (50)$$

The parameter $\hat{\omega}$ is estimated as before, equation (46). The forecast errors are

$$\mathcal{E} \equiv \ln c_{m+\tau} - \ln \hat{c}_{m+\tau} = (\omega - \hat{\omega}) \sum_{i=m+1}^{m+\tau} X_i + \sum_{i=m+1}^{m+\tau} \eta_i. \quad (51)$$

Substituting $\hat{\omega}$ from equation (46),

$$\mathcal{E} = \left(-\frac{\sum_{i=1}^{m} X_i \eta_i}{\sum_{i=1}^{m} X_i^2} \right) \sum_{i=m+1}^{m+\tau} X_i + \sum_{i=m+1}^{m+\tau} \eta_i,$$

$$\mathcal{E} = \sum_{i=1}^{m} \left[X_i \left(\frac{-\sum_{i=m+1}^{m+\tau} X_i}{\sum_{i=1}^{m} X_i^2} \right) \eta_i \right] + \sum_{i=m+1}^{m+\tau} \eta_i,$$

~385~

$$\mathcal{E} = \sum_{i=1}^{m} H_i \eta_i + \sum_{i=m+1}^{m+\tau} \eta_i, \quad (52)$$

where I have defined

$$H_i \equiv X_i \left(\frac{-\sum_{i=m+1}^{m+\tau} X_i}{\sum_{i=1}^{m} X_i^2} \right)$$

$$= \left(\frac{-\tau}{m} \cdot \frac{r_{(f)}}{r_{(p)}^2 + \sigma_{z,(p)}^2} \right) X_i \equiv \xi X_i. \quad (53)$$

Exact variance of the forecast errors. From (52) we can now carefully separate independent noise terms ("method 1" in sec. A),

$$\mathcal{E} = \sum_{i=1}^{m} H_i(\epsilon_i + \rho\epsilon_{i-1}) + \sum_{i=m+1}^{m+\tau} (\epsilon_i + \rho\epsilon_{i-1}),$$

$$= \left\{ \rho H_1 \epsilon_0 + \sum_{i=1}^{m-1} (H_i + \rho H_{i+1})\epsilon_i + H_m \epsilon_m \right\}$$

$$+ \left\{ \rho \epsilon_m + \sum_{i=m+1}^{m+\tau-1} (1+\rho)\epsilon_i + \epsilon_\tau \right\},$$

so that the variance of the forecast errors is

$$\text{Var}(\mathcal{E})_{\text{exact}} = \sigma_\epsilon^2 \left(\rho^2 H_1^2 + \sum_{i=1}^{m-1} (H_j + \rho H_{j+1})^2 \right.$$

$$\left. + (\rho + H_m)^2 + (\tau - 1)(1+\rho)^2 + 1 \right). \quad (54)$$

Justifying an approximation. Let us rewrite equation (54) as

$$\frac{\text{Var}(\mathcal{E})_{\text{exact}}}{\sigma_\epsilon^2} = \underbrace{\rho^2 H_1^2 + \sum_{i=1}^{m-1}(H_i + \rho H_{i+1})^2 + H_m^2 + 2\rho H_m}_{(1)}$$

$$+ \underbrace{\rho^2 + (\tau - 1)(1 + \rho)^2 + 1}_{\approx (1+\rho)^2 \tau, \text{ see } (40)},$$

$$(55)$$

If experience grew at fairly similar rates year after year in the past, $X_j \approx X_{j'}$ for any j and j', so $H_j \approx H_{j'}$. In particular, if we just assume that $X_m \approx X_1$, we have

$$(1) \approx \sum_{i=1}^{m}(H_i + \rho H_{i+1})^2 = \xi^2 \sum_{i=1}^{m}(X_i + \rho X_{i+1})^2.$$

using (53) in the last step. This approximation becomes very good as m grows large, as only one out of m terms is approximated. Expanding, we have

$$(1) \approx \xi^2 \left(\sum_{i=1}^{m} X_i^2 + \rho^2 \sum_{i=1}^{m} X_{i+1}^2 + 2\rho \sum_{i=1}^{m} X_i X_{i+1} \right). \quad (56)$$

To get to a simple formula, the useful final approximation is

$$\hat{r}_{(p)}^2 + \hat{\sigma}_{(p)}^2 = \frac{1}{m}\sum_{i=1}^{m} X_i^2 \approx \frac{1}{m}\sum_{i=1}^{m} X_{i+1}^2 \approx \frac{1}{m}\sum_{i=1}^{m} X_i X_{i+1}.$$

$$(57)$$

Pre-multiplying (56) by m/m and using (57), we have

$$(1) \approx m(1 + \rho)^2 \xi^2 (\hat{r}_{(p)}^2 + \hat{\sigma}_{(p)}^2) = (1 + \rho)^2 \frac{\tau^2}{m} W, \quad (58)$$

where I have used (53) and (49). Substituting (58) into (55) and using $\sigma_\epsilon^2 = \sigma_\eta^2/(1 + \rho^2)$ (27),

$$\text{Var}(\mathcal{E})_{\text{approx}} = \sigma_\eta^2 \frac{(1 + \rho)^2}{1 + \rho^2} \left(\tau + \frac{\tau^2}{m} W \right), \quad (59)$$

which is the formula quoted in the main text.

Error of the simulation method. Again, the simulation method would draw ω from its distribution, and draw future noise terms independently. We would thus have

$$\text{Var}(\mathcal{E})_{\text{sim}} \equiv \text{Var}(\ln c_{t+\tau})$$

$$= \left(\sum_{i=m+1}^{m+\tau} X_i \right)^2 \text{Var}(\hat{\omega}) + \text{Var}\left(\sum_{i=m+1}^{m+\tau} \eta_i \right), \quad (60)$$

where the second term, the variance of future noise, is as in Moore's law, equation (42). For the first term, from looking at (46),

$$\hat{\omega} = \omega + \frac{1}{\sum_{i=1}^{m} X_i^2}\left(\rho X_1 \epsilon_0 + \sum_{i=1}^{m-1}(X_i + \rho X_{i+1})\epsilon_i + X_m \epsilon_m \right),$$

so its variance is

$$\text{Var}(\hat{\omega}) = \frac{\sigma_\epsilon^2}{[\sum_{i=1}^{m} X_i^2]^2}\left((\rho X_1)^2 + \sum_{i=1}^{m-1}(X_i + \rho X_{i+1})^2 + X_m^2 \right).$$

As for Moore's law, the simulation method (59) is only approximate because, starting from (51), we should express the variance of forecast errors as the sum of a term linked to parameter estimation, a term linked to future noise, *and* a covariance term ("method 2" in sec. A),

$$\text{Var}(\mathcal{E})_{\text{exact}} \equiv \left(\sum_{i=m+1}^{m+\tau} X_i \right)^2 \text{Var}(\hat{\omega}) + \text{Var}\left(\sum_{i=m+1}^{m+\tau} \eta_i \right)$$

$$- 2\left(\sum_{i=m+1}^{m+\tau} X_i \right) \text{Cov}\left(\hat{\omega}, \sum_{i=m+1}^{m+\tau} \eta_i \right), \quad (61)$$

which can be compared to equation (41). The covariance term can be calculated as

$$\text{Cov}\left(\hat{\omega}, \sum_{i=m+1}^{m+\tau} \eta_i \right) = E\left[\left(\epsilon_m \frac{X_m}{\sum_{i=1}^{m} X_i^2} \right)(\rho \epsilon_m) \right]$$

$$= \sigma_\epsilon^2 \rho \frac{X_m}{\sum_{i=1}^{m} X_i^2}. \quad (62)$$

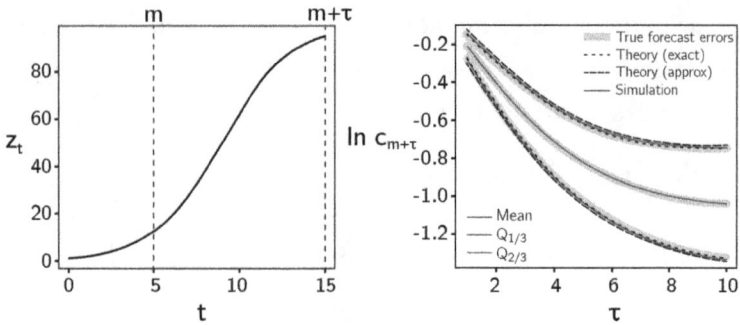

Figure 1. Distributional forecasts for costs conditional on future experience, comparing three methods. The left panel shows the evolution of experience, assumed to be a logistic curve, and highlights the assumption for the sample size (m) and forecast horizon (τ). The right panel shows the distributional forecasts, using equation (54), equation (59), and the "simulation" method (simulating forward paths after drawing from the distribution of estimated parameters). This is compared to the actual distribution of forecast errors obtained by simulating the stochastic process, making forecasts, and recording the errors. The quantiles shown are $1/3$ and $2/3$; see text for detailed values of the parameters.

Comparing the definition for the exact and simulated variance, equations (60) and 61, their difference is

$$
\mathrm{Var}(\mathcal{E})_{\mathrm{sim}} = \mathrm{Var}(\mathcal{E})_{\mathrm{exact}} - 2\left(\sum_{i=m+1}^{m+\tau} X_i \right) \mathrm{Cov}\left(\hat{\omega}, \sum_{i=m+1}^{m+\tau} \eta_i \right),
$$

$$
= \mathrm{Var}(\mathcal{E})_{\mathrm{exact}} - 2\sigma_\epsilon^2 \rho \frac{\sum_{i=m+1}^{m+\tau} X_i}{\sum_{i=1}^{m} X_i^2} X_m,
$$

$$
= \mathrm{Var}(\mathcal{E})_{\mathrm{exact}} - 2\sigma_\epsilon^2 \frac{\tau}{m} \rho W \frac{X_m}{r_f},
$$

where the second step uses equation (62), and the last step makes it easier to compare to the equivalent for Moore's law, equation (44), remembering that W is defined in equation (49) and equals 1 in this case.

Figure 1 compares the various formulas. To highlight that Wright's law is different from Moore's law, I assume that experience is a (deterministic) logistic curve, so the growth rates are not constant (eq. 22, $L = 100$, $k = 0.5$, $t_0 = m + 5$). I take $\sigma_\epsilon^2 = 0.1$, and, to try to highlight the differences between the formulas, a very high autocorrelation ($\rho = 0.9$) and a very small sample size ($m = 5$). The "true" forecast errors are from generating 10^6 true series and forecasts, and the "simulation" is using 10^6 simulated paths.

The figure shows that the simulation method produces almost exact results. In general, it is difficult to find reasonable examples where the simulation method will deviate significantly. By contrast, the intervals based on $\text{Var}(\mathcal{E})_{\text{approx}}$ are perceptibly different, although still very close. A case where they differ dramatically from the exact result is when $\rho < 0$, as one can check that $\text{Var}(\mathcal{E})_{\text{approx}} \to 0$ as $\rho \to -1$.

B   On the Volatility of Sums of Lognormals

If production is a geometric random walk, what are the time series properties of *cumulative* production (experience)?

Let production be a random walk with drift,

$$\Delta \ln q_t = g + \sigma_q u_t,$$

where $u_t \sim \mathcal{N}(0,1)$. Thus, q_t is lognormal, and for future reference note that the variance of its growth rate (its volatility) is σ_q^2 while its ("ensemble" or "cross-sectional") variance grows linearly with time,

$$\text{Var}(\ln q_t) \sim \sigma_q^2 t.$$

To avoid any confusion, let me define the empirical counter-parts of the population moments (which will be used in simulations below). The "variance" is the cross-sectional variance of the levels of the log variable

$$\text{Var}(\ln q_t) \equiv \frac{1}{N} \sum_{i=1}^{N} \left(\ln q_{it} - \langle \ln q_t \rangle \right)^2,$$

with $\langle \ln q_t \rangle \equiv \frac{1}{N} \sum_{i=1}^{N} \ln q_{it}$. It is computed using N different time series, taken at their time step t.

In contrast, the "volatility" is the variance of the growth rate of one time series. It is computed as

$$\text{Var}(\Delta \ln q_{it}) \equiv \frac{1}{t} \sum_{s=1}^{t} \left(\Delta \ln q_{is} - \hat{g}_i \right)^2,$$

where the average growth rate is the estimated drift, $\hat{g}_i = \frac{1}{t} \sum_{s=1}^{t} \Delta \ln q_{is}$. In simulations I will report the average of this quantity over the ensemble.

Now, define experience as cumulative production,

$$z_t = \sum_{j=1}^{t} q_j.$$

Lafond *et al.* (2018) derived the approximation equation (15) in the main text,

$$\sigma_z^2 \approx \sigma_q^2 \tanh(g/2).$$

To test how well it works, I simulate 5,000 time series of production of 110 periods (for each different values of g and σ_q); compute the cumulative sum of each time series to construct "experience;" remove the initial 10 periods, as a "burn-in;" and finally, compute the volatility of each of the 5,000 time series, and average over all simulations.

Figure 2 (left) shows the results, demonstrating a good agreement between the simulations and the theoretical results for most reasonable parameter values. R. Zadourian and A. Klümper (2018) go a lot further, and derive the distribution of experience. Let me now comment on two further results.

Experience is not volatile, but it is uncertain. First, Lafond *et al.* (2018) also derived an approximation for the variance of the levels as

$$\text{Var}(\ln z_t) \approx \sigma_q^2 \left(\frac{2e^g + 1}{1 - e^{2g}} + t \right).$$

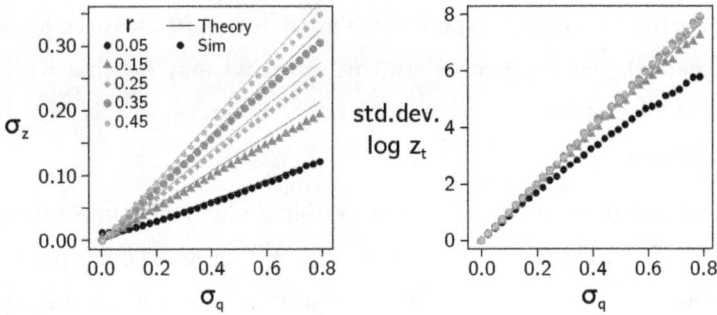

Figure 2. Empirical moments of experience against their predicted value.

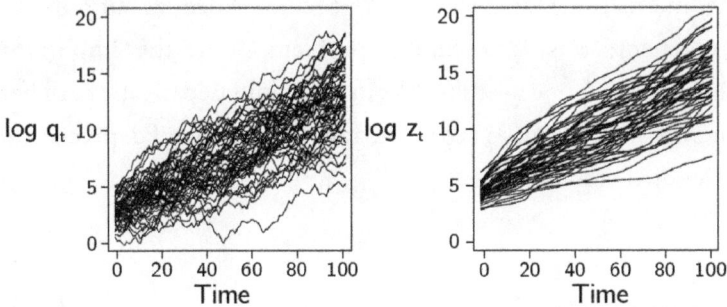

Figure 3. The cumulative (z_t, right) of a geometric random walks with drift (q_t, left) has much lower volatility, but similar cross-sectional dispersion.

This is interesting because since the first term disappears as $t \to \infty$, this implies

$$\text{Var}(\ln z_t) \sim \text{Var}(\ln q_t),$$

where $\sim$ here means that the variables scale together as time goes to infinity (their ratio tends to 1). In other words, the *ensembles* of production and experience spread out in the same way (their cross-sectional variance is almost the same), even though, as we have seen, their volatility is much different. Figure 2 (right) shows that this formula provides a good approximation.

To drive the point home, figure 3 shows 50 simulated time series of production, and the associated time series of experience ($r = 0.1$ and $\sigma_q = 0.3$). The figure makes it clear that while the volatility of experience is much lower, its cross-sectional dispersion remains similar. In this sense, we may say that while experience is much less volatile than production, it is just as uncertain.

Depreciation weakens the smoothing effect of cumulating. This phenomenology is interesting well beyond our specific application, given the prevalence of random walks and cumulative sums in various domains of science and engineering. Taking a view from economics, consider that we want to understand the fluctuations of the capital stock, defined as cumulative investment; this is a similar problem, with the important difference that one needs to take into account depreciation. In her PhD thesis, Zadourian (2018) further derived that if depreciation is denoted δ, so that

$$z_t = (1 - \delta)z_{t-1} + q_t,$$

then equation (15) becomes

$$\sigma_z^2 \approx \sigma_q^2 \tanh\left(\frac{g - \ln(1 - \delta)}{2}\right) \approx \sigma_q^2 \tanh\left(\frac{g + \delta}{2}\right),$$

where the last approximation holds for $|\delta| \ll 1$.

This shows that more depreciation leads to more volatility of the growth of the capital stock, and thus, thinking in terms of growth accounting equations, more volatility of labor productivity. This potentially has some relevance to the current landscape, where modern economies are shifting from traditional capital (which may have a depreciation $\delta = 1\% - 20\%$), to "intangible" capital like software, which depreciates very quickly ($\delta \approx 20\% - 50\%$, see Goldin *et al.* 2024, table 6). This equation predicts that, everything else being equal, the shift toward intangible capital should lead to higher aggregate fluctuations, or, to phrase it in the context of this paper, higher prediction intervals for predictions of technological progress.

Similarly, due to overinvestment in fossil fuels in the last decades, it is likely that some assets will need to be retired earlier than originally planned (Pfeiffer *et al.* 2018). These stranded assets effectively correspond to higher depreciation, and thus, everything else equal, higher uncertainty of future productivity growth.

C Spurious Regressions and Experience Curves

If both costs and experience were independent random walks with drifts, how would various estimators of their relationship perform? Specifically, which estimator would pick up that this is a spurious regression ($\omega = 0$)? Our goal is to show that the only estimator that works, the first-difference estimator allowing a non-zero intercept, also has very large standard errors, making it very hard to properly test for spurious regression.

Data generating process. Let

$$\Delta \ln c_t \equiv Y_t = \mu + u_t, \qquad (63)$$

$$\Delta \ln z_t \equiv X_t = r + v_t. \qquad (64)$$

To denote the variances of u and v, which will come up in calculations, I will directly use σ_Y^2 and σ_X^2.

The level estimator. It is defined as the OLS estimator of ω in the equation

$$\ln c_t = \alpha + \omega \ln z_t + \epsilon_t. \qquad (65)$$

H. Entorf (1997) shows that $E[\hat{\omega}] \to \mu/r$. This is the well-known "spurious regression" result: performing a regression with two independent random walks returns the ratio of their drifts, rather than 0, with a high degree of statistical significance.

Entorf (1997) also shows that asymptotically, $\hat{\omega}$ is normal with variance

$$\mathrm{Var}(\hat{\omega}) = \frac{1}{m}\left(\frac{6}{5} \cdot \left(\frac{\mu}{r}\right)^2\left[\left(\frac{\sigma_Y}{\mu}\right)^2 + \left(\frac{\sigma_X}{r}\right)^2\right]\right). \qquad (66)$$

So precision increases when $\sigma_X \to 0$, meaning that in our case of interest, the estimator becomes increasingly precisely wrong.

The first difference (FD) estimator with an intercept. It is

defined as the OLS estimator of ω in the equation

$$Y_t = \alpha + \omega X_t + \epsilon_t. \qquad (67)$$

In this case, the ϵ_t are stationary, so the OLS regression gives "correct" results, $E[\hat{\omega}] = 0$, but with variance

$$\mathrm{Var}(\hat{\omega}) = \frac{\sigma_Y^2}{m\sigma_X^2}, \qquad (68)$$

where I have used the classic result for when regressors are non-stochastic, and substituted $\hat{\sigma}_X$ by σ_X. These standard errors will be huge if σ_X is small, which we should expect (see Appendix B): experience fluctuates very little so it is hard to distinguish it from "time ticking." Indeed, this model is not our stochastic Wright's law, because the intercept in difference implies a time trend in levels,

$$\ln c_t = \mathrm{cstt} + \alpha t + \omega \ln z_t,$$

that is, a "mix" of Moore's and Wright's laws. When we think that the data-generating process is our stochastic Wright's law, the OLS estimator of (67) is both an estimator of the incorrect DGP, and an estimator with very poor precision. The right estimator in this case is discussed next.

The first-difference estimator without a constant. It is the OLS estimator of ω in the equation

$$Y_t = \omega X_t + \epsilon_t. \tag{69}$$

This is the model discussed in the main text, equation (11). The estimator is defined in equation (46), and Appendix A studies its distribution when model (69) is correct.

Here we are interested in the properties of the estimator (46) when the model (69) is *not* correct, but instead, the data is generated as two independent random walks equations (63)–(64). We can easily find the behavior of $\hat{\omega}$ heuristically, as follows. By definition of $\hat{\omega}$ (46), inserting the DGP equations (63)–(64), we have

~ 395 ~

$$\hat{\omega} = \frac{\sum Y_i X_i}{\sum X_i^2} = \frac{\mu r + r\left(\frac{1}{m}\sum u_i\right) + \mu\left(\frac{1}{m}\sum v_i\right) + \left(\frac{1}{m}\sum v_i u_i\right)}{r^2 + 2r\left(\frac{1}{m}\sum v_i\right) + \left(\frac{1}{m}\sum v_i^2\right)}, \tag{70}$$

where m is the sample size. Let $m \to \infty$ and replace $\frac{1}{m}\sum u_i \to 0$ and $\frac{1}{m}\sum v_i \to 0$. The sums with the v_i^2 is just a consistent estimator of the volatility of X, $\frac{1}{m}\sum v_i^2 \to \sigma_X^2$. By assumption the noises of the two times series are independent, so $\frac{1}{m}\sum v_i u_i \to 0$. Plugging these four results into equation (70), we have

$$\hat{\omega}_{|m\to\infty} = \frac{\mu/r}{1 + (\sigma_X/r)^2}. \tag{71}$$

From this it becomes clear that whether the asymptotic $\hat{\omega}$ is "correct" or "spurious" depends on σ_X,

$$\hat{\omega}_{|m\to\infty} \to 0 \text{ as } \sigma_X \to \infty \quad \text{[correct]},$$

$$\hat{\omega}_{|m\to\infty} \to \mu/r \text{ as } \sigma_X \to 0 \quad \text{[spurious]}.$$

For the standard errors, a heuristic is to derive it conditional on X, $\text{Var}(\hat{\omega}|X) = \frac{\sigma_Y^2}{\sum_i X_i^2}$, and then, taking expectation over X and assuming that the expectation of the inverse is well approximated by the inverse of the expectation,

$$\mathrm{Var}(\hat{\omega}) = \frac{\sigma_Y^2}{m(r^2 + \sigma_X^2)}. \tag{72}$$

In contrast to the first difference with a constant, equation (68), the denominator includes the term r^2, which prevents the standard errors from diverging as $\sigma_X \to 0$. So while the estimator

that gives a "correct" result is highly imprecise, this one, somewhat like the spurious regression, is precisely wrong. When $\sigma_X \to \infty$, however, the expectation approaches the correct result, and the estimator becomes more precise.

Numerical results. To show numerically that equation (71) works well, I simulate independent random walks and estimate ω according to three methods: level, difference with and without intercept.

The simulation setup is similar to the values reported for solar photovoltaics (PV) by Lafond *et al.* (2018): 41 periods, the mean and standard deviation of Y equal -0.121 and 0.153, and the mean of X is 0.318 (Lafond *et al.* 2018, report 0.318 for cumulative production, and 0.315 for production). I use various values for the variance of X, to see its effects, and run 10,000 replications for each value of σ_X.

To test the formulas, the first set of simulation follows the assumption made for the calculations, that is, that X is a random walk with drift. Next we will see if the formulas still work in the realistic case where X is the growth of the *cumulative* of a geometric random walk with drift.

Figure 4 (left) shows how each estimator performs at different values of σ_X. Dots show the mean across replications, and error bands show the 0.025–0.975 quantiles. To avoid clutter, the theoretical results for the standard errors are not shown, as they

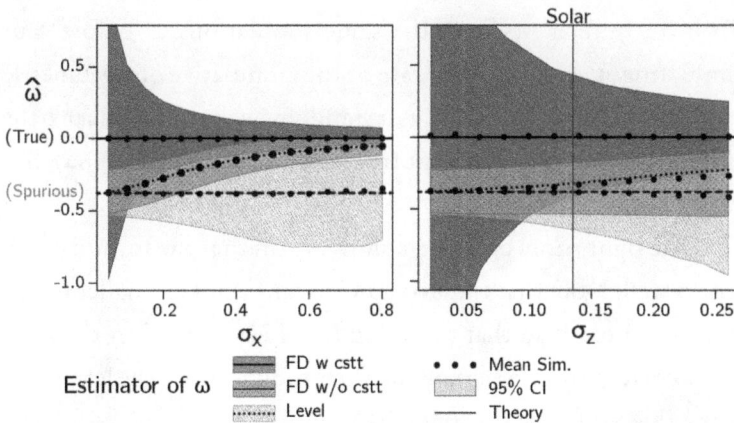

Figure 4. Properties of three different estimators of ω as a function of the variance of the regressor, when the DGP is two independent random walks (left). On the right panel, the regressor is "experience," that is, cumulative of geometric random walks.

do not work perfectly for small sample sizes, but I have checked that they work well for larger sample sizes.

As seen in the theoretical discussion, the first-difference estimator with an intercept, in black with a solid line, is correct on average, but features large errors when the variance of the regressor is small, as intuitively known from regressions: a larger range of the regressor is better to pin down the correct slope.

The level model, in light gray with dashed lines, gives on average the spurious result. A large volatility of the regressor makes it worse, as has been shown by Entorf (1997). Finally, for the estimator of interest, the first-difference without constant, the mid gray with dotted lines shows that the theoretical result (71) agrees very well with the simulations, and the variance of the estimator decreases slightly with more variance of the regressor. For small volatility, there is no chance that it is able to pick up the correct value (zero), but it is substantially less biased than the level estimator. So the key question is whether in practice, the variance of the regressor (the volatility of experience) is "high enough."

To investigate, I first run the same simulations as before, but simulating X as the growth rate of the cumulative of a geometric random walk, rather than as a random walk. This means the simulations are now different from the DGP assumed in (64), but closer to the real-world.

The right panel of figure 4 shows again that the formulas still works well. Note that the x-axis now spans a much smaller range; in fact I chose it so that the volatility of experience on the right panel corresponds to the volatility of production on the left panel, using the result (15; see appendix B).

Doing this makes it possible to check where "real technologies" lie. I take the value of σ_z measured for solar by Lafond *et al.* (2018). Unfortunately, for a value of σ_z comparable to empirical data for solar, the difference estimator without intercept is not in the good regime: it still gives a spurious answer. In this regime, the first-difference estimator with a constant is hardly very useful, as its standard errors are so large that the spurious answer is within its confidence interval. Thus, in this regime, none of the two estimators would be very useful to detect whether the regression is spurious.

WHY ARE NEW IDEAS
GETTING HARDER TO USE?

Diane Coyle, University of Cambridge

Abstract

Ideas drive productivity growth, yet productivity growth has slowed in recent decades despite the wave of innovation in digital, information-carrying technologies. Prior work focusing on economic and knowledge complexity as indicators of geographically located capabilities has considered the role of social networks in conveying ideas between people, particularly the tacit knowledge for which person-to-person contact is needed. This chapter builds on this approach by introducing underpinning infrastructure as an essential, common-resource asset that determines people's ability to use ideas productively. Infrastructure, broadly defined, shapes the "adjacent possible" of economic activity in any location. The social network transmitting ideas between individuals is layered on top of built, physical networks; these have a history and a geography whose affordances and constraints shape innovation and ultimately productivity growth. Broad-based economic growth rests on the possibilities afforded by glass, steel, and concrete.

Ideas drive productivity growth—the increase in economic value created using the inputs available—and thus rising living standards over time. Both economic history (e.g., DeLong 2022; McCloskey 2016) and growth theory (Aghion and Howitt 1992) underline the importance of new ideas and innovation for progress. Yet since around 2007, when the advent of the smartphone, wireless networks, and apps launched the current pervasively digital era, productivity growth has slowed dramatically in the OECD economies. Although there are many other contributory factors, it seems a paradox that progress has ground to a halt despite amazing technological leaps ranging from artificial intelligence to biomedicine. What Will Baumol (2002) vividly characterized as the "free market innovation machine" has stalled in the twenty-first century. The impressive recent innovations have not translated into productivity growth and improved living standards.

Can the productivity paradox be overcome? There is a pessimistic macroeconomic literature arguing that ideas are getting "harder to find" (Bloom *et al.* 2020), that modern innovations are less important than those of the early twentieth century (Gordon 2016), and that the dynamics of growth mean a slowdown is inevitable (Vollrath 2019). However, firm-level evidence from across the OECD economies indicates that a minority of businesses whose productivity levels are already high have been able to increase their productivity even further, including through the use of digital technologies. That is, there is mounting evidence that the highest-productivity firms are those using digital tools (Cathles, Nayyar, and Rückert 2020; Coyle *et al.* 2022; Tambe *et al.* 2020) and that they are pulling ever farther away from the rest of the pack (Andrews, Criscuolo, and Gal 2015; De Loecker, Obermeier, and Van Reenen 2022).

Yet if some firms are using data and digital tools to become greatly more productive, can others catch up? This chapter builds on prior work describing how ideas spread in person-to-person social networks (Manski 2005; Young 2005). It discusses knowledge complexity as an index of geographically located ideas, just as economic complexity indexes activities or industries, and argues that people's ability to use ideas ultimately depends on an area's underpinning infrastructure. This form of common resource capital asset—which I define broadly—determines the capabilities available to businesses and people in an area, and therefore the potential for knowledge to expand into the adjacent possible. The social network transmitting ideas between individuals is layered on built, physical networks that have a history and a geography whose affordances and constraints shape innovation and ultimately economic growth. In other words, although ideas are fundamental to economic growth, they are not disembodied. The ability of people and firms to use ideas depends on social networks shaped by the affordances of physical networks—on the system of systems.

~401~

Causes?

Pessimism about the prospects for productivity growth to return to the rates experienced in the 1990s and early 2000s embraces several arguments.

Robert Gordon (2016) argues that recent digital innovations are trivial compared to the wave of early twentieth-century practical innovations such as electricity, indoor plumbing, and the internal combustion engine, all of which had dramatic effects on the quality of life. A more recent influential paper (Bloom *et al.* 2020) points to the decreasing productivity of research; both in the aggregate and at the level of individual technologies, the marginal increase in economic output per researcher has declined, such that more and more researchers are needed to produce a constant growth rate, leading them to claim that ideas are getting harder to find. A third argument is that the slowdown in growth is inevitable due in large part to the importance of services, whose productivity potential is limited because of their requirement for labor input (Vollrath 2019; Baumol 1967).

A more optimistic perspective sees the absence of necessary complements to innovations as potential explanations for productivity growth below the potential created by technological advances.

One missing complement may be tacit knowledge, drawing on a literature (dating in economics back to (dating in economics back to Griliches 1957) that links technology adoption to person-to-person connections, or to the need for physical proximity to share tacit engineering or practical knowledge among employees of different firms (Tassey 2014). Another complement is organizational capital, a firm's capacity to restructure its processes in ways that give employees the scope to use new information flows enabled by digital technology. This features in the concept of the "productivity J curve," namely that adopting some new technologies will decrease productivity before increasing it because of the need to reorganize production (Brynjolfsson, Rock, and Syverson 2021). The tacit knowledge gap or the organization gap may be larger in the case of complex modern software tools than with older generations of technology; James Bessen (2022) argues that using digital technology and the associated software, artificial intelligence (AI), and data science has become sufficiently challenging that relatively few firms can adopt them successfully, while the more they manage to do so, the harder it is for their competitors to catch up.

There is a third complement, rarely noted in the relevant literatures: infrastructure. I refer not to a specific innovation infrastructure (consisting of features such as standards, accreditation, the intellectual property regime, or research institutions) but to the broad system of built infrastructure that characterizes every place. Infrastructure has a geography, and also a history, as a system of systems that layer onto each other at different times and embodying a specific vintage of technology. The quantity and quality of infrastructure will determine social connections and thus affect the capacity of ideas to jump from one person to another. The social network of people is another layer in the system of systems.

The Adjacent Possible

One way to frame the question analytically is to adopt the biological metaphor of the adjacent possible (Kauffman 2000) for the domain of economic activity and consider what it implies for measures of potential expansion. How does this apply to the adoption of ideas that drive innovation and productivity growth? It represents the economy as a complex adaptive system, whose adjacent possible comprises activities sufficiently close to current activities. In the growing economic complexity literature, these are generally measured in terms of the network relatedness of industrial sectors. For example, in Penny Mealy and Coyle (2022), we found for the United Kingdom that local authority areas with a low Economic Complexity Index (ECI) were specialized in certain low-value-added manufacturing activities, implying a set of capabilities that constrained the adjacent possible activities they might expand into.

A complementary approach addressing an area's knowledge base more directly is the Knowledge Complexity Index (KCI). Like the ECI, the analogous KCI orders locations by an index representing their ideas capability set, comprising the diversity of their knowledge (how many types of knowledge the place has a comparative advantage in) and ubiquity (how many places have the same comparative advantage).

A location can have a high KCI if it has a diverse range of specialisms, or unique specialisms. Some types of frontier knowledge are locationally specific, often anchored around universities. KCI measures can be constructed using patent classes to define different types of formal knowledge. In Coyle and Lucy Hampton (2024), we calculate this KCI for UK local authorities using patent data. Like the ECI, it is positively (although more weakly) correlated with local economic outcomes such as gross value added (GVA) per hour and growth in GVA per hour. The

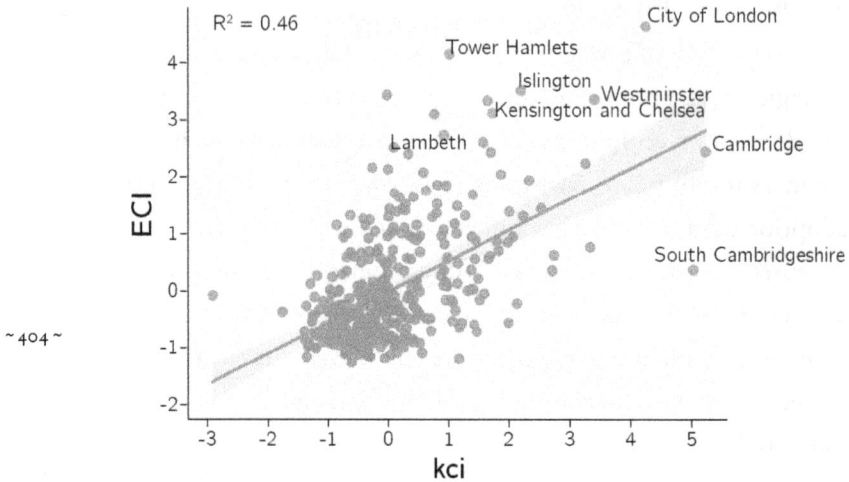

Figure 1. Local economic activity network, Cambridge region. *(Source: Coyle and Hampton (2024))*

KCI and ECI are thus positively (relatively weakly) correlated with each other, although they evidently capture different aspects of the local economies (fig. 1). The United Kingdom's well-known spatial inequalities are reflected in the presence of the golden triangle (Cambridge, Oxford, and London) in the south and east in figure 1, with the London local authorities in which the financial districts are located scoring high on the ECI and Cambridge (the university and its biomedical campus) scoring particularly high on the KCI. (Patenting is relatively rare in financial services, which rely substantially on tacit knowledge exchange.)

The ECI, KCI, and similarly Product Complexity Index (PCI) orderings can be compared for insight into the adjacent possible for different localities (tab. 1). For example, the Cambridge region does not feature in the first ten ECI places (in fact, no local authority outside Greater London does); nor do the activities that contribute to its high KCI figure feature much in the first

ECI RANK (LOCAL AUTHORITY)	KCI RANK (LOCAL AUTHORITY)	PCI RANK (INDUSTRY)
1. City of London	Cambridge	Reinsurance
2. Tower Hamlets	South Cambridgeshire	Fund management activities
3. Islington	City of London	Television programming
4. Westminster	Westminster	Trusts, funds, other financial
5. Southwark	Vale of White Horse	Motion picture, video
6. Camden	City of Edinburgh	Advertising
7. Hammersmith and Fulham	South Oxfordshire	Market research
8. Kensington and Chelsea	West Berkshire	Other information services
9. Hackney	Three Rivers	Management consultancy
10. Lambeth	Oxford	Computer services

~ 405 ~

Table 1. Top ten ECI, KCI, and PCI in the United Kingdom. *(Source: Author's own data, based on Mealy and Coyle 2022; Coyle and Hampton 2024)*

ten industries by PCI. While similar places have high KCI and ECI metrics, the places with low outcomes on each index differ: On average, postindustrial locations have a low ECI ordering, and rural places have a low KCI ordering. These measures contain different information that together can give a clearer sense of the adjacent possible for each area.

These complexity metrics are calculated at an aggregated level; network analysis is useful to illuminate a locality's specific knowledge strengths in more detail. For example, using real-time classifications of activity (constructed from language clusters in web data linked to other available datasets) to investigate the relatedness of firms in the Cambridge region, Owen Garling and Burcu Sevdi Selvi (2024) calculate the average weighted degree and betweenness centrality of the business network. They find that life sciences and associated activities and services related to engineering, physical sciences, and environmental sciences are the most densely connected; AI and computer science–related activities are also important, with the region having a large

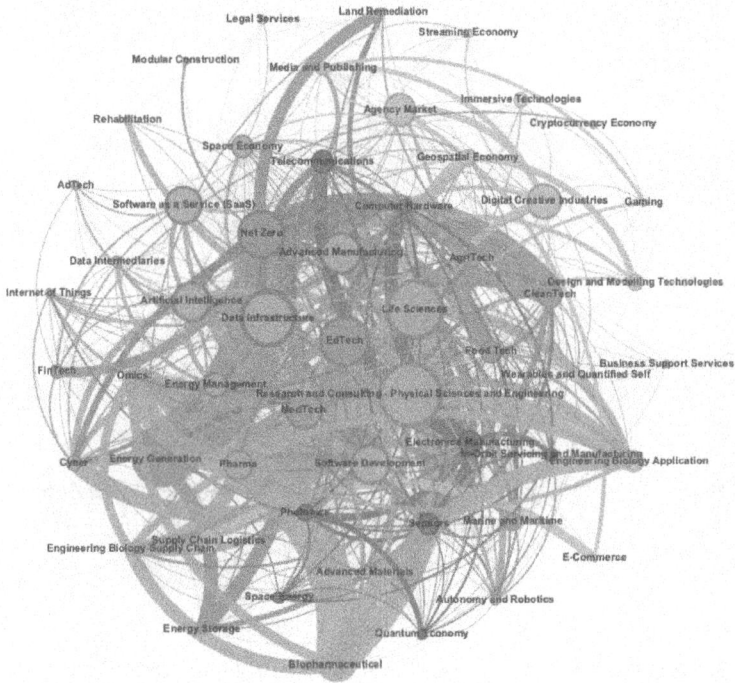

Figure 2. Local economic activity network, Cambridge region. *(Source: Garling and Selvi 2024)*

number of companies undertaking these, but they are less central and less densely connected (fig. 2).

Infrastructure

The complexity and network analyses are useful diagnostic tools for insight into the knowledge types and economic activities that characterize different localities, and therefore shed light on a place's adjacent possible. These results underline the important role of local networks in shaping the different types of capabilities. Capabilities depend on stocks of both formal and tacit knowledge, which (as well as patents or other codifiable knowledge) could include for example know-how about supply chains and markets for innovations or practical engineering tips.

A place's strengths and networks will have been shaped by its economic history, with substantial path dependence. Path dependence in innovation has been widely discussed (Arthur 1994). However, places and social networks through which ideas are exchanged are enabled or constrained by their physical and built environment. Infrastructure is needed to actualize the adjacent possible of ideas and capabilities—yet it is not (as far as I have been able to identify) much considered in the complexity literature. It features in some of the older development literature, particularly Albert Hirschman's (1977) concept of "backward and forward linkages."

César Hidalgo (2023) does emphasize the importance of "where" in using complexity analysis to inform policy, noting the potential for rail and telecommunications connections to accelerate spillovers: "Where approaches are about understanding the geographic constraints, and opportunities, implied by the spatial position of an economy."

However, the role of "where" needs to be considered in the round for specific places, rather than trying to identify average effects of rail or broadband links across the whole of the economy, as is standard in the empirical literature. The relevant policy question in this context is not "How much transport investment does the UK need?" but rather "What does Cambridge (or anywhere) need in order to grow?" For example, the UK government's current plans to see significant economic growth in Cambridge are being challenged locally not because its residents do not want the city to expand but because local businesses have identified infrastructural capacity limits such as inadequate water supplies and electricity generation (Foster 2024). Different types of infrastructure may be complements or substitutes for each other, and different places have great variation in their inherited stocks of such assets.

Koen Frenken and Frank Neffke (2026, ch. 29 in this volume) and Luís Bettencourt *et al.* (2007) note that components of physical infrastructure scale sublinearly with urban growth, meaning the dynamics differ from those of the social networks and knowledge exchange thanks to economies of scale. At the same time, existing infrastructure may imply inefficient allocation of resources so that large returns to additional investment may be possible (Coyle 2022).

Infrastructure should be capaciously defined as location-specific tangible collective (although either privately or publicly owned) assets that either enable or constrain knowledge spillovers, innovation, and productivity growth. Expanding on Brett Frischmann (2012), infrastructure has the following characteristics:

- It consists of long-lived assets expected to be of use for many years and often involving an upfront cost of investment so marginal costs of supply are low.

- The assets are collective, with a presumption that access to them is either universal or does not depend on personal relationships or identity.

- They are generally nonrival (up to the scale where congestion occurs).

- They provide generic capital services that can be used as inputs into a wide range of other activities.

- Different infrastructure types may be complements or substitutes for each other, and the affordances of the whole portfolio will vary.

- On the demand side, demand for their use is often derived, with economic value created by downstream activities using them as inputs.

- Relatedly, as they involve spillovers or externalities (often due to network effects), there will be nonlinearities in demand when tipping points are reached.

This set of characteristics points to a broader definition of infrastructure than is traditional. The concept has usually been applied to physical networks such as telecommunications and broadband, rail, or energy networks. Increasingly, it includes social infrastructure (Alexandrova *et al.* 2024; Kelsey and Kenny 2021), or in other words the physical collective assets such as hospitals and schools, or cafes and stores, where people meet and can exchange ideas. The bundle of assets that comprise a locality's infrastructure shapes the environment in which its residents and firms form networks and undertake economic activities. Postwar reconstruction led to significant infrastructure investment in a number of OECD countries, but the rate of investment in recent decades has been low and the available estimates point to substantial gaps (Woetzel *et al.* 2017; Coyle 2022).

Infrastructure types might be directly decisive for a locality's specialisms; for instance, data centers need to be located for energy sources and cooling possibilities, and mining villages are located where the relevant minerals are. Transport and communication networks, and social infrastructures, are what shape both the person-to-person contact and encounters with other people that seem vital for idea generation (e.g., Clancy; Agrawal, McHale, and Oettl 2017; Roche 2020) and for continuing collaboration between people (e.g., Agrawal, McHale, and Oettl 2015; Freeman, Ganguli, and Murciano-Goroff 2014). Some of these empirical studies of the role of face-to-face encounters include elements of social infrastructure such as cafes and bars.

There is limited macroeconomic evidence regarding the impact of infrastructure on economic growth, for several reasons including not only lack of data but also the inherent challenge of identifying the effect when demand is derived rather than direct. However, there are persuasive microeconomic studies that point to the efficiency gains possible from factor reallocation enabled by new transport links or communications investments (see Coyle 2022 for an overview). Highly productive companies have the in-house capabilities that enable them to overcome some infrastructure limitations, and are more likely to be at the apex of supply chains or ecosystems that link them to others and thus to the flow of ideas. For the majority of firms in OECD countries, however, infrastructure as an important enabler of innovation has been degrading for decades.

The challenge for both research and policy is not only to combine the what (economic activities or products), who (social actors), when (timing of policy pushes), and where (which localities)—borrowing Hidalgo's (2023) categories—as they will be jointly determined. It is also to anchor the complexity and network analysis in time and space. As Mealy and Coyle (2022) noted, places with a low ECI are likely to have a low ECI adjacent possible, and vice versa. This is due to the path dependence and spatial anchoring of capabilities. One explanation for the stickiness of ideas, and therefore local trajectories, is that people do not move far or often; but the infrastructure that affects how and where they can move, who they meet, and what economic activities they can undertake is just as important as it will literally shape the adjacent possible.

Conclusion

Ideas drive innovations and growth, so the network of innovators through which ideas spread from one person to another is key for the evolution of the economy. Recent digital technologies do not seem to be diffusing in the same way as earlier generations, however. A minority of firms (in OECD countries) are pulling ahead of the rest in terms of productivity, a growing divergence empirically related to the use of digital tools. The pace of technological advance in digital and other fields seems inconsistent with the claim that new ideas are getting scarcer, but perhaps they are getting harder to use.

This chapter has argued that complexity analysis illuminating the adjacent possible for an economy, through measures of economic or knowledge complexity and network analysis, should be augmented by taking account of the infrastructure—the physical network or system of systems on which all social and economic networks rely. Social networks are shaped and constrained by physical networks, and economic analysis needs to take into account the specific characteristics of places at each level. In many OECD countries, infrastructure maintenance and investment is considered to have been too low for some decades, while upgrades in energy and communication networks are needed in the years ahead to embed new technologies. Traditional and social infrastructure forms a portfolio of collective assets that are important for ideas to spread outside the boundaries of the already-productive firms or places. Economic policies and strategies aimed at increasing the lackluster recent rate of productivity growth must take into account for the relevant geographies characteristic of the whole system of systems, from physical substrates to the resulting social networks to the path-dependent capabilities and knowledge captured by complexity indices. The face-to-face exchange of ideas in social networks, and thus broad-based economic growth, rests on the possibilities afforded by glass, steel, and concrete. ✦

REFERENCES

Aghion, P., and P. Howitt. 1992. "A Model of Growth Through Creative Destruction." *Econometrica* 60 (2): 323–351. https://doi.org/10.2307/2951599.

Agrawal, A., J. McHale, and A. Oettl. 2015. "Collaboration, Stars, and the Changing Organization of Science: Evidence from Evolutionary Biology." In *The Changing Frontier: Rethinking Science and Innovation Policy*, 75–102. Chicago, IL: University of Chicago Press.

———. 2017. "How Stars Matter: Recruiting and Peer Effects in Evolutionary Biology." *Research Policy* 46 (4): 853–867. https://doi.org/10.1016/j.respol.2017.02.007.

Alexandrova, A., S. Coulter, D. Coyle, O. Garling, and M. Kenny. 2024. *Measurement of Social and Cultural Infrastructure: Vision and Approach.* Bennett School of Public Policy Cambridge. https://www.bennettinstitute.cam.ac.uk/wp-content/uploads/2024/03/Measurement-ofsocial-and-cultural-infrastructure.pdf.

Andrews, D., C. Criscuolo, and P. N. Gal. 2015. *Frontier Firms, Technology Diffusion and Public Policy: Micro Evidence from OECD Countries.* https://www.oecd-ilibrary.org/economics/frontier-firms-technology-dibusion-and-public-policy_5jrql2q2jj7b-en.

Arthur, W. B. 1994. *Increasing Returns and Path Dependence in the Economy.* Ann Arbor, MI: University of Michigan Press. https://doi.org/10.3998/mpub.10029.

Baumol, W. J. 1967. "Macroeconomics of Unbalanced Growth: The Anatomy of Urban Crisis." *American Economic Review* 57 (3): 415–426. http://www.jstor.org/stable/1812111.

———. 2002. *The Free-Market Innovation Machine: Analyzing the Growth Miracle of Capitalism.* Princeton, NJ: Princeton University Press.

Bessen, J. 2022. *The New Goliaths: How Corporations Use Software to Dominate Industries, Kill Innovation, and Undermine Regulation.* New Haven, CT: Yale University Press.

Chapter 27: Why Are New Ideas Getting Harder to Use?

Bettencourt, L. M. A., J. Lobo, D. Helbing, C. Kühnert, and G. B. West. 2007. "Growth, Innovation, Scaling, and the Pace of Life in Cities." *Proceedings of the National Academy of Sciences* 104:7301–7306. https://doi.org/10.1073/pnas.0610172104.

Bloom, N., C. I. Jones, J. Van Reenen, and M. Webb. 2020. "Are Ideas Getting Harder to Find?" *American Economic Review* 110 (4): 1104–1144. https://doi.org/10.1257/aer.20180338.

Brynjolfsson, E., D. Rock, and C. Syverson. 2021. "The Productivity J-curve: How Intangibles Complement General Purpose Technologies." *American Economic Journal: Macroeconomics* 13 (1): 333–372. https://doi.org/10.1257/mac.20180386.

Cathles, A., G. Nayyar, and D. Rückert. 2020. *Digital Technologies and Firm Performance: Evidence from Europe.* EIB Working Papers 2020/06. European Investment Bank. https://ideas.repec.org/p/zbw/eibwps/202006.html.

Clancy, M. *New Things Under the Sun.* https://mattsclancy.substack.com/.

Coyle, D. 2022. "Shaping Successful Mega-Project Investments." *Oxford Review of Economic Policy* 38 (2): 224–236. https://doi.org/10.1093/oxrep/grac003.

Coyle, D., and L. Hampton. 2024. *The Role of Knowledge Production in UK Economic Divergence.* Bennett Institute Working Paper, forthcoming.

Coyle, D., K. Lind, D. Nguyen, and M. Tong. 2022. *Are Digital-Using UK Firms More Productive?* Economic Statistics Centre of Excellence. https://www.escoe.ac.uk/are-digital-using-uk-firms-more-productive/.

De Loecker, J., T. Obermeier, and J. Van Reenen. 2022. *Firms and Inequality.* Discussion Paper No. 1838. Centre for Economic Performance (CEP). https://eprints.lse.ac.uk/117827/1/dp1838.pdf.

DeLong, J. B. 2022. *Slouching Towards Utopia: An Economic History of the Twentieth Century.* New York, NY: Basic Books.

Foster, P. 2024. *Cambridge Innovation Hub at Risk from Lack of Infrastructure, Warn Businesses.* Financial Times. https://www.ft.com/content/905e048b-c903-45c3-929a-550dd7294bcf.

Freeman, R., I. Ganguli, and R. Murciano-Goroff. 2014. "Why and Wherefore of Increased Scientific Collaboration." In *The Changing Frontier: Rethinking Science and Innovation Policy,* 17–48. Chicago, IL: University of Chicago Press.

Frenken, K., and F. Neffke. 2026. "Economic Geography and Complexity Theory." In *The Economy as an Evolving Complex System IV,* edited by R. M. del Rio-Chanona, M. Pangallo, J. Bednar, E. D. Beinhocker, J. Kaszowska-Mojsa, F. Lafond, P. Mealy, A. Pichler, and J. D. Farmer. Santa Fe, NM: SFI Press.

Frischmann, B. M. 2012. *Infrastructure: The Social Value of Shared Resources.* Oxford, UK: Oxford University Press. https : / / doi . org / 10 . 1093 / acprof : oso / 9780199895656.001.0001.

Garling, O., and B. Selvi. 2024. *Exploring Sectoral Relatedness in East Anglia: A New Approach.* Bennett Institute Working Paper. https://www.bennettschool.cam. ac.uk/publications/exploring-sectoral-relatedness-in-east-anglia/.

Gordon, R. J. 2016. *The Rise and Fall of American Growth: The U.S. Standard of Living since the Civil War.* Princeton, NJ: Princeton University Press.

Griliches, Z. 1957. "Hybrid Corn: An Exploration in the Economics of Technological Change." *Econometrica* 25 (4): 501–522. https://doi.org/10.2307/1905380.

Hidalgo, C. A. 2023. "The Policy Implications of Economic Complexity." *Research Policy* 52 (9). https://doi.org/10.1016/j.respol.2023.104863.

Hirschman, A. O. 1977. "How Economic Expansion was Expected to Improve the Political Order." In *The Passions and the Interests: Political Arguments for Capitalism before Its Triumph,* 67–114. Princeton, NJ: Princeton University Press. https://doi.org/10.1515/9781400848515-007.

Kauffman, S. A. 2000. *Investigations.* Oxford, UK: Oxford University Press.

Kelsey, T., and M. Kenny. 2021. *Townscapes: The Value of Social Infrastructure.* Bennett Institute for Public Policy Cambridge. https://www.bennettschool. cam.ac.uk/publications/social-infrastructure/.

Manski, C. 2005. "Social Learning and the Adoption of Innovations." In *The Economy as an Evolving Complex System III: Current Perspectives and Future Directions,* edited by L. E. Blume and S. N. Durlauf. Oxford, UK: Oxford University Press.

McCloskey, D. N. 2016. *Bourgeois Equality: How Ideas, Not Capital or Institutions, Enriched the World.* Chicago, IL: University of Chicago Press.

Mealy, P., and D. Coyle. 2022. "To Them That Hath: Economic Complexity and Local Industrial Strategy in the UK." *International Tax and Public Finance* 29:358–377. https://doi.org/10.1007/s10797-021-09667-0.

Roche, M. P. 2020. "Taking Innovation to the Streets: Microgeography, Physical Structure, and Innovation." *Review of Economics and Statistics* 102 (5): 912–928. https://doi.org/10.1162/rest_a_00866.

Tambe, P., L. Hitt, D. Rock, and E. Brynjolfsson. 2020. *Digital Capital and Superstar Firms.* National Bureau of Economic Research. https://doi.org/10.3386/w28285.

Tassey, G. 2014. "Competing in Advanced Manufacturing: The Need for Improved Growth Models and Policies." *Journal of Economic Perspectives* 28 (1): 27–48. https://doi.org/10.1257/jep.28.1.27.

Vollrath, D. 2019. *Fully Grown: Why a Stagnant Economy is a Sign of Success.* Chicago, IL: University of Chicago Press.

Woetzel, L., N. Garemo, J. Mischke, P. Kamra, and R. Palter. 2017. *Bridging Infrastructure Gaps.* McKinsey Global Institute. https://www.mckinsey.com/capabilities/operations/our-insights/bridging-infrastructure-gaps-has-the-world-made-progress.

Young, H. P. 2005. "The Diffusion of Innovations in Social Networks." In *The Economy as an Evolving Complex System III: Current Perspectives and Future Directions,* edited by Lawrence E. Blume and Steven N. Durlauf. Oxford, UK: Oxford University Press.

THE EVOLUTIONARY ECOLOGY OF SOFTWARE: CONSTRAINTS, INNOVATION, AND THE AI DISRUPTION

Sergi Valverde, Institute of Evolutionary Biology (CSIC-UPF);
Blai Vidiella, Theoretical and Experimental
Ecology Station (CNRS); and
Salva Duran-Nebreda, Institute of Evolutionary Biology (CSIC-UPF)

Abstract

This chapter investigates the evolutionary ecology of software, focusing on the symbiotic relationship between software and innovation. An interplay between constraints, tinkering, and frequency-dependent selection drives the complex evolutionary trajectories of these socio-technological systems. Our approach integrates agent-based modeling and case studies, drawing on complex network analysis and evolutionary theory to explore how software evolves under the competing forces of novelty generation and imitation. By examining the evolution of programming languages and their impact on developer practices, we illustrate how technological artifacts co-evolve with and shape societal norms, cultural dynamics, and human interactions. This ecological perspective also informs our analysis of the emerging role of AI-driven development tools in software evolution. While large language models (LLMs) provide unprecedented access to information, their widespread adoption introduces new evolutionary pressures that may contribute to cultural stagnation, much like the decline of diversity in past software ecosystems. Understanding the evolutionary pressures introduced by AI-mediated software production is critical for anticipating broader patterns of cultural change, technological adaptation, and the future of software innovation.

Introduction

Since the dawn of the digital age, there has been a strong mutual influence between biologists and computer scientists. Computer scientists have attempted to model computers after biological processes using a variety of approaches, including cellular automata, neural networks, and evolutionary algorithms. In contrast, biologists have used computational metaphors to illustrate how biological systems operate. For example, geneticists have linked DNA to software, and neuroscientists have claimed that brain functions are similar to those performed by computers.

In spite of this mutual influence, there is a palpable, sharp divide between biology and computer science. Evolutionary algorithms, like genetic algorithms, are inspired by organismic evolution, although they have evident limitations in terms of complexity and open-endedness. On the other hand, biologists opposed computational analogies as early as 1951, when neuroscientist Karl Lashley argued that "we are more likely to find out how the brain works by studying the brain itself, and the phenomena of behaviour, than by indulging in far-fetched physical analogies" (Beach *et al.* 1960).

To deepen the debate about the differences and similarities between software and biology, it is crucial to move beyond the superficial assumption that technology is different from living systems mainly because it is built by humans. Several examples, such as the present climate crisis, demonstrate the limits of technological planning. This is relevant when projecting the long-term uses of technology, as advances in software are not always the result of well-planned, dependable, and managed systems. Instead, all technologies evolve via a cumulative process based on previous, empirically-tested practices (Richerson and Boyd 2008). Software is a well-documented example of cultural evolution, which is the study of how ideas, behaviors, technologies, and practices change, spread, and adapt within societies over time (Vidiella *et al.* 2022; Solé *et al.* 2013).

We will examine the evolutionary and ecological drivers of software innovation. Our methodology departs from previous approaches that depend on qualitative biological metaphors, since we adopt the quantitative techniques of empirical and theoretical network analysis. With this, we do not aim to demonstrate that software and biology are the same, but rather to highlight that they can be analyzed using similar tools. As society becomes more dependent on software, it is critical to develop a technologically oriented evolutionary approach capable of identifying the causes of constraints, enabling collaborative problem-solving and facilitating technological advances.

Software Networks Are Scale-Free

Software is an integral part of our daily life, yet it often introduces unexpected complexity, even though software engineers are constantly refining system design and structure, providing "patches" that fix any flaws (Valverde 2021). One of the main goals for software designers is to create systems that are easier to understand, handle, and update. To accomplish this, they divide the system into components with predictable interactions while adhering to modular and hierarchical design principles (Baldwin and Clark 2000). This approach has worked well in electronics because understanding the circuit as a whole does not necessitate understanding the internal details of the underlying components. However, why aren't these principles fully applicable to software?

The outputs of planned design must be considered highly optimized systems (Valverde, Ferrer-i-Cancho, and Solé 2002), although design goals might come into conflict with the practical requirements of dealing with environmental complexities, which are often mirrored in the internal structure of technological networks (McNerney *et al.* 2011). To measure the level of structural complexity, we examine the software network represented as a graph $G = (V, E)$, where V denotes the software elements (such as classes, files, or machine symbols) and connections $(i, j) \in E$ depict semantic relationships among classes (see fig. 1a), dependencies between source code files (see fig. 1b), or associations between symbols and sentences within source code files (see fig. 1c).

Many real-world networks, including software networks, have a structure that is highly heterogeneous (fig. 1d), with a small number of hub nodes having many connections, while the majority have only a few links. For example, in software dependency networks, the probability that a random node has k incoming links (or in-degree distribution) follows a power-law (see fig. 2a):

$$P(k) \sim k^{-\gamma},$$

where the exponent $\gamma \approx 2$ (Valverde and Solé 2005a; de Sousa, de Menezes, and Penna 2009). Similar scale-free degree distributions are seen in class diagrams as well (Valverde, Ferrer-i-Cancho, and Solé 2002; Valverde and Solé 2007a). This heterogeneous organization, which is not intentionally imposed by software engineers, significantly impacts the development of software systems (Lakos 1996), suggesting that we must work around complexity constraints to successfully design and manage these systems.

These heterogeneous degree distributions, a signature of emergent complexity, may not capture all aspects of software

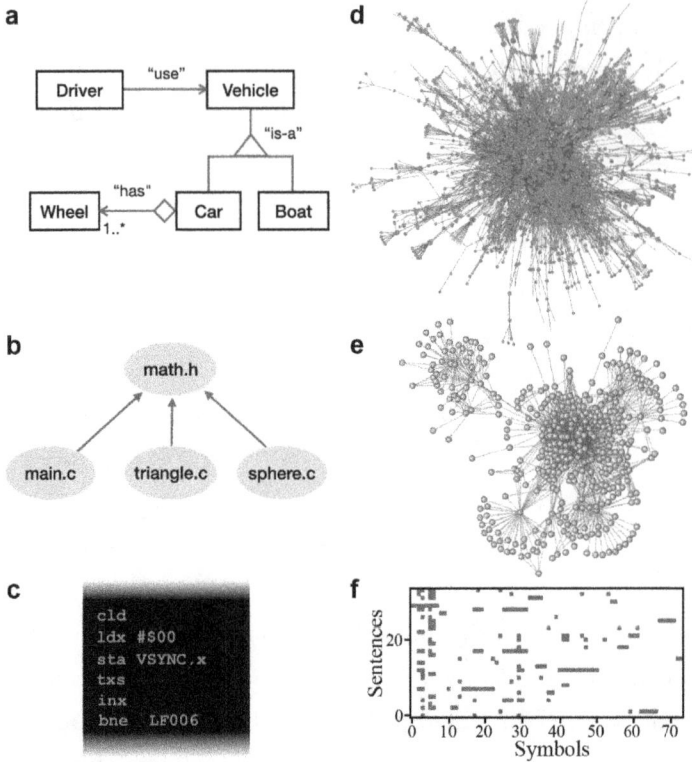

a

Driver — "use" → Vehicle

Vehicle — "is-a"

Wheel ← "has" — Car   Boat
1..*

b

math.h

main.c   triangle.c   sphere.c

c

```
cld
ldx #$00
sta VSYNC,x
txs
inx
bne  LF006
```

d

e

f

Sentences / Symbols

Figure 1. Network representations of software systems. (a) Software engineers use class diagrams, a type of semantic map described in unified modeling language (UML) notation, to organize software components and their interactions. We can see part of the class diagram used to describe the elements in a racing game, including several types of vehicles ("is-a" relationships) and the association between a car and its wheels (a "has" relationship). (b) A dependency network distributes software functions into a directed acyclic graph of source code files and their dependencies on other code files. (c) Source code is a text file containing the software instructions written in a language of machine symbols, including arithmetic operations, register names, and memory addresses. (d) Software network for the class diagram used in the development of the console game Pro Rally 2002 (Ubisoft, 2002). Node size represents the in-degree. (e) The dependency network of the XFree86 X Window System exhibits scale-free behavior (code files from the version published on May 15, 1993). (f) Every network may be represented using an adjacency matrix, including the bipartite network that shows the relationship between sentences and machine symbols in source code.

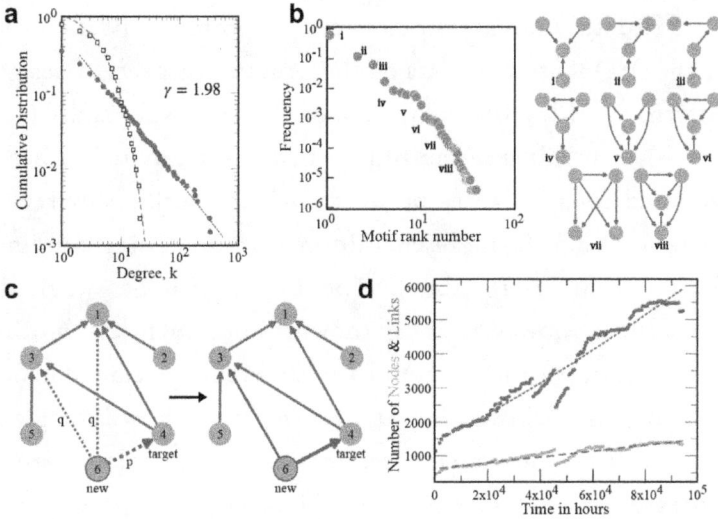

Figure 2. Tinkered evolution of software networks. (a) Cumulative in-degree (filled circles) and out-degree (white squares) distributions for the project XFree86. The power-law fit of the in-degree distribution yields $P_>(k) \sim k^{-\gamma+1}$ with $\gamma = 1.97 \pm 0.01$ while the out-degree distribution is exponential (Valverde and Solé 2005a). (b) Frequency-rank distribution of 4-subgraphs in the software network for the project Exult (Valverde and Solé 2005b). The frequency $P(R)$ decays rapidly with subgraph rank k indicating how common subgraphs (like i or ii) are sparser than less common ones, which are more dense (like vii or viii). (c) Copying rules used in the model of software network growth. Each node is labeled with an age (number 1 is the oldest). A new node v_6 links to target node v_4 with probability p. This new node inherits every connection from the target node (dashed links) with probability q. This model predicts topological characteristics of software networks, such as the exponent $\gamma = 2$ of power-law in-degree distributions and observed subgraph frequencies (Solé and Valverde 2006), as well as (d) the evolutionary pattern of logarithmic scaling in software (Valverde and Solé 2005a).

design. Engineers integrate multiple components to develop functionalities that are too complex to be contained within a single piece of software. For example, a "design pattern" is a template that includes interacting software parts that may be reused to address common design problems (Gamma *et al.* 1995). Quantitative data on the structural aspects of design patterns, such as the frequency of software subgraphs (see fig. 2b), may aid in establishing their utility, as it has been proposed for regulatory networks, where specific subgraphs (or network motifs) represent information-processing building blocks (Milo *et al.* 2002). The importance of subgraph abundances, however, is unknown, since identical motifs may perform various functions in different systems (Knabe, Nehaniv, and Schilstra 2008), demonstrating how biological and software components cannot be totally isolated from contextual factors. To disentangle these factors, a proper null model is needed.

Software Evolves by Tinkering

In software development, "tinkering," or playful, unguided learning, refers to the process of experimenting with code. An informal and iterative approach to learning promotes curiosity and flexibility, often leading to unexpected discoveries and innovative solutions (Martocchio and Webster 1992; Webster and Martocchio 1993). Tinkering (also known as "bricolage;" see Turkle and Papert 1992) relies on experimenting with new combinations (and recombinations) of existing software elements.

A tinkering-based model can predict the abundances of motifs in software networks (Valverde and Solé 2005b), challenging the conventional assumption that functionality is the main driver of design processes (Solé and Valverde 2006;

Brunswicker and Mukherjee 2023). This network model, which is not reliant on any specific function, is able to accurately predict the evolution of average degree over time and the asymmetrical patterns in the distribution of degrees.

Starting with a small group of randomly linked nodes, we can simulate the tinkered evolution of a software network via the following copying rules. We grow the network one node at a time. A new node is linked to m randomly chosen target nodes with probability p, as well as all ancestor nodes of each target with probability q (see fig. 2c). This process continues until a network of size N is formed. The associated mathematical model for the total number of connections $L(N)$ is:

$$\frac{dL}{dN} = mp + mq\frac{L}{N}.$$

The solution of this equation defines three possible behaviors for the average degree $\langle K \rangle = L/N$ depending on the parameter values. For $mp < 1$, the network maintains a constant average degree:

$$\langle K \rangle \sim \frac{mp}{1 - mq}.$$

While $mp > 1$ causes faster growth,

$$\langle K \rangle \sim N^{mq-1}$$

resulting in a fully linked network. Software networks seem to be situated precisely at a critical point $mp = 1$, which serves as a boundary between a lack of growth in average degree and a highly interconnected state. At this point, average degree grows logarithmically with the number of nodes (see fig. 2d):

$$\langle K \rangle \sim \log(N).$$

In addition, the in-degree distribution follows the scaling equation $P(k) \sim k^2$ with an exponent that is independent of parameter values, whereas the out-degree distribution decays exponentially (Krapivsky and Redner 2005).

The above exposes how some statistical properties of software networks are independent of particular selection forces while some are influenced by cultural evolutionary mechanisms. Although software structure is created by humans, it cannot be free of the constraints that come with evolutionary processes. For many years, we have argued that engineering differs from biology in terms of our ability to forecast the outcomes of our actions. However, when designing complex software systems, continuous experimentation is needed to determine what is correct, and it is very difficult (if not impossible) to anticipate the necessarty changes ahead of time (Soergel 2014). This scenario resembles organismic evolution, in which random changes (mutations) are filtered according to the selection pressure created by environmental conditions. However, a deeper parallel between organisms and software may extend beyond the driving role of selection (either natural or directed by human goals), as both systems have traits influenced by neutral evolution (Lynch 2007). In other words, both organisms and software exhibit complexity that cannot be solely attributed to adaptation.

Eco-Evolutionary Feedbacks in Software

Besides internal constraints and for-free complexity afforded by tinkering, software displays clear signatures of eco-evolutionary feedbacks underlying its evolution. In this section we will explore some key structural and temporal patterns relating to various kinds of ecological interactions among technological agents. This classification is necessarily a simplification of a complex hierarchy of firms, programming languages, individual programmers and code. Quantifying diversity and structure across scales is crucial for understanding this complex web of interactions, reflecting a balance between cultural mechanisms of innovation, reinforcement, and replacement (Richerson and Boyd 2008).

PARASITISM

Programming languages, which are comparable to human languages but designed for algorithm execution, are a main driver of software evolution. Programming languages are a set of rules that govern grammar and semantics used to write software, as well as a "runtime environment," which includes a compiler and libraries for translating the "high-level" code into actual hardware instructions. Because of their evolving traits, transmission via social learning, and selective spread of certain dialects or variants over others, natural and artificial languages are both paradigmatic examples of cultural evolution (Mace and Holden 2005; Valverde and Solé 2015b).

~425~

Language differs from organism evolution in that it lacks a cultural genome, making it difficult to apply traditional genetic methods to reconstruct its evolution (Mace and Holden 2005). However, we can still infer information flows using influence or similarity between languages (Valverde and Solé 2015b). Furthermore, the links between ancestor and descendant languages reveal ecological interactions when these coexist in the same technological niche, which may include antagonistic relationships. For example, TypeScript and Clojure are "parasitic" programming languages built on top of the popular JavaScript, leveraging its stability, infrastructure, and, more importantly, its large user base (Hickey 2020). Hence, influence links capture both ecological and evolutionary dimensions of cultural evolution.

The phylogenetic network reconstruction of the evolution of programming languages detects events of rapid diversification (Valverde and Solé 2015b; Valverde 2016) (fig. 3a). After

1972, there is a larger rate of linguistic trait recombination (horizontal transmission links), especially between the two major programming language families: imperative (descending from Fortran) and functional (descending from Lisp). In line with the pattern of punctuated equilibria found in the fossil record (Eldredge 2015; O'Brien *et al.* 2024), external factors could have accelerated abrupt changes in language evolution—for example, the wide adoption of microprocessor technologies as a democratizing factor in software technologies, as well as opening up new niches.

Conversely, key features developed in the most prolific languages find their way into unrelated ones, which could be interpreted as purely internally driven. For instance, language diversification may be facilitated via ecological interactions. Parasitic languages, as they evolve to better exploit hosts, have the potential to cause evolutionary changes in their host languages (i.e., prompting an evolutionary arms race between hosts and parasites; Hickey 2020; Smith and Benkman 2007). This phenomenon may result in the divergence of languages, with significant differences between those that experience high levels of parasitism and those that do not. However, parasitism in software evolution is no longer limited to programming languages alone. With the rise of AI-driven development, LLMs have introduced a new form of parasitism—one that operates at the level of knowledge production rather than syntax and execution environments.

In recent years, LLMs have introduced a new layer of parasitism within the software ecosystem. Unlike traditional programming languages, which evolve through direct human intervention, LLMs do not generate new syntax or execution environments. Instead, they "feed" on existing human-generated code, learning from repositories, forums, and software documentation to generate

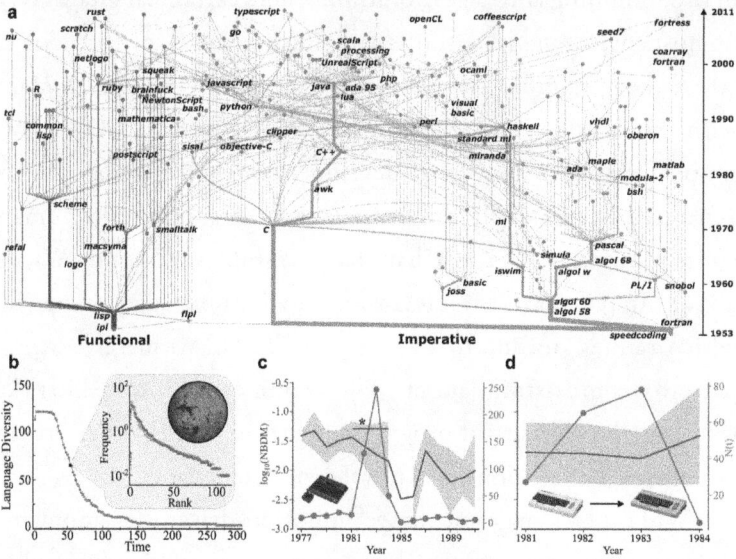

Figure 3. Long-term evolutionary trends in software systems. (a) The phylogenetic tree of programming languages exhibits a punctuated pattern (Valverde and Solé 2015b) with substantial variations in the number of descendants on distinct branches (link thickness). Key innovations in programming languages such as C and Java led to evolutionary radiations. More recently, languages coming from the two primary language families, namely functional (left branch) and imperative (right branch), are converging due to increasing trait recombination rates (gray horizontal links). (b) An ecological perspective on technological competition forecasts the collapse of programming language diversity (squares), using simple rules of competitive exclusion and an upper bound to the number of known languages per user (Valverde and Solé 2015a). A spatially explicit population-dynamics model (top spheres, darker tones represent higher language diversity) reproduces the log-linear rank-popularity relationship (inset), with good agreement between the model (dark circles) and empirical (light circles) popularity. (c) Average yearly Kolmogorov–Chaitin complexity of Atari 2600 video games (solid line) and the number of games released each year (solid circles). (d) Equivalent plot for VIC-20 code complexity (line), as well as productivity (solid circles). The significant decrease in code complexity precedes the economic collapse of 1983, suggesting a causal link between innovation and product value. Similar trends in lexical diversity and code compressibility indicate significant increases in code redundancy due to imitation (Duran-Nebreda *et al.* 2022).

new outputs. This process mirrors the parasitic relationship seen in programming language evolution, where certain languages rely on host environments without contributing novel infrastructure.

A key example of this dynamic is how LLMs interact with knowledge-sharing platforms such as Stack Overflow. Empirical studies show that developers increasingly rely on AI-generated responses, leading to a measurable decline in human contributions (del Rio-Chanona, Laurentsyeva, and Wachs 2024). In contrast to human-mediated knowledge exchange, which refines and improves best practices, LLMs merely extract patterns from existing datasets. This asymmetric relationship risks reducing the diversity of programming techniques by reinforcing established conventions over novel experimentation.

While LLMs may encourage imitation-driven development, they also have the potential to expand the space of possible software innovations. By lowering entry barriers, facilitating hybridization of programming paradigms, and assisting in optimization, LLMs might accelerate software evolution rather than merely reinforcing established norms. Unlike past examples of stagnation due to over-imitation, AI-assisted development may function more like an evolutionary "catalyst," introducing syntactic and structural variations that human programmers can refine and select. The key determinant of whether LLMs lead to stagnation or progress may lie in how developers engage with these tools—as passive consumers or active collaborators.

From an evolutionary perspective, LLMs may be seen as a new form of horizontal knowledge transfer, akin to how parasitic languages introduce foreign syntactic elements into host languages. LLMs have quickly grown since the dominance of decoder-only architectures like GPT-3 and GPT-4 (Yang *et al.* 2024). Unlike traditional programming languages, which undergo gradual divergence and recombination, LLMs evolve in a highly centralized manner, controlled by a few major research labs. This shift raises fundamental questions about whether AI-driven code generation will foster continued software innovation or lead to increasing uniformity and stagnation. If LLMs shape software development in the same way parasitic languages influence their hosts, will they ultimately accelerate evolution (Betts *et al.* 2018)—or will they gradually erode the diversity that makes software ecosystems resilient?

~429~

COMPETITION

The adoption and use of programming languages frequently results in the formation of communities (Valverde and Solé 2007b; Schueller *et al.* 2022), shared practices, and even cultural norms centered on their application. These interactions and collaborations contribute to the social dimension of software, often neglected but crucial in understanding its evolution. Interoperability and ease of dissemination are major driving forces in the development of new programming language features, and allow for large-scale standardization across the software landscape (Valverde 2021). Moreover, programmers tend to learn those languages that are more useful to them, that is, those that are more widely adopted by their peers and contain larger user bases.

At a higher level, the necessity for individual programmers to collaborate translates into a competition by the programming languages, which vie for a limited amount of agents. Cultural-transmission models, integrating an ecological perspective on the underlying social fabric and cultural norms can offer some insights on the pattern of diversification and extinction of programming languages (Valverde and Solé 2015a). The empirical popularity of coexisting programming languages follows a discrete generalized beta distribution (DGBD; Martínez-Mekler *et al.* 2009, inset, fig. 3b), linking a language frequency (f) to its rank (r):

$$f(r) = \frac{A}{r^a}(R + 1 - r)^b,$$

where R is the maximum rank value, A is a normalization constant and a, b the two fitting exponents (here $a \sim 1.44$, $b \sim 0.46$). Martínez-Mekler *et al.* proposed a general model for the DGBD in various cultural systems with an stochastic growth model incorporating two opposed forces: reinforcement and removal of cultural variants (Martínez-Mekler *et al.* 2009). These two processes map to the fitting parameters of DGBD (a, b respectively), creating steep, long-tailed popularity distributions when reinforcement dominates ($a > b$), and flatter more "disordered" distributions in the opposite case.

An alternative explanation for the DGBD relies on competition between cultural variants (Valverde and Solé 2015a). This view considers programmers not as agents but as a finite resource, that programming languages "infect" at the expense of other languages. The growth rate of any given language ($d\rho_i/dt$) depends on its current popularity share (ρ_i), following the general set ODEs:

$$\frac{d\rho_i}{dt} = \mu_i \rho_i \left(\rho_i - \sum_{j \neq i} \rho_j \right) - \mu_i \rho_i \phi(\overrightarrow{\rho}),$$

where μ_i is the intrinsic growth rate of the ith language and $\phi(\overrightarrow{\rho})$ stands for the competition function that considers the frequency of the focal language i as well as all putative competitors. This system can be made spatially explicit (inset, fig. 3b), adding new terms for language transmission according to local density and the discovery of new languages. These rules represent a simple cultural diffusion process, in which variant fitness is defined by its popularity share. In ecological terms, the system dynamics are driven by competitive exclusion, converging towards n languages shared by all programmers (fig. 3b). The number of final languages

n is the precisely the size of the niche, that is, how many different languages are programmers typically proficient in.

COOPERATION

Antagonism is not the only mode of ecological interaction among technological agents that can generate diversity. Cooperation— through coordination strategies and the maintenance of public goods—can increase diversity and complexity, while failure to cooperate can lead to a collapse in both. Understanding the interplay between reward structures, population dynamics, and sociality requires evolutionary models that integrate multiple-choice selection with social learning.

Let's define the probability $\Pi(z)$ of choosing a variant $z \in \{z_1, z_2, z_3, ...\}$ of a trait as follows:

$$\Pi(z) \sim \Phi(z) \times s(p_z),$$

where $\Phi(z)$ is the fitness of the variant (a phenotype-fitness map), $s(p_z)$ is the frequency-dependent selection coefficient, $p_z = n_z/N$ is the frequency of the trait in the population, n_z is the density of the trait, and N is the number of individuals in the population. This model describes the interaction of different selection pressures in cultural evolution. Directional selection implies that fitness $\Phi(z) = e^{\beta z}$ rises exponentially with trait value z, mediated by pay-off transparency (β) (Lande 1983). Conversely, frequency-dependent selection (FDS) emphasizes the social dimension of cultural evolution by increasing the fitness of a trait as it becomes more common (Ayala and Campbell 1974). FDS follows the scaling relationship $s(p_z) \sim p_z^J$, capturing negative ($J > 0$), positive ($J > 0$), and frequency-independent ($J = 0$) selection, where the exponent J quantifies social imitation (Vidiella *et al.* 2022).

This model, which includes directional selection and FDS, may help explain the diversity of behaviors seen in software development even in the absence of external factors. For example, the model predicts an endogenous origin of punctuated evolution linked to positive FDS (O'Brien *et al.* 2024). In this case, the transition from stasis to punctuation is not due to external shocks; rather, it's the result of accumulating many gradual advances that, over time, overcome adoption barriers associated with conformity bias and imitation (Vidiella *et al.* 2022). The height of these barriers is defined by the minimal size $\Delta z = z_1 - z_0$ of an adaptive step:

$$\Delta z \geq \frac{J-1}{\beta} \log(N),$$

where z_1 is the mean trait after the step, and z_0 is the main trait before the step. Although imitation can be beneficial to speed up cultural evolution (Richerson and Boyd 2008), no new traits can be easily discovered with exceedingly large J/β ratios; instead, individuals only reinforce the popularity of current information, regardless of how obsolete it may be.

The balance between imitation and innovation also shapes software resilience and adaptability. While code reuse reduces development costs, excessive "copy-paste" programming can lead to bug propagation (Li *et al.* 2006), higher maintenance costs (Eick *et al.* 2001), unnecessary complexity (Valverde 2017), and code "bloating" (Langdon and Poli 1998), particularly in novelty-driven markets (Dewett and Williams 2007). However, history shows that over-exploitation of successful but repetitive strategies can contribute to cultural stagnation and collapse. Lehman and Stanley argue that abandoning fixed design objectives in favor of novelty prevents stagnation (Lehman and Stanley 2011), yet an analysis of Atari 2600 video-game development (1977–1982) suggests the opposite pattern (Duran-Nebreda *et al.* 2022). Before the video game industry crash of 1983, rampant code reuse led to declining lexical diversity and complexity (fig. 3c).

This trend, quantified through the Kolmogorov–Chaitin complexity (Chaitin 1966) of code structures (see fig. 1f), is typically uncomputable; however, it can be approximated via the Coding Theorem (Zenil *et al.* 2018):

$$K(x) = -\log m(x) + O(1),$$

where $m(x)$ is the probability that string x is produced by a random program, and $O(1)$ is a constant independent of x (Zenil *et al.* 2018). Frequent strings have lower complexity, meaning widespread imitation can systematically reduce software diversity. In anticipation of the impending collapse, an increasing number of Atari 2600 games were produced as clones, detectable by the complexity analysis of their code. The Commodore VIC-20 followed a similar rise-and-fall trajectory in game production, but its software maintained complexity (see fig. 3d). Unlike Atari's imitation-driven collapse, the VIC-20 became obsolete through technological succession (Strotz and Lieberman 2023), replaced by the more advanced Commodore 64.

A major challenge to cooperative knowledge-sharing in software development is the risk of self-referential learning loops introduced by AI-generated content. Recent studies suggest that when LLMs are trained on their own generated outputs, they begin to lose diversity and accuracy, a phenomenon known as model collapse (Shumailov *et al.* 2024). Just as cultural evolution depends on a balance between imitation and genuine innovation, software ecosystems require a continuous influx of diverse human contributions to remain adaptive. However, as AI-generated code and documentation proliferate, newer models may increasingly be trained on synthetic data, reinforcing established patterns rather than fostering novel solutions. Over time, this feedback loop may erode the adaptive capacity of software development, making it more fragile to external shocks and less capable of generating truly innovative solutions.

This mirrors past cultural collapses where over-reliance on imitation led to stagnation, such as the Atari 2600 software ecosystem, where excessive code reuse ultimately contributed to the industry's decline (Duran-Nebreda *et al.* 2022). If AI-generated content dominates software development practices, a similar fate may await software engineering, where innovation is replaced by the blind reinforcement of existing conventions. Unlike human-driven cooperation, which refines and expands knowledge, AI-mediated learning risks amplifying its own biases, accelerating the homogenization of programming practices rather than promoting diversity.

SYMBIOSIS

Symbiotic interactions in software emerge when two systems merge, typically when a larger project absorbs a smaller or discontinued one, or when a project integrates external codebases. These interactions resemble biological symbiosis, where species co-evolve in mutually dependent relationships. In software, symbiosis can take different forms. In some cases, a dominant system extracts functionality from another without major modifications, resembling parasitism. In others, a project may benefit from another without significantly altering it, a dynamic closer to commensalism. However, the most productive forms of symbiosis are mutualistic, where two systems evolve together, improving performance, stability, or adaptability.

A common example of software symbiosis occurs when an open-source project incorporates a third-party library, introducing complex co-evolutionary dynamics. Initially, the host system exhibits a transition from endogenous (internally driven) to exogenous (externally driven) scaling dynamics, while the imported library remains relatively inactive (Valverde and Solé 2005a; Valverde 2007). As the library becomes fully integrated, it accumulates modifications and begins to co-evolve with the host system, resulting in coupled development cycles. These interactions shape the long-term trajectory of software evolution by determining how different components interact and adapt to changes in their environment.

Software activity fluctuations reveal a central tension between internal maintenance tasks and external requirements. At the individual developer level, non-homogeneous activity patterns suggest self-organization, indicating that the social structure of development teams may influence long-term software evolution. Specifically, the distribution of time delays between consecutive modifications in a software project follows a Weibull distribution:

$$P_>(T) \sim e^{-(T/\langle T \rangle)^\alpha},$$

where $\alpha \sim 0.6$ (Challet and Valverde 2008). This distribution differs from the pure power-law behavior observed in financial markets and other technical systems (Eisler and Kertész 2006). The presence of non-Poissonian statistics suggests that software and financial systems share a key feature: strong agent interactions that induce long-term memory effects. In software, this implies that past development decisions influence future modifications, leading to path-dependent evolution (Solé *et al.* 2013). This persistence of historical structures is a crucial factor in understanding how software ecosystems remain stable or adapt over time. Just as symbiotic relationships in biological systems can shape evolutionary outcomes, software symbiosis influences the long-term sustainability and resilience of technological artifacts.

Discussion

Understanding the evolution of software requires a holistic approach that incorporates both neutral processes and an ecological perspective. Common network properties like scale-free behavior and the heterogeneous distribution of motifs evidence the widespread reuse of selected components. Contrasting these empirical observations with theoretical predictions can reveal underlying feedback loops between software adaptation and environmental constraints. When software components interact with human agents, they create an artificial ecosystem characterized by elements such as parasitism, competition, collaboration, and symbiosis. Similar to natural ecosystems, cooperation and mutualism among software components can enhance the tempo and mode of software innovation. For example, collaborative development processes often lead to faster and more creative solutions (Gloor 2006).

Large language models (LLMs) introduce a new dynamic to this artificial ecosystem. LLMs offer developers quick access to technical information while also introducing new selective pressures that shape software evolution. A key concern is that their widespread use may disrupt the traditional balance between cooperation, imitation, and innovation. By providing immediate AI-generated solutions, LLMs reduce the need for developers to engage in collaborative problem-solving and knowledge refinement (del Rio-Chanona, Laurentsyeva, and Wachs 2024). If this trend continues, it could alter the cultural transmission mechanisms that have historically governed software development, fundamentally reshaping how knowledge and innovation propagate within the industry.

Instead of an ecosystem driven by the exchange of novel solutions, software innovation may increasingly rely on imitation and AI-reinforced conventions, accelerating a shift toward a cultural homogenization trap. Its effects can already be seen in the prevalence of repetitive coding patterns and the widespread adoption of standardized AI-generated solutions (Wang *et al.* 2023). This trend is consistent with the dilution of expertise hypothesis, which suggests that when a domain like software development expands and becomes more accessible to a broad, non-expert audience, there is a danger of over-reliance on imitation, which is harmful to innovation (Duran-Nebreda *et al.* 2022). In the past, software diversity has been sustained by a dynamic equilibrium between exploration and exploitation, where developers refine solutions through iterative feedback. LLMs, by making common solutions immediately accessible, may weaken the incentives for deep technical exploration. Over time, this could lead to a narrowing of software diversity, as developers converge on AI-suggested implementations rather than independently experimenting with alternatives. However, this outcome is not inevitable. The same mechanisms that drive imitation could also be leveraged to expand creative possibilities, depending on how LLMs are used in software development.

~437~

LLMs may act as innovation catalysts, enabling software to evolve through syntactic recombination and novel hybridization. By exposing developers to unfamiliar programming styles, unconventional optimizations, and emergent design patterns, LLMs could paradoxically increase the tempo of software evolution. Whether LLMs serve as catalysts for innovation or engines of stagnation depends largely on how they are integrated into development workflows. If used passively, they may reinforce conventions. However, if leveraged as collaborative augmentation tools, they could enrich software evolution, much like recombination accelerates genetic diversity in living organisms.

Ultimately, the future trajectory of AI-driven software development may be determined not just by the capabilities of LLMs, but by how developers, educators, and industry leaders choose to integrate AI into software engineering practices—whether as a tool for creative exploration or as an automated shortcut that reinforces existing conventions.

This chapter provides empirical and theoretical evidence indicating that software complexity and innovation cannot be solely reduced to our capacity for purposeful action in the environment. Instead, software is an emergent property shaped by both directed changes and eco-evolutionary feedbacks. Software, while a machine-based representation of a mathematical algorithm, also serves as a nonmaterial support for social interactions that foster innovation and diversity. The dual nature of software, serving as both a technical product and a social phenomenon, significantly influences cultural evolution, despite being understudied. With the rising prominence of AI-mediated knowledge production, a crucial question arises: will LLMs drive a new era of software evolution, fostering unprecedented creativity and discovery? Or will they instead lead to a cultural collapse, where imitation surpasses innovation and the diversity of software stagnates? The answer may depend not on the technology itself, but on how we choose to wield it. ⸙

Acknowledgments

The authors thank François Lafond and Doyne Farmer for their kind invitation to participate in this book. S. V. acknowledges his colleagues in the video-game industry, in particular José Paredes, Alex Rodriguez, Francisco José García-Ojalvo, José Andreu, and Eduardo Arancibia, for all the shared lessons and conversations over the years. S. V. is supported by the Spanish Ministry of Science and Innovation through the State Research Agency (AEI), grant PID2020-117822GB-I00/AEI/10.13039/501100011033. S. D-N. is supported by the Beatriu de Pinós postdoctoral program, from the Office of the General Secretary of Research and Universities and the Ministry of Research and Universities (2019 BP 00206) and the support of the Marie Sklodowska-Curie COFUND (BP3 contract no. 801370) of the H2020 programme.

REFERENCES

Ayala, F. J., and C. A. Campbell. 1974. "Frequency-Dependent Selection." *Annual Review of Ecology and Systematics* 5 (1): 115–138. https://doi.org/10.1146/annurev.es.05.110174.000555.

Baldwin, C. Y., and K. B. Clark. 2000. *Design Rules: The Power of Modularity*. Vol. 1. Cambridge, MA: MIT Press.

Beach, F. A., D. O. Hebb, C. T. Morgan, and H. W. Nissen. 1960. *The Neuropsychology of Lashley. Selected Papers of K. S. Lashley*. New York, NY: McGraw-Hill.

Betts, A., C. Gray, M. Zelek, R. C. MacLean, and K. C. King. 2018. "High Parasite Diversity Accelerates Host Adaptation and Diversification." *Science* 360 (6391): 907–911. https://doi.org/10.1126/science.aam9974.

Brunswicker, S., and S. Mukherjee. 2023. "The Microstructure of Modularity in Design: A Design Motif View." *Industrial and Corporate Change* 32 (1): 234–261. https://doi.org/10.1093/icc/dtac051.

Chaitin, G. J. 1966. "On the Length of Programs for Computing Finite Binary Sequences." *Journal of the ACM* 13 (4): 547–569. https://doi.org/10.1145/321356.321363.

Challet, D., and S. Valverde. 2008. *Fat Tails, Long Memory, Maturity and Ageing in Open-Source Software Projects*. arXiv preprint: 0802.3170. https://doi.org/10.48550/arXiv.0802.3170.

de Sousa, O. F., M. A. de Menezes, and T. J. P. Penna. 2009. "Analysis of the Package Dependency on Debian Gnu/Linux." *Journal of Computational Interdisciplinary Sciences* 1 (2): 127–133. https://doi.org/10.6062/jcis.2009. 01.02.0015.

del Rio-Chanona, R. M., N. Laurentsyeva, and J. Wachs. 2024. "Large Language Models Reduce Public Knowledge Sharing on Online Q&A Platforms." *PNAS Nexus* 3 (9): pgae400. https://doi.org/10.1093/pnasnexus/pgae400.

Dewett, T., and S. D. Williams. 2007. "Innovators and Imitators in Novelty-Intensive Markets: A Research Agenda." *Creativity and Innovation Management* 16 (1): 80–92. https://doi.org/10.1111/j.1467-8691.2007.00421.x.

Duran-Nebreda, S., M. J. O'Brien, R. A. Bentley, and S. Valverde. 2022. "Dilution of Expertise in the Rise and Fall of Collective Innovation." *Humanities and Social Sciences Communications* 9 (1): 1–10. https://doi.org/10.1057/s41599-022-01380-5.

Eick, S. G., T. L. Graves, A. F. Karr, J. S. Marron, and A. Mockus. 2001. "Does Code Decay? Assessing the Evidence from Change Management Data." *IEEE Transactions on Software Engineering* 27 (1): 1–12. https://doi.org/10.1109/32.895984.

Eisler, Z., and J. Kertész. 2006. "Size Matters: Some Stylized Facts of the Stock Market Revisited." *The European Physical Journal B-Condensed Matter and Complex Systems* 51:145–154. https://doi.org/10.1140/epjb/e2006-00189-6.

Eldredge, N. 2015. *Eternal Ephemera: Adaptation and the Origin of Species from the Nineteenth Century Through Punctuated Equilibria and Beyond.* New York, NY: Columbia University Press.

Gamma, E., R. Helm, R. Johnson, and J. Vlissides. 1995. *Design Patterns: Elements of Reusable Object-Oriented Software.* Boston, MA: Pearson.

Gloor, P. A. 2006. *Swarm Creativity: Competitive Advantage through Collaborative Innovation Networks.* Oxford, UK: Oxford University Press.

Hickey, R. 2020. "A History of Clojure." *Proceedings of the ACM on Programming Languages* 4 (HOPL): 1–46. https://doi.org/10.1145/3386321.

Knabe, J. F., C. L. Nehaniv, and M. J. Schilstra. 2008. "Do Motifs Reflect Evolved Function?—No Convergent Evolution of Genetic Regulatory Network Subgraph Topologies." *Biosystems* 94 (1-2): 68–74. https://doi.org/10.1016/j.biosystems.2008.05.012.

Krapivsky, P. L., and S. Redner. 2005. "Network Growth by Copying." *Physical Review E* 71 (3): 036118. https://doi.org/10.1103/PhysRevE.71.036118.

Lakos, J. 1996. *Large-Scale C++ Software Design.* Reading, MA: Addison-Wesley.

Lande, R. 1983. "The Response to Selection on Major and Minor Mutations Affecting a Metrical Trait." *Heredity* 50 (1): 47–65. https://doi.org/10.1038/hdy.1983.6.

Langdon, W. B., and R. Poli. 1998. "Fitness Causes Bloat." In *Genetic Programming: First European Workshop, EuroGP '98,* edited by W. Banzhaf, R. Poli, M. Schoenauer, and T. C. Fogarty, vol. 1391. Lecture Notes in Computer Science. Berlin, Germany: Springer.

Lehman, J., and K. O. Stanley. 2011. "Abandoning Objectives: Evolution through the Search for Novelty Alone." *Evolutionary Computation* 19 (2): 189–223. https://doi.org/10.1162/EVCO_a_00025.

Li, Z., S. Lu, S. Myagmar, and Y. Zhou. 2006. "CP-Miner: Finding Copy-Paste and Related Bugs in Large-Scale Software Code." *IEEE Transactions on Software Engineering* 32 (3): 176–192. https://doi.org/10.1109/TSE.2006.28.

Lynch, M. 2007. "The Frailty of Adaptive Hypotheses for the Origins of Organismal Complexity." *Proceedings of the National Academy of Sciences* 104 (suppl_1): 8597–8604. https://doi.org/10.1073/pnas.0702207104.

Mace, R., and C. J. Holden. 2005. "A Phylogenetic Approach to Cultural Evolution." *Trends in Ecology & Evolution* 20 (3): 116–121. https://doi.org/10.1016/j.tree.2004.12.002.

Martínez-Mekler, G., R. A. Martínez, M. B. del Río, R. Mansilla, P. Miramontes, and G. Cocho. 2009. "Universality of Rank-Ordering Distributions in the Arts and Sciences." *PLoS One* 4 (3): e4791. https://doi.org/10.1371/journal.pone.0004791.

Martocchio, J. J., and J. Webster. 1992. "Effects of Feedback and Cognitive Playfulness on Performance in Microcomputer Software Training." *Personnel Psychology* 45 (3): 553–578. https://doi.org/10.1111/j.1744-6570.1992.tb00860.x.

McNerney, J., J. D. Farmer, S. Redner, and J. E. Trancik. 2011. "Role of Design Complexity in Technology Improvement." *Proceedings of the National Academy of Sciences* 108 (22): 9008–9013. https://doi.org/10.1073/pnas.1017298108.

Milo, R., S. Shen-Orr, S. Itzkovitz, N. Kashtan, D. Chklovskii, and U. Alon. 2002. "Network Motifs: Simple Building Blocks of Complex Networks." *Science* 298 (5594): 824–827. https://doi.org/10.1126/science.298.5594.824.

O'Brien, M. J., S. Valverde, S. Duran-Nebreda, B. Vidiella, and R. A. Bentley. 2024. "Punctuated Equilibrium at 50: Anything There for Evolutionary Anthropology? Yes; Definitely." *Evolutionary Anthropology: Issues, News, and Reviews* 33 (1): e22009. https://doi.org/10.1002/evan.22009.

Richerson, P. J., and R. Boyd. 2008. *Not by Genes Alone: How Culture Transformed Human Evolution.* Chicago, IL: University of Chicago Press.

Schueller, W., J. Wachs, V. D. P. Servedio, S. Thurner, and V. Loreto. 2022. "Evolving Collaboration, Dependencies, and Use in the Rust Open Source Software Ecosystem." *Scientific Data* 9 (1): 703. https://doi.org/10.1038/s41597-022-01819-z.

Shumailov, I., Z. Shumaylov, Y. Zhao, N. Papernot, R. Anderson, and Y. Gal. 2024. "AI Models Collapse when Trained on Recursively Generated Data." *Nature* 631 (8022): 755–759. https://doi.org/10.1038/s41586-024-07566-y.

Smith, J. W., and C. W. Benkman. 2007. "A Coevolutionary Arms Race Causes Ecological Speciation in Crossbills." *The American Naturalist* 169 (4): 455–465. https://doi.org/10.1086/511961.

Soergel, D. A. W. 2014. "Rampant Software Errors May Undermine Scientific Results." *F1000Research* 3. https://doi.org/10.12688/f1000research.5930.2.

Solé, R. V., and S. Valverde. 2006. "Are Network Motifs the Spandrels of Cellular Complexity?" *Trends in Ecology & Evolution* 21 (8): 419–422. https://doi.org/10.1016/j.tree.2006.05.013.

Solé, R. V., S. Valverde, M. R. Casals, S. A. Kauffman, J. D. Farmer, and N. Eldredge. 2013. "The Evolutionary Ecology of Technological Innovations." *Complexity* 18 (4): 15–27. https://doi.org/10.1002/cplx.21436.

Strotz, L. C., and B. S. Lieberman. 2023. "The End of the Line: Competitive Exclusion and the Extinction of Historical Entities." *Royal Society Open Science* 10 (2): 221210. https://doi.org/10.1098/rsos.221210.

Turkle, S., and S. Papert. 1992. "Epistemological Pluralism and the Revaluation of the Concrete." *Journal of Mathematical Behavior* 11 (1): 3–33. https://www.learntechlib.org/p/146817/.

Valverde, S. 2007. "Crossover from Endogenous to Exogenous Activity in Open-Source Software Development." *Europhysics Letters* 77 (2): 20002. https://doi.org/10.1209/0295-5075/77/20002.

—. 2016. "Major Transitions in Information Technology." *Philosophical Transactions of the Royal Society B: Biological Sciences* 371 (1701): 20150450. https://doi.org/10.1098/rstb.2015.0450.

—. 2017. "Breakdown of Modularity in Complex Networks." *Frontiers in Physiology* 8:497. https://doi.org/10.3389/fphys.2017.00497.

—. 2021. "The Long and Winding Road: Accidents and Tinkering in Software Standardization." *Metode Science Studies Journal* 0 (11): 91–97. https://doi.org/10.7203/metode.11.16112.

Valverde, S., R. Ferrer-i-Cancho, and R. V. Solé. 2002. "Scale-Free Networks from Optimal Design." *Europhysics Letters* 60 (4): 512. https://doi.org/10.1209/epl/i2002-00248-2.

Valverde, S., and R. V. Solé. 2005a. "Logarithmic Growth Dynamics in Software Networks." *Europhysics Letters* 72 (5): 858. https://doi.org/10.1209/epl/i2005-10314-9.

—. 2005b. "Network Motifs in Computational Graphs: A Case Study in Software Architecture." *Physical Review E* 72 (2): 026107. https://doi.org/10.1103/PhysRevE.72.026107.

—. 2007a. "Hierarchical Small-Worlds in Software Architecture." Special Issue on Software Engineering and Complex Networks, eds K. L. Teo and X. Liu, *Dynamics of Continuous, Discrete & Impulsive Systems, Series B: Applications & Algorithms* 14:1–11.

—. 2007b. "Self-Organization Versus Hierarchy in Open-Source Social Networks." *Physical Review E* 76 (4): 046118. https://doi.org/10.1103/PhysRevE.76.046118.

—. 2015a. "A Cultural Diffusion Model for the Rise and Fall of Programming Languages." *Human Biology* 87 (3): 224–234. https://doi.org/10.13110/humanbiology.87.3.0224.

—. 2015b. "Punctuated Equilibrium in the Large-Scale Evolution of Programming Languages." *Journal of The Royal Society Interface* 12 (107): 20150249. https://doi.org/10.1098/rsif.2015.0249.

Vidiella, B., S. Carrignon, R. A. Bentley, M. J. O'Brien, and S. Valverde. 2022. "A Cultural Evolutionary Theory that Explains Both Gradual and Punctuated Change." *Journal of the Royal Society Interface* 19 (196): 20220570. https://doi.org/10.1098/rsif.2022.0570.

Wang, Y., Y. Pan, M. Yan, Z. Su, and T. H. Luan. 2023. "A Survey on ChatGPT: AI-Generated Contents, Challenges, and Solutions." *IEEE Open Journal of the Computer Society,* https://doi.org/10.1109/OJCS.2023.3300321.

Webster, J., and J. J. Martocchio. 1993. "Turning Work into Play: Implications for Microcomputer Software Training." *Journal of Management* 19 (1): 127–146. https://doi.org/https://doi.org/10.1177/014920639301900109.

Yang, J., H. Jin, R. Tang, X. Han, Q. Feng, H. Jiang, S. Zhong, B. Yin, and X. Hu. 2024. "Harnessing the Power of LLMs in Practice: A Survey on ChatGPT and Beyond." *ACM Transactions on Knowledge Discovery from Data* 18 (6): 1–32. https://doi.org/https://doi.org/10.1145/3649506.

Zenil, H., S. Hernández-Orozco, N. A. Kiani, F. Soler-Toscano, A. Rueda-Toicen, and J. Tegnér. 2018. "A Decomposition Method for Global Evaluation of Shannon Entropy and Local Estimations of Algorithmic Complexity." *Entropy* 20 (8): 605. https://doi.org/10.3390/e20080605.

ECONOMIC GEOGRAPHY AND COMPLEXITY THEORY

Koen Frenken, Utrecht University; and
Frank Neffke, Complexity Science Hub

Abstract

The global economy operates as a complex system that allocates resources in a decentralized way across myriad agents. Over time, it exhibits an impressive rate of collective learning as evidenced by its growing productivity and the expanding variety of output it generates. However, growth, productivity, and learning are not distributed equally across locations. On the contrary, wealth, opportunity, economic activity, and innovation all tend to concentrate in a relatively small number of affluent places. Various strands of complexity science have contributed to our understanding of these phenomena. However, they have done so in disconnected debates and communities. In this chapter, we use the framework of economic complexity to synthesize insights derived from three distinct literatures: urban scaling, evolutionary economic geography, and global production networks. Economic complexity proposes that production requires access to capabilities, such that increasing the variety of economic production necessitates acquiring or accessing new capabilities. From this synthesis, we derive a research agenda that aims to understand how local economies develop, not only as individual units exploring their adjacent possible, but as parts of a system that allows local economies to mix their capabilities with those of distant counterparts by relying on the interplay of multinational corporations, global value chains, and institutions to coordinate interactions at the local and global scales.

Introduction

Modern economies combine a large range of inputs from various places to produce a wide variety of highly complex goods and services. Moreover, they manage to do so in quantities that meet consumer demand surprisingly accurately. The self-organized nature of this process has fascinated generations of economists since the works of Adam Smith. An early explanation for capitalist economies' success pointed to prices as an efficient information-organizing principle (Hayek 1945) that allowed a system without central control or planning to constantly adjust to changing consumer preferences and producer technologies. However, with time, evidence gathered that the bandwidth of price signals is too narrow for the complex coordination tasks that today's production processes require. Accordingly, economies are more than just abstract marketplaces where anonymous buyers and sellers meet. Instead, economies employ a mixture of narrow- and high-bandwidth communication, using markets, networks, corporate hierarchies, and institutions to structure these interactions within and across territories.

Here, we discuss recent complexity-theory-based advances in the field of economic geography that start from an explicit notion of complexity, namely, the complexity of products and services that a city or region produces. Following this literature, complexity is here taken to mean the number of inputs or capabilities required for an output to be produced. This starting point brings the role of firms to the fore—as well as that of the value chains they participate in—as principal vehicles to coordinate an increasingly fine-grained division of labor. In doing so, it helps us understand the diverse trajectories of urban and regional development that we observe in the real world as a result of differences in the complexity of goods that companies are capable of producing and of the territorial institutions that support the division of labor within and across companies. In its explicit representation of "recipes" that transform inputs into outputs, this complexity approach differs from past contributions in complexity theory. In early theorizing, complexity scholars adopted the view of the economy as a self-organizing system (Krugman 1997) in which the historical evolution of either transportation technology or entrepreneurship generates core–periphery structures in space. In the former case, geographic clustering is understood as a nonlinear response to a fall in transportation costs, causing production to concentrate geographically (Krugman 1991). In the latter case, geographic clustering is driven by a cumulative process of firm formation in which entrepreneurs establish spinoff companies close to their parent companies (Klepper 2010). Instead, the more recent complexity-theoretical contributions in economic geography follow an evolutionary approach, modeling the growth of economies in terms of expanding capability bases that allow them to produce increasingly varied and complex products.[1]

~ 447 ~

Here, we review this literature to identify neglected questions and directions for future research.

Economic Complexity

In the late 1990s and early 2000s, a new research program emerged that was inspired by evolutionary economics (Nelson and Winter 1982). This so-called evolutionary economic

---

[1] Evolutionary economics has traditionally embraced metaphors from evolutionary biology. In the present case, capabilities are often regarded as defining an economy's genotype, whereas the concrete products and services that they produce are analogous to phenotypes (see Schetter *et al.* 2024). As in biology, whereas genotypic information is hard to observe, the phenotypical information is immediately available from the structure of its output.

geography (EEG; see Boschma and Frenken 2006) approach built on concepts taken from the literature on innovation and industrial dynamics. For instance, it analyzed the spatial consequences of industry lifecycles (Klepper 2010), showing that geographic concentrations and clusters undergo lifecycle dynamics (Menzel and Fornahl 2010; Neffke *et al.* 2011). This literature also borrowed the biological metaphors of mutation and selection. For instance, like industries, geographical clusters are assumed to start with an expansion of novelty ("mutations") to later undergo rationalization in a so-called shake-out period ("selection"). Another example is the work that stresses the value of variety in economic growth and, in particular, related variety (Frenken, Van Oort, and Verburg 2007).

One particularly prominent idea in EEG is that regional development is path-dependent (Martin and Sunley 2006). When this idea is applied to the economic composition of a local economy—for instance, to describe the economy's export, industrial, or occupational composition—it implies that regions diversify into activities that build on their historical strengths. That is, regional diversification can be seen as a branching process (Frenken and Boschma 2007), a proposition that was later verified empirically (Neffke and Henning 2008; Neffke, Henning, and Boschma 2011).

The idea of economic development as branching along paths of related activities mirrored work that emerged in parallel in complexity science by a group of scholars working on what they termed economic complexity (see also ch. 7 in this volume).[2] A core argument of this new generation

---

[2] EEG and the work in economic complexity differ in a subtle way in how they motivate the prediction of related diversification. In the EEG literature, which emerged from the literature in evolutionary economics about innovation dynamics, related diversification is an expression of learning

of economic-complexity scholars holds that the total body of collective knowledge in a society exceeds by far the cognitive capacities of individual workers (Hidalgo *et al.* 2007; Hidalgo and Hausmann 2009). In response, societies distribute knowledge across an increasing array of experts that specialize in different yet complementary tasks (Neffke 2019). To organize this distributed knowledge, societies need to orchestrate the interactions between individuals in teams (e.g., firms) and teams of teams (e.g., value chains). The depth of the division of knowledge that can be achieved in this way is limited not by the extent of the market as in Adam Smith but by the costs of coordination (Becker and Murphy 1992). From this perspective, spatial concentration can help lower coordination costs, because face-to-face interactions make it much easier to coordinate complex distributed knowledge over short distances than over long distances.

~449~

Ricardo Hausmann and César Hidalgo (2011) model economies using the notion of capabilities as the set of inputs that are needed to produce a specific output. These capabilities are strictly complementary—as in a Leontief production function—such that production fails even when a single capability is unavailable, as for instance in Michael Kremer's (1993) O-ring model. Consequently, regions move up the development ladder when their economies acquire a new capability. This new capability can be combined with existing capabilities in new combinations to allow for the production of new products, expanding the economy's variety of economic activities in a way that is consistent with empirical evidence (van Dam and Frenken 2022; Inoua 2023).

---

between technologically or cognitively related activities. In the literature on economic complexity, related diversification was originally motivated through economies of scope in production, where activities are related if they can share similar inputs, or "capabilities."

Moreover, with a growing number of capabilities, products that are added to an economy's portfolio will on average be more complex than existing products, raising the economy's complexity. The greater number of capabilities that complex products require also make them harder to imitate. Complex products therefore often command higher prices. Provided that workers have some bargaining power, this increased profitability will be shared through higher wages. This explains why the average complexity of products in a city tends to be closely related to average incomes, as well as why complexity is often regarded as a measure of economic development (Hidalgo and Hausmann 2009).

Following this logic, in Koen Frenken, Frank Neffke, and Alje van Dam (2023) we argue that, because diversification is essentially a process of capability acquisition, the process of diversification itself tends to take the shape of related diversification. Moreover, capability acquisition is unlikely to be random. This is because the more complementary a new capability is—in terms of how easily it can be combined with existing capabilities—the greater the number of new products that can be produced. Note, however, that these new products will be related to existing ones, making diversification even more prone to be related rather than unrelated.

Conceptually, the relatedness between two industries is defined as the number of capabilities that two industries have in common. However, directly measuring this relatedness is challenging. Consequently, capabilities themselves often remain unobserved in economic complexity frameworks. Instead, scholars have developed indirect ways to measure relatedness using co-occurrence analysis as pioneered by Hidalgo *et al.* (2007) and further developed in an information-theoretic framework by Alje van Dam *et al.* (2023). Moreover, recently some efforts have been undertaken to observe capabilities directly (e.g., Schetter *et al.* 2024).

Regarding estimating the complexity of an economy, substantial debate remains about the best way to infer the number of capabilities in an economy from data on the structure of economic output (e.g., Hidalgo and Hausmann 2009; Tacchella *et al.* 2012; Mealy, Farmer, and Teytelboym 2019; McNerney *et al.* 2021; Inoua 2023, see also ch. 24 in this volume)

Urban Scaling

Another approach to make sense of the spatial concentration of economic activities emerged in urban complexity research, where scholars identified striking empirical regularities in the spatial concentration of economic activity: urban scaling laws (Pumain *et al.* 2006; Bettencourt *et al.* 2007). Urban scaling laws describe how the size of a local economic activity grows with city size. In a log–log plane, basic services tend to scale linearly with city size. That is, the per-capita intensity of such services tends to be similar across cities of different sizes, reflecting that such services locate close to demand due to high transportation costs. Infrastructure, instead, tends to grow less than proportionally with the size of a city. That is, infrastructure tends to scale sublinearly with city size, indicating that there are economies of scale in keeping a city connected. By contrast, knowledge-intensive activities grow more than proportionally with city size. Indeed, R&D, patents, and total wage sums all scale superlinearly with city size.

Despite having developed in a disconnected manner, urban scaling and the new work on economic complexity are not in contradiction. On the contrary, Andres Gomez-Lievano, Oscar Patterson-Lomba and Ricardo Hausmann (2016) show that urban scaling laws can in fact be derived from an economic complexity model that centers on capabilities. To do so, Gomez-Lievano and his coauthors propose that different types of social activities require different capabilities.

Here, we follow the presentation of a closely related model in Gomez-Lievano and Oscar Patterson-Lomba (2021). In this model, for an individual to engage in an activity, they must have access to all capabilities that the activity requires. However, they need not possess all capabilities themselves but can borrow some from the urban environment in which they reside. Formally, the authors propose that the probability that an individual i in city c participates in activity p can be modeled as:

$$P\left(X_{icp} = 1 | D_c\right) = s_i^{M_p - D_c} \tag{1}$$

where M_p is the total number of capabilities that activity p requires, which can be thought of as the activity's complexity. Furthermore, s_i is the probability that individual i has a certain capability (which is here assumed to be the same for all capabilities) and D_c represents the number of capabilities required by p that are available in city c.

In other words, equation 1 states that the likelihood that an individual participates in an activity, conditional on their city offering access to D_c of the capabilities that this activity requires, equals the likelihood that the individual has all other required capabilities themselves. Furthermore, let us assume that city c offers access to capabilities at constant probability r_c. Generally, r_c will be a function of city size and Andres Gomez-Lievano, Oscar Patterson-Lomba, and Ricardo Hausmann (2016) argue that the number of capabilities that can be accessed in a city grows linearly with the logarithm of its population size.[3]

[3] The authors offer two explanations for this functional form. The first relies on models of skill-biased social learning with incomplete inference developed in evolutionary anthropology (Henrich and Boyd 2002). The second assumes

~452~

Now, conditioning out D_c yields the following expression for the unconditional probability that i participates in activity p:

$$P\left(X_{icp} = 1\right) = \sum_D s_i^{M_p - D} \binom{M_p}{D} r_c^D \left(1 - r_c\right)^{M_p - D} \quad (2)$$

This simplifies to $\left(r_c + s_i \left(1 - r_c\right)\right)^{M_p}$, which, for small s_i and r_c can be approximated by:

$$P\left(X_{icp} = 1\right) = e^{\ln\left(P(X_{icp}=1)\right)} \cong e^{-M_p(1-s_i)(1-r_c)} \quad (3)$$

This simple setup predicts that the size of an activity in a city scales with population size exactly according to the scaling laws documented in the urban scaling literature.[4] Moreover, taking the derivative with respect to the activity's complexity, M_p, shows that the more complex an activity is (i.e., the more capabilities the activity requires), the steeper the scaling relation gets. This proposition was later confirmed by Pierre-Alexandre Balland *et al.* (2020).

Value Chains

What are capabilities? Gomez-Lievano *et al.*'s (2016) paper offers a useful clue: Capabilities of cities need to be accessible to actors within but not outside the city. Furthermore, in Neffke

---

that cities draw capabilities proportionally to their number of inhabitants. Under certain assumptions, the expected number of different capabilities that cities draw increases linearly with the logarithm of population size.

[4] This would be captured by the fact that population size raises the probability that a city has any capability, i.e., $r_c \sim \log\left(population_c\right)$. Gomez-Lievano, Patterson-Lomba, and Hausmann (2016) derive further expressions for the intercept and variance around a scaling law, showing that these also depend on the complexity of the activity. In particular, more complex activities will have lower intercepts, meaning that they are relatively rare, and exhibit higher variance around the fitted regression line between participation levels and city size, predictions that hold empirically for a wide range of social activities, ranging from crime and health to innovation and economic activities.

et al. (2018) we argue that capabilities share a commonality with resources in the resource-based view of the firm as developed in management science. Accordingly, for something to count as a capability, it needs to be valuable, rare, nonsubstitutable, and hard to imitate (Barney 1991). For regional capabilities, much of the same holds: They need to be valuable and rare. Moreover, they need to be hard to substitute, a central assumption in economic complexity as we have seen above, and they need to be specific to economic activities. What sets them apart from firm-level capabilities is that they must be hard to access from outside the region but be nonrivalrous among firms inside the region. Plausible candidates are skilled pools of workers, specific types of infrastructure, and specialized local suppliers of goods and services with high transaction costs.

In Frenken, Neffke, and Alje van Dam (2023), however, we point out that, while the economic-complexity framework is consistent with evolutionary patterns toward increasing variety and complexity in cities and regions, the framework remains limited in that it views "regions as 'containers' of capabilities without explicitly accounting for the relational structures between firms operating in value chains within and across regions." Instead, urban and regional economic development needs to account for the fact that modern production is organized in value chains that connect firms that may be, but generally are not all, colocated in the same city or region. Through these multilocational firms, local actors can tap into capabilities that reside in other cities.

Furthermore, more complex products will tend to have longer value chains, aggregating knowledge that is distributed across greater numbers of firms and their workforces. As value chains spread across sectors and geographies, urban and regional development becomes driven by more than the set of locally available capabilities and, increasingly, comes to depend on a city's or region's ability to participate in complex value chains. To do so, local economies require effective institutions that reduce transaction costs in value chains and collaboration costs in collective knowledge production.

While economic-complexity theory emphasizes that local economies tend to diversify and to increase their variety, adding a value-chain perspective also allows theorizing about specialization. By inserting local firms into multiple value chains, a city can exploit a regional focus on capabilities in support of certain common components of different value chains, such as R&D, production, logistics, marketing, and information technology (IT). This type of specialization is known as functional specialization in urban economics (Duranton and Puga 2005). In this way, a region can sustain a large degree of product diversification while at the same time maintaining only a limited set of capabilities associated with specific functions (Frenken, Neffke, and van Dam 2023). Examples of this are logistical hubs such as Rotterdam, financial centers like London, or IT hot spots like Silicon Valley.

A value-chain perspective on economic complexity also allows integration of theoretical questions related to development and trade. The more open a local economy is to trade, the less it needs to rely on a local presence of capabilities for participating in high-value-added, complex production processes. However, the same openness that supports development through value-chain participations also exposes it to value-chain disruptions. Our understanding of such trade-offs is currently limited but will benefit from efforts to map high-resolution supply networks by exploiting detailed, high-frequency transaction data derived from, for instance, value-added tax data (Pichler *et al.* 2023).

Conclusion

The economic-complexity framework as applied in economic geography reasons from local capabilities as the genotypes that express themselves in phenotypes of specific products or services derived from these genotypes. In this framework, urban and regional economic development can be modeled as a process of related diversification, where locations acquire capabilities that raise their economy's complexity. Moreover, urban scaling laws can be derived from this same framework. However, as economic geographers have long stressed, production is nowadays often organized in value chains that span across multiple regions worldwide. Consequently, economic development is not just conditioned by local capabilities but also dependent on the institutions that support local firms to participate in value chains that coordinate production across localities. This points to the value of an augmented capability framework as an analytical basis on which evolutionary and network approaches in economic geography can be integrated. Connecting work in complexity science on supply networks to the capability-based framework that studies how capabilities are coordinated across local economies through value chains should therefore present a particularly promising direction for future research. 𝔶

REFERENCES

Balland, P. A., C. Jara-Figueroa, S. G. Petralia, M. P. Steijn, D. L. Rigby, and C. A. Hidalgo. 2020. "Complex Economic Activities Concentrate in Large Cities." *Nature Human Behaviour* 4 (3): 248–254. https://doi.org/10.1038/s41562-019-0803-3.

Barney, J. 1991. "Firm Resources and Sustained Competitive Advantage." *Journal of Management* 17 (1): 99–120. https : / / doi . org / 10 . 1177 / 014920639101700108.

Becker, G. S., and K. M. Murphy. 1992. "The Division of Labor, Coordination Costs, and Knowledge." *The Quarterly Journal of Economics* 107 (4): 1137–1160. https://doi.org/10.2307/2118383.

Bettencourt, L. M. A., J. Lobo, D. Helbing, C. Kühnert, and G. West. 2007. "Growth, Innovation, Scaling, and the Pace of Life in Cities." *Proceedings of the National Academy of Sciences* 104:7301–7306. https : / / doi . org / 10 . 1073 / pnas . 0610172104.

Boschma, R. A., and K. Frenken. 2006. "Why is Economic Geography not an Evolutionary Science? Towards an Evolutionary Economic Geography." *Journal of Economic Geography* 6 (3): 273–302. https://doi.org/10.1093/jeg/lbi022.

Duranton, G., and D. Puga. 2005. "From Sectoral to Functional Urban Specialisation." *Journal of Urban Economics* 57 (2): 343–370. https://doi.org/10.1016/j.jue.2004.12.002.

Frenken, K., and R. A. Boschma. 2007. "A Theoretical Framework for Evolutionary Economic Geography: Industrial Dynamics and Urban Growth as a Branching Process." *Journal of Economic Geography* 7 (5): 635–649. https://doi.org/10.1093/jeg/lbm018.

Frenken, K., F. Neffke, and A. van Dam. 2023. "Capabilities, Institutions and Regional Economic Development: A Proposed Synthesis." *Cambridge Journal of Regions, Economy and Society* 16 (3): 405–441. https://doi.org/10.1093/cjres/rsad021.

Frenken, K., F. Van Oort, and T. Verburg. 2007. "Related Variety, Unrelated Variety, and Regional Economic Growth." *Regional Studies* 41 (5): 685–697. https://doi.org/10.1080/00343400601120296.

Gomez-Lievano, A., and O. Patterson-Lomba. 2021. "Estimating the Drivers of Urban Economic Complexity and their Connection to Economic Performance." *Royal Society Open Science* 8 (9): 210670. https://doi.org/10.1098/rsos.210670.

Gomez-Lievano, A., O. Patterson-Lomba, and R. Hausmann. 2016. "Explaining the Prevalence, Scaling, and Variance of Urban Phenomena." *Nature Human Behaviour* 1:0012. https://doi.org/10.1038/s41562-016-0012.

Hausmann, R., and C. A. Hidalgo. 2011. "The Network Structure of Economic Output." *Journal of Economic Growth* 16:309–342. https://doi.org/10.1007/s10887-011-9071-4.

Hayek, F. A. 1945. "The Use of Knowledge in Society." *The American Economic Review* 35 (4): 519–530. https://www.jstor.org/stable/1809376.

Henrich, J., and R. Boyd. 2002. "On Modeling Cognition and Culture: Why Cultural Evolution does not Require Replication of Representations." *Journal of Cognition and Culture* 2 (2): 87–112. https://doi.org/10.1163/156853702320281836.

Hidalgo, C. A., and R. Hausmann. 2009. "The Building Blocks of Economic Complexity." *Proceedings of the National Academy of Sciences* 106 (26): 10570–10575. https://doi.org/10.1073/pnas.0900943106.

Hidalgo, C. A., B. Klinger, A. L. Barabási, and R. Hausmann. 2007. "The Product Space Conditions the Development of Nations." *Science* 317 (5837): 482–487. https://doi.org/10.1126/science.1144581.

Inoua, S. 2023. "A Simple Measure of Economic Complexity." *Research Policy* 52 (7): 104793. https://doi.org/10.1016/j.respol.2023.104793.

Klepper, S. 2010. "The Origin and Growth of Industry Clusters: The Making of Silicon Valley and Detroit." *Journal of Urban Economics* 67 (1): 15–32. https://doi.org/10.1016/j.jue.2009.09.004.

Kremer, M. 1993. "The O-Ring Theory of Economic Development." *The Quarterly Journal of Economics* 108 (3): 551–575. https://doi.org/10.2307/2118400.

Krugman, P. 1991. "Increasing Returns and Economic Geography." *Journal of Political Economy* 99 (3): 483–499. https://www.jstor.org/stable/2937739.

———. 1997. "How the Economy Organizes Itself in Space: A Survey of the New Economic Geography." In *The Economy as a Complex Evolving System II*, edited by W. B. Arthur, S. N. Durlauf, and D. A. Lane, 239–262. Boca Raton, FL: CRC Press.

Martin, R., and P. Sunley. 2006. "Path Dependence and Regional Economic Evolution." *Journal of Economic Geography* 6 (4): 395–437. https://doi.org/ 10.1093/jeg/lbl012.

McNerney, J., Y. Li, A. Gomez-Lievano, and F. Neffke. 2021. "Bridging the Short-Term and Long-Term Dynamics of Economic Structural Change." *Nature Communications* 16:10225. https://doi.org/10.1038/s41467-025-65043-0.

Mealy, P., J. D. Farmer, and A. Teytelboym. 2019. "Interpreting Economic Complexity." *Science Advances* 5 (1): eaau1705. https://doi.org/10.1126/ sciadv.aau1705.

Menzel, M.-P., and D. Fornahl. 2010. "Cluster Life Cycles—Dimensions and Rationales of Cluster Evolution." *Industrial and Corporate Change* 19 (1): 205–238. https://doi.org/10.1093/icc/dtp036.

Neffke, F., M. Hartog, R. Boschma, and M. Henning. 2018. "Agents of Structural Change: The Role of Firms and Entrepreneurs in Regional Diversification." *Economic Geography* 94 (1): 23–48. https://doi.org/10.1080/00130095.2017. 1391691.

Neffke, F., M. Henning, and R. Boschma. 2011. "How Do Regions Diversify over Time? Industry Relatedness and the Development of New Growth Paths in Regions." *Economic Geography* 87 (3): 237–265. https://doi.org/10.1111/j. 1944-8287.2011.01121.x.

Neffke, F., M. Henning, R. Boschma, K.J. Lundquist, and L.O. Olander. 2011. "The Dynamics of Agglomeration Externalities Along the Life Cycle of Industries." *Regional Studies* 45 (1): 49–65. https://doi.org/10.1080/ 00343401003596307.

Neffke, F., and M.S. Henning. 2008. *Revealed Relatedness: Mapping Industry Space*. Technical report. Papers in Evolutionary Economic Geography 08.19. DRUID, Copenhagen Business School, Department of Industrial Economics and Strategy/Aalborg University, Department of Business Studies.

Neffke, F. M. H. 2019. "The Value of Complementary Co-Workers." *Science Advances* 5 (12): eaax3370. https://doi.org/10.1126/sciadv.aax3370.

Nelson, R., and S. Winter. 1982. *An Evolutionary Theory of Economic Change.* Cambridge, MA: Belknap Press.

Pichler, A., C. Diem, A. Brintrup, F. Lafond, G. Magerman, G. Buiten, T. Y. Choi, V. M. Carvalho, J. D. Farmer, and S. Thurner. 2023. "Building an Alliance to Map Global Supply Networks." *Science* 382 (6668): 270–272. https://doi.org/10.1126/science.adi7521.

Pumain, D., F. Paulus, C. Vacchiani-Marcuzzo, and J. Lobo. 2006. "An Evolutionary Theory for Interpreting Urban Scaling Laws." *Cybergeo* 343:20. https://doi.org/10.4000/cybergeo.2519.

Schetter, U., D. Diodato, E. Protzer, F. Neffke, and R. Hausmann. 2024. *From Products to Capabilities: Constructing a Genotypic Product Space.* Technical report 19369. CEPR Discussion Papers. https://cepr.org/publications/dp19369.

Tacchella, A., M. Cristelli, G. Caldarelli, A. Gabrielli, and L. Pietronero. 2012. "A New Metrics for Countries' Fitness and Products' Complexity." *Scientific Reports* 2 (723): 1–7. https://doi.org/10.1038/srep00723.

van Dam, A., and K. Frenken. 2022. "Variety, Complexity, and Economic Development." *Research Policy* 51 (8): 103949. https://doi.org/10.1016/j.respol.2020.103949.

van Dam, A., A. Gomez-Lievano, F. Neffke, and K. Frenken. 2023. "An Information-Theoretic Approach to the Analysis of Location and Co-Location Patterns." *Journal of Regional Science* 63:173–213. https://doi.org/10.1111/jors.12621.

PART VII

*Political Economy &
Public Policy*

THE POLITICAL ECONOMY OF COMPLEX EVOLVING SYSTEMS: THE CASE OF DECLINING UNIONIZATION AND RISING INEQUALITIES

Giovanni Dosi, Scuola Superiore Sant'Anna;

Marcelo C. Pereira, Universidade Estadual de Campinas
and Scuola Superiore Sant'Anna;

Andrea Roventini, Scuola Superiore Sant'Anna and OFCE Sciences Po;

Maria Enrica Virgillito, Scuola Superiore Sant'Anna
and Università Cattolica del Sacro Cuore

Abstract

This chapter presents an application of the multisector labor-augmented Schumpeter Meeting Keynes (K+S) agent-based model to two contemporary challenges in political economy, namely declining unionization and rising inequality, with reference to medium-term evidence in the United States. What has been the effect of declining unionization? The model proves to be a promising tool to confront different scenarios emerging from the interaction of an endogenous dynamic competition between union and non-union firms, the latter arriving at a specific time. The arrival of non-union firms induces direct first-order effects, in the form of rising inequality in the workplace and at the macro level, but also indirect second-order effects, in the form of lower rates of labor absorption, and demand patterns skewed toward luxury consumption goods for the wealthy. In that, complexity economics proves to be a promising avenue to incorporate and confront the grand challenges of contemporary capitalism.

Introduction

This chapter discusses the link between political economy and agent-based macro models, drawing upon the multisector (Dosi *et al.* 2022) labor-augmented Schumpeter Meeting Keynes (K+S) family of models (Dosi *et al.* 2017, 2018, 2020). Capitalist forms of socioeconomic organization have always been characterized by ubiquitous heterogeneity among economic agents, conflicts among social groups, and coordination hurdles. Consequently, the system has always generated structural imbalances, fluctuations, and crises. However, recent trends point at an increasing fragility of the system, together with deepening inequalities and the erosion of many forms of public intervention and institutions. In the post–World War II era, institutions had guaranteed relatively stable patterns of income distribution and the provision of both public goods and relatively universal access to social welfare. Indeed, the relationship between the state and the economy has radically changed, as the state has increasingly given up its role of socioeconomic coordinator and basically taken up that of protector of corporate interests.

How can economists analyze, model, and identify such alternative modes of socioeconomic organization and their properties? The dominant macroeconomic theory is bound to be silent on the subject. The litmus test was the 2008 financial crisis, whose very possibility was ruled out by construction, given its solipsistic agents and the commitment to equilibrium (Colander *et al.* 2008; Krugman 2011). Standard macroeconomics is even less able to address the political-economy issues related to changes in the broad institutional setup, mostly restricted to economic institutions rewarding innovation efforts (Acemoglu and Robinson 2013). This is further demonstrated in this book (Beinhocker and Bednar 2026, ch. 31).

Since the 1990s, agent-based models (ABMs), built on the convergence between evolutionary and complexity paradigms (Dosi and Roventini 2019; Dosi 2023), have been an important source of scientific knowledge to advance our understanding of the dynamics of capitalism. The Santa Fe Institute series *The Economy as a Complex Evolving System*, now in its fourth volume, is a testament to this process. Evolutionary ABMs have proved to match an impressive ensemble of stylized facts, that is, basic statistical regularities—ranging from the microlevel distributions of firm sizes and growth rates, the pattern of evolution of industries, all the way to macroeconomic fluctuations and crises. In addition, they represent a powerful tool to scenario analysis. We are in the middle of a multipronged effort to understand and formalize some fundamental *general properties* of the "anatomy and physiology" of the capitalist socioeconomic fabric.

The socioeconomic fabric is subject to profound *phase transitions* shaped by the coevolution of technologies, institutions, and economic processes. This includes also transitions toward self-cannibalization (Fraser 2023) and the self-destruction of the system. Indeed, such dynamics is the domain of analysis that we call the *political economy* of agent-based macro models. This, we suggest, is the next frontier that ABMs are just beginning to tackle. Those models are powerful policy laboratories (Dosi *et al.* 2020) in that they are consistent simplified worlds, wherein experiments with different policy measures and institutional set-ups can be configured. As such, they can be precious instruments for exploring alternative political economy scenarios. This goes well beyond counterfactual exercises concerning the marginal impact, *ceteris paribus*, of single policies upon specific variables, say, the rate of growth or the overall level of functional inequality. Rather, the exploration of different scenarios also involves the painstaking search for *combinations of institutions and policies* able to reverse the current trends toward dramatically increasing inequalities in the distribution of income and power, and, relatedly, toward social and environmental catastrophe.

In this chapter we address two fundamental challenges in contemporary capitalism: the decline in unionization rate and the rise in income inequality. What have been the micro- and macro-level effects of the declining unionization rate? The historical counterpart of such phenomena, which we use to highlight the empirical plausibility of the analysis, is the US experience. There, one observes the repeated defeats of unions in disputes and the growing anti-union legislation, including right-to-work (RTW) laws, disfavoring union firms and paving the way for anti-labor practices. We present an application of the multi-sector, labor-augmented K+S agent-based model addressing the declining unionization and rising inequality. The model proves to be an important tool to confront different scenarios emerging out of the endogenous dynamic competition between union and non-union firms. The arrival of the latter induces direct first-order effects, as rising inequality at both the workplace and the macro level. Indirectly, it drives second-order effects, as lower rates of employment absorption, and demand patterns skewed toward luxury consumption goods for the wealthy.

In the following, drawing upon our work on Dosi *et al.* (2022) and Dosi *et al.* (2021), we first discuss the two challenges of political economy we would like to explore. We then move to the agent-based model application, presenting our model properties and results. We conclude by discussing our findings and some avenues for future research.

Two Grand Challenges for Contemporary Political Economy: Rising Inequality and Declining Union Power

The rise of inequality is certainly one of the predominant trends documented in contemporary capitalism. Inequality has increased (i) in wage dispersion among similar occupations in different establishments (Barth *et al.* 2016); (ii) across occupations in the same companies, between CEOs and the rest of the workforce (Gabaix and Landier 2008); (iii) in terms of functional income inequality (Dosi and Virgillito 2019); (iv) in terms of personal income or wealth (Piketty 2015); and (v) within and across countries (Milanovic 2024). Its multidimensional effects have propagated from economic to political spheres (Stiglitz 2015), from definition of property rights to access to public goods (Dosi, Fanti, and Virgillito 2024).

The extant literature has mostly attributed individual wage inequality to the skill- and routine-biased nature of technological change (Autor and Dorn 2013). According to such research streams, the determination of wage and the ensuing origin of inequality are a market-based issue. Therefore, the dynamics of labor remuneration is mainly due to technology-related causes, driven by changes in the elasticity of substitution among inputs, yielding "biases" in the demand for different types of jobs. In turn, such biases are matched by the "wrong" educational attainments, and the corresponding skill mismatch, with a rising demand for college-educated workers (Tinbergen 1974; Katz and Murphy 1992). Under that perspective, the *skill-bias* interpretation is deemed as the dominant explanation for inequality. It has been gradually adopted to analyze job tasks and technological-based factors according to the *task-biased* or *routine-biased* technical change approach (Acemoglu and Autor 2011). In practice, this trend has been primarily attributed to the rise in computer adoption, until the Great Recession, or, more recently, to a general "robotization age" (Restrepo 2023). In a nutshell, technologically driven factors are held responsible for a change in the composition of occupational structure, leading to the disappearance of intermediary occupations, and also for the polarization in wages. More recently, artificial intelligence (AI), with its growing diffusion, has been also taken on board (Acemoglu *et al.* 2022).

However, a growing number of researchers are questioning the technology-driven origin of inequality (Dosi *et al.* 2022; Mishel 2022; Cetrulo, Guarascio, and Virgillito 2024). The need to account for deeper and persistent nontechnological drivers has refocused scholars' attention toward other factors that could impact the determination of wages and inequality. This certainly requires a departure from simplistic neoclassical premises, based on (perfectly) competitive labor markets able to (fairly) reward individuals for their skills and productivity. Alternative candidates to explain wage levels, inequality, and the associated dynamics must consider the socio-institutional dimensions embedded in the occupational class structure (Hugrée, Penissat, and Spire 2020; Goedemé *et al.* 2021), the rise of the care economy (Dwyer 2013; Folbre 2021), and the weakening of labor market institutions (Stansbury and Summers 2020).

Increasing wage disparities are usually linked with the widespread decline in the labor share of income. A declining share is not only a signal of wage compression and functional inequality but, behind that, the reorganization of capitalism in favor of managerial-shareholder power. Such rise in power has been a force pushing managerial remuneration, including in terms of shares and stock options, up to the point, documented by Josh Bivens and Jori Kandra (2022), of a rise of almost 400 times in the CEO–average worker compensation ratio in the companies present in the Compustat dataset. Such an increase represents a dramatic process of income redistribution that certainly cannot be ascribed to the relative worker productivities.

The decline of labor share has come together with, or because of, a reduction of the *bargaining power* of workers. Under nondecreasing returns and asymmetric power relations between employers and employees, the distribution of income might well be the outcome of a negotiation process between firms and workers, possibly represented by unions and mediated by labor market institutions. Workers, whenever protected by strong unions and pro-labor legislation, are likely better able to negotiate wage increases in line with productivity gains, helping to maintain a stable labor share.

Empirically, there is a growing consensus on the role of labor market institutions in affecting the share dynamics through the bargaining power channel. Several studies have found that factors such as strike activity, collective bargaining arrangements, minimum wages, and union density, affect the labor share (Kristal 2010; Bentolila and Saint-Paul 2003; Argitis and Pitelis 2001). In particular, union density—the percentage of unionized workers within a given worker population—has been shown to have a positive effect on the labor share at the country level (Guschanski and Onaran 2021; Stockhammer 2015; Bengtsson 2014; Stockhammer 2013; Jaumotte and Osorio Buitron 2020). In addition, the evidence (Dao, Das, and Koczan 2020; Dimova 2019) suggests that unions may have different effects on the wage-setting process for dissimilar skill groups, protecting in particular low-skilled workers, thus reducing wage inequality. A piece of long-run historical evidence on the positive effects of unionization for taming inequality is in Henry S. Farber *et al.* (2021).

Historically, the rise of union power in the United States has been described as a spurt dynamics (Freeman 1998), with a rapid increase from the 1930s up to the mid-1950s, reaching a peak value of 36%. Two laws were important in that phase. The first was the National Labor Relations Act (NLRA) in 1935, also known as the Wagner Act, which provided an institutional framework for union workplaces. It ensured the right to unionize, including collective bargaining, the right to strike, and the institution of a federal commission, the National Labor Relations Board, responsible for prosecuting unfair labor practices. With the approval of this law, the initial phase of the spurt started (see fig. 1). A subsequent anti-labor policy, the Taft–Hartley Act in 1947, was introduced to limit the space of action of unions and stop the ascending unionization. The act allowed each state to pass RTW laws, which exempt workers in unionized plants from paying fees even if they benefit from the union activity (Fortin, Lemieux, and Lloyd 2023). Historically, Southern and Midwestern states have adopted RTW laws, and that has been associated with lower unionization rates. More recent legislation, post-2010, in five states around the Great Lakes, has accelerated deunionization rates, with stronger declines in more unionized sectors (Shierholz *et al.* 2024; Fortin, Lemieux, and Lloyd 2023). Figure 1 shows the dynamics of union density in the US and marks the timing of different laws, accounting for the rise and decline in unionization.

More generally, the decline in union membership, a socio-institutional trend since the 1970s, has been found to account for the rising wage inequalities. While unions have always been considered to reduce wage inequality for unionized workers, Bruce Western and Jake Rosenfeld (2011)

~471~

also highlight the positive effects for non-union workers by means of the complementary effect on their wages. The decline in unionization has been linked to two main drivers: structural-economic forces, due to the rise in employment outside historically cohesive union industries, and institutional forces, due to increasing employer power and anti-union practices. This trend intensified following the US Reagan moment, with the defeat of air-traffic controllers strike in 1981 as a pivotal symbolic event, and the appointment of the Reagan Labor Board in 1983, as the institutionalization of a new anti-labor role for the board (Farber and Western 2002; Tope and Jacobs 2009). Coming to the first group of explanations, Barry T. Hirsch (2008) shows that much of the decline has been driven by within-industry dynamics, due to a progressive increase in the share of non-union firms. Similar evidence is presented in Farber and Western (2002). Market competition between union and non-union firms has favored the latter: unionized firms, paying more equal and higher wages, face progressively lower-cost competitors, and they are not able to pass the higher costs to consumers by rising prices, and eventually are forced to leave the market.

Needless to say, we are still far from accounting for all such institutional richness into any agent-based model. However, in the following, we present an instantiation of such phenomena, illustrating the endogenous coevolution between deunionization and market-driven competitive forces, with non-union firms entering into the market and competing with incumbent union ones. While the end outcome of such dynamics is fully endogenous, the specific arrival time of non-union firms can be interpreted as the exogenous introduction of a RTW-type law, favoring deunionization (Fortin, Lemieux, and Lloyd 2023; Shierholz *et al.* 2024). This way, the model

~472~

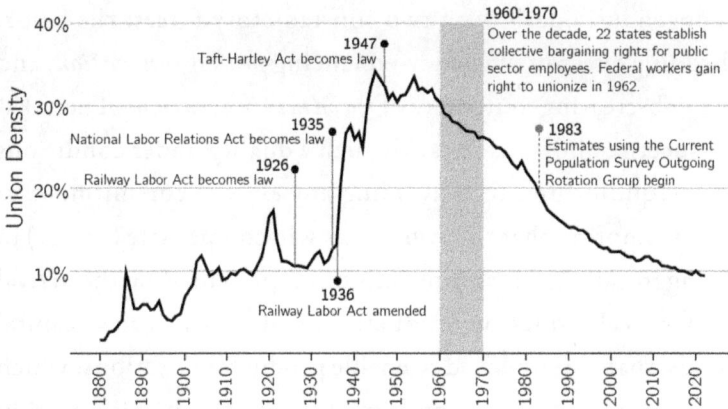

Figure 1. Union density 1880–2022. (*Source: Figure 1 in Romero and Whittaker 2023*)

can account for both structural and institutional drivers. In addition, considering that unionization is an industry-specific attribute, the effects of the introduction of a RTW law are expected to be industry-specific as well. Notably, Nicole Fortin, Thomas Lemieux, and Neil Lloyd (2023) show that the introduction of RTW laws have induced faster decline in unionization, notably in previously high-unionization industries.

The Multisector K+S Model Facing Political Economy

We present a *general-disequilibrium*, stock-flow-consistent, agent-based model, populated by heterogeneous workers, firms, and banks that behave according to heuristic rules.[1]

In a nutshell, the multi-sector, labor-augmented K+S model analyzes the long-term pattern of labor demand under the fundamental duality of technical change. Therefore, the model

---

[1] The section draws upon Dosi *et al.* (2022), to which the reader is referred for all technical details.

endogenously deals with two contradictory forces: the labor-shedding effect of efficiency-enhancing *process innovation*, and the job-creating outcome of *product innovation*. The ABM perspective allows us to tackle such a duality under conditions of disequilibrium, thus avoiding any *ex-ante* commitment to the assumption that the two effects will compensate (or not) in the aggregate. Process innovation is represented by the arrival of new techniques of production, embedded in new capital goods, that are employed to enable product innovations, which diffuse across producers and among users. Product innovation in final goods here is modeled by means of the emergence of new industries.

The model economy is composed by five populations of heterogeneous agents, namely, L^S workers/consumers, F_t^1 capital-good firms, F_t^2 consumption-good industries with $F_{h,t}^2$ firms in each, and B banks, plus the central bank and the government.[2] The basic structure of the model is depicted in figure 2.

Consumer–workers demand goods in a hierarchical order starting from basic and moving to luxury ones. Consumers split their income between basic- and luxury-good budgets, entirely allocating it to basic goods up to a given threshold corresponding to the median of income distribution, and the excess, if any, to luxury consumption. The budget for (divisible) basic goods is (tentatively) spent every period, and split among basic-good industries according to the respective products attributes (price, quality, novelty, and complexity). Luxury goods, which are not divisible, are acquired whenever three conditions are met: (i) a minimum period from last acquisition

[2]Subscript t stands for (discrete) time $t = 1, 2, ..., T$. Agent-specific variables are denoted by subscript h, in case of industries, i, for capital-good firms, j, for consumption-good firms, k, for banks, and ℓ, for workers.

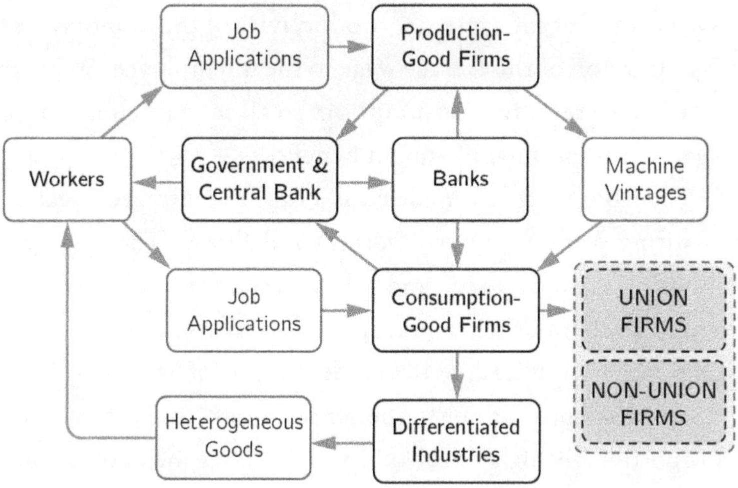

Figure 2. The overall model structure. Bold text represents the model's agents.

passed; (ii) at least one not-recently-bought good is obtainable; and (iii) the available luxury budget (current plus accumulated) is enough to buy at least one unit of the chosen good. If these conditions are not met, the available luxury budget is saved for the next period. So the consumption bundle is comprised by a set of heterogeneous basic goods, each one supplied by a different industry and firm, plus possibly one or more units of a single luxury good. If total supply is insufficient to satisfy the resulting demands for basic and luxury goods, the excess is saved in banks, and turns into additional consumption demand in the next period(s).

Workers consume part of their income and save the rest for acquiring more expensive luxury goods or to smooth consumption in case of unemployment. On top of wages, paid to all employees, there is a profit-sharing mechanism that allows firms with above-average profits to distribute bonuses as a fixed share of current wages. The government enforces a minimum wage indexed to the aggregate productivity of the economy and pays a fraction of the average wage to the unemployed. Workers do not take credit for consumption, so all income comes from wage, bonus, or unemployment benefit.

The labor market is modeled as a fully decentralized, search-and-hiring process between workers and firms.[3] The aggregate supply of labor is fixed, and all workers are available to be hired in any period. When unemployed, workers submit a certain number of job applications to a random subset of firms. Employed workers may apply or not for better positions. Larger firms have a proportionally higher probability of receiving job applications, which are organized in separated, firm-specific application queues. The labor market is also characterized by imperfect information as firms only observe workers' skills and wage requests on their own queues, and workers are aware only of the wage offers they may receive from firms where they applied for a job.

Firms, on the grounds of machine orders received, the expected consumer demand, and the current labor productivity levels, decide whether to (i) hire new workers; (ii) fire some of the existing ones; or (iii) keep the current labor force. Each hiring firm defines a unique wage offer for the best applicants, based on firm- and economy-wide productivities. Workers select the best wage offer they get from firms to which they submitted applications, if any. When already employed, they may quit the current job if a better offer is received. There are no further rounds of bargaining between workers and firms in the same period. Thus, firms have no guarantee of filling all the open positions, workers may not find a job even when there are still unfilled ones, and no labor market clearing is ever guaranteed. Moreover, there are no firing or hiring transaction costs.

---

[3]For simplicity, banks, the central bank, and the government occupy no workers.

Capital-good firms invest in R&D and produce heterogeneous machine-tools whose stochastic productivity evolves endogenously over time. Less frequently, new generations of machines are discovered, enabling the emergence of new consumption goods and industries. Downstream consumption-good firms combine machines bought from capital-good firms and labor in order to produce differentiated goods for final consumers. Across industries with heterogeneous products, consumption-good firms compete for consumers' expenditures. Workers search for jobs, and firms hire them according to their individual demand expectations. The banking sector is represented by a fixed number of banks that take deposits and provide interest-paying loans to finance firms' production and investment plans. The central bank manages the monetary policy, imposes regulatory reserves to the banks, and bails out the failing ones. Government levies taxes on firm and bank profits, pays unemployment benefits, imposes a minimum wage, absorbs excess profits and losses from the central bank, and keeps a nonexplosive public-debt trajectory in the long run.

The capital-good industry is the locus of endogenous innovation in the model. Capital-good firms innovate by developing new machine-embodied techniques or imitate the ones of their competitors in order to produce and sell more productive and cheaper machinery. Innovation is of two types, *incremental* or *radical*. Incremental innovation gradually increases productivity of existing technologies, both on new machine construction and their usage. Radical innovation introduces a new, qualitatively different generation of machines, associated with a new technological paradigm, which is more productive to use but also more expensive to produce and is possibly associated with the arrival of new industry producing "luxury" goods (see below). Machine prices are set using a fixed mark-up over (labor) costs of production.

Consumption-good firms in each industry produce a single, quality-, novelty-, and complexity-differentiated good, employing capital (composed by different "vintages" of machine-tools) and labor, under constant returns to scale. Desired production is determined according to adaptive (myopic) demand expectations. Given the actual inventories, if the current capital stock is not sufficient to produce the desired output, firms order new machines to expand their installed capacity, paying in advance — drawing on their retained past profits or, up to some limits, on bank loans. Moreover, they replace non-economical machines according to a payback-period rule. As new capital embeds state-of-the-art technology, the labor productivity of consumption-good firms increases over time according to the mix of (employed) vintages in the capital stocks. Firms choose the capital-good supplier comparing price and productivity of the machines they are aware of. They fix their output prices applying a variable mark-up rule on their (labor) production costs, balancing profit margins and market shares, increasing mark-ups and prices whenever expanding or reducing otherwise. Imperfect information is also the normal state of the consumption-good markets, so consumers do not instantaneously switch to the most competitive producer. Market shares evolve according to a replicator dynamics: More competitive firms expand, while less competitive firms shrink or exit the market.

Consumption-good firms group into different industries. Firms in the same industry produce a novelty-homogeneous but quality-differentiated good. New industries introduce novel products, which tend to be preferred by consumers. This introduces a lifecycle dynamics due to inter-industry competition for demand. From the consumer perspective, there are two broad categories of goods: basic (non-durable) and luxury (durable). Luxury goods require more stages of production, resulting in more complex products and so demanding more labor and capital, resulting in higher prices relative to single-stage basic goods, but increased attractiveness to consumers.

The entry–exit process for industries and firms is entirely endogenous. Industries disappear and firms leave whenever market shares get close to zero or (total) net assets turn negative (bankruptcy). There is a positive probability of a new luxury-good industry entering the economy after each new machine generation introduction, due to a successful radical innovation in the capital-good sector. New basic-good industries enter randomly, with probability inversely proportional to the number of incumbent basic industries. At the firm level, the (stochastic) number of entrants in an industry depends on the quantity of incumbents and the prevailing financial conditions.

Firms in an industry may be unionized or not, depending on the current institutional set-up at the moment of entry. Table 1 contrasts the wage-setting and other agents' behaviors for union and non-union cases.

Union firms pay equal wages to all workers and change wages collectively as aggregate and market productivity evolve. They fire employees only when profits become negative. In hiring and firing, union firms try to keep the more skilled employees. Union workers seek alternative jobs less frequently than non-union ones, consistent with the exit-voice trade-off in the labor market (Freeman 1980).

Conversely, non-union firms set wages according to individual worker skills and labor-market conditions. Wages are set by an asymmetric negotiation process where firms have the last say. There are no hiring/firing protections, and unemployed

Table 1. Differentiated behaviors of union and non-union firms and workers.

AGENT BEHAVIOR	UNION	NON-UNION
Differentiated wages	no	yes
Wage sensitivity to unemployment	low (rigid)	high (flexible)
Wage indexation to average productivity	full	partial
Labor-firing restrictions	under losses only	none
Worker-hiring rule	higher skills	lower wage-to-skill ratio
Worker-firing rule	lower skills	higher wage-to-skill ratio
Worker new-job search intensity	low	high

workers must adjust downward wage demand up to the individual "satisficing" level. Employed non-union workers actively search for better paid jobs, and firms frequently fire excess workforce because of shrinking production. Hiring and firing of workers is based on the (individual) wage-to-skill ratio.

To focus on the decline in unionization, we configure the model so that, after an initial phase of just union firms in the market, from time $\hat{t} = 100$,[4] only non-union firms enter the market. From there, both types of firms compete in each industry according to an evolutionary process. After a grace period, at $\hat{t} = 200$ the likelihood of union or non-union firms entering the consumer-good market is proportional to their shares in each industry.

Our primary focus here is on the relationship between deunionization and rising inequality. The validation procedure follows the so-called *output validation* approach (Fagiolo *et*

---

[4]In the following, we present the MC time series excluding a model "warm-up" period, as explained later. Therefore, all time plots refer to relative $\hat{t} = 1, ..., 400$, corresponding to absolute simulated $t = 101, ..., 500$ after the warm-up.

al. 2019), which is progressively becoming the most adopted empirical validation strategy in agent-based models. According to this approach, the model properties at different levels of disaggregation are contrasted with the empirical evidence. That is, the model is judged in terms of its ability to robustly reproduce an ensemble of stylized facts, at different scales of disaggregation. The list of stylized facts and model properties is presented in table 2, and is in line with the set of micro- and macroeconomic stylized facts discussed in Andrew G. Haldane and Arthur E. Turrell (2019). Table 3 shows more details about the new properties introduced by the current model, together with references to the associated empirical evidence.

~481~

Notice that the proposed validation approach is quite different from the ones based on *moment-matching* or *strict parameter calibration* on single time series, as discussed in this book (Pangallo and del Rio-Chanona 2026, ch. 10). The employed procedure avoids both the scaling problems involving direct moment comparison, and the "trap" of *ex post* fitting of *ex ante* strictly calibrated models. Notwithstanding the common belief, estimating the parameters of single time-series independently (one at a time) is epistemologically problematic, an utterly undisciplined exercise potentially compatible with undesirable theoretical settings.[5] A commonly cited problem of the output validation approach lies in the weak performance of non-calibrated models for quantitative forecasting. However, ABMs, employed as a representation of evolving complex sys-

---

[5] An exemplary case is the common practice of parameter estimation in DSGE models: Although it might fit some empirical moments of specific time series, these are hardly metaphorical models able to explain processes and mechanisms (Bouchaud 2023).

Table 2. Stylized facts matched by the K+S model at different aggregation levels, with newly added facts in bold.

MICROECONOMIC STYLIZED FACTS	MACROECONOMIC STYLIZED FACTS
Skewed firm size distribution	Endogenous self-sustained growth with persistent fluctuations
Fat-tailed firm growth rates distribution	Fat-tailed GDP growth rate distribution
Heterogeneous productivity across firms	Endogenous volatility of GDP, consumption and investment
Persistent productivity differentials	Cross-correlation of macro variables
Lumpy investment rates of firms	Pro-cyclical aggregate R&D investment and net entry of firms in the market
Heterogeneous skills distribution	Persistent and counter-cyclical unemployment
Fat-tailed unemployment time distribution	Endogenous volatility of productivity, unemployment, vacancy, separation and hiring rates
Fat-tailed wage growth rates distribution	
Cross-sectional Engel's law	Unemployment and inequality correlation
Heterogeneous propensity to save and consume	Pro-cyclical worker's skills accumulation
	Beveridge curve
	Okun curve
	Wage curve
	Matching function
	Engel's law
	Non-satiation in luxury goods

TECHNOLOGY-LEVEL STYLIZED FACTS	SECTORAL-LEVEL STYLIZED FACTS
Stepwise increase in technological frontier	**Product lifecycle**
Lower rate of radical versus incremental innovation	**Exponential age distribution**
	Sectoral wage and productivity differentials
Fast diffusion of dominant techniques	

tems, emerged in economics with the main objective of providing interpretation, rather than precise forecasting.[6]

We next present a battery of model simulation results substantiating our findings concerning labor relations and labor-market institutions. The model was coded and simulated using the LSD framework (Valente and Pereira 2023), and the produced simulation results were analyzed using the R platform (R Core Team 2024).[7] The figures presented below are the outcomes of a Monte Carlo (MC) experiment, to properly consider across-run stochastic effects, comprising 100 realizations of 500 discrete time periods ($t = 1, ..., 500$) each.[8] The model is parametrized so that one time period roughly corresponds to one quarter. Initial setup is kept to a minimum: All industries, firms, and workers start equal, departing from balanced supply and demand, under full utilization.[9] The employed values for the model parameters and initial conditions, including an extensive analysis of the model sensitivity to the chosen values, are available in Dosi *et al.* (2022). The sensitivity analysis shows that the results below are robust to significant parametric changes.

Starting with figure 3a, the spurt dynamics in deunionization is presented for the ensemble of consumption-good in-

---

[6]In epistemological terms, long-term, quantitative forecasting of complex systems properties is a "doomed" proposition irrespective of the modeling methodology employed (see, e.g., Arthur 2015; 2026, chapter 2 in this volume).

[7]Other than these, several auxiliary third-party open-source libraries were used under the respective license terms. Please refer to https://github.com/SantannaKS/LSD for code and licensing details.

[8]The MC design of experiment (DoE) was validated to capture the behavior of most model variables under a significance level of at least 5%, and more typically at 1%.

[9]The objective of this *light-touch* approach is to let the model structure, which induces significant heterogeneity among agents, find an endogenous initial regime, usually achieved before $t = 100$, the warm-up period. Therefore, results are analyzed from $t = 101$ (or $\hat{t} = 1$).

dustries. The spurt is quite evident as the share of non-union firms after a relative short time interval *endogenously* reaches 80%. Notably, non-union firms populate all industries, but they are not able to dominate the entire market, and a percentage of union firms remain alive, however progressively declining over time. The decline in unionization maps into macro-level inequality as shown by the rise in the Gini index from less than 0.15 up to 0.30. Most of the rise is due to the bonus distributed by more profitable firms, as shown by the upper line in figure 3b.

Figure 3c looks at the process of wage growth across industries. At the industry level, considering inter-firm wage heterogeneity, wage-growth rates under both institutional scenarios present tent-shaped distributions. This is in line with the general and robust empirical evidence on growth rates in landscapes characterized by any type of competition process (Dosi, Pereira, and Virgillito 2017). However, the distribution support widens whenever non-union firms arrive, with more frequent extreme firm-cases at *both* tail sides.

Figure 3d presents the heterogeneous unionization rate by industry. A U-shaped pattern in terms of incidence of union firms appears, showing the endogenous emergence of both highly unionized and non-unionized industries in the model. More mixed degrees of unionization across industries are less probable (note the log vertical scale), but still possible scenarios. Accordingly, the prevalence of union firms deeply affects the wage dispersion across firms and industries. Different wage-distribution patterns in the unionized vs. mixed scenario emerge, with a wider support in the second case which reaches substantially more extreme boundary (log) values. This is shown in figures 3e and 3f. In general, the higher the share of unionized firms in a given industry, the higher the average real wage rate,

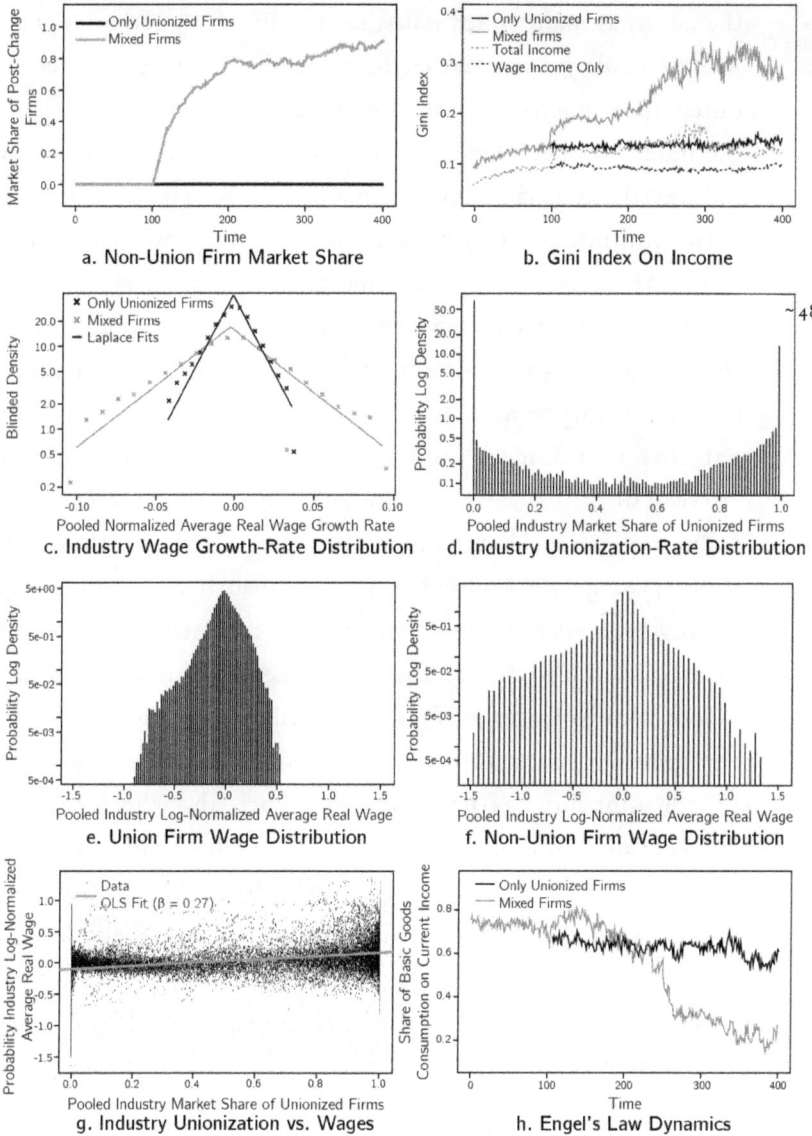

a. Non-Union Firm Market Share

b. Gini Index On Income

c. Industry Wage Growth-Rate Distribution

d. Industry Unionization-Rate Distribution

e. Union Firm Wage Distribution

f. Non-Union Firm Wage Distribution

g. Industry Unionization vs. Wages

h. Engel's Law Dynamics

~485~

Figure 3. Selected temporal and distributional model results presenting the declining unionization and the rising inequalities at the macro- and industry-level, and the change in consumption patterns. Series MC median computed for 100 runs in period $\hat{t} \in [1, 400]$. Distributions evaluated from 100 runs in $\hat{t} \in [301, 400]$.

as shown in figure 3g. It is important to notice, however, that the latter, as many other statistical results of properly designed ABMs, are *emergent properties*, that is, results that are the aggregate outcomes of micro-level interactions and *not* assumed *ex ante* in the model design. Therefore, the property that deunionization induces (i) rising macro-level inequality; (ii) rising wage dispersion between firms; and (iii) polarization in wage growth dynamics represents an industry-specific emergent attribute.

The effects of deunionization are deep and reverberate into the structural core of the model, that is, into the dynamics of labor absorption, technological change, and consumption patterns. Our model's industries display the typical S-shaped curve of diffusion (Franses 1994), presenting the characteristic industrial lifecycle dynamics (Klepper 1997). In the peak industry stage, the number of workers absorbed in a unionized setting is *higher* when compared to coexisting non-union firms (about 17,000 vs. 14,000 workers). This result holds across Monte Carlo average and median statistics. In turn, the different labor absorption levels are due to the pattern of consumption, as presented in figure 3h, where Engel's law is evaluated in each scenario. These curves show a direct interaction between the structure of income distribution and the consumption pattern over time. In a more egalitarian unionized setup, the share of basic goods on the worker income decays over time at a significantly more tamed pace. Conversely, in the scenario populated also by non-union firms, the share of basic goods rapidly shrinks, leaving more space to luxury (durable) goods, accessible mostly to the richer workers. Therefore, as an endogenous property, the model is able to link inequality from two distinct perspectives, income and consumption. In a more unequal society, as wealthy individuals consume and desire more luxury goods—say, mansions, yachts,

Table 3. Model emergent properties and supporting references on empirical literature.

MODEL PROPERTIES	EMPIRICAL EVIDENCE
Spurt dynamics in unionization/ deunionization	Freeman (1998)
Positive correlation between unionization and inequality	Farber *et al.* (2021)
Deunionization as a result of within-industry dynamics and competition	Hirsch (2008)
Higher wage in union vs. non-union establishments	Lemieux (1998)
More homogeneous wages in union vs. non-union establishments	Fortin, Lemieux, and Lloyd (2023)
Industry-level heterogeneous unionization rates	Fortin, Lemieux, and Lloyd (2023)
Positive correlation of unionization rate and wages at the industry level	Western and Rosenfeld (2011)

airplanes—the more costly and less accessible those goods become to budget-constrained workers.

Figure 4 presents the macroeconomic feedback effects in terms of gross domestic product (GDP) growth (4a) and unemployment rate (4b). The presence of mixed firms affects the macroeconomic growth-rate distribution, shifting downward its support, that is, increasing the possibility of lower-growth episodes, and conversely, even if the medians are similar. The effects on employment are far more substantial, as the median unemployment is about 10 p.p. higher in the mixed-firms scenario, and around 15 p.p. over in the worst realizations. Unfortunately, these results seem in line with the historical trend.

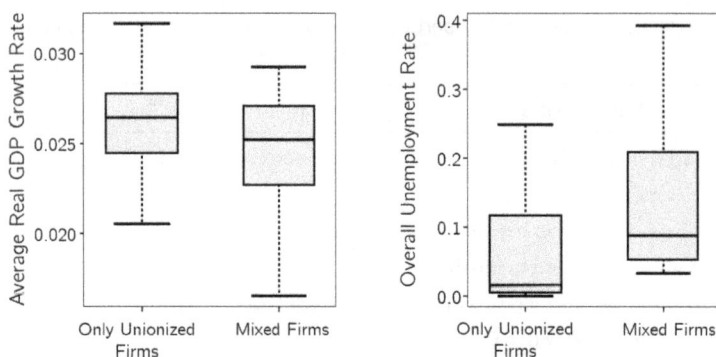

a. GDP Growth-Rate Distribution   b. Unemployment Rate Distribution

Figure 4. Selected distributional model results presenting the macroeconomic second-order effects. Evaluated from 100 MC runs in period $\hat{t} \in$ [201, 400]. Bar: median, boxes: 2nd and 3rd quartiles, whiskers: maximum and minimums.

Conclusions

There are four fundamental features of the K+S family of agent-based models. The first is the complementarity between a Schumpeterian engine of innovation and a Keynesian driver of demand generation. Second, the models entail the intrinsic duality of wages, which are an item of cost for individual firms but also an essential component of aggregate demand. Third, there is a permanent dualism between the labor-shedding effects of technical change, via productivity improvements, and its employment-generation drive, by the introduction of new products. Finally, fourth, ubiquitous institutions shape the behavior of individual agents and their pattern of interaction.

In this chapter, we provide a new instantiation of the institutional embeddedness of the model architecture, focusing, as an illustrative example, on the coupling dynamics of competitive market forces and regulatory change in fostering deunionization. Our modeling exercise is quite in tune with the historical evidence. In fact, since 2010, five states in the US have introduced right-to-work laws, an institutional change disfavoring unionization. Empirical evidence has shown that such laws weaken workers' unionization rights. These five states joined numerous states, mostly in the South and Midwest, that have adopted RTW laws since the introduction of the Taft–Hartley Act in 1947. The recent adoption of RTW laws has been accompanied by two macro long-run structural and institutional trends, namely, declining unionization and increasing inequality. How does one interpret such a pattern? Can complexity economics provide a coherent representation of the effects of declining unionization? Can deunionization be a driver of increasing inequalities, both at the workplace and at the macroeconomic level? What is the dynamics of labor absorption when non-union firms prevail? May wage inequality also be reflected in the consumption realm?

These are some of the questions that we try to answer using the multi-sector, labor-augmented K+S model. The proposed model is able to reproduce phase transitions with tipping points, such as the spurt dynamics in deunionization, but also to account for cumulative, long-lasting propagation mechanisms, at different aggregation levels and time scales. Such features are essential to properly model complex systems exhibiting self-organizing criticality, a concept described in the present book (Bouchaud 2026, ch. 9). Deunionization does not simply affect the wages workers receive in the firm where they are employed. It also propagates to the macro level, affecting the lifecycle pattern of industries, and the long-run dynamics of the consumption structure, via the Engel's law. In this respect, macro-evolutionary, agent-based models appear to be a formidable tool to assess the transformation mechanisms of the capitalist machine, a multilevel, multiscale structure of production and exchange, whose feedbacks propagate with mixed speeds, and manifest in erratic ways.

Other applications of the current model include the analysis of the relationship between product market concentration versus labor market performance, consumption-pattern change and inflation dynamics, the hysteretic impact of firing and plant closures during crises, and monopsony in the labor market due to the rise of giant firms. They also include, more generally, the effects of changes in union power and quit rates, or labor regulation reforms, as the introduction/abolition of a minimum wage. New avenues of research certainly include embedding multidimensional forms of inequality, such as the ones linked to distinct group attributes, that is, gender, race, exposure to diseases, and pollution. Extensions of the model able to describe the changing role of social institutions, particularly the role of the welfare state and the provision of public goods, are other complementary lines of research.

In general, the capitalist system rapidly changes, at an unpredictable pace, at least in its details and timing. This means that any interpretation of such dynamics in terms of equilibrium models will be unavoidably badly off the mark. Conversely, evolutionary ABMs seem to be promising candidates to face such a challenge. ✶

Acknowledgments

The authors acknowledge the editors for their helpful comments and suggestions. G. Dosi acknowledges support from the Italian Ministry of University and Research (MUR) PRIN2022 project "TELI—Technology, Labor, Inequality," number 2022W2R55L. M. C. Pereira acknowledges support of

Chapter 30: The Political Economy of Complex Evolving Systems

Fundação de Amparo à Pesquisa do Estado de São Paulo (FAPESP), process no. 2015/24341 – 7.

REFERENCES

Acemoglu, D., and D. Autor. 2011. "Skills, Tasks, and Technologies: Implications for Employment and Earnings." Chap. 12 in *Handbook of Labor Economics,* edited by D. Card and O. Ashenfelter, vol. 4B, 1043–1171. Amsterdam, Netherlands: Elsevier. https://doi.org/10.1016/S0169-7218(11)02410-5.

Acemoglu, D., D. Autor, J. Hazell, and P. Restrepo. 2022. "Artificial Intelligence and Jobs: Evidence from Online Vacancies." *Journal of Labor Economics* 40 (S1): S293–S340. https://doi.org/10.1086/718327.

Acemoglu, D., and J. A. Robinson. 2013. *Why Nations Fail: The Origins of Power, Prosperity, and Poverty.* New York, NY: Crown Currency.

Argitis, G., and C. Pitelis. 2001. "Monetary Policy and the Distribution of Income: Evidence for the United States and the United Kingdom." *Journal of Post Keynesian Economics* 23 (4): 617–638. https://doi.org/10.1080/01603477.2001.11490302.

Arthur, W. B. 2015. *Complexity and the Economy.* Oxford, UK: Oxford University Press.

———. 2026. "Combinatorial Evolution." In *The Economy as an Evolving Complex System IV,* edited by R. M. del Rio-Chanona, M. Pangallo, J. Bednar, E. D. Beinhocker, J. Kaszowska-Mojsa, F. Lafond, P. Mealy, A. Pichler, and J. D. Farmer. Santa Fe, NM: SFI Press.

Autor, D. H., and D. Dorn. 2013. "The Growth of Low-Skill Service Jobs and the Polarization of the US Labor Market." *American Economic Review* 103 (5): 1553–1597. https://doi.org/10.1257/aer.103.5.1553.

Barth, E., A. Bryson, J. C. Davis, and R. Freeman. 2016. "It's Where You Work: Increases in the Dispersion of Earnings Across Establishments and Individuals in the United States." *Journal of Labor Economics* 34 (S2): S67–S97. https://doi.org/10.1086/684045.

Beinhocker, E. D., and J. Bednar. 2026. "Complexity and Paradigm Change in Economics." In *The Economy as an Evolving Complex System IV,* edited by R. M. del Rio-Chanona, M. Pangallo, J. Bednar, E. D. Beinhocker, J. Kaszowska-Mojsa, F. Lafond, P. Mealy, A. Pichler, and J. D. Farmer. Santa Fe, NM: SFI Press.

Bengtsson, E. 2014. "Do Unions Redistribute Income from Capital to Labour? Union Density and Wage Shares Since 1960." *Industrial Relations Journal* 45 (5): 389–408. https://doi.org/10.1111/irj.12065.

Bentolila, S., and G. Saint-Paul. 2003. "Explaining Movements in the Labor Share." *The B.E. Journal of Macroeconomics* 3 (1): 1–33. https://doi.org/10.2202/1534-6005.1103.

Bivens, J., and J. Kandra. 2022. *CEO Pay has Skyrocketed 1,460% Since 1978: CEOs Were Paid 399 Times as Much as a Typical Worker in 2021.* Technical report. Economic Policy Institute. https://epi.org/255893.

Bouchaud, J.-P. 2023. "From Statistical Physics to Social Sciences: The Pitfalls of Multi-Disciplinarity." *Journal of Physics: Complexity* 4 (4): 041001. https://doi.org/10.48550/arXiv.2308.02895.

———. 2026. "The Self-Organized Criticality Paradigm in Economics and Finance." In *The Economy as an Evolving Complex System IV,* edited by R. M. del Rio-Chanona, M. Pangallo, J. Bednar, E. D. Beinhocker, J. Kaszowska-Mojsa, F. Lafond, P. Mealy, A. Pichler, and J. D. Farmer. Santa Fe, NM: SFI Press.

Cetrulo, A., D. Guarascio, and M. E. Virgillito. 2024. *Two Neglected Origins of Inequality: Hierarchical Power and Care Work.* Technical report. LEM Papers Series 2024/04. Laboratory of Economics and Management (LEM), Sant'Anna School of Advanced Studies.

Colander, D., P. Howitt, A. Kirman, A. Leijonhufvud, and P. Mehrling. 2008. "Beyond DSGE Models: Toward an Empirically Based Macroeconomics." *American Economic Review* 98 (2): 236–240. https://doi.org/10.1257/aer.98.2.236.

Dao, M. C., M. Das, and Z. Koczan. 2020. "Why is Labour Receiving a Smaller Share of Global Income?" *Economic Policy* 34 (100): 723–759. https://doi.org/10.1093/epolic/eiaa004.

Dimova, D. 2019. *The Structural Determinants of the Labor Share in Europe.* IMF Working Papers 2019/067. International Monetary Fund. https://doi.org/10.5089/9781498302920.001.

Dosi, G. 2023. *The Foundations of Complex Evolving Economies: Part One: Innovation, Organization, and Industrial Dynamics.* Oxford, UK: Oxford University Press.

Dosi, G., L. Fanti, and M. E. Virgillito. 2024. "Attributes and Trends of Rentified Capitalism." *Italian Economic Journal* 10 (2). https://doi.org/10.1007/s40797-024-00279-1.

Dosi, G., R. B. Freeman, M. C. Pereira, A. Roventini, and M. E. Virgillito. 2021. "The Impact of Deunionization on the Growth and Dispersion of Productivity and Pay." *Industrial and Corporate Change* 30 (2): 377–408. https://doi.org/10.1093/icc/dtaa025.

Dosi, G., M. C. Pereira, A. Roventini, and M. E. Virgillito. 2017. "When More Flexibility Yields More Fragility: The Microfoundations of Keynesian Aggregate Unemployment." *Journal of Economic Dynamics and Control* 81:162–186. https://doi.org/10.1016/j.jedc.2017.02.005.

———. 2018. "Causes and Consequences of Hysteresis: Aggregate Demand, Productivity, and Employment." *Industrial and Corporate Change* 27 (6): 1015–1044. https://doi.org/10.1093/icc/dty010.

———. 2020. "The Labour-Augmented K + S Model: A Laboratory for the Analysis of Institutional and Policy Regimes." *EconomiA* 21 (2): 160–184. https://doi.org/10.1016/j.econ.2019.03.002.

———. 2022. "Technological Paradigms, Labour Creation and Destruction in a Multi-Sector Agent-Based Model." *Research Policy* 51 (10): 104565. https://doi.org/10.1016/j.respol.2022.104565.

Dosi, G., M. C. Pereira, and M. E. Virgillito. 2017. "The Footprint of Evolutionary Processes of Learning and Selection Upon the Statistical Properties of Industrial Dynamics." *Industrial and Corporate Change* 26 (2): 187–210. https://doi.org/10.1093/icc/dtw044.

Dosi, G., and A. Roventini. 2019. "More is Different . . . and Complex! The Case for Agent-Based Macroeconomics." *Journal of Evolutionary Economics* 29 (1): 1–37. https://doi.org/10.1007/s00191-019-00609-y.

Dosi, G., and M. E. Virgillito. 2019. "Whither the Evolution of the Contemporary Social Fabric? New Technologies and Old Socio-Economic Trends." *International Labour Review* 158 (4): 593–625. https://doi.org/10.1111/ilr.12145.

Dwyer, R. E. 2013. "The Care Economy? Gender, Economic Restructuring, and Job Polarization in the US Labor Market." *American Sociological Review* 78 (3): 390–416. https://doi.org/10.1177/00031224134871.

Fagiolo, G., M. Guerini, F. Lamperti, A. Moneta, and A. Roventini. 2019. "Validation of Agent-Based Models in Economics and Finance." In *Computer Simulation Validation*, edited by C. Beisbart and N. Saam, 763–787. Cham, Switzerland: Springer. https://doi.org/10.1007/978-3-319-70766-2_31.

Farber, H. S., D. Herbst, I. Kuziemko, and S. Naidu. 2021. "Unions and Inequality Over the Twentieth Century: New Evidence from Survey Data." *The Quarterly Journal of Economics* 136 (3): 1325–1385. https://doi.org/10.1093/qje/qjab012.

Farber, H. S., and B. Western. 2002. "Ronald Reagan and the Politics of Declining Union Organization." *British Journal of Industrial Relations* 40 (3): 385–401. https://doi.org/10.1111/1467-8543.00240.

Folbre, N. 2021. *Gender Inequality and Bargaining in the US Labor Market*. Technical report. Economic Policy Institute. https://epi.org/209716.

Fortin, N. M., T. Lemieux, and N. Lloyd. 2023. "Right-to-Work Laws, Unionization, and Wage Setting." In *Research in Labor Economics: 50th Celebratory Volume*, edited by S. W. Polachek and K. Tatsiramos, 50:285–325. Leeds, UK: Emerald Publishing Limited. https://doi.org/10.1108/S0147-912120230000050011.

Franses, P. H. 1994. "Fitting a Gompertz Curve." *Journal of the Operational Research Society* 45 (1): 109–113. https://doi.org/10.2307/2583955.

Fraser, N. 2023. *Cannibal Capitalism: How Our System is Devouring Democracy, Care, and the Planet and What We Can Do About It*. New York, NY: Verso Books.

Freeman, R. B. 1980. "The Exit-Voice Tradeoff in the Labor Market: Unionism, Job Tenure, Quits, and Separations." *The Quarterly Journal of Economics* 94 (4): 643–673. https://doi.org/10.2307/1885662.

———. 1998. "Spurts in Union Growth: Defining Moments and Social Processes." In *The Defining Moment: The Great Depression and the American Economy in the Twentieth Century*, edited by M. Bordo, C. Goldin, and E. White, 265–296. Chicago, IL: University of Chicago Press.

Gabaix, X., and A. Landier. 2008. "Why Has CEO Pay Increased So Much?" *The Quarterly Journal of Economics* 123 (1): 49–100. https://doi.org/10.1162/qjec.2008.123.1.49.

Goedemé, T., B. Nolan, M. Paskov, and D. Weisstanner. 2021. "Occupational Social Class and Earnings Inequality in Europe: A Comparative Assessment." *Social Indicators Research* 159:215–233. https://doi.org/10.1007/s11205-021-02746-z.

Guschanski, A., and Ö. Onaran. 2021. "The Decline in the Wage Share: Falling Bargaining Power of Labour or Technological Progress? Industry-Level Evidence from the OECD." *Socio-Economic Review* 20 (3): 1091–1124. https://doi.org/10.1093/ser/mwaa031.

Haldane, A. G., and A. E. Turrell. 2019. "Drawing on Different Disciplines: Macroeconomic Agent-Based Models." *Journal of Evolutionary Economics* 29:39–66. https://doi.org/10.1007/s00191-018-0557-5.

Hirsch, B. T. 2008. "Sluggish Institutions in a Dynamic World: Can Unions and Industrial Competition Coexist?" *Journal of Economic Perspectives* 22 (1): 153–176. https://doi.org/10.1257/jep.22.1.153.

Hugrée, C., É. Penissat, and A. Spire. 2020. *Social Class in Europe: New Inequalities in the Old World.* New York, NY: Verso Books.

Jaumotte, F., and C. Osorio Buitron. 2020. "Inequality: Traditional Drivers and the Role of Union Power." *Oxford Economic Papers* 72 (1): 25–58. https://doi.org/10.1093/oep/gpz024.

Katz, L. F., and K. M. Murphy. 1992. "Changes in Relative Wages, 1963-1987: Supply and Demand Factors." *The Quarterly Journal of Economics* 107 (1): 35–78. https://doi.org/10.2307/2118323.

Klepper, S. 1997. "Industry Life Cycles." *Industrial and Corporate Change* 6 (1): 145–182. https://doi.org/10.1093/icc/6.1.145.

Kristal, T. 2010. "Good Times, Bad Times: Postwar Labor's Share of National Income in Capitalist Democracies." *American Sociological Review* 75 (5): 729–763. https://doi.org/10.1177/0003122410382640.

Krugman, P. 2011. "The Profession and the Crisis." *Eastern Economic Journal* 37:307–312. https://doi.org/10.1057/eej.2011.8.

Lemieux, T. 1998. "Estimating the Effects of Unions on Wage Inequality in a Panel Data Model with Comparative Advantage and Nonrandom Selection." *Journal of Labor Economics* 16 (2): 261–291. https://doi.org/10.1086/209889.

Milanovic, B. 2024. "The Three Eras of Global Inequality, 1820–2020 with the Focus on the Past Thirty Years." *World Development* 177:106516. https://doi.org/10.1016/j.worlddev.2023.106516.

Mishel, L. 2022. "How Automation and Skill Gaps Fail to Explain Wage Suppression or Wage Inequality." *Industrial and Corporate Change* 31 (2): 269–280. https://doi.org/10.1093/icc/dtac004.

Pangallo, M., and R. M. del Rio-Chanona. 2026. "Data-Driven Economic Agent-Based Models." In *The Economy as an Evolving Complex System IV*, edited by R. M. del Rio-Chanona, M. Pangallo, J. Bednar, E. D. Beinhocker, J. Kaszowska-Mojsa, F. Lafond, P. Mealy, A. Pichler, and J. D. Farmer. Santa Fe, NM: SFI Press.

Piketty, T. 2015. "Putting Distribution Back at the Center of Economics: Reflections on Capital in the Twenty-First Century." *Journal of Economic Perspectives* 29 (1): 67–88. https://doi.org/10.1257/jep.29.1.67.

R Core Team. 2024. *R: A Language and Environment for Statistical Computing*. Vienna, Austria: R Foundation for Statistical Computing. https://www.R-project.org/.

Restrepo, P. 2023. *Automation: Theory, Evidence, and Outlook*. Technical report. National Bureau of Economic Research. https://doi.org/10.3386/w31910.

Romero, P. D., and J. M. Whittaker. 2023. *A Brief Examination of Union Membership Data*. Congressional Research Report R47596. Congressional Research Service.

Shierholz, H., C. McNicholas, M. Poydock, and J. Sherer. 2024. *Workers Want Unions, but the Latest Data Point to Obstacles in Their Path*. Technical report. Economic Policy Institute. https://www.epi.org/publication/union-membership-data/.

Stansbury, A., and L. H. Summers. 2020. *The Declining Worker Power Hypothesis: An Explanation for the Recent Evolution of the American Economy*. Technical report. National Bureau of Economic Research. https://doi.org/10.3386/w27193.

Stiglitz, J. 2015. *The Great Divide*. London, UK: Penguin UK.

Stockhammer, E. 2013. "Why Have Wage Shares Fallen? An Analysis of the Determinants of Functional Income Distribution." In *Wage-Led Growth: An Equitable Strategy for Economic Recovery*, edited by M. Lavoie and E. Stockhammer, 40–70. London, UK: Palgrave Macmillan.

————. 2015. "Rising Inequality as a Cause of the Present Crisis." *Cambridge Journal of Economics* 39 (3): 935–958. https://doi.org/10.1093/cje/bet052.

Tinbergen, J. 1974. "Substitution of Graduate by Other Labour." *Kyklos: International Review for Social Sciences,* 217–226. https://doi.org/10.1111/j.1467-6435.1974.tb01903.x.

Tope, D., and D. Jacobs. 2009. "The Politics of Union Decline: The Contingent Determinants of Union Recognition Elections and Victories." *American Sociological Review* 74 (5): 842–864. https : / / doi . org / 10 . 1177 / 000312240907400508.

Valente, M., and M. C. Pereira. 2023. *LSD: Laboratory for Simulation Development.* Aquila, Italy and Campinas, Brazil: Università degli Studi dell'Aquila and Universidade Estadual de Campinas. https://www.labsimdev.org/.

Western, B., and J. Rosenfeld. 2011. "Unions, Norms, and the Rise in US Wage Inequality." *American Sociological Review* 76 (4): 513–537. https://doi.org/10.1177/0003122411414817.

COMPLEXITY AND PARADIGM
CHANGE IN ECONOMICS

Eric D. Beinhocker, University of Oxford and Santa Fe Institute; and
Jenna Bednar, University of Michigan and Santa Fe Institute

Abstract

Since the first volume in this series (Anderson, Arrow, and
Pines 1988), a variety of scholars have claimed that complexity
economics presents a fundamentally different and more
scientifically grounded way of explaining and modeling the
economy than more traditional perspectives. Looking back at
over thirty-five years of development in the field, this essay argues
that complexity economics is not merely an alternative and
advantageous set of methods for understanding the economy
but could play a critical role in the construction of a new
economic paradigm. Complexity economics is part of a broader
interlocking set of ideas—what we refer to as an ontological
stack—that has the potential to supplant the dominant economic
paradigms of the twentieth century. The development of such a
paradigm would have major implications for economic policy
and politics. The essay concludes with a discussion of what can
be done to advance the complexity economics agenda and how
such a paradigm might be developed.

Introduction

Research fields often have founding origin stories. In the case
of complexity economics, the story usually starts with a ten-
day meeting that was held at the Santa Fe Institute in 1987.
While the intellectual roots of complexity economics are deep and
varied—ranging from Thorstein Veblen famously asking "Why
is economics not an evolutionary science?" to Friedrich Hayek's

insights on economic self-organization and Thomas Schelling's pioneering agent-based model of housing discrimination—the Santa Fe meeting is often credited with launching the field.

The meeting, the papers of which are collected in the first volume in this series, was convened to explore whether ideas and methods from complexity science might contribute to economics. The meeting was vividly described by popular science writer M. Mitchell Waldrop (1992) as a clash of intellectual titans. Participants included a clutch of Nobel laureates, such as the physicists Murray Gell-Mann and David Pines and economists Kenneth Arrow and (later laureate) Thomas Sargent; complexity-theory pioneers W. Brian Arthur, Stuart Kauffman, and John Holland; and (then) young up-and-coming physicist J. Doyne Farmer. While the meeting did not produce anything like a consensus, it raised a set of fundamental questions about the nature of the economy and launched a program of research at SFI. Catalyzed by that program, an interdisciplinary community of scholars coalesced around a body of work that Brian Arthur would later label "complexity economics."[1] (See ch. 1 for a definition of complexity economics. Papers and accounts of subsequent SFI economics meetings can be found in Arthur, Durlauf, and Lane 1997; Blume and Durlauf 2005; and Arthur, Beinhocker, and Stanger 2020.)

Some three and a half decades later, that community has grown and become global, and its work has started to have important impacts on topics ranging from financial crises to economic development, climate change, labor markets, supply chains, and macroeconomics (e.g., Iori and Hommes 2015; Farmer 2024; Axtell and Farmer 2025; Bednar *et al.* 2025).

---

[1]The term *complexity economics* first appeared in print in Arthur (1999), while Arthur (2021) provides a broad overview of the complexity-economics perspective.

During this same period, economics changed significantly. The field is no longer dominated by the largely fact-free body of neoclassical theory that the Santa Fe Institute scientists criticized in 1987. Economics has taken a major turn toward empirical work, embraced behavioral economics, rediscovered the importance of institutions, recognized the failures of standard dynamic stochastic general equilibrium (DSGE) macroeconomic models, and expanded its methodological toolbox to include structural models, Heterogeneous Agent New Keynesian (HANK) models, principal-agent models, microsimulation, and field experiments. It has also taken a more rounded and realistic view of markets, increasingly incorporating information asymmetries, frictions, externalities, endogenous preferences, power relations, cultural norms, identity, and various forms of market failure into its theories and models.

But as economists have attempted to grapple with the messy complexity of the real-world economy, they have increasingly run into the limits of historical tools and methods. In particular, analytical models typically require simplifications (such as utility-maximizing agents) to produce closed-form solutions. The complex-systems community, meanwhile, has significantly advanced the development of tools and methods that can model such complex economic phenomena in highly realistic and empirically validated ways. These methods, which include statistical-physics models, network models, agent-based models, and machine-learning and other forms of AI models, have ridden the wave of advances in computation and data, providing researchers with powerful tools the scholars at the 1987 meeting could have only dreamed of.

This chapter argues that bringing such complex-systems ideas and methods into the theoretical and methodological heart of economics has the potential not just to advance the field and deliver new insights, but to reshape the economic paradigm much more broadly.

Economic paradigms play a role in society that is different from physical science paradigms. Like physical science paradigms, economic paradigms attempt to explain phenomena with empirically supported theories and models. But unlike physical science paradigms, economic paradigms also provide guidance as to how the system could and *should* work according to some set of normative criteria. This normative function means that economic paradigms themselves influence the behavior of the system through policy, politics, business, the law, and the broader culture.

~ 501 ~

The twentieth century was dominated by three major economic paradigms: Marxist socialism, Keynesian social democracy, and what we will refer to as the neoliberal consensus. We argue that all three of these historical paradigms failed in the face of various crises, losing both intellectual credibility and popular support. Most recently, support for the neoliberal consensus, which dominated policy and politics in the United States and much of the West from the 1970s, collapsed in the wake of the 2008 global financial crisis. This created a paradigm vacuum into which populist, authoritarian politicians have stepped in many countries, threatening not just their domestic economies and democracies but causing breakdowns in the international order.

Various groups in academia, as well as in civil society and business, have been calling for a new economic paradigm that can address the failures of the neoliberal consensus, provide a compelling alternative to the populists, and restore trust in liberal democracy (see, e.g., Naidu, Rodrik, and Zucman 2019; Boushey 2019; Wong 2022). Our concern, and a central thesis of this chapter, is that, while economic issues are not the only issues that underpin support for authoritarian populists, the problems created by neoliberal policies created fertile ground for that support. Without alternative economic explanatory frames, policies, and political narratives, those who wish to uphold liberal democracy—both conservatives and progressives—will struggle to regain support from the authoritarian populists. A new paradigm is needed to address the failures of the twentieth-century paradigms (e.g., inequality, financial crises, "left behind" communities) but also to confront urgent twenty-first-century challenges such as climate change and the impact of technologies like artificial intelligence.

Important progress has been made on this agenda, with contributions from economists, political scientists, sociologists, historians, philosophers, policy experts, legal scholars, and many others, but this broad, ambitious project remains incomplete. This chapter endeavors to make three contributions:

1. Define more specifically what constitutes an economic paradigm and use that framework—what we call an *ontological stack*—to identify why the neoliberal consensus failed.

2. Argue that a new paradigm is indeed emerging, but there are critical gaps in the scientific explanatory layers of that paradigm that complexity economics can help fill.

3. Outline an agenda for more closely integrating complexity economics into economics and the crossdisciplinary project of paradigm construction.

We conclude that by integrating complexity economics into the broad structure of a new paradigm, there is potential for new answers to some of our greatest challenges, and perhaps even a healthier politics that can help heal some of our deepest divisions.

Paradigm Change in Economics

The most well-known use of the term *paradigm* comes from Thomas Kuhn's (1962) landmark work, in which he describes the progress of science not as a steady accumulation of knowledge but as episodic, following distinct phases: "normal science," where researchers solve puzzles within an established, communally shared framework; "crisis," where anomalies, inconsistencies, and falsifications of the established framework accumulate; and "paradigm shift," where a new framework emerges that both better explains the anomalies and incorporates the successes of the previous framework. This shift is then complete when it is adopted by the community and becomes the new framework for "normal science."

While Kuhn's theory is recognized as a simplification of the messy human endeavor of science, and glosses over important epistemological, methodological, and cultural differences across scientific fields, it is nonetheless a useful way to think about the broad historical pattern of scientific advance. Historians of economic thought likewise tend to take an episodic view of the development of economics, identifying distinct historical eras such as classical economics, the marginalist revolution, and neoclassical synthesis (e.g., Ekelund and Hébert 2013).

All sciences have both an explanatory and an applied role— for example, the relationships between physics and engineering, or between biology and medicine. So, too, does economics in its relationship with business, finance, law, and public policy. However, there is a fundamental difference between economics and the physical sciences. While changes in physical-science paradigms often have major impacts on the world through their application, which particular paradigm is held by scientists *does not affect or change the fundamental laws or behaviors of the system itself.* Whether physicists believe in Newtonian mechanics or Einsteinian relativity does not affect or change the laws of gravity. Nor does whether biologists accept Darwinian or Lamarckian theories of evolution affect how species evolve. Physical scientists observe, model, and theorize about natural laws and regularities that operate independently of human action.[2]

Social systems such as economies, in contrast, are created by human action. The "physics" of such systems, or "rules of the game," are products of human thought. The order in such systems emerges from what humans believe and think and how they behave. Such human-created orders are constrained and shaped by physical and biological laws—we can't make products that violate the laws of physics, and human behaviors are strongly influenced by biology and our evolutionary history—but the emergent behaviors of social systems are largely shaped by human-created norms, beliefs, customs, knowledge, institutions, and technologies.

This creates a reflexive feedback loop between our beliefs about the system and how the system behaves (Soros 2013; Beinhocker 2013). Throughout history, humans have tried to understand and explain their social systems (positive theories) and then used that understanding to devise views (normative theories) as to how the system *should* work, whether for the betterment of society or for the betterment of themselves or their

---

[2]One might question whether the measurement problem in physics is an exception. But this, too, is a general physical law independent of human thought or belief. Any interaction with the outside world in a way that records or distinguishes one probabilistic outcome from another causes the collapse of a quantum wave function into a single state, not just a human observer. It occurs regardless of our views on the theories of Werner Heisenberg and Niels Bohr.

group. People furthermore use that understanding to construct narratives to convince others of the rightness of their views, and then individuals and groups take actions based on those views that change the behavior of the system. Again, this is a distinctive feature of social-science theories. Physicists do not have a theory of how the universe *should* work, nor do their theories influence how it *does* work.

For most of history, these reflexive feedback loops between beliefs and system behavior were based on religious, philosophical, and political views. For example, a society's religious beliefs and cultural norms might strongly influence how individuals behave and how its institutions are organized, both of which would influence how its economic system performed. The performance of the economic system, in turn, would influence the evolution of beliefs and norms over time in a reflexive loop.

As economics began to develop as a field in the eighteenth and nineteenth centuries, it also began to play a reflexive role in not just describing *how* the economic system works but shaping how it *does* work. For example, Adam Smith's arguments against the mercantilist system of his time and advocacy of free trade were influential in the 1846 repeal of the Corn Laws in Britain and Prime Minister Robert Peel's pro-trade policies. Likewise, David Ricardo's theories had important impacts on the taxation, trade, and monetary policies of that era.

Perhaps the most dramatic illustration of this reflexive feedback loop between economic ideas and economic reality was the influence of Karl Marx and Friedrich Engels. In the twentieth century, their theories of socialism provided the intellectual inspiration for revolutions around the world that led to radical experiments in running economies on communist principles. Those experiments resulted in disaster (it is estimated that the collectivization of agriculture led to five to eight million deaths from starvation in the Soviet Union and fifteen to forty-five million deaths in China), and those failures in turn fed back into economic theory, stimulating critiques of central planning and helping motivate the rise of the neoliberal free-market ideology in the West (Burgin 2012).

This reflexive interplay between positive and normative economics means we need to take a broader view of what is meant by a "paradigm" than is typically applied in the natural sciences. We must think of a paradigm in an economic context as not just a set of explanatory theories, models, and methodologies, but as a broad set of interlocking ideas that also includes moral values, normative analysis, policies, and political and public narratives.

The Ontological Stack

With both these positive, normative, and reflexive roles of economics in mind, we can now more carefully define what constitutes a paradigm in economics. In Beinhocker (2020), one of us introduces the concept of an *ontological stack*—a set of mutually reinforcing, interlocking concepts that form the basis of an economic paradigm.

Samuel Bowles and Wendy Carlin (2021) introduce a related framework for decomposing economic paradigms in their analysis of the challenges faced by modern capitalism and their call for a new paradigm. Building on and combining these two frameworks, we propose a revised ontological stack that explicates the levels and elements of an economic paradigm (table 1):[3]

---

[3] This framework also draws on Beinhocker's work with Nick Hanauer in their forthcoming book, *Market Humanism.* Note that Bowles and Carlin (2021) use *paradigm* in two senses: The first is in the Kuhnian sense referring to a scholarly discipline, and the second is a "policy paradigm." We have combined the two meanings in our ontological stack framework due to the reflexive interplay between them.

Table 1. The ontological stack of an economic paradigm.

FUNCTIONAL LEVELS	LAYERS OF THEORY AND PRACTICE	EXPLANATION
Values	Moral foundations	Moral values and philosophical traditions that define "good" and "bad" in the system
Scientific	Behavioral theory	Theories of human motivations and decision-making
	Economic systems theory	Theories of agent interactions and collective economic behavior
	Processes of change	Theories of how the economic system changes over time
	Metrics	How we measure economic performance and change
Normative	Normative analysis	How we evaluate relative performance or change in the system
	Political economy and ideology	How we should organize the economy and society to maximize performance
	Emblematic policies	Key policies that would make the system perform better
	Public and political narratives	Stories that explain how the system works and how it could perform better

~ 507 ~

Following our discussion, an economic paradigm can be viewed as having three functional levels:

1. A set of values that define what is "good" and "bad" in the system;

2. A set of scientific theories and models that explain how the system works; and

3. A set of normative functions that connect the values and explanations to derive actions and changes that would make the system "better" or "worse."

These three functional levels are in turn composed of multiple layers of theory and practice: The values are built on moral foundations from philosophy, religious traditions, and cultural norms. The scientific explanations include theories of human behavior, economic systems, processes of change, and metrics for measuring system performance. And the normative layers include frameworks for normative analyses of change in the system (i.e., will this change make things better?); political economy, and ideological theories as to how the system should be organized; emblematic policies (a term borrowed from Bowles and Carlin 2021) that exemplify the values, explanations, and normative frameworks in action; and narratives to explain the paradigm and justify its political and policy implications to the public.

We refer to such a collection of interrelated ideas as an ontological stack because it provides a systematic vocabulary and structure for how people think about entities and relationships in the economic domain and is used for organizing knowledge and framing debates.[4]

The easiest way to see how such an ontological stack works, and how the different levels interrelate and support each other, is to illustrate it with an example. Table 2 provides the ontological stack for what we refer to as the *neoliberal consensus.* This paradigm is a constellation of ideas on the workings and performance of market economies. These ideas have intellectual roots in the eighteenth and nineteenth centuries that were then mathematically formalized during the twentieth century. The ideas then rose to political prominence in the United States, United Kingdom, and many other countries, as well as international institutions, helping shape the global economic

---

[4]Our use of the term *stack* is analogous to and inspired by how the term is used in software engineering: a bundle of technologies used to build and run an application, where each "layer" handles a function for part of the system (e.g., operating system, server, database, user front end, etc.). Similarly, in the ontological stack, the ideological, policy, and narrative "front ends" sit atop deeper layers of ideas.

order from the 1970s into the 2010s, playing a reflexive organizing role in the economy and society.

This paradigm is often popularly referred to simply as *neoliberalism*, but we feel it is more accurate to call it the neoliberal consensus because it is in fact a fusion of multiple intellectual strands, including eighteenth-century utilitarianism, nineteenth-century marginalist economics, twentieth-century neoclassical theory, and twentieth-century neoliberal political economy and ideology, along with influences from libertarian philosophy. These strands came together powerfully in the latter half of the twentieth century to form a broad consensus in the political, policy, business, finance, and legal communities on the workings and organization of free-market economic systems (sometimes also referred to as the *Washington consensus* or *Davos consensus*).

This ontological stack was then used to justify major structural changes in Western economies in the late twentieth and early twenty-first centuries, including privatization, deregulation, the globalization of capital markets, free-trade agreements, shifts in tax policy, a reduction in union power, a *laissez-faire* approach to technological change, a reduction in antitrust action, and shifts in corporate governance practices to prioritize shareholders over other stakeholders. While the political version of this paradigm is often associated with conservative figures such as Ronald Reagan and Margaret Thatcher, there was also a center–left version represented by figures such as Bill Clinton and Tony Blair.

In table 2, one can see how each level built on and reinforced the others. Utilitarian philosophy provided a foundation for utility theory and the rational-actor behavioral model. The utility-maximizing rational-actor model was in turn essential in enabling the mathematics of general equilibrium theory to develop. That model then yielded welfare theorems (rooted in utilitarian ethics) that supported normative neoclassical views on institutions and

Table 2. The ontological stack of the neoliberal consensus paradigm.

LAYER IN THE ONTOLOGICAL STACK	NEOLIBERAL CONSENSUS	EXAMPLE FIGURES
Moral foundations	Hedonism, utilitarianism, individual rights, liberty	Epicurus, Hobbes, Bentham, Nozick
Behavioral theory	Self-interest, utility max, rational actor, methodological individualism	Jevons, Marshall, Robbins
Economic systems theory	General equilibrium, neoclassical	Walras, Samuelson, Arrow, Hicks
Processes of change	Exogenous forces and shocks, competitive pressure, incentives	Solow, Ramsey, Cass, Koopmans, Hayek
Metrics	GDP, productivity, return on capital	Kuznets, Stone, Meade
Normative analysis	Welfare economics	Pareto, Pigou, Kaldor
Political economy and ideology	Neoliberalism; markets are efficient, government only for limited "market failures"	Friedman, Hayek, Buchanan
Emblematic policies	Tax cuts, deregulation, free trade, shareholder value maximization	Feldstein, Stigler, Becker, Ohlin, Friedman
Public and political narratives	Trickle-down, small government, growth, freedom	Ronald Reagan, Bill Clinton, Margaret Thatcher, Tony Blair

policies. Those neoclassical views were often congruent with neoliberal ideas on political economy, which in turn were used to support free market policies, political agendas, and public narratives.

It is important to note that while the ideas in the paradigm interrelate and broadly cohere, this does *not* mean there were not disagreements and inconsistencies within it. For example, we have placed both Paul Samuelson and Milton Friedman within this paradigm, even though they often disagreed (most publicly in their respective *Newsweek* columns), particularly on issues of policy. Samuelson, for example, supported an active role for government in addressing various market failures while Friedman advocated a minimalist role for the state. But their arguments were occurring *within* the same broad ontological framework—such disagreements are what Kuhn would have called "normal science." They shared many values, assumptions, and theories from deeper levels of the ontological stack—for example, assumptions about human behavior and theories about the basic workings of markets—but they differed on many details of economic theory or whether specific issues constituted market failures requiring government intervention or not.

There were also debates across levels of the stack. For example, Austrian political economy theorists such as Friedrich Hayek were vocal critics of neoclassical economic theory. But Hayek and neoclassical economists such as Thomas Sargent also had much in common, such as their critique of Keynesianism, skepticism of government intervention, respect for market mechanisms, and shared values around individual freedom. Likewise, at the political level of the stack, there were important policy disagreements between figures such as Ronald Reagan and Bill Clinton, but they and their respective technocratic advisers were arguing within a shared economic framework with much they agreed on (e.g., the benefits of free trade).

While the neoliberal consensus is a big tent, it is also distinct from other identifiable paradigms. One could, in principle, create an ontological stack for the Marxist socialist paradigm. Such a stack might include moral foundations rooted in egalitarianism, behavioral theories based on class identity, economic systems theories that include the labor theory of value, processes of change based on historicism, political economy implications for worker ownership of the means of production, and so on. And again, while there are varieties of Marxist thought and many disagreements among Marxists, their debates are within a common paradigmatic framework; their worldview is shaped and defined by their stack.

Similarly, one could create a distinct paradigm stack for Keynesian social democracy, with values of social justice at its base, extending through Keynes's General Theory, and into normative implications and policies for countercyclical spending, the welfare state, and full employment. Keynesian social democracy is also a big tent encompassing strands from leftist Fabians to centrist social democrats, to more market-oriented ordoliberals in Germany. Keynesianism also illustrates how paradigms cross and interconnect. For example, Paul Samuelson made fundamental contributions to neoclassical economics and thus we have cited him in table 2, but he was also an important advocate of Keynesianism (not least through his highly influential textbook).

Looking at other systems of economic thought, one could also say that China's state-led capitalist economy that evolved following Deng Xiaoping's reforms in the 1970s and '80s is yet another paradigmatic model, which draws on China's own intellectual and political history as well as elements from each of the three paradigms above. Finally, the "America First" economic nationalism promoted by Donald Trump and his supporters could also be seen as still another distinct paradigm (although arguably less developed and coherent than the examples above), with roots in historical right-wing nativist and populist traditions and drawing some elements from the neoliberal consensus (e.g., tax cuts) and other elements from older modes of thinking (e.g., trade tariffs and mercantilism).

Evaluating Economic Paradigms

This leads to an important point: Not all paradigms are created equal. Some are better than others. But what constitutes "better"? How should we evaluate an economic paradigm? Paradigms in the natural sciences are typically evaluated based on their explanatory and predictive powers, supported by empirical tests (Popper 1959;

Table 3. Evaluating an economic paradigm.

FUNCTIONAL LEVELS: EVALUATION CRITERIA	LAYERS IN THE ONTOLOGICAL STACK
Values: Broadly accepted and ethically defensible	Moral foundations
Scientific: Rigorous explanatory theories and models making empirically testable predictions; falsifiable	Behavioral theory
	Economic systems theory
	Processes of change
	Metrics
Normative: The impact of recommended behaviors, policies, and institutional structures on system performance and individual outcomes as evaluated by the values	Normative analysis
	Political economy and ideology
	Emblematic policies
	Public and political narratives

Kuhn 1962). However, the positive, normative, and reflexive nature of economic paradigms requires us to think differently about how to evaluate them.

Table 3 presents a proposal noting that different functional levels of the ontological stack require evaluation by different criteria. The first layer in the stack is a set of moral values for which there isn't an objectively right or wrong answer. Instead, we can ask whether the values are broadly accepted in society and whether they are ethically defensible (i.e., do they hold up to scrutiny and are they consistent with basic ethical principles)? The former test is necessary because a system that is not based on broadly shared values will not be seen as legitimate. The latter test is necessary as history shows it is possible for societies to have broadly shared values that are morally indefensible (e.g., support for slavery).

There are then four layers of the ontological stack that are comprised of positive explanatory theories—a behavioral theory, economic systems theory, theory of economic change, and metrics. These can and should be evaluated from a scientific standpoint and subject to Popperian falsification tests (Popper 1959). Have the theories been rigorously defined and articulated (often by means of mathematical or computational formalization)? Are they logically coherent and mutually consistent? Do they make testable, falsifiable predictions? What have the results of those empirical tests been?

The next four layers then provide the normative end of the stack: How do we analyze whether a change will result in good or better economic outcomes? How do we organize the system to deliver good or better outcomes? What are the specific policies? How do we explain and build support for such changes? These normative elements should be evaluated on their performance in the world: Have the recommended behaviors, policies, and institutions had a positive impact on human well-being? Have they delivered the good or better outcomes (consistent with the moral values) that they promised? Have there been negative consequences or side effects? What have the trade-offs been?

The Failed Paradigms of the Twentieth Century

Three of the paradigms described above dominated the twentieth century: Marxist socialism, Keynesian social democracy, and the neoliberal consensus. But by the early twenty-first century, all three had failed. All three faced crises, lost their intellectual credibility, and lost popular support.

Marxist socialism hit its high-water mark in the 1970s, when it was the governing ideology for about 1.5 billion people—nearly a third of the world's population. While some might point to claimed successes in industrialization, healthcare, rights for women, and other social conditions, the overall historical economic record was calamitous. Deprivation, shortages, inefficiencies, corruption, and political oppression were endemic in Marxist socialist economies around the world. From the 1970s onward, populations rejected these economies and political systems, whether through migration, revolution, or reform. This culminated in *glasnost* in the USSR, the collapse of the Berlin Wall, and Deng Xiaoping's "Reform and Opening Up" in China. By the 1990s, Marxist socialism had lost its grip on countries around the world.

Meanwhile, Keynesian social democracy dominated the economic discourse and politics of the most economically powerful nations of the world, from New Deal America in the 1930s through Western European and Japanese postwar reconstruction in the 1940s–1960s. During this period, the paradigm delivered increasingly inclusive growth, social protections, and rapidly rising living standards across broad populations. There is debate as to how much of this success was attributable to the unique conditions of postwar reconstruction versus the policies pursued. Yet from the 1970s, the paradigm was seen as failing in the face of high inflation, unsustainable expansion of the social welfare state, and a loss of economic dynamism. With the collapse of the Bretton Woods system, oil shocks, stagflation, labor unrest, government debt crises, and painful recessions, by the 1980s, Keynesian social democracy was subject to intense intellectual criticism and had lost much of its political and electoral support.

As support for Marxism and Keynesianism faded, the neoliberal consensus appeared to be the last paradigm standing. It took hold of the economic and political agendas of many Western countries in the 1980s and 1990s and guided international institutions such as the International Monetary Fund, World Bank, and World Trade Organization, thus inspiring John Williamson's (1989) label, the "Washington Consensus." Through the 1990s, the paradigm was viewed as a success: Many countries pursuing these policies enjoyed a "Goldilocks" period of high growth, low inflation, and low interest rates as global markets opened and technology innovation accelerated.

However, these perceived successes hid darker multidecade trends in wage stagnation, declining social mobility, expanding income and wealth inequality, greater economic insecurity, and the capture of most of the gains of growth by the wealthiest members of society (Nolan 2018). The neoliberal consensus faced its own crisis in 2008. The global financial collapse not only caused misery around the world but also cracked confidence that the neoliberal politicians and technocrats knew what they were doing. This loss of confidence, along with long-simmering tensions over other issues (e.g., immigration, race, gender, culture), created an ideological vacuum into which stepped opportunistic authoritarian populists in countries around the world.

But arguably the most consequential failure of all three twentieth-century paradigms has been climate change. While the economic records of the three paradigms have differed considerably, all three oversaw periods of massive industrialization and exponentially increasing energy use, emissions, and waste production, leading to the global environmental crisis we face today. To be truly successful, an economic system must deliver the twin goals of high standards of living for people *and* operate within planetary biophysical boundaries (Raworth 2017; Beinhocker 2023). But research shows that *no* current economic paradigm in operation in the world today delivers on these twin goals of high standards of living *and* sustainability (O'Neill *et al.* 2018).

These failures in real-world performance (albeit to varying degrees) lead one to ask, why? While it is beyond the scope of this chapter to delve deeply into the ontological stacks of each paradigm and provide a critique, we can surmise that something went wrong in the transmission between each paradigm's professed values—many of which were both widely accepted and defensible (e.g., Marxist socialism's promotion of egalitarian values, Keynesian social democracy's championing of social justice, and the neoliberal consensus's advocacy for individual rights, freedom, and meritocracy)—through the scientific layers and into practical applications in the real world. None of the three dominant twentieth-century paradigms succeeded in creating the worlds they promised.

While it is too high a standard to expect any paradigm to deliver utopia, we should, however, expect the scientific layers of a paradigm to help us at least steer toward better (Popper 1945). But if one's causal explanation of how the economy works is not correct—if it is not rigorously articulated, modeled, falsifiable, and empirically tested—then attempts to translate values, no matter how meritorious, into good or better real-world outcomes via policies and institutions will inevitably go awry. Instead of creating a more equal society, collectivizing agriculture killed millions. Instead of helping the poorest succeed, the welfare state created dependency. Instead of creating trickle-down growth, tax cuts for the rich enabled plutocracy. And instead of creating prosperity for future generations, all three paradigms have endangered the future of life on Earth.

But history shows that from paradigm failure, new paradigms emerge. Marx and Engels presented their ideas as a theoretical counter to classical economics and as an alternative to the injustices of nineteenth-century *laissez-faire* capitalism; Keynes was attempting to offer an alternative to both *laissez-faire* capitalism and revolutionary socialism; and the neoliberals emerged in response to Cold War threats from communism and the perceived failures of Keynesianism.

So, the question is, can a new paradigm be created with scientific layers that better explain economic reality? A paradigm that connects strong moral foundations to better outcomes? And what contribution to such a program could complexity economics make?

Building a New Paradigm and the Role of Complexity Economics

Since the 2010s, motivated by the collapse of the neoliberal consensus and alarmed by the rise of authoritarian nationalist populism, multiple groups of scholars have been engaged in work to develop an alternative paradigm. Examples include the Emergent Political Economies Network (of which SFI is a member), the Institute for New Economic Thinking (INET), Economics for Inclusive Prosperity (EfIP), the London Consensus initiative, the Global Fund for a New Economy, and a growing number of research centers, think tanks, NGOs, and funders.

Drawing on our framework, we would observe that much of the energy in these efforts has been focused on the bottom and upper layers of the ontological stack. There has, for example, been productive debate and work on the moral foundations of the economy (e.g., Bowles 2016; Collier and Kay 2020; Sandel 2020). Potential contributions to alternative moral foundations come from a variety of figures and philosophical traditions—for example, Amartya Sen (1999) and Martha Nussbaum's (2013) work on capabilities, Elizabeth Anderson's work on inequality (1999), John Ahlquist and Margaret Levi's (2014) concept of "communities of fate," Danielle Allen's (2023) writing on power and justice, Alasdair MacIntyre's virtue ethics (1999), and Daniel Chandler's (2024) modern interpretations of Rawls. There has also been promising work on new frameworks for normative analysis (e.g., Beinhocker *et al.* 2023), political economy (e.g., Levi and Farrell 2023; Naidu, Rodrik, and Zucman 2019; Besley and Persson 2023), and policies (e.g., Rodrik 2025; Besley, Bucelli, and Velasco 2025).

There has also been progress on the scientific layers stemming from the significant changes in economics discussed in the introduction. There have also been important efforts to synthesize this progress, most notably in the CORE project (core-econ.org), a global effort by over thirty authors to create a modern introductory economics text that is substantively different from previous standard texts (Bowles and Carlin 2020).

Yet, despite this progress, significant gaps remain. The reason, we believe, is that economics is increasingly running into the limits of its historical and current methodological toolkit. Economists are asking the right questions. For example: How do we incorporate greater behavioral realism into our models? How do we model profoundly disequilibrium events like financial crises or climate change? And how can we better understand structural changes, such as those driven by technology? But the field has not necessarily had the right tools, methodologies, and conceptual frames to answer them.

This is where the complex-systems community can contribute. Specifically, there are eight types of problems for which complexity economics has a track record of employing methodologies that provide empirically supported insights that are differentiated from more conventional methods. This volume has a number of examples illustrating work on these issues, but below we have provided additional examples from the literature:

1. **Behavioral realism:** While utility maximization may be a reasonable simplification for some types of problems, greater agent behavioral realism is essential for others. Modern behavioral science portrays humans as often

pursuing multiple goals, making decisions employing a variety of heuristics, engaging in heuristic switching, and learning and adapting (Gigerenzer and Selten 2001). While such behavioral richness may be impossible to collapse into a single utility function, it can be represented computationally in agent-based simulations. For example, Cars Hommes (2013) estimates the heuristics used by subjects in asset-pricing decisions in laboratory experiments and then simulates heterogeneous agents employing those heuristics and engaging in heuristic switching learning behavior in an empirically validated agent-based model. The model shows how financial instabilities can be created through the dynamic interactions of ecologies of heuristics, an insight that cannot be generated by models with homogeneous, utility-maximizing agents.

2. **Institutional realism:** Analytical models are often highly limited in the institutional detail they can portray. Yet those details can be critical to explaining the phenomena of concern. For example, standard models of financial markets assume random arrivals of buy and sell orders and that markets automatically and instantaneously clear those orders. These assumptions then underpin analyses showing market efficiency. Yet Fabrizio Lillo and J. Doyne Farmer (2004) showed empirically that order flows are not random and obey a long-memory process. Lillo, Szabolcs Mike, and Farmer (2005) then hypothesized that this long memory in order flows was due to a set of institutional details in real-world markets, specifically delays in market clearing, the common practice of traders splitting large orders and executing them incrementally, and the distribution of investor sizes (from Warren Buffet–size investors to individuals with small retirement

accounts). Using methods from statistical physics, the authors built a stochastic process model of the market microstructure, which they then simulated and used to make quantitative macroscopic predictions about order flows. Those predictions were then empirically validated eighteen years later by Yuki Sato and Kiyoshi Kanazawa (2023), who were able to obtain a previously unavailable detailed nine-year dataset from the Japanese stock market. Further work by Farmer and colleagues (2013) showed how order-splitting behaviors interact with the structure of limit-order books to impact prices and market efficiency, with implications for market design and regulation.

3. **Market disequilibrium:** Economists use the term *equilibrium* in two ways: First is in the sense of market clearing, where supply equals demand and a price is discovered. The second is in game theory, where agents understand the strategy space and have reached a point where their strategies are no longer changing. The first sense is often not a bad assumption in real-world markets, particularly over longer time scales. But even so, there are situations, such as financial crises, depressions, or other major economic dislocations, where markets can remain out of equilibrium for extended periods of time. Or situations (per above) where behavioral and institutional factors cause markets to deviate from equilibrium. Conventional models typically have little to say about such situations; as the most widely used graduate text Mas-Colell, Whinston, and Green (1995, 620) puts it, "Economists are good (or so we hope) at recognizing a state of equilibrium but are poor at predicting precisely how an economy in disequilibrium will evolve." Agent-based models (ABMs) provide a means to simulate the evolution of such systems out of equilibrium. Alan Kirman and Nicolaas

Vriend (2001), for example, provide an empirically informed microeconomic example in their study of the Marseille fish market (which also includes behavioral and institutional realism), while Sebastian Poledna and colleagues (2023) provide a macroeconomic example that compares out-of-sample forecasts of their ABM with standard DSGE models.

4. **Strategy disequilibrium:** The second type of equilibrium/disequilibrium in economics, the nonconvergence of games in a strategy space, is also amenable to study using complex systems methods. In a result of highly general importance, Marco Pangallo, Torsten Heinrich, and Farmer (2019) show that in a computationally large space of possible games, games where strategies converge to equilibrium are exceedingly rare. In games with more than a few players, and with strategies that include learning (derived from experiments with human players), the games generate endogenous oscillations in best-reply cycles that don't converge. Most games in the real-world economy involve more than a handful of players and feature heterogeneous strategies with learning and adaptation, in which case, as the authors put it, "equilibrium is typically an unrealistic assumption." Drawing on techniques from biology, complexity researchers model strategy spaces as dynamic ecologies, showing, for example, how this can lead to market malfunction (e.g., Scholl, Calinescu, and Farmer 2021).

5. **Networks:** Economies are composed of various kinds of networks, from supply chains to financial networks, labor market networks, and so on, and their influence on economic phenomena has been of growing interest to economists (e.g., Jackson 2014; Carvalho 2014). Crossdisciplinary studies of

networks have long been a core subject of complexity economics. For example, Anton Pichler and colleagues (2020) introduced a dynamic input–output model with micro detail on the UK supply chain and occupations that was used to make real-time forecasts of the economic impacts of the COVID-19 pandemic. Later analysis (Pichler *et al.* 2022) found that the forecasts produced by that model were significantly more accurate than those provided by standard aggregate macroeconomic models, such as those used by the Bank of England.

6. **Emergence:** Complexity theorists view the economy as a system where macro behaviors emerge bottom up from lower-level heterogeneous micro- and meso-level behaviors and structures, and emergent patterns and structures can exhibit collective behaviors (and, in biological and social systems, agency) that are distinct from lower-level units. Philosophically, this stance bridges the longstanding debate in social science between methodological individualism (e.g., Weber, Schumpeter, Elster) and methodological holism (e.g., Durkheim, Marx). Practically, instead of assumptions of representative agents linearly adding up to generate macro phenomena, as in most standard macroeconomic models, ABMs explicitly model heterogeneous micro- and meso-level behaviors and structures and the macro phenomena emerge from the bottom up. For example, Yuki Asano and colleagues (2021) developed a macroeconomic model that loosens the representative rational agent constraint and models the dynamics of myopic heterogeneous households in a social network. The model generates emergent macro business cycles and inequality consistent with stylized facts and

demonstrates critical transition points in system behavior that could be relevant to policymaking.

7. **Evolution:** Economics has had a long tradition of evolutionary theorizing and modeling (e.g., Nelson and Winter 1982); however, it has historically sat outside the mainstream of the field (it is interesting that no Nobel Prize has yet been awarded for evolutionary economics). There are two senses in which evolution is central to a complex systems view of the economy (Wilson and Kirman 2016): First, humans themselves are products of evolution, and this has influenced important aspects of both our individual and social behavior, notably how multilevel selection has shaped humans to be prosocial and highly cooperative (Bowles and Gintis 2011; Wilson *et al.* 2023), which is an essential fact in explaining the large-scale, cooperative order creation among nonkin that characterizes the economy (and is counter to traditional assumptions of individual, self-regarding rationality). Second, human social systems themselves evolve according to generalized Darwinian principles (Hodgson and Knudsen 2010; Beinhocker 2011), including human culture broadly (Henrich 2015), technology (Arthur 2009; ch. 3 in this volume), and institutions (Hodgson 2004; Nelson 2005). Advances have also been made in formalizing evolutionary perspectives in economics. Peyton Young (1993, 1998) uses evolutionary game theory to model how stable social norms and structures can evolve through evolutionary processes. Herbert Gintis (2017) provides both a unifying theoretical perspective and formal models using evolutionary game theory and Markov processes to explore evolutionary interactions

between individual and collective system behaviors. Giovanni Dosi and colleagues (2017) use ABM to bring an evolutionary perspective into macroeconomics, integrating Schumpetarian technology dynamics with a Keynesian model of demand fluctuations and examining implications for policy.

8. **Environment:** The standard approach to integrating environmental concerns into economics has been to treat the environment as an externality—an infinite source of resources and infinite sink for waste, outside the bounds of the economy itself. This perspective has anchored much of the research in models of market failure, Pigovian taxes, shadow prices, cost–benefit analysis, etc. But this perspective fails to capture the two-way dynamics of interactions between the environment and economy, as well as the nonmarginal, structural transformations required to create an economy that operates within biophysical limits compatible with life flourishing on Earth (Beinhocker 2023). The complex-systems perspective, however, sees the economy as an open thermodynamic system, embedded in the physical environment, with flows of energy, materials, and information inputs leading to order creation and entropy reduction within the system, and the exporting of higher-entropy waste heat, gases, and materials back into the physical environment—the "metabolism of civilization" as Farmer (2024, 48–72) puts it. This entropic perspective has been core to the development of ecological economics (Georgescu-Roegen 1971; Daly 1977) but, like the evolutionary perspective, has sat outside the mainstream. But if economics is to fully grapple with the profound issues of climate change,

ecosystem destruction, and their implications for the economy, policy, and society, it must move beyond its narrow frame of market failure. Researchers have shown that the economy as metabolism is not just a metaphor but can be studied and modeled empirically (Schandl *et al.* 2024) with implications for how equitable and high living standards can be achieved within biophysical boundaries (O'Neill *et al.* 2018). One of those implications is deep structural changes in our technologies and institutions. Rupert Way and colleagues (2022) provide an empirically grounded model showing how a dynamic view of technology change upends standard (e.g., Nordhaus 2017) cost-benefit analyses and conclude that a rapid transition to net-zero energy technologies yields significant economic benefits, even absent the benefits of avoided climate damage.

If we step back and look across this list—behavioral realism, institutional realism, market and strategic disequilibrium, networks, emergence, evolution, and environment—what we see is an opportunity to make economics more capable of scientifically capturing the complexity of economic phenomena, and more relevant to addressing complex real-world challenges.

These eight points cover much of the agenda of modern economics, where cutting-edge work is both needed and being done. This volume, and the literature cited, shows that the interdisciplinary complex-systems community can now claim to have a multidecade record of using tools, methods, and perspectives that are differentiated from those historically used in economics, to generate new, empirically validated insights.

Mapping back to our framework of economic paradigms, we can see how the complex-systems community is making crucial contributions to what we have called the four scientific layers of the ontological stack:

Behavioral theory: Incorporating a crossdisciplinary perspective on real human behavior, including heuristic decision-making and learning, prosociality and cooperation, multiple goals, social norms, and culture, into economic models.

Systems theory: A systems theory rooted in the idea of the economy as a complex adaptive system of networks within networks, that exhibits both equilibrium and disequilibrium behaviors, where macro patterns emerge from dynamic interactions at the micro and meso levels, and that is intertwined with the physical environment.

~527~

Processes of change: Where much change is endogenous, evolutionary, and multilevel, with the evolution and coevolution of technologies and institutions (within the broader evolution of human culture) driving the longterm self-creation, unfolding, and development of the system—or, borrowing a term from evolutionary biology, what Brian Arthur has referred to as economic "autopoiesis."[5]

Metrics: New multidimensional measures of well-being and performance "beyond GDP."

Putting these pieces together with the other layers in the broader project of new paradigm construction, we can begin to see a sketch of what such a new paradigm might look like (table 4).

As we have noted, important progress has been made on the bottom (moral foundations) layer and upper normative layers of such a new ontological stack. We believe that, by strengthening and building the scientific layers with tools, methods, and ideas

[5]From a presentation by W. Brian Arthur to Nanyang Technical University, February 29, 2012.

Table 4. An emerging new paradigm.

LAYER IN THE ONTOLOGICAL STACK	A NEW 21ST-CENTURY PARADIGM	COMMENTS
Moral foundations	Alternatives to Benthamite utilitarianism	e.g., capabilities; moral and democratic equality; virtue; communities of fate; modern interpretations of Rawls
Behavioral theory	Modern behavioral science with a cross-disciplinary perspective	e.g., costly cognition; heuristic decision-making; adaptive learning; multimotivated prosociality; role of norms, culture, and identity; social nature of knowledge
Economic systems theory	Complex adaptive systems	Diverse agents, networks, nonlinearities, dynamics, multilevel, emergent, nonergodic, embedded, open
Processes of change	Endogenous, evolutionary	Universal Darwinism, multilevel and multidomain evolution (biology, culture, technologies, institutions)
Metrics	Beyond GDP and shareholder value	Multidimensional measures of well-being and performance (e.g., SAGE, OPHI, OECD Better Life, B Corp Impact Assessment)
Normative analysis	Individual and social flourishing	Empirically based conceptions of individual well-being and human social flourishing
Political economy and ideology	New political economy	New theories of value creation, distribution, roles of markets, states, and civil society (e.g., Bowles and Carlin "shrinking capitalism," Besley and Chandler "cohesive capitalism," Rodrik "productivism," Beinhocker and Hanauer "market humanism")
Emblematic policies	Policies to align markets with human well-being and environmental sustainability	e.g., job guarantees, place-based policies, investments in capabilities, new forms of labor power, balanced stakeholder corporate governance, modern competition policy, green industrial policy, circular economy
Public and political narratives	Middle-out economics; enabling state; freedom to flourish	e.g., from greed is good to cooperation is good; from equality vs. merit to fairness; from big trade-offs to big win–wins; from growth to progress

from the complex-systems community, we will begin to see greater coherence across the stack and new insights as to how policies and institutions might better translate the values of a new paradigm into better outcomes in the real world.

Toward a New Paradigm

While there is a long way to go, complexity economics is already contributing novel scientific insights to such an agenda.

Much complexity-economics work has normative implications for major policy and political challenges, including the function of the financial system (e.g., Poledna and Thurner 2016), economic inequality (e.g., Berman, Peters, and Adamou 2021), macroeconomics (Wiese *et al.* 2024), economic growth and development (Hidalgo *et al.* 2007), climate change (Way *et al.* 2022), diversity (Page 2010), political institutions and democracy (Bednar and Page 2018, 2025), political polarization (Bednar 2021), and institutional robustness and adaptability (Bednar 2009).

We should also note that there is potential for this progress to accelerate rapidly in the coming years. Complexity-economics methods tend to heavily utilize computing power and data—both of which continue to become exponentially cheaper and more available. And the AI revolution will unlock new possibilities in the development of complexity economics. AI is already being used to accelerate model coding, parameterization, sensitivity testing, data cleaning, analysis, and forecasting. Potential exists to combine AI with ABMs to create highly detailed and realistic "digital twins" of economic systems with micro-level data on all relevant agents (e.g., Axtell 2016) and to explore possible policy spaces (e.g., Agrawal *et al.* 2025).

So, what needs to be done to advance the agenda of new paradigm construction? In our view, there are five priorities:

1. **Scaling the complexity-economics community:** The progress that has been made to date has been driven by a relatively small, interdisciplinary community of scholars. There are a number of research centers focused on complexity economics, including INET Oxford, Harvard's Growth Lab, the University of Vienna Complexity Science Hub, George Mason's Computational Social Science department, the Institute of Economics at the Sant'Anna

School for Advanced Studies, the Complexity Lab in Economics at Cattolica University, the Econophysics and Complex Systems group at École Polytechnique, the Center for Nonlinear Dynamics in Economics and Finance at the Amsterdam School of Economics, and of course the Santa Fe Institute. But most scholars are scattered in institutions around the world, and the scale of activity is small relative to more traditional economic research. Robert Axtell of George Mason University roughly estimates that traditional equilibrium-based macroeconomic models alone have had about a million person-years of cumulative effort invested in them to date, while complexity economics models across all topics have had something like 100,000 person-years.[6] Furthermore, additional integration is needed between the complex-systems and evolutionary perspectives within the complexity-economics community (Wilson and Kirman 2016).

2. **Developing a new welfare economics:** There needs to be more two-way engagement between the complexity economics community and scholars working on the moral foundation layers, as well as those working on the normative and policy layers of a new paradigm. In the neoliberal consensus stack, welfare economics provides critical connective tissue between moral foundations, formal models, normative findings, and policy analysis. Such connective tissue is missing in the new paradigm (Beinhocker *et al.* 2023). And many scholars working on these issues are unfamiliar with the complexity-economics approach and vice versa.

---

[6]Axtell's presentation to the Google Modeling Talk Series is available at: https://sites.google.com/modelingtalks.org/entry/agent-based-modeling-of-economic-phenomena-at-very-large-full-scale

3. **More interdisciplinary collaboration between economists and the complex-systems community:** A new generation of economists trained in empirical approaches, comfortable with computational methods, and interested in tools such network theory, multiagent models, and AI presents an opportunity for closer engagement. There are important methodological and scientific issues to be debated between the economics and complex-systems communities, but to date that debate and engagement has been limited. Many economists remain unaware of the complex-systems literature, and complexity researchers would benefit from the deep domain knowledge of economists. The need for new answers at the normative and policy ends of the stack should drive innovation and openness to nontraditional approaches in both communities.

4. **More engagement with policymakers and political leaders:** Some of the most important progress in complexity economics, and development of a new paradigm more generally, has been driven by the needs of policymakers. For example, since the 2008 crisis, there has been significant engagement with complexity economists by central banks (Borsos *et al.* 2025), as well as policymakers working on climate change, labor market policies, trade, supply chains, and other topics. Furthermore, by viewing political systems as networks of people and interconnected institutions, complexity science builds our understanding of the robustness and efficacy of governance structures. By exploring these networks and interdependencies, complexity science can illuminate "sensitive intervention points" where interventions can yield outsize positive outcomes (Farmer *et al.* 2019). Complexity science also emphasizes the interconnectedness of political actions and public responses, enabling the design

of policies that are not only supported and effective but also adaptable to future challenges.

5. **Development of new public narratives:** The use of terms from complexity science such as *leverage points, feedback loops,* and *interdependence* is becoming common in discussions about global issues such as financial stability and climate change. These are no longer just academic terms; they are becoming part of everyday language for practitioners and the public alike. But we need to go much further in developing compelling narratives that connect the moral foundations of a new paradigm with scientific insights from complexity economics and normative calls to action. Such narratives were key to the popular support for and political adoption of the three twentieth-century paradigms (despite their later failures). Humans are storytelling animals, and a new paradigm needs good stories.

As complexity economics advances, it holds the potential to provide a crucial layer of scientific explanations, connecting moral ideas on what constitutes a good or better economy with normative political economy ideas on how the system should be organized and the policies, practices, and institutions to get us there. By fostering interdisciplinary collaboration and continued methodological innovation, the complexity economics community could help lead the development of new tools and frameworks that enable societies to better manage the enormous challenges we face in a complex, interconnected world. The failed economic paradigms of the twentieth century are not up to this challenge. It is time to build a twenty-first-century paradigm that is. 🖑

Acknowledgments

We are deeply grateful for feedback from Tim Besley, Wendy Carlin, Daniel Chandler, Doyne Farmer, Nick Hanauer, Margaret Levi, Scott Page, Dennis Snower, David Sloan Wilson, our co-editors on this volume, and especially to Sam Bowles, who was particularly generous with his time, guiding us to a significant improvement in our argument. We thank everyone for their wise input, and we are solely responsible for all errors that remain.

REFERENCES

Acemoglu, D., and J. A. Robinson. 2019. *The Narrow Corridor: States, Societies, and the Fate of Liberty.* London, UK: Penguin.

Agrawal, A., J. Dyer, A. Glielmo, and M. Wooldridge. 2025. "Robust Policy Design in Agent-Based Simulators Using Adversarial Reinforcement Learning." In *The First MARW: Multi-Agent Artificial Intelligence in the Real-World Workshop at the Association for Advancement of Artificial Intelligence 2025.* https : / / openreview.net/forum?id=vPzij1AYf2.

Ahlquist, J. S., and M. Levi. 2014. *In the Interest of Others: Organizations and Social Activism.* Princeton, NJ: Princeton University Press.

Akerlof, G. A., and R. J. Shiller. 2009. *Animal Spirits.* Princeton, NJ: Princeton University Press.

Allen, D. 2023. *Justice by Means of Democracy.* Chicago, IL: University of Chicago Press.

Anderson, E. S. 1999. "What is the Point of Equality?" *Ethics* 109 (2): 287–337. https: //doi.org/10.1086/233897.

Anderson, P. W., K. J. Arrow, and D. Pines. 1988. *The Economy as an Evolving Complex System.* Redwood City, CA: Addison-Wesley.

Arthur, W. B. 1999. "Complexity and the Economy." *Science* 284 (5411): 107–109. https://doi.org/10.1126/science.284.5411.107.

———. 2009. *The Nature of Technology.* New York, NY: Free Press.

———. 2013. *Complexity and the Economy.* Oxford, UK: Oxford University Press.

———. 2021. "Foundations of Complexity Economics." *Nature Reviews Physics* 3:136–145. https://doi.org/10.1038/s42254-020-00273-3.

Arthur, W. B., E. D. Beinhocker, and M. S. Stanger, eds. 2020. *Complexity Economics: Proceedings of the Santa Fe Institute's 2019 Fall Symposium.* Santa Fe, NM: SFI Press.

Arthur, W. B., S. N. Durlauf, and D. A. Lane, eds. 1997. *The Economy as an Evolving Complex System II.* Reading, MA: Addison-Wesley.

Asano, Y. M., J. J. Kolb, J. Heitzig, and J. D. Farmer. 2021. "Emergent Inequality and Business Cycles in a Simple Behavioral Macroeconomic Model." *Proceedings of the National Academy of Sciences* 118 (27): e2025721118. https://doi.org/10.1073/pnas.2025721118.

Axtell, R. I.. 2016. "120 Million Agents Self-Organize into 6 Million Firms: A Model of the US Private Sector." In *Proceedings of the 15th International Conference on Autonomous Agents and Multi-Agent Systems,* edited by J. Thangarajah, K. Tuyls, C. Jonker, and S. Marsella, 806–816. International Foundation for Autonomous Agents and Multiagent Systems.

Axtell, R. L., and J. D. Farmer. 2025. "Agent-Based Modeling in Economics and Finance: Past, Present, and Future." *Journal of Economic Literature* 63 (1): 197–287. https://doi.org/10.1257/jel.20221319.

Bednar, J. 2009. *The Robust Federation: Principles of Design.* Cambridge, UK: Cambridge University Press.

———. 2021. "Polarization, Diversity, and Democratic Robustness." *Proceedings of the National Academy of Sciences* 118 (50): e2113843118. https://doi.org/10.1073/pnas.2113843118.

———. 2023. "Governance for Human Social Flourishing." *Daedalus* 152 (1): 31–45. https://doi.org/10.1073/pnas.2113843118.

Chapter 31: Complexity and Paradigm Change in Economics

Bednar, J., R. M. del Rio-Chanona, J. D. Farmer, J. Kasowska-Mojsa, F. Lafond, P. Mealy, M. Pangallo, and A. Pichler, eds. 2025. "Complex System Approaches to 21st Century Challenges: Inequality, Climate Change, and New Technologies." Special Issue, *Journal of Economic Behavior and Organization* 235. https://doi.org/10.1016/j.jebo.2025.107049.

Bednar, J., and S. E. Page. 2018. "When Order Affects Performance: Culture, Behavioral Spillovers, and Institutional Path Dependence." *American Political Science Review* 112 (1): 82–98. https://doi.org/10.1017/S0003055417000466.

———. 2025. "Institutions and Cultural Capacity: A Systems Perspective." *Journal of Economic Behavior and Organization* 234:106990. https://doi.org/10.1016/j.jebo.2025.106990.

Beinhocker, E. D. 2006. *The Origin of Wealth: Evolution, Complexity and the Radical Remaking of Economics.* Boston, MA: Harvard Business School Press.

———. 2011. "Evolution as Computation: Integrating Self-Organization with Generalized Darwinism." *Journal of Institutional Economics* 7 (3): 393–423. https://doi.org/10.1017/S1744137411000257.

———. 2013. "Reflexivity, Complexity, and the Nature of Social Science." *Journal of Economic Methodology* 20 (4): 330–342. https://doi.org/10.1080/1350178X.2013.859403.

———. 2020. "Toward a New Ontological Framework for the Economic Good." *Global Perspectives* 1 (1). https://doi.org/10.1525/gp.2020.17578.

———. 2023. "Biophilic Markets." *Daedalus* 152 (1): 94–99. https://doi.org/10.1162/daed_a_01965.

Beinhocker, E. D., W. B. Arthur, R. Axtell, J. Bednar, J.-P. Bouchaud, D. Colander, M. Crockett, *et al.* 2019. *Inclusive Economics is Complexity Economics.* Boston Review. https://www.bostonreview.net/forum/suresh-naidu-dani-rodrik-gabriel-zucman-economics-after-neoliberalism/complexity-economists-economics-needs-embrace-transdisciplinary/.

Beinhocker, E. D., T. Besley, D. Coyle, M. Fabian, and M. Stevens. 2023. "Is It Time to Reboot Welfare Economics? Overview." *Fiscal Studies* 44 (2): 109–121. https://doi.org/10.1111/1475-5890.12334.

Berman, Y., O. Peters, and A. Adamou. 2021. "Wealth Inequality and the Ergodic Hypothesis: Evidence from the United States." *Journal of Income Distribution* 30 (1). https://doi.org/10.25071/1874-6322.40455.

Besley, T., I. Bucelli, and A. Velasco. 2025. *The London Consensus: Economic Principles for the 21st Century*. London, UK: LSE Press.

Besley, T., and T. Persson. 2023. "The Political Economics of Green Transitions." *The Quarterly Journal of Economics* 138 (3): 1863–1906. https://doi.org/10.1093/qje/qjad006.

Blume, L. E., and S. N. Durlauf, eds. 2005. *The Economy as an Evolving Complex System III: Current Perspectives and Future Directions*. Oxford, UK: Oxford University Press.

Borsos, A., A. Carro, A. Glielmo, M. Hintershweiger, J. Kaszowska-Mojsa, and A. Uluc. 2025. *Agent-Based Modeling at Central Banks: Recent Developments and New Challenges*. Working Paper 2025-05. INET Oxford. https://oms-inet.files.svdcdn.com/production/files/Agent_based_modeling_at_central_banks_WP_Feb_2025.pdf?dm=1741021620.

Boushey, H. 2019. "A New Economic Paradigm." Symposium: Beyond Neoliberalism, Summer 2019, *Democracy*, no. 53.

Bowles, S. 2016. *The Moral Economy: Why Good Incentives Are No Substitute for Good Citizens*. New Haven, CT: Yale University Press.

Bowles, S., and W. Carlin. 2020. "What Students Learn in Economics 101: Time for a Change." *Journal of Economic Literature* 58 (1): 176–214. https://doi.org/10.1257/jel.20191585.

———. 2021. "Shrinking Capitalism: Components of a New Political Economy Paradigm." *Oxford Review of Economic Policy* 37 (4): 794–810. https://doi.org/10.1093/oxrep/grab029.

Bowles, S., and H. Gintis. 2011. *A Cooperative Species: Human Reciprocity and Its Evolution*. Princeton, NJ: Princeton University Press.

Burgin, A. 2012. *The Great Persuasion: Reinventing Free Markets Since the Depression*. Cambridge, MA: Harvard University Press.

Carvalho, V. M. 2014. "From Micro to Macro via Production Networks." *Journal of Economic Perspectives* 28 (4): 23–48. https://doi.org/10.1257/jep.28.4.23.

Castle, J., and D. F. Hendry. 2024. "What a Puzzle! Unravelling Why UK Phillips Curves Were Unstable." *Oxford Bulletin of Economics and Statistics*, https://doi.org/10.1111/obes.12615.

Cengiz, D., A. Dube, A. Lindner, and B. Zipperer. 2019. "The Effect of Minimum Wages on Low-Wage Jobs." *Quarterly Journal of Economics* 134 (3): 1405–1454. https://doi.org/10.1093/qje/qjz014.

Chandler, D. 2024. *Free and Equal: What Would a Fair Society Look Like?* London, UK: Penguin UK.

Collier, P., and J. Kay. 2020. *Greed Is Dead.* London, UK: Allen Lane.

Daly, H. E. 1977. *Steady-State Economics.* San Francisco, CA: W. H. Freeman.

Dhami, S. 2016. *The Foundations of Behavioral Economic Analysis.* Oxford, UK: Oxford University Press. ~537~

Dosi, G. 1982. "Technological Paradigms and Technological Trajectories." *Research Policy* 11 (3): 147–162. https://doi.org/10.1016/0048-7333(82)90016-6.

Dosi, G., M. Napoletano, A. Roventini, and T. Treibich. 2017. "Micro and Macro Policies in the Keynes+Schumpeter Evolutionary Models." *Journal of Evolutionary Economics* 27, no. 1 (January): 63–90. https://doi.org/10.1007/s00191-016-0466-4.

Ekelund, R. B., and R. F. Hébert. 2013. *A History of Economic Theory and Method.* Long Grove, IL: Waveland Press.

Farmer, J. D. 2024. *Making Sense of Chaos: A Better Economics for a Better World.* London, UK: Penguin UK.

Farmer, J. D., A. Gerig, F. Lillo, and H. Waelbroeck. 2013. "How Efficiency Shapes Market Impact." *Quantitative Finance* 13 (11): 1743–1758. https://doi.org/10.1080/14697688.2013.848464.

Farmer, J. D., C. Hepburn, M. C. Ives, T. Hale, T. Wetzer, P. Mealy, R. Rafaty, S. Srivastav, and R. Way. 2019. "Sensitive Intervention Points in the Post-Carbon Transition." *Science* 364 (6436): 132–134. https://doi.org/10.1126/science.aaw7287.

Georgescu-Roegen, N. 1971. *The Entropy Law and the Economic Process.* Cambridge, MA: Harvard University Press.

Gigerenzer, G., and R. Selten, eds. 2001. *Bounded Rationality: The Adaptive Toolbox.* Cambridge, MA: MIT Press.

Gintis, H. 2017. *Individuality and Entanglement: The Moral and Material Bases for Social Life.* Princeton, NJ: Princeton University Press.

Hall, P. A., and D. Soskice, eds. 2001. *Varieties of Capitalism: The Institutional Foundations of Comparative Advantage.* Oxford, UK: Oxford University Press.

Hendry, D. F. 2020. "A Short History of Macro-Econometric Modelling." *Journal of Banking, Finance, and Sustainable Development* 1:1–32.

Henrich, J. 2015. *The Secret of Our Success: How Culture Is Driving Human Evolution, Domesticating Our Species, and Making Us Smarter.* Princeton, NJ: Princeton University Press.

Hidalgo, C. A., B. Klinger, A.-L. Barabási, and R. Hausmann. 2007. "The Product Space Conditions the Development of Nations." *Science* 317 (5837): 482–487. https://doi.org/10.1126/science.1144581.

Hodgson, G. M. 2004. *The Evolution of Institutional Economics: Agency, Structure and Darwinism in American Institutionalism.* London, UK: Routledge.

Hodgson, G. M., and T. Knudsen. 2010. *Darwin's Conjecture: The Search for General Principles of Social & Economic Evolution.* Chicago, IL: University of Chicago Press.

Hommes, C. 2013. *Behavioral Rationality and Heterogeneous Expectations in Complex Economic Systems.* Cambridge, UK: Cambridge University Press. https://doi.org/10.1017/CBO9781139094276.

Iori, G., and C. Hommes, eds. 2015. "Crises and Complexity." Special Issue, *Journal of Economic Dynamics and Control* 50:1–202. https://doi.org/10.1016/j.jedc.2014.09.026.

Jackson, M. O. 2014. "Networks in the Understanding of Economic Behaviors." *Journal of Economic Perspectives* 28 (4): 3–22. https://doi.org/10.1257/jep.28.4.3.

Jones, C. I. 1995. "Time Series Tests of Endogenous Growth Models." *Quarterly Journal of Economics* 110 (2): 495–525. https://doi.org/10.2307/2118448.

Kirman, A. P., and N. J. Vriend. 2001. "Evolving Market Structure: An ACE Model of Price Dispersion and Loyalty." *Journal of Economic Dynamics and Control* 25 (3–4): 459–502. https://doi.org/10.1016/S0165-1889(00)00033-6.

Kuhn, T. S. 1962. *The Structure of Scientific Revolutions.* Chicago, IL: University of Chicago Press.

Levi, M., and H. Farrell, eds. 2023. "Creating a New Moral Political Economy." Special Issue, *Daedalus* 152 (1). https://direct.mit.edu/daed/issue/152/1.

Chapter 31: Complexity and Paradigm Change in Economics

Lillo, F., and J. D. Farmer. 2004. "The Long Memory of the Efficient Market." *Studies in Nonlinear Dynamics and Econometrics,* http://www.long-memory.com/other/LilloFarmer2004.pdf.

Lillo, F., S. Mike, and J. D. Farmer. 2005. "Theory for Long Memory in Supply and Demand." *Phys. Rev. E* 71 (6): 066122. https://doi.org/10.1103/PhysRevE.71.066122.

Lucas, Jr., R. E. 1976. "Econometric Policy Evaluation: A Critique." In *The Phillips Curve and Labor Markets,* edited by K. Brunner and A. H. Meltzer, 19–46. Amsterdam: North-Holland.

MacIntyre, A. 1999. *Dependent Rational Animals: Why Human Beings Need the Virtues.* Chicago, IL: Open Court Press.

Mas-Colell, A., M. D. Whinston, and J. R. Green. 1995. *Microeconomic Theory.* New York, NY: Oxford University Press.

Mizon, G., and D. F. Hendry. 2014. *Why DSGEs Crash During Crises.* CEPR VoxEU. https://cepr.org/voxeu/columns/why-dsges-crash-during-crises.

Naidu, S., D. Rodrik, and G. Zucman. 2019. *Economics After Neoliberalism.* Boston Review. https://www.bostonreview.net/forum/suresh-naidu-dani-rodrik-gabriel-zucman-economics-after-neoliberalism/.

Nelson, R. R. 2005. *Technology, Institutions, and Economic Growth.* Cambridge, MA: Harvard University Press.

Nelson, R. R., and S. G. Winter. 1982. *An Evolutionary Theory of Economic Change.* Cambridge, MA: Belknap Press.

Nolan, B., ed. 2018. *Inequality and Inclusive Growth in Rich Countries.* Oxford, UK: Oxford University Press.

Nordhaus, W. D. 2017. "Revisiting the Social Cost of Carbon." *Proceedings of the National Academy of Sciences of the United States of America* 114:1518–1523. https://doi.org/10.1073/pnas.1609244114.

Nussbaum, M. C. 2013. *Creating Capabilities: The Human Development Approach.* Cambridge, MA: Harvard University Press. https://www.hup.harvard.edu/books/9780674072350.

O'Neill, D. W., A. L. Fanning, W. F. Lamb, and J. K. Steinberger. 2018. "A Good Life for All Within Planetary Boundaries." *Nature Sustainability* 1 (2): 88–95. https://doi.org/10.1038/s41893-018-0021-4.

Page, S. E. 2010. *Diversity and Complexity*. Princeton, NJ: Princeton University Press.

Pangallo, M., T. Heinrich, and J. D. Farmer. 2019. "Best Reply Structure and Equilibrium Convergence in Generic Games." *Science Advances* 5:eaat1328. https://doi.org/10.1126/sciadv.aat1328.

Pichler, A., M. Pangallo, R. M. del Rio-Chanona, F. Lafond, and J. D. Farmer. 2020. *Production Networks and Epidemic Spreading: How to Restart the UK Economy?* arXiv preprint: 2005.10585. https://doi.org/10.48550/arXiv.2005.10585.

———. 2022. "Forecasting the Propagation of Pandemic Shocks with a Dynamic Input–Output Model." *Journal of Economic Dynamics and Control* 144:104527. https://doi.org/10.1016/j.jedc.2022.104527.

Poledna, S., M. G. Miess, C. Hommes, and K. Rabitsch. 2023. "Economic Forecasting with an Agent-Based Model." *European Economic Review* 151:104306. https://doi.org/10.1016/j.euroecorev.2022.104306.

Poledna, S., and S. Thurner. 2016. "Elimination of Systemic Risk in Financial Networks by Means of a Systemic Risk Transaction Tax." *Quantitative Finance* 16 (10): 1599–1613. https://doi.org/10.1080/14697688.2016.1156146.

Popper, K. 1945. *The Open Society and Its Enemies*. Princeton, NJ: Princeton University Press. https : / / press . princeton . edu / books / paperback / 9780691210841/the-open-society-and-its-enemies.

———. 1959. *The Logic of Scientific Discovery*. London, UK: Hutchinson.

Raworth, K. 2017. *Doughnut Economics: Seven Ways to Think Like a 21st-Century Economist*. White River Junction, VT: Chelsea Green Publishing.

Richerson, P. J., and R. Boyd. 2005. *Not by Genes Alone: How Culture Transformed Human Evolution*. Chicago, IL: University of Chicago Press.

Rodrik, D. 2007. *One Economics, Many Recipes: Globalization, Institutions, and Economic Growth*. Princeton, NJ: Princeton University Press.

———. 2025. *Shared Prosperity in a Fractured World: A New Economics for the Middle Class, the Global Poor, and Our Climate*. Princeton, NJ: Princeton University Press.

Sandel, M. J. 2020. *The Tyranny of Merit*. New York, NY: Farrar, Straus / Giroux.

Sato, Y., and K. Kanazawa. 2023. "Inferring Microscopic Financial Information from the Long Memory in Market-Order Flow: A Quantitative Test of the Lillo-Mike-Farmer Model." *Phys. Rev. Lett.* 131 (19): 197401. https://doi.org/10.1103/PhysRevLett.131.197401.

Schandl, H., R. Marcos-Martinez, J. West, A. Miatto, S. Lutter, M. Lieber, S. Giljum, *et al.* 2024. "Global Material Flows and Resource Productivity: The 2024 Update." *Journal of Industrial Ecology* 28 (6): 2012–2031. https://doi.org/10.1111/jiec.13593.

Scholl, M. P., A. Calinescu, and J. D. Farmer. 2021. "How Market Ecology Explains Market Malfunction." *Proceedings of the National Academy of Sciences* 118 (26): e2015574118. https://doi.org/10.1073/pnas.2015574118.

Sen, A. 1999. *Development as Freedom.* New York, NY: Alfred A. Knopf.

Sober, E., and D. S. Wilson. 1998. *Unto Others: The Evolution and Psychology of Unselfish Behavior.* Cambridge, MA: Harvard University Press.

Soros, G. 2013. "Fallibility, Reflexivity, and the Human Uncertainty Principle." *Journal of Economic Methodology* 20 (4): 309–329. https://doi.org/10.1080/1350178X.2013.859415.

Vines, D., and S. Wills. 2018. "The Rebuilding Macroeconomic Theory Project: An Analytical Assessment." *Oxford Review of Economic Policy* 34 (1–2): 1–42. https://doi.org/10.1093/oxrep/grx062.

———. 2020. "The Rebuilding Macroeconomic Theory Project Part II: Multiple Equilibria, Toy Models, and Policy Models in a New Macroeconomic Paradigm." *Oxford Review of Economic Policy* 36 (3): 451–501. https://doi.org/10.1093/oxrep/graa066.

Waldrop, M. 1992. *Complexity: The Emerging Science at the Edge of Order and Chaos.* New York, NY: Simon & Schuster.

Way, R., M. C. Ives, P. Mealy, and J. D. Farmer. 2022. "Empirically Grounded Technology Forecasts and the Energy Transition." *Joule* 6 (9): 2057–2082. https://doi.org/10.1016/j.joule.2022.08.009.

Wiese, S., J. Kaszowska-Mojsa, J. Dyer, J. Moran, M. Pangallo, F. Lafond, J. Muellbauer, A. Calinescu, and J. D. Farmer. 2024. *Forecasting Macroeconomic Dynamics Using a Calibrated Data-Driven Agent-Based Model.* arXiv preprint:2409.18760. https://doi.org/10.48550/arXiv.2409.18760.

Williamson, J. 1989. "What Washington Means by Policy Reform." In *Latin American Readjustment: How Much Has Happened?*, edited by J. Williamson, 7–20. Washington, DC: Institute for International Economics.

Wilson, D. S., and A. Kirman. 2016. *Complexity and Evolution: Toward a New Synthesis for Economics.* Cambridge, MA: MIT Press. https://mitpress.mit.edu/9780262035385/complexity-and-evolution/.

Wilson, D. S., G. Madhavan, M. J. Gelfand, S. C. Hayes, P. W. B. Atkins, and R. R. Colwell. 2023. "Multilevel Cultural Evolution: From New Theory to Practical Applications." *Proceedings of the National Academy of Sciences* 120 (16): e2218222120. https://doi.org/10.1073/pnas.2218222120.

Wong, F. 2022. "Overview: Post-Neoliberalism at a Crossroads." Symposium: Beyond Neoliberalism Part II, Spring 2022, *Democracy*, no. 64, https://democracyjournal.org/magazine/64/overview-post-neoliberalism-at-a-crossroads/.

Young, H. P. 1993. "The Evolution of Conventions." *Econometrica* 61 (1): 57–84. https://www.jstor.org/stable/2951778.

———. 1998. *Individual Strategy and Social Structure: An Evolutionary Theory of Institutions.* Princeton, NJ: Princeton University Press.

Protektorat Böhmen und Mähren
Protektorat Čechy a Morava
THE JAPANESE GOVERNMENT
TEN DOLLARS
MP
REICHSBANKNOTE
2 MILLIONEN MARK
Eine Krone
JEDNA KORUNA
10 sen in silver.

THE ART IN THESE VOLUMES

Both volumes of *The Economy as an Evolving Complex System IV* feature public-domain imagery of numerous forms of currency spanning time and space, an acknowledgment of how technological developments and innovation impact economies and societal norms. All images are out of copyright and were sourced via The New York Public Library, the Internet Archive, and Wikimedia Commons.

བྱ

VOL. I
TABLE OF CONTENTS

CONTRIBUTORS TO THESE VOLUMES

Joos Akkerman, *Delft University of Technology*

Pia Andres, *Durham University and Centre for Economic Performance*

W. Brian Arthur, *Santa Fe Institute and SRI International*

Robert Axtell, *George Mason University and Santa Fe Institute*

Stefano Battiston, *University of Zurich, Ca' Foscari, University of Venice, and CEPR*

Paul Beaudry, *University of British Columbia and NBER*

Jenna Bednar, *University of Michigan and Santa Fe Institute*

Eric D. Beinhocker, *University of Oxford and Santa Fe Institute*

András Borsos, *Magyar Nemzeti Bank, Complexity Science Hub, and University of Oxford*

Jean-Philippe Bouchaud, *Capital Fund Management and Académie des Sciences*

William Brock, *University of Wisconsin, Madison, and University of Missouri, Columbia*

Fabio Caccioli, *University College London and Systemic Risk Centre, London School of Economics and Political Science*

Adrian Carro, *University of Oxford and Banco de España*

Diane Coyle, *University of Cambridge*

Herbert Dawid, *Bielefeld University*

Domenico Delli Gatti, *Università Cattolica del Sacro Cuore*

R. Maria del Rio-Chanona, *University College London*

Giovanni Dosi, *Sant'Anna School of Advanced Studies*

Marion Dumas, *London School of Economics and Political Science*

Salva Duran-Nebreda, *Institute of Evolutionary Biology (CSIC-UPF)*

Steven N. Durlauf, *University of Chicago*

J. Doyne Farmer, *University of Oxford and Santa Fe Institute*

Luca Eduardo Fierro, *International Institute for Applied Systems Analysis*

Tatiana Filatova, *Delft University of Technology*

Morgan R. Frank, *University of Pittsburgh*

Koen Frenken, *Utrecht University*

Dana Galizia, *Carleton University*

John Geanakoplos, *Yale University and Santa Fe Institute*

Aldo Glielmo, *Banca d'Italia*

Omar Guerrero, *University of Helsinki*

Marc Hinterschweiger, *Bank of England*

Cars Hommes, *Bank of Canada, University of Amsterdam, and Tinbergen Institute*

Jagoda Kaszowska-Mojsa, *University of Oxford, Narodowy Bank Polski, and Institute of Economics, Polish Academy of Sciences*

Sharon Kozicki, *Bank of Canada*

François Lafond, *University of Oxford*

Francesco Lamperti, *Sant'Anna School of Advanced Studies, RFF-CMCC European Institute on Economics and the Environment, and Euro-Mediterranean Center on Climate Change (CMCC)*

Rosario N. Mantegna, *Università degli Studi di Palermo and Complexity Science Hub*

David McMillon, *Emory University*

Penny Mealy, *University of Oxford, Santa Fe Institute, and Monash University*

Irene Monasterolo, *Utrecht University, CEPR, and Wirtschaftsuniversität Wien*

José Moran, *Macrocosm Inc., University of Oxford, and Complexity Science Hub*

Esteban Moro, *Northeastern University and Massachusetts Institute of Technology*

Ljubica Nedelkoska, *Complexity Science Hub and Central European University*

Frank Neffke, *Complexity Science Hub*

Scott E. Page, *University of Michigan–Ann Arbor and Santa Fe Institute*

Marco Pangallo, *CENTAI Institute*

Marcelo C. Pereira, *Universidade Estadual de Campinas and Scuola Superiore Sant'Anna*

Anton Pichler, *Vienna University of Economics and Business and Complexity Science Hub*

Sebastian Poledna, *Austrian Institute of Economic Research*

Franck Portier, *University College London and CEPR*

Massimo Riccaboni, *IMT School for Advanced Studies Lucca and Scuola Superiore IUSS*

Matteo Richiardi, *University of Essex*

Andrea Roventini, *Sant'Anna School of Advanced Studies and OFCE Sciences Po*

Angelica Sbardella, *Enrico Fermi Research Center*

Ulrich Schetter, *University of Pavia*

Andrea Tacchella, *Enrico Fermi Research Center*

Arthur Turrell, *Bank of England*

Arzu Uluc, *Bank of England*

Sergi Valverde, *Institute of Evolutionary Biology (CSIC-UPF)*

Justin van de Ven, *University of Essex*

Blai Vidiella, *Theoretical and Experimental Ecology Station (CNRS)*

Maria Enrica Virgillito, *Scuola Superiore Sant'Anna and Universitá Cattolica del Sacro Cuore*

Yang Zhang, *Bank of Canada*

COORDINATING EDITORS

R. MARIA DEL RIO-CHANONA is a lecturer in computer science at University College London. Her research draws from large language models, network science, and agent-based modeling and focuses on the net-zero transition and the impact of new technologies in the economy, with a particular focus on labor markets.

Del Rio-Chanona completed her BSc in physics at UNAM, Mexico and her PhD in mathematics at the University of Oxford, where she was part of the complexity economics group at the Oxford Martin School's Institute for New Economic Thinking. She was a JSMF research fellow at the Complexity Science Hub in Vienna and a visiting scholar at the Harvard Kennedy School. Maria has worked alongside international policy organizations, including the International Monetary Fund, the World Bank, and the International Labour Organization. She is currently a member of the CEPR Artificial Intelligence Research Policy Network.

MARCO PANGALLO is a senior researcher at the Center for Artificial Intelligence (CENTAI), where he leads the complexity economics team. Previously, he was a James S. McDonnell Foundation postdoctoral fellow at the Sant'Anna School of Advanced Studies, Italy. Pangallo obtained his PhD in mathematics at the University of Oxford and was part of the complexity economics group at the Oxford Martin School's Institute for New Economic Thinking.

Pangallo is generally interested in understanding the economy quantitatively through a combination of data-driven and theoretical approaches. He believes that traditional economic models—based on optimization and equilibrium—are not well suited to quantitatively account for the complexity of the economy. Instead, agent-based models are the best tool to assimilate increasingly available granular data and produce more reliable economic forecasts.

EDITORS

JENNA BEDNAR is a professor of political science and public policy at the University of Michigan, a member of the external faculty at the Santa Fe Institute, and serves in the provost's office as the inaugural faculty director of UMICH Votes and Democratic Engagement. She leads a campus-wide collaborative effort to elevate democracy-related research, curriculum, and engagement. Her research focuses on how collective action builds social goods and the role that institutions play in that collaboration. Bednar's current work includes robust system design, especially of federal democracies; the interdependence of norms, culture, and institutions; and place-based public policy to support human social flourishing. Her book *The Robust Federation: Principles of Design* (2009) was awarded the APSA Martha Derthick Best Book Award in recognition of its enduring contribution to the study of federalism. In 2020, she was named the APSA Daniel Elazar Distinguished Federalism Scholar Award. She earned her BA from the University of Michigan and MA and PhD from Stanford University.

ERIC D. BEINHOCKER is a professor of public policy practice at the Blavatnik School of Government, University of Oxford. He is also the founder and executive director of the Institute for New Economic Thinking at the University's Oxford Martin School. INET Oxford is an interdisciplinary research centre dedicated to the goals of creating a more just, sustainable, and prosperous economy. Beinhocker is also a Supernumerary Fellow in economics at Oriel College, Oxford, and an external professor and chairman of the Science Board at the Santa Fe Institute.

Prior to joining Oxford, Beinhocker had an eighteen-year career as a partner at McKinsey & Company, where he held leadership roles in McKinsey's Strategy Practice, its Climate Change and Sustainability Practice, and the McKinsey Global Institute. Beinhocker writes frequently on economic and public-policy issues; his work has appeared in the *Financial Times, The Wall Street Journal, Bloomberg, The Times, The Guardian, The Atlantic,* and *The Washington Post.* He is the author *The Origin of Wealth: The Radical Remaking of Economics and What It Means for Business and Society* (2007). Originally from Boston, Massachusetts, Beinhocker is a graduate of Dartmouth College and the MIT Sloan School.

JAGODA KASZOWSKA-MOJSA is an economic expert at the National Bank of Poland and a Research Associate at the Institute for New Economic Thinking and the Oxford Smith School of Enterprise and the Environment. She also works as a research fellow at the Institute of Economics, Polish Academy of Sciences, and as a lecturer at Cracow University of Economics in Poland. Her research focuses on systemic risk, financial (in)stability, macroprudential policies and regulations, and agent-based modeling.

Kaszowska-Mojsa has degrees in economics from the University of Alcalá and mathematics from Jagiellonian University, as well as a PhD in economics and finance from Cracow University of Economics. Her dissertation was nominated for the Prime Minister's Award in Economics for the best doctoral dissertation, and also won the Central Statistical Office's competition for outstanding doctoral dissertation. As a Fulbright Scholar, she conducted her PhD research in the United States. Her research was funded by the National Bank of Poland, Ministry of Education in Poland, National Science Centre, European Commission (H2020) and Santander Bank.

FRANÇOIS LAFOND is deputy director of the complexity economics group at the Institute for New Economic Thinking, University of Oxford; senior researcher at the Smith School for Enterprise and the Environment; an Oxford Martin fellow; an associate member of Nuffield College, Oxford; and external faculty at the Complexity Science Hub in Vienna.

Lafond's main areas of research are in the economics of innovation and productivity, environmental economics, complex systems, and forecasting. Currently, his research interests lie in the macroeconomics of the net-zero transition, the structure and evolution of production networks, and the future of technology. His research has appeared in economics and interdisciplinary journals, and has been featured in books, news articles, and public-sector reports.

PENNY MEALY is a senior economist at the World Bank, a research associate at the Institute for New Economic Thinking (INET) and the Oxford Smith School of Enterprise and the Environment, an adjunct senior research fellow at SoDa Labs at the Monash Business School, and an external Applied Complexity Fellow at the Santa Fe Institute. Her work applies various methods from complex systems and data science to analyze the interrelated challenges of climate change and economic development. Her research has developed novel, data-driven approaches for analyzing structural change, occupational mobility and the future of work, and the transition to the green economy.

Mealy completed a PhD at INET, University of Oxford. She has held various research fellow roles at the Oxford Martin School, the Oxford Smith School of Enterprise and the Environment, the Bennett Institute for Public Policy at Cambridge University, and SoDa Labs, Monash University. Penny has also frequently advised international organizations, governments, and businesses on green growth and development strategies.

ANTON PICHLER is an assistant professor in supply-chain analytics at the Vienna University of Economics and Business. Previously, he was a James S. McDonnell Foundation postdoctoral fellow at the Complexity Science Hub in Vienna. He holds a PhD in mathematics from the University of Oxford, as well as degrees in quantitative finance, economics, and political science.

His current research focuses on the economics of the energy transition and modeling the impacts from climate-induced disasters. In his research, Pichler builds on and contributes to various quantitative methods including agent-based simulations, mathematical optimization, time-series analysis, machine learning and complex network theory. He has published research papers on topics spanning the propagation of economic shocks in production networks, forecasting technological change, systemic risk in financial networks, and energy supply security.

J. DOYNE FARMER is director of the complexity economics program at the Institute for New Economic Thinking and Baillie Gifford Professor of Complex-Systems Science at the Smith School of Enterprise and the Environment, University of Oxford. He is also an external professor at the Santa Fe Institute and chief scientist at Macrocosm.

Farmer's current research is in economics, including agent-based modeling, financial instability, and technological progress. He was a founder of Prediction Company, a quantitative automated trading firm that was sold to UBS in 2006. His past research includes complex systems, dynamical systems theory, time-series analysis, and theoretical biology. His book, *Making Sense of Chaos: A Better Economics for a Better World*, was published in 2024.

ABOUT THE SANTA FE INSTITUTE

THE SANTA FE INSTITUTE is the world headquarters for complexity science, operated as an independent, nonprofit research and education center located in Santa Fe, New Mexico. Our researchers endeavor to understand and unify the underlying, shared patterns in complex physical, biological, social, cultural, technological, and even possible astrobiological worlds. Our global research network of scholars spans borders, departments, and disciplines, bringing together curious minds steeped in rigorous logical, mathematical, and computational reasoning. As we reveal the unseen mechanisms and processes that shape these evolving worlds, we seek to use this understanding to promote the well-being of humankind and of life on Earth.

ᶳPR🖋•SS

THE SANTA FE INSTITUTE PRESS

The SFI Press endeavors to communicate the best of complexity science and to capture a sense of the diversity, range, breadth, excitement, and ambition of research at the Santa Fe Institute.

To provide a distillation of work at the frontiers of complex-systems science across a range of influential and nascent topics.

To change the way we think.

SEMINAR SERIES
New findings emerging from the Institute's ongoing working groups and research projects, for an audience of interdisciplinary scholars and practitioners.

ARCHIVE SERIES
Fresh editions of classic texts from the complexity canon, spanning the Institute's four decades of advancing the field.

COMPASS SERIES
Provocative, exploratory volumes aiming to build complexity literacy in the humanities, industry, and the curious public.

SCHOLARS SERIES
Affordable and accessible textbooks and monographs disseminating the latest findings in the complex-systems science world.

— ALSO FROM SFI PRESS —

Complexity Economics:
Proceedings of the Santa Fe Institute's 2019 Fall Symposium
W. Brian Arthur, Eric D. Beinhocker, and Alison Stanger, eds.

Foundational Papers in Complexity Science
David C. Krakauer, ed.

For additional titles, inquiries, or news about the Press, visit us at
www.sfipress.org

COLOPHON

The body copy for this book was set in EB Garamond, a typeface designed by Georg Duffner after the Ebenolff-Berner type specimen of 1592. Headings are in Kurier, created by Janusz M. Nowacki, based on typefaces by the Polish typographer Małgorzata Budyta. For footnotes and captions, we have used CMU Bright, a sans serif variant of Computer Modern, created by Donald Knuth for use in TeX, the typesetting program he developed in 1978. Additional type is set in Cochin, a typeface based on the engravings of Nicolas Cochin, for whom the typeface is named

The SFI Press complexity glyphs used throughout this book were designed by Brian Crandall Williams.

SANTA FE INSTITUTE
COMPLEXITY
GLYPHS

ZERO

ONE

TWO

THREE

FOUR

FIVE

SIX

SEVEN

EIGHT

NINE

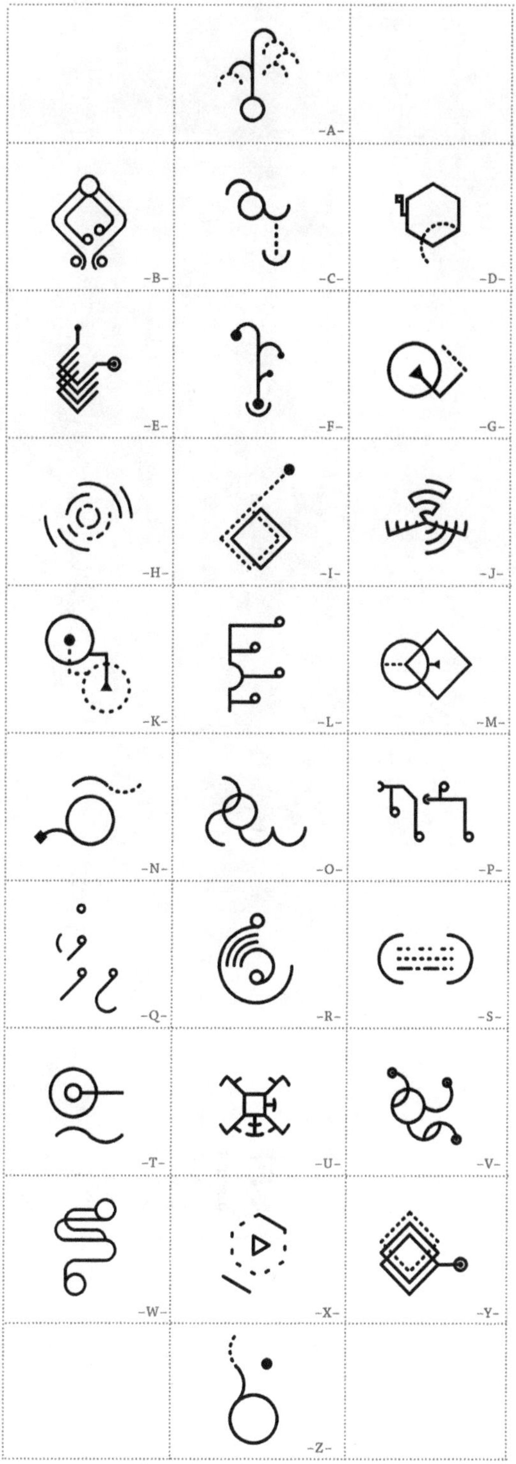

-A-
-B- -C- -D-
-E- -F- -G-
-H- -I- -J-
-K- -L- -M-
-N- -O- -P-
-Q- -R- -S-
-T- -U- -V-
-W- -X- -Y-
-Z-

SFI PR**SS

SEMINAR SERIES